Teacher Preparation Classroom

See a demo at
www.prenhall.com/teacherprep/demo

Your Class. Their Careers. Our Future. Will your students be prepared?

We invite you to explore our new, innovative and engaging website and all that it has to offer you, your course, and tomorrow's educators! Preview this site today at www.prenhall.com/teacherprep/demo. Just click on "go" on the login page to begin your exploration.

Organized around the major courses pre-service teachers take, the Teacher Preparation site provides media, student/teacher artifacts, strategies, research articles, and other resources to equip your students with the quality tools needed to excel in their courses and prepare them for their first classroom.

This ultimate on-line education resource will provide you and your students access to:

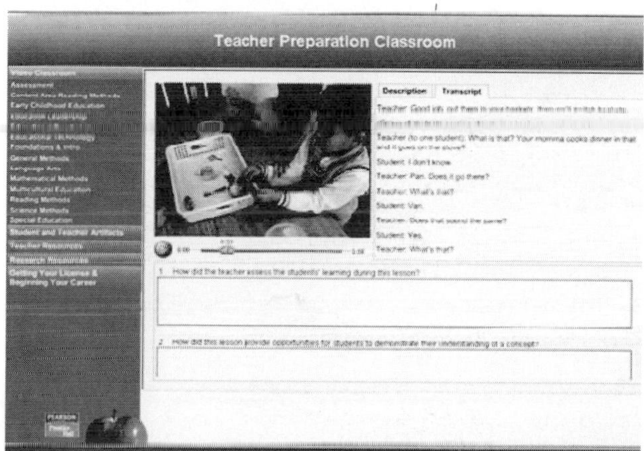

Online Video Library. More than 250 video clips—each tied to a course topic and framed by learning goals and Praxis-type questions—capture real teachers and students working in real classrooms.

Student and Teacher Artifacts. More than 200 student and teacher classroom artifacts—each tied to a course topic and framed by learning goals and application questions—provide a wealth of materials and experiences to help your students observe children's developmental learning.

Lesson Plan Builder. Step-by-step guidelines and lesson plan examples support students as they learn to build high-quality lesson plans.

Articles and Readings. Over 500 articles from ASCD's renowned journal *Educational Leadership* are available. The site also includes *Research Navigator,* a searchable database of additional educational journals.

Strategies and Lessons. Over 500 research-supported instructional strategies appropriate for a wide range of grade levels and content areas.

Licensure and Career Tools. Resources devoted to helping your students pass their licensure exam; learn standards, law, and public policies; plan a teaching portfolio; and succeed in their first year of teaching.

How to ORDER *Teacher Prep* for you and your students:

- For students to receive a *Teacher Prep* Access Code with this text please provide your bookstore with ISBN 0-13-614931-6 when you place your textbook order. The bookstore must order the text with this ISBN to be eligible for this offer.

Upon ordering *Teacher Prep* for their students, instructors will be given a lifetime *Teacher Prep Access Code.* To receive your access code, please email: **Merrill.marketing@pearsoned.com** and provide the following information:

- Name and Affiliation
- Author/Title/Edition of Merrill text

PARENTS AS PARTNERS IN EDUCATION

Families and Schools Working Together

SEVENTH EDITION

EUGENIA HEPWORTH BERGER
Professor Emerita, Metropolitan State College of Denver

Upper Saddle River, New Jersey
Columbus, Ohio

Library of Congress Cataloging-in-Publication Data

Berger, Eugenia Hepworth.
Parents as partners in education: families and schools working together / Eugenia Hepworth Berger. — 7th ed.
p. cm.
Includes bibliographical references and index.
ISBN 978-0-13-228670-1 (pbk.)
1. Home and school—United States. 2. Education—Parent participation—United States. I. Title.
LC225.3.B47 2008
371.19'2—dc22 2007003550

Vice President and Executive Publisher: Jeffery W. Johnston
Publisher: Kevin M. Davis
Acquisitions Editor: Julie Peters
Editorial Assistant: Tiffany Bitzel
Production Editor: Linda Hillis Bayma
Production Coordination: Thistle Hill Publishing Services, LLC
Design Coordinator: Diane C. Lorenzo
Photo Coordinator: Valerie Schultz
Cover Designer: Ali Mohrman
Cover image: SuperStock
Production Manager: Laura Messerly
Director of Marketing: David Gesell
Marketing Manager: Amy Judd
Marketing Coordinator: Brian Mounts

This book was set in New Caledonia by Integra Software Services. It was printed and bound by Hamilton Printing Company. The cover was printed by Phoenix Color Corp.

Pearson Education Ltd.
Pearson Education Singapore Pte. Ltd.
Pearson Education Canada, Ltd.
Pearson Education–Japan
Pearson Education Australia Pty. Limited
Pearson Education North Asia Ltd.
Pearson Educación de Mexico, S.A. de C.V.
Pearson Education Malaysia Pte. Ltd.

10 9 8 7 6 5 4 3 2 1
ISBN-13: 978-0-13-228670-1
ISBN-10: 0-13-228670-X

To the memory of my husband, Glen Berger.
To the rest of my extended family,
my parents, Gladys and Richard Hepworth
and Anna and Henry Berger
my children, Dick, Debra, and John
my grandchildren, Jevon, Jeni, Caroline, and Andrea, and
my sisters, Cora, Marian, and Jo.

It was through my participation in an extended family that I became aware of the importance of support, nurturance, and love.

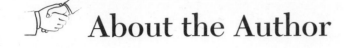

About the Author

Eugenia Hepworth Berger became interested in parent involvement when she and her husband, Glen, became the parents of three children who attended public schools. A professional in early childhood education, sociology, family life education, and parent education for 35 years, she has two master's degrees and a Ph.D. in sociological foundations of education. Eugenia is active in many professional organizations, including the Association for Childhood Education International, the National Association for the Education of Young Children (life member), and the National Council for the Social Studies. In 1994 she served on the board for the National Association of Early Childhood Teacher Educators. She has been a board member of the Colorado Association for Childhood Education, served as president of the Rocky Mountain Council on Family Relations for three years, and served on the board of the Colorado Association for the Education of Young Children from 1998 to 2006. She conducted many conferences, ranging from the Colorado Year of the Child in 1979 to ACEI and RMCFR state conferences in the 1980s and 1990s. Before becoming a college professor, she was a public school teacher and director of a parent education program. While finishing her doctorate at the University of Denver, she taught for two years in the Sociology Department. In 1968, she became a faculty member at Metropolitan State College, where she wrote the early childhood education certification program and the minor in early childhood and coordinated the early childhood education program for 8 years. She retired in December 1997 and is now professor emerita of education.

Eugenia has been elected to a variety of honorary associations, including Pi Kappa Lambda, Mortar Board, Mu Phi Epsilon, Pi Lambda Theta, and Kappa Delta Pi. She was included in several editions of *Who's Who in the West* and *Who's Who of American Women.* She received the Distinguished Service Award from Metropolitan State College of Denver.

Preface

The turmoil of the decade increases the need to have families and schools working in a partnership for a secure and supportive environment for children. Fortunately, there has been a movement toward engaging families and communities more completely as partners in education. A look at today's families, schools, and communities shows that they continue in their roles of nurturing and educating children.

The No Child Left Behind Act includes a focus on parents and families. This focus should continue in the future. No longer do we question whether parents should collaborate with schools. Now we try to design an appropriate and successful partnership that meets the needs of children, parents, individual schools, and school districts.

When I wrote the first edition of *Parents as Partners,* I did so because of my great interest in parent–school collaboration. This developed from my roles as a parent, a public school teacher, and a college professor as well as my experience as director of a Parent Education and Preschool Program. It was my aim to project this enthusiasm for parent–school partnerships to preservice teachers, school personnel, and parents.

CHANGES TO THIS EDITION

This edition includes updated material and additional coverage of many subjects. Of particular interest are:

- **Research on the brain** and the environment needed by infants and young children in order for them to grow optimally (chapter 1).
- Update on current research and previous research concerning the **developing child** (chapter 1).
- Chapter 3, The Family and Community, from the previous edition, was divided into two chapters: chapter 2, Families and Communities: Overview, Trends, and Insights, and chapter 3, Working with Culturally Diverse Groups. These chapters together provide students with a broad understanding of the **changing population** of children and families they might be working with, an understanding of why population shifts are occurring, a deeper understanding of various cultural groups, and insights and strategies for **working with diverse ethnic groups.**
- Expanded content throughout on the **diverse ethnicities of children and families** living in the United States, and the implications of diverse people in schools today for teaching professionals. There is more coverage of Native Americans, African Americans, Latinos, and other ethnic groups.
- A **streamlined history chapter,** now chapter 4, with a focus on understanding general trends.
- Research on school-based programs (chapter 8).
- Research on home-based programs (chapter 9).
- **Update on IDEA 2004** and help for the child with disabilities (chapter 10).
- Intervention in **bullying** in schools and neighborhoods (chapter 11).
- **Update of legal rights** and responsibilities of parents and other adults (chapter 12).
- **Ombudsmanship** in the United States and abroad (chapter 12).
- New annotated **Web sites** appear at the end of every chapter.
- Resources for Home and School Programs, which was an Appendix in the last edition, was moved to the *Online Instructor's Manual.*

GUIDELINES AND STRATEGIES FOR WORKING WITH FAMILIES

The tried and true how-to ideas and means to help parents and educators join together include

- Communication, an essential element in order to provide an environment where learning and caring coexist

- Ideas to help build a partnership of home and school
- The ability to set up an environment where learning can take place
- Historical development of family life and changes in living styles, which provides background information and encourages deeper understanding on the part of preservice teachers of the rich and long history of groups of people from around the world
- Activities and programs to enrich parent-school collaboration
- Methods needed to recruit volunteers for the school
- Practices necessary to develop working relationships

ORIENTATION TO THE TEXT

Interdisciplinary. The text studies parent involvement from an interdisciplinary approach and looks at home–school collaboration using historical, educational, psychological, ethnic-social diversity, and sociological perspectives. In this edition there is a strong effort to include immigration patterns and the history of diversity in the United States, as well as recognition of the original inhabitants, the Native Americans.

Theory and Research. Theory and research underpin each chapter of the text. New research emphasizes the need for collaboration between families and schools.

Practical Application. A parent, student, teacher, or administrator can pick up this book and find suggestions and descriptions of specific programs that will enable collaboration between families and schools.

Readability. Reviewers and students have commented on the readability of the text and its comprehensive coverage. It is written in an easy-to-read style.

Figures and Tables. Many tables and figures are included in the text. Enlargements of certain tables and figures are included in the Instructor's Manual so that transparencies can be made easily.

Illustrations. Chapter 4 includes many classical paintings from leading art museums that illustrate the history of families and children. In addition, more than 100 photographs enrich the narrative throughout the book.

SPECIAL FEATURES

Situational Vignettes. Vignettes bring alive situations that typically occur in parent–school relationship.

Advocacy. Preparation and suggestions on advocating for children, plus facts about ombudsmanship for children in the United States, give parents and educators the knowledge they need to encourage them to be active in involvement in advocacy issues.

Historical Outline. An outline in chapter 4 of historical highlights of parent education and education succinctly illustrates parent involvement.

INSTRUCTOR'S RESOURCES

All ancillaries are available for download at **www.prenhall.com** in the Instructor's Resource Center. Register for an access code in the IRC. Contact your Prentice Hall representative for additional assistance if needed.

Online Instructor's Manual. Ideas for the instructor include a Study Guide (discussion questions), Objectives, Class Activities and Discussions (repeated from the text as well as additional ones), and some additional resources. The Appendix, Resources for Home and School Programs, which appeared in the previous edition of the textbook, is now included here and provides information and reference materials.

Online Test Bank. The manual includes multiple-choice, short-answer, and essay questions to be used for tests.

Test Management Software. The assessment items in the Online Test Bank are provided electronically within a test management program, TestGen.

WebCT and Bb. Course cartridges in WebCT and Blackboard format are available to upload to your online course.

ACKNOWLEDGMENTS

This text developed over the years and in doing so I worked with many persons over the 25 years of publication. I would like to thank them all. Everyone was cooperative and gracious and their encouragement helped me to continue.

Professionals and organizations—Susan Blosten, Phyllis Levenstein, Joyce Epstein, Don Davies, Julia Herwig, Marion M. Wilson, Bettye Caldwell, Miriam Westheimer, Cynthia Franklin, Loretta Fuddy, Virginia Plunkett, Romie Tobi, Virginia Castro, Kevin Swick, Colorado Department of Education, Parents as Partners, Parent Education and Assistance for Kids (PEAK) Parent Center, and Utah Parent Center—all have shared materials with me in the past or present. Kelly and Bruce Stahlman wrote about their experiences with twins who have cerebral palsy, and Bruce updated information about the children for this edition. Clark E. Myers used his law expertise and contributed to chapter 11. Pat Welch and David Denson of the C. Henry Kempe Center for the Prevention and Treatment of Child Abuse and Neglect gave me information and the Barton Schmitt photographs that appear in chapter 10. Although I am no longer teaching, I am still indebted to my students; two of the case studies were written by Bretta Martinec and Rosina Kovar, students at MSCD. My family has also been an essential ingredient in the entire project each time around, for they embodied what is best in families.

I also want to show my appreciation to all of the many organizations and government agencies for their continued efforts to benefit children and share information with others. A look at the Bibliography will show how many there are.

The Metropolitan Museum of Art, the Saint Louis Art Museum, and the Denver Art Museum allowed me to use prints from their collections. Audrey Gilden, Debra MClave, John and Elena Machina Berger, Catherine Smith, and Andrea Berger graciously shared photographs.

I want to thank the staff of Merrill/Prentice Hall for their continued support. Most supportive were my editor, Julie Peters, who guided the revision and suggested changes, and Karen Banks, an early childhood educator and consultant, who contributed revisions to several chapters. I would also like to extend special thanks to production editor Linda Bayma, who was instrumental in guiding this edition, and to Thistle Hill Publishing Services for the production services provided.

Finally, I want to thank the following individuals for their comments and suggestions during the development of this text: Susan Matoba Adler, University of Illinois at Urbana–Champaign; Ann C. Barbour, California State University, Los Angeles; Beth N. Quick, Tennessee State University; Donna Rafanello, Long Beach City College; and Sharla Snider, Texas Woman's University.

Brief Contents

Contents

CHAPTER 8

School-Based Programs 239

CHAPTER 9

Home-Based Programs 280

CHAPTER 10

Working with Parents of a Child with Disabilities 315

CHAPTER 11

The Abused Child 357

Note: Every effort has been made to provide accurate and current Internet information in this book. However, the Internet and information on it are constantly changing, so it is inevitable that some of the Internet addresses listed in this textbook will change.

1 Family Involvement—Essential for a Child's Development

Research on the brain makes it clear that children must have a loving, warm, interactive environment. Communities and schools can enable families to flourish by providing support and caring.

E. H. Berger

In partnerships, educators, families, and communities members work together to share information, guide students, solve problems, and celebrate successes.

Epstein, 2001, p. 4

The question today is not whether early experience matters, but rather how early experiences shape individual development and contribute to children's continued movement along positive pathways.

Shonkoff & Phillips, 2000, p. 6

In this chapter on the importance of parents, you will read about needs and successes when parents, schools, and communities collaborate and advocate together. After completing the chapter, you should be able to do the following:

- Discuss the increase in collaboration among families, communities, and schools.
- Cite research that supports the significance of education and family, school, and community involvement.
- Identify and explain research on attachment that illustrates the need for early attachment of children with a parent or significant caregiver.
- Discuss breakthroughs in neuroscience research on brain development and what it means for families and education.
- Discuss the developmental theories of Piaget and Vygotsky and Hunt's book *Intelligence and Experience* as they describe development and challenge the assumption of fixed intelligence and predetermined development.
- Cite examples, such as Reggio Emilia, Comer's program, and Brazelton's Touchpoints, that focus on emergent development and family involvement in the positive development of children.
- Define *developmental continuity* and *discontinuity* and explain why it is important for families, schools, and social agencies to work together.

INTRODUCTION

Throughout the world, parents, educators, political leaders, professionals, and concerned citizens of all ages, socioeconomic groups, and ethnic backgrounds recognize that strong families are essential for society. Although there is no consensus on specific needs of families, there is agreement that families are important and that society must give families the time and resources necessary to provide the support and attention their children need. Resources include child-care centers, preschools, as well as schools and community support. (The term *school* is used throughout this book to include child-care centers, preschools, and schools. School is defined as an organization that provides instruction and as an institution for the teaching of children [Merriam-Webster, 2002]. Child-care centers, preschools, and schools all help families raise and educate their children. Although a prime concern for child-care centers is the care children receive and how children are guided, if the environment is rich they learn while attending child-care centers and preschools. When the discussion focuses specifically on child-care centers, that term will be used.)

As society becomes increasingly dependent on technology and members of extended families are separated from one another, it becomes apparent that schools and communities must help parents and families provide a caring environment for children. Throughout this text, the term *parents* includes those who act in a primary caregiver or parent role whether they are the biological parent, a relative, adoptive parent, foster parent or a nonrelated caregiver. The need to promote human interactions becomes even stronger than in previous generations, when extended families and parents had more time to provide for the caring of children. Currently, with many mothers and fathers working outside the home, the need for other caregivers to provide the parental role is expanded. A rallying cry for collaboration among schools, families, and communities has spread across the nation. Ingredients for successful collaboration include adequate and supportive child care, small class sizes in the early years to ensure individual attention for children, and the active involvement of parents and caregivers in the children's development and education. To create a literate society, we must care for children and give them the opportunity to develop skills and become educated citizens.

CHALLENGES

The challenges that our society faces include (1) promoting caring schools and communities, (2) encouraging caring family environments, (3) providing adequate and enriching child care, (4) providing positive before- and after-school care, (5) creating and supporting collaboration among parents, teachers, and the community, and (6) creating an educational environment that meets the needs of children with diverse culture and backgrounds.

CARING SCHOOLS AND COMMUNITIES

When teachers, parents, and members of the community reach out to children in a caring, supportive way, children know that they belong. They are able to form attachments and respond positively. Parents, child-care providers, and teachers must recognize the need for children to have a caring environment. Schools, families, and communities are called on to increase their involvement and collaboration to support the children. This reflects an ecological approach to child caring. In order to understand and support the child, child-care centers and schools need to be aware of and responsive to the family and community.

What temperaments do caregivers need to enable them to provide a caring environment? They must see themselves as caring, capable individuals who have a positive sense of identity. Swick states that four sets of dispositions are needed by individuals to provide caring environments for their students: (1) healthy sense of self, (2) caring skills and behavior, (3) prosocial relationships with others, and (4) helping and serving skills and relationships (2001, p. 131). The first, a healthy sense of self, develops from relationships with significant others—parents, caregivers, teachers, role models, and those who had an impact on the child.

The development of caring skills and behavior is strengthened further by interactions, modeling, and guidance with other caring individuals. Children

Todd Yarrington / Merrill

Silver Burdett Ginn

Shirley Zeiburg / PH College

Krista Greco / Merrill

EMG Education Management Group

Parents are their children's first and most important caregivers, nurturers, socializers, and educators.

model what they experience; prosocial behaviors are learned through prosocial relationships with others.

The acquisition of caring and serving skills is a constructionist process in which the child's involvement with parents and other significant adults is critical to the child's continued growth in becoming a caring individual (Swick, 2001, p. 132). The process includes modeling when children are involved in caring and service; educators are role models and need to build mutual trust and respect with the students. Suggestions for becoming a caring, competent caregiver and teacher include

(1) building mutual trust—be honest; (2) cultivating communication skills—be a role model; (3) adjusting the schedule—be flexible; (4) altering perspectives—be empathetic; (5) promoting humor—be human; and (6) promoting a positive self-image—be kind (Krall & Jalongo, 1998–1999).

Comer (2004) sees schools as social organizations in which the environment enables students to develop a sense of fairness and belonging. In providing a secure, caring environment schools can encourage and help restore a feeling of wellness. Comer describes the "common threads" that result in successful schools: "positive school relationships; caring, responsible, predictable adults in the lives of students; a sense of belonging in constructive groups engaged in challenging learning and activities; and opportunity for students to sense direction and purpose" (1997, p. 72).

There is a need for a more caring community for children and youth from early childhood to young adulthood. The use of illicit drugs, alcohol, and tobacco by young people illustrates this need. Involved, caring adults who offer alternatives such as social activities, programs devoted to music and the arts, health, physical fitness and recreational opportunities, as well as educational enrichment can help children grow into physically and emotionally healthy young adults. These alternatives can help reduce the temptation to use these harmful substances, despite their widespread availability.

How can schools and families develop a caring environment? Teachers and parents can reach out to one another with genuine interest and support. They can take time to get to know one another and to recognize and respect one another's beliefs, values, and concerns. Most important, if parents and teachers show respect for one another, they can develop a caring partnership (Berger, 1996a, 1996b; Comer, 2004; Swick, 1997).

Debra McClave

Teachers, reaching out to children in a caring, supportive way, let children know that they matter and that they belong.

CARING FAMILIES

The importance of parents giving attention, support, love, and encouragement to children is well established. Findings show that the primary causal factor in a child's success or lack of success in school is not socioeconomic status (Epstein, 1996, 2001; Zill, 1996), but the caring support and encouragement given by others. Concern about finances makes it difficult to provide for housing and nutrition, let alone concentrate on emotional and educational needs of the family. Low-income families who provide caring for their children supply the base for their educational and social needs. It is shown that caring about school attendance beginning with the early grades is important for the child's success. Encouraging and supporting attendance enables children to be successful in school (Epstein & Sheldon, 2002). At every level of income, in all cultures, and in different family forms, it is essential that children have enriching and loving families that guide and help them as they grow.

Boyer (1991) states, "There is no evidence that today's parents are less committed or less caring" (p. 4). Parents have not changed, but the "loss of community, the increased fragmentation of family life, the competing, often conflicting, pressures" affect their ability to provide the family life children so desperately need (p. 4). It is recognized that having children who are "ready to learn" does not mean they come to school with specific academic skills in place. It also means that children have the care, conditions, environment, health provisions, and nutrition that allow them to be ready to learn.

The eight parenting skills recommended by Galinsky (1999) include caring attitudes that parents and other caregivers should use with their charges.

1. Making the child feel important and loved
2. Responding to the child's cues and clues
3. Accepting the child for who he or she is but expecting success
4. Promoting strong values
5. Using constructive discipline
6. Providing routines and rituals
7. Being involved in the child's education
8. Being there for the child (pp. 18–26)

These skills provide the child with a base on which they can grow and develop emotionally and cognitively.

Adequate and Enriching Child Care

The family is the most important child-care provider. A national survey of employed mothers found that nearly half of children younger than 5 were cared for by the respondent's parents or other relatives when the mother worked outside the home. Twenty-two percent of parents preferred having a relative care for their children, especially for very young children (Larner, 1996). Other options included family child-care providers and child-care centers. Those who used child-care centers and home-based child care were most concerned about safety, the attention children receive, cleanliness, communication with the parent, and the provider's warmth (p. 30). The discussion of Reggio Emilia in this chapter illustrates how a child-care provider can work with parents to provide a rich, caring environment.

The increased use of child-care centers requires that care providers work with parents to provide a loving, supportive environment for the children. Parents must also provide loving care when they are with their children, recognizing that the child is their most important responsibility and asset.

Debra McClave

Children are curious, capable, and strong.

Child-Care Providers

The urgent need for child care when parents work outside the home is evident. Parents worry most about the quality of care, the expertise and caring ability of providers, and the turnover rate of staff members. Children need continuity in caregivers to develop caring relationships, and parents want providers who show caring and warmth to their charges. Because child-care providers generally are poorly paid, the turnover rate of workers is high. It is necessary to recognize the importance of high-quality child care and acknowledge that child-care providers require a sufficient income to stay in the profession.

Positive Before- and After-School Care

Over the past decade, there has been growing concern about the increasing amount of time that school-age children spend unsupervised and often alone, before and after school. It is recognized that unsupervised after-school time not only fails to support children's development, intellectually and emotionally, but also creates an opportunity for children to become involved with drugs, smoking, and other illegal activities. Collaboration among schools, recreation services, human services, and/or arts in residence needs to occur so that children have a safe environment before and after school. "It is a demand for care, first, all day from birth to school age; second, after school every day until parents return from work; and, third, all summer" (Coleman, 1994, p. 36).

Collaboration Among Parents, Teachers, and the Community

The demand for schools to work with families and communities to become involved has exploded on the education scene. The question is no longer whether there is a need for collaboration between schools and parents, but what is the most effective way to work together and how should it be accomplished (Epstein, 1996, 2001; Epstein & Sheldon, 2002).

Schools that have reached out to parents are guideposts for those schools that have not begun to do so. Parents, schools, and communities may access information from the U.S. Department of Education by telephone, fax, correspondence, and the Internet. The department offers videos, articles, booklets, and newsletters concerning family and school partnerships. Schools need to be innovative in their effort to reach families. If they need help, information is available. Schools have an obligation to take the lead in developing partnerships.

REGGIO EMILIA

After World War II throughout Europe, many women entered the workforce outside the home. They needed and wanted a positive environment and experience for their young children. In addition, the end of the war brought hope of more freedom and a better quality of life, so excellent care and education for their young children was important to both parents. In Reggio, Italy, following the end of the war in 1945, mothers and fathers and other community members worked to develop a new type of school. "It was Loris Malaguzzi who was ready and able to support the school started by commonpeople in Reggio in 1945 and who carried the battle to get the city government to take upon itself the running of the people's schools and open the best municipal school in 1963" (Henrick, 1997, p. 5). From these beginnings the philosophy and educational tenets developed in Reggio Emilia have influenced early childhood education programs throughout the United States.

What Can We Learn from Reggio Emilia?

Parents can become positively involved as partners with caregivers in the rearing of children. A natural alliance among children, parents, and caregivers forms. In Reggio Emilia, caregivers usually stay with the same children over a 3-year span, often starting when the child is only 6 or 7 months old (Edwards & Gandini, 2001). "The school, the infant–toddler center, is a system of relationships. It is for children, but you cannot separate them from family and society, the places where they live" (Rinaldi, 2001, p. 53). This continuity of relationships, child, caregiver, and family, underlies the great success of the programs.

Some of the other elements of the Reggio Emilia experience that contribute to its being an important model include parents' and children's orientation to the program, the physical setting, a responsive curriculum that includes exploration and discovering, and documentation of children's activities and work.

Physical Setting

The school must be one where child, teacher, and family feel comfortable. The physical setting should be healthy, safe, inviting, and warm. It needs to provide space not only for the children's work and play and but also room for adults to rest, socialize, and work. "It should promote children's daily life, feelings of well-being in aesthetic surroundings and learning experiences" (Edwards & Gandini, 2001, p. 222).

Parents' and Children's Orientation

The center must be one where child, teacher, and family feel comfortable with one another in an interconnected system. The space is organized so that the child, family, and teachers feel welcomed. "Programs for children should communicate to parents the primary contribution they make to the child's development and provide space, time, and opportunities for occasions that help parents feel and become competent participants in the life of the center" (Edwards & Gandini, 2001, p. 222).

Responsive Curriculum

A natural alliance forms among children, parents, and caregivers. If followed, infants and toddlers have a hand in the curriculum development because it naturally flows from their interests and investigations. Children are curious, capable, and strong. Following the child's lead aids in emerging curriculum development and the child's heightened interest.

Documentation

Documentation is a process of inquiring and reflecting the children's interests and understandings. It serves as a positive tool in understanding the child and helps in designing the environment to meet the child's interests and needs. It is gained through observing, listening, collecting, interpreting, examining, and recording through note taking, audiotapes, and video recording. Displaying children's works and documenting their interests and achievements shows respect for the children's work and engages parents and children as well as teachers (Gandini & Goldhaber, 2001; Goldhaber & Smith, 2002). Documentation can serve as a method of communication by showing parents the work that is being achieved. It also tells children that their work is valuable and worthy to be shared (Edwards & Gandini, 2001).

Catherine Smith

Eye contact of father and child fosters human attachment, a necessary component for health development.

How Do Many Child-Care Centers in the United States Differ?

One of the major differences between care for infants and toddlers in Reggio Emilia and the United States is the support provided by paid parental leave. This results in the caregiver being able to stay home with the infant until the child is approximately 6 months of age, whereas infant care in the United States is often needed by the time the infant is 6 or 7 weeks of age. "A second clear distinction is the way the care of the young is conceptualized. In Italy it is seen as an appropriate activity, socially and intellectually enriching, to be carried out for the benefit of all the children in the community. In the United States, it is usually seen as a service to free families to do something other than care for their child (Lally, 2001, p. 19). A third difference is the belief that caregiving for toddlers and infants is a profession rather than a baby-sitting position. One journal article's title, "Here, We Call It 'Drop Off and Pickup': Transition to Child Care, American-Style," by Rebecca S. New, reflects the difference between many early child-care centers in the United States and those in Reggio Emilia (1999, p. 34).

Family Ecological Systems

Just as schools are systems with teachers, principals, superintendents, students, caregivers, and ancillary personnel interacting with the goal to educate, so the families they serve are entities or ecological systems. Each child and parent is affected by the family system in which they participate. The family is embedded in the social system in which it developed and the child is embedded in that family system (Hamilton, Roach, & Riley, 2003). The family has been described as "an example of an open, ongoing, goal-seeking, self-regulating, social system . . . shaped by its own particular structural features (size, complexity, composition, life stage, the psychobiological characteristics of its individual members) . . . and its socio-cultural and historic position in its larger environment" (Broderick, 1993, p. 37). Family systems are guided and influenced by their cultural and historical backgrounds as well as by the composition of the members of the family with their own psychobiological characteristics and structure.

Ecological Systems Vary

Family system theories are derived from diverse sources and are varied (Rosenblatt, 1994). A family that lives in a rural area will have a structure different from a city family's. On a farm, the family needs to work as a team to accomplish the tasks of caring for animals and producing crops. Children participate within the system as necessary cogs in the operation. In the city, many children are unable to contribute to the family's well-being. There is no role that helps them feel productive, so the systems that result are different.

Families native to the area where they live will have a different frame of reference from new arrivals. Immigrant families may have systems derived from their place of origin. They may adapt to the new society or they may prefer to keep their original system intact. If children live with a prescribed frame of behavior in their own family system that is at odds with the families of their classmates, they may have great difficulty adjusting to the opposing systems.

Changes in a System

When a family undergoes a transitional event such as the birth of a child, a move to a new location, or an illness of a family member, the system will need to adapt to accommodate the change. Change occurs in a variety of ways. It may be sudden or gradual, positive or negative. The change may be minimal or shattering. Divorce causes children to lose the family system as they knew it and adapt to an entirely new one. Teachers need to know what is happening in a student's family so that they can respond in an appropriate manner and be helpful to the child.

Three Levels of Ecological Systems

The child's development is related to experiences in the entire environment. Bronfenbrenner (1979, 1986) recognized three levels of systems:

1. The microsystem includes face-to-face relations with family and peers, with parents as the major influence on a child's interactive ecological system (O'Callaghan, 1993).
2. The mesosystem involves face-to-face relationships with more formal organizations such as schools, scouting groups, recreation facilities, and religious groups.
3. The ecosystem, which if further removed from personal interaction, still influences children through their parents and the parents' employment and government actions. The total ecological system is related to the care given to children; see Figure 1.1.

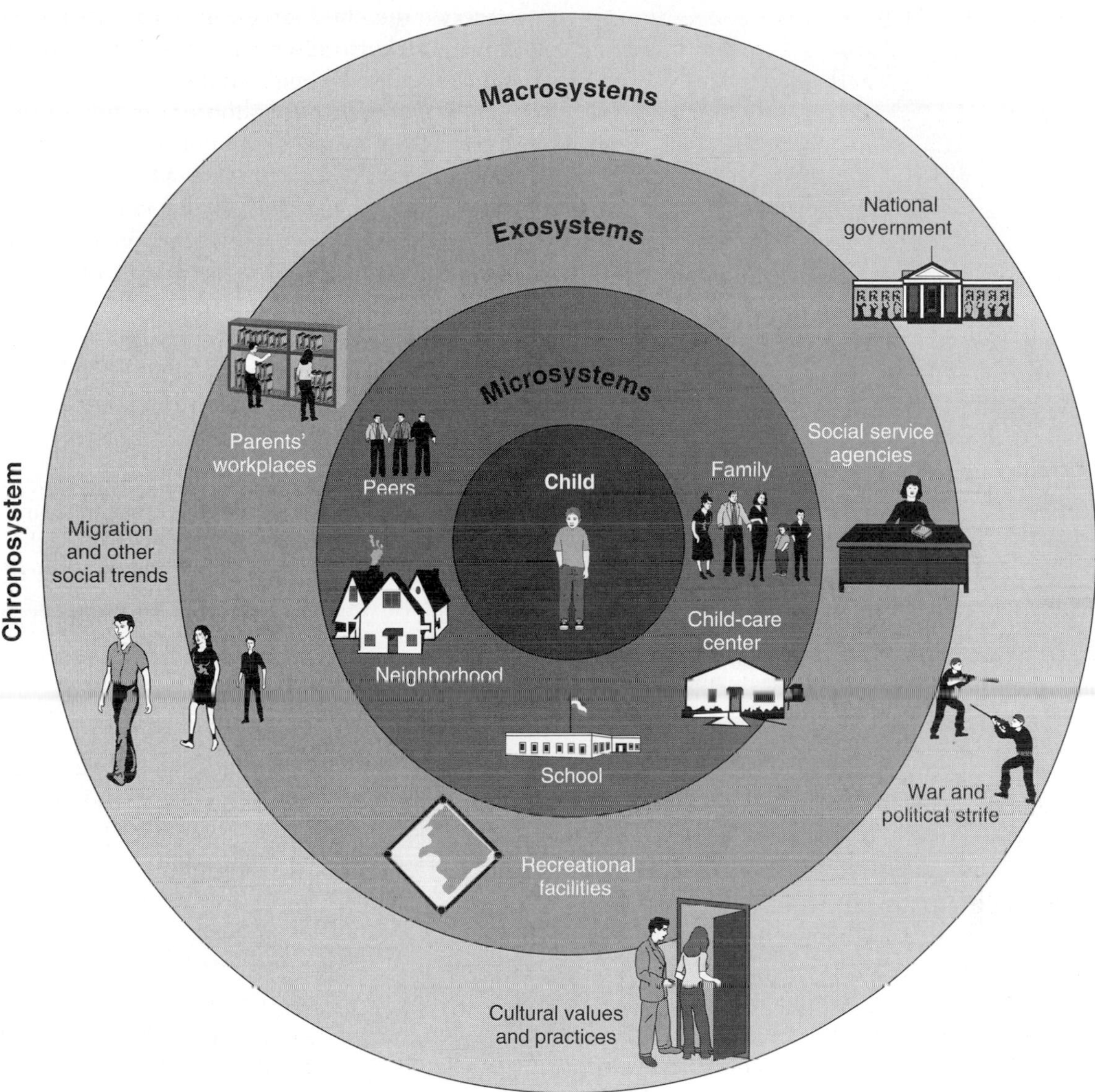

FIGURE 1.1 Bronfenbrenner's Ecological Theory.

Source: Based on *Making Human Beings Human: Bioecological Perspectives on Human Development,* by U. Bronfenbrenner, 2005, Thousand Oaks, CA: Sage.

Parents: First Educators

Parents are the first nurturers, socializers, and educators of their children. It is almost impossible to overemphasize the significance of the role of parents. The parents' role in their children's early years is significant in many ways, but it has these essential aspects: (a) Society would not survive if a culture stopped procreating or rearing its young. (b) Children who do not have the opportunity to form attachment to a significant other during the first 2 years of life find it difficult or impossible to overcome the lack of that emotional bond. (c) Brain research shows that experiences, both good and bad, during the first 3 years of life affect the connections and the "wiring" of the child's brain. (d) In addition to their importance as first educators, parents continue to be essential nurturers, socializers, and educators of their children throughout their childhoods.

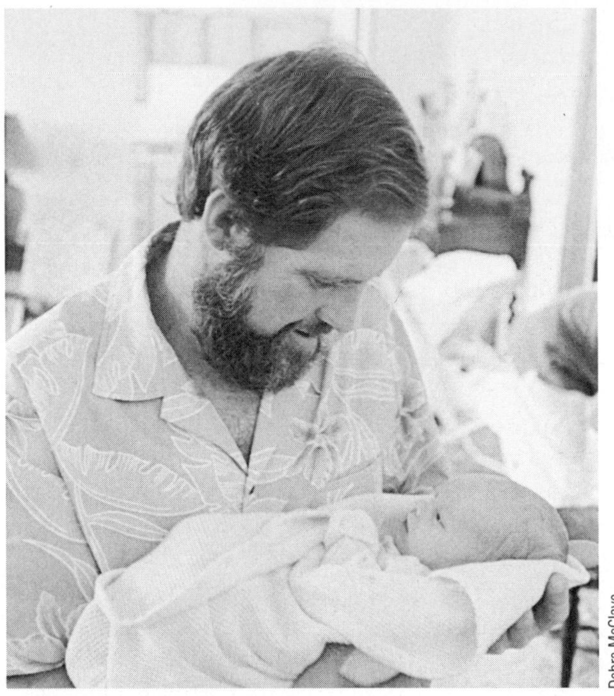

Debra McClave

Father and infant begin the attachment process through caring and eye-to-eye contact.

ATTACHMENT

The ability to nurture does not blossom automatically when one gives birth to a child. It involves many diverse variables, ranging from parent–child attachment to previous modeling experiences to environmental conditions that allow and encourage a positive parent–child relationship. Many parents have not had the good fortune to learn from a positive role model. They need advice and a support system of family, friends, and professionals.

Issues related to readiness to learn are the child's feelings of attachment, security, and well-being. An area of research of paramount importance to parents is that of human attachment. Since the 1930s there has been increasing research on bonding and attachment. Experts recognize attachment as an essential ingredient for a healthy personality. *Attachment* is defined as a form of behavior that has its "own internal motivation distinct from feeding and sex, and of no less importance for survival" (Bowlby, 1988, p. 27). Attachment behavior is the behavior that a person exhibits to obtain and maintain proximity to the attachment figure, generally the mother but also the father and, in their absence, someone the child knows. It is strongest when the child is sick, tired, or frightened. Human attachment is crucial throughout the life cycle.

The recognition of the importance of the first few years in the development of attachment came through studies of children who did not thrive. Skeels, Spitz, and Bowlby did *not* do controlled studies that gave some children love and withheld it from others. Instead, they looked at what had happened to children who had failed to thrive. Why had this happened? What did these children lack that the other children had?

Skeels

It was during the 1930s that questions about the importance of human attachment in the young child were raised. Harold Skeels, a member of the Iowa group of child researchers, studied the effect of environment on the development of children during a period when most researchers (e.g., Gesell and Watson) were studying maturation or behaviorism. One study, a *natural* history investigation, had startling findings (Skeels, 1966). Skeels placed 13 infants and toddlers from an orphanage in an institution for people with mental retardation. The 13 children—10 girls and 3 boys—ranged in age from 7.1 to 35.9 months and had IQs from 36 to 89, with a mean IQ score of 64.3. Children in the control group of 12, also chosen from children in the orphanage, between 12 and 22 months old, had IQs of 50 to 103, with a mean IQ of 86.7 points. The children placed in the wards for mental retardation were showered with attention by the attendants and supervisors. They were cared for, played with, loved, and allowed to go along on excursions. Almost every child developed an attachment to one person who was particularly interested in the child and his or her achievements. The control group of children in the orphanage, however, received traditional care with no special treatment. When retested, after varying periods from 6 to 52 months, the children in the institution for mental retardation had gained 27.5 IQ points, but those left in the orphanage had lost an average of 26.2 IQ points.

Although the research could be criticized because variables were not controlled—there were more girls than boys placed in the wards—and changes in IQ can be partially explained by statistical regression, the results were so dramatic and unexpected that the effect of early environment had to be considered.

Skeels (1966) followed up on the subjects of this research almost 20 years later and found evidence to reinforce his initial findings. Of the 13 children in the experimental group who had been transferred to the mental institution, 11 had been adopted and reared as "normal" children. Twelve of the 13 had become self-supporting adults, achieving a median educational level of 12 years of schooling. Of the control group children who had been left in the orphanage, four were still in institutions; one was a gardener's assistant; three were employed as dishwashers; one was a floater; one was a part-time worker in a cafeteria; and one had died. Only one individual had achieved an educational level similar to that of the experimental group—a man who as a child had received different treatment from the others. He had been transferred from the orphanage to a school for the deaf, where he received special attention from his teacher. The children who had been placed in a mental institution and later adopted received love and developed human attachments; they had achieved a lifestyle more typical of children outside the orphanage, whereas those left in the orphanage had only a marginal existence. Evidence strongly supports the importance of a nurturing early environment and also indicates that a poor initial environment can be reversed by enriched personal interaction (Skeels, 1966).

Spitz

René Spitz, a physician, also became involved in the observation of infants during the 1930s. In *The First Year of Life* (1965) he described his research and observations of the psychology of infants. He studied babies in seven situations: private families, foster homes, an obstetrics ward, an Indian village, a well-baby clinic, a nursery, and a foundling home.

Both the nursery and foundling home were long-term institutions that guaranteed constancy of environment and dramatically illustrated the necessity of human attachment and interaction. Both institutions provided similar physical care of children, but they differed in their nurturing and interpersonal relationships. Both provided hygienic conditions, well-prepared food, and medical care. The foundling home had daily visits by a medical staff, whereas the nursery called a doctor only when needed. The nursery was connected to a penal institution where delinquent girls, pregnant on admission, were sent to serve their sentences. Babies born to them were cared for in the nursery until the end of their first year. The mothers were primarily delinquent, psychopathic, or socially maladjusted minors. In contrast, some of the children in the foundling home had well-adjusted mothers who were unable to support their children. Others were children of unwed mothers who were asked to come to the home and nurse their own and one other child during the first 3 months.

Spitz (1965) filmed a representative group of the children he studied in both institutions. He studied 203 children in the nursery and 91 in the foundling home. The major difference in the care of the two sets of children was the amount of nurturing and social interaction. The nursery, which housed 40 to 60 children at a time, allowed the mothers or mother-substitutes to feed, nurse, and care for their babies. The infants had at least one toy; they were able to see outside their cribs and to watch the activities of other children and the caregiving mothers. The babies thrived.

In the foundling home, however, the babies were screened from outside activity by blankets hung over the sides and ends of their cribs, isolating them from any visual stimulation. They had no toys to play with, and the caretakers were busy tending to other duties rather than mothering the children. During the first 3 months, while they were breast-fed, the babies appeared normal. Soon after separation, however, they progressively deteriorated. Of the 91 foundling home children, 34 died by the end of the second year.

Spitz (1965) continued to follow up on 21 children who remained in the foundling home until they were 4 years old. He found that 20 could not dress themselves; 6 were not toilet trained; 6 could not talk; 5 had a vocabulary of two words; 8 had vocabularies of three to five words; and only 1 was able to speak in sentences. Spitz attributed the deterioration of the infants to lack of mothering. Although the children in the nursery had mothering, those in the foundling home did not.

> Absence of mothering equals emotional starvation. . . . This leads to progressive deterioration engulfing the child's whole person. Such deterioration is manifested first in an arrest of the child's psychological development; then psychological dysfunctions set in, paralleled by somatic changes. In the next stage this leads to increased infection liability and eventually, when the emotional deprivation continues into the second year of life, to a spectacularly increased rate of mortality. (Spitz, 1965, p. 281)

Eugenia Hepworth Berger

The interplay between a child's genetic makeup and positive experiences enables the brain to develop.

Bowlby

In 1951, John Bowlby reviewed studies of deprivation and its effects on personality development. In a systematic review for the World Health Organization, he described those works that supported theories on the negative aspects of maternal deprivation. In a monograph, Bowlby (1966) stated: "It is submitted that the evidence is now such that it leaves no room for doubt regarding the general proposition that the prolonged deprivation of the young child of maternal care may have grave and far-reaching effects on his character and so on the whole of his future life" (p. 46).

Development of Attachment

Bowlby (1982) described attachment in a family setting. Most babies about 3 months old show more attention and are more responsive to their primary caregiver than to others by smiling at, vocalizing to, and visually following their parent or other primary caregiver. At about 6 to 8 months of age, infants develop stranger anxiety. They become concerned about being near their caregiver and fearful of those they do not know. This attachment to primary caregivers continues and strengthens in intensity from 6 to 9 months, although when the child is ill, fatigued, hungry, or alarmed, the intensity increases. During the same period the infant demonstrates attachment to others as well, primarily the father, siblings, and caregivers. Attachment to others does not reduce the attachment to the mother or primary caregiver. At 9 months, most children try to follow primary caregivers when they leave the room, greet them on return, and crawl to be near them. This behavior continues throughout the second year of a child's life and on into the third. When children reach about 2 years 9 months to 3 years of age, they are better able to accept a parent's temporary absence.

Bowlby (1966) emphasized that the greatest effect on personality development is during the child's early years. The earliest critical period was believed to be during the first 5 or 6 months, while mother-figure and infant are forming an attachment. The second vital phase was seen as lasting until near the child's third birthday, during which time the mother-figure needs to be virtually an ever-present companion. During a third phase, the child is able to maintain the attachment even though the nurturing parent is absent. During the fourth to fifth year, this tolerable absence might extend from a few days to a few weeks; during the seventh to eighth years, the separation could be lengthened to a year or more. Deprivation in the third phase does not have the same destructive effect on the child as it does in the period from infancy through the third year.

ORPHANAGES IN ROMANIA

Research in the 1990s on infants raised in Romanian orphanages reaffirmed the findings of Spitz, Skeels, and Bowlby and furthered the study of causal factors. "Evidence began accumulating that sensory stimulation plays a crucial role not only in the early development of the brain's sensory- and motor- and memory-processing circuitry, but also in the development of the neural and hormonal systems that regulate our response to stress" (Carlson, 2002). The researchers looked specifically at the dismal patterns of cortisol secretion. "Touch is critical to the establishment of this mechanism for maintaining the body's homeostatic balance" (Carlson, 2002). Thirty of the children were in the control group of standard orphanage care, where one caregiver would look after 20 children. Many of these children were withdrawn and exhibited repetitive movements. Although they received adequate care and medical attention, they were not called by name and were moved frequently from caregiver to caregiver. "Clearly, the social networks in which children grow up bear on the development of the neural networks that mediate memory, emotion, and self" (Carlson, 2002).

Children in Romania still need help. It is suggested that 6,000 are without a home, but it is questionable whether they will have the option of finding new homes outside of Romania. In June 2004, Romania, with the possible exception of pending cases and grandparents, closed its adoption program.

MATERNAL OR HUMAN ATTACHMENT?

Rutter (1981) and Bower (1982) questioned whether the term *maternal deprivation* was too restrictive to cover a wide range of abuses and variables. They suggested that maternal deprivation was too limited a concept—that human attachment and multiple attachment should be considered, and that warmth as well as love be regarded as vital elements in relationships. Rutter suggested that the bond with the mother was not different in quality or kind from other bonds. In addition, individual differences among children resulted in some children being more vulnerable to "mother deprivation."

Tizard and Hodges

Questions regarding the irreversibility of deprivation were raised. Would sound childrearing reverse early deprivation? It appeared that good childrearing practices and a good environment would help the child, but early deprivation continued to be a problem and deprived infants often remained detached. Tizard and Hodges (1978) studied children raised in an institution to see if the lack of personal attachment had lasting effects. Children who were adopted did form bonds as late as 4 or 6 years of age, but they exhibited the same attention and social problems in school as those who remained in the institution. "Being one in a class of many other children may for the child have repeated some of the elements of the nursery 'family group,' leading to a similar pattern of competitive attempts to gain the attention of the teacher and poor relationships with other children" (Hodges, 1996, p. 71).

Ainsworth

Ainsworth (1973) wrote that parent–child attachment is necessary for the development of a healthy personality, but that attachment may occur beyond the early "sensitive period." Ainsworth identified three classifications of attachment: avoidant/insecure, ambivalent/insecurely, and securely attached (Shore, 1997).

Brazelton and Yogman

In their extensive studies of infants, Brazelton and Yogman (1986) analyzed the process of early attachment and wrote specifically about the interaction between infant and parent, covering even the effects of experiences in utero. The child appears to be born with predictable responses, including the ability to develop a reciprocal relationship with the caregiver.

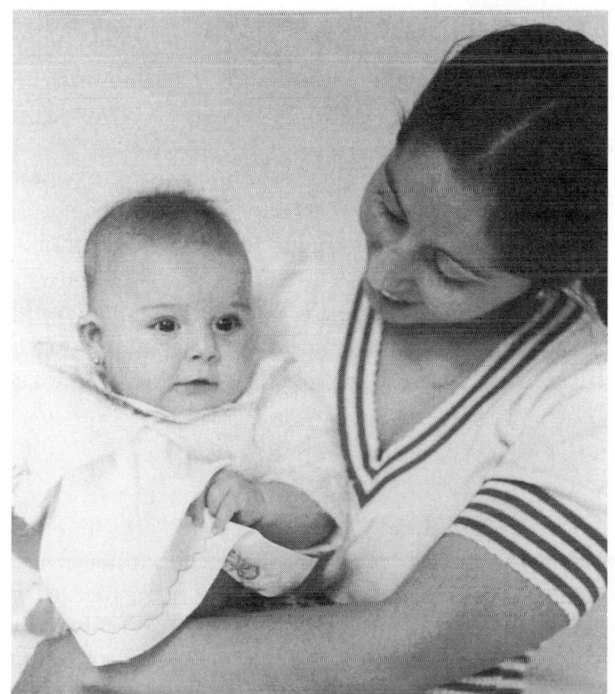
Eugenia Hepworth Berger

The brain is affected by nourishment, care, and stimulation. Early attachment and nurturing is essential to a child's development.

The authors described four stages vital to the parent–infant attachment process, which lasts from birth to 4 or 5 months. In the first stage the infant achieves homeostatic control and is able to control stimuli by shutting out or reaching for stimuli. During the second stage the infant is able to use and attend to social cues. In the third stage, usually at 3 and 4 months, the reciprocal process between parent and child shows the infant's ability to "take in and respond to information" as well as to withdraw. During the fourth stage the infant develops a sense of autonomy and initiates and responds to cues. If the parent recognizes and encourages the infant's desire to have control over the environment, the infant develops a sense that leads to a feeling of competence. This model is based on feedback and reciprocal interaction and allows for individual differences.

Brazelton Institute

The Brazelton Institute has continued to study infant behavior. Findings include the development of the Newborn Behavioral Observation (NBO). Early months of infancy, from birth until the third month, are important periods in the infants' adaptation to their environment. The NBO is a family centered observation set that is designed to be used by clinicians as they focus on individual infants and observe their individuality and competencies. In addition to strengthening the relationships between infant and parent as well as parent and clinician, the NBO provides information to the parents that helps them make positive caregiving. The parents learn to read their baby's communication cues, understand their baby better, and are able to respond with appropriate care (Brazelton Institute, 2005, p. 1).

Concerns

Three groups of parents may pose particular concern when developing parent–child attachments. The first is made up of parents who have never had models of good parenting or have been reared in abusive homes. They need help in learning how to care for children. The second group contains parents who tend to be isolated and insecure and do not have a support system. These groups could be helped by home-based programs such as Parents as Teachers, HIPPY, and Project CARE. (See chapter 8.) The third group includes parents who are busy and away from home for extended periods. The importance of early bonding and attachment development is such that these parents should be aware of the consequences of not devoting time to their young children.

Maltreatment of children, from infancy on, may have enormous effects on their social interaction. These children are often aggressive in their relationships with other children in a school setting. Youngblade and Belsky (1989) describe the effects that maltreatment might have on toddlers and older children, extending into adulthood. It sometimes results in dysfunctional relations not only between parent and child with insecure attachments, but also with peers. The authors state that "maltreated toddlers are, on average, more aggressive, less prosocial, and more disturbed in interaction with age-mates than are comparison children" (p. 11). Therapy can ameliorate the effects on children of dysfunctional parenting and maltreatment. Intervention with parents who may be prone to abusing their children is also essential.

Parents who are at risk for abusing children can be helped. Bowlby (1988) described a Home Start program in Leicester, England, in which volunteers visited parents in their homes and helped them with their roles as parents. The C. Henry Kempe Center in Denver and Hawaii's Healthy Start Program have also worked with parents who were likely to become child abusers and with parents who had already abused their children. Having good child-care models and support during periods of stress helps parents develop more appropriate childrearing skills.

The attachment process and the early life of a child are the first steps to the child's total growth. They provide the necessary emotional trust that allow the child to continue to develop relationships.

Children Speak Out

Children are responding to the increasing violence in schools. Galinsky and Salmond (2002) of the Families and Work Institute of New York published a booklet containing the results of a study they conducted with the support of the Colorado Trust. One thousand twelve students in the fifth through twelfth grades in Colorado and 1,001 young people of a nationally representative group were interviewed. Thirty-five percent of those interviewed suggested that students in the schools need to "stop or change the smaller things that lead to more extreme violence" (p. 5). They suggested stopping the acts of emotional violence such as bullying, meanness, insults, gossiping, teasing, and making fun of each other. In addition, they responded that students need to be nice and friendly and get along with each other, and that the physical violence must stop—no more fighting, hitting, pushing, or shoving. Instead, there should be tolerance, respect, and an end to hatred and racial discrimination. The children suggested getting young people to "talk it out" with one another and having adults talk with them about alternatives and consequences.

Hospitalism

Bowlby (1982) also cited research that illustrates the need for concern for young children who must go to a hospital for an extended length of time or who must have institutional care. His research revealed that when children ages 15 to 30 months are placed in residential nurseries or hospitals in a strange environment away from the mother-figure and other familiar people, they commonly go through three stages: (a) protest, (b) despair, and (c) detachment. The phases do not start and stop abruptly, but may involve days or weeks of transition or shifts back and forth.

The first phase, protest, may last from a few hours to a week or more. The child reacts to the environment and may cry, display distress and anger, and seem to be looking for the missing parent. The second phase is a period of despair when the child withdraws, makes no demands, and appears to be in a state of mourning. The final stage is the detachment period, which may appear to be adjustment and recovery but is actually a withdrawal from the parent and an absence of the attachment behavior that is normal for the child's age. The child becomes more sociable, accepting food and toys from nurses, but withdraws from the former attachment figures. If separation continues, the child may not attach to anyone and may appear to care for no one. The child will become detached. Most hospital staff members are concerned about children's attachment to their parents and thus will encourage a parent to stay with the child or visit often.

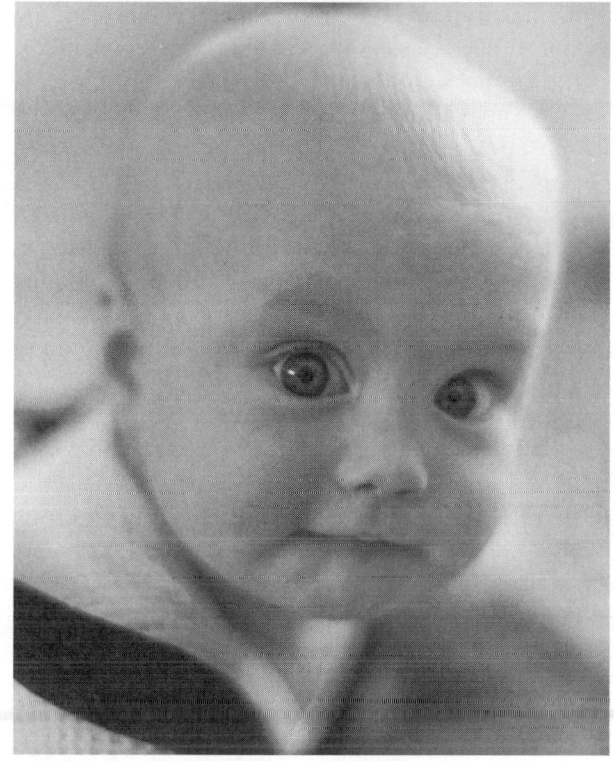
Eugenia Hepworth Berger

The brain of an infant develops at an exhilarating rate.

RESEARCH ON THE BRAIN

Theories on attachment and brain development emphasizing the importance of the first years of life have gained support from recent research (Brazelton & Greenspan, 2000; Carnegie Corporation of New York, 1994; Education Commission of the States, 1996; Greenspan, 2002; F. Newman, 1996; Shonkoff & Phillips, 2000; Shore, 1997; Zero to Three, 1998–2001). Scientists use ultrasound to study fetal brain development and neural functioning and scanning techniques such as magnetic resonance imaging (MRI) and positron emission tomography (PET) to learn how the brain works postnatally.

"Functional MRI provides information about changes in the volume, flow, or oxygenation of blood that occur as a person undertakes various tasks, including not only motor activities, such as squeezing a hand, but also cognitive tasks, such as speaking or solving a problem" (Shore, 1997, p. 8). Another noninvasive way of studying activity in the brain can be through the use of neuropsychological tools such as electroencephalogram and magnetic encephalography. The brain is studied indirectly by giving a child a task and observing which part of the brain are active and the child's level of activity in response to different stimuli (Shonkoff & Phillips, 2000).

A PET scan, employed when a child is thought to have neurological problems, requires an injection of a tracer chemical, making it an invasive procedure, which researchers generally avoid. Since PET scans cannot be considered noninvasive, the research comes from situations in which the child has needed the scan for medical reasons. By analyzing the results of PET scans researchers have furthered scientific knowledge: "Scientists can visualize not only the fine structures of the brain, but also the level of activity that is taking place in its various parts" (Shore, 1997, p. 9). Prior to these technological advances, brain research was accomplished only when operations were performed or people had strokes, and neither situation revealed what was happening in the brain at specific times.

Brain Development

The brain and spinal cord begin their developmental journey just a few days after conception. It develops in overlapping phases with the brain cells multiplying and migrating according to where they are needed. "Once nerve cells are formed and finished migrating they rapidly extend axons and dendrites and begin to form connections with each other, called synapses" (Shonkoff & Phillips, 2000, p. 186). The nerve cells are able to communicate with one another. The synapses are refined through maturation and pruning followed by myelination, a protective and supportive tissue surrounding the cells.

The brain does not develop one area and then the next in a straight, linear pattern. It develops in an integrated and overlapping fashion. Structures that control cognition (thinking), perception (sensing), and action (moving) develop at the same time, though not in lock-step fashion. They are linked by a network of interconnections, separate but functioning parallel to one another (Goldman-Rakic, 1996). "Genes and environment interact at every step of brain development, but they play very different roles. Generally speaking, genes are responsible for the basic wiring plan—for forming all of the cells (neurons) and general connections between different brain regions—while experience is responsible for the fine-tuning these connections, helping each child adapt to the particular environment (geographical, cultural, family, school, and peer-group) to which he belongs" (Zero to Three, 1998–2001, p. 1).

The development of the brain proceeds at an exhilarating rate. The number of neurons peaks before birth, and new neurons are produced throughout life though far less rapidly. Brain size also increases more gradually. A newborn's brain is only about one quarter the size of an adult's. It grows to 80 percent of adult size by 3 years of age and 90 percent by 5. Their growth is largely due to changes in individual neurons, which are structured like trees. Thus, each brain cell begins as a tiny sapling and only gradually sprouts its hundred of long, branching dendrites. Brain growth, measured either by weight or volume, is largely due to the growth of these dendrites, which serve as the receiving point of synaptic input from other neuron. Another way of measuring brain growth is speed processing. Newborns are considerably slower than adults—16 times less efficient—and the brain does not reach maximum size until about 15 years of age. Most of the increases in speed are due to myelin (Zero to Three, 1998–2001).

It is estimated that the number of synapses reaches adult level by age 2, and by age 3, a child's brain is two and one half times more active than the brain of an adult. For the first 3 years, production of synapses is greater than elimination. (Shore, 1997, p. 210). It is estimated that by age 3, the child's brain has a quadrillion synapses. The number holds steady for the first decade. After approximately 10 years, the synapses decline in density, and by late adolescence half of the synapses have been discarded and 500 trillion remain (Shore, 1997). Elimination varies related to the area of the brain. Huttenlocker researched the production of synapses and the pruning that reduces the amount of synapses to adult level. He estimated that various areas of the brain have different patterns of synapse development and pruning. The visual cortex production occurs about midway of the first year followed by a gradual reduction by the middle of the preschool period. The part of the brain responsible for language and hearing is similar but somewhat later. In the prefrontal area which contains higher level cognition the proliferation of synapses begins around the first year, but adult level is not reached until the middle to late adolescence (Shonkoff & Phillips, 2000).

A look at the development of vision illustrates one journey of growth. Infant vision is still developing when the child is born. At 1 month the infant has poor contrast sensitivity and relatively poor color recognition. By 2 months the baby can distinguish between many colors such as red, blue, and green. Their visual acuity and sensitivity to contrast has improved but is still about 20 times less developed than adults and has immature focus. By the third month dramatic changes help the infant see shapes clearer, although depth perception is not fully developed. Color vision is similar to that of an adult's color vision. The baby has also developed a sense of recognition so that when a parent picks up and holds the infant, the child is aware and recognizes the parent. By 6 months of age there is rapid improvement in eye development. The baby can focus at different distances as well as an adult can. Infants can tell differences in depth, and their motion detection continues to improve (Restak, 2001).

Wiring of the Brain

The proliferation of synapses occurs around the sixth month and reduces to adult amount later in early childhood. Experience is critical in the "wiring" of a child's brain. When a stimulus activates a neural path, the synapses receive and store a chemical signal. If synapses are used repeatedly, they are strengthened, reach a threshold level, and become permanent. If not used repeatedly, they are pruned and eliminated (Shore, 1997).

> In the first decade of life, a child's brain forms trillions of connections synapses. Axons hook up with dendrites, and chemicals called neurotransmitters facilitate the passage of impulses across the resulting synapses. Each individual neuron may be connected to as many as 15,000 other neurons, forming a network of neural pathways that is immensely complex. This elaborate network is sometimes referred to as the brain's "wiring" or "circuitry" (p. 17).

Early interactions directly affect the way the brain is wired. When an infant or young child consistently uses one eye over the use of the other eye, it will seriously damage the other eye. Visual experience is necessary for the visual cortex to become functional. If one eye gets all or most of the visual stimulation, the other eye does not develop properly. Patching the good eye in order to force the other eye to receive visual stimulation is often done to correct the problem.

It appears that if synapses are not used they are probably eliminated. "It is reasonably clear that building the organized neural systems that guide sensory and motor development involves the production of excess connections followed by some sort of pruning that leaves the system in a more precisely organized pattern (Shonkoff & Phillips, 2000, p. 189).

Eugenia Hepworth Berger

For children to achieve their potential, it is essential for families and educators to show support and caring.

INHERENT CAPACITIES: LANGUAGE DEVELOPMENT

Children are primed to acquire language and basic skills, but not to learn to read or solve complex arithmetic problems. Inherent capacities of children are speech, language, movement, and emotional development. Watching children as they learn to crawl and walk without being taught to do so makes it clear that certain developments are inherent. The ability to acquire language illustrates the inherent nature of language development.

Within the first 6 months, as infants listen to a caregiver's speech, their perceptual systems are configured to their native tongue. Kuhl (1996) described the process as "language magnets" that attract infants to their native language. "Babies are born with an ability to distinguish among all vowel sounds, but if a sound doesn't occur in the baby's language the ability to discern it will decline" (p. 13). For example, the Swedish language has 16 vowel sounds; English, 8 or 9; and Japanese, 5. "Babies learn to categorize their languages' specific vowel sounds simply by listening to their parents' speech. At 6 months, even before they can produce and understand words, infants' perceptual systems are configured to acquire their native languages" (pp. 13–14). This ability to hear and learn language at a young age illustrates why the prime time to teach children multiple languages is when they are infants and toddlers with caregivers who speak different languages.

Learning is part of memory. "Learning is what happens when information is presented; memory is the gradual process of manipulating that information into a form it will maintain over time, so that it can be consciously retrieved and applied" (LeDoux, 1996, pp. 16–17).

Interacting with Infants

Children learn and develop with their own developmental timetable, but they need interaction with their caregivers, mothers, fathers, and others to help in that development. When one realizes how rapidly the newborn infant's brain develops, a question emerges. How should the mother, father, and caregivers respond? Babies need holding, gentle touching, and eye contact. They need to hear a voice whether singing or talking to them while they are being dressed or fed. It is important to develop a secure and positive relationship with the infant through holding or rocking the baby in a loving and comforting manner. Talk together—respond to the baby's sounds. Babies try to imitate the sounds that they hear. Young children enjoy looking at colorful picture books and reading books with the caregiver. It is also important to respond to the infant's cues when they show that they are tired and need to disengage for a while. Engaging with the infant and young child enables the child to develop emotionally and intellectually. (Zero to Three, 2006; U.S. Department of Education, 2002). For a comprehensive description of the infant's development, go to zerotothree.org or call the organization, 1-800-899-4301.

Emotion and Intellect

Six levels of developing emotional and intellectual health in children are described by Greenspan (2002). At the first level, when a familiar caregiver touches and talks with the infant, the child responds with interest and pleasure. This helps the child develop a feeling of security and also helps the child organize his or her senses and motor responses. When children do not receive interaction from their caregiver, they withdraw and become apathetic and despondent.

The second level of development occurs by 4 months when infants begin to respond to a parent's smile. Emotional responses precede the child's motor ability. These emotional responses can be observed by watching a 4- or 5-month-old baby smile in response to another's smile. By 9 months there are early forms of communication and thinking. Two-way communication with the mother talking and the baby responding occurs.

The emotional abilities developed earlier become the building blocks in the third level at 12 to 18 months. The child has greater ability to problem solve. The fourth level focuses on the toddler who needs to increasingly develop the use of emotional cueing, more often referred to as affect cueing.

The fifth level includes symbols that have purpose and meaning such as seen in preteen play. The sixth level finds the child able to use cause-and-effect thinking, recognizing the ideas of someone else with his or her own intent and feelings. This level allows impulse control, judgment, and reality testing (Greenspan, 2002).

Effect of the Environment

The brain is affected by the environment. As the previous discussions have shown, children's brain development is not fixed at birth. The brain's development is a dynamic interplay between nature and nurture. The brain is affected by the nourishment, care, and stimulation it receives.

- How a brain develops hinges on a complex *interplay* between the *genes* you're born with and the *experiences* you have.
- *Early experiences* have *decisive impact* on the architecture of the brain and on the nature and extent of adult capacities.
- *Early interactions* don't just create a context; they *directly affect* the way the *brain is "wired."*
- Brain development is *nonlinear*. There are prime times for acquiring different kinds of knowledge and skills.
- By the time children reach age 3, their brains are twice as active as those of adults. Activity levels drop during adolescence. (Shore, 1997, p. 18)

See chapter 11 for a discussion of the negative effects of maltreatment on infants and children.

The dynamic relationship between nature and nurture shapes human development (Shore, 1997, p. 15). The brain is affected by care, nourishment, stimulation, and environmental conditions.

Even before birth the environment has an impact. Trauma and abuse can harm the brain and interfere with its development. Exposure to nicotine, alcohol, or other drugs affects the child before and after birth. It influences not only the child's general development but also the wiring of the brain.

The implication inherent in recognizing the important role of experiences in children's development is the need to promote nourishing, caring, responsive environments for children.

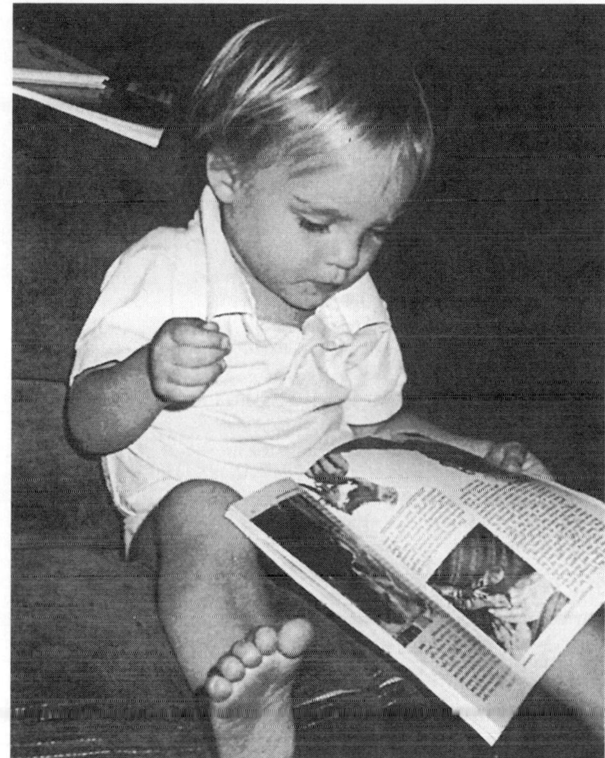

Eugenia Hepworth Berger

Infants and young children are primed for learning.

Early Experiences

Children are primed for learning during the early years. Their experiences in the first 3 years affect their growth and abilities for the rest of their childhood and as adults. "Early stimulation is essential to normal development" (L. Newman, 1996, p. 15). Early care and nurturing have an impact on how children develop and learn as well as on the state of their emotional development. Parents must be able to read their babies' cues and respond to infants' feelings, knowing when they need stimulation, when they need to be left alone, and when they need comforting. Nurturing is essential to a child's development and helps protect the child against stress (Education Commission of the States, 1996; Shore, 1997).

Coupled with a discussion of brain development and reading is the continuing need for emotional attachment. When the environment is nurturing and stimulating, it results in both neurological brain development and human attachment (Brazelton & Greenspan, 2000).

EARLY THEORIES CONCERNING INTELLECTUAL DEVELOPMENT

Theories developed by Hunt, Piaget, and Vygotsky were not based on neuroscientific evidence, yet much of their work supports the findings now available through brain scans.

Piaget and Vygotsky

Piaget (1896–1980) and Vygotsky (1896–1934) were both born in 1896, but Piaget's work began influencing American education in the late 1950s; Vygotsky's influence occurred later. Both believed that children construct their own understanding. Piaget emphasized that knowledge is constructed as a result of the child's interaction with physical objects, whereas Vygotsky focused on language and the child's interaction with adults. Piaget believed that children progressed through their intellectual developmental level independent of a cultural context; Vygotsky wrote that the culture in which a child lives influences the child's development. For Vygotsky, "competence is developed through language and through interaction with adults and other children in everyday problem-solving activities. Adults and capable peers provide a child with guidance and 'scaffolding,' as well as support calibrated to the child's abilities" (Kagan, Moore, & Bredekamp, 1995, p. 37). The major difference would be obvious while watching teachers interact with students. The Vygotsky theorist would aim at skills the child is developing, not those already developed. Scaffolding a child to an emerging concept would be appropriate in a Vygotsky classroom. "When kindergarten teachers help children to develop self-regulation skills, Vygotskians believe children will be able to learn cognitive skills and concepts effectively and be prepared for the learning activity that is the leading activity for the next stage of their development" (Bodrova & Leong, 2007, p. 162). A Piagetian, on the other hand, would be working with the child's current development.

Hunt

Hunt was one of the first theorists in the United States to raise questions concerning the development of intelligence in children. He recognized that children are not born with fixed intelligence. In *Intelligence and Experience* (1961), Hunt challenged the assumptions of fixed intelligence and predetermined development. The belief in fixed intelligence had far-reaching implications for education and childrearing. If IQ were fixed, intellectual growth could not be affected. The role of parents, therefore, had been to allow intellectual growth to unfold naturally toward its predetermined capacity. Hunt noted that, between 1915 and 1935, parents were even warned against playing with their infant, lest overstimulation interfere with the child's growth. Hunt's belief that IQ is *not* fixed led to a change in perception of the parental role from one of passive observation to one of facilitation.

Piaget

Hunt (1961) focused on the effects of experience on the development of intelligence. He thoroughly reviewed research on the development of intelligence in children. He devoted a large portion of his book to the works of Jean Piaget, a genetic epistemologist who wrote a prodigious number of books and articles on knowledge and cognitive development.

Piaget emphasized that development involves the interaction of the child with the environment. Piaget's book *To Understand Is to Invent* (1976) succinctly illustrates his basic concept of the importance of activity on the part of the learner—the need to act or operate on the environment in the process of developing knowledge. It is through this interaction with the environment that the child develops intelligence. Piaget saw this as an adaptive process that includes *assimilation* of experiences and data into the child's understanding of the world; *accommodation*, by which the child's thought processes are adjusted to fit the new information into the schemes or models already constructed; and finally *equilibrium*, which results from the adaptive process. This model of acquiring new knowledge was important to the cognitive theorists and affected the educator's curriculum because it emphasized the importance of experience to the developing child. A child without a rich environment was at a disadvantage.

Another aspect of Piagetian theory that reinforces his description of the developmental process of learning is his analysis of the developmental stages of the child's thought. In the process of acquiring intellect, children differ from adults in the way they form concepts. Children relate to experience at their own levels of understanding. Hunt (1961) described these three major stages—sensorimotor, preconceptual, and formal:*

SENSORIMOTOR

The first period of intellectual development, the sensorimotor, lasts from birth till the child is roughly between 18 months and 2 years old. The reflexive sensorimotor schemata are generalized, coordinated with each other, and differentiated to become the elementary operations of intelligence which begin to be internalized and which correspond to the problem-solving abilities of sub-human animals. During this period, the child creates through his continual adaptive accommodations and assimilations, in six stages, such operations as "intentions," "means-end" differentiations, and the interest in novelty (Piaget, 1936). On the side of constructing reality, the child also develops the beginnings of interiorized schemata, if not actual concepts, for such elements as the permanence of the object, space, causality, and time (Piaget, 1937).

CONCRETE

The second period of concrete operations in intellectual development, beginning when the child is about 18 months or 2 years old, lasts till he is 11 or 12 years old. It contains, first, a preconceptual phase during which symbols are constructed. This lasts to about 4 years of age, and during it the child's activity is dominated by symbolic play, which imitates and represents what he has seen others do, and by the learning of language. The accommodations forced by the variation in the models imitated along with the assimilations resulting from repetitions of the play-activities gradually create a store of central processes which symbolize the actions imitated (Piaget, 1945). As the images are established, the child acquires verbal signs for those which correspond to the collective system of signs comprising language. At this point the child comes under dual interaction with the environment, i.e., with the world of things and the world of people. The child's action-images greatly extend the scope of his mental operation beyond the range of immediate action and momentary perception, and they also speed up his mental activity, for the sensorimotor action is limited by the concrete sequence of perceptions and actions. This period contains, second, an intuitive phase. This is a phase of transition that lasts till the child is 7 or 8 years old. In the course of his manipulations and social communications, he is extending, differentiating, and combining his action-images and simultaneously correcting his intuitive impressions of reality (space, causality, and time). It contains, third, the phase of concrete operations. As the child interacts repeatedly with things and people, his central processes become more and more autonomous. Piaget (1945, 1947) speaks of his thought becoming "decentred" from perception and action. With greater autonomy of central processes come both differentiations and coordinations, or groups, of the action-images into systems which permit classifying, ordering in series, numbering. . . . The acquisition of these "concrete operations," . . . bring a distinctive change in the child's concrete conceptions of quantity, space, causality, and time.

FORMAL OPERATIONS

The third period of formal operations starts at about 11 and 12 years when the child begins to group or systematize his concrete operations (classifications, serial ordering, correspondences, etc.) and thereby also to consider all possible combinations in each case.

Piaget's theories clearly indicate that intellectual development is a process that commences in infancy and continues throughout childhood. The early years are important even though the development of intelligence in young children differs from that in older children.

Hunt's book kindled interest in Piaget as well as in the importance of experience for young children during the time when their parents are the prime caregivers and teachers.

The time was ripe for consideration of intervention and parent involvement. Equal educational opportunity was a high priority. The nation had been aroused by the Soviet Union's launching of *Sputnik* in 1957. Many people wondered if children were learning as well as they should, and there was concern that the United States was falling behind the Soviets in scientific discovery. It was hoped that an emphasis on early childhood

*From *Intelligence and Experience* (pp. 113–115), by J. M. Hunt, 1961. New York: John Wiley & Sons. Copyright 1961, John Wiley & Sons. Reprinted by permission of John Wiley & Sons, Inc.

Caring support helps the child develop cognitive competencies such as representational thought, program solving mathematical knowledge, social knowledge, and imagination.

Eugenia Hepworth Berger

education would help overcome learning and reading deficiencies. These considerations supported arguments for early intervention in education.

Appropriate Practices in Early Development

Elkind (1987a) warned against pressured learning in early childhood. He described the scores of intelligence tests at age 4 as predicting with an accuracy of 50 percent what a child's scores will be at age 17. This does not mean, however, that children at age 4 must have half of all the skills they will gain by age 17. Nor does it mean that "this calls for formal, teacher-directed learning. . . . We serve [children] best by providing an environment rich in materials to observe, explore, manipulate, talk, write, and think about" (p. 10). Neurological researchers and educators echo this warning (Brazelton & Greenspan, 2000; Carnegie Corporation of New York, 1994; Education Commission of the States, 1996; Greenspan, 2002; F. Newman, 1996; Shore, 1997).

Although research guides and describes the brain, there is both promise and peril in its use. "The peril rests in believing that these 'windows of opportunities' are so absolute that failing to take advantage of one will lead to unfavorable outcomes for children" (Puckett, Marshall, & Davis, 1999, p. 8). These authors see the promises, but warn that the focus should continue to be on the whole child with continuing best practices and that the research on the working of the brain not be misused. Yet, the brain research supports the understanding developed in earlier studies, and can, if used wisely and appropriately, strengthen childhood programs. "Much of what scholars and practitioners in child development and early childhood education have been proposing for years finally can enjoy the confirmation of scientific 'hard' data" (Puckett et al., p. 12).

IMPLICATIONS FOR PARENTS AND OTHER CAREGIVERS

1. *First, do no harm* (Shore, 1997). Parents must not subject their children, born or unborn, to tobacco, alcohol, or other drugs.

   Parents and other caregivers must not abuse their children emotionally, sexually, or physically.

   Parents and caregivers should follow a child's cues. Do not overstimulate, cause stress by expecting too much, or encourage overkill of the child's potential. Respond to the child's signals of interest and physical condition.

2. *Give your child quality time.* Tune in to your child's interests and needs. Echo the sounds of an infant; listen and respond to the toddler;

ensure language development by listening and talking with children at all ages.

Encourage inquisitive, discovery behavior. Provide objects that the child can manipulate safely. Provide language, music, movement, and enriching experiences. Continue to have an appropriate environment for older children. Use positive reinforcement and love to guide the child. Have behavior parameters for older children that allow them freedom within the boundaries.

3. *Share the knowledge.* Implications for childrearing challenge all parent educators. New parents should be encouraged to become actively involved with and responsive to their infants. To achieve these goals, all high schools should offer child development and family life courses that include information on attachment and intellectual development. Continuing or adult education programs should offer childrearing classes for parents who are no longer in school. Innumerable channels exist for disseminating information to a wide audience through health services, schools, television, and social agencies.

A more comprehensive discussion of these issues with suggestions for improving school–home collaboration is found in the following chapters.

DEVELOPMENTAL CONTINUITY AND DISCONTINUITY

Throughout childhood, many caregivers—teachers, child-care workers, doctors, and administrators—are involved with the child and family. Ideally, they can provide a stable environment where each of society's institutions contributes to the child's growth in an integrated and continuous approach. *Developmental continuity* is defined as a coherent whole or an uninterrupted succession of development. *Discontinuity* means a lack of continuity or logical sequence and refers to changes or disruptions in a child's development.

From a population that finds strength in its diversity, it is impossible to produce a curriculum that ensures perfect developmental continuity for all, but it is possible to work toward support systems that foster the child's continuous development. To provide continuity, the professional must look beyond the individual to the social system in which the child lives. Children whose parents come from a different country experience great differences between their home experience and school. It is particularly difficult for children from non-Western cultures who attend a Western school (Kellaghan, Sloane, Alvarez, & Bloom, 1993):

> Other groups of children who are likely to experience cultural discontinuities at school are minority and subordinate group children. Examples of such groups in the United States are blacks, American Indians, Chicanos, and Puerto Ricans. . . . The result is that, even though they may know a good deal about the culture of the dominant group, they do not accept it for themselves because of its negative associations in their history and experience. (pp. 22–23)

Change pervades all parents' lives. High mobility, a decrease in extended families living nearby, an increase in poverty, and the devastating effect of drugs are some concerns of today's parents. Parents, schools, child-care programs, recreation centers, and public agencies must work together to ensure continuity of provisions, discipline, and nurturing.

Parents can more easily adapt to new conditions, and children can handle change better, if they can depend on some stability in their environment. Families, child-care programs, and schools are the first line of defense in the provision of this stability. Those who work with children need to know what provisions, discipline, and nurturing the child is receiving from each of the other providers—family, schools, recreation facilities, churches, child-care providers, and public agencies. Only then can they offer the continuity that children need.

Lombardi (1992) proposes three elements to ensure continuity. The first is a developmentally appropriate curriculum that will fit the needs of the child. The second is parent involvement with the school at all levels of collaboration, such as support groups, parent education, volunteers, decision makers, and staff. The third requires community support and services offered by social agencies in collaboration with the school.

Concerns—Continuity and Responsiveness in School Environment—Developmentally Appropriate Curriculum

Early childhood education has been influenced over the past decades by research and practical experience concerning the best ways to meet the needs of children. *Developmentally Appropriate Practices in Early Childhood Programs* (Bredekamp & Copple, 1997) addressed and guided these concerns. Traditionally, early childhood has focused on the development of the "whole" child. In reaching the child, there has been a focus on responding to the child's interest. Historically, many early childhood practices in the United States have centered on the child's needs and emerging development similar to the beliefs of Italy's Reggio Emilia. Some of these practices are found in constructivist theory, the project method, Minnesota Early Literacy Training, the Carolina Abercedarian Project, and High/Scope.

Continuity and Responsiveness

First, it is the school's responsibility to create an environment that enables children to succeed while providing enough continuity so that the children feel as though they belong. This is important for both young children and adults. The school should be culture sensitive and respond positively to the language and culture of the home.

A curriculum that provides developmental continuity is based on the "whole" child, including social, emotional, physical, and intellectual development, and is adjusted so that children experience success. Artificial barriers are eliminated and the curriculum provides a smooth transition from preschool through the grades (Barbour & Seefeldt, 1993). "The curriculum is designed to provide learning experiences that are linked to children's prior knowledge, that flow in a natural progression across the preschool and primary grades toward more sophisticated and complex content, and that permit progress according to each child's rate and style of learning" (p. 11). If schools provide a positive environment with a developmentally appropriate curriculum, they will enable the child to be successful.

Is all continuity beneficial? Silvern (1988) and Kontos (1992) point out that continuity in and of itself is not always positive. Discontinuity is clearly appropriate for children from sterile or abusive homes. Rather than continue an oppressive situation, the school must provide a nurturing environment, including lunches and/or breakfasts when necessary.

If children come from culturally diverse homes, they will feel more comfortable if the school acknowledges cultural diversity and enriches the curriculum by incorporating aspects of their home cultures into the school setting. This will help children make the transition from home to school. If children come from an ideal home environment, they will benefit from an educational climate that incorporates the positive aspects of a nurturing

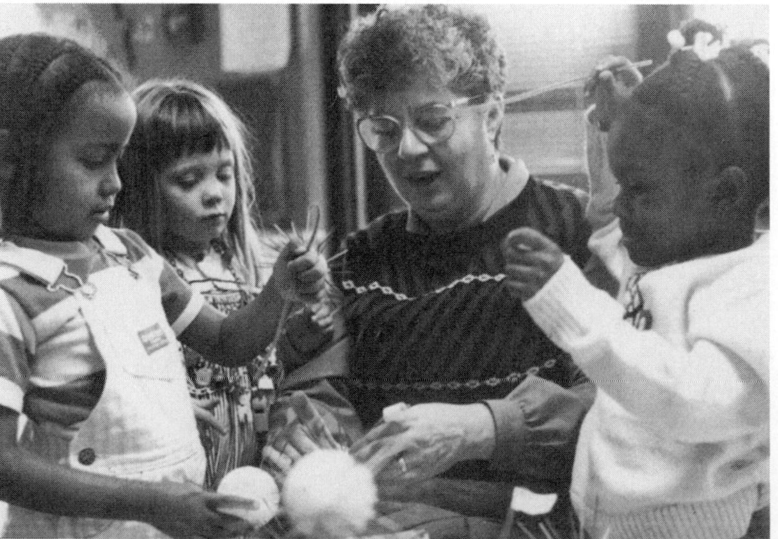

Eugenia Hepworth Berger

Families, child-care programs, and schools are the first line of defense in the provision of a stable environment.

home environment and parental involvement. In both instances school personnel need to become familiar with the children's home environment and parental involvement in order to determine how best to support children's development. Some preschool and early elementary school programs encourage and support home visits by teachers to achieve this outcome.

Elementary, middle, and secondary schools provide additional challenges. For primary school children, the change from one teacher to another may cause a change in continuity. Students in middle and secondary schools routinely have a variety of teachers, each with their own methods and personalities. Children at all ages have to make these transitions. Are they able to do it successfully? In addition, children whose first language is not English come to school as experienced users of another language.

> Children do not acquire language skills out of context or despite a cultural milieu; rather, language is embedded in that context. When the tasks, demands, and interactions of a young child's everyday experiences are similar to and continuous with those of the school, then the child's prior experiences facilitate success in school. But when the child's experiences differ from those encountered in school—when they are discontinuous—it is more difficult for children to apply previously acquired abilities in school and to acquire new ones. (Kagan et al., 1995, p. 34)

Ensuring continuity for children is an enormous challenge to families, schools, and communities and is an issue that will require continued efforts.

Developmentally Appropriate

What guides developmentally appropriate curriculum? Some of the qualities of a good program include the following:

1. Knowledge of child development and learning is used as a predictor and guide for the educational experiences, activities, and interactions.
2. The environment is safe and healthy, and at the same time it challenges the child to accomplish achievable goals.
3. Individual children will be taught in ways that recognize and support their strengths and abilities as well as their social, family, and cultural background.
4. Parent participation is encouraged in both assessment and educational activities. Families are a significant part of early childhood education (Berger, 1996b, 1998; Bredekamp & Copple, 1997).

Programs for young children should not be seen as either play oriented or academic. Whether in preschool or in a primary classroom, developmentally appropriate practice should respond to the natural curiosity of young children, reaffirm a sense of self, promote a positive disposition toward learning, and help build increasingly complex skills in the use of language, problem solving, and cooperation (Lombardi, 1992, p. 1).

Although children progress through similar stages of development as they move across the preschool and primary grades, this development is not equal or identical. Children learn best as they are allowed to construct knowledge and schools—whether child-care centers, preschools, or public schools—must provide environments that ensure that children's educational experiences will support their growth, development, and different modes of learning.

No Child Left Behind

The No Child Left Behind Act of 2001 was signed into law in 2002. Beginning in 2005 schools were required to test math and reading in grades 3 through 8 and at least once during grades 10 through 12. By 2007–2008 science was included in the testing. The goal of the program is to have all children successful in education.

NCLB has been criticized for stressing standardized achievement tests with time lines that do not allow enough time to achieve the goals and for lacking adequate funding to be successful (Epstein, 2005).

Many school districts, in an effort to improve test scores and reading ability, have added more and more rote academics to the young child's educational experience. This has to be done with great care to ensure the growth of the child, and not the failure. Many early childhood professionals feel that if the curriculum is not developmentally appropriate, the environment may cause many children to fail, unable to accomplish their tasks.

The recognition of parents as important to achievement of the goals was reflected in Section

118, which added greater emphasis on parent involvement (Epstein, 2005). The following parental involvement principles are included:

1. Multilevel leadership: Professional development that helps both the educators and the parents know and support the practices and goals of educator–parent partnerships.
2. Parent involvement as a component of both classroom and school: "Parental involvement as an essential component of school improvement, linked to the curriculum, instruction, assessments, and other aspects of school management" (pp. 179, 180).
3. Shared responsibility by both families and educators for children's education: Shared information about achievement tests, quality of schools and staff, options to change, and shared responsibility of parents for children's success. Epstein cites her six parent types of parent involvement, which are "parenting, communication, volunteering, learning at home, decision making, and collaborating with the community" (p. 180).
4. All families must be included: Information must be disseminated and communication needs to be in languages the parents can understand. Epstein cautions that engaging all parents needs increased research and programs to engage all parents.

Although preschools and the first two grades do not have to give NCLB tests to their students, children are tested in third grade, a part of early childhood education, and the pressure to pass the test results in third grade puts pressure on the earlier grades.

The U.S. Department of Education has developed a number of publications featuring the most effective practices in academic subjects. In addition there is an effort to involve parents. *No Child Left Behind: What Parents Need to Know* includes the following tips to help children succeed in school:

> 1. Encourage Your Child to Read. It's the single most important thing you can do to help your child succeed in school. Read aloud to your baby right from the start. Babies love to hear your voice, look at pictures, and touch the pages. As your child grows older, make reading together part of your daily routine.
> 2. Talk With Your Child. Take advantage of everyday opportunities to talk with your child, for example, as you walk or ride in a car together, have dinner or shop. Children who don't hear a lot of talk and who aren't encouraged to talk themselves often have problems learning to read, which can lead to other problems in school.
> 3. Monitor Homework. Have a special place for your child to study, set a regular time and check in once in a while to see if your child needs help.
> 4. Monitor TV Viewing and Video Game Playing. Set limits on the amount of time your child spends watching TV and playing video games. Spend time watching TV with your child and talking about what you are watching together.
> 5. Encourage Your Child to Use the Library. Go to your local library together, get a library card for your child, introduce your child to the children's librarian, and check out books for both of you.
> 6. Help Your Child Learn to Use the Internet Properly and Effectively. Help your child choose activities that build his or her knowledge, responsibility and independence, and monitor what your child does after school, in the evenings and on weekends.
> 7. Encourage Your Child to Be Responsible and to Work Independently. Help your child choose activities that build his or her knowledge, responsibility and independence, and monitor what your child does after school, in the evenings and on weekends.
> 8. Encourage Active Listening. Listen to your child's ideas and respond. This time of give-and-take at home is likely to help the child participate and be interested at school. (U.S. Department of Education, Office of Communications and Outreach. *No Child Left Behind: What Parents Need to Know*, Washington, DC, 2005, pp. 10, 11)

PROGRAMS ACROSS THE NATION

Many programs show what can be done to improve the lot of children. Some of these programs have been replicated, encouraging the adaptation of successful efforts. One highly successful program based on parental involvement is the Parents as Teachers (PAT) programs developed in Missouri. (Please refer to chapters 8 and 9 for a discussion of a variety of programs.)

In many cases, parents need to be empowered before they can participate fully with the schools. Both Comer (1997, 2004), who developed a program in New Haven, Connecticut, and Epstein (Epstein, 1996, 2001, 2002, 2005), who did research in Baltimore schools, found that meaningful activities in the schools helped parents become involved with schools in a productive way.

Comer's Program in New Haven

One school system that reached out to parents turned around poor parent participation so well that the program has been extended to more than 50 schools. Comer (1988, 1997, 2004; Comer, Haynes, Joyner, & Ben-Avie, 1996) and the Yale University Child Study Center started working with two schools in the New Haven school system in 1968. Initially, Comer found a misalignment between home and school. This was overcome by involving parents in restructuring the school. Parents were involved on three levels: as aides in the classroom, as members of governance and management teams, and as general participants in school activities. Parents' distrust of the school needed to be overcome, and this could happen only when they and the school cooperated.

Students were viewed as having unmet needs rather than as being uninterested, having behavior problems, or being bad children. These children were served by a mental health team that attempted to understand their anxiety and conduct. A Discovery Room encouraged children to regain an interest in learning, and a Crisis Room provided positive alternatives to children who had behavior problems. The greatest turnaround in intellectual development occurred when social skills were incorporated into the program. Parents were able to join in as partners, and the school became a force for increased self-esteem and desire for learning.

Comer's Leave No Child Behind

Comer's program has been replicated in schools across the nation. In a discussion of the reasons for its success, Comer (2004) recognized the need to involve parents and community with the schools. He sees schools as social organizations where the environment helps restore community and parent support for the child's development. "Too many parents do not understand that the way they rear their children greatly influences development and learning" (p. 23). When parents, schools, and community work together they help the child develop positively. In Comer's School Development program, six pathways are considered critical. These are psychological–emotional, ethical, cognitive–intellectual, physical, and linguistic (p. 74). If the school provides a caring and supportive environment, a sense of belonging develops and positive development occurs. Schools, with help from parents and community, could be the leading social organization in restoring a reasonable degree of parental and community support for youth development (p. 72).

The BrazeltonTouchpoints Center

Parents need friends and professionals who can support them as they raise their children. In *The Irreducible Needs of Children,* Brazelton and Greenspan (2000) list questions that parents, caregivers, and others can use to appraise the child's emotional and intellectual developmental level from 3 months to 12 years. The irreducible needs include the need for ongoing nurturing relationships, which encourage emotional and intellectual development. Children need the security of warm and dependable relationships with significant others. The experiences need to fit the individual differences of children especially in the early years. They need discipline and structure as well as structure with limits that enable them to channel aggression and solve problems. Their need for physical protection includes safety and regulation. The children need to live in a stable supportive environment and community with experiences that are appropriate to each child's stage of development. Children also need to live in a society that protects their future, including "The security of having physical needs met, . . . a philosophy that fosters ongoing human relations that preserve and support families and communities, and families, educational settings, and communities that help children become communicative reflective members of society" (pp. 181, 182).

Table 1.1 shows the development of infancy to 36 months. Early Child Care and Education (ECCE) promotes child-care providers as allies with parents in the positive development of children. "Based on Dr. T. Berry Brazelton's extensive clinical practice and research, the Touchpoint approach emphasizes the building of supportive alliance between parents and providers around key points in the development of young children" (Brazelton Touchpoint Center, 2005, p. 1). Brazelton developed the Touchpoints program,

TABLE 1.1 Each Touchpoint corresponds to a specific age and focus.

Touchpoint	Age	Focus
1	Prenatal	Imagining the baby, the parent, considering the realignment of relationships, and preparation
2	Newborn	Health, parental emotions, the baby's characteristics, and attachment
3	3 weeks	Parental exhaustion, feeding, individuality, and relationships
4	6–8 weeks	Sociability, parental self-confidence, and relationships
5	4 months	Attachment, interest in the world patterns of care, baby's demands, and father engagement
6	7 months	Motor abilities, feeding, sleeping, and object permanence
7	9 months	Mobility, social referencing, person permanence, and control
8	12 months	Independence, motor skills, learning, and irritability
9	15 months	Autonomy, play, motor skills, dependence, and language are the areas of discussion
10	18 months	The parents and staff are concerned with cognition, language, sense of self, and battles for control
11	24 months	Pretend play, language, autonomy, and motor skills
12	36 months	Imagination, fears and phobias, language, peer relations, and social understanding

Source: Based on *The Irreducible Needs of Children: What Every Child Must Have to Grow, Learn, and Flourish,* by T. B. Brazelton and S. I. Greenspan, 2000, Cambridge, MA: Perseus.

which covers the first 3 years of the child's development (see Table 1.1) to use as a guide. "Touchpoints are like a map of child development that can be identified and anticipated by parents and providers" (Brazelton & Greenspan, 2000, p. 184).

Brazelton and Greenspan (2002) also developed a three-level training program—individual level, community level, and faculty level—to implement the Touchpoints program. For more information, contact touchpoints@tch.harvard.edu. Each of the Touchpoints is based on child development, and the training is essential to perform the guidance and leadership that is necessary to accomplish the aim of Touchpoints.

Involvement of parents (or parent substitutes) in their children's care and education from infancy on is essential for the growth, education, and mental health of all children.

SUMMARY

Parenthood is an essential role in society. The support given by parents, interrelated with agencies—particularly the school—should be integrated and continuous. Programs that respond to parents' needs range from infancy, preschool, and primary and intermediate grades to secondary and young adult programs.

Five areas are considered: caring schools and communities, caring families, adequate and enriching child care, positive before- and after-school care, and collaboration among parents, teachers, and the community.

Families are social systems that impact and impart their history and culture. Systems vary, and they change related to the circumstances in the family.

Parents are their child's first educators and, as such, are responsible for the child's survival and for providing an environment that facilitates attachment and brain development in their child. All three responsibilities are extremely important for the child's subsequent development. The chapter discusses brain development from infancy through 3 years of age.

The renewed interest in parental involvement, which manifested itself in concern over the child's intellectual development, was reinforced by the writings of Piaget, Vygotsky, and Hunt.

Studies on human attachment, including those by Skeels, Spitz, Bowlby, Ainsworth, and Tizard, emphasized the significance of a nurturing and warm parent-figure.

Developmental continuity with a caring environment, an appropriate curriculum, and smooth transitions is important. Discontinuity is needed when the child comes from an abusive or sterile environment. The concepts of

No Child Left Behind are being incorporated into the regular early childhood education program. The chapter closes with the Touchpoint table, which covers the first 3 years of a child's development.

SUGGESTED CLASS ACTIVITIES AND DISCUSSIONS

1. Survey a preschool, elementary school, or middle or high school in your area to find out how the school involves parents.
2. Visit a child-care center or primary-grade classroom and survey the variety of families in a class. How many are two-parent families, single-parent families, or foster-parent families? What ways would you suggest that the school could work with families to provide caring environments for the children? How can families help the teacher enrich the caring classroom?
3. Describe how you can defend the importance of parents as teachers of their own children and parents as partners with the school.
4. Review the information on brain development. How would you relay this information to parents?
5. Look into the research on attachment. How are both parents important to the infant?
6. Give Piagetian-type tests to children at ages 3 months to 9 years. Focus on the way the children think and the differences in ability. Add a scaffolding activity (Vygotsky) with a child. Did the child respond positively to the help or did the child show discouragement?
7. Visit an infant center or nursery. Observe the extent to which children are actively involved in their environment. Are some more actively involved than others?
8. Discuss the importance of Hunt's book *Intelligence and Experience.* How has it helped change the belief in fixed IQ?
9. Invite a social worker to discuss the problems involved in foster home and institutional placements.
10. Visit a Head Start center. How are parents involved in the program?
11. Visit a preschool cooperative organized and run by parents—a parent cooperative. Talk with some parents about their responsibilities in the preschool program. Interview the director and discuss the roles parents play in the total program.
12. Investigate and analyze the goals of *Call for Action for American Education in the 21st Century.*
13. Visit a school and ask teachers and/or administrators about their thoughts and analysis of NCLB.

WEB SITES

Center on School, Family, and Community Partnerships
www.csos.jhu.edu/p2000/center.htm

Joyce Epstein, director of the Center on School, Family, and Community Partnerships at Johns Hopkins University, offers information on a variety of topics related to family–school partnerships.

Especially for Parents
www.ed.gov/parents/landing.jhtml

This site provides parents with information on homework, how to help their child in school, and a variety of resources including a monthly online TV show for parents.

North American Reggio Emilia Association: Schools of Reggio
http://www.reggioalliance.org/schools/

This site provides information on Reggio Emilia, listing and describing programs in the United States.

Parent Information Center
www.parentinformationcenter.org

Information on this site offers help in finding resources and in building strong family–school relationships.

U.S. Department of Education
www.ed.gov

Research and statistics, information on No Child Left Behind, and other relevant publications are available on this site.

2 Families and Communities: Overview, Trends, and Insights

The people strengthen themselves as they become a mosaic of diverse shapes and colors bound together in a supportive, cooperative whole, more complete combined than segregated.

Berger, 1998

All of our children ought to be allowed a stake in the enormous richness of America.

Kozol, 1991

In this chapter on the diversity of families you will find information that will help you examine the strengths and needs of families and enable you to do the following:

- Define the term *family*.
- Cite population changes in the United States.
- List and discuss social needs of families in the United States.
- Describe changes occurring in society that affect families.
- Discuss the greater involvement of fathers in rearing their children.
- Discuss poverty in the United States and the effect it has on families.
- Identify considerations that should be given to various types of family structures—for example, single-parent, recently divorced, and blended families.
- Identify strengths that allow families to have positive, constructive, and enabling lives.

FAMILIES

Families in the United States and around the world are living with change, but the essence of the family remains stable, with family members needing a permanent relationship on which they can count for consistency, understanding, and support.

The importance of the family unit in the socialization of children cannot be overstated. It is essential that children have a supportive interactive environment that provides a loving, caring relationship. Families can provide the necessary caring that enables children to develop emotionally, intellectually, and physically.

The family is the most stable component of society. Countries emerge and disintegrate, but the family remains—changed in form, but not in essential functions. If there is a bond among its members, with young children receiving nurturing as well as shelter and food, the family unit will survive. If the family is connected, reducing isolation and alienation, the family and those within it will flourish. As it bends with the winds of time, its basic structure and functions are amazingly secure. As the provider for and socializer of children, the family has no match. It might be a nuclear two-parent family, a single-parent family, or an extended family, but as long as it gives the

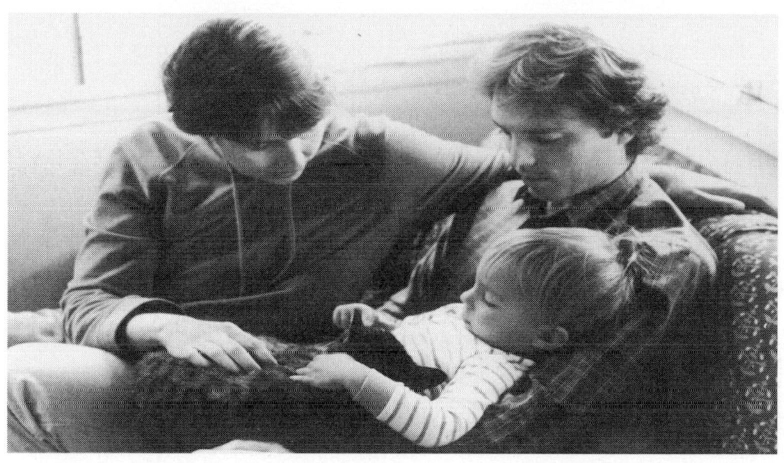

Eugenie Hepworth Berger

Families provide the necessary caring that enables children to develop emotionally, intellectually, and physically.

nurture and support needed by its members, it is a viable, working unit.

If you walked down a street in the United States today and knocked on a door, would you find a mother, father, and at least one child in the house with the mother working as a homemaker? Probably not. In 2006, only one in five families fit that description. What was once considered a typical family—two parents and children—is not the average family in the United States.

Survival of Society Depends upon Families

Infants cannot survive without being nurtured. The manner of nurturing infants varies within each subculture as well as across cultures. A child's well-being is affected by both the quality of care and the child's resiliency. One child may thrive whereas another may deteriorate in environments that seem identical. The child, the caregiver, and the environment intertwine in the childrearing process, making each child's experiences unique.

The essential commitment between caregiver and child emphasizes the significance of the parent's role. Other roles such as breadwinner, food gatherer, or food producer are necessary but can be filled in a variety of ways, depending on the culture. In child rearing, however, certain obligations and responsibilities transcend all groups of people. Every child must be fed, touched, and involved in communication—verbal and nonverbal—for it to grow and develop. Childrearing, whether by parents or alternative caregivers, requires a nurturing environment. Perhaps the ease with which most men and women become parents diminishes the realization that parenthood is an essential responsibility. Many have assumed that parenthood is a natural condition and that simply becoming a parent or caregiver transforms the new mother or father into a nurturing parent. As a result, society has not demanded that parents have the prerequisite knowledge that would ensure competence in one of the most important occupations—childrearing. Some basic understanding of child development on which to base parenting skills, allowing for individualization and cultural diversity, should be expected.

GROWTH OF A NATION

The first United States census in 1790 reported a population of only 4 million (3,939,326 to be exact). By the 1940s, the country had grown to a bustling, heterogeneous land of 131,409,119 (Kaplan, Van Valey, & Associates, 1980, p. 25). During this period, the nation changed from small and rural to large, industrial, and urban. From 1940 to 1990, about 118 million more inhabitants were added to the United States. The Bureau of the Census gave a total of 249,632,692 people in 1990, an increase of 10.21 percent over the 1980 census (U.S. Bureau of the Census, 1991a), 282,125.000 in 2000 (U. S. Census Bureau. 2004), and over 300 million in the fall of 2006 (U. S. Census Bureau. 2006).

The resident population increased dramatically during the 20th century (Figure 2.1). The population grew from 76 million in 1900 to 300 million in 2006. The resident population numbers differ

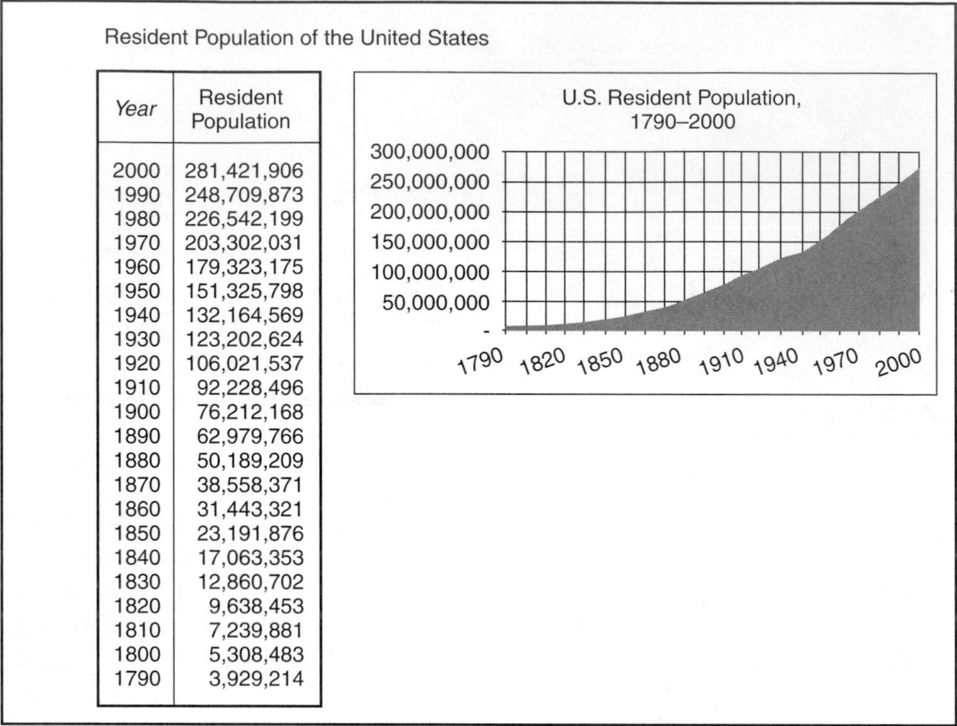
Resident Population of the United States

Year	Resident Population
2000	281,421,906
1990	248,709,873
1980	226,542,199
1970	203,302,031
1960	179,323,175
1950	151,325,798
1940	132,164,569
1930	123,202,624
1920	106,021,537
1910	92,228,496
1900	76,212,168
1890	62,979,766
1880	50,189,209
1870	38,558,371
1860	31,443,321
1850	23,191,876
1840	17,063,353
1830	12,860,702
1820	9,638,453
1810	7,239,881
1800	5,308,483
1790	3,929,214

FIGURE 2.1 The 20th century has seen a dramatic increase in resident population.

Source: From the U.S. Census Bureau, 2000. Retrieved February 14, 2003, from www.census.gov/dmd/www/resapport/states/unitedstates.pdf

slightly from the population numbers, but both figures dramatically illustrate the change.

In just 50 years, from 1940 to 1990, the population nearly doubled. Most of the increase was from the net increase of births over deaths rather than from immigration. Infant mortality was reduced, and people were living longer. During the 1970s the birth rate declined to about 13 million, but with the arrival of refugees and immigrants and the increased number of senior citizens, the population steadily grew. In the 1990s, as indicated previously on the information on population count, natural increase of birth over death accounted for 61 percent, but immigration was also high at 39 percent.

In the 1980s, children of the baby boom era—those born from 1946 to 1964—began having children. Many had delayed marriage and childrearing, and their children were in school in the 1990s. This increase in the number of children attending school continued into the first decade of the 21st century.

IMMIGRATION

Many of the children who attend schools in the United States come from families who migrated here. At the middle of the decade, in March 2005, the number of immigrants, legal and illegal combined, reached the highest number ever recorded. Between 2000 and March 2005, 7.9 million new immigrants had settled in the United States, with 3.7 million of these estimated to be illegal (Center for Immigration Studies, 2005). The states most affected by the increase in immigrants are California, 10 million (28 percent of the nation's total); New York, 11 percent; Texas, 10 percent; and Florida, 9 percent. Schools have a challenge and a responsibility to educate the 10.3 million school-aged immigrant children. They will find that one third of the families lack health insurance. Twenty-nine percent use at least one welfare program. Almost one out of four lives in poverty. "The low educational attainment of many

Eugenia Hepworth Berger

At the middle of the decade, in March 2005, the number of immigrants, legal and illegal, reached the highest ever recorded.

immigrants and resulting low wages are the primary reason so many live in poverty or lack health insurance, not their legal status or an unwillingness to work" (Center for Immigration Studies, 2005, p. 1).

POPULATION COUNT

The 2000 census surprised the demographers with the increase in population. Although the projection had been for 275 million people, the census identified 281,421,906 people in the United States. On July 1, 2001, there were 284,796,887 people, an increase of over 3 million, or 1.2 percent. This was partially due to a 61 percent natural increase of births over deaths; however, immigration (international migration) was responsible for 30 percent (U.S. Census Bureau, 2001b). The population is varied. Some are young; some are senior citizens; some are middle-aged; and any of these may be single, divorced, widowed, or married.

Table 2.1 is divided into two sections. The top section shows the total population, with the White category including Hispanics initially and then with the Hispanic population alone. The lower section gives the percentage of each category. Note that the total number of 282,125,000 reported in 2000 is slightly different from that reported in 2001 (see Table 2.1). Whites (Hispanics and other Whites)

TABLE 2.1 Projected population of the United States by race and Hispanic origin.

Population or percent and race or Hispanic origin	2000	2010	2020	2030	2040	2050
Population total	282,125	308,936	335,805	363,584	391,946	419,854
White alone	228,548	244,995	260,629	275,731	289,690	302,626
Black alone	35,818	40,454	45,365	50,442	55,876	61,361
Asian alone	10,684	14,241	17,988	22,580	27,992	33,430
All other races	7,075	9,246	11,822	14,831	18,388	22,437
Hispanic (of any race)	35,622	47,756	59,756	73,055	87,585	102,560
White alone, not Hispanic	195,729	201,112	205,936	209,176	210,331	210,283
Percentage of total population	100.0	100.0	100.0	100.0	100.0	100.0
White alone	81.0	79.3	77.6	75.8	73.9	72.1
Black alone	12.7	13.1	13.5	13.9	14.3	14.6
Asian alone	3.8	4.6	5.4	6.2	7.1	8.0
All other races	2.5	3.0	3.5	4.1	4.7	5.3
Hispanic (of any race)	12.6	15.5	17.8	20.1	22.3	24.4
White alone, not Hispanic	69.4	65.1	61.3	57.5	53.7	50.1

"All other races" includes American Indian and Alaska Native alone, Native Hawaiian and Other Pacific Islander alone, and Two or more races

Source: U.S. Census Bureau, 2004, "U.S. Interim Projections by Age, Sex, Race, and Hispanic Origin," www.census.gov/ipc/www/usinterimproj Internet Release Date: March 18, 2004.

accounted for 228,548,000, or 81 percent of the population. Of this number, 12.6 percent, or 35,622,000, were Hispanic. Black alone had 35,818,000, or 12.7 percent, and Asians had 10,684,000, or 3.8 percent of the population. All other races accounted for 2.5 percent, or 10,684,000 persons. As the nation progresses through the years, the projection of percentage of Whites gradually falls in comparison with the other groups. For example, in 2030, although the number of Whites is expected to increase, their proportion is experted to fall to 75.8 percent. The U.S. population will become more diverse.

DEFINITIONS OF RACE

The categories of race and Hispanic origin were changed in the 2000 census to include persons who view themselves as more than one race. In addition, Pacific Islanders were removed from the Asian category and joined with Native Hawaiians.

Six categories of persons from one race alone and a new category for those from two or more races were included. The addition of a category for those with multiracial identification was important. There are 15 separate response categories and 3 areas that allow the respondents to write in their choice of race. These categories follow five questions that classify persons of Spanish/Hispanic/Latino race. Figure 2.2 illustrates how the 2000 census offered the respondents opportunities to describe how they defined their racial background.

The categories of race and Hispanic/Latino status in Table 2.2 are defined as follows:

American Indian and Alaska Native. A person having origins in any of the original peoples of North America, who maintains cultural

→ Note: Please answer BOTH Questions 5 and 6

5. Is this person Spanish/Hispanic/Latino? *Mark* ☒ *the "No" box if not Spanish/Hispanic/Latino*

☐ No, not Spanish/Hispanic/Latino ☐ Yes, Puerto Rican

☐ Yes, Mexican, Mexican Am., Chicano ☐ Yes, Cuban

☐ Yes, other Spanish/Hispanic/Latino—*Print group*

6. What is this person's race? *Mark* ☒ *one or more races to indicate what this person considers himself/herself to be.*

☐ White

☐ Black, African Am., or Negro

☐ American Indian or Alaska Native–*Print name of enrolled or principal tribe.*

☐ Asian Indian ☐ Japanese ☐ Native Hawaiian

☐ Chinese ☐ Korean ☐ Guamanian or Chamorro

☐ Filipino ☐ Vietnamese ☐ Samoan

☐ Other Asian—*Print race* ☐ Other Pacific Islander–*Print race*

☐ Some other Race

FIGURE 2.2 2000 Census questions on race and Hispanic origin.

Source: From Census 2000, by the U.S. Census Bureau, retrieved August 21, 2002, from www.census.gov/dnd/www/pdf/do2p

TABLE 2.2 Households, families, subfamilies, and married couples: 1980 to 2003.

Type of unit	1980	1990	1995	2000	2001	2002	2003	Percent change 1980–1990	Percent change 1990–2000	Percent change 2000–2003
Households	80,776	93,347	98,990	104,705	108,209	109,297	111,278	16	12	6
Average size	2.76	2.63	2.65	2.62	2.58	2.58	2.57	(X)	(X)	(X)
Family households	59,550	66,090	69,305	72,025	73,767	74,329	75,596	11	9	5
Married couple	49,112	52,317	53,858	55,311	56,592	56,747	57,320	7	6	4
Male householder[1]	1,733	2,884	3,226	4,028	4,275	4,438	4,656	66	40	16
Female householder[1]	8,705	10,890	12,220	12,687	12,900	13,143	13,620	25	17	7
Nonfamily households	21,226	27,257	29,686	32,680	34,442	34,969	35,682	28	20	9
Male householder	8,807	11,606	13,190	14,641	15,345	15,579	16,020	32	26	9
Female householder	12,419	15,651	16,496	18,039	19,097	19,390	19,662	26	15	9
One person	18,296	22,999	24,732	26,724	28,207	28,775	29,431	26	16	10
Families	59,550	66,090	69,305	72,025	73,767	74,329	75,596	11	9	5
Average size	3.29	3.17	3.19	3.17	3.14	3.15	3.13	(X)	(X)	(X)
With own children[2]	31,022	32,289	34,296	34,605	35,355	35,705	35,968	4	7	4
Without own children[2]	28,528	33,801	35,009	37,420	38,412	38,623	39,628	18	11	6
Married couple	49,112	52,317	53,858	55,311	56,592	56,747	57,320	7	6	4
With own children[2]	24,961	24,537	25,241	25,248	25,980	25,792	25,914	−2	3	3
Without own children[2]	24,151	27,780	28,617	30,062	30,612	30,955	31,406	15	8	4
Male householder[1]	1,733	2,884	3,226	4,028	4,275	4,438	4,656	66	40	16
With own children[2]	616	1,153	1,440	1,786	1,836	1,903	1,915	87	55	7
Without own children[2]	1,117	1,731	1,786	2,242	2,438	2,535	2,741	55	30	22
Female householder[1]	8,705	10,890	12,220	12,687	12,900	13,143	13,620	25	17	7
With own children[2]	5,445	6,599	7,615	7,571	7,538	8,010	8,139	21	15	8
Without own children[2]	3,261	4,290	4,606	5,116	5,362	5,133	5,481	32	19	7
Unrelated subfamilies	360	534	674	571	568	474	525	48	7	−8
Married couple	20	68	64	37	44	43	34	(B)	(B)	(B)
Male reference persons[1]	36	45	59	57	70	59	84	(B)	(B)	(B)
Female reference persons[1]	304	421	550	477	455	371	407	39	13	−15
Related subfamilies	1,150	2,403	2,878	2,984	3,118	2,986	3,089	109	24	4
Married couple	582	871	1,015	1,149	1,202	1,129	1,232	50	32	7
Father-child[1]	54	153	195	201	251	269	260	(B)	31	29
Mother-child[1]	512	1,378	1,668	1,634	1,665	1,588	1,596	169	19	−2
Married couples	49,714	53,256	54,937	56,497	57,838	57,919	58,586	7	6	4
With own household	49,112	52,317	53,858	55,311	56,592	56,747	57,320	7	6	4
Without own household	602	939	1,079	1,186	1,246	1,172	1,266	56	26	7
Percent without	1.2	1.8	2.0	2.1	2.2	2.0	2.2	(X)	(X)	(X)

[In thousands, except as indicated (80,776 represents 80,776,000). As of March. Excludes members of Armed Forces except those living off post or with their families on post. Beginning 2001 population controls based on Census 2000 and an expanded sample of households. Based on Current Population Survey. Minus sign (−) indicates decrease.]

B Not shown; base less than 75,000. X Not applicable. [1] No spouse present. [2] Under 18 years old.

Source: U.S. Census Bureau, Current Population Reports, P20-547 and earlier reports; and unpublished data.

identification through tribal affiliation or community recognition.

Asian. A person having origins in any of the original peoples of the Far East, Southeast Asia, and the Indian subcontinent. This area includes, for example, China, India, Japan, Korea, and the Philippine Islands.

Black or African American. A person having origins in any of the Black racial groups of Africa.

Hispanic or Latino. A person of Mexican, Puerto Rican, Cuban, Central or South American, or other Spanish culture or origin, regardless of race.

White. A person having origins in any of the original peoples of Europe, North Africa, or the Middle East.

Some other race. A person who identifies with a race not listed. (Day, 1996a, p. 31; U.S. Census Bureau, 2000)

Those who chose more than one race were referred to as two or more races or more than one race (see Figure 2.2). "The concept of race the Census Bureau uses reflects self-identification by respondents; that is the individual's perception of his/her racial identity. The concept is not intended to reflect any biological or anthropological definition" (U.S. Department of Commerce, 2000).

HOUSEHOLDS

Parents who collaborate with teachers and child-care workers are a varied group. Some belong to two-parent families; others are never-married single parents. Some may be same-gender couples, divorced single parents, or single parents whose spouses have died. Most parents who divorce soon remarry, so blended or reconstituted families may involve joint custody, stepparents, stepbrothers and stepsisters, half-brothers and half-sisters, and brothers and sisters.

Census reports include two groups of household types: family household and nonfamily household. The *family household* is one in which the householder and at least one other person are related, categorized as married couple, female with no spouse present, or male with no spouse present. The *nonfamily household* may have only one person or may have others, but none are related. It is categorized as either female nonfamily or male nonfamily.

The number of both types, family and nonfamily, of households cited in 2003 was 111,278,000 with family household accounting for 75,596,000 (74 percent). Married couples live in 57,320,000 houses; male householders in 4,656,000, and female householders in 13,620,000 (see Table 3.2). Of both of these householders, 35,968,000 were families who lived with their own children. Close to 26 million of these were married couples, 4,656,000 were male householders, and 8,139,000 female householders. The average size of a family in 2003 was 3.13 persons, slightly lower than the 3.29 persons recorded in 1980. Families with no children account for 39,628,000 householders. Of these, there were 31,406,000 married couples, 2,741,000 male householders, and 5,481,000 female householders (U.S. Census Bureau, 2003).

Household Composition

Figure 2.3 illustrates family composition in 2000. Almost one fourth, 24.1 percent, were married couples with children, and 8.9 percent were other families with children, for a total of 33 percent of families with children. Just over one fourth, 25.5 percent, were nonfamily householders who lived alone. Seven percent were other families without children. The largest group was married couples without children (28.7 percent).

Roles of Parents

Although their forms vary, families provide similar functions. It is expected that the roles within families provide for the needs of the children and that parents have rights and responsibilities. Swick (1986) described these roles as "(1) nurturing, (2) guiding, (3) problem solving, and (4) modeling" (p. 72). Cataldo (1987) described similar roles providing "care, nurturance, and protection"; socialization; "monitoring the child's development as a learner"; and supporting "each youngster's growth into a well-rounded, emotionally healthy person" (p. 28).

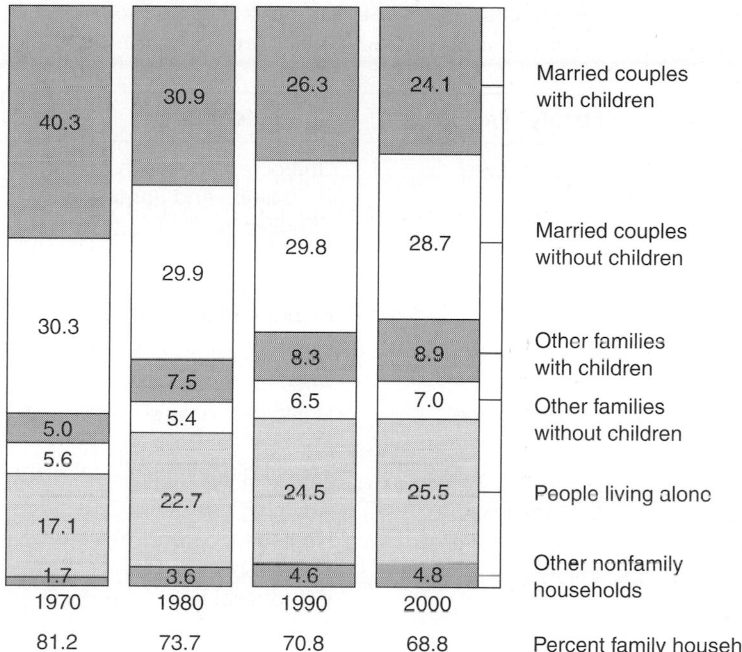

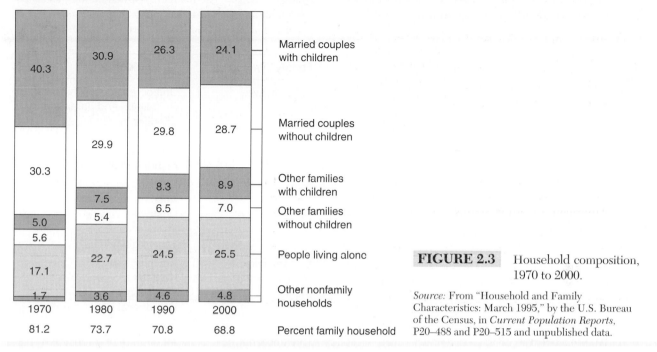

FIGURE 2.3 Household composition, 1970 to 2000.

Source: From "Household and Family Characteristics: March 1995," by the U.S. Bureau of the Census, in *Current Population Reports*, P20–488 and P20–515 and unpublished data.

The first function of a family is to nurture and supply nutrition, protection, and shelter. Families provide interaction, love, and support. The family has a right to rear the child as it sees fit and a responsibility to see that the child receives adequate care.

Parents socialize their children to follow the norms of society in accordance with the parents' cultural beliefs. Socialization varies, depending on the culture. Families in some cultures demand respect toward their elders; others socialize their children in a democratic style that depends on mutual respect. There are also variations within cultures that often result from how the parents were raised. In the rearing process, most children learn and internalize their parents' value system.

Parents also have the obligation to see that the child is educated both at home and at school. In some families, education is not recognized as a function of the family, but learning or lack of learning is very much a part of any family system. Parents are the first educators of their children, so the child's ability to function well in school rests to a great extent on the home's nurturance and environment.

Therapists have come to recognize that it is a mistake to send an emotionally disturbed child back into the same ecosystem in which the disturbance developed. Therapists must work with the family as well as the child. Therapists also need to understand the larger community in which the family lives. How does the larger community affect the family? Are there cultural norms that influence their communication skills? Is the family under stress? Is under- or unemployment a factor? Only when therapists arrive at an understanding of the concerns and culture are they able to guide the family and child toward healthier relationships. Working with children at school is similar. Teachers need to know their school neighborhood and the issues and problems that parents face to understand the children under their charge.

Stages in Family Life

In addition to recognizing the many family forms, professionals find it helpful to view parenthood as divided into stages. Sometimes families are in several stages simultaneously, such as families with a large number of children whose births are spread over 20 or more years. The stages developed by Galinsky (1987) divide parenthood into six levels of development, much like the child's stages of development. The first stage, the *image making* stage, takes place before the birth of a child. Images are formed and preparation is made for the birth. The second stage is the *nurturing* period, when attachment develops during infancy. In the third period, the *authority* stage, families help their child understand the norms of the society. During the fourth stage, from preschool to adolescence, parents offer *guidance* and children learn to interpret their social reality. The *interdependent* years, the teens, make up the fifth stage of family development. When the children are ready to go out into the world for themselves, parents enter their last stage: *departure*. During each of these stages, parents provide the guidance necessary for that stage of development.

Parenting Styles

Ideally, families provide a support system that allows the child to grow into a healthy, responsible person. Parenting styles (some of which are more effective than others) are often identified as *authoritative, authoritarian,* or *laissez-faire* (see Table 2.3).

Each of these types has different ways of handling issues and concerns within the family. In addition, depending on the circumstance, responses in families may vary. The style recommended by parent educators is the authoritative, democratic style, because it is thought that children raised under that style will achieve, be dependable and responsible, and feel good about themselves.

Children raised with authoritative parents will be allowed to analyze and recognize the issues confronting them. Guidance will be available but will not be dictated. Children will learn to make decisions. Working and talking together, they will be able to learn why angry, quick decisions do not work.

Children with authoritarian parents are expected to mind their parents without any question about what precipitated the issue. The children do not get an opportunity to resolve an issue or learn from actions except to learn that punishment will follow no matter what the situation. They receive little training in decision making. Children may learn to mind, but they also learn to avoid being caught and, perhaps, to lie when they are.

TABLE 2.3 The manner in which families socialize their children varies. Three major theories, authoritative, authoritarian, and laissez-faire, include a multitude of styles.

Family Type	Characteristics
Authoritative	Democratic decision making Guidelines and parameters Effective communication Problem solving Self-discipline and responsibility
Authoritarian (might be overprotective)	Demanding parent Absolute rules Restrictive environment Punitive control Strong guidelines
Laissez-faire (might be very indulgent)	Anything goes Neglectful parent No one cares Withdrawal from parental responsibilities
Dysfunctional (includes authoritative, authoritarian, and laissez-faire families)	Alcohol- or drug-addicted Neurotic or mentally ill Abusive

Children of laissez-faire rearing often think that their parents are not interested in them. The children may be depressed, act out, or take risks because they do not feel their parents care. In addition, they get no guidance to help them make decisions. Too much freedom makes it possible for children to think that they do not matter.

Eating meals together, at dinner or breakfast, with open discussion is important. It helps families know each other and bond. In addition, a weekly family meeting with shared leadership (each person taking a turn) helps families understand one another and make satisfactory and fair decisions. It can be a time when children and parents can share their feelings, help make decisions, and receive encouragement. See "Building Family Strengths" in chapter 5 for more discussion of strong families.

Two subtypes do not fit into the three major types. The overprotective parent can often become authoritarian; the indulgent parent may not guide the child. Dysfunctional families—including those that are abusive, addicted to drugs or alcohol, mentally ill, or neurotic—may fluctuate between authoritarian to the point of abuse, and laissez-faire, with abdication of parental roles. One of the most difficult issues that children face is the inconsistency in dysfunctional families. Dependable families in which children understand the guidelines and can communicate with and rely on their parents are extremely important to children's mental health.

If the types of families are multiplied by the number of configurations of families (single, two-parent, and blended) and the individual personality differences of each child and parent, it becomes apparent that to work effectively with parents, teachers and child-care workers must individualize their suggestions and responses.

Children who arrive at the school's door represent these many varieties of families. Nearly 15 percent are born to unmarried mothers, half of whom are teenagers. It is estimated that 90 percent of unwed women keep their children and raise them alone or with help from their families. This results in many children being raised by grandparents or aunts and uncles. This "skip-generation parenting" results in children growing up in an extended family with cousins and a variety of interrelationships. The National Center for Lesbian Rights estimates that 2 million children are being raised by lesbian or gay mothers or fathers. "Most gay couples . . . describe themselves and their families as conventional in most ways, even boring" (Johnston, 1990, p. 5).

FAMILY FORMS

Traditional two-parent families, unmarried couples, skip-generation households, widowed parents, single-parent families, gay and lesbian couples, and singles make up a vast array of family forms (Johnston, 1990). "To judge one kind of family structure as 'right' and another as 'wrong' creates a distance" (p. 7) between the parents and the school and makes it difficult if not impossible to create the kind of working relationship essential for parent–school collaboration.

Some commonalty stands out. Both men and women questioned in polls placed importance on the family and were willing to adapt and make sacrifices to keep the family together. Keep in mind that parents often view their child as an extension of themselves. If parents are approached in a way that lets them know the teacher wants the child to succeed as much as the parents do, a true collaboration can take place.

The structure, stage of family development, family size, and ages and gender of the children all figure in to the makeup of each unique family. The families described here are representative of the many types of families. Add to the list with your own descriptions.

Catherine Smith

Traditional two-parent families, unmarried couples, single parents, skip-generation households, singles, gay and lesbian couples, and widowed parents make up the vast array of family forms.

Single-Parent Family

Tina is a young divorced mother with one son, Tommy, age 3. They live with Tina's parents. In addition to working part time at a department store, Tina takes 6 hours of classes at the community college. Each morning she prepares breakfast for Tommy and herself, bundles him into his coat during cold weather, hopes that her aging automobile will start, and heads into her long day. First, she deposits Tommy with her sister, who runs a family child-care home. She feels fortunate to have a relative who enjoys children to care for Tommy. He has been anxious ever since his father left, and the security of spending his days at Aunt Georgia's helps compensate for his loss.

Tina figures that with family help and her part-time college work she will be able to graduate in a little more than 2 years, just about the time Tommy will start school. Her ex-husband, Ted, does not send support money consistently, and Tina knows her parents can help only so much. As she works as a clerk in the department store, she dreams of the time when she will make enough to give Tommy the home and opportunities he needs.

Unwed Single Teenage Mother

As Sherrill thinks back, she can't remember when she didn't want a baby. "When I have a baby," she thought, "I'll be treated like an adult by my mother, and I'll also have a baby all my own who will love me." At 3 months, though, Gerald, has already become a real handful.

Sherrill turned 15 yesterday, and instead of being able to bum around with her friends, she had to take care of Gerald. "If only my mother hadn't had to work," Sherrill complained, "I would have had a couple of hours between feedings just to get out. I never dreamed a baby would be so demanding. What makes him cry so much?"

The school down the street offers a program for teen mothers and their infants. Sherrill is on the waiting list and plans to enroll at the end of summer. "I never thought I'd want to go back to school," she says, "but they help out by caring for my baby while I'm in class and my mother says that I need to be able to make a living for Gerald. Temporary Assistance to Needy Families (TANF) will help me for only 24 months. I really don't like school, but I guess I'd better go. If only Gerald would start being more fun."

Two-Parent Family Experiencing Homelessness

When Barbara married Jed, the future looked good. Young, handsome, and willing to work, Jed thought his job at the plant would last forever. Who would have expected the layoffs? Jed's father worked at the plant for 25 years before he retired. Now Jed and Barbara, along with Jessie, age 2, and Bob, age 6, are moving west in hopes of finding work.

It's hard to live out of a car. Barbara worries about Bob because he is missing first grade. She and Jed put him in school whenever they are in a city for any length of time, but schools want his permanent address. It embarrasses Barbara to say their family is homeless, so she finds out the name of a street near the school and pretends they live there. Bob doesn't like school anyway. He says the children make fun of him and the teacher gives him seatwork that he doesn't understand.

Jed feels as if he has failed as a father and provider for his family. If he could just find a good job. Minimum wage doesn't give him enough to pay for rent, let alone buy clothing and food. Last month they spent time at a church-run mission for the homeless. Jed was glad that they were in a town far from home so that none of his old school friends recognized him and Barbara. Maybe a good factory job will turn up.

Two-Income Family

"Joe, the alarm. It's your turn to get up and start breakfast." Maria turns over to get 10 more minutes of sleep before the drive to school. Each day Maria teaches 28 second graders in the adjoining school district. Joe teaches mathematics at the local middle school. It works exceedingly well for them. The children, Karen and Jaime, stay with a neighbor until it is time for them to walk to school. Joe and Maria take turns dashing home early enough in the afternoon to supervise the children after school.

At times, the stress of work and the demanding days get to Joe and Maria. Some days their schedules do not blend, and they scurry to find someone to care for the children after school. Karen and Jaime occasionally have been latchkey children, providing for themselves. Neither Joe nor Maria want their children to be left on their own. They see too many children in their classrooms in similar situations who feel as if no one cares. Joe tries to be a nurturing father who helps with the home, but he relies on Maria to clean, shop, and cook.

Summers are the best time for the family. Joe works for a summer camp, but Maria is able to spend more time at home, enjoying the children and organizing for the coming year. Periodically she thinks about how much easier it would be for her to quit teaching and be a full-time homemaker, but then reality sets in. They could not make the house payments if they were not a two-income family—and a family needs a home.

GREATER AMOUNT OF EDUCATION FOR PARENTS

Today, many workers need more education because of the large number of technical jobs. These better educated parents are generally comfortable in their dealings with the school. In 1940, only 36 percent of men and 40 percent of women (24 to 29 years old) had completed high school, and only 7 percent of men and 5 percent of women had completed college (Howe, 1988). By 1999, 83 percent of both men and women had completed high school. Whites had the highest percentage with 84.3 percent; Blacks, 77 percent; Asian and Pacific Islanders, 64.7 percent; and Hispanics, 56 percent. Those 25 years and older who had completed 4 years of college included 27.5 percent of men and 23.1 percent of women. Of these, 25.9 percent were White, 15.49 percent were Black, 42.4 percent were Asian and Pacific Islander, and 10.9 percent were Hispanic (U.S. Department of Commerce, 2000).

Parents who have not had educational opportunities are often very supportive of the schools and want an education for their children, but some feel uncomfortable with teachers and principals. Parents who have had to quit school or who had an unpleasant experience in their own schooling may fear the schools and find it difficult to become a partner with the professional. The school must reach out to these reluctant parents.

CHILD COUNT AND CHILD WELFARE

The number of children in the United States in 2000 was 72,293,812, a 14 percent increase since 1990 (Annie E. Casey Foundation, 2001). Table 2.4 illustrates the number of children according to race. Sixty-one percent, or 44 million, are White; 15 percent, or 10.6 million, are Black; 17 percent, or 12.3 million, are Hispanic, 3 percent, or 2.5 million, are Asian/Pacific Islander; and 1 percent, or 686,000, are American Indian/Alaska Native. Three percent, or almost 2 million, chose more than one race, and

TABLE 2.4 Number of children by race and Hispanic origin: 2000 Census.

	Number	Percent
Total population under age 18	72,293,812	100%
One race only*	58,045,361	80.3%
White*	44,027,087	60.9%
Black or African American*	10,610,264	14.7%
American Indian or Alaska Native*	685,911	0.9%
Asian*	2,420,274	3.3%
Native Hawaiian or other Pacific Islander*	109,499	0.2%
Some other race*	192,326	0.3%
More than one race*	1,906,192	2.6%
Hispanic	12,342,259	17.1%

*Non-Hispanic races are marked with asterisks.

Source: From Census 2000 data, in the *KIDS COUNT Data Book* (p. 24), by the Annie E. Casey Foundation, 2001.

192,326 chose some other race (Annie E. Casey Foundation, 2001).

These figures illustrate the "largest increase in the number of children living in the United States since the 1950s, foreshadowing major new challenges to the nation's schools and social services (Annie E. Casey Foundation, 2001). Improvements in the last decade include decreases in infant mortality, teenage and children's death rates, and the high school dropout rate. Poverty rates declined to 16.9 percent in 2000 from a high of 22.7 percent in 1992. Births to teenagers declined from 37 percent in 1990 to 25 percent in 2003 (Annie E. Casey Foundation, 2004). However, *KIDS COUNT* found that 10 million children have employed parents who struggle to make ends meet. Infant mortality (deaths per 1,000 live births) rates were reduced from 16.1 percent in 1975 to 6.8 percent in 2003. Child death rates were also reduced. For children aged 1–14 the rate was 44 per 100,000 in 1975, which was reduced to 22 in 2003 (Annie E. Casey Foundation, 2004).

Other encouraging data on children's welfare include the rate of teen deaths due to accident, homicide, or suicide. For teenagers aged 15–19, the rate fell from 73 per 100,000 in 1975 to 50 in 2003. The high school dropout rate was also reduced for teenagers aged 16–19 from 12 percent in 1975 to 9 percent in 2003. The number of children who live in families that have no parent with full-time, year-round employment fell from 33 in 1975 to 25 in 2003. However, the increase of single-parent families rose from 17 percent in 1975 to 29 percent in 2001 (Annie E. Casey Foundation, 2004).

Working parents of preschool children provide child care in a variety of ways. The Families and Work Institute survey of 1997 found 55 percent of the parents of preschoolers relying on parents or other relatives to care for their preschoolers (Bond, Galinsky, & Swanberg, 1998). In 1997 the Census Bureau reported that 41 percent of parents of preschoolers in families with employed mothers counted on relatives to help out; 35 percent used family child-care homes or child-care centers; 12 percent used both relatives and child care; 30 percent used a relative (grandparents or other relatives); and 12 percent used fathers. A few mothers (4 percent) used siblings to care for their children while they worked. Generally these mothers either worked from their home or administered their own business (U.S. Census Bureau, 1997).

In the 21st century, similar child-care arrangements for preschoolers were necessary. Information (Ehrle & Tout, 2001) on infants and toddlers under the age of 3 shows that parent care (27 percent) and relative care (27 percent) provide the greatest percent of child-care arrangements. This is followed by center-based care (22 percent); family child care, is similar to family child-care homes cited above (17 percent); and nanny care (7 percent). The percentages, although they differ, show that parents continue to rely heavily on relatives and on adjusting their own time schedules so that they can help care for their young children.

Working Mothers

Today, mothers who work outside the home outnumber mothers who work solely in the home. In 1996 more than half (68 percent) of married women living with a spouse and children younger than 6 were in the labor force, with 28 percent employed full time, year-round. For married mothers living with a spouse and school-age children (6–17), 80 percent worked, with 44 percent working full time year-round (Bianchi & Spain, 1996, p. 21). The school-age children will need before- and after-school care or they will be latchkey children.

Since 1940 there has been dramatic changes in workforce patterns. In 1940 almost 70 percent were breadwinner/homemaker families, and both parents worked in less than 10 percent of families (Ahlburg & De Vita, 1992). In 2000, 60 percent of families with children under 6 years of age had both parents in the labor force (U.S. Bureau of Labor Statistics, 2001). The changes are continuing.

Insights for Teachers and Administrators

1. Parents of school-age children rely heavily on schools to provide care for the children with school hours and after-school programs or after-school child-care programs. Some children become latchkey children. Other children are cared for in their own homes or in other homes with relatives and neighbors providing before- and after-school care.
2. A mother working full time does not have the opportunity to volunteer in the classroom

The number of single parents increased from 9 percent in 1970 to 29 percent in 2001.

during the week, so offer her other ways in which she can contribute. A form with options and with room for suggestions that can be answered by a parent and returned to school can help parents connect with the school.

3. Adopt before- and after-school programs that offer enriching activities for the child and safe child care for the family.
4. Keep the parents informed on the progress of their child. Set aside some time each week during which the parents can telephone you.
5. Initiate telephone calls at a convenient time for both you and the parents to share something positive about the child. Hold a get-acquainted evening program for parents. Ask them to fill out a chart so they may share needs with others. Allow parents to decide on the extent of their participation.
6. Use the Internet to share class information. E-mail individual parents to share positive comments about the class or the child. Take digital photos and e-mail them to parents (make sure you have permission to photograph).
7. Videotape class activities or programs that are important to the children so that the parents who were unable to attend may view them later.
8. Make home visits at a time convenient for the family.

Today, women are not as likely as they once were to leave the labor force when they have children. Mothers with one or two children are most likely to work outside the home; as family size increases, outside employment decreases.

GREATER INVOLVEMENT OF FATHERS WITH THEIR CHILDREN

Roles of fathers have changed and increased in the past two centuries. From the Puritan times until industrialization, a "good" father was the breadwinner and provider of moral guidance. Fathers have long held these two roles, but in the 20th century the importance of fathers' roles in their children's development underwent change based on social conditions and beliefs as well as research in child development. In the 21st century fathers exhibit willingness to provide expanded roles as companions, standard-setters, guidance counselors, play partners, teachers, providers, caregivers, and role models.

The Children's Bureau, established in 1912, provided information to families about caring for their infants in the publication *Infant Care*. Although fathers were mentioned in the publication, the advice was directed to mothers. Fathers were not considered as important to the child's development until the 1940s. Awareness of the father as a gender-role model came about toward the end of World War II, but it was not until the 1970s that the role of nurturant father was emphasized (Lamb, 1997).

Some advocates for fathers argue that in the 20th century fathers were viewed as superfluous. "The retreat from fatherhood began in the 1960s, gained momentum in the 1970s, and hit full stride in the 1980s" (Horn, 1997, p. 24). In the 1990s, however, organizations that focused on fathers included the National Institute for Responsible Fatherhood and Family Development, Promise Keepers, National Centers for Fathering, and the National Fatherhood Initiative. These groups responded to data about the negative aspects of being raised without a father, including the fact that such children are "three times more likely to fail at school, two to three times more likely to experience emotional or behavioral problems requiring psychiatric treatment . . . three times more likely to commit suicide as adolescents . . . five times more likely to be poor" (p. 27). When income was controlled, children without a father present fared worse than those who had both parents (Horn, 1997). In two-parent families, it is important that family members are supportive of one another and that conflict and abuse be absent.

Research

In the 1980s, 1990s, and continuing in the 2000s, research shows that the fathers' more physical style of interacting with their children supports and adds to the nurturing and verbal style of the mother (Horn, 1997; Lamb, 1997). If the parents have supportive relationships with one another and their children, the children thrive. "Children who have secure, supportive, reciprocal, and sensitive relationships with their parents are much more likely to be well-adjusted psychologically than individuals whose relationships with their parents—mothers or fathers—are less satisfying" (Lamb, 1997, p. 13). A parent's feelings and attitudes, when projected onto the child, impact the child's feelings of well-being. It is the characteristics of the man as a father, not as a man, that influence the child's development (Pruett, 1996). Studies show that children do better cognitively and emotionally if both parents are involved, rather than just one.

The National Center on Fathers and Families has developed the Fathering Indicator Framework, which has six fathering indicator categories. The categories include father presence, caregiving, children's social competence, cooperative parenting, father's healthy living, and material and financial contribution. The operational categories accompany the fathering indicator categories to be used by programs to guide research (National Center on Fathers and Families, 2002).

Although many boys without fathers develop normally, if the combination of mother and father support each other, provide a better economic base for the family, and provide a nurturing environment for their children, that combination is preferred over a single-parent family.

Father Involvement

Heightened interest in fatherhood goes hand in hand with the increasing number of women who work outside the home. More than ever, mothers need a cooperating husband to help with all the duties of homemaking. More important, many young fathers see the expression of love toward their children as a way of fulfilling their own lives with meaningful relationships. Some fathers are full-time homemakers and care for the children while their wives work outside the home.

Single parents, both men and women, often substitute a network of friends and kin to handle emergencies and everyday obligations. This extended network helps parents meet the demands of nurturance and role model.

Fathers in two-parent families tend to be playmates with the children, rather than being responsible for children's care and rearing or obtaining child care for the children. Although fathers and mothers are similar rather than dissimilar in their connection with their children, fathers tend to be more physically stimulating with unpredictable play, whereas mothers tend toward containment and soft, repetitive verbal expression. Both types of interaction are beneficial for the child (Lamb, 1997).

In the National Association for the Education of Young Children (NAEYC) accredited child-care programs, fathers preferred involvement in (a) family activities, (b) Daddy and Me programs, (c) activities for both parents to learn about their child's future, (d) activities for both parents to learn about child development, and (e) sporting events (Turbiville, Umbarger, & Guthrie, 2000, p. 77).

A survey conducted by the Families and Work Institute in 1997 found that fathers had increased their interaction with their children. Fathers spent an average of 2.3 workday hours doing things with or caring for their children, an increase of 30 minutes per workday since a 1977 survey was conducted. Working mothers spent another hour each day, but the total time spent caring for children had not increased. On days off, fathers spent 6 hours with their children, and women, 8. Even with the new emphasis on father nurturance, 56 percent of employed mothers wished that fathers would spend more time with the children, and 43 percent wished that fathers would help more with household chores. Both parents would like more time with their children: 70 percent felt that they do not have enough time with children. The amount of personal time dropped to 1.6 hours a day for men—a decrease of 36 minutes from the 1977 survey—and 1.3 hours for women—a decrease of 24 minutes. In caring for sick children or other needs, 22 percent of fathers said they take time off from work, compared to 83 percent of employed mothers. On average, however, men work longer hours than women, with men working 50.9 hours a week and women, including part-time workers, averaging 41.4 (Bond et al., 1998). The amount of paternal involvement depends on (a) motivation; (b) skills and self-confidence; (c) support, especially from the mother; and (d) institutional practices.

Positive suggestions include:

1. *Be there.* Engage in activities with your child from the early caregiving, bathing and bedroom routine, to later when you can read to your child, share your own stories, and play together.
2. *Accept your child.* Accept your child for who she or he is. Each child has an individual personality. Trying to change a quiet child into a boisterous one or an uncoordinated child into an outstanding athlete, makes the child feel unaccepted.
3. *Use positive parenting.* Praise is better than punishment in guiding children. Help the child express anger constructively.
4. *Share parenting.* Work as a team with your spouse.
5. *See fathering as worthwhile and satisfying.* "Children need their fathers to help them with skills and decision making, and to feel competent and good about themselves" (Ballantine, 1999/2000, p. 105).
6. *Be there for your children.* Listen and be involved in their education from early childhood on.

Involving Fathers in Schools and Centers

Research shows that children whose fathers are positively involved in their school activities complete more school and have stronger emotional and cognitive development (Byrne, 1997; Engle & Breaux, 1998; Lamb, 1997, 2003; Levine, Murphy, & Wilson, 1993). The reverse is true for children without father involvement. They are three times more likely to fail, have more emotional problems that need psychiatric treatment, have more behavioral problems, have lower reading scores, and are three times as likely to commit suicide (Horn, 1997; Levine et al., 1993).

Many schools and centers have developed ways to involve men. Fourteen of these programs are described in *Getting Men Involved* (Levine et al., 1993).

The National Fathering Network has affiliates in 35 states. The Kindering Center in Bellevue, Washington, is a model for a support group of fathers who meet and share. Support groups hold weekly meetings for fathers who have children with special needs. Other examples include father centers that provide group meeting for parents who are

Audrey Gilden

At the turn of the 21st century, fathers exhibit willingness to provide expanded roles as companions, standard setters, guidance counselors, play partners, teachers, providers, caregivers, and role models.

new to the United States and the English language. The Parents as Teachers program in Ferguson-Florissant, Missouri, has established programs for high school teenage parents and parents to be. The FRED program (Fathers Reading Every Day) focuses on reading. Research shows that parents who read to their children strengthen their child's love of reading. This carries over into the child's own interest and ability in reading. "Parents who read to their children on a regular basis tend to have children who are superior readers and who perform better in school" (Green, 2002, p. 1).

The first step in getting fathers, brothers, uncles, and interested high school seniors and juniors involved is to create a father-friendly environment. The term *father* extends to all father-substitutes. Because many children do not have a father in the home, encouragement and inclusion of father-substitutes are extremely important. Encourage family friends, uncles, grandfathers, stepfathers, and interested others to become family substitutes. The term *father* includes any father or father-substitute.

Insights for Teachers and Administrators

1. When fathers drop off or pick up their children at school, make an effort to talk with the father as well as the mother.
2. Encourage fathers to participate in the classroom.
3. Send newsletters to fathers and other male relatives. Send a newsletter to noncustodial fathers, unless the courts object to contact with the noncustodial parent. Include a picture and an article about a father participating in the classroom.
4. Schedule conferences at times that are convenient for both parents. Encourage the father to come and participate.
5. Have a special conference with the noncustodial parent, if the courts permit, if it appears to be counterproductive for both custodial and noncustodial parents to be present at the same time.
6. Make telephone calls letting both parents know about something the child has done that was interesting and positive.
7. Ask a father who participates to recruit another. Or pair up two fathers so that the new father can model the father who is familiar with the classroom.
8. Make home visits at a time when both parents will be there.
9. Videotape children in the classroom to share with parents. Include fathers working in the

classroom in the video so that fathers see they are welcome to participate.

10. Include activities that appeal to fathers. Let them help with all types of classroom involvement, but also have activities such as games, exercise, or physical activities that some fathers would feel comfortable overseeing.
11. Present a workshop that allows parents to participate in the class so they become familiar with the expectations and activities. Encourage them to attend workshops on helping in the classroom, parenting skills, and conflict resolution.
12. Plan field trips such as visits to a zoo, farm, or museum. Ask parents to accompany and participate.
13. Plan a family evening where parents come and read with their children.
14. Learn from and listen to the fathers. Appreciate their contributions.

DIVORCE

Divorce involves change for both parents and children. The effects of divorce on children are related more to the previous situation and the subsequent events that affect the child than on the divorce itself. Children are usually ashamed of the divorce and feel rejected because of a parent's departure. On the other hand, divorce may improve the situation for a child in cases where a successful reestablished single family or a remarriage provides the child with a good quality of life. The initial effect of divorce is reduced over time. Children adjust to it, and their risk at school is much lower a year after the divorce than immediately following it. Shaw (1992) listed conditions that affect the adjustment of children to divorce:

- Relationships of parents following divorce. Are the parents amicable, or do they use the children as ammunition against each other?
- Separation from a parent who is significant to the child.
- The parenting skills and relationship of the children with the custodial parent.
- The relationship of children to the nonresidential parent.
- Economics and financial ability to keep a standard of living. (p. 182)

Children's Responses

Children of all ages respond to the divorce of their parents. Wallerstein (1985) found that younger children seem to suffer the most at the time of the divorce, but in a 10-year follow-up, older girls still harbored feelings of betrayal and rejection by men, making commitment to their own relationships difficult. If the quality of life after the divorce was good, children did well. If parents continued to fight over the children or burdened their children with too much responsibility, "in short, if stress and deprivation continue after the divorce—then children are likely to suffer depression and interrupted development" (p. 8).

Children need to be reassured that they are not the cause of the divorce. They also need to know by the parents' actions and words that they will continue to have their parents' love. Adapt your caring for children to their level of development. Their understanding and response is related to their age and maturity.

1. Older infants and toddlers realize that one of their parents no longer live with them. Infants need reassurance and tender caregiving.
2. Toddlers need reassurance of their parent's love. There may be evidence of regression in some of their skills but, with support, they can regain their development.
3. Preschool and early elementary children are more likely to blame themselves for the divorce. They need reassurance, support, and connection with the parent who no longer lives at home (Leon & Cole, March 2004).

For more information, try the Web site www.fatherhood.org listed at the end of the chapter.

Insights for Teachers and Administrators

1. Children do better following a divorce if they know that a positive relationships with both parents will continue.
2. Parent hostility versus parent cooperation causes major problems for children who may

be buffeted between the two parents. Research that compared intact homes with marital conflict to single homes without conflict have shown that children in the conflict-free homes have fewer emotional problems (Lamb, 1997; Shaw, 1992).

3. Teachers and administrators must also recognize that during the period of divorce, the family may be in turmoil. Children will bring their distress with them to the classroom.
4. The school can offer the child a stable and sensitive environment—one the child can count on—during that period. The school may be the only environment during this period that remains the same, so it may be the only place where children can count on structure and guidance to offer security. This is especially important for children going through a recent divorce. When they come to school, they do not want to be singled out as if there were something different about them because a divorce has occurred in their family, but they do need support and understanding.
5. Especially during the first year of divorce, children experience not only change and feelings of loss, but also the disorganization and reorganization of their parents' lives. Parents are sometimes distant; at other times they may be more possessive of their children. Children are affected if they perceive abandonment by one parent (Lamb, 1997). If parents use their children as part of their conflict, the children suffer.
6. Children often yearn for their parents to reconcile and may blame themselves for the divorce. Children may respond to divorce by externalizing or internalizing problems or experiencing cognitive deficits. Boys, more than girls, show early negative reactions by being more quarrelsome and acting out. They externalize their change and loss. Children who are unhappy in their life situations, whether a divorce or not, tend to internalize their concerns and/or become less successful in school.
7. Keep positive expectations for the children. Be kind, but encourage them to keep up with their classwork. Find ways that the child can contribute to the class. Use special projects or activities that may interest the child.
8. Support the child by maintaining consistency and discipline. Make children feel confident, listen to the child's point of view, and advocate for the child (Sammons & Lewin, pp. 104, 105).
9. Make phone calls to both parents to share a school activity or a positive contribution the child has made to the class.

Decline of Economic Well-Being

A concrete change, and one of the most significant, is the decline in economic well-being of women who have custody of their children after divorce. Women and their children experience a loss of income and economic well-being after a divorce. After divorce, about half of eligible women receive some child support. There are a variety of reasons that child support is not available. In a survey by the U.S. Census Bureau, only 26 percent of women received the full amount to which they were entitled. Twelve percent who were supposed to receive payment received none, and another 12 percent received a partial amount. Forty-four percent were not awarded any support; 27 percent of these women wanted support but were not awarded any (U.S. Bureau of the Census, 1991d, 1995). Men did not fare any better when they were the sole support of a family. Fifty-nine percent were not awarded any support money; 28 percent were to receive support, but only 18 percent of those received any (U.S. Bureau of the Census, 1995).

If the woman is dependent on her own salary, she has the disadvantage of earning less income based on her gender. Women earn less than men no matter what their educational level. The wage gap continues. In 1996 women's median annual earnings for year-round, full-time jobs were 73.8 percent of men's salaries (U.S. Census Bureau, 1998).

SINGLE-PARENT FAMILIES

The 1970 census showed that 9 percent of children lived with a single parent. In 2003, 30 percent did. Two factors have increased single parenthood. One is the increase in birth to unmarried women, and the other is the increase in the divorce rate. In the early 1990s the trend toward an increase in single parents continued, and in 2003, the percentage was at 30 percent (Annie E. Casey Foundation, 2006).

Single-parent families are not a new phenomenon. From the 1860s until the mid-1960s, there was no increase in the proportion of single parents because the growing divorce rate was offset by the declining death rate. Young children in the last half of the 1800s and first half of the 1900s were raised in single-parent families most often because the mother was widowed. Twenty-five percent lost a parent to death (Amato, 1994). Single-parent mothers worked hard to raise their children by taking in boarders, doing laundry, and somehow managing—with help from their children—to rear the family.

By the 1960s, however, the divorce rate had risen to such a degree that the number of single-parent families increased because of divorce rather than death (Furstenberg, 1994; Thornton & Freedman, 1983). The divorce rate doubled from 1963 until 1979, but it appeared to have stabilized by the 1990s. Nearly half of all recent first marriages will end in divorce, with most children (88 percent) having their mothers as the custodial parent (Bogolub, 1995; Norton & Glick, 1986; Shiono & Quinn, 1994). Most divorced parents remarry, however, making it possible for 80 percent of children to live in two-parent homes most of the time they are in school.

During the period that a mother is raising her children alone, she has a much higher risk of poverty. Twelve percent of the single parents who work full time find themselves in poverty; 49 percent of those who work part time were also poor. Almost 74 percent of the single parents who did not work are in poverty. Seventy-nine percent of single parents are in the labor force (Litcher & Crowley, 2002).

OUT-OF-WEDLOCK BIRTHS

One and a half million infants were born to unwed mothers in 2004. There is great concern about the alarming number of out-of-wedlock births; in 2004, 35.7 percent of all births were to unmarried women. Fifty-five percent of unwed women, 20 to 24 years of age had births; 28 percent of women 25 to 29 had births. The birthrate for unmarried teenagers ages 15 to 19 was 24 percent (Jayson, 2005). Girls now do not marry as young as their counterparts in the 1950s, and teenagers and young adults are continuing to having babies without marrying the fathers. For many young mothers, marrying the father is not a viable option; many of these young men are unable to obtain employment that would bring the family out of poverty.

Two factors—an increase in births out of wedlock and decreases or delays in births to married women—increased the percentage of births to unmarried mothers from 5 percent in 1970 to 14.2 percent in 1975, 18 percent in 1980, and 35.7 percent in 2004 (Children's Defense Fund, 1997; Thornton & Freeman, 1983; Jayson, 2005). These startling figures point to the need for more family life education in the schools, especially for young mothers, and it also calls for an educational system that meets the needs of low-income families.

One in every five females with below-average educational skills who lives in a below-poverty-level home becomes a mother while still a teenager. No matter whether young people are White, Black, or Hispanic, they are more likely to become pregnant if they are below average in academic skills. Higher infant mortality rates and greater risks to the child are just two of the problems associated with teenage pregnancies. Very young women are not prepared emotionally, economically, or physically to take on the challenge of childrearing.

Insights for Teachers and Administrators

What does this mean for a teacher? First, schools must accept the fact that single-parent families can supply the components necessary for a flourishing, functioning family. However, single parents have special needs. Unless they have established a strong network of friends or family, they may have difficulty meeting all the requests and obligations in their involvement with the school.

1. If children become part of a single parent family through the death of one parent, they also need the teacher to recognize the change that is happening to them.
2. Opportunities for talking with teachers and counselors or attending group sessions with other children who have lost a parent through death or divorce can be helpful (Lewis, 1992).
3. Parents and teachers need to communicate throughout a child's education, but it is essential during periods of change to know what is happening both at home and at school and to help

children overcome the isolation and distress they feel. Although only one in every five children will probably be from a one-parent family at any given time, half of all children will spend part of their childhood in a one-parent family.

4. Offer convenient times for parent–teacher conferences. Single parents (and many two-parent families) need early morning, evening, or weekend times for their conferences. A form such as the one suggested in Figure 5.8 will help teachers find out when parents are available. Single parents may also need child care while they attend a conference. This service is helpful for two-parent families as well, as it allows both parents to attend.
5. Acknowledge and communicate with noncustodial parents. If noncustodial parents receive report cards and other information, they likely will be more interested in the child's work and better able to be involved with the child. Most noncustodial parents are men, and the percentage of men who pay child support is low. Schools can help sustain or even increase the father's interest by keeping him informed. Most fathers already have a keen interest in their child's schooling. They want to know what is happening without questioning the child. Honor their position; send them frequent reports unless the courts have specified that the noncustodial parent should not have contact or information about the child.
6. Learn parents' names. Always check the records to determine the names of the children and the parents, because they may not be the same. This applies equally to two-parent families, because half of them will have had a divorce. Calling the parents by their correct names is a simple gesture of courtesy.
7. Help parents become involved easily. Find ways that single parents can be involved without putting great stress on the family. Parents who work outside the home might be able to attend early morning breakfasts, especially if child care is provided and the children get breakfast, too. Keep the number of parents at each breakfast small so you can talk with each parent individually. Find out how they would like to be involved, what their needs are, and if they have any ideas for their partnership with the school. Acknowledge their suggestions for improved home-school collaboration.
8. Encourage communication among parents. Establish a newsletter that allows parents to communicate with other parents. Let the parents include what they want to say in the newsletter. Better yet, make it a parent-to-parent newsletter, so they can establish their own networks.
9. Use care in communication. In all partnerships with parents, one of the most important elements of cooperation and understanding is the ability to communicate. The first objective is to have effective communication. The second objective is to prepare written materials that project positive and knowledgeable feelings toward the parent. Take care when preparing invitations to programs. Perhaps you may wish to emphasize one group, but make sure the child and parent know that they do not need to have a father, mother, or grandparent to attend. For example, saying "Bring your grandparent or a grand friend to class next week" implies that the visitors, not their titles, are important. At the program make sure you have some get-acquainted activities so that no one feels left out or alone. Activities also encourage networking among parents, and may be the best opportunity for new single parents in the neighborhood to become acquainted with others. (See chapter 5 for more school activities, and chapter 7 for ways to make group meetings work.)
10. Reach out. To involve both single and working parents, Moles (1996a) suggests: "Develop a single unobtrusive system to keep track of family changes, such as these examples: At the beginning of the year ask for the names and addresses of individuals to be informed about each child and involved in school activities. At mid-year send a form to each child's parents or guardians to verify that the information is still accurate. Invite the parents or guardians to indicate any changes. . . . Work with local businesses to arrange released time from work so that parents can attend conferences, volunteer or in other ways spend time at their child's school when it is in session" (p. 49).

In addition, reach out to unwed single parents in a supportive way to determine if they have special needs such as economic needs and resources that are available in your school and in the school distict.

Based on a study of seventh- and eighth-grade children and their parents, Wanat (1992) recommended that the school, in addition to providing stability, acceptance, and parent involvement, provide students with special attention from teachers, counselors, and administrators. The single parents wanted to be the parent and did not want the school to assume that they had abdicated that role, but they could be helped by offering (a) extra educational help, (b) tutoring for the children, and (c) before- and after-school study time.

If the parent remarries, the child is affected again, and concerns arise regarding the following:

- The loss of the parent as the sole caregiver and the strong relationship that may have developed between parent and child.
- The relationships between the stepparent and the children. These are discussed in the following section.

BLENDED FAMILIES

School personnel tend to view families as they have in the past. They look to the residential family—the family and children located within their school district—as the one family involved with the school and children. School policies must recognize the unique concerns of the blended family and avoid detrimental effects on the growing number of stepchildren.

There is a complex social organization in blended families. In the remarried families, some children may be offspring of the mother, some of the father, and the remaining may be born to the remarried couple. A child may be living in a home with a brother or sister, a stepbrother or stepsister whose biological parent is the mother or father in the home, and a half-sister or half-brother who is the child of the remarried couple. In addition, they may have visitation with their other biological parent and have the same types of configurations when they are living or visiting there. Families may have as many as 30 configurations (Manning & Wootten, 1987). In addition, there is an increase in families that have blended cultures.

Blended Family Cycle

When two people marry and one or both have children from a previous relationship, the road to a secure, happy family is difficult. They come with different backgrounds, have no family history together, and no shared way of doing things. Newly blended families need to recognize and mourn their losses, develop the ability to make decision as a family, support each other, nurture the parent–child relationship, and foster new relationship among their new stepparent and other stepchildren as well as their own parent and siblings (American Academy of Child and Adolescent Psychiatry, 2004). Building a strong new family can be accomplished, but the original thoughts of delight on the part of the children and acceptance of the new arrangement by ex-spouses are complicated by the realities of the situation. One of the complicating circumstances occurs because both parent and child have come from single-parent family status. During the single-parent stage, parent and child tend to become extremely close. The parent may have turned to the children for emotional support and decision-making help in the absence of the former spouse. Children of the newly married couple often see the remarriage as a double loss. First they lost a parent through divorce. Now they are losing their special relationship with the other parent by having to share their custodial parent with a new stepparent.

Thus begins the blended family. Initially, the newly married couple fantasize that all the children will enjoy one another and both adults. The children, however, come into the remarriage generally hoping their biological parents will get back together. Therefore, fantasy is the first stage of the blended family cycle.

The cycle of the blended family as developed by Papernow (1993, 1998) starts with an early stage in which family members move from fantasy to recognizing their problems and needs. The cycle moves to a middle or restructuring stage, and then enters a final stage of solidifying the new family. In the first three stages, the family is generally divided according to biological line. The early stage includes three components: fantasy, immersion, and awareness.

During the fantasy stage, parents visualize that the new marriage will provide a supportive, loving family, although the children probably want their biological parents back together. "Both partners may imagine that because the adults in the new family adore each other, stepparents and stepchildren will also" (Papernow, p. 13). In the second stage, immersion, the nonbiological parent becomes the outsider parent, not able to relate in the same way a biological parent does to the biological children. It is a period of sinking versus swimming. During immersion, the parents may be concerned about the family with negative feelings occurring. During the awareness stage, parents become more able to understand the dynamics of the new relationship. The bond between biological parent and child is acknowledged by the outsider parent, and they are ready to go to the next stage. If parents can recognize the areas of concerns of the first three stages and deal with them in the next, the family will probably thrive, but, if they get stuck in the first three stages, the family will probably dissolve.

The middle or restructuring stage includes mobilization, during which the airing of differences occurs, and action—power struggles are resolved and new agreements are made, with changes in family structure and new boundaries. "Every family activity is no longer a potential power struggle between insiders and outsiders" (Papernow, 1993, p. 16).

The final stage includes contact, during which intimacy and authenticity in real relationships are forged. "The marital relationship becomes more of a sanctuary and source of nourishment and support, even on step issues" (Papernow, p. 16). Finally, resolution occurs. Although issues may recur and the family may reexperience the stepparenting cycle, the family is able to go forward. Differences no longer threaten the family.

The entire cycle affects the children. During the first stage, while the children are still feeling a loss, their participation in school often suffers. They may go through stages of grief similar to those experienced after divorce, death, or moving away from loved ones. Children may act out in class; they may be despondent, and they may have no interest in schoolwork. For school-age children, the school is a stable environment and can be a support for them. Staying in the same school with their friends can ease the transition.

During the early stage, stepparents become aware that they are not able to nurture children in the same way that biological parents do. Biological parents already have a strong bond with their children. Parents develop an awareness of these family pressures. Both partners recognize what they can handle and which attitudes need to be changed. In some cases the family is never able to restructure their lives, and many of these marriages do not succeed.

The restructuring period of stepfamily development allows for more openness in discussion of change. Parents and children continue to have strong biological ties, but the differences lead to action. In this action phase, family boundaries are clarified and the couple attempts to work together to find solutions.

In the final stages, the roles of each stepparent have been more clearly defined. The stepparent has a specific role relationship with the stepchildren. Acceptance of the new family structure is evident.

Blended family stages cannot be rushed. Papernow (1993) found that from 4 to 7 years were needed to complete the entire cycle, and some families were never able to develop their blended family into a strong family.

Visher points out that "learning how to work as a team is crucial to stepfamily integration, and usually essential for a close couple relationship to develop and grow" (2001, p. 4). The adult who has the most power is the parent rather than the stepparent. The parent's children love him or her, not the stepparent, and the parent can help the stepparent become part of the family by showing understanding of the stepparent's position. "Requiring civility within the household allows relationships to have the opportunity to develop, and demonstrating love and caring for both his or her children and new partner is an important element in the success of the family" (p. 3). When issues are resolved and the blended family develops into a strong family, the student at school will not have the emotional drain that may have hindered the student from participating fully in the educational program.

Insights for Teachers and Administrators

Support for blended families may be provided by implementing the following practices (adapted from American Academy of Child & Adolescent Psychiatry, 2004; Crosbie-Burnett & Skyles, 1989; Kelly, 1995; Manning & Wootten, 1987; Visher, 2001; Visher & Visher, 1979).

1. Provide workshops for teachers to explain the varying configurations and the developmental stages of blended families. Review the possible effects on children according to age, gender, and needs.

2. Provide workshops on developing family traditions that strengthen families.
3. Eliminate the use of terms like *broken home* that may offend remarried or single families. Survey the parents to determine whether *reconstituted*, *step*, or *blended* are preferred terms. Children can devalue themselves if they hear terms that appear to be derogatory. Other children might conclude that some students are different and inferior.
4. Mail report cards, newsletters, and other informational items to both custodial and noncustodial parents.
5. Include noncustodial parents on field trips, in special programs, and in school activities.
6. Be aware of days when the student is likely to go on a visitation. Time messages accordingly.
7. Encourage children to make more than one Mother's Day or Father's Day card if they have more than one parent of the same gender.
8. Appoint parents from blended and single-parent families to serve on advisory councils, Parent Teacher Associations, or other organizations.
9. Be sensitive to a child whose parent has just remarried. This is a period of stress for both the child and the family. Children may act out and need special handling during the transition.
10. Include family information and positive stories about children in blended families or single-parent families within the curriculum.
11. Provide peer support groups for stepchildren or single-parent children where they can meet, talk, and realize that they are not the only ones in a blended family. Allow children to question and express their feelings and concerns.
12. Offer books, articles, and lists of resources about stepfamilies and single-parent families for parents and school personnel. Subscribe to the *Stepfamily Bulletin* from the Stepfamily Association of America.

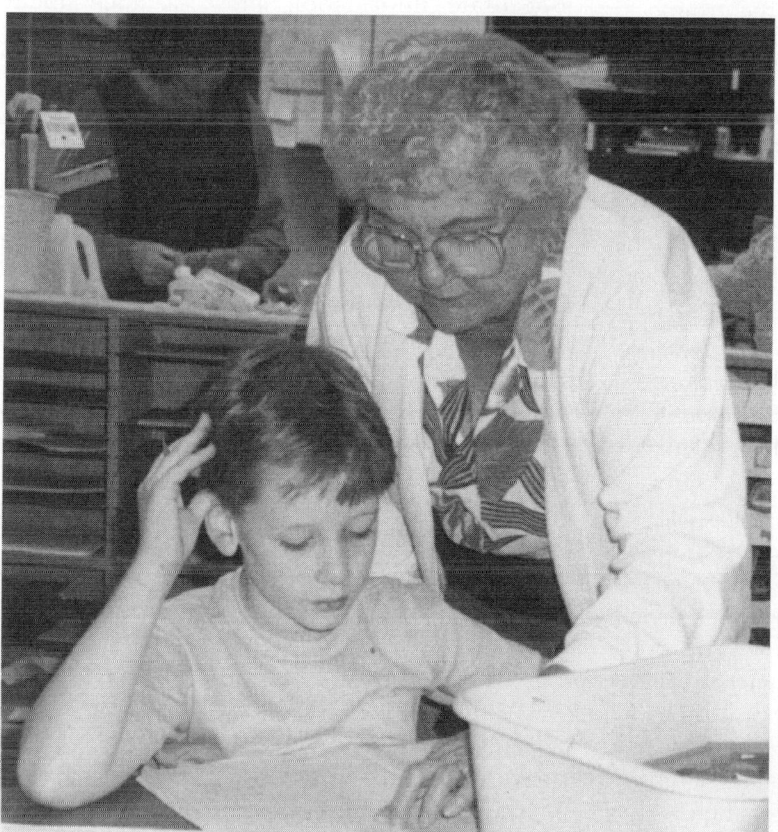

Eugenia Hepworth Berger

Grandparents maintaining families have increased from 2.2 million in 1970 to 4.5 million in 2000.

GRANDPARENT MAINTENANCE FAMILIES

In the 2000 census, for the first time, many questions regarding the responsibility for children under the age of 18, in particular grandparent caregivers, were ascertained. The number of grandparents maintaining families doubled from 2.2 million in 1970 to 4.5 million in 2000. Care for grandchildren was maintained by 2.4 million grandparent caregivers. They accounted for 3.9 percent of all households in 2000. Of these families, 19 percent had incomes below poverty. These are families in which parents may live with the family, but where the grandparents provide the financial support, different from the families who have a grandparent move in with them. They account for 3.9 percent of all households in 2000. Of these, 19 percent had incomes below the poverty level (Simmons & Dye, 2003). This means that schools will have some families in which those who are responsible for the children are the children's grandparents.

The families included different ethnic groups and differences in the proportion of the ethnic group who had grandparents caring for grandchildren. The largest number of children living with their grandparents are White, although the percentage is lower than other groups. These percentages are 2 percent non-Hispanic White; 6 percent Asian; 8 percent each for Black, American Indian and Alaska Native, and Hispanic; and 10 percent of Pacific Islanders. Thirty-five percent of the grandparent caregivers were aged 50–59 with only 7 percent of the grandparents in their thirties. Most (94 percent) of the grandparent caregivers were householders or were married to a householder. Of these, 35 percent were "skipped-generation households," living with the grandchildren without the parents living there (Simmons & Dye 2003). Schools will have grandparents who are responsible for their grandchildren. How long were children with the grandparent caregivers? Only 12 percent had their grandchildren less than 6 months. Eleven percent cared for their grandchildren from 6 to 11 months; 23 percent for 1 to 2 years; 15 percent for 3 to 4 years, and the most, 39 percent, for 5 or more years.

The research indicates that the majority of grandparent-maintained families differ from households maintained by parents. These differences include the educational level of the grandparent who may not have graduated from high school and who is unable to obtain a high-income job. Even when grandparents work and have health insurance, the insurance programs often do not cover grandchildren living with them. Children cared for in grandparent homes are younger, the grandparent is older, and they are likely to be living in the central city, to be poor, and to be uninsured. "Grandparents and their grandchildren would benefit greatly if policies and programs intended to help traditional parent-child families in times of need could be uniformly extended to grandchildren" (Casper & Bryson, 1998, p. 12).

Insights for Teachers and Administrators

1. When grandparents drop off or pick up their grandchild or grandchildren at school, be available to talk with them.
2. Send newsletters and other notices home to the grandparents.
3. Grandparents may need help in obtaining accurate information and assistance about support services for them and their grandchildren. These issues may include counseling, mentoring, and tutoring for the children. The grandparents may need counseling as well as information on legal and financial aid. Information given should be easy to understand. The information needs to be geared so all grandparents, regardless of their ethnicity or educational background, can understand and use the information.
4. Make telephone calls to share something the grandchild has done that was a positive contribution. This could include such things as a painting, drawing, story, or just an interest in a subject.
5. Invite the grandparent to programs and "back to school night."
6. Invite them to visit the class and, if appropriate, share with a group of students.
7. Treat grandparents as you would treat the other parents.
8. If there is a grandparent support group, encourage the grandparents with children in your class or school to attend. If there isn't

a support group in your school, start one or find one nearby.

9. "Teachers can use projects to strengthen young children's motivation to master a wide variety of academic skills" (Helm & Lang, 2003 p. 97). They can help their students begin to master their own environment by "maximizing opportunities for self-initiated learning" (p. 94).

POVERTY

Poverty is defined in the United States according to the income of the person or family. In 1990 a family of four who earned less than $13,359 was classified as in poverty (U.S. Bureau of the Census, 1991c). In 1996 the poverty threshold was $16,036 for a family of four. In 2000, the poverty threshold for a family of four was $17,603 annual income; for a family of three, the threshold was $13,738 (U.S. Census Bureau, 2002). With inflation, the poverty threshold increases by the same annual average as the Consumer Price Index.

The poverty rate for children in 2000 was 16.2 percent, down from 22.7 percent in 1993. Children under 18 have a higher poverty rate than any other age group. Children make up 39 percent of the poor, but they are only 26 percent of the population (U.S. Census Bureau, 2000c).

Prevalence of Poverty

The number of poor in 2000 was 31.1 million—1.1 million fewer than in 1990, even though there was a population increase (Figures 2.4 and 2.5). The overall poverty rate was 11.3 percent, down from 11.8 percent in 1999 (Current Population Reports, 2000). However, in 2002, the Census Bureau reported that the percentage of families with children had increased from 12.7 percent in 2000 to 13.4 percent in 2001 (U.S. Census Bureau 2002a). Black families with children had the highest rate, with 26.6 percent in poverty. Hispanics followed with 23.7 percent. In 2000, the median household incomes of the following groups were: Blacks, $30,439; Hispanics, $33,447; non-Hispanic Whites, 45,904; Asian and Pacific Islanders, $55,521; and a 3-year average for American Indian and Alaska Natives, $31,799. The income for Blacks and Hispanics was at an all-time high. Women with no husband present had median incomes of

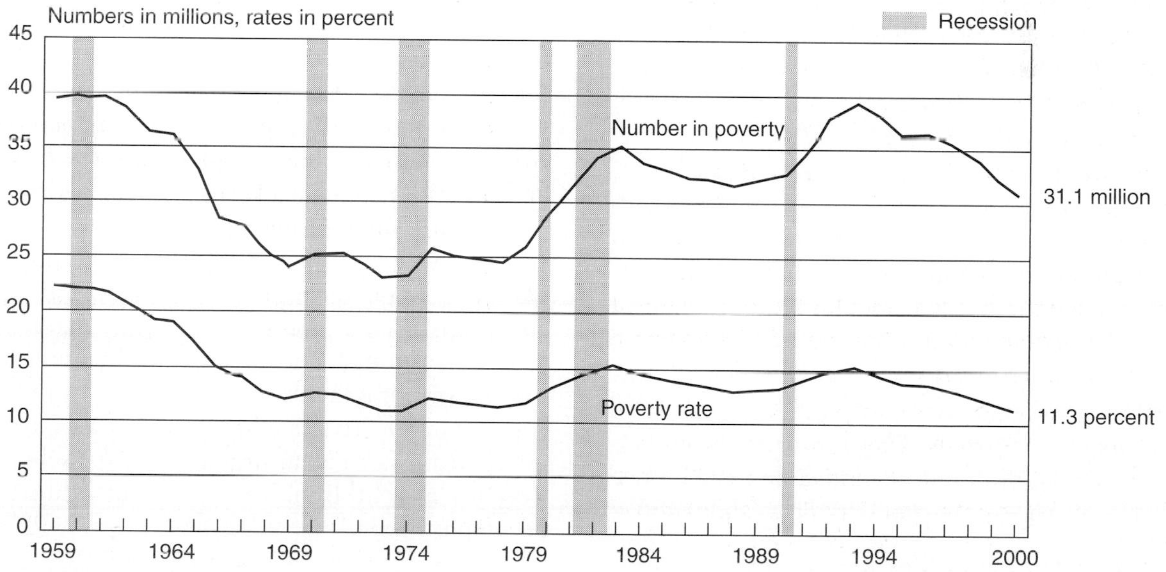

FIGURE 2.4 Number of poor and poverty rate: 1959 to 2000.

Note: The data points represent the midpoints of the respective years. The latest recession began July 1990 and ended in March 1991; data do not include the 2002 recession.

Source: From the *Current Population Survey*, by the U.S. Census Bureau, March 1960–2001, retrieved August 22, 2002, from *www.census.gov/hhes/poverty/poverty00/pov00.html*

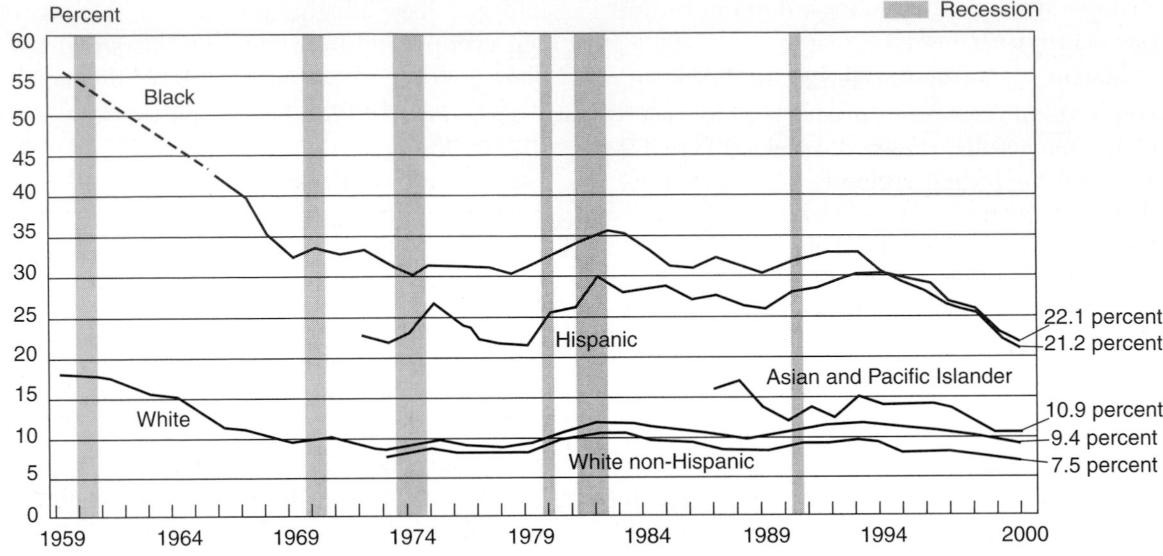

FIGURE 2.5 Poverty rates by race and Hispanic origin: 1959 to 2000.

Note: The data points represent the midpoints of the respective years. The latest recession began July 1990 and ended in March 1991. Data for Blacks are not available from 1960 to 1965. Data for the other race and Hispanic origin groups are shown from the first year available. Hispanics may be of any race.

Source: From the *Current Population Survey*, by the U.S. Census Bureau, March 1960–2001, retrieved August 22, 2002, from *www.census.gov/hhes/poverty/poverty00/povrac00.html*

$28,116 (U.S. Census Bureau, September 25, 2001). Median income points to the middle of incomes rather than the average; half of each group was below the median income, and half was above.

Destructive Nature of Poverty

To exist in the culture of poverty means to feel depressed, powerless to effect change, and unable to control one's destiny. Alienation, anomie, isolation, and depression are common partners of poverty. Parents who are depressed and unable to control their own world pass that feeling on to their children.

Children in poverty are likely to have poor health, inadequate maternal care, and negative educational experiences. They score poorly on standardized tests, drop out of school, and experience violence, and many are prone to die in childhood.

Length of Time Families Are in Poverty

Contrary to popular belief, only a portion of the impoverished are poor for 8 years or longer. Most people who become poverty stricken move back out of poverty in 1 to 2 years. In the 1990s one in three children spent at least 1 year in poverty. For poorly educated, young, minority, or disabled persons, poverty may remain for long periods.

Long-term poverty is rare among White children, however: less than 1 percent are in poverty for more than 10 years, and 6 percent for 5 or more years. But long-term poverty affects 29 percent of African American children for more than 10 years, and almost half for more than 5 years. Children who live in extreme poverty or are in poverty for long periods suffer the most. If poverty occurs during early childhood years, the consequences are more severe than if it occurs in a child's later years (Brook-Gunn & Duncan, 1997). Education influences whether a family is in poverty and whether it remains in poverty. As education increases, poverty decreases. There is an urgent need for schools to prepare all children for successful educational accomplishments.

Whom Does Poverty Affect?

Poverty is not as prevalent now as when the War on Poverty began in 1966. At that time, one in every five families—39.5 million people—earned so little they fell below the poverty level. This was reduced to

24.1 million in 1969. It remained fairly constant throughout the 1970s, until the 1980s, when 4.8 million more became impoverished. In 1986, 32.4 million people lived below the poverty level (Shapiro & Greenstein, 1988). In 2000, 33.1 million people lived below the poverty level. See Figure 2.4, which shows the total number of poor and the poverty rate for 1959–2000, and Figure 2.5 which reflects the poverty rate by race and Hispanic origin.

In 2000, poverty rates were 21.2 percent for Hispanic children and 22.1 percent for African American children. The 3-year average poverty rate for American Indians and Alaska Natives was 25.9 percent. Poverty rates for all groups except Whites were at their historic low (U.S. Census Bureau, 2000c).

"Children living in mother-only families were more than five times more likely to be poor than those living in two-parent families: 38 percent compared with 7 percent" (Corcoran & Chaudry, 1997, p. 41). Although African Americans and Hispanics have a greater chance of being in poverty, more Whites are below the poverty level because there is a greater number of Whites in the United States. Numerically, 60 percent of all poor people are White children, but proportionately, 90 percent of the children in long-term poverty are African American (pp. 45, 47).

African Americans, with a 22.1 percent poverty rate, have over 8 million in poverty; Hispanics have a 21.2 percent poverty rate with 7.5 million people living in poverty. Non-Hispanic Whites with a 7.5 percent poverty rate have 14.5 million in poverty. The two groups that are hardest hit by poverty in the United States are Black children and children of female-headed single-parent families. There has been a significant reduction of children living in families where no parent has full-time, year round employment. It was reduced from 33 percent in 1975 to 23 percent in 2000 (see Figure 2.6).

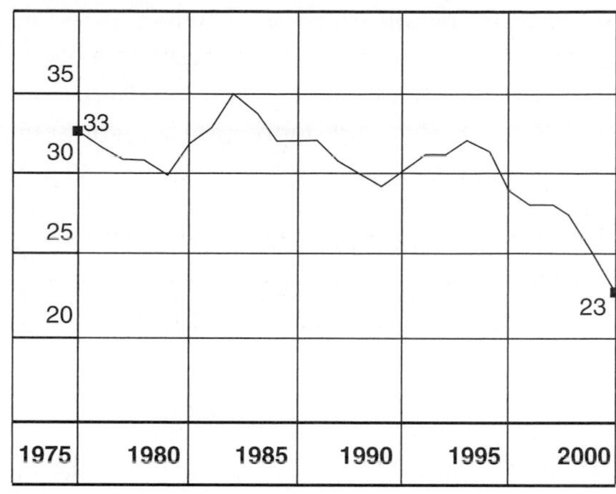

FIGURE 2.6 Percentage of children living in families where no parent has full-time, year-round employment, 1975–2000.

Source: From Census 2000 data, in the *KIDS COUNT Pocket Guide* (p. 6), by the Annie E. Casey Foundation, 2002.

Insights for Teachers and Administrators

1. One of the greatest problems that half of all single mothers face is insufficient income. When working with these mothers, teachers should recognize not only their time constraints but also their financial bind and avoid pressure in either area.
2. Find ways to involve parents, for they need to know that they are important and wanted.
3. Parents who are depressed and unable to control their own world pass that feeling on to their children.
4. Children in poverty are likely to have poor health and inadequate care. Before viewing a child as being neglected, however, find out the source of the problem.
5. Teachers in a central city are likely to have many pupils who are in low socioeconomic levels. A higher percentage of children who live in the central city are in poverty, but no matter where they work teachers will find children from families having financial problems.
6. Families who have always been self-sufficient and suddenly find themselves without employment face tremendous psychological adjustments as well as difficulty in providing shelter and food.
7. For some, using social welfare is an acknowledgment of defeat and they would rather do without some necessities than accept such help. If they are open to suggestions, help by providing information on social services. The school can also provide exchange options where outgrown clothes may be substituted for ones that fit.

8. To exist in the culture of poverty means to feel depressed, powerless to effect change, and unable to control one's destiny. Alienation, anomie, isolation, and depression are common partners of poverty.

Ways to Counteract Poverty

To counteract the stress of poverty on families, parents and children need at least the following:

- A decent standard of living (jobs that pay enough to adequately rear children)
- More flexible working conditions so children can be cared for
- An integrated network of family services
- Legal protection for children outside and inside families

Family Support Programs

Programs to support families are being offered across the United States. They range from family resource centers to family literacy programs. These programs will be discussed in more detail in chapters 7 and 8.

HOMELESSNESS

Over 3 million persons (women, children, and men) were homeless in 2001. Since early 2005, demand for shelter rose 13 percent, according to the U.S. Conference of Mayors' December 2001 report on homelessness. The Department of Housing and Urban Development found that 4.9 million low-income households paid more than 50 percent of their income on rent, an amount much too high to allow them adequate income for other necessities (National Law Center on Homelessness & Poverty, 2002a).

The U.S. Conference of Mayors revealed the following data on the families without homes:

40 percent are families with children
57 percent are single-parent families
22 percent are mentally disabled
20 percent work
4 percent are unaccompanied children

Of these

50 percent are African American
35 percent are White
12 percent are Hispanic
2 percent are Native American
1 percent are Asian (National Law Center on Homelessness & Poverty, 2002a, Overview, p. 1)

Only 38 percent of the single young women who are mothers have ever held a job longer than six months. They are generally undereducated, have few job skills, probably have abused alcohol and other drugs, and are the victims of domestic violence. Those without homes lack more than just housing (Home for the Homeless, Institute for Children and Poverty, 2004).

Other people without homes, in addition to young single mothers with children, include unemployed two-parent families; single men and women; jobless people with mental illness; people with mental and physical disabilities; homeless independent children and young adults; alcoholics; and transients. It is estimated that families with children make up 40 percent of the homeless. Schools are directly concerned with single- or two-parent families with children who should be in school and runaway children who have dropped out of school.

McKinney-Vento Homeless Education Assistance Act

The Stewart B. McKinney Homeless Assistance Act of 1987 (P.L. 100-77) was reauthorized in January 2002 as the McKinney-Vento Amendment. The act was designed to ensure that homeless children have access to education. Although it offers incentives and nominal grants to encourage states to provide for homeless children, the responsibility is left to each state (National Law Center on Homelessness & Poverty, 2002b; Stronge & Helm, 1991). The authorized federal funding is $70 million. The minimum amount of funding any state receives is $150,000 (National Law Center on Homelessness & Poverty, 2002b).

Authorized Rights for Students Who Are Experiencing Homelessness

Children and youth who are eligible for special consideration include those who are living with someone who cannot afford or has lost their home, be they a friend, relative, or someone else. It also includes those staying in a motel, hotel, or emergency shelter because they do not have adequate accommodations (National Law Center on Homelessness & Poverty, 2002b).

The reauthorization has the following requirements with guidelines for academic achievement, school selection enrollment, dispute resolution, transportation, liaison, and segregation.

Students in homeless situations have the following protections in school selection:

- Local educational agencies (LEA) must keep students in the school they attended when they had a permanent home or the school they last attended if at all feasible and if it is not against the parent's or guardian's desire.
- Students may stay at their original school until the end of the school year in which they move into permanent housing.
- If the LEA does not enroll the students in their school of origin, a written explanation to the parent/guardian is required and may be appealed. Dispute resolution is available.
- Students in homeless situations without a guardian or parent must be helped in choosing a school and enrolling.
- States must have a McKinney-Vento plan that describes how students in homeless situations will be given the same opportunity to reach academic standards as other students.
- Students in homeless situations should have access to education and services they might need to ensure that they meet the academic standards.
- Students in homeless situations must be enrolled even if they do not have all the required documents needed.
- At the parent's or guardian's request, transportation must be provided to transport the child to and from the school of origin. To ensure that the children and youth in homeless situations are able to access the availability of education, the LEA must have a designated appropriate staff person to help them with information and assistance in obtaining services and education (National Law Center on Homelessness & Poverty, 2002b, pp. 1–6).

The McKenney-Vento Act states that children without homes must have the same educational services that are provided to other students. These include Head Start availability, Individuals with Disabilities Education and Child Find for early identification of needs, Title I for those at risk of failing in school, and free and reduced-price meals.

A more complete copy of the reauthorization can be obtained on the Internet at www.nationalhomeless.org/publications/facts/McKinney.pdf.

The National Law Center for Homelessness & Poverty recognized some issues that need to be addressed to help persons who are homeless. Less than 30 percent of the people eligible for low-income housing receive low-income housing. Only 11 percent of the 40 percent eligible for disability receive disability. Only 37 percent have food stamps even though most are eligible for them. Similarly, most are eligible for welfare benefits, but only 52 percent receive them. Regrettably, in spite of the law, 12 percent are still denied their education (National Law Center for Homelessness & Poverty, 2002a, pp. 1–2).

Concern for Children Experiencing Homelessness

When families are dislocated because of losing their home, they may move to various locations, such as shelters or relatives' homes in other school districts. Not only do the children lack the security of living in a stable environment, but they also face uncertainty, moving time and again. It is a problem for these children to continue their schooling if the school will not accept them because of residency requirements. Concern of administrators and teachers for the welfare of children who are homeless should include (a) the opportunity for education, (b) acceptance by staff and peers, and (c) referrals as needed for special services.

Teachers found learning difficulties, speech delays, behavioral problems, depression and anxiety, short attention span, aggression, and withdrawal in homeless children (Bassuk & Rubin, 1987; Klein, Bittel, & Molnar, 1993; McCormick & Holden, 1992). Children who are without homes have a higher risk of nutritional deficiency and other health problems including delayed immunization, poor iron levels, and developmental difficulties. In a study of children without homes compared with low-income children who had homes, it was found that the children without homes were delayed in their growth (Fierman et al., 1991). It may be a combination of factors—malnourishment, diarrhea, asthma, elevated lead levels, or social factors including family violence, drug-exposed babies, alcohol abuse, mental disorders, and child abuse and neglect—that affect the child's growth (Bassuk, 1991; Fierman et al., 1991).

Children experiencing homelessness who come to school are usually ashamed of not having a home, of living out of a car, tent, or shelter. They need support, not blame; they need acceptance, not rejection or shame; and they need a curriculum that allows them to succeed. They may need special tutoring and a buddy assigned to help them learn the routine. If they are continuing in the same school that they attended before becoming homeless, they need to be assured that they are still valued.

Because the family and children are under a lot of stress, it is better to let them offer information than to inquire into personal concerns. Children without homes revealed their feelings in interviews by Berck (1992): "If being a poor child living in a rich city is a crime, I'm guilty. . . . People have no right to punish me for something I have no control over" (p. 32).

Parents' Desires

In a research survey (McCormick & Holden, 1992), parents without homes indicated they would like assistance with transportation; developmentally appropriate child care; opportunities to share with others; flexible opportunities to be involved; respite opportunities; mental health self-esteem groups; information on services; an easy intake process for preschool participation; and classes.

The McKinney-Vento Act (Sec. 722(g)(4)) offers the following standards for parents:

> Standard 4. Parents or persons acting as parents of homeless children and youth will participate meaningfully in their children's education.
>
> 4.1 Parents or persons acting as parents will have a face-to-face conference with the teacher, guidance counselor, or social worker within 30 days of enrollment.
>
> 4.2 Parents or persons acting as parents will be provided with individual student reports informing them of their child's specific academic needs and achievement on academic assessments aligned with state academic achievement standards.
>
> 4.3 Parents or persons acting as parents will report monitoring or facilitating homework assignments.
>
> 4.4 Parents or persons acting as parents will share reading time with their children (i.e., parent reads to child or listens to child read).
>
> 4.5 Parents who would like parent skills training will attend available programs.
>
> 4.6 Parents or guardians will demonstrate awareness of McKinney-Vento rights.
>
> 4.7 Unaccompanied youth will demonstrate awareness of McKinney-Vento rights.

Children's Feelings

Walsh (1992) pictured children experiencing homelessness through their conversations. Sam writes about how he feels about losing his pet dog, Ralphy, when he had to move to a shelter:

> I had a dog for a long time before I came here. We had to give him to a friend because we couldn't bring him down ere wit us. The shelter say "No animals." And, even if we move out of here, we can't get him back because he likes the people he's with right now. And me and him were best friends. His name was Ralphy. I always still remember him. I just hope he remembers me. (p. 77)

Juan expresses his feelings of sadness, not just for himself, but also for his parents:

> Being here makes me sad but I don't cry. I feel sad about it by myself. Sometimes I talk to my mother about it. I tell her how sad I am. She says she knows I'm sad. She knows because she feels the same way. I don't know if she cries about it. If she does I never see her. I think she does though. I don't like to talk about this stuff too much. (p. 82)

Insights for Teachers and Administrators

Teachers cannot solve the problems of families without homes, but they are in a position to greatly ameliorate the damage done to children.

1. Establish a buddy system in the classroom. Assign a buddy to all children new to the room (not just the homeless). Make it a classmate-friendly room.

2. Have clear, simple outlines that allow children to fit into the class schedule. (For children enrolling for the first time, let a buddy discuss the routine with the new child, mentor and guide the child through the procedures.)
3. Have a procedure for transitions from one activity to another. Music, rhythm, and movement give children extra creative activities as well as providing organized transitions.
4. Provide a place where children can keep their school materials and a supervised area where homework or enrichment activities can be completed at school.
5. Help the new child catch up, and individualize the assignments for the new child.
6. Provide health provisions (toothbrushes, soap, etc.) and clothes.
7. Encourage parents to become involved. Let the parents of homeless children participate in the classroom. As with all parents, they will need to know how you want them to participate. Plan a workshop for parents, or mentor them individually. Their involvement will not only provide extra help in the classroom, but it can also become an educational program for parents. They may learn more about how they can help their children.

All these suggestions can help the family, but families need time to develop skills and stability. The way homeless shelters are usually set up, the family can stay only a limited time. Some programs have begun to recognize that this does not provide homeless families enough time to gain skills for employment or enough stability to provide for the family. Nuñez (1996) described the American Family Inns, where parents and children can live for a year, establishing stability in the family and allowing the parents to become self-sufficient. The American Family Inn meets the educational needs of each parent, children have supplemental help to compensate for skills they need to develop, and infants and preschoolers go to child development centers, giving the children a jump-start. Recreation and cultural programs are also provided. Similar programs have been established across the country. They provide single mothers and two-parent families time to develop skills and establish stable lifestyles.

The extra effort works. After a family moves from the American Family Inn to their own permanent housing, they are provided with after-care services for an additional year. Studies show that approximately 94 percent who lived in an American Family Inn were still self-sufficient and living independently 2 years later (Nuñez, 1996, p. 76).

The continuing concerns for families and the children without homes affected by homelessness requires giving top priority to schools and programs that help these families survive and flourish. The United States has a challenge from other nations:

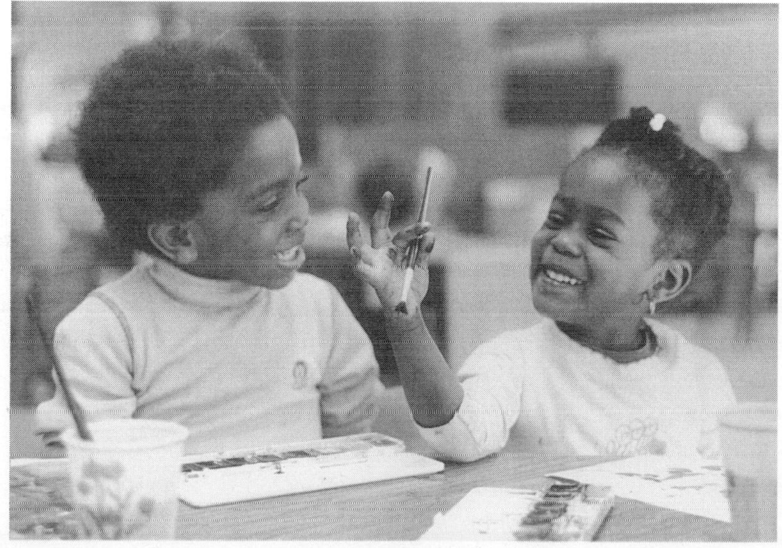

Debra McClave

The 72 million children in 2000 illustrate a 14 percent increase since 1990. Of these, 61 percent were White, 15 percent Black, 17 percent Hispanic, 3 percent Asian American, and 1.5 percent Native American.

The United States ranks 12th among industrialized countries in living standards for our poorest one fifth of children, 14th in efforts to lift children out of the poverty level, 18th in the percentage of children living in poverty, 18th in the narrowest gap between rich and poor, and 25th in infant mortality (Children's Defense Fund, 2005).

SUMMARY

Families around the world are living with change, but the family, the most stable component of society, flourishes. Marriage and family life are important.

The population of the United States has increased dramatically in the last 50 years. Along with growth in numbers, several trends are evident. Many mothers are working outside the home. More people are completing high school and college. Out-of-wedlock births, especially to teenagers, have increased alarmingly. Twenty-nine percent of children live with single parents. Fathers are getting more involved with their children; thus, in the 1990s and 2000s, the emphasis was on families and father involvement.

Poverty in the United States increased in the last decade and leveled off by 2000. The greatest proportions are among children of single-parent mothers and children in Black families.

SUGGESTED CLASS ACTIVITIES AND DISCUSSIONS

1. Count the number of moves the members of your class have made. Why have they moved? Where have they moved? How many times have they moved?
2. Survey your class members. How many different cultural lifestyles are represented in your class? Discuss.
3. How can teachers support fathers' involvement with and support of their children?
4. Interview a single parent. Find out the advantages and disadvantages of rearing children alone. Which support systems do they need?
5. How is family life changing in the United States? How does this affect parent education programs? Discuss the changes that have occurred during your lifetime.
6. Monitor the food stamp program, changed by the 1996 welfare law, the Personal Responsibility and Work Opportunity Reconciliation Act (PRWORA). Is it working? Is it causing hardship for children? Has it been changed?
7. Research the effect of Temporary Assistance for Needy Families (TANF) on child care and families. Has it been helpful? Are there any concerns?

WEB SITES

Association for Childhood Education International (ACEI)
www.acei.org
ACEI's web site includes easy access to important childhood questions.

Involving Fathers at School
www.teachersfirst.com/fathers.html
The site offers a list of programs and their programs for father involvement.

National Association for the Education of Young Children
www.naeyc.org
This national organization focuses on young children.

National Fatherhood Initiative
www.fatherhood.org
This program promotes active fatherhood. Two of their books of interest include *Coaching for Fatherhood* and *Multicultural Counseling with Teenage Fathers.*

3 Working With Culturally Diverse Groups

Children are like snowflakes.
At first they appear to be alike,
But on close examination
they are all different.
Focus on their similarities,
But understand their differences.

In this chapter on working with diverse cultural groups, you will find information that will help you understand distinctions and similarities in the cultural groups with which you might be working and enable you to do the following:

- Explain what the term *culture* means and what it encompasses.
- Explain why examining one's own ancestry, culture, and values is important before beginning to work with diverse families and children.
- Describe some ways that children learn about appreciating differences through an antibias curriculum.
- Discuss strategies for working with children and families who have a Native American culture.
- Discuss the history of Spanish explorers, the terms that should be used when describing the various groups of Hispanic peoples, and the diversity of present-day Hispanics.
- Explain the importance of understanding children and their families as individuals and not to assuming that you know their heritage.
- Discuss strategies for working with children and families who are African American.
- Discuss the various countries that Asian Americans come from, what countries are considered the Indochinese region, and strategies for working with children and families whose heritage is Asian American.

INTRODUCTION

What is the best way teachers can meet the needs of children? How can they help children accept themselves and others in an environment that is fair regardless of ability, gender, or race? How can they encourage all children to achieve their potential in a supportive environment? Four approaches to one's work with children are included here. Those who help children develop—teachers and other personnel—should:

1. *Focus on self.* Know their own biases, beliefs, and culture. Why do they feel the way they do? What do they value? What would they change? Teachers must examine their own lifestyles and beliefs.

2. *Focus on children's understanding and appreciating themselves.* Encourage children to know themselves through an environment of acceptance, encouragement, and inquiry. Interactions with children should be based on knowledge of child development in order for the interaction among children and adults to be appropriate and enabling.
3. *Focus on collaboration with parents and community, acceptance of others, and understanding of cultural history as well as individual family history.* Recognize history and culture and its influence on the lives of children and families.
4. *Focus on caring and teaching.* Strive for practices that acknowledge the child's development and needs. Recognize that there are a variety of learning styles that can be enhanced through teaching strategies that individualize for the strengths and needs of the students.
5. *Focus on helping children whose home language is not English.* Support and encouragement help children adapt and learn.

FOCUS ON SELF

Examine family history. What internalized values really came from childhood and the manner in which children are socialized? How much do you model after your parents, other relatives, or friends? Examine the lives of those who have been significant to you—family, teachers, friends, or someone famous. What was their cultural background? What did they believe? What values did they live by? Have they influenced you?

When did your family or ancestors move to the United States? How easy or hard was the transition from their native country? What are the beliefs that carried down to your generation? What changes were made? How did they influence you, or did they influence you? Or, if you are American Indian, where did your ancestors live? How did they fare when settlers from other countries arrived? What was their value system? Table 3.1 illustrates the diversity in the United States. Many residents have different values and life experiences.

The questions you can ask yourself are endless. If you find some prejudicial feelings, you may be able to examine them, recognize that they are not based on fact, and work them out so that you can be prejudice-free.

Activities

One activity that may help you on your journey to understanding yourself is the answer to the question, "Who am I?" Make a list of who you are. List the points of how you see yourself, as the thoughts come to mind. Do not dwell on what the answers mean. Make the list five to ten items long. Now you can look at the list and see what you placed first. Was it teacher, mother, father, husband, or wife? When you think of yourself, what roles are paramount? Your view of who you are may change depending on what stage of life you are in. You may not even agree with the list you just made. Are there other roles more important to you? The list is unimportant. What is important is your review of the roles and thinking about what they mean to you.

Another activity is something both you and your students can work on. Make a family history. Talk with relatives and find out what you can about the family. Record the stories they share.

If you have a computer, you can use a family history computer program, or you can write a narrative about the family. Use a scanner to include pictures of your ancestors and living relatives. You will learn a lot about your family and yourself.

FOCUS ON CHILDREN AND CULTURE

Many books written since the late 1960s examine multicultural education. Each has its own positions and strengths. Each focuses on its beliefs on how teachers can approach diversity within the classrooms. The focus on children and culture is defined by De Gaetano, Williams, and Volk (1998):

> *Kaleidoscope* is deeply rooted in an understanding that children are intimately connected to their family, their ethnicity, religion, race, gender, abilities, and disabilities, sexual orientation, and life experiences—in short, their culture. This approach requires that

TABLE 3.1 Languages spoken at home by language: 2003.

Language	Number (1,000)	Language	Number (1,000)
Total population 5 years and over	263,230	Other Indic languages	524
Speak only English	214,809	Other Indo-European languages	376
Spanish or Spanish Creole	29,698	Chinese	2,193
French (incl. Patois, Cajun)	1,379	Japanese	475
French Creole	483	Korean	967
Italian	782	Mon-Khmer, Cambodian	163
Portuguese or Portuguese Creole	560	Miao, Hmong	175
German	1,094	Thai	112
Yiddish	142	Laotian	174
Other West Germanic languages	311	Vietnamese	1,104
Scandinavian languages	136	Other Asian languages	525
Greek	333	Tagalog	1,262
Russian	705	Other Pacific Island languages	300
Polish	601	Navajo	136
Serbo-Croatian	234	Other Native North American languages	166
Other Slavic languages	284	Hungarian	90
Armenian	195	Arabic	558
Persian	360	Hebrew	168
Gujarathi	280	African languages	503
Hindi	396	Other and unspecified languages	142
Urdu	335		

263,230 represents 263,230,000. Covers population 5 years old and over. The American Community Survey universe is limited to the household population and excludes the population living in institutions, college dormitories, and other group quarters. Based on a sample and subject to sampling variability.

Source: U.S. Census Bureau, American FactFinder, 2003 American Community Survey Summary Table, P034. Language Spoken at Home for the Population 5 Years and Over. http://factfinder.census.gov, accessed July 10, 2005.

> teachers observe children carefully, seeking the essence of who and what students are, their strengths, and their world. (p. 5)

One book written for preschool teachers and their charges is *Anti-Bias Curriculum: Tools for Empowering Young Children* by Derman-Sparks and A.B.C. Task Force (1989). It focuses on ways to help children see themselves and others in a positive light.

The authors point out that children notice gender and racial differences as early as the second year of life. By age 3 they may have been exposed to biases that are "preprejudice." By ages 3 and 5 they are sorting out aspects of their own self, their gender, and race. For these reasons an antibias curriculum program for young children is important (Derman-Sparks & A.B.C. Task Force, 1989):

> Bicultural, bicognitive education means children (1) learn the beliefs, values, rules, and language of their own culture in the learning/teaching style appropriate to their culture, and also (2) learn the beliefs, values, rules, language, and learning style of the dominant culture.
>
> The ideal early childhood program would incorporate both an anti-bias approach . . . and, where appropriate, bicultural, bicognitive curriculum. (p. 6)

Basic principles that undergird the teaching of children include:

- Affirming the cultures of all children, not simply those of the dominant culture.
- Integrating the experiences and culture of all children into the content and process of schooling to motivate and promote learning.
- Weaving cultural diversity into the transmission of values, knowledge, and skills that occurs in schools.
- Enabling students to become socially and politically responsible people. (De Gaetano, Williams, & Volk, 1998, p. 12)

The *Anti-Bias Curriculum* book helps early childhood educators provide the opportunity for preschool children to examine their gender and cultural identities. When children ask questions, their questions are not ignored. They are answered directly and given opportunities so that they are able to develop their understanding of self and others. Color and cultural blindness and ignoring the questions would be fine if these realities did not exist, but they do. Rather than rejecting the examination of our gender and culture, it is best to recognize it and learn to appreciate differences.

The antibias curriculum seeks to avoid the trap of tourist examination of cultures, in which holidays and customs are the only adventures into cultural identity. A preschool curriculum includes:

1. Many books that reflect differences in gender, race, disabilities, geographic location, and socioeconomic class.
2. Opportunities for dramatic play with costumes, clothing, and equipment that allow for diversity.
3. Identity books such as *I Am Special* or *All About Me.*
4. Music of all countries.
5. Art from all countries.
6. Diversity in the types of dolls.
7. Visuals so that all groups are represented on posters, in pictures, videos, and computers. (Derman-Sparks & A.B.C. Task Force, 1989)

"The first step in implementing an anti-bias approach is establishing the valuing of differences as well as commonalities and fostering respectful, fair treatment of the children in the class" (Derman-Sparks, 2004, p. 27). After children are comfortable with sameness and difference and recognize that the environment is supportive, diversity can be extended beyond the classroom to the neighborhood. The four goals for antibias are (a) to nurture every child's construction of knowledge, self-identity, and group identity; (b) to promote each child's emphatic interaction with people from diverse backgrounds; (c) to foster each child's critical thinking about bias; and (d) to cultivate each child's ability to take action against bias (Derman-Sparks, 2004, p. 35).

The number of multiracial infants has increased 260 percent since the 1970s. Focusing on a single race when many children are multiracial or multiethnic can cause confusion and negative feelings. "Assist these children in integrating their diverse and complex heritage into a unified, healthy self esteem and identity" (Wardle, 2003, p. 34).

Children need to have multiracial and multiethnicity examples in their books, songs, classroom articles and pictures, as well as in the curriculum.

GET ACQUAINTED WITH THE COMMUNITY

Because of the influx of new minority groups into the United States, teachers are realizing they need to increase their understanding of different cultures. This is not an easy task, and it requires an essential commitment. The first and most important thing to remember when working with culturally diverse groups is to avoid stereotyping. Although it is essential to understand a group's culture, it is also necessary to allow them to be individuals. Every group is composed of individuals, and those individuals may or may not fit the norm.

The only way to get to know the families in the community, in addition to inviting them to the school, is to go out into the community to meet them on their territory.

School personnel should get acquainted with the school neighborhood before school starts. Take "block walks" with small groups in nice weather. A complete, integrated study unit may also be developed on the neighborhood early in the school year.

Eugenia Hepworth Berger

Strengths found in African American families include strong kinship bonds and a strong work and achievement orientation.

CULTURAL DIVERSITY

"Citizens in a diverse democratic society should be able to maintain attachments to their cultural communities as well as participate effectively in the shared national culture" (Banks, 2003 p. xxi). It is important that diversity is looked upon as an enrichment to the national culture, but it is even more important that all citizens share allegiance and identity with the national culture. "Diversity without unity leads to Balkanization and the fracturing of the nation-state" (Banks, 2003, p. xxi). Throughout the generations of immigrants arriving on the shores of the United States, many have taken time to assimilate into the national culture, but the intent, and later, the transition and transformation was accomplished. The number of ethnic groups arriving in the United States has increased in recent years so that some school systems have many immigrant groups with varying languages and customs. In addition, there are cultural groups who are already citizens who have not prospered in the educational systems. It is imperative that the educational system respond to the needs of new arrivals as well the needs of cultural groups already here. Our nation is culturally diverse. It includes diverse family configurations, many ethnic groups, varying socioeconomic levels, and religious differences, as well as rural and urban influences. For over 300 years, men and women in North America have been marrying others who have different countries of origin. Our society is made up of Irish Americans, Italian Americans, Asian Americans, Polish Americans, Albanian Americans, Native Americans, German Americans, African Americans, English Americans, French Americans, Spanish Americans, Arab Americans, and many others. Most of these have a multi-American cultural background such as French American, Native American, African American, and Irish American combined, or Irish American, German American, and Italian American combined.

Most of the new arrivals (85 percent of foreign-born) are legal residents. Of this group, most (78 percent) of the children attend school in five states (California, 45 percent; Illinois; Texas; New York; and Florida). Schools will find an increase in the number of students as well as children from many countries. It is projected that the number of children in school will grow from 34 million in 1990 to 42 million in 2010. Of these, 9 million will be children of immigrants, 22 percent of the school-age population (Board on Children and Families, 1995, p. 75). School personnel should be aware of and ready to respond to the cultural diversity.

Culture: A Way of Life

School personnel and parents may not understand the cultures that make up the school population. The term *culture* is most easily understood when viewed as a way of life. Other descriptions are "blueprints for living" and "guidelines for life." Culture includes the way in which life is perceived. It is the knowing, perceiving, and understanding one brings to a situation. Culture may include artifacts such as housing, clothing, and utensils. It is easier to recognize that different artifacts stem from different lifestyles than it is to discern that individuals are perceiving information differently—viewing a situation or communication with varying interpretations.

Culture is both *learned* and *internalized* by the child. Children of any ethnic background learn the cultural patterns in which they are raised. They come to school with those perceptions. For example, the concept that a child should be seen and not heard is common in various cultures. Such a child is usually well behaved but does not offer to answer questions or is not comfortable talking in class. This trait does not work to the child's advantage in school when the student is called upon. Teachers should be aware of this cultural pattern and make sure that the child has many opportunities for expression in an encouraging, safe environment. They must be aware that the child has internalized the quiet behavior. It will be difficult for the student to change, but acceptance of the child's positive behavior plus encouragement and reinforcement of the desired behavior will help the child participate. High expectations based on knowledge and understanding of each child sets the stage for growth.

The teacher and the class have an opportunity to build an effective community of children who work together in a respectful manner. Recognition and acceptance of diversity allows individuals and groups to interact effectively. Being culturally attuned to the members of a class requires a response "that demonstrates openness and authentic responsiveness to the heritage values and expressions of each cultural group represented in the student population" (Lindsay, Roberts, & Campbelljones, 2005, p. 54).

Exploring Your Culture

A look at the ancestry groups of those who live in the United States shows how diverse the population is. The United States is a nation made up of many ancestry groups. In Table 3.2 you will not find those from Asia listed because their increase in population is recent rather than distant ancestry. Native Americans as well as those from Mexico and other Latin and South American countries are included under United States or American. The figure illustrates the descendents of early immigration into the United States. The greatest number of immigrants were of German ancestry with the Irish being the second highest. English is the third largest group of ancestry and those from North and South America is fourth. The message behind Table 3.2 is the recognition of the United States as a multicultural nation.

When people first arrive in the United States, intermarriage with those from other countries of origin may or may not have occurred. But the mixture in the United States increases as people interact with one another. Children in a classroom may not even be aware of their ethnic background. Encouraging them to explore their ancestors results in greater understanding of culture with its historical and geographical background.

Challenges

Two challenges face the schools as they work with culturally diverse students. One is accepting, understanding, and working with each child. The other is helping the children to accept themselves. The more the school and home become involved with each other in a positive relationship, the greater the opportunities for understanding the family and reducing discrimination.

TABLE 3.2 Population by selected ancestry group and region: 2003.

Ancestry group	Total (1,000)	Percent distribution by region: Northeast	Midwest	South	West
Total population	282,910	19	22	36	23
Arab	1,258	25	24	27	24
Austrian	790	31	24	22	23
British	1,153	17	17	38	28
Canadian	698	32	17	24	27
Czech	1,426	12	45	26	17
Danish	1,435	8	33	15	44
Dutch	5,059	16	37	27	21
English	28,403	17	22	37	24
European	2,164	13	19	31	36
Finnish	778	10	59	10	20
French (except Basque)	9,678	26	24	31	19
French Canadian	2,188	42	20	23	16
German	47,842	16	39	25	19
Greek	1,229	34	22	24	20
Hungarian	1,495	33	31	20	17
Irish	33,992	26	24	31	18
Italian	16,726	47	16	21	16
Lithuanian	720	41	28	18	13
Norwegian	4,494	6	50	11	33
Polish	9,304	34	38	17	11
Portuguese	1,349	47	3	12	38
Russian	2,975	38	18	20	24
Scotch Irish	5,099	14	20	45	21
Scottish	5,811	18	20	36	26
Slovak	811	46	35	11	8
Sub-Saharan African[1]	1,884	25	17	42	15
African	1,144	19	17	48	15
Swedish	4,254	14	40	15	31
Swiss	984	14	35	18	33
Ukrainian	870	44	21	17	18
United States or American	19,677	10	20	54	16
Welsh	1,890	20	24	30	26
West Indian[1,2]	2,129	50	4	42	4
Haitian	666	43	2	53	2
Jamaican	825	52	5	39	4

In thousands (282,910 represents 282,910,000). Covers single and multiple ancestries. The American Community Survery universe is limited to the household population and excludes the population living in institutions, college dormitories, and other group quarters. Based on a sample and subject to sampling variability.

[1] Includes other groups not shown separately.

[2] Excludes Hispanic origin groups.

Source: U.S. Census Bureau, American FactFinder, 2003 American Community Survey Summary Tables. PCT023 Ancestry; and PCT026 Ancestry (Total Categories Tallied) For people With One Or More Ancestry Categories Reported. http://factfinder.census.gov, accessed August 4, 2005.

Since the Vietnam War, refugees from most of Indochina—Laotians, Hmongs, Cambodians, Chinese, and Vietnamese—have entered our schools. In addition, many new arrivals have come from Mexico, Latin America, and South America. Immigration has continued from other countries as well, so you may find children in the schools speaking languages from Europe, Asia, Africa, and the Americas.

Caring Strategies

Some teaching and caring strategies may be more effective than others in working with children. Consider (a) group problem solving; (b) peer reading and tutoring; (c) cooperative learning; (d) group pride, sharing, and replacing competition against others with self-competition; (e) culturally relevant materials; (f) parent volunteers; (g) flexibility in timed events, and (h) dramatizations, sharing of folk tales, and journal writing (Berger, 1997; Gilliland, 1988; Little Soldier, 1985). Observe the children and analyze their learning strengths and interests. As you learn about your students, adapt your class to the best ways of learning for individual children and the class as a group.

Glenn Morris

When studying American Indians (Native Americans), it becomes clear that there is diversity as well as commonalities among the nations. Visit with families or attend a powwow. Get to know the parents and grandparents of the child.

THE FIRST INHABITANTS OF NORTH AMERICA

American Indians, the Native Americans, are indigenous to what is now the United States. The most prominent theory of their origin asserts that their ancestors crossed a land bridge across the Bering Strait from Siberia into North America as early as 40,000–10,000 B.C. (Kullen, 1994). Although often portrayed as a homogeneous people, they are diverse both culturally and physically. Their facial features, height, and hair textures vary; skin colors range from dark brown to very light (Banks, 2003).

When the Europeans first came to the Americas, as many as 18 million Native Americans were living in North America (John, 1988). Estimates of the number of spoken languages range from 300 (John, 1988) to 2,000 (Banks, 2003). Anthropologists have attempted to group the Indian nations who resided in what is now the United States. These groupings include the following areas: Eastern Woodland, Great Lakes Woodland, Southeastern, North Central Plains, South Central Plains, Southwest, California, Northwestern Plateau, and Northwest Pacific Coast.

Native Americans share many values and characteristics, including spirituality with a deep respect for the land, and living things. In early days Native Americans did not recognize ownership of land. They believed that the land could be used as long as you respect it, but people did not own the land (Banks, 2003). But in addition to similarities, many nations and groups have varying cultural traits. Table 3.3 shows the self-identification of 39 tribes,

TABLE 3.3 American Indian and Alaska Native population by tribe: 2000.

American Indian and Alaska Native tribe	Number	American Indian and Alaska Native tribe	Number
Total persons[1]	4,119,301	Osage	15,897
Apache	96,833	Ottawa	10,677
Blackfeet	85,750	Paiute	13,532
Cherokee	729,533	Pima	11,493
Cheyenne	18,204	Potawatomi	25,595
Chickasaw	38,351	Pueblo	74,085
Chippewa	149,669	Puget Sound Salish	14,631
Choctaw	158,774	Seminole	27,431
Colville	9,393	Shoshone	12,026
Comanche	19,376	Sioux	153,360
Cree	7,734	Tohono O'odham	20,087
Creek	71,310	United Houma Nation	8,713
Crow	13,394	Ute	10,385
Delaware	16,341	Yakama	10,851
Iroquois	80,822	Yaqui	22,412
Kiowa	12,242	Yuman	8,976
Latin American Indian	180,940	Alaskan Athabascan	18,838
Lumbee	57,868	Aleut	10,548
Menominee	9,840	Eskimo	54,761
Navajo	298,197	Tlingit-Haida	22,365

As of April. This table shows data for American Indian and Alaska Native tribes alone or in combination of tribes or races. Respondents who identified themselves as American Indian or Alaska Native were asked to report their enrolled or principal tribe. Therefore, data shown here reflect the written tribal entries reported on the questionnaire. Some of the entries (for example, Iroquois, Sioux, Colorado River, and Flathead) represent nations or reservations. The information on tribe is based on self-identification and includes federally or state-recognized tribes, as well as bands and clans.

[1]Includes other tribes not shown separately.

Source: U.S. Census Bureau, *The American Indian and Alaska Native Population: 2000*, Census 2000 Brief (C2KBR/01–15), February 2002.

bands, and clans. The total person category lists a population of 4,119,301 American Indians and Alaska Natives. This includes other tribes that are not shown separately. The Cherokee list of 729,533 members includes a variety of tribes, bands, or clans living in different areas. The second largest group, the Navajo, have 298,197 members, who primarily live on a reservation. The number of self-identified Native Americans illustrates the diversity of Native Americans from the smallest tribe listed, the Cree, with 7,734 members to the largest, the Cherokee.

When studying the American Indian (Native American), it becomes clear that there is diversity as well as commonality among the nations.

Contributions to Civilization

Native Americans have made important contributions to the U.S. and world cultures. Their contributions to agriculture, architecture, irrigation, and government are outstanding. As early as 10,000 B.C. the Native Americans had domesticated corn. They were accomplished horticulturists. In addition to corn, some of the more common foods developed by the Indians of North and South America are potatoes, peppers, tomatoes, peanuts, squash, maple sugar, and beans. (The Irish potato originated with Native Americans.) These foods are used extensively in the world today. Indians in the Southwest developed an elaborate irrigation system. The pyramids of Teotihuacan in Mexico, the Tikal pyramids in Guatemala, and the Cahokia pyramids in the Mississippian culture as well as the Taos pueblos illustrate their architectural achievements (Kullen, 1994; Weatherford, 1988, 1991).

Their concept of representative government, which was practiced by the Iroquois confederacy of Five Nations (Mohawks, Oneidas, Onondagas, Cayugas, Senecas, and later the Tuscaroras) had great influence on the establishment of the U.S. government. Benjamin Franklin studied this confederacy and learned about their representative government before the U.S. Constitution was written (Weatherford, 1988). These and other contributions help show a more accurate picture of the Native American.

By the time Cristoforo Colombo (Christopher Columbus) arrived, there were more than 300 nations established in all parts of North America. The population estimates ranged from 2 or 3 million to 18 million.

Movement West

Within each area, numerous Indian tribes flourished. As Europeans settled the eastern portion of the United States, those people indigenous to the East were pushed westward.

Indian tribes were placed on reservations with most of the reservations in the midwestern and western parts of the United States. The treatment of the Native American is characterized by broken treaties, genocide, and persecution—an oppressive chapter of American history.

Most descriptions of the European expansion into North America misrepresent the resistance of the Native American. This distortion of history influences the view other Americans hold about Native Americans, as well as erodes the Native American's self-esteem. A study of different Indian nations, including the people indigenous to the area

Debra McClave

A study of Indian nations, including people indigenous to the area in which you live, will provide a more accurate picture of Native Americans.

in which you live, will provide a more accurate picture of the history of the Native American.

Education for Native Americans

In the 1990s two landmark efforts were made to describe Indian education and to make specific recommendations for its improvement. Two groups working toward these aims were the Indian Nation a Risk Task Force and the White House Conference on Indian Education (WHCIE). Suggested basic research included the study of bilingualism, the inclusion of Native American languages, and research into the health issue of fetal alcohol effects. It was also recommended that Native Americans should do more research—that an insider view is essential.

Suggestions include:

- Alternative assessment or unbiased standardized tests to assess student achievement and abilities
- Effective parent support programs (WHCIE)
- Instruction, curriculum, and program administration for exceptional American Indians and Alaska Natives of all ages (WHCIE)

Insights for Teachers and Administrators

1. Although Native Americans come from diverse cultures, they are similar in many ways. It is important that teachers who have these children in their classes learn as much as possible about their specific cultures and backgrounds. "The acculturation of Native Americans should be looked upon as a continuum ranging from 'traditional orientation' to 'assimilated' " (Little Soldier, 1985, p. 186).
2. As is the case in all ethnic groups, individual preferences and values exist. Use the background on culture as a guide to help you understand the individual child, not as a stereotypical absolute.
3. Visit in the neighborhood, talk with parents in informal settings, attend a powwow (unless it is a closed ceremony), and visit the parents in their homes after they feel comfortable having you there.
4. In working with the parents of Native American children, teachers need to show interest and acceptance. Teachers must expect to reach out to the parents and the extended family. Help them feel comfortable with you and the classroom. When they are at ease, invite them to share their specialties, perhaps crafts and folklore, with the class.
5. Curriculum in the schools needs to include an accurate history of Native Americans to overcome the stereotypical misrepresentation of them as savage hunters of the plains. The study of Indian nations that represent a variety of lifestyles and governmental forms can show the diversity and accomplishments of American Indians prior to the coming of the Europeans.
6. Some cultural traits that may cause misunderstanding unless the teacher is aware of them include (Gilliland, 1988):
    a. *Eye contact.* To many Indians, looking down is a sign of respect. In some Indian groups, a person looks another in the eye only to show defiance.
    b. *Time.* Time has a different meaning for many Indians, far different from the way many European Americans view the concept. For example, European Americans "say 'time flies.' To the Mexican 'time walks.' However, the Indian tells, 'time is with us' " (p. 26). Patience is a highly valued characteristic.
    c. *Family.* The extended family is important to the Native American child, so grandparents may be the ones to attend parent–teacher conferences. If the child is separated from the extended family by a move to the city or some other circumstance, the child may experience a loss of the sense of security.
    d. *Nature and spirituality.* Native Americans respect nature, and spirituality is an important part of the Indian culture. "Harmony with nature, and spirituality, are also necessary to good health" (p. 31).
    e. *Age and wisdom.* The focus in the dominant U.S. society is on youth; in the Native American tradition, there is respect for age and the wisdom associated with elderly people.

ARRIVAL OF OTHER ETHNIC GROUPS

Some believe that artifacts in Mexico indicate that Africans were the first to "discover" America, but no settlement or lasting impact occurred. It is known that around A.D. 1000, Norse explorers Leif Ericsson and Thorwald Ericsson made voyages to Newfoundland. Since Norse settlements did not survive, their impact on the continent did not continue. The next group of people to explore the Americas were the Spanish. The Portuguese, French, and British followed.

SPANISH AMERICAN FAMILIES

When the Europeans came to the Americas there were two continents that already had 300 nations, each designated by individual names and each with its own culture developed in response to the environment and to answer its people's questions about life and death. The continents were named after Amerigo Vespucci, a navigator and explorer, because German cartographer Martin Waldesmuller published a map with the name *America* on it.

Christopher Columbus, sailing for Spain and searching for Asia, reached the Caribbean in 1492. He landed on the island of San Salvador in the Bahamas, explored Cuba and Hispaniola, made three more voyages, and claimed all the land for Spain. In 1496 Santo Domingo was established by Columbus on the southwestern shore of Hispaniola, the earliest continuously inhabited settlement of Europeans in America. Spanish explorations included present-day Puerto Rico, Florida, Mexico, and the southwestern United States. In 1559, Arellano became governor of La Florida. One thousand colonists and 500 soldiers brought 240 horses and settled near present-day Pensacola. In 1560, Durango in north-central Mexico was founded. Others were becoming interested in the new land. In 1564 French Huguenots built Fort Caroline on the St. Johns River in Florida. The Spanish drove out the Huguenots, destroyed Fort Caroline, and in 1565 established a colony at St. Augustine.

The Spanish explorations were far flung. Missions were established as far north as present-day San Francisco and beyond.

Throughout the 1500s the Spanish explorers continued to develop a Spanish empire in the Americas. Coronado marched north into Arizona and New Mexico. De Soto reached the Mississippi River in 1542. Spanish explorers including Ponce de Leon, Cortes, Coronado, and Balboa explored what is now Florida, Mississippi, New Mexico, and other parts of the western and southern United States as well as Mexico and South America.

One area in the United States that was settled as early as 1581 and still retains the beauty of some of its early culture is southern Colorado and New Mexico. In 1581, Juan de Onate helped found a settlement and Franciscan missions in the Rio Grande Valley of New Mexico. In 1600 the colonists moved to San Gabrielle on the Rio Grande. Onate served as governor until 1607. The city of Santa Fe, the first capital in the United States, was established in 1609. Many of the descendants of the early conquistadors and families who were given Spanish land grants still live in Colorado and New Mexico.

Debra McClave

The Hispanic American population is heterogeneous with varied social status and educational levels, isolation or hardships encountered on arrival, desire to acculturate, and the length of time they have resided in the United States. Many in the Southwest are descendants of early settlers.

This first group of Spanish-surnamed citizens in the United States were in North America before the Pilgrims arrived. Hardly immigrants, they had settled and lived with the Pueblo Indians long before the United States was interested in the territory. These Spanish colonialists, given land grants by the Spanish viceroys, continued their Spanish lifestyle in areas including Santa Fe, San Antonio, and San Diego. Missions, Spanish-style architecture, their methods of ranching, and irrigation systems show their contributions to the lifestyle of the Southwest. Many of these people do not want to be called Mexican American or Chicano; their heritage is Spanish and the terms *Spanish American, Hispanic,* or *Latino* better fit their culture and their heritage.

Diversity in Present-Day Hispanics

Although the Spanish-surnamed residents of the United States share some linguistic and cultural traits, each wave of immigrants from Spain, Cuba, Latin America, and Mexico, as well as U.S. citizens from Puerto Rico, has brought unique attributes. Varied social status and educational levels in their countries of origin, the isolation or hardships encountered on arrival, their desire to acculturate, and the length of their family's residence in the United States all contribute to a heterogeneous Hispanic American population. Teachers must work to dispel any stereotypical ideas they may have about their Spanish-surnamed students.

The southwestern United States was Spanish territory until 1821, when Mexico gained independence from Spain. The Southwest was part of Mexico until Texas gained freedom in 1836 and was annexed by the United States in 1845. Arizona, New Mexico, Nevada, and parts of California and Colorado were acquired by the United States as the result of the Mexican-American War. Thus, by 1848 many people whose ancestors had lived in traditionally Spanish-speaking areas since the 1600s suddenly became citizens of the United States.

The great influx of Mexican Americans did not begin in the United States until about the time of the Mexican Revolution in 1910. Many of the first immigrants were upper-class Mexicans, refugees escaping for political reasons. Their assimilation into U.S. society was relatively easy. A second influx of immigrants occurred in 1916, when Mexicans were hired to help maintain the railroad system across the United States. They were expected to work and return home, but many remained. They suffered bitter discrimination, especially from those who felt that they were taking jobs from U.S. citizens. Nonetheless, the descendants of this group of Mexican Americans are now assimilated into the society.

During World War II the United States needed help with its farm crops, so the *bracero* program was instituted. Mexicans were invited to work temporarily in the gardens of California and other states. In 1951, the Migratory Labor Agreement (P.L. 78) established a new *bracero* program (Banks, 1997).

After World War II many Spanish-surnamed people migrated to cities and northern states to work. Some came from Mexico, but many were U.S. citizens who moved from New Mexico, Texas, and southern Colorado to work in cities and on ranches. These included the natives of the Southwest who were forced off their land when the mines closed and farms were automated. They were a rural people, trying to assimilate into an urban culture.

The use of *braceros* and migrant workers set a pattern for Mexican workers to come to the United States. Many began crossing the border illegally. In 1954 U.S. immigration authorities began deporting illegal Mexicans, but thousands of Mexicans continued to pour across the borders (Banks, 1997). An amnesty bill passed by Congress and implemented in 1988 allowed illegal residents who could prove they had lived in the United States for 5 years to become citizens.

Illegal immigration continues today. The economies in Mexico and other Latin American countries are poor. Many of these immigrants are grasping at an opportunity to provide for their families. In the 1990s and first decade of the 21st century, the influx of illegal immigrants, along with legal immigration, was extremely high. The children come to school knowing little or no English. These children need special care and help to succeed in our educational system. This new group of Spanish-speaking Americans, coupled with the rural-to-urban movement of longtime citizens of Hispanic background, present a challenge to the schools to provide both bilingual education and a strong program in language enrichment.

Insights for Teachers and Administrators

It should be remembered that Spanish Americans were the first to settle in America—in New Mexico, Texas, Colorado, Arizona, Florida, and California—so there are many levels of assimilation and diversity. Sharing the knowledge of the contributions of all Hispanic groups helps children respect and honor that heritage.

1. Children of Hispanic heritage seem to work best in a cooperative, rather than competitive, atmosphere.
2. For the newly arrived Hispanic, opportunities for language expression need to be encouraged at all levels of education. Small group discussions, cooperative games that increase language skills, use of language on the computer, role playing, creative dramatics, puppetry, and general encouragement of language use are all essential for language development. Classrooms in which children are encouraged to talk with one another also promote language development. If children are not allowed to talk in the lunchroom, the importance of language development is being ignored.
3. As is the case with all children, teachers working with Spanish-surnamed children must get to know the parents and work with them and their children to meet their needs.
4. Recently arrived immigrants may be reluctant to get involved in the school—many fear being identified as illegal immigrants, even though schools are required to educate all children and are not responsible for determining who is legal and who is not. Many of these parents have not had a good experience in school themselves and feel threatened by the school. See chapters 5, 8, and 9 for ideas on how to involve this challenging group of parents.
5. Education of Latinos varies from bilingual to English emersion. Some recent data recommended focus on English with substantial support for the learner. An important ingredient is the teacher. Excellent teachers provide the environment that produces excellent results.

AFRICAN AMERICAN FAMILIES

African Americans have been a part of the Americas since Diego el Negro sailed with Columbus in 1502. Blacks helped Coronado explore present-day Kansas in 1541 and helped establish St. Augustine, Florida, in 1565 (Banks, 1991). As indentured servants, Blacks landed on the eastern shores of the United States in 1619. When they were brought over as slaves, their culture was eradicated as much as possible. (Refer to chapter 4 for a discussion of slavery.) Family life was discouraged, and families were broken up if the master wanted to sell one member of the family and not the others. Children were most often left with their mother until they were old enough to be on their own.

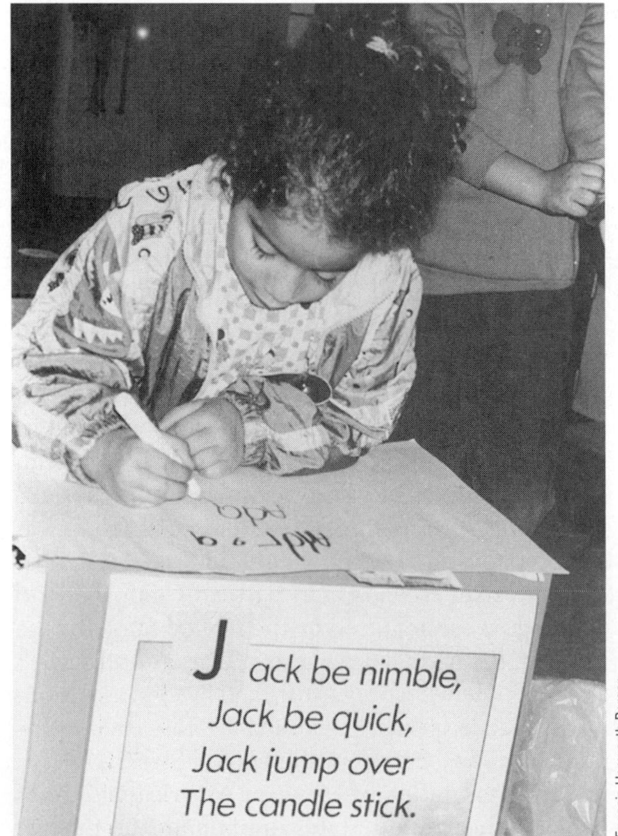

The strengths found in African American families include strong kinship bonds, an achievement orientation, a strong work ethic with a desire for upward mobility, adaptable family roles, and an emphasis on religion.

Most were not allowed to learn to read; schooling was usually forbidden.

Achievements of African Americans

Throughout the history of the United States there have been African Americans who were free, and many who were slaves educated themselves. Those who were free worked for the emancipation of African Americans who were under the bondage of slavery. African Americans contributed to the growth and development of the United States. They were leaders, teachers, and scientists. In 1770 Crispus Attucks, the first to die for independence, was killed during the Boston Massacre. Benjamin Banneker (1731–1806) was an inventor and mathematical genius. Harriet Tubman (1826–1913) conducted the Underground Railroad, a system of helping slaves escape bondage. Frederick A. Douglass (1817–1895), a great orator, denounced the evils of slavery. James P. Beckwourth (1798–1867) was a pioneer in the West. Early members of Congress included many African American men who served from 1870 and beyond.

African Americans continued to contribute as scientists, artists, business leaders, agronomists, musicians, educators, and authors. Elijah McCoy (1843–1929) was an inventor who had 57 patents; Dr Daniel Hale Williams (1856–1931) was the first person to perform heart surgery; Dr. Ernest E. Just (1883–1941) was a noted biologist; and Charles Drew (1904–1950) was a pioneer in blood plasma preservation. Children know about Martin Luther King Jr., but many do not know the heritage of other African Americans. The African American heritage includes a high development of music, art, literature, and an emphasis on religion. There is a strong commitment to church—most African Americans have a church affiliation—so children grow up in families where faith and religion are important. Many Black leaders have been ministers (for example, Martin Luther King Jr. and Jesse Jackson). Music is an essential expression in their religion. Black musicians developed jazz. Although many Blacks have a remarkable creative ability in music, this does not mean that all Blacks are great musicians, nor do all Blacks use the church as a focal point in their lives.

The strengths found in African American families include strong kinship bonds, an achievement orientation, a strong work orientation with a desire for upward mobility, adaptability of family roles, and an emphasis on religion (Banks, 2003; Billingsley, 1992; Hale-Benson, 1986; Hill, 2001). Roles are flexible, egalitarian, and adaptable. Although mothers have a special place in the family, the extended family allows parenting roles to be shared by family members, relatives, or friends. African Americans gain strength through extended family relationships (Weaver, 2005). These strengths encourage parent–teacher cooperation, and school personnel should approach the collaboration with a winning attitude. The extended family, along with flexible family roles, allowed families to survive the hardships and trials that have been a part of their lives in the United States.

The "church and community-based culture" of African Americans . . . "serve protective and promotive functions," providing a "sense of adequacy and belonging. This softened the effects of mainstream abuse and exclusion" (Comer, 2004, p. 87). Earlier, Comer (1997) recommended that for African Americans to become part of the "Good Society," the first step was that scapegoating of Blacks and others must decrease. This is necessary so that all can focus on and handle the problems and opportunities that exist. Second, schools must help solve the cultural and societal problems of the nation rather than reflect them. Last, it is possible to have a "win-win culture," still competitive but also enabling and caring (pp. 14–15).

In order for families to thrive in a democracy, Comer (1997) states that the society must (a) develop a sound and growing economy that permits the participation of all its citizens, and (b) maintain sound community and family functioning so that critical tasks, particularly childrearing, can be performed well. The culture must value families, allowing them to participate in a strong economy and facilitating a sound family and community (p. 11). African American students need to have a caring school community and a supportive family. They also need the opportunities for their families to participate fully in the society.

Insights for Teachers and Administrators

Sharing the knowledge of the contributions of African Americans helps children respect and honor their heritage. Focus on discovering the many contributions made by African Americans and other ethnic groups. Help children know the dream.

1. Each child, of any cultural group, is unique. Culture depends in great part on the location and socioeconomic status of the family. The culture—regardless of race—in a lower-income neighborhood is much different from that in a middle-class and upper-class area. Middle- and upper-class African Americans tend to have culture similar to that of others in middle- and upper-class society in the United States.
2. Impoverished Black families have different strengths and different problems. Black parents in ghettos face problems of poverty, powerlessness, alienation, and a negative environment. Their children rarely see models of financial success as a result of education and hard work. A good standard of living is impossible if the parent is unemployed or earning only minimum wage. These children are raised in a culture of dropouts and school failure, as well as with the love of their extended family.
3. Encourage parents and compliment their effort to encourage their children to achieve. Clark (1983) and Comer (1997, 2004) suggest that family lifestyle is a stronger indicator of a child's success in school than socioeconomic level. Clark found that children who were high achievers came from homes that supported and helped their children achieve, regardless of their income. The interpersonal communications within these families showed encouragement in their academics, nurturing interaction with frequent dialogue, established rules and clear guidelines, and monitoring of their learning activities.
4. Collaboration with parents can encourage success for both the child and the parent. When parents participate in decision making and learning activities, it allows them to be involved with the schools in positive ways. "When engaged in task-oriented activities with stipulated objectives and expected outcomes, the individual experiences his or her effort as being valued and accumulates strength that is generated by the realization that he or she is able to make things happen. In a society in which one is defined by what one does, a mother's identity and self-worth begins to be reaffirmed by virtue of her work in schools" (Winters, 1993, p. 99).
5. Children who speak a Black dialect of English at home will come to school knowing different language patterns than those who are surrounded by standard English. They will have to practice standard English, which is not always an easy task. Have the room share stories and chants. Encourage listening, sharing, initiating, and labeling, along with language activities encouraged in an early childhood classroom. There should be ample opportunity for all children to enjoy them.
6. A model early childhood classroom for all children includes (a) a supportive environment with frequent touching and lap sitting; (b) an emphasis on the development of self-concept through success experiences, compliments, and display of work; (c) opportunities for creative expression in music, dramatics, and visual arts; (d) involvement in arts and crafts with African American and African art as part of the curriculum; (e) activities that involve physical movement, play, and dance with as much self-direction as feasible; (f) exposure to artifacts, stories, and other aspects of African culture; (g) extracurricular activities that include bringing the community into the school and taking field trips; and (h) celebration of holidays that include the holidays of many cultural groups (Hale-Benson, 1986). A child-care center, Visions for Children, founded by Hale in a Cleveland suburb, is based on the program described here:

> Visions for Children's focus is on language skills. This includes expressive as well as receptive language; too often children receive language through listening but do not have enough opportunity to engage in expressive language. Expressive language includes holding conversations with adults, telling stories for pictures, engaging in sociodramatic play, and responding to questions in complete sentences. (Hale, 1994, p. 175)

The teacher must be aware of body language and be sensitive to its cues, model standard English, encourage the children to talk, emphasize group learning, incorporate music into the curriculum, and have a variety of learning activities that reach children with a variety of learning styles.

Until prejudice and discrimination are eliminated in the United States, most Black children will receive mixed messages. Schools that include their parents as active partners, recognizing their contributions, will enable children to feel acknowledged and accepted. At school, children need to receive one message: All children will succeed because they are first-class citizens.

ASIAN-AMERICAN FAMILIES

"The term, Asian, refers to people having origins in any of the original peoples of the Far East, Southeast Asia, or the Indian subcontinent (for example, Cambodia, China, India, Japan, Korea, Malaysia, Pakistan, the Philippine Islands, Thailand, and Vietnam)" (U.S. Census Bureau, 2002, p. 1). Since 1965 and the passage of the Immigration and Nationality Act Amendments of 1965 and the end of the Vietnam War in 1975, many immigrants have arrived from Asia. Most (70 percent) came to the United States after 1970 (Lee, 1998). Those coming from Southeast Asia were primarily refugees from the Vietnam War. One of the easiest mistakes for teachers to make is to presume all Southeast Asians—from Vietnam, Laos (including the Hmong), Cambodia, and Thailand—share a common background. The first major group of refugees arrived from South Vietnam in 1975 after the fall of the country to the North Vietnamese. This group included wealthy and poor people and highly educated scholars and professionals as well as unskilled workers. Most were literate, but 18 percent had no education (Banks, 1991). The second wave of Indochinese refugees was more diverse and included Hmong, Laotians, and Kampucheans (Cambodians). They were more homogeneous in their lack of education and their inability to speak English.

Eugenia Hepworth Berger

The term *Asian* refers to people who originated from the Far East, Southeast Asia, or the Indian subcontinent.

The largest Asian ethnic group in the United States is from China and in 2002 had a total of 2.7 million persons living here. Of this number, 15.4 percent of the total identified themselves as one of a multiple group, for example, Chinese and Filipino. The second largest group was Filipino, with 2.4 million persons; 2.4 percent had multiple ethnicity. Third were the Asian Indians with 1.9 million, and 1.6 percent reported multiple identification. These three groups emigrated to the United States for various reasons, including the opportunity to obtain work and the ability to send money to their families left in their homeland.

Chinese men migrated to the United States in the 1840s to work on the transcontinental railroad. Later, they were able to bring their families over. Immigration was highly restrictive until the Immigration and Nationality Act was passed in 1965 and extended in 1990, allowing a dramatic increase in immigration from Asians. The fourth largest group of immigrants had a very different migration push. The Vietnamese began coming to the United States in the 1970s as refugees from the Vietnam War. Their population reached 1.2 million, with 8.3 percent having multiple ethnicity. Cambodians, Hmong, and Laotians also emigrated following the Vietnam War (U.S. Census Bureau, 2002; Weaver, 2005).

French Indochina, proclaimed the Indochinese Union by the French in 1893, was made up of Vietnam, Cambodia, and Laos. Until that time, the countries were separate political entities; after the union they continued to differ from one another in language, history, and culture. The term *Indochinese* was given by the French and may be used to describe an area but should not be used to designate individual countries. Laos, Cambodia, and Thailand were influenced by India; Vietnam and the Hmong regions (the mountains of Laos) were influenced by China. However, these countries do not view themselves as one area; they are separate countries. Throughout their long history, these countries were often enemies, controlled by one or the other as one empire thrived and was then destroyed. When working with children from this area of Asia, find out which country was the parent's homeland.

Language differences in these countries are illustrated in Figure 3.1 and Table 3.1. These children will have to use English as a second language to communicate with each other. Indochinese families also have different placement of names.

The Vietnamese, Cambodians, and Laotians are addressed by their first name, although many of the refugees have adapted their names to fit name placement traditionally found in the United States. Schools may not find as much confusion in 2008 as they did in the 1970s.

During the 2,000-year history of Indochina, its inhabitants were influenced by Chinese, Indian, Oceanic, and European cultures. The variety of religious traditions are indicative of the many cultures in the region. Buddhism spread from India; Taoism and Confucianism originated in China; and Christianity was introduced much later. An Indochinese person may believe in more than one religion because Eastern religions are based on philosophies of behavior more than deification of their leaders. In addition to the major religions, animism and ancestor worship are practiced in many rural areas. Polytheism is accepted. Most Eastern religions share an emphasis on the individual's search for peace and harmony, a reverence for ancestors, and a respect for elderly persons.

Insights for Teachers and Administrators

It will be necessary for the teacher to determine whether the families of students who are from Asia have lived in the United States 20 to 30 years or whether they are new arrivals.

1. If children come from a culture where there is no formal education, they may have problems adjusting to school. Teachers need to recognize these children's experiences and backgrounds and plan a curriculum to address their strengths and needs.
2. Southeast Asian children who were in school before coming to the United States were taught largely through lecture and memorization; active participation in the learning process may be new to them. Others may not have attended school at all.
3. Most Indochinese families form close-knit extended families. They often try to reunite when they arrive in the United States. They also work hard to save money, often sacrificing, to bring other members of their families to their new home. Use journals for older children and creative art for younger and older children to help them express feelings.
4. Teachers should be sensitive to gestures and mannerisms that may have unintended meanings. For example, Southeast Asian students may not look steadily in the eyes of the teacher because such behavior is a sign of disrespect. A pat on the child's head may be meant as a kindly gesture, but it is likely to offend. Be sure not to criticize children in front of others; they need to be able to "save face." Indochinese pupils may come to school with small round bruises on the arm, but *coining* (pressure by coins) is used as a method to reduce illness or pain and is not a sign of abuse.
5. Most Asian American families value education, and generally Vietnamese, Cambodian, Chinese, and Laotian students work hard to obtain an education. Often parents or siblings will tutor young children or others before school. Their respect for education extends to teachers, so most Indochinese parents will not question the teacher's decisions or expertise.

This chapter points out many of the diverse challenges that face teachers, parents, and schools. The changing world—accompanied by the birth and growth of a new generation and the arrival of newcomers from other lands—requires dedication to the task.

Families are like blossoms
in a wild flower garden
Mixed in color, size, and configuration
All the flowers lend to the beauty
of the garden
So it is with families
Each adds to the beauty of the community

Hmong (Hmong)	Lus tshaj tawm: kom teb cov teebmeem hauv qab no ua lus hoob. tom qab, yog koj teb tau kom teb cov teebmeem uas pom hauv no ua lwm yam lus. 1. koj lub npe hu li cas? ________ 2. koj nyob qhov twg tuaj? ________
ພາສາລາວ (Lao)	ຄໍາອະທິບາຍ: ຈົ່ງຕອບຄໍາຖາມສອງຂໍ້ຢູ່ລຸ່ມນີ້ເປັນພາສາລາວ. ແຕ່ຖ້າວ່າທ່ານຫາກສາມາດຕອບເປັນພາສາອື່ນໄດ້ ກໍ່ໃຫ້ຕອບຄໍາຖາມທຸກໆພາສາທີ່ທ່ານຕອບໄດ້ນັ້ນພ້ອມ. 1. ທ່ານຊື່ຫຍັງ? ________ 2. ທ່ານມາຈາກປະເທດໃດ? ________
Tiếng Việt (Vietnamese)	Lời Chỉ Dẫn: Trả lời hai câu hỏi dưới đây bằng tiếng Việt. Sau đó, nếu có thể, trả lời những câu hỏi trên thẻ này bằng các ngoại ngữ khác. 1. Em tên họ là gì? ________ 2. Em từ đâu tới? ________
中文 (Chinese)	指示：請用中文回答下列兩個問題。如可能的話，請用卡片上其他語言回答其他問題。 1. 你貴姓名？________ 2. 你從那裏來？________

FIGURE 3.1 These examples illustrate the variety of language of the Indochinese people.

Source: From *Indochinese Students in U.S. Schools: A Guide for Administrators* (pp. 49–50), by the Language and Orientation Resource Center, 1981, Washington, DC: Center for Applied Linguistics.

SUMMARY

It is necessary to focus on one's self as well as on understanding others. Encourage children to focus on understanding and appreciating themselves. With the increase of different ethnicities in schools, professionals need to be aware of different cultures and work positively with children of all cultures. Immigrant children will be involved in their primary culture and the American culture. Banks (2003, p. xxi) stated that "citizens in a diverse society should be able to maintain attachments to their cultural communities as well as participate effectively in the shared national culture."

"Insights for Teachers and Administrators" have been included to present the opportunity to think about and acknowledge the culture and contributions of various cultural groups. In each of the cultures, special contributions or history are briefly examined. The Native Americans, Spanish Americans, Black Americans, and Asians (as well as other groups that were not included) have made special contributions to the United States. These discussions are meant to be a springboard for a more complete examination of the cultural groups that make up each school's population.

The first inhabitants of North America were the Native Americans. This chapter attempts to acknowledge their important contributions in agriculture, irrigation, and culture and provide information about the many different groups, nations, or tribes.

Spanish Americans' ancestors developed a Spanish empire in the western and southwestern United States as well as in Mexico, Latin America, and South America. Texas gained freedom from Mexico in 1836 and was annexed to the United States in 1845. Arizona, New Mexico, Nevada, and parts of Colorado and California were acquired as the result of the Mexican-American War. Families of Hispanic origin are a part of the American culture. Current immigration to the United States requires that schools help children adapt and feel comfortable with the new culture and also provide bilingual education and a strong language enrichment programs.

The history of African Americans in the United States begins as early as 1619 when a few arrived as servants. Then Africans were brought to the country under the bondage of slavery. Despite the hardships, African Americans have contributed as scientists, artists, business leaders, educators, musicians, agronomists, and authors.

Immigration remained steady during the late 20th century. The United States has seen an influx of Chinese, Filipino, Asian Indian, Vietnamese, Korean, Japanese, Cambodian, Hmong, and Laotian immigrants since 1965.

Although it is important to understand cultural differences, teachers will encourage success in their students when they focus on the strengths of each child.

SUGGESTED CLASS ACTIVITIES AND DISCUSSIONS

1. What is an ideal family? Discuss. List the values and strengths you look for in an ideal family. Why did you choose them?
2. Discover your heritage by researching your family's past. If you were adopted and your heritage is not revealed to you, make up a heritage that you would like to have.
3. Invite parents of different cultures to share with the class how they celebrate different holidays. Encourage them to share family traditions.
4. Visit various places of worship. Invite ministers, priests, or clerics to share beliefs and ideas with the class.
5. Have a class discussion of family traditions and beliefs.
6. Visit museums in the area. What is revealed about beliefs or cultures of different time periods?
7. Investigate methods that school districts are using to help Asians (e.g., Vietnamese, Cambodians, Thais, etc.), Cubans, Chicanos or Latinos, and other immigrant students acculturate into the school system, child care, or preschool. Ask for materials from your school district that are being used by teachers to help students acculturate and integrate into the school system.
8. Investigate methods and curriculum that schools are using to help children with learning disabilities, Native American and African American students, and other students who might need special consideration and curriculum.

WEB SITES

National Association of Elementary School Principals (NAESP)

www.naesp.org

NAESP has published a book titled *Leading Early Childhood Learning Communities: What Principals Should Know and Be Able to Do.*

National Association for Bilingual Education (NABE)

www.nabe.org

NABE addresses the needs of bilingual students.

Southern Poverty Law Center—Fight Hate and Promote Tolerance

www.tolerance.org/index.jsp

The center discusses a variety of issues on tolerance and assault.

North American Indian History
http://americanindian.net
Site archives historical data about the indigenous peoples of North America.

National Museum of the American Indian: Visitor Information
www.nmai.si.edu/subpage.cfm?subpage=visitor
The National Museum of the American Indian has locations in New York City, Washington, DC, and Suitland, Maryland.

Smithsonian Institution: African American History Resources
www.si.edu/resource/faq/nmah/afroam.htm
The Smithsonian Institution Web site has African American History and Culture links addressing many historical and cultural issues related to African American heritage.

The African-American Mosaic: A Library of Congress Resource Guide for the Study of Black History and Culture
www.loc.gov/exhibits/african/intro.html
The Library of Congress has a resource guide for the study of Black history and culture. It includes colonization, abolition, migration, and the WPA.

Internet Resources for Latin America
http://lib.nmsu.edu/subject/bord/lagulia
Site contains many links for learning about Latin American cultures.

PBS—*Ancestors in the Americas*
www.pbs.org/ancestorsintheamericas/aahistorysites.html
The site for PBS's *Ancestors in the Americas* series has resource classroom guides plus media support. It includes general Asian history and resources as well as specific national groups.

4 Historical Overview of Family Life, Diverse Families, and Parent Involvement

As each decade passes, society goes through changes in feelings, beliefs, and goals. Each time reflects its own color, shape, and sound. With the passing of the 20th century, it is time to reflect on the goals, standards, and beliefs that are needed for the 21st century. What will the future reflect?

E. H. Berger

In this chapter you will learn the history of parent education and involvement through the years. After completing the chapter you should be able to do the following:

- Recognize that theories on parent education and child development change as the political climate and beliefs of the culture evolve.
- Enumerate societies in ancient times that were concerned with childrearing and identify their characteristics.
- Identify Plato, Aristotle, and Cicero, their lands of origin, and their beliefs about families and childrearing.
- Describe how children were educated during the Middle Ages.
- Identify and discuss major advancements or changes in society during the 15th and 16th centuries that affected children's education.
- Describe childrearing in Europe during the 17th and 18th centuries.
- Describe the religious zeal of the New England Puritans and the childrearing practices in the early colonies.
- Identify the contributions of Comenius, Locke, Rousseau, Pestalozzi, and Froebel.
- Identify Elizabeth Peabody and Henry Barnard and their contributions to early childhood education and the kindergarten movement.
- Describe the early civilizations in the Americas and the Europeans' treatment of the native population.
- Describe the growth of parent education and the development of women's associations.
- Describe childrearing in the United States from the 1890s to the present.
- Discuss patterns of immigration and migration in the United States.
- Discuss current issues and concerns in family life and education.
- Recognize that movement in political thought results in changes in education and family life.

Children reflect the beliefs and social conditions of the times in which they live. These children show peace and harmony as one child listens while the other plays a flute in a lovely pastoral scene.

William Adolphe Bouguereau, *Childhood Idyll,* 1900
Denver Art Museum Collection: The Gift of the Lawrence C. Phipps Foundation: 1958.115

INTRODUCTION

It is meaningful to compare the emergence of educational programs with the economic conditions and social thought of corresponding historical periods, for there is a relationship between a time's societal developments and its childrearing practices and educational theories. Note the effect the Russian *Sputnik* success had on the U.S. emphasis on cognitive development during the 1960s. Or go back further into history and relate the needs of poverty-stricken children in Switzerland in the 1700s to the educational beliefs and practices of Pestalozzi. The history of parent education and involvement can be pictured as the ebb and flow of the ocean's tide. Some eras portray a calm; others are characterized by tumult. As rapid changes, social problems, poverty, and political unrest produce turbulence for families, their need for stabilizing forces increases. So in the 1960s with the calls for a War on Poverty and the Great Society, there emerged a focus on the family as one institution that could affect the lives of millions of disadvantaged children. The powerful call resulted in renewed interest in programs in child-care centers, home-based education, and combined home–school intervention projects. Meeting the challenges of the 21st century requires that children be educated, and that can be accomplished only if families and schools work together.

PREHISTORIC PARENT EDUCATION

Since the beginning of civilization, family groups and parents have been involved with the rearing of their young. Before the development of written records, which is believed to have occurred between 6000 and 5000 B.C., early human beings had developed a primitive culture. To ensure survival they had to develop means to obtain food and water for sustenance and provide protection from harsh weather and predators. Picture a primitive family group with children modeling their parents' actions. Children accompanied their parents on forays, learning to obtain food through hunting, fishing, and gathering wild foods, or, in later periods, by growing crops. Parents also taught their children rules for participating as members of both the family group and the larger society. A study of contemporary primitive groups in Brazil and Indonesia substantiates the fact that nonliterate people use the oral tradition to pass on time-tested wisdom and practices.

Primitive societies did not develop schools; the prime educators were the family and community. Children were valued for their contribution to survival and for their implied continuance of society. They were the future—they would carry on the traditions of the culture as well as provide for the basic needs of the group.

For thousands of years, children have learned and internalized the important customs, rules, values, and laws of their society so they could function within their cultural groups. This process of socialization is prevalent in all groups, primitive or highly developed. Without it, children do not develop into functioning human beings as defined by the culture in which they live. During prehistoric times, just as today, the first teachers—the socializers—were parents and families.

FORMAL EDUCATION IN EARLY SOCIETIES

Our knowledge of education in ancient civilizations with written records is more extensive. In the valleys of the Tigris–Euphrates and Nile rivers, where the ancient civilizations of Sumeria, Babylon, Assyria, and Egypt flourished, formal learning joined forces with informal learning. During the Old Kingdom in Egypt, 5510–3787 B.C., children were educated at home. During the Middle Kingdom, 3787–1580 B.C., there are indications that school outside the home developed (Frost, 1966; Osborn, 1991). Artwork depicts Egyptians as holding their children in high esteem. Adults showed affection for their children by holding them on their laps and embracing them. Children were also portrayed in art as carefree—running, playing with balls, dolls, board games, and jumping at leapfrog and hopscotch (Bell & Harper, 1980; Osborn, 1991). In Sumeria, both boys and girls were important to the family and were given opportunities to learn (Chambliss, 1982). Formal systems of education also existed in ancient India, China, and Persia, as well as in the pre-Columbian Americas, especially in the cultures of the Mayas, Aztecs, and Incas.

Egyptian boys were educated at home during the Old Kingdom. During the Middle Kingdom, schools developed outside the home.

Portrait of a Boy, 2nd century C.E.
The Metropolitan Museum of Art, Gift of Edward S. Harkness, 1918 (18.9.2)

PARENT INVOLVEMENT IN EDUCATION AND FAMILY LIFE IN GREECE

The Athenian state produced philosophy and social thought that is still studied in schools. As far back as the 6th century B.C., regulations governed schools. Parents were responsible for teaching their sons to read, write, and swim; schools were to be in session for a certain number of hours; a public supervisor was appointed; and free tuition was provided for sons of men killed in battle. Schools were nonetheless private, and parents had the right to choose the pedagogue or school they desired for their children.

Greeks viewed children as children but also as a link to the future, the conveyors of culture and civilization, as well as valued members of the family. They focused on close supervision rather than physical punishment as the way to guide children (Bell & Harper, 1980).

Plato

Real concern over education blossomed during the golden age of Greece. Plato (427–347 B.C.)

questioned theories of childrearing in his dialogues in the *Republic.*

> And shall we just carelessly allow children to hear any casual tales which may be devised by casual persons, and to receive into their minds ideas for the most part the very opposite of those which we wish them to have when they are grown up? We cannot. (Plato, 1953, p. 221)

Plato even believed the games children played should be controlled. He believed strongly that a child could be molded to fit the needs of society. In his ideal city–state, genetics and procreation would be controlled by the state to produce children who, when grown, would be capable of administering affairs of state (Chambliss, 1982). Parent education was not for the benefit of the family or its individual members; it was designed to strengthen the communal state.

Aristotle

Although Aristotle (384–323 B.C.) disagreed with Plato about the desirability of a communal ideal state, he agreed that education was too important to be determined by the financial ability of the parents. Like Plato, he believed that education did not exist for the benefit of the family or its individual members but to strengthen the state.

Families were important to Romans; fathers placed high priority on their sons' education.

Domenico Ghirlandaio (Domenico di Tommaso Curradi di Doffo Bigordi), *Francesco Sassetti (1421–1490) and His Son Teodoro,* ca. 1487?
The Metropolitan Museum of Art, The Jules Bache Collection, 1949 (49.7.7)

PARENT INVOLVEMENT AND FAMILY LIFE IN ROME

During the same period, family life in Rome was flourishing, and parents were actively involved in their children's education. The high priority placed on children resulted in concern for their development, with the parents being their children's first educators.

Mother as First Teacher

In Rome and Sparta, the mother was the first teacher of her children, but the Roman mother had a greater role in academic education than the Spartan mother and taught the children to read. The mother taught her daughters the obligations, responsibilities, and skills necessary to be a homemaker. The father encouraged his sons to read and write, develop physical skills as well as business acumen, and practice citizenship. This changed in the middle of the second century B.C. when schools were established and fathers began to use tutors or schoolteachers (Bell & Harper, 1980; Frost, 1966; Osborn, 1991).

Infanticide

It should be noted that from primitive times through Greco–Roman days to modern times, laws and customs illustrate that infanticide, abandonment to exposure, and sale of children have been common practices (see deMause, 1974, pp. 25–33). Roman children had few rights. Roman fathers held the power of determination over their children, even to the extent of deciding upon life or death. The need for survival became a guide for practices of infanticide. In most societies in which infanticide or similar practices occurred, once the decision was made to keep children, they were raised in the same way as the other children within the culture.

Concern for eradication of child desertion, infanticide, and the selling of children began to grow about the first century A.D. In 318 in Rome, Emperor Constantine decreed that killing infants was a crime (Osborn, 1991). Rewards were offered to those who reared an orphan. Refuge and asylum for abandoned children were offered by the Catholic church, which further testified to the emergence of concern for children (Bossard & Boll, 1966). Finally, in 374, an imperial edict prohibited the exposing and consequent death of infants (Bell & Harper, 1980).

Education and family life had become important during the golden civilizations of Greece and Rome and in early Christian times. A subsequent decline in the importance of the family occurred during the Middle Ages, and the concern for parent involvement did not emerge again until many centuries later.

EUROPEAN CHILDREN DURING THE MIDDLE AGES

As the Roman Empire declined, turmoil, famines, and warfare made family life difficult, if not impossible. The major concern was for survival. Adults and children were not given different treatment (Bell & Harper, 1980).

Feudal System

The emergence of the feudal system provided a protective though restrictive social order for the people. During the Middle Ages, about 400–1400, children were very low among society's priorities. There was no system of education and, due to the lack of privacy, very little family life. Living conditions did not provide the poor with an opportunity for privacy or time with their families. Thus, learning came through working with parents to fulfill the menial tasks required to subsist on feudal estates (Aries, 1962; Frost, 1966). As children worked and participated in everyday life, they were socialized into the way of life—the values, customs, and means of existence—for the poor.

Noble children, dressed as young adults, were treated very much like adults.

Hyacinthe Rigaud, *Louis XV (1710–1774) as a Child*
The Metropolitan Museum of Art, Purchase, Mary Wetmore Shively Bequest, in memory of her husband, Henry L. Shively, M.D., 1960 (60.6) Image © The Metropolitan Museum of Art

Children of Nobility

By contrast, children of nobility were reared and taught in their homes until the age of 7. Life in a medieval castle, built for defense rather than for family life, was difficult for children.

The children of nobles were precursors of the emerging middle- and upper-class families of the 17th and 18th centuries. They inherited property and were educated for their future duties. They, too, were socialized into the values and social graces of their families, but beyond that they were also taught reading, ciphering, and penmanship. Because the men were often away on missions and women were left to run the estates, both genders were taught the practical skills needed to care for the household and land. After the age of 7, boys were sent to work as apprentices with another family.

Boys from the upper classes learned skills and duties befitting a noble and the art of chivalry, while commoners were apprenticed to learn a craft, a trade, or agriculture. The custom of education by apprenticeship existed for many centuries.

PEOPLE IN OTHER PARTS OF THE WORLD

Great civilizations were in progress in Asia, Africa, and the Americas during Europe's Middle Ages, A.D. 400–1400. The following incomplete descriptions of the ancient civilizations are included to illustrate that the multicultural makeup of the United States includes many people whose ancestors had great learning and civilizations. Children were raised by their families within the traditional cultural expectations of the time period. Children in classrooms come from a variety of cultural backgrounds. Recognition of their heritage helps make the classroom family friendly.

Africa

The Egyptian calendar has a recorded date of 4241 B.C. People began to settle along the Nile around 4000 B.C. The Kush kingdom of Nubia (Sudan) was established in 1600 B.C. Between A.D. 400 and 900 several kingdoms developed on the African continent (Kullen, 1994, p. 17). The civilizations that flourished before and during the period of world explorations were Ghana (A.D. 1000); Mali (A.D. 1300); Kongo, Swahili, and Monomotapa (A.D. 1400); and Songhai, Kanem-Bornu, Bunyoro, and Luanda (A.D. 1500). The Songhai Empire reached it zenith under Askia Muhammad I in the mid-1500s (p. 34).

Asia

The Xia dynasty ruled China from 2205 to 1766 B.C., a period of improvement in farming, irrigation, and writing. The Zhou Dynasty, 1066–221 B.C., was the period in which the teachings of Confucius became important. The Great Wall of China was begun in 256 B.C. The Han Dynasty ruled China from 206 B.C. until A.D. 220. "The writing brush, paper and ink come into wide usage, and the first dictionary is compiled" (Kullen, 1994, p. 13).

Americas

As early as 10000 to 5000 B.C., villages were built in the Americas. Although the first year of the Mayan calendar was 3111 B.C., the golden age of the Mayans was 600–500 B.C. The civilization continued until the abandonment of their cities in A.D. 1400–1450.

The Olmec civilization developed near Veracruz, Mexico, in 2000 B.C. and flourished from 1250 to 1200 B.C. Through much of Central America the Olmecs established "trade routes, highly developed art and architecture, and a form of writing" (Kullen, 1994, p. 4).

Other civilizations in the Americas included the Toltecs in central Mexico (A.D. 850–900), the Hohokam and Anasazi in present-day Arizona and New Mexico (A.D. 100–900), the Mochica and Nazca civilizations in Peru (A.D. 100–900), and the Aztec and Incan empires (A.D. 1200–1500). The Incan Empire ruled over an estimated 16 million people and stretched through the Andes from present-day Ecuador to Santiago, Chile. It continued until 1553, almost 60 years after Columbus came to the Americas (Kullen, 1994).

INFLUENCE OF THE PROTESTANT REFORMATION AND INVENTION OF THE PRINTING PRESS

The Reformation of the 16th century, coupled with the invention of the printing press, brought about great change in Europe. An awareness of childhood began to evolve in the 12th century, gaining ground through the 17th century. The invention of movable type for printing in 1439 by Johannes Gutenberg made books available to a much larger segment of the population, even though only the wealthy were able to purchase them for personal use. By 1500 "there were nearly 2,000 printing establishments in Europe and more than three million books had been produced" (Osborn, 1991, p. 21). The increased number of books brought about great change in society and also revealed the changing times. Children's lives between the 14th century, when children were still tied to apprenticeship systems, and the 17th century, when the family was organized around children, were illustrated by the

Adults had ambivalent feelings about children in the 17th and 18th centuries. Change was taking place in society as well as in the family.

Francisco de Goya y Lucientes, *Manuel Osorio Manrique de Zuñiga (1784–1792),* possibly 1790s
The Metropolitan Museum of Art, The Jules Bache Collection, 1949 (49.7.41)
Image © The Metropolitan Museum of Art

This painting of mother and child depicts loving care of parents to children throughout the centuries.

Jean-Baptiste-Camille Corot, *Mother and Child,* probably 1860s
The Metropolitan Museum of Art, H. O. Havemeyer Collection, Gift of Mrs. P. H. B. Frelinghuysen, 1930 (30.13) Image © The Metropolitan Museum of Art

change in etiquette books. Those published in the 1500s were restricted to etiquette for adults, while *La Civilitie Nouvelle,* written in 1671, included children as part of the family system. One of the very early parent education books contained directives for parents to use as they taught children their letters. It even included the proper way to discipline and control children (Aries, 1962). For the first time in history, authors were speaking directly to parents.

Religion

European societies, emerging from a time of suffering and hardship and influenced by the Protestant Reformation and the Catholic Counter-Reformation, viewed the child as one in whom evil must be suppressed and the soul nourished (Bell & Harper, 1980). Throughout the Middle Ages, the Catholic church had been a primary influence on people's behavior. Martin Luther (1483–1540) opened the floodgates for religious change in 1517, and the Protestant Reformation was born. People were expected to learn to read and study the Bible for themselves and thereby find their own salvation. Luther believed people should be able to read the Bible in their own language. He took his beliefs to the people and wrote the Sermon on the Duty of Sending Children to School, in which he pointed out to parents that they should educate their children. He recommended that children learn their catechisms, and he encouraged the use of Aesop's fables for the teaching of morals.

The Catholic Counter-Reformation saw the founding of the Jesuit Order, which made much progress in religious education. These advancements in education permeated educational practices both in Europe and the United States. The religious tenor of the times also influenced social thought and, consequently, childrearing practices for centuries.

THE BEGINNINGS OF MODERN PARENT EDUCATORS AND CHILD DEVELOPMENT THEORISTS

The modern parent educator began to emerge during the 17th and 18th centuries, but the general population was not affected until the 19th century. New ideas about education and the importance of the home in the education of children were developed by social thinkers such as Comenius, Locke, Rousseau, Pestalozzi, and Froebel, all of whom rejected the concepts of original sin and depraved children.

John Amos Comenius (1592–1670)

Born in Moravia in 1592, Comenius was a member and bishop of the Moravian Brethren who believed in the basic goodness of each child as opposed to the concept of original sin. This idea is reflected in his writing about education methodology; his thinking was more advanced than that of many others who lived during the same period. In *Didactica Magna,* a large treatise on education, he discussed the importance of the infant's education: "It is the nature of everything that comes into being, that while tender it is easily bent and formed, but that, when it has grown hard, it is not easy to alter. Wax, when soft, can be easily fashioned and shaped; when hard it cracks readily" (Comenius, 1967, p. 58). In the *School of Infancy,* written in 1628, he emphasized that education begins at home and described in detail the manner in which young children should be educated. Comenius also wrote textbooks for children. *Orbis Pictus* (The World in Pictures) is considered the first picture book for children (Morrison, 1991). Although a prolific writer, Comenius was unable to change the direction of education during his lifetime.

John Locke (1632–1704)

Locke, an Englishman, had far-reaching and innovative ideas concerning government and education. He probably is best known for the concept that the newborn's mind is a *tabula rasa,* or blank slate, at birth. All ideas develop from experience; none are innate. Therefore, it is incumbent upon family and

Poverty and deprivation caused the underclass to resort to begging.

Master of the Béguins (possibly Abraham Willemsens), *Beggars at a Doorway,* 17th century
The Metropolitan Museum of Art, Purchase, 1871 (71.80)

teacher to provide the optimum environment and valuable experiences for the child's mind to thrive.

Locke, who lived during the period when "hardening" of the child was in vogue, was a staunch supporter of the concept. If children were exposed to cold baths and other methods of hardening, according to the belief, they would become more resistant to diseases and ailments. "A sound Mind in a sound Body is a short, but full Description of a Happy State in this World" (Locke, 1989, p. 83).

Jean Jacques Rousseau (1712–1778)

Rousseau, a Frenchman, was another giant in the development of changing European social thought. As thoughts of greater freedom for human beings evolved, stirrings of freedom for children also emerged. As a political analyst, Rousseau wrote *Social Contract* in 1762, in which he described government through consent and contract with its subjects. This desire for freedom extended into his writings concerning children. In *Emile,* written in 1762, he urged mothers to "cultivate, water the young plant before it dies. Its fruits will one day be your delights. . . . Plants are shaped by cultivation and men by education" (Rousseau, 1979, p. 38).

Johann Heinrick Pestalozzi (1747–1827)

Pestalozzi believed in the natural goodness of children and struggled for many years teaching and caring for poor children in his home in Switzerland. He was so impressed by Rousseau's *Emile* that he used it as a guide for the education of his own child.

Pestalozzi based his teaching on use of concrete objects, group instruction, cooperation among students, and self-activity of the child. To teach mathematics, he used beans and pebbles as counters and divided cakes and apples to demonstrate fractions. The child's day also included recreation, games, and nutritious snacks and meals (Gutek, 1968). Pestalozzi is remembered primarily for his writings; in his first successful book, *How Gertrude Teaches Her Children,* he emphasized the importance of the mother and included teaching methods for parents. It was the first comprehensive education book for parents. Pestalozzi can be hailed as the father of parent education.

Friedrich Wilhelm Froebel (1782–1852)

Froebel, known as the father of kindergarten, was born in Germany in 1782, 35 years after Pestalozzi. Froebel is most noted for his development of a curriculum for the kindergarten, but he also recognized the importance of the mother in the development of the child. He saw the mother as the first educator of the child and wrote a book for mothers to use with their children at home. The book, *Mother Play and Nursery Songs with Finger Plays,* included verses, pictures, songs, and finger plays still used today, such as "pat-a-cake, pat-a-cake." Froebel's plan for education grew around a concept of unity. He organized his curriculum to follow the natural unfolding of the child with the mother assisting in the development.

Froebel's development of kindergarten curriculum had a significant effect on the current philosophy of education. Instead of a prescribed curriculum designed by the adult to teach the child to read, write, and be moral, the curriculum was developed from the needs of the child. The concept of child development and teaching to the individual levels of each child was a radical departure from lock-step education.

EUROPEAN CHILDREN IN THE 17TH AND 18TH CENTURIES

Ambivalent feelings about children and their place in the social system were reflected during the 17th and 18th centuries in Europe. The well-to-do commonly employed wet nurses to breast-feed their children. Although sometimes necessary, the practice separated the mother from her infant. Another characteristic of the period was the swaddling of young infants, which seems to have been done primarily to provide warmth, because buildings were damp and drafty. The infants were bound from head to toe in a cloth band (a maillot) about 2 inches wide with their arms at the sides and legs extended. Later, between the first and fourth months, the arms were released and the child could use them. Usually at 8 or 9 months, the infant was unswaddled. Babies also were unwrapped when it was necessary to clean them. Although it may seem that swaddling would have retarded growth and development, this does not appear to be the case.

Families tended to fit into one of three categories: The wealthy, the emerging middle class, or the poor and poverty stricken.

John Hoppner, *The Sackville Children,* 1796
The Metropolitan Museum of Art, Bequest of Thomas W. Lamont, 1948 (53.59.3)
Image © The Metropolitan Museum of Art

After they were unswaddled, babies were soon encouraged to walk. Louis XIII, who had been swaddled, was running by 19 months of age and playing the violin and drum at about 18 months (Hunt, 1970).

Social Change

The 18th century was one of tremendous upheaval, filled with social change and restlessness. In France this political and social unrest resulted in the French Revolution. In England, growth in industry created a demand for labor. In the latter half of the 18th century and during much of the 19th century, the Industrial Revolution created an atmosphere of poverty and misuse of children as laborers.

Families tended to fit into one of three categories: the wealthy, who allowed others to rear their offspring and who exhibited indifference to children; the emerging middle class, who wanted to guide, direct, and mold their children in specific patterns (Lorence, 1974); or the poor and poverty stricken, who lacked the means to have much semblance of family life.

Wet Nurses

The lack of interest of the wealthy in their children encouraged the continued use of wet nurses. In France and England some mothers placed their children with countrywomen to be cared for until they were 2 or 3 years of age. Or, if very wealthy, they hired nurses to come into their homes.

Parental Guidance

These writings and those of Comenius, Rousseau, Pestalozzi, and Froebel illustrate a new spirit of humanism and a recognition of children as human beings with some rights. Sometimes these rights were subjugated to the belief that children must be totally obedient to their parents to grow properly. These parents represent the second category of families, the emerging middle class who wanted to guide, direct, and mold their children in very specific patterns.

Susanna Wesley, mother of John Wesley, the founder of the Methodist religious movement in England, could never be criticized for overindulgence. Regarding her childrearing beliefs, she wrote:

> I insist upon conquering the will of children betimes, because this is the only strong and rational foundation of a religious education, without which both precept and example will be ineffectual. (Moore, 1974, p. 33)

Children of poor families were often sent to workhouses or foundling homes, and these were hardly nurturing environments for the young. As soon as the child was old enough to work, apprenticeships were found and, most often, the child was misused as a source of cheap labor.

Children's Recreation

Despite the strict discipline imposed on the young of all classes, there were some light and free times for some children in England. The theater was immensely popular, and upper-class children

Rhymes, Mother Goose, and fairy tales have provided reading material for mothers reading to their children throughout the years.

James Jebusa Shannon, *Jungle Tales (Contes de la Jungle)*, 1895
The Metropolitan Museum of Art, Arthur Hoppock Hearn Fund, 1913 (13.143.1) Image © The Metropolitan Museum of Art

Life was not all work and no play. Cards, blindman's bluff, and blowing bubbles were some recreational diversions.

Jean Siméon Chardin, *Soap Bubbles*, 18th century
The Metropolitan Museum of Art, Wentworth Fund, 1949 (49.24) Image © The Metropolitan Museum of Art

occasionally accompanied their parents. More often, however, children attended puppet shows. They also played organized games, including many that are still popular today, such as blindman's bluff, hide-and-seek, teeter-totter, cricket, hockey, and football (Bossard & Boll, 1966). Rhymes and fairy tales prevailed. Mother Goose tales, published in 1697, gave parents a collection of rhymes and stories to read to their children. Many of the favorite nursery rhymes read to children today originated during this period, including, "To Market, to Market," "Little Boy Blue," "Baa, Baa, Black Sheep," "Jack and Jill," "Who Killed Cock Robin?," "Tom, Tom, the Piper's Son," and "The House That Jack Built." Many of the rhymes were political statements of the times but were used then, as today, as poems to amuse children.

Such were the diverse methods of childrearing in Europe at the time of the settling and colonization of the future United States. Depending on their station in life in the old country, settlers had varied childrearing practices, but there was some homogeneity within the colonies. More consistency developed as colonists faced common conditions in a new frontier.

THE FAMILY IN COLONIAL NORTH AMERICA

Colonists settled three major areas: New England, the middle colonies, and the southern colonies. In the new country, the concept of the family had unique importance. Children were valued in the frontier because cutting home sites from raw land, constructing houses and outbuildings, tilling the soil, and harvesting the crops required great physical efforts. Eager hands were needed to survive.

Puritans

The religious zeal of the New England Puritans permeated family life and influenced childrearing practices as it defined the duties of parents and children, husbands and wives, and masters and servants. Benjamin Wadsworth, in a 1712 essay titled *The Well Ordered Family: Or Relative Duties,* gave directives on proper marital relationships. Husbands and wives were to be supportive of and loving toward each other.

Wadsworth further advised parents on their relationships with their children. Mothers were expected to nurse their children. Parents were required to provide religious instruction, pray for their children, and see that they were well "settled in the World" (Wadsworth, 1712/1972, p. 58). Although parents were to care for their children, they were not to be overindulgent. Children were to be brought up with diligence and to have respect for the law.

Children were not "to laugh or jeer at natural defects in any, as deafness, blindness, lameness, or any deformity in any person but teach them rather to admire God's mercy; that they themselves don't labour under such inconveniences" (p. 87). Children were to love, fear, revere, and honor their parents. They were to be obedient and faithful, for "when children are stubborn and disobedient to Parents, they're under awful symptoms of terrible ruine [sic]" (p. 97).

Wadsworth's essay was followed by Eleazar Moody (1775/1972) in *The School of Good Manners.* In the preface a quotation from Proverbs 22:6 supported his theme: "Train up a Child in the Way he should go, and when he is Old he will not depart from it." The complete title explains the purpose of the essay: *The School of Good Manners: Composed for the Help of Parents in Teaching Children How to Behave During Their Minority.* The second chapter contained 163 rules for children, including rules governing behavior at the meeting house, at home, at school, and in the company of others. Following are a few of the rules:

> Never sit in the presence of thy Parents without bidding, tho' no stranger be present. (p. 8)
>
> Approach near thy Parents at no time without a Bow. (p. 8)

Schools

New England schools reinforced stern discipline and instruction in good manners, as well as providing religious teachings. Breaking the will of obstinate young pupils was handled through corporal punishment. The birch rod, the flapper (a 6-inch-wide leather strap with a hole in the center), ferules (flat pieces of wood used to smart the palms), and the cat-o'-nine-tails were used in schools to enforce discipline (Bossard & Boll, 1966).

Three Regions: North, Middle, and South

The essays of Cotton Mather, Benjamin Wadsworth, and Eleazar Moody, all published in Boston, reflected the lifestyle in New England. Childhood in the northern colonies implied adherence to a strict and complicated code. The families in the middle colonies were a more heterogeneous group, ranging from the Dutch in New York to the Quakers in Pennsylvania and the Catholics in Maryland. Those who settled in the south had not come because of religious persecution and, though as concerned about their children, were more gentle and solicitous in their guidance. The families in all three regions were patriarchal: the father's word was law for children. Colonial laws supported parental authority.

EARLY EDUCATION IN THE SPANISH SOUTHWEST

While family life on the eastern seaboard of North America was developing, Spain was extending its settlement of Mexico and the American Southwest. Spain's initial reason for exploring north and west of the Rio Grande was to seek wealth. Later, settlements were established to claim the land for Spain and spread the Catholic faith.

Life in these settlements developed quite differently from the structures of the eastern colonies of the northern Europeans. Some of the Spaniards had been given land for their military service; others obtained their land by "squatters' rights." Spanish colonists included continentals (those born in Spain), Spaniards born in the New World, mestizos (offspring of Spanish and Indian marriages), Indians, and slaves. Each of the first three classes looked down on the other classes. Wealthy Spaniards, who received land grants from the viceroys, seldom mixed with the mestizos or Indians except to employ them as overseers for their haciendas. The major educational force was the family, with religious guidance coming from Catholic missionaries. Families resulting from intermarriage, however, tended to mix religious customs. The parents of the Indian child, as well as the parents of the mestizo and the Spanish child, were the major educators of their children.

Jesuit and Franciscan priests, who wanted to convert all people to Catholicism and teach Spanish to the Indians, were not encouraged by the viceroys from Spain to establish schools, so no formal system of education was developed during the early days in the Southwest. Uneducated settlers were easier to control than those who had an education. Children did not need to learn to read the scriptures because priests cared for their religious needs.

Outdoor activities were enjoyed by children.

Sir Henry Raeburn, *The Drummond Children,* ca. 1808–09
The Metropolitan Museum of Art, Bequest of Mary Stillman Harkness, 1950 (50.145.31) Image © The Metropolitan Museum of Art

DEVELOPMENT OF THE FAMILY CONCEPT

Concurrent with a view of the child as a unique individual was the development of the family into a more cohesive and private unit. In 18th-century Europe, however, this evolution was limited to families of means. In the early 19th century, the greatest proportion of families, those who were poor, lived as they had in medieval days, with children often separated from their parents.

Living conditions were crowded, and there was little privacy. Children were either apprenticed at a young age or remained with their parents and labored from dawn to dusk to earn their keep. Between the 18th and 20th centuries, the European concept of family did not change, but the ability to have a family life extended to those who were not wealthy (Aries, 1962).

Families in the New World

In this respect, the pattern in the colonies and in the Southwest differed from that in Europe. Families were able to become cohesive social entities in early colonial life. They were able to establish homes and work together to provide food for the table.

African Americans

The land of opportunity did not exist, however, for people brought to the New World as slaves. Family life was not allowed to develop; mothers and children were separated from fathers at the whim of their owners. It was not until after the Civil War that former slaves were free to redefine their family roles and structures. This early loss of human rights had a complex and continuing effect on the economic and social history of the African American family in the United States.

NATIVE AMERICANS IN THE 1700s AND 1800s

The Native American nations had similarity in their reverence for nature, but each nation developed its own culture. From the time of the arrival of the Europeans, their lives were disrupted by clashes among the British, French, and Spanish, with some Indian nations collaborating with the French and others the English in the wars. Their expectations, after fighting with the European nations, were to benefit from the success in battle. This did not occur. As time progressed the European settlers moved the Native Americans to the Indian Territory west of the Mississippi River.

Settlements

The Native Americans in the east and south tended to live in permanent residences, where they farmed and hunted. Many in the west were migratory, foraging for food and using movable homes such as the teepee. In the southwest, pueblos served as permanent residences.

The Iroquois and the Cherokee are two fine examples of Indian culture. The Iroquois confederation was found in what is now upstate New York. The Cherokee settled in and around present-day Georgia and the mountains of North and South Carolina and Tennessee.

Resistance

There are many examples of resistance by the Native people. In 1680 the Pueblo Indians, led by Pope, a medicine man, destroyed 21 missions and drove 2,300 Spanish colonists out of New Mexico and Arizona. These settlers fled to El Paso, but the Spanish returned and reconquered New Mexico and its capital, Santa Fe, in the 1690s.

The tales of cowboys and Indians reflect the Native people protecting their land.

American Indian Removal

Although the Supreme Court recognized the rights of American Indians to use their property at their own discretion, they could not sell their land to anyone other than the U.S. government. This was followed in 1829 by a policy established for removal of Native Americans to lands west of the Mississippi River. In 1830 Congress passed the Removal Act, and five southeastern tribes were forcibly marched to west of the Mississippi.

The Cherokee, fearing they would follow, took their case, *Cherokee Nation v. Georgia,* to the Supreme Court. The court found that the Cherokee had a right to their land. The land was settled by the Cherokee, who had homes, schools, government, and a newspaper. However, gold had also been found in the area, and White settlers wanted the land. In 1838 the entire nation (except for those who fled to the hills) was forcibly marched to Indian Territory in present-day Oklahoma. Many died along the route, known as the Trail of Tears.

The removal of Native people continued. The Winnebago ceded lands to the government and moved west to Iowa in 1840. In 1848 and 1849 they were moved again, this time to Minnesota. The Potawatomie were moved to a 30-square-mile reservation in Indian Territory in present-day Kansas. The Shawnee, who had dominated trade with the European Americans in South Carolina, met the same fate and were relocated in Indian Territory near the Potawatomie.

It is difficult to move from this inhuman practice of uprooting families and relocating them to reservations to discussing the theories of childrearing of the families settling in former American Indian country. Were the now-dominant Whites unable to see that strong families and the opportunity to rear their young were just as important to those earliest Americans as it was for the newest settlers in the New World?

CHILDREARING IN THE 1800s IN THE UNITED STATES

The colonies declared independence from England in 1776. Soon, the first hard years of recovering from the war for independence, of building a new nation, and fighting the War of 1812 would be past. Instead of looking to Europe, considering the Native peoples, or relying on the religious guides of the clergy, families began to develop their own beliefs in childrearing. There were steadily increasing publications on the topic in the United States.

Music continued to be important to families and their children. Lutes, violins, and the piano in this painting were some of the instruments that were enjoyed.

Pierre-Auguste Renoir, *The Daughters of Catulle Mendès, Hughette (1871–1964), Claudine (1876–1937), and Helyonne (1879–1955)*, 1888
The Metropolitan Museum of Art, The Walter H. and Leonore Annenberg Collection, Gift of Walter H. and Leonore Annenberg,1998, Bequest of Walter H. Annenberg, 2002 (1998.325.3) Image © The Metropolitan Museum of Art

Early Literature

Robert Sunley analyzed this period by drawing from original works concerning childrearing in 19th-century magazines, journals, reports, children's books, medical books, and religious texts. Mothers were encouraged to breast-feed their children. Babies were to be weaned between 8 and 12 months of age, and mothers were not to extend the period by many months. Loose, light clothing was recommended, but heavy layers seemed to be prevalent, and swaddling was customary in some areas. Cradles were used, although mothers were not to rush to the side of the cradle if the baby cried. Immediate response to a baby's crying was thought to encourage more crying.

Early toilet training was recommended as a means of "establishing habits of cleanliness and delicacy" (Sunley, 1955, p. 157). Standards for personal neatness and cleanliness were high, and children were expected to wash often.

Childrearing advice consistently emphasized the significance of the mother's role in the care and upbringing of the child. Fathers were, for the most part, ignored in the childrearing literature. Articles advised strict moral training, reflecting the Calvinist doctrine of infant depravity, which required strict guidance reminiscent of earlier days. Children were not to be spoiled, and parents were to expect total and immediate obedience.

Three Theories of Childrearing

Mothers were intent on their responsibilities of childrearing. Brim (1965) cited parent group meetings as early as 1815 in Portland, Maine. Mother study groups were formed before 1820 in other parts of the country as well. Called Maternal Associations, these parent groups generally consisted of middle-class members of Protestant–Calvinist religious groups. They were interested in proper moral training and discussed methods of childrearing that included discipline and breaking the child's will.

Sunley pointed out that there were two theories of childrearing besides the religious moral emphasis discussed earlier. One was the idea of "hardening" the child, which probably stemmed from Locke and Rousseau. "Children should become strong, vigorous, unspoiled men like those in early days of the country" (Sunley, 1955, p. 161).

A third theory had the more modern ring of nurturing. Sunley cited the theory as being rooted in Europe. Children were treated in a gentle and persuasive manner with "understanding and justice" and with "consistency and firmness" underlying the nurturing. This guidance was thought to enable children to reach their potential.

In 1856, Margaretha Schurz, having migrated from Germany, founded the first kindergarten in the United States in Watertown, Wisconsin (Weber, 1969). This school, based on Froebelian theory, was in marked contrast to the authoritarian and rigid traditional schools of the period.

IMMIGRATION AND ANNEXATIONS

Between 1820 and 1930 about 38 million people immigrated to the United States. In addition, there were 2.9 million African Americans, including 386,000 who were free, as reported in the 1840 U.S. Census.

Journey to the New World

Whether it was made on sailing ships like those that Columbus sailed or, later, on crowded steamers, the journey across the Atlantic was extremely hard on the immigrants. For those who were forced by religious intolerance, social upheaval, or lack of opportunities in their homelands, the decision to come to the United States to find their freedom or fortune was difficult.

First, they were leaving the society and home they knew. Many never saw their loved ones again. Second, they had to save up money and gather food in order to afford the trip. Many were forced to travel by foot to a port city where they might wait months before a ship was ready to sail.

As they waited they used resources and food planned for the voyage. Ship owners wanted to make as much money as possible, so ships were crowded. Many of the immigrants became ill on the voyage. Some suffered from hunger. When they arrived in the Americas, they might already be ill and destitute. Many of those who had few resources stayed in the cities where they landed, trying to accrue enough so they could move on. Those with more money were able to journey on and obtain land.

Each group of immigrants had its trials. Those who arrived after the country obtained independence also found discrimination. When new arrivals differed from the established settlers, they were considered less desirable. There was great discrimination against the Irish who arrived after the potato famine (1845–1849) in Ireland. Chinese immigrants felt great discrimination when they arrived on the West Coast in the 1850s. In 1882 the Chinese Exclusion Act, which barred Chinese laborers, was enacted. Subsequently, it was extended for years. Later, Italians and other people from southern and eastern Europe (1890–1924) faced prejudice. As time passed, those who looked like the original settlers faced less discrimination; those who were physically identifiable have had a continuing battle for equality. Teachers today need to be aware of the struggles that early and present-day immigrants face and exhibit sensitivity and understanding for them.

Immigration from Germany and Ireland

In the 1840s, there was a large amount of political unrest in Germany. When reform they desired did not take place, thousands of Germans with liberal political beliefs fled to the United States. They had enough capital to be able to settle beyond the coastal cities. They established German-speaking schools and tried to retain their culture. They and the Irish, who also came in huge numbers in the 1840s but for a different reason, are the two largest ethnic groups, besides the British, to immigrate to the United States.

The Irish had been coming to the United States over the years, but the potato famine of the 1840s sent huge numbers of starving, poverty stricken Irish streaming to the United States. An estimated 800,000 Irish refugees came during the 1840s; more than 105,000 came in 1847 alone. Unlike the Germans, most of whom had financial backing, most of the Irish were poor. Many spoke Gaelic, wore homemade clothes, and had to settle in coastal cities because they could not afford to move inland.

People of Irish descent were persecuted in the United States for their differences, one of which was their Roman Catholic faith. Since the Puritans (Protestants) had fled because of religious persecution, they did not want the Roman Catholic Church to have any influence in the United States. This persecution continued with killings and church burnings until the Civil War took the focus off the Irish Catholics.

Texas and the Mexican-American War

Texas revolted against Mexico in 1835 and won its independence. Ten years later it was annexed to the United States. This was one of the factors contributing to the subsequent Mexican-American War, which began in 1845. In the 1848 Treaty of Guadalupe Hildalgo, Mexico ceded California, Nevada, Utah, and parts of New Mexico, Arizona, Wyoming, and Colorado to the United States. The region's inhabitants were allowed to move to Mexico or stay in the United States. Residents were supposed to retain all rights and property; however, many lost their land due to taxes they were unfamiliar with as well as through illegal land dealings.

Thus, shortly before the Civil War, many people in the Southwest, new to the laws and rules of the country, became U.S. citizens.

CIVIL WAR

In the 1860s, the country was torn apart by the Civil War. Although the slave trade had been outlawed in 1808, slavery continued in the United States. States' rights, including the related issue of slavery, resulted in the Southern states seceding from the union.

Slavery

Slavery—the practice of owning another person, providing their keep but using their labor—has existed for thousands of years. The earliest slaves were either captured in war or were in debt and forced to pay off their debts as slaves. Rules controlled the practice of slavery. According to the laws of Moses, slaves of their own people were to be freed after 6 years and foreign slaves, twice every century. Greeks obtained slaves through war and bought them from pirates. The Romans had slavery throughout the period when they conquered other countries. But the practice of slavery did not sanction lifetime slavery or ownership of a slave's offspring.

Eugenia Hepworth Berger

The Civil War tore the country apart and changed it forever.

In 1418, Portuguese Prince Henry the Navigator began the exploration of Africa. As Portugal continued exploring Africa and building forts, it began trading with the kingdom of Benin and became involved in the slave trade. In 1442 the Portuguese explorer Antam Goncalvez kidnapped some African nobility. As ransom he received 10 Africans, whom he sold into slavery. Thus began the slave trade that would later impact the Americas (Kullen, 1994, p. 2). The Portuguese exploration of Africa and the wealth resulting from obtaining slaves and selling them, mixed with the discovery of North and South America, led to the horrendous practice of slavery in the Americas.

By 1518 there was extensive slave trade in San Juan Bautista (Puerto Rico). By the late 1800s, almost 4 centuries later, as many as 30 million people had been taken from Africa and forced into slavery in North and South America.

When the Spanish first came to the New World, they expected to use the indigenous people as slaves. The practice of providing a grant of land with accompanying unpaid, forced labor—called *encomienda*—did not work out because the slaves knew the territory and were able to run away. In addition, many died from diseases of European origin. They were extremely susceptible to these diseases because they had not developed resistance to them.

Africans were able to handle the climate, the environment, and the heavy work—positive attributes that contributed to a devastating and sad period in American history. Slavery was used because it was profitable. Laws were made that restricted African Americans. In 1663 in Maryland, all imported Africans were considered to be slaves and, if a free European American woman married a slave, she also lost her freedom.

Even after emancipation, African Americans had a difficult life and worked long hours while they attempted to keep their families together and cared for.

Thomas P. Anshutz, *The Way They Live*, 1879
The Metropolitan Museum of Art, Morris K. Jesup Fund, 1940 (40.40) Image © The Metropolitan Museum of Art

In 1664, enslavement was for life and transferred to the children through the mother (Kullen, 1994).

Changes for African Americans

During the Civil War and Reconstruction, change came about for African Americans. In 1865 the 13th Amendment to the Constitution abolished slavery. A year later, the 14th Amendment made African Americans U.S. citizens. In 1870 the 15th Amendment gave them the vote. These changes held great promise of freedom for African Americans, but reality delivered continued prejudice and restrictions. In 1896 the U.S. Supreme Court ruled in *Plessy v. Ferguson* that separate but equal facilities were constitutional.

Changes for Women

During the Civil War, women began to take over farm work and carry out the obligations generally reserved for their husbands. Women also filled the void left by men who resigned from teaching to fight in the war (Calhoun, 1960), and their experience with children brought forth a more nurturing environment in the educational system.

After the Civil War, women did not return to the same subservient positions they had held previously. Calhoun described the change:

> The whole movement signifies an extension of woman's economic independence of man, and the breaking down of that barrier of inequality that had so long served to keep woman in a subordinate place in the household. While the Civil War did not start the movement, it did greatly stimulate, and . . . helped to unsettle the foundation of "mediaeval" family which was now passing out and through a transition of storm and stress yielding to the new family of equality and comradeship. (Vol. 2, pp. 361–362)

The change in the woman's role in the family and the new feeling of equality encouraged the formation of women's clubs and the resultant emphasis on parent education within those organizations.

CHANGE IN EDUCATION

Change was coming to education as well as to family life. During this same period, the mid-1800s, the kindergarten movement was gaining strength. Henry Barnard, secretary of the Connecticut Board of Education and later U.S. commissioner of education, became enthused by Froebelian materials at the International Exhibit of Education Systems in London in 1854. Barnard disseminated information in the *American Journal of Education* and a volume that he edited, *Kindergarten and Child Culture Papers*. He became recognized as the father of the kindergarten movement in the United States.

Elizabeth Peabody

Elizabeth Peabody was a sister-in-law of Horace Mann, a prominent reformer who led the movement to establish public elementary schools. Peabody was also a staunch supporter of the

Change was coming to education. Women were called upon to teach in the schools and take the place of male teachers who left to fight the war.

Winslow Homer, *The Country School*, 1871
Saint Louis Art Museum, Museum Purchase (123:1946)

kindergarten movement and helped spread the "good word" about the kindergarten methods of Froebel. Most important, Peabody crusaded to introduce kindergarten throughout the land and spread her beliefs about the natural goodness of children. Throughout her life, she was an apostle of Froebelian kindergarten.

Froebel's *Mother Play and Nursery Songs* was translated into English, giving parents an opportunity to use Froebelian activities in their homes. In 1870 there were only four books on kindergarten, but by the end of the decade five more had been translated, four more had been written, many articles had been printed and distributed, and two journals, *The Kindergarten Messenger* and *The New Education*, were flourishing (Vandewalker, 1971).

Peabody and Barnard firmly established Froebelian kindergarten in the United States. Pestalozzi and Froebel influenced the educational roles of parents with the belief that parents are integral components of education. In this climate of change, the possibility of the perfectibility of humans, and reverence for motherhood prevailed. Thus, the time was ripe for the parent education movement to begin.

Table 4.1 highlights the events and people who influenced ideas about children and childrearing from early times until the 1880s.

Parent education and childrearing practices reflect the times in which they occur. The first parent education programs in Maine in 1815 reflected the concern of the time—breaking the will of the child. In the United States, children were still viewed as willful and depraved, in need of having their sinfulness banished.

The free kindergarten programs of the 1890s reflected the perceived need for immigrant and poor children to learn the ways of the establishment, particularly in regard to health habits and cleanliness. Many of the parent education programs established in the 1920s were the consequence of the tuberculosis epidemic and the need to spread information about health.

As you read the rest of this chapter, reflect on the changes in childrearing practices. Note the effects of Hall, Freud, Watson, Skinner, Erikson, Spock, and Piaget. As their theories became known, childrearing practices changed. Relate that to today as the process of sharing information continues to change. The remainder of this chapter is divided into decades that reflect the changing parenting skills and childrearing practices.

TABLE 4.1 Events and people who influenced ideas about children and childrearing, 6000 B.C.–A.D. 1800.

6000–5000 B.C.	Primitive cultures developed. Parents modeled behavior for children to learn.
5510–3787 B.C.	Egyptian children were educated in their homes in the Old Kingdom of Egypt.
3787–1580 B.C.	Schools outside the home developed in Egypt.
427–347 B.C.	Life of Plato, who questioned theories of childrearing, suggesting that a controlled environment would promote good habits. Infanticide was practiced by Greeks, Romans, and others.
384–323 B.C.	Life of Aristotle, father of the scientific method, who promoted childrearing and education by the state.
204–122 B.C.	Life of Polybius, who noted the importance of the family in developing good Roman citizens.
106–43 B.C.	Life of Cicero, who emphasized the family's role in the development of the Roman citizen.
A.D. 318	Emperor Constantine declared infanticide a crime.
A.D. 400–1400	The Roman Empire declined and the feudal system emerged. Wealthy children were apprenticed to nobles; commoners were apprenticed to tradesmen. Peasants worked in the fields.
A.D. 1450	The printing press was invented, but books were available only to the wealthy.
1483–1540	Life of Martin Luther, who introduced the Ninety-five Theses and began the drive for all to learn to read the Bible.
1500–1671	Etiquette books began to include etiquette for children.
1592–1670	Life of John Amos Comenius, a Moravian educator, who wrote books on progressive educational theories.
1632–1704	Life of John Locke, who believed the newborn's mind was like a blank slate—everything is learned.
1697	Mother Goose tales were published.
17th and 18th centuries	Wealthy European children were cared for by wet nurses. Colonial American children were taught to follow Puritanical religious beliefs and were trained to be obedient and faithful. Spanish-Indian Catholic children in the Southwest United States were reared in extended, close-knit families.
1703–1791	Life of John Wesley, founder of Methodism, who was raised by his mother, who believed in breaking the will.
1712–1778	Life of Jean Jacques Rousseau, author of *Emile,* who wrote that children should grow up untainted by society.
1747–1827	Life of Johann Heinrich Pestalozzi, father of parent education, who developed a curriculum based on concrete objects and group instruction, cooperation among students, and self-activity.
1782–1852	Life of Friedrich Froebel, who developed a curriculum for the young child based on the concept of unity. He is regarded as the father of kindergarten.
19th century	American parents began to rely on American publications in addition to European ideas and the tenets of the church.
1815	Parent group meetings were held in Portland, Maine.
1854	Henry Barnard, U.S. commissioner of education, supported Froebelian concepts.
1856	A German-speaking kindergarten was established in Wisconsin by Margaretha Shurz.
1860	Elizabeth Peabody established the first English-speaking kindergarten in the United States.
1860–1864	During the Civil War, women were encouraged to replace men as teachers.
1870	The National Education Association was founded.
1870–1880	A great extension of the kindergarten movement and parent education occurred.
1871	The first public kindergarten in North America was established in Ontario, Canada.
1873	Susan Blow directed the first public kindergarten in the United States, opened by Dr. William Harris in St. Louis.

Childrearing practices reflect the times in which they occur. Toward the close of the 19th century, there was a growing belief in the perfectibility of mankind.

Sir Thomas Lawrence, *The Calmady Children (Emily, 1818–?1906, and Laura Anne, 1820–1894),* 1823
The Metropolitan Museum of Art, Bequest of Collis P. Huntington, 1900 (25.110.1) Image © The Metropolitan Museum of Art

1880 TO 1890

Toward the close of the 19th century there was a growing belief in the perfectibility of humans and society. Education was viewed as an avenue to that end. Kindergarten was believed to be an excellent instrument to reach children while they were still young enough to be guided in their moral development.

Settlement Houses

Settlement houses were established in the 1880s and 1890s for the urban immigrant groups who arrived in the new land destitute and without a livelihood. The kindergarten was used by the settlement houses to alleviate the suffering of children. "Industry, neatness, reverence, self-respect, and cooperation were seen as results of the properly directed Froebelian kindergarten, and these moral beliefs were linked to both individual and societal advancement" (Weber, 1969, p. 39).

The Women's Christian Temperance Union (WCTU) also supported the kindergarten movement and education of parents by establishing WCTU kindergartens in at least 20 cities (Weber, 1969). Free Kindergarten Associations were formed throughout the United States. By 1897, more than 400 of these associations were actively involved in the education of young children and parents. The WCTU developed a course using Froebel's belief in unity with a sequential curriculum for use with mothers of young children. Settlement houses and Free Kindergarten Associations worked with the lower socioeconomic groups and new immigrants. The concern and interest shown the poor and the philanthropic commitment to alleviate suffering reflected the awakening of renewed social conscience. The kindergarten movement and parent education were strengthened by the development of humanism and the belief in the child's innate goodness (Weber, 1969).

Women's Associations

By the 1880s, the growing emphasis on childrearing and education emerged from two additional sources, women's associations and the child study movement. The Child Study Association of America (CSAA) was formed in 1888 by a group of New York City mothers; the American Association of University Women (AAUW) was founded in 1882 by college graduates; the National Congress of Mothers, later changed to the National Congress of Parents and Teachers, the PTA, was organized by women who gathered from across the nation at a meeting in 1897; and the National Association of Colored Women was established in 1897.

The associations founded in the 1880s and 1890s had a lasting effect on parent education in the United States. Throughout its history, the CSAA has emphasized child study and parent education; it was the oldest and largest organization solely committed to the study of children. Its earliest programs were studies by authorities of the time: Spencer, Rousseau, Froebel, and Montessori (Brim, 1965). The organization engaged in a variety of activities and services—all related to children and parents (Brim, 1965; Fisher, 1933; National Society for the Study of Education, 1929; Schlossman, 1976).

The American Association of University Women implemented a diverse educational program, including the study of children and parent education. The PTA has been concerned with parent–school relationships since its inception. The National Association of Colored Women has focused on civic service, social service, and education with committees on home and the child, mothers, and legislation. Another group, the General Federation of Women's Clubs, formed in 1889, ushered in an even greater interest in women's roles as leaders. These organizations, with the exception of the CSAA, are still actively involved in the field of education.

Child Study Movement

When G. Stanley Hall, a charismatic psychologist at Clark University, was elected president of the university in 1889, he founded a child study center. Children had not been the center of scientific research before then. Hall wanted to determine what was in children's minds. Using a questionnaire method of research, he first used associates and assistants at the university to gather data. As his research progressed, he extended the use of questionnaires to teachers throughout the country and then to thousands of parents. To answer the questions, parents needed to observe their child's speech and behavior. Hall and his associates—Patty Smith Hill and Anna Bryan—compiled some provocative recommendations. "Above all, he counseled parents, be indulgent with young children; treat them as young animals, who simply have to behave as they do. Childhood was an easygoing, cavorting stage which youngsters must pass through peaceably if they were eventually to become mature, self-controlled adults" (Schlossman, 1976, p. 443).

Even though Hall's child study movement was short lived, replaced by the research of Thorndike, Cattell, and Watson in the 1900s, he remains important to parent education for his institutionalization of child study and his influence on the founding of the PTA. Since then, the development of effective childrearing practices and parent education has become no longer the effort of just a few individuals. Hall made child study part of a college program, and strong organizations, founded and sustained by dedicated men and women, are actively involved in parent education today.

1890 TO 1900

The 1890s centered on the family, with well-defined roles for mother, father, and children. The father's duty was to financially support the family while the mother controlled the home. Women's clubs flourished. Well-to-do mothers were able to join the many clubs available to them. Those who were on a lower socioeconomic level were served by settlement houses and the Free Kindergarten Association.

Stendler (1950) analyzed the first year of every decade from 1890 until 1950 in articles in three popular magazines, *Good Housekeeping, Ladies' Home Journal,* and *Woman's Home Companion.* He found an immense amount of interest in childrearing in the 1890s and early 1900s. The home environment was recognized as important in the formation of character. Mothers were idolized as the epitome of purity and goodness, and children were thought to model the mother in their character development. It was important then that the mother be the right kind of person. The father was earning the family fortune, and the mother was looked up to as knowledgeable and capable of rearing children. The articles reflect those who were financially secure, not the many who were poverty stricken.

Native Americans

At the same time that the home environment was recognized as important for formation of character,

The Hatch family illustrates the extended family, which emphasizes the importance of mothers to nurture and care for the children while the fathers were providers.

Eastman Johnson, *The Hatch Family*, 1870–71
The Metropolitan Museum of Art, Gift of Frederic H. Hatch, 1926 (26.97) Image © The Metropolitan Museum of Art

American Indian children were being removed from their homes and placed in boarding schools. In 1894, Hopi children were forcibly gathered and placed in European American-type schools. In 1911, the U.S. Army entered the Navajo and Hopi reservations and captured more than 60 Hopi children to take them to boarding schools (Kullen, 1994, p. 258). This separation of families was damaging to both child and parent.

In 1901 citizenship was conferred on people in more than 30 tribes in Indian Territory: Apache, Arapaho, Caddo, Cheyenne, Comanche, Creek, Delaware, Iowa, Kaw (Kansa), Kickapoo, Kiowa, Modoc, Miami, Navajo, Osage, Otoe and Missouria, Ottawa, Pawnee, Peoria, Ponca, Potawatomi, Quapaw, Sac (Sauk) and Fox (Mesquakie), Seneca and Cayuga, Shawnee, Tonkawa, Wichita, and Wyandotte (Kullen, 1994, p. 246).

Immigration

In the late 1890s and the early 1900s, immigrants continued arriving. In 1892 Ellis Island was opened, replacing Castle Gardens (New York City) as the port of entry for immigrants. More than 12 million immigrants were processed through its gates, which were open through 1954. Officials gave cursory examinations to determine who could enter the United States and who would be deported. As each wave of immigrants arrived in the United States, it was believed that they needed to discard their old cultures and adapt to the culture in America. It was not uncommon for families to be separated at Ellis Island. If a child was found to be ill, the family was allowed to enter the United States, but the child was expected to return, alone, to his or her country of origin. Likewise, children could be admitted, but an ill parent might be turned back. Names of immigrants were changed by the agents if the name was too difficult to spell or too long to write. The impact on immigrants could be devastating.

Spanish American War

At the conclusion of the Spanish-American War in 1898, Spain ceded the Philippines, Guam, and Puerto Rico to the United States under the Treaty

Eugenia Hepworth Berger

Many immigrants settled in the cities. The country, however, was primarily rural with families living in small towns or on farms like the one pictured here.

of Paris; Spain received $20 million in consideration of its losses.

1900 TO 1910

The first decade of the 19th century continued focusing on the family. In 1908 the American Home Economics Association was formed. Primarily an organization of teachers of home economics in colleges, public schools, and after 1914, extension programs, the association emphasized home management skills related to homemaking and parenthood, such as food preparation and nutrition. Emphasis gradually included child development and family enrichment (Brim, 1965; National Society for the Study of Education, 1929). In 1909 the National Committee on Mental Hygiene was formed. Because there was concern with improving mental hygiene, the emphasis on mental health increased during succeeding decades. In 1950 this group merged with others to form the National Association of Mental Health.

Changes in Education

This period saw change emerging in education as well as in childrearing. John Dewey, along with Hall, emphasized the need for change in childhood education. Dewey, William Kilpatrick, Francis Parker, and Patty Smith Hill drew away from traditional structured educational practices toward a curriculum that included problem solving, learning by doing, purposeful activity, and social aspects of education.

Montessori

While educators in the United States were moving toward a child-oriented, problem-solving curriculum, Maria Montessori was establishing another educational form in Italy. Concern for poverty-stricken children prompted Montessori, a physician, to establish Casa dei Bambini, a children's home in a tenement section of Rome. In 1907, she designed a specific program, structured so that children learn by doing. By teaching children precisely how to use equipment, she was able to help children overcome their impoverished environment. Her methodology—more structured than that of American theorists—did not find wide acceptance in the United States until the 1960s.

First White House Conference

Poverty-stricken children in the United States were often forced to work under horrendous conditions at a very young age. These children, who were undernourished, neglected, or abused, prompted a rising social concern. As a result, the first White House Conference on Care of Dependent Children was called in 1909. The Children's Bureau was created in 1912 as a consequence of the conference, a first step in government concern for children.

Immigration

In the late 19th century and the beginning of the 20th century, immigration continued at a high rate. Between 1890 and 1914, 15 million Europeans, mostly from southern and eastern Europe, arrived. Their customs and physical appearance differed from those of people already in the United States, and were, therefore, considered inferior. These immigrants experienced discrimination, "but the racism they experienced never reached the proportions it did in the South against African Americans or on the West Coast when Asian immigrants started arriving there in the 1800s" (Banks, 2003, p. 83).

1910 TO 1920

Soon after the 1909 White House conference, the government began disseminating information on child care. The first *Infant Care,* which would become a popular parent education book on child care for infants, was published in 1914 by the federal agency that is now the U.S. Department of Health and Human Services.

College Research Centers

Colleges and universities also became involved by establishing research and teaching centers devoted to the study of children. The State University of Iowa instituted a child-study center in 1911. Its purpose was the "investigation of the best scientific

Country schools educated many of the youth in the primarily rural United States during the 19th and early 20th centuries. This famous 1872 painting depicts young men playing snap the whip during recess.

Winslow Homer, *Snap the Whip*, 1872
The Metropolitan Museum of Art, Gift of Christian A. Zabriskie, 1950 (50.41) Image © The Metropolitan Museum of Art

methods of conserving and developing the normal child, the dissemination of the information acquired by such investigation, and the training of students for work in such fields" (National Society for the Study of Education, 1929, p. 286).

First Parent Cooperative

Twelve faculty wives at the University of Chicago—with guidance from the university—established the first parent cooperative in the United States in 1916. The women wanted high-quality child care for their children, parent education, and time to work for the Red Cross during the war (Taylor, 1981). This cooperative, the only one established in that decade, followed the tradition of English nursery schools established in 1911 by Margaret McMillan.

Ethalynn Fortescue

The period between 1890 and 1920 witnessed an explosion of population interest in children, as evidenced by the great number of magazine articles on child development. G. Stanley Hall, who felt children should be kept out of school until they were 7 or 8, represented the growing academic interest in children.

Nursery School

McMillan originally designed an open-air school for the poor in England. She emphasized health, education, play, and parent education, rather than mere child watching. The concept of the nursery school was welcomed by middle-class American families, as illustrated by the first parent cooperative in Chicago. Thus, parent cooperatives and the growth of nursery schools in the United States strengthened and promoted parent education.

Change in Discipline

Although authorities during the 1890s and early 1900s had emphasized love and affection in the formation of character, a new trend suggested that discipline through punishment was necessary to ensure character development. Parents were advised to use more discipline in the establishment of character in their children. The increased attention to strict childrearing was illustrated by the first issue of *Infant Care.* Autoerotic activities, such as thumb sucking and masturbation, were thought to be extremely dangerous. It was felt that if such activities were not brought under control, they could permanently damage the child. "While he was in bed, he was to be bound down hand and foot so that he could not suck his thumb, touch his genitals, or rub his thighs together" (Wolfenstein, 1953, p. 121). During the day, thumb sucking was handled by covering the hand with cotton mittens or making the hand inaccessible to the child (Wolfenstein, 1953).

A drastic change in attitude was reflected by scheduling the infant's activities rather than responding to the baby's needs. In 1890 the infant's life was loosely scheduled. In 1900, 22 percent of the articles recommended tight scheduling for infants; in 1910, 77 percent of the articles called for rigid scheduling (Stendler, 1950). Although breast-feeding was still highly recommended, a supplemental bottle could be given at 5 months, and the child was supposed to be completely weaned by the end of the first year (Wolfenstein, 1953). Mothers were told to expect obedience, ignore temper tantrums, and restrict physical handling of their children. These severe attitudes continued into the 1920s, when all magazine articles on the topic recommended strict scheduling of infants (Stendler, 1950).

Throughout these periods there were exceptions to every trend (Brim, 1965). Even though the period of 1890 to 1910 stressed love and freedom, the period of 1910 to 1930 emphasized strict scheduling and discipline, and self-regulation appeared in the late 1930s and 1940s, while other theories were interwoven with these during the same periods.

1920 TO 1930

Early childhood as an important period for character formation was stressed in the 1920s. This belief was at the other end of the spectrum from Hall's belief in allowing the child to grow free and unrestricted. Behaviorists warned that parents should "do it right early or else" (Schlossman, 1976, p. 462).

Child-Care Beliefs

During the 1920s many teenagers and young adults were viewed as reckless, overindulged, and spoiled (Schlossman, 1976). To reverse this scandalous situation, children were to be trained early to be responsible, well-behaved individuals. Watsonian behaviorism was beginning to be felt. This childrearing theory was mixed in the 1920s with the learning-by-doing theories of Dewey, a small portion of Freudian psychology, and Gesell's belief in natural maturation and growth. Although each theorist had a different approach, all recognized the importance of early experiences and the influence of the environment on the child's development.

The 1923 edition of *Infant Care*, issued by the Children's Bureau, admonished parents that "toilet training may begin as early as the end of the first month. . . . The first essential in bowel training is absolute regularity" (Vincent, 1951, p. 205). Although breast-feeding was recommended for 6 to 9 months, once weaning was commenced it was to be accomplished in 2 weeks. If the parents insist on substitution to "artificial food . . . the child will finally yield" (Wolfenstein, 1953, p. 125).

An explosion of parent programs accompanied the prosperity of the 1920s. The era reflected a swing from parent education offered by settlement houses for immigrants and free kindergartens for the underprivileged to the involvement of many middle-class parents in study groups for their own enlightenment and enjoyment.

Parent Cooperatives

Parent cooperatives emerged in five locations in the 1920s: (a) Cambridge, Massachusetts; (b) the University of California at Los Angeles; (c) Schenectady, New York; (d) Smith College in Northampton, Massachusetts; and (e) the American Association of University Women in Berkeley, California.

The parent cooperative movement, which developed rapidly in California but grew more slowly elsewhere until after World War II, was a way for parents to obtain high-quality education for their children (Osborn, 1991). To participate, parents must share responsibilities—an excellent example of parent involvement.

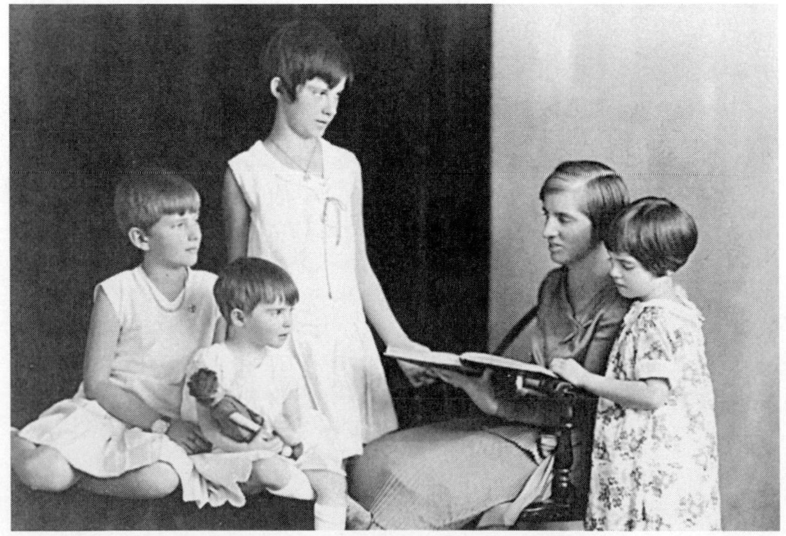

Eugenia Hepworth Berger

This mother reading to her children illustrates the emphasis on parent education, which expanded in the 1920s and continued into the 1930s.

Parent Education

Organizational membership growth also illustrated increased interest in parent education. PTA membership expansion depicted, in terms of sheer numbers, the growth in interest in parent programs. The organization grew from 60,000 in 1915 to 190,000 in 1920, to 875,000 in 1925, to nearly 1.5 million in 1930 (Schlossman, 1976). AAUW membership rose to 35,000 in the 1920s, and each issue of its journal contained a column on parent education. Concurrently, the Child Study Association of America, recognized as the educational leader in parent education during the 1920s, grew from 56 parent groups in 1926 to 135 in 1927 (National Society for the Study of Education, 1929).

Child-Study Manual

In the 1920s Benjamin Gruenberg published *Outlines of Child Study: A Manual for Parents and Teachers*, a text on childrearing that many parent groups used as a study guide. Succinct discussions on issues of child development were included in each chapter (Gruenberg, 1927).

Across the country many school systems implemented parent education and preschool programs. The Emily Griffith Opportunity School (Denver public school system) initially funded a parent education and preschool program in 1926. Its early emphasis on health education for families expanded to childrearing theories and other parent skills as interests and needs changed.

Special Concerns

Concern for children with mental retardation emerged during the 1920s, with separation and custodial care seeming to be the answer. "In regard to all mentally deficient children, it may be said that while we cannot improve their mentality we have reached the point where, by recognition of their capabilities and limitations, we can so place them in our social scheme that they may lead happy and useful lives" (Gruenberg, 1927, p. 230). This thinking has gradually changed over the years to the positions supporting mainstreaming for children with disabilities in the 1970s and inclusion in the 1990s and 2000s along with increased parent involvement and advocacy by parents of children with exceptionalities.

The effect of early childhood concerns and parent education was so great during the 1920s that the National Society for the Study of Education (1929) devoted its *Twenty-Eighth Year Book* to preschool and parent education. This issue described programs and listed conferences and agencies engaged in parent education during the 1920s. Refer to the *Twenty-Eighth Year Book* for a comprehensive report on the 1920s.

Restrictive Legislation on Immigration

Fear of the rapid increase of immigrants during the late 19th century and the first two decades of the 20th century resulted in restrictive legislation. The Johnson Reed Act in 1924 established a quota system for immigration from each country that was based on a percentage of those who lived in the United States in 1890. The Chinese Exclusion Act of 1882 had closed down Chinese immigration. The 1924 act extended this ban and made all Asians ineligible for citizenship. Paradoxically, in the same year, the Citizenship Act granted Native Americans full citizenship, along with the right to vote, a right that should have been theirs since the independence of the nation.

The Coming of the Depression

As the 1920s drew to a close, middle-class parents were active in parent groups, optimistic about the future, and concerned about health, nutrition, and shaping their children's actions. The financial crash of 1929 brought a tremendous change in the lifestyle of many families and set the stage for the Great Depression of the 1930s.

1930 TO 1940

The 1930s ushered in the depression era with a necessary response to the needy and a broadening of concern for the family and family relationships as well as for the individual child (Fisher, 1933; Gruenberg, 1940). The decade began with the White House Conference on Child Health and Protection in November 1930.

Childrearing Practices

The 1930s reflected varying viewpoints on childrearing, ranging from strict scheduling to self-regulation. Character formation began to take on broader meanings. Whereas it had meant moral development earlier in the 1900s, articles in magazines now included personality development (Stendler, 1950).

Poverty made it very difficult for families to provide for their children during the depression years. In rural communities, families had gardens to help with nutrition for the children. Being poor was not unusual, so a family in poverty was no disgrace. All or most of the child's friends were also poor.

Parent education continued at a high level of participation during the first half of the decade. The Pennsylvania Department of Public Instruction's (1935) Bulletin 86, *Parent Education,* reported that parents were being reached through study groups, with more than 700,000 parents involved in group participation. Parents in the United States also were receiving information through the mass media: radio series, lectures, magazines, and distribution of more than 8 million copies of *Infant Care.* The following statement from Bulletin 86 emphasized the importance of parent education:

> The job of the school is only half done when it has educated the children of the nation. Since it has been demonstrated beyond doubt that the home environment and the role played by understanding parents are paramount in the determination of what the child is to become, it follows that helping the parent to feel more adequate for his task is fully as important from the point of view of public education and the welfare of society as is the education of the children themselves. Moreover, an educated parenthood facilitates the task of the schools and insures the success of its educational program with the child. (p. 12)

Social and economic conditions were having an effect on family life and, consequently, on children within the family. The depression and a need to support families by offering information on budget, clothing, health, physical care, and diet precipitated parent education for the poor. Rehabilitation projects of the 1930s, such as the Works Progress Administration (WPA), offered a forum for mothers who were not active in women's clubs or parent–teacher associations to learn about home management practices. Established in October 1933, the Federal Emergency Relief Administration (FERA) authorized work-relief wages for unemployed teachers and others to organize and direct nursery schools; about 75,000 children were enrolled during 1934 and 1935 (Goodykoontz, Davis, & Gabbard, 1947). It was the intention of FERA that the nursery programs be taken over by the schools when funds from the federal government were terminated. "It is my desire that . . . schools shall be so administered in the states as to build toward a permanent and integral part of the regularly established public school program" (pp. 60–61). Few, however, were taken over by the schools.

Treatment of Minorities

Minority children had a double handicap to overcome: prejudice against children of color prevailed. In many areas, children of Spanish heritage were not allowed to speak in their family's native language, a problem that continued for many decades. This told them that their background was not acceptable. Much of the United States followed the separate-but-equal doctrine, operating separate, usually substandard programs for African Americans. It was not until 1954 that the U.S. Supreme Court declared the practice a violation of the Constitution.

1940 TO 1950

The tendency of parents in the 1920s and early 1930s to follow the specific rules of behaviorists changed in the 1940s when parents began to recognize that no one answer could work for all situations (Brim, 1965). The emotionally healthy child was the goal for professionals and parents. "The swing from the 'be-tough-with-them, feed-on-schedule, let them cry-it-out' doctrines of the twenties and thirties was almost complete" (Brim, 1965, pp. 130–131). Self-regulation allowed the development of trust and automony in the young child.

Baby Decade

Vincent (1951) suggested that the decade between 1935 and 1945 could be called "baby's decade" with the mother "secondary to the infant care 'experts' and the baby's demands" (p. 205). By the early 1940s, mothers were told that children should be fed when hungry, and bowel and bladder training should not begin too early. Babies were to be trained in a gentle manner after they developed physical control. The latest version of *Infant Care* depicted children as interested in the world around them and viewed exploring as natural.

Mead and Wolfenstein described the change in attitude toward the basic nature of human beings:

> One of the most striking changes in American thinking about children from the nineteenth and early twentieth centuries to the more recent past and the present is the radical change in the conception of the child's nature. From the 19th-century belief in "infant depravity" and the early 20th-century fear of the baby's "fierce" impulses, which, if not vigilantly curbed, could easily grow beyond control and lead to ruin, we have come to consider the child's nature as totally harmless and beneficent. (Mead & Wolfenstein, 1963, p. 146)

Eugenia Hepworth Berger

Two world wars were fought in the 20th century: World War I(1914-1918) and World War II (1939–1945). After World War II, soldiers returned home and many returned to school on the GI bill.

Spock

Shifts in beliefs about children were reflected in the childrearing practices of the period. In 1946 Benjamin Spock, a best-selling author and parent educator, published *The Common Sense Book of Baby and Child Care.* He believed the rules and regulations imposed on parents during the 1920s and 1930s caused undue pressure, and he advised parents to enjoy their children and the role of parent.

Spock's book answered questions on feeding, sleeping, clothing, toilet training, management, and illnesses; he had answers for almost all the questions a new parent might have. It continued to have great influence on childrearing through the 1950s and beyond as children raised by Spock's methods became parents.

Parent Groups

The 1940s, although consumed by the outbreak of World War II, saw no reduction in offerings in parent education. Parent groups continued in public schools, and county extension programs prospered. Although services continued and emergency-relief nursery schools for workers involved in the war effort expanded, research and training in child development declined (Brim, 1965).

Both the Great Depression and World War II brought federal support for children's services at younger ages. FERA regulated the child care funds originally, followed by WPA, and, during World War II, the Federal Works Agency (Goodykoontz et al., 1947). The need to provide child care for families during the depression emanated from the necessity for parents to work to get back on their feet and support their families. During World War II, women needed child care services so they could join the war effort.

Parent education found added direction in the 1940s through the mental health movement. In 1946 the National Mental Health Act authorized states to establish mental health programs and related parent education (Goodykoontz et al., 1947). The need to understand oneself and one's children was recognized as necessary for healthy parent–child interaction.

1950 TO 1960

World War II was over, and the 1950s were years of relative calm, with emphasis on children and family life. Schools were feeling the increase in numbers of children and were rapidly expanding to meet their needs. Many young adults had postponed marriage and family during the war. But now, the "baby boom" began gathering ever more steam. The PTA had more than 9 million members and thousands of study groups among its 30,000 local chapters. Parents were involved with the schools as room parents and fundraisers for special projects. The view "Send your child to school, we will do the teaching; your responsibility as a parent is to be supportive of the teachers and schools" prevailed as the basic philosophy between school and parents. The formal learning of reading, writing, and arithmetic started when the child entered first grade, as it had for many decades.

Emphasis on Family Life

A survey by the National Education Association revealed that family life was the topic of 32 percent of adult education classes (Brim, 1965). Parent education and preschool programs, part of adult education in many school districts, continued as a vital source of childrearing information. Pamphlets from the Child Study Association, the Public Affairs Committee, Science Research Associates, and the Parent Education Project of Chicago, plus books by authorities such as Arnold Gesell, Erik Erikson, B. F. Skinner, Benjamin Spock, Lawrence Frank, and Sidonie Gruenberg, were used as curriculum guides. During the 1950s James L. Hymes wrote his first book on home–school relations.

Orville Brim, sponsored by the Russell Sage Foundation and the Child Study Association, examined the issues involved in parent education in *Education for Child Rearing* (1965). His analysis of the effects of parent education continues to be relevant to the study of parent education today. *Your Child from 6 to 12*, published by the U.S. Department of Health, Education and Welfare (1949), illustrated the attitude that prevailed in the 1950s and beyond. The preface of the booklet reflected the change from the absolutism of the 1920s and 1930s: "There are many more things that we don't know than we know about children. . . . Every child is unique in temperament, intelligence, and physical make-up" (p. 39). In the early 1950s, thumb sucking was viewed as a natural occurrence rather than a negative one. A baby "may try to get pleasure out of his thumb or fingers. Sucking is a poor substitute for being held, or talked to, or fed; but it is better than nothing" (Wolfenstein, 1953, p. 124). Concern for mental health gave parents double messages; it was difficult to combine firm guidance and advice on emotional health. One such view on emotional health stated, "Any action that causes children to feel guilty . . . should be avoided. It is often better to say nothing whatever to the children, for fear of saying too much, or the wrong thing. Instead, divert their minds, give them new interests" (U.S. Department of Health, Education and Welfare, 1949, p. 38).

Eugenia Hepworth Berger

The 1950s were characterized by fathers working and mothers staying home to care for the children. The need for parent education was recognized. Programs were offered by schools, hospitals, and social agencies.

Erikson

Erikson (1986) popularized the eight stages of personality development in *Childhood and Society,* first published in 1950. His neo-Freudian theories emphasized social and emotional development based on interdisciplinary theories from biology, psychology, and sociology. His theory outlines eight stages of growth from infancy to old age. The stages begin with development of trust versus mistrust for infants, autonomy versus shame and doubt for toddlers, initiative versus guilt for preschoolers, and industry versus inferiority for school-age children. The later stages involve adolescents forming identity versus identity diffusion; for young adults, intimacy versus isolation; for adults, generativity versus self-absorption; and for mature adults, integrity versus despair. Erikson and the childrearing practices of the 1950s reflected the belief that social and emotional health were of utmost importance to the child.

Analysis of Parent–Child Relations

In a content analysis of *Ladies' Home Journal, Good Housekeeping,* and *Redbook* from 1950 to 1970, Bigner (1985) found articles primarily concerned with parent–child relations, socialization, and developmental stages. Spanking was condoned by some in the early 1950s, but by the end of the decade it was consistently discouraged and described as an inefficient and barbaric method that does no more than show the youngster that parents can hit. Most articles encouraged self-regulation by the child. Parents were told it was important that children feel loved and wanted. Parents were advised to hold, love, and enjoy their children and to rely on their own good judgment in making childrearing decisions. Parents were also encouraged to provide a home life that was supportive of individual differences and allowed each child to grow into a well-adjusted adult. Development was a natural process, and maturation could not be pushed. Gesell's work on development in psychomotor and physical areas supported the theory that children proceed through innate developmental stages. As a consequence, parents were encouraged to provide a well-balanced, nutritional diet and an environment that allowed children to grow and learn at their own rate.

Toward the end of the 1950s, the nation's calm was disturbed. Russia's success in launching *Sputnik* into space caused ripples across the United States. Why had the Soviets achieved a feat not yet accomplished by the United States? Americans looked for an answer.

1960 TO 1970

The 1960s was a decade of sweeping changes in parent involvement, social and civil rights, and family characteristics. The family had been gradually changing since the early part of the century, when the family was viewed with great sentimentality, mothers were revered, and the family was a sacred institution that few dared to question. By the 1960s it was common for all institutions—family, education, religion, economics, and government—to be criticized and questioned. Great changes in the American family took place between 1890 and 1960 as the country changed from a basically rural nation to an urban nation. The majority of families had been self-sufficient rural families with authoritarian parents; now most became dependent on others for income. As a mobile society evolved, one person in five moved each year for a better job or a better education. Children were no longer economic assets who helped their parents with the family farm or business; instead, they became financial liabilities, costing $20,000 to raise from infancy to 18 years of age (Hill, 1960). The many women who had continued working after World War II were joined in the 1960s by many more who entered the labor force to supplement their husband's income or increase their own economic freedom. For many other women, who were single parents or were a supporting member of a two-parent family, working was an economic necessity.

Immigration Policies

Immigration policies were reformed in 1965, effective in 1968, when original national quotas were removed. Since that time there has been a great increase in immigration from Asia, South America, and Latin America.

Father Involvement

The importance of the father's relationship with his children was stressed and, although his obligations to his children were not the same as the mother's,

John and Elena Machina Berger

The importance of fathers in the child's development began to be emphasized in the 1960s and 1970s and continued into the 21st century.

early interaction with his newborn baby was recognized as very beneficial. "Fathers who feel comfortable giving physical attention to their babies at the start are lucky" (U.S. Department of Health, Education and Welfare, 1962, p. 29).

Publications

Parents had many child-care books and booklets from which to choose. Publications from the Child Study Association and Science Research Associates and public affairs pamphlets covered many of the problems parents faced. Benjamin Spock continued to publish books on child care, and in them he advised firm, consistent guidance of the child. Spock's efforts were aided by psychologist Haim Ginott (1965), who offered parents a method for talking about feelings and guiding the child in a manner that avoided placing guilt and helped the child understand the parents' feelings, thus disciplining the child in a positive manner.

Piaget

Professionals working with children and parents were greatly influenced by Piaget's theories of cognitive development. His ideas, clearly discussed by Hunt in his book *Intelligence and Experience* (see chapter 1 of this book), emphasized active involvement of the child with the environment. Parents became much more concerned about their child's intellectual development and were no longer satisfied that development would unfold naturally.

White House Conferences

The time was ripe to meet the needs of all people—not just the dominant social class. When the Golden Anniversary White House Conference on Children and Youth convened in 1959, it delved into concerns about the family and social change, development and education, and problems and prospects for remediation (Ginsberg, 1960). This conference was followed by a White House Conference on Mental Retardation in 1963.

The Great Depression of the 1930s and World War II in the 1940s had kept the country occupied with emergencies. The affluent 1950s, impaired by the Korean War and the Cold War with the Soviet Union, gave cause for reflection. The 1960s brought forth many questions. Was the United States able to provide advantages for all its people? Were democracy and the free enterprise system capable of providing the best life for the most people? Could the United States surpass the Soviets in the space challenge? These were some of the difficult questions, concerning millions of people, that faced the nation.

Equal Educational Opportunity

The social climate of the nation during the 1960s mandated a concerted effort to provide equality of opportunity, as reflected in the Civil Rights Act of 1964. Researchers found that school curricula and expenditures on facilities and materials did not affect school achievement, but the quality of teachers did. The students who achieved believed they had some control over their own destiny. "Minority pupils, except for Orientals, have far less conviction than whites that they can affect their own environment and futures" (Coleman et al., 1966, p. 23). The most important factor shown to affect achievement was family background. Notable variables included the home's effective support of education, number of children in the family, and parents' educational levels.

War on Poverty

Although prosperity was within reach for most U.S. citizens and the standard of living had steadily improved to the highest in the world, minorities, people with disabilities, and the economically disadvantaged were still underemployed, often poverty stricken, and largely ignored. The government had high hopes for a Great Society in which poverty would be eliminated for all citizens. In the War on Poverty programs, children of the poor—who were undernourished, in ill health, without proper housing, and lacking educational opportunities—were chosen as a major target to realize hope for the future.

The works of behavioral scientists and educators presented overpowering evidence that early environment has a profound effect on a child's development (Bloom, 1964; Hunt, 1961; Skeels, 1966; Spitz, 1965; see chapter 1). These reports, along with the national mood of the mid-1960s supporting equal rights and opportunity, propelled the country to respond to the needs of the poor and disadvantaged. One of the most effective responses was to provide educational intervention for the children of the poor. If children could be given equal environmental opportunities, the cycle of poverty could be broken. The stage was set for the birth of Head Start. As research indicated that parent involvement and family background were positively correlated with academic success, the inclusion of parents in their child's education program was entrenched from the beginning of the Head Start program.

Head Start

In 1965 the Office of Economic Opportunity began an 8-week summer program for preschool children from low-income families. The proposed projects had a two-pronged approach. The child would benefit from an enriched early education program, and the parents would be an integral part of the programs as aides, advisory council members, or paraprofessional members of the team. As a result of these beliefs, the first Head Start centers were opened in the summer of 1965 as part of the War on Poverty. Head Start was a comprehensive program of health, nutrition, and education as well as a career ladder for economically disadvantaged families. Migrant Head Start had the first center-based infant–toddler program.

ESEA

Shortly after the formation of Head Start, the Office of Education, Department of Health, Education, and Welfare undertook direction for the Elementary and Secondary Education Act (ESEA) of 1965. Two of the title projects under ESEA were:

1. Title I, which assists school districts in improving the education of educationally deprived children. From its inception, parents were involved in the program.
2. Title IV-C (formerly Title III), which promoted the innovative programs that enrich educational opportunities. Many of these projects included home visitation programs for preschool children, identification of children with developmental delays before school entry, and working with the parents for the benefit of their children.

Concern about continuity of educational success after Head Start resulted in the implementation of the Follow Through program as part of the 1967 Economic Opportunity Act. Designed to carry the benefits of Head Start and similar preschool programs into the public school system, parent participation was a major component of the program, and, as with the Head Start program, parent advisory councils were mandated.

Civil Rights Act of 1965

Although not directly connected with parent education, the Civil Rights Act of 1965 had great influence on the role of minorities and women during subsequent decades and, through this, affected the family. Affirmative action, requiring minorities and women to be treated equally in housing, education, and employment, resulted in psychological as well as empirical, observable changes in conditions for these populations.

Vietnam War

Throughout most of this decade the Vietnam War affected family relationships, values, and social change. The war diminished the opportunity for success of the Great Society by funneling money and energy away from domestic programs. It also had an immense effect on family unity because many families were torn apart over diverse values concerning drug use, participation in the war, and moral responsibilities. The decade closed with greater emphasis on parent involvement and education for families of low socioeconomic levels than in any previous era.

1970 TO 1980

The enormous number of programs implemented in the 1960s came of age in the 1970s. Development occurred in both private and public sectors with churches, local agencies, public schools, and clubs, as well as state and federal agencies, showing concern for families caught in the stream of social change. The country was still confronted with the Vietnam War at the beginning of the decade. With the end of U.S. involvement in 1973, one of the major disruptive forces on family unity was resolved.

Advocacy

The decade could be described as the era of advocacy. Groups were no longer willing to sit and wait for someone to do something for them; they had learned in the 1960s that the way to help is through self-help and self-determination. Parents of children with disabilities, individually and through organizations such as the Association for Retarded Children, the Council for Exceptional Children, and the Association for Children with Learning Disabilities, advocated equal rights for the special child and won (see chapter 10). Advocate groups for children sprang up across the land with training sessions on political power and the means to implement change and protection for children.

The public schools were not immune. Parents began to question programs and their participation with schools and teachers. Forced integration and required busing were issues confronting schools and parents.

Research

Studies conducted in the 1970s consistently demonstrated the importance of an enriched early home environment to the child's school success (Hanson, 1975; Shipman, Boroson, Bidgeman, Gart, & Mikovsky, 1976; White, Kaban, Attanucci, & Shapiro, 1973). Shipman et al. (1976) studied African American children of low socioeconomic status. The mother's educational aspirations and expectations were higher for children who scored high in reading than for those who scored low in reading. A higher level of parental education was also associated with children's overall academic success.

In 1975 the Consortium for Longitudinal Studies (1983) set out to determine the effect of the experimental early intervention programs of the 1960s on children. The consortium selected 11 research groups for analysis. Although the programs differed, they were all well designed and well monitored, so there was an excellent database.

The consortium's findings emphasized the importance of early intervention (Consortium for Longitudinal Studies, 1983; Gray, Ramsey, & Klaus, 1982; Lazar et al., 1982; Levenstein, 1988; Spodek, 1982). In a summary of the consortium's findings, Lazar (1983) discussed two important points. First, a good preschool program pays off in two ways: benefits for children's development and financial savings as a result of less special education placement. Second, "closer contact between home and school and greater involvement of parents in the education of their children are probably more important" than generally realized by administrators (p. 464).

A follow-up study of Weikart's Perry Preschool Program vividly illustrated the effect that early educational intervention can have on children's lives (Berrueta-Clement, Schweinhart, Barnett, Epstein, & Weikart, 1984). The Perry Preschool Program followed children to age 19, 4 years beyond the report published by the consortium. Berrueta-Clement et al. compared children who had attended the Perry Preschool with children who had not. The researchers found that former Perry Preschool students grew up with more school success, placed a higher value on school, had higher aspirations for college, had fewer absences, and spent fewer of their school years in special education than children in a control group.

In 1972, 16 Home Start programs serving 1,200 families were launched. Eleven Child and Family Resource programs serving 900 families were started in July 1973. "These programs, all built around a Head Start program, promote continuity of service by including all children in the participating family from prenatal stage through age 8, and broaden the program focus from the age-eligible child, to the entire family" (U.S. Department of Health, Education and Welfare, 1974, p. iii).

Developmental Continuity

Concern about the link between Head Start and the public school resulted in funding for developmental continuity. Two program designs were investigated. One was based on a cooperative model with both Head Start and the schools working out a continuous educational program for the child. The other caused change within the existing school system and included programs for children 3 years and up as part of the school system as well as a curriculum structured for preschool ages through age 8. Both programs involved parents throughout preschool and school years.

Children in the 1970s, according to the experts, continued to need love, consistent guidance, and an enriched and responsive environment. Concern over parent–child separation, particularly in a required hospital stay, was evident in advice given to parents. They were told to stay with the child if hospitalization was necessary. Bonding and the importance of early child–parent interaction was reflected in the research of Ainsworth (1973), Bowlby (1966, 1982, 1988), Brazelton (1987), Klaus and Kennell (1982), and Spitz (1965).

Child abuse and neglect were recognized as debilitating and destructive forces against children, and the concerns of the 1960s became a mandate to report all suspected cases of child abuse and neglect (see chapter 11).

Sexist references in texts, which implied innate differences between boys and girls or referred to children in masculine terms only, became noticeable by their absence. Feminists joined civil rights activists and advocates of rights for disabled persons in elimination of stereotypes and inequality of opportunity.

The decade closed with school, government, social agencies, and families concerned with educational programs and support systems for children and parents. Over the years, parent involvement in school decision making had diminished. Families in earlier centuries had the prime responsibility for education of their children. When formal education joined with informal education, parents still had decision-making rights in regard to their child's schooling. In colonial days the church and family were the major institutions for the socialization of children. During the 18th and 19th centuries the community school increased in importance, but parents were still involved in decision making. Schools were small. Many country schools were dispersed across the nation, and schoolteachers were hired by the local school board, lived in the community, and were responsible to the school district. Between 1890 and 1920 there was a shift from community to urban schools (Butts & Cremin, 1953; Goodson & Hess, 1975). The dramatic shift from a rural society to an urban society resulted in a change in the control of schools. The process transferred control of schools from the community to professionals. Consolidation of rural schools into larger, centrally located schools improved equipment, facilities, and diversity of staff, but it took away parent influence. From the 1920s until the 1970s the steady flow from rural to urban areas increased the separation of school and families, with minorities and the poor being the most alienated from the educational process.

1980 TO 1990

White House Conference

The 1980s commenced with the White House Conference on Families, which took place in July 1980 at three locations: Baltimore, Minneapolis, and Los Angeles. Interest was high. Families were important to the citizens, but divisive interests complicated the work. Despite this, the conference approved 20 recommendations to support families, including flexible work schedules, leave policies, job sharing, more part-time jobs, and more child care services. However, it did not have a great impact on reducing divorce or improving marital harmony.

The decade ended with little movement toward achievement of these recommendations. Few companies offered flexible work schedules and job sharing. Congress defeated the Family and Parental Leave Act in 1988.

Family Concerns

Families in this decade were under stress caused by financial pressure, lack of available time, high mobility, lack of an extended family in proximity, drugs, abuse, violence on the streets and on television, health concerns, inadequate nutrition, and difficulty in obtaining or providing adequate child care. On the positive side, inflation steadied in the 1980s. Those who did not have housing, however, were caught in a crunch. Home buyers were faced with high down payments or extremely high monthly payments. Many could not afford any housing, and the number of homeless increased to become a national disgrace.

Poverty existed in all parts of the United States—32.5 million people were poor, 12.5 million of whom were children. One child out of five lived in poverty. The ratios were even higher for two minority groups: Nearly one in two Black children and one in three Hispanic children lived in poverty (Children's Defense Fund, 1989). Poverty was most evident in the core cities. Shelters and churches offered warmth to the homeless on cold nights, and food lines were set up by many private and church groups. In rural areas where poverty was not so evident, little hope was available. Many children attended school without their basic nutritional needs being met. School lunches were a necessity for them.

In sharp contrast, the 1980s were also characterized by greater affluence. High salaries were available for those in business, technology, and communication. Education was recognized as one way out of poverty. Dealing drugs was another. Children and families living in central cities with high crime rates and widespread drug abuse needed comprehensive support to enable them to realize a more promising destiny (Schorr & Schorr, 1988). Poverty, social programs, and education were intertwined in an effort to lower the high risk of poverty.

Two concerns that contributed to high risk for children were the increased numbers of teenage pregnancies and unmarried mothers. Very young mothers are not prepared physically, educationally, or mentally to rear children, yet one in five infants was born to an unmarried teenager in the 1980s (Hymes, 1987). The increased numbers of single mothers due to divorce, death of the husband, or preference also heightened the risk of poverty. In addition, acquired immunodeficiency syndrome (AIDS) frightened the entire society. This deadly disease was first recognized in the early 1980s.

In more than half of two-parent families in the United States, both parents worked (O'Connell & Bloom, 1987). This gave families a higher standard of living. However, time became a precious commodity, and some families found it difficult to save time for themselves and their children. Articles on handling stress and programs for stress reduction continued to grow in popularity. Parent education programs such as STEP, PET, and Active Parenting were offered by schools, hospitals, and social agencies (see chapter 6).

Many baby boomers began families of their own, and some chose to use birthing rooms in hospitals so that parents and infants could have time together when the infant was first born. Lamaze classes helped prepare parents for the birth, and La Leche League helped mothers with nursing. Many baby boomers had waited to start having children and were eager recipients of the parent education offered by these and other groups.

Parent Education

The need for more parent education for teenagers and all parents was recognized. The country was divided throughout the 1980s, just as it had been during the White House Conference on Families. The far right decried public interference in rearing of children, but polls showed that most people favored family life education. Abortion clinics were bombed as the "right to life" faction demonstrated against the "right to choice" faction. "Pro-family" had different meanings for different people.

Developmentally Appropriate Practice

The National Association for the Education of Young Children (NAEYC) prepared a position statement that outlined the components of developmentally appropriate curricula to guide schools, programs, and teachers of young children.

Interest in programs for 4-year-olds increased in individual states, and states began to fund programs that would meet the needs of 4-year-olds who were at risk. The federal government, in the form of

P.L. 99-457, offered incentive grants to support programs for children with physical and learning disabilities from birth until age 2.

Child Development Associate

An issue was the lack of qualified child-care staff. The Child Development Associate (CDA) program continued. It was developed to credential individuals to work in child-care centers. These included Head Start parents who began to be employed as paraprofessionals in Head Start positions. More than 31,000 people were credentialed by the end of the 1980s.

1990 TO 2000

Focus on Family

The 1990s could be called the Decade of Focus on the Family. Parent involvement changed to family involvement. From focusing on mothers in the 1950s and both fathers and mothers in the 1960s and 1970s, a shift occurred toward viewing family environment as the most important factor in a child's education. The Department of Education emphasized the strengthening of families and issued a paper, *Strong Families, Strong Schools: Building Community Partnerships for Learning* (1994). Family partnerships with school were encouraged. In 1990, the Center on Children, Schools, Families, and Children's Learning was established.

Federal influence on schools continued with federal programs such as Title I, Even Start, and the Elementary and Secondary School Act. The introduction of *Goals 2000: Educate America* and the development of national standards were criticized by some as taking away the constitutional rights of states to control education. At the same time, parents were given more power to influence the education of their children. Many schools began restructuring and turned to site-based management, an educational design that had parents working with school personnel in the establishment of goals and direction. There was also a movement for choice in school selection. Charter schools became available in many states commencing in 1996 and 1997. Parents could elect their own board and choose their own curriculum for their charter schools, funded by the school district in which they were located. Early childhood had great interest in constructivism and Reggio Emilio philosophy.

Family Resource Centers

Family resource centers were funded. Their goals were to strengthen and empower families. The centers designed their programs according to the needs of their populations with offerings that might include parent education, programs for children, and literacy programs. Family literacy programs were established to help those who could not read. The classes helped newcomers who did not speak or read English well, as well as those who had not learned to read in school. Family literacy programs recognized that parents could help their children more if the parents were able to read and support their children.

Homeschooling

Homeschooling became more popular during this decade, and support groups helped parents who wanted to teach their children at home. States enacted certain requirements for parents to continue homeschooling. For example, children must take tests every 3 years and place no lower than the 19th percentile. It was recommended that schools work with homeschooling parents so that children could participate in activities that the home is unable to offer, such as band, chorus, and athletics.

Family and Medical Leave Act

Congress finally passed the Family and Medical Leave Act in early 1993, providing 12 weeks of unpaid leave for employees with such family concerns as childbirth, adoption, or a serious illness of a child, spouse, or parent. The bill required all companies with 50 or more employees to guarantee jobs and provide health benefits to workers when they returned after the leave.

Temporary Assistance for Needy Families

Welfare was revamped in 1996 with the Personal Responsibility and Work Opportunity Reconciliation Act. AFDC (Aid to Families with Dependent

Children) had provided assistance for poor, single-parent families since 1935. It was replaced with Temporary Assistance for Needy Families (TANF), which provides block grants to states who run their own programs within federal guidelines. The law requires mothers to join the workforce if they receive assistance for more than 2 years. It places a 5-year lifetime limit on eligibility for assistance. In carrying out the law some concerns have emerged, including child care, health care, poor job skills of some former AFDC recipients, and child-care workers who earn low wages.

Pro-life and Pro-choice

Advocates for stronger families and better conditions for children were strong in their positions. The two largest camps were those in favor of no abortions and those who favored abortion under certain circumstances. Although both groups were strong advocates, the pro-life advocates differed from the pro-choice advocates in their approach to strengthening families.

IDEA 97

The Individuals with Disabilities Education Act, IDEA 97 (P.L. 105–17) was reauthorized in 1997. It addressed the participation of parents in the development of their child with disability's program.

The new century arrived with the country strong in spirit. Will it support its schools and families?

2000 TO 2008

Response to Terrorism

On September 11, 2001, the Twin Towers at the World Trade Center in New York City and a section of the Pentagon in Washington were destroyed by terrorists. The focus on education continued in schools, home, and community, but the national focus changed to a war on terrorism. Special forces were sent to Afghanistan to conduct a war against Al Qaeda and Osama bin Laden, their leader. The war on terrorism, however, would continue to be a concern throughout the decade because it was recognized that there were terrorist cells in various countries with attacks in Spain and other countries throughout the decade. The United States invaded Iraq in March 2003, citing a fear that Saddam Hussein was developing nuclear and biological weapons. The invasion went quickly with little resistance to the American forces, but securing the peace continued to be a difficult challenge. It was found that Hussein did not have materials to develop nuclear weapons. Internal conflicts among the Shiites, Sunnis, and Kurds hampered the efforts to develop a democracy and peace.

Emphasis on Education—No Child Left Behind Act

The 21st century opened with continued emphasis on education. Programs that had originated in the 1960s from the War on Poverty, such as the Elementary and Secondary Education Act and Head Start, continued into the new century. The importance of families in the education of children was emphasized, and programs for the very young child were increased. A new law, No Child Left Behind Act of 2001, was signed into law on January 8, 2002. "The new law is considered to be the most sweeping reform of the Elementary and Secondary Education Act since it was enacted in 1965" (U.S. Department of Education, 2002). The law required that states test third through eighth graders annually in reading and mathematics. The object of testing is to require that states and school districts develop systems of accountability. States were required to provide annual report cards on school performance and statewide results. At the same time, states and school districts have more local control and flexibility in decision making on how increased learning and testing will be obtained. Parents of children in schools that are designated as failing may transfer their child to another school, traditional or charter, that is performing better. When schools continue to fail, supplemental service such as after-school programs, tutoring, and summer school may use Title I funds. More federal funding in reading instructional materials and in improving teacher quality was also approved (U.S. Department of Education, 2002).

White House Summit on Early Childhood

The government focused on improving education. A White House Summit on Early Childhood was held on July 26 and 27, 2001. Its focus was to raise public awareness of the importance of early childhood. The topics covered were varied, with speakers who discussed brain development, poverty and how it affects children, and intervention skills. Prior to the summit, the National Education Association (NEA), a professional organization with 2.6 million members, had challenged the focus on literacy, recommending that health, nutrition, and brain and social development of infants and young children must also be included.

The previous White House Conference on Early Childhood Development and Learning on April 17, 1997, made many educators aware of the importance of the early years on brain development. Programs that were specially developed to help families with young children included the Child Care Development Fund and Early Head Start. In addition, individual school districts continued a trend toward funding all-day kindergartens.

Partnerships for Family Involvement in Education

The U.S. Department of Education offered information and support through the establishment of Partnerships for Family Involvement in Education. In addition, the Center on Families, Communities, Schools, and Children's Learning, which was established at Johns Hopkins University, continued to provide research, policy, and the National Network of Partnerships.

The National Education Goals Panel, created in 1990 as a bipartisan group was dissolved in 2002 by a congressional mandate. A number of Promising Practices Policies resulted in various improvements in the schools during the panel's existence. The two goals most related to early childhood were Goal l, All Children Ready to Learn and Goal 8, Parental Involvement.

Charter Schools

By 2006, 40 states, the District of Columbia, and Puerto Rico had enacted laws for charter schools. In 1992 only two states had charter schools which, although public schools, are organized differently and offer an alternative type of education for parents and students. Charter schools may be a part of a local school district or serve as their own district. Charter schools find and develop their own facilities, hire their own teachers, and design their own curriculum. They are usually smaller than traditional public schools, are popular with parents, and have a more diverse population than the traditional school. Charter schools vary widely. Whether the charter schools are accomplishing better education is unclear. Those connected to the local school district had higher scores than those that were idependent. Students taught by certified teachers in either traditional or public schools had comparable scores. Current research has not found that charter schools have higher academic achievement than traditional schools. More research comparisons will be available in the future (Dervarics, 2001; National Education Association, 2006; U.S. Charter Schools, 2004).

Family and Medical Leave Act

The Family and Medical Leave Act, which offers 12 weeks of unpaid leave from work, was favored by most citizens. It was found, however, that 78 percent of those who needed leave were unable to take it because one salary was not enough to support their families. Some states are looking at options that would supplement the one salary by allowing the parent staying home with the infant to take out unemployment benefits or temporary disability insurance. In 2000, the U.S. Department of Labor adopted regulations encouraging states to provide unemployment benefits to working parents who take leave to care for newborns or newly adopted children (Asher & Lenhoff, 2001).

Technology

"Computer technology has transformed society in profound ways. For better or worse, the increasing persuasiveness of computer technology is a reality no one can ignore" (Shields & Behrman, 2000). The number of computers in the schools has increased from 250,000 in 1983 to 8.6 million in 1997. Access to computers at home ranges from 22 percent of families with less than $20,000 income to 91 percent of families with incomes of $75,000, according to a 1998 survey (Becker, 2000).

Making computers a useful tool in the early childhood classroom requires that the teacher be knowledgeable and supportive. Children should be 3 or 4 years of age before they explore and use appropriate computer software. Kindergarten and primary-grade

Eugenia Hepworth Berger

Pleasurable experiences together strengthen the parent-child bond.

children continue with exploration, using developmentally appropriate software, but as they become more familiar with computers, their explorations may lead to composing short stories. With the explosion of computer use, and the information available through the Internet, it is essential in the 21st century that older children become competent computer users.

Population Diversity

Schools' student populations show increased diversity in the 21st century. During the 1990s and early 21st century, immigration rose to its highest level since the beginning of the 20th century. Early in the 20th century, 1 million immigrants arrived each year. Since 1992, almost 1 million immigrants have arrived each year as well, accounting for 9 percent of the total population. The greatest number of immigrants come from Asia and Latin America. Those migrating from Asia are often from China and the Philippines, whereas the majority of Latin Americans come from Mexico (Martin & Midgley, 1999; Martin & Widgren, 2002). This influx of immigrants and refugees (through both legal and unauthorized entry) impacts the schools, with enrollment of many English Language Learners. In 2000, the foreign-born population in the United States totaled almost 30.5 million: 15.5 million Latin Americans; 8.3 million Asians; 4.7 million Europeans; 836,000 Africans; 835,000 North Americans; and 181,000 Oceanians (U.S. Census Bureau, 2001). These students enhance the diversity of the schools, but they also require special programs, such as English as a Second Language (ESL) and English Language Learners (ELL), to help them adjust to education in the United States. Immigration continued as an issue throughout most of the decade.

Living with Change

The nation looks forward to a new century with many changes happening around the world. To understand the future, it is also necessary to understand the past. Tables 4.1 and 4.2 offer an overview of important ideas about children over the centuries. As the new century begins, the nation faces the need for a continued response to terrorist threats, conflict with Iraq, nuclear concerns, and continued unrest in the Israel-Palestine area. Around the world, many live in dire conditions that need to be ameliorated. Challenges abound. How will the nation respond to make the world a better place for all children?

SUMMARY

Parental involvement in the education of children has been present since prehistoric times. The family provided the first informal education for the child through modeling, teaching, and praise or discipline. From the times of early Egyptian, Sumerian, Hebrew, Greek, and Roman days, parents were actively involved in the selection of teachers and the education of their children.

During the Middle Ages (A.D. 400–1400), at 7 years of age children of nobility were sent to live in another noble's home, and others became apprentices in trades. Children were treated as miniature adults rather than children. It was not until the 15th to 17th centuries that the concept of family began to develop.

Strict discipline was imposed on all classes of children. This philosophy prevailed until the writings of Rousseau, Pestalozzi, and Froebel in the 18th and early 19th centuries brought a touch of humanism to the rearing of children.

Family life in the United States was able to flourish from the early days. Childrearing practices varied

TABLE 4.2 Highlights of events and people who influenced ideas about children, early education, and childrearing, 1880–2004.

1882	The American Association of University Women was established.
1884	The Department of Kindergarten Instruction of the National Education Association was formed (later the Department of Elementary-Kindergarten-Nursery Education; dissolved in the mid-1970s).
1888	The Child Study Association of America was founded.
1889	The General Federation of Women's Clubs was founded. G. Stanley Hall began the first child study center.
1890–1900	Settlement houses were established to aid the poor and new immigrants.
1892	The International Kindergarten Union (now the Association for Childhood Education International) was established.
1895	Patty Smith Hill and Anna Bryan studied with G. Stanley Hall.
1896	The Laboratory School at the University of Chicago was started by John Dewey. The National Association of Colored Women was established.
1897	The Parent Teachers Association (PTA) was founded.
1898	*Kindergarten Magazine* was first published.
1905	Maria Montessori established Casa dei Bambini in Rome. Sigmund Freud wrote *Three Essays of the Theory of Sexuality.*
1909	The First White House Conference on Care of Dependent Children was held.
1911	Margaret McMillan designed an open-air nursery for children of the poor in England. Gesell started the Child Development Clinic at Yale University.
1912	The Children's Bureau was established. It published the first edition of *Infant Care* in 1914.
1916	The first parent cooperative was established in Chicago.
1917	The Smith-Hughes Act was passed. The Iowa Child Welfare Research Station was established.
1920s	Twenty-six parent education programs were established.
1920	The Child Welfare League of America was founded. Watson, a behaviorist, believed that children should be strictly scheduled and should not be coddled.
1922	A nursery school was established in Boston by Abigail Elliot. Benjamin Gruenberg wrote the *Child Study Manual.*
1925	The National Council of Parent Education was established. Patty Smith Hill began the National Committee on Nursery Schools (now the National Association for the Education of Young Children).
1927	The first Black nursery school in the United States was founded by Dorothy Howard in Washington, DC.
1928	The nursery school movement expanded from 3 schools in 1920 to 89 in 1928.
1930	The White House Conference on Child Health and Protection recommended parent education as part of the public school system.
1932	Parent education courses were offered in 25 states.
1933	The Federal Emergency Relief Administration authorized work-relief wages for nursery school teachers.
1934–1938	*Parent Education,* the journal of the National Council of Parent Education, was published.
1940s	A new emphasis on mental health for children emerged.
1940	The Lanham Act provided money for child care so that mothers could join the war effort.
1946	Benjamin Spock published *The Common Sense Book of Baby and Child Care.*
1949	*Your Children from 6 to 12* was published by the Children's Bureau.
1950	Erik Erikson wrote *Childhood and Society,* which included the eight stages of personality growth. James Hymes wrote *Effective Home-School Relations.*
1952	Jean Piaget's work *The Origins of Intelligence in Children* was translated into English.

(Continued)

TABLE 4.2 Continued

1957	After the launching of *Sputnik,* new emphasis was placed on children's intellectual development. *Parenthood in a Free Nation* was published by the Parent Education Project of the University of Chicago.
1960	The Golden Anniversary White House Conference on Children and Youth was held. The Parent Cooperative Preschools International was founded.
1960	The Day Care and Child Development Council of America was founded.
1962	J. McVicker Hunt wrote *Intelligence and Experience,* which questioned the concept of fixed IQ.
1963	The White House Conference on Mental Retardation was held.
1964	The Economic Opportunity Act of 1964 began the War on Poverty.
1965	The Civil Rights Act was passed. Head Start was established. The Elementary and Secondary School Act was passed; Title I provided money for educationally deprived children.
1967	The Follow Through program was begun to provide continuity for former Head Start students.
1970	The White House Conference on Children and Youth was held.
1972	The National Home Start program, which involved parents in teaching, was initiated.
1975	The Education for All Handicapped Children Act, P.L. 94–192, was passed.
1980	The White House Conference on Families was held.
1987	PL 99–457; designed to serve handicapped children with disabilities up to age 2, was passed.
1990	National Education Goals 2000 was established.
1993	The Family and Medical Leave Act of 1993 was passed.
1996	Temporary Assistance for Needy Families (TANF) replaced Aid to Families with Dependent Children (AFDC).
1997	The White House Summit on Early Childhood was held July 26 and 27.
1997	The Individuals with Disabilities Education Act of 1997 was reauthorized.
2001	The No Child Left Behind Act of 2001 was passed.
2001	On September 11, the Twin Towers of the World Trade Center in New York City was destroyed by terrorists.

according to country of origin, but they were basically tied to the religious background of the family. The nation is culturally diverse with immigrants from many countries arriving from the 1600s to the present time. The major exceptions were the indigenous population and Black families brought from Africa to serve as slaves; they were not allowed to have a normal family life. The indigenous people (American Indians) were also mistreated and moved to reservations by the late 1800s, a destructive process for their family lifestyles.

Childrearing practices of the former Europeans were reflected by the Puritan belief in breaking the will of the child and the need for perfect behavior. The parent education groups in the early 1800s were based on the need to rear children according to these religious principles.

The modern parent education movement began in the 1880s and 1890s. Prominent women founded the National Congress of Mothers, later known as the National Congress of Parents and Teachers (PTA), the Child Study Association, and the American Association of University Women. Each included childrearing as a part of its program. G. Stanley Hall created the first child-study center in the United States at Clark University. In addition, philanthropic organizations included parent education in their settlement schools and Free Kindergarten Association programs.

The federal government became involved in family life with the first White House Conference on Care of Dependent Children in 1909. As a result, the Children's Bureau was established in 1912, and the first issue of *Infant Care* was published in 1914. Colleges and universities showed their concern for research in child development by the establishment of research and child study centers.

The 1920s were the most productive in terms of the establishment of parent education programs. Twenty-six parent education organizations were founded during the decade, and many parent education groups emerged across the nation. Change had also come in terms of childrearing practices. Although authorities in the 1890s and the early 1900s emphasized love and affection in the formation of character, the 1920s focused on strict scheduling and discipline.

During the 1940s parent education programs continued, bolstered by child-care money for mothers working in the war effort.

The 1950s showed more concern for the mental health of the child. The writings of Freud and Erikson on social–emotional growth, plus Benjamin Spock's famous child-care book, helped shift attitudes from the strict scheduling of the 1920s to the "on demand" feedings and concern for mental health of the 1950s.

In the late 1950s the Soviet Union launched *Sputnik*. Suddenly, there was concern for the intellectual development of American youth. This forecast the emphasis toward cognitive development in the 1960s and 1970s. The total child—emotional, social, intellectual, and physical—was the focus of many professionals, and although cognitive development was emphasized and Piaget's theories on cognitive development had a great effect on education, this developmental theory complemented the belief in the need for physical, social, and emotional health. Head Start, Follow Through, and Title I programs looked toward the child's total needs. The family was brought into the development and ongoing commitments of federal programs.

In the 1960s and 1970s Americans were confronted with great social change. The 1980s began with the first White House Conference on Families, attended by men and women representing diverse philosophic beliefs about families.

Parent involvement was recognized as an important element in a child's success at school. Monetary support for family support programs, however, decreased in the 1980s. Head Start continued but served only one fifth of the eligible children. Societal problems included increased drug and alcohol abuse by school-age children and poverty for one in five children. Families were faced with a shortage of time and increased stress in a turbulent world.

In 1987, P.L. 99-457—legislation to serve exceptional young children—was passed. The 1990s saw the Family Medical Leave Act pass in 1993. Family resource centers, family literacy, and Even Start supported parents in their search for literacy and family strengths.

In 1996, welfare was revamped as Temporary Assistance for Needy Families (TANF) which replaced Aid to Families with Dependent Children (AFDC).

In 2002, the No Child Left Behind Act of 2001 was passed. All third and eighth graders are required to be tested annually in mathematics and reading.

Iraq in 2003 was invaded by the United States and allies thinking that Hussein was developing an atomic bomb. This was found to be untrue, and the development of a democracy became the ultimate target. The 21st century arrived with many challenges.

SUGGESTED CLASS ACTIVITIES AND DISCUSSIONS

1. Ask a librarian to help you find books from art museums throughout the world. Examine these for trends in childrearing practices and beliefs.
2. Find a library that has federal publications. Look through books published by the Children's Bureau. Examine the changes in beliefs about child development.
3. Get a copy of the *Twenty-Eighth Year Book, Parts I and II, Preschool and Parent Education* by the National Society for the Study of Education. Compare the programs on parent education in the 1920s with the programs in 2006.
4. Concern about the poor was strongest during the 1890s, the early 20th century, the 1930s, and the 1960s. What were the differing causes of poverty? Why did the concern seem to lessen in intervening decades?
5. Why did nursery schools serve the poor in England? Why do they tend to serve middle-class parents in the United States? How did their origins differ?
6. Identify some of the Native Americans' nations. How has their way of life changed over the past 150 years?
7. Discuss federal intervention. Trace its history from the hands-off approach of Spencer to the start of the Children's Bureau. How has federal involvement grown since 1910?
8. Examine your community. How many types of programs for children have begun since Head Start was initiated in 1965?
9. Describe the changes in immigration. How have various immigrant groups differed in their treatment after arriving in the United States?
10. Ask school officials how they have implemented the Individuals with Disabilities Education Act requirements.
11. Discuss with school officials the changes in education that have occurred since they became involved.
12. E-mail or call with requests for information on education and family involvement.

WEB SITES

When this chapter on history was originally written, Web sites were not as numerous as they currently are. The information was primarily acquired from books and journals, and the subject matter changed with each decade. I recommend that any specific information desired be found in individual Web sites such as those that accompany the rest of the chapters or in history Web sites.

National Society for the Study of Education: Yearbooks
www.nsse-chicago.org/yearbooks.asp
The National Society for the Study of Education archives its yearbooks all the way back to 1900.

***On Writing Childhood History* by Lloyd deMause**
www.psychohistory.com
An interesting account of Lloyd deMause's (a psychohistorian rather than an early childhood educator) study of psychiatry. Written in 1988, deMause illustrates the challenge of childhood history.

Smithsonian Education
www.smithsonianeducation.org
Site details school pograms and tours at the National Museum of American History.

Smithsonian National Museum of American History: Kids
www.americanhistory.si.edu/kids
Site offers child-centered activities and information related to American history.

U.S. National Archives and Records Administration
www.archives.gov
The archives of the United States are quite extensive, but the site allows you to select a subject. For example, there are 186 multi-page letters received by teacher Clara D. True of Santa Clara Day School, a Santa Fe Indian School, from August 29, 1902 until September 17, 1906.

5 Effective Home–School–Community Relationships

Education should consist of a series of enchantments, each raising the individual to a higher level of awareness, understanding, and kinship with all living things.

Anonymous (Frank, 2001, p. 232)

Where can anyone find an opportunity to impact a child's world as easily and as well as in a school or home, leading children to discover their own distinct way to grow and develop?

Know you what it is to be a child? . . . It is to believe in love, to believe in loveliness, to believe in belief; it is to be so little that the elves can reach to whisper in your ear; it is to turn pumpkins into coaches, and mice into horses, lowness into loftiness, and nothing into everything, for each child has its fairy godmother in its own soul.

Thompson, 1988, p. 300

In this chapter on parent involvement in schools, which include child-care centers, preschools, and primary grades, you will learn about ideas and programs that will enable you to collaborate successfully with parents and also do the following:

- Set up a program that encourages parents to participate.
- Develop a school, child-care center, or preschool that welcomes parents.
- Inform parents of their importance and role in the school–home partnership.
- List and explain services that schools, child-care centers, and preschools can offer to help families accomplish the task of parenting.
- List and explain services that help parents become partners with their child-care centers, preschools, or schools.
- Provide parents with access to information about school and homework.
- Provide a family resource center.
- Develop a parent advisory council.

In reading the chapter, please recognize that all early childhood, whether in child-care centers, preschools, primary or upper elementary grades, parents, providers, and teachers need partnerships to accomplish the task of helping children grow and develop. In order to make the discussion flow more smoothly, schools will often be used to include all levels of care and education.

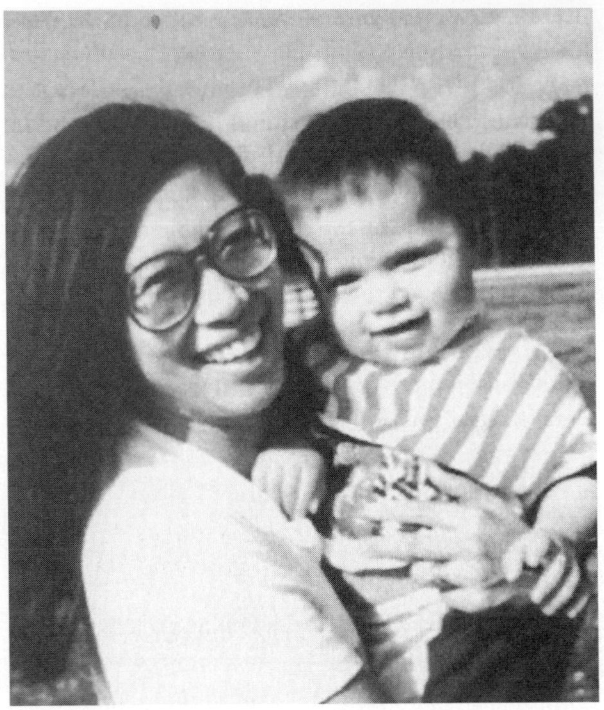

Schools and centers must be support systems working cooperatively with the home. The importance of parent involvement in their child's growth and education has been recognized for many years.

PARENT–SCHOOL COOPERATION

Parent–school cooperation brings the strengths of the home and the expertise of the center or school into a working partnership. Every issue, concern, and educational goal involves the family of the child. Separation of the child from the family is impossible, because every child is socialized into a family culture. Even those reared in an institution are affected by the culture of the institution—their substitute family. Children bring the ideas, feelings, strengths, and weaknesses of the home into their life at school. If homes and centers are connected through the children, clearly a working partnership will strengthen the effectiveness of the center or school. Home–school partnerships are an essential step forward. Working together, schools and homes will succeed in educating the next generation.

Recent research emphasizes increased opportunities for children's success when the home and school work together. More parent–school involvement is needed from birth through high school (Epstein 1996, 2001, 2005b; Epstein et al., 2002; Epstein & Sheldon, 2002; Loucks, 1992; Meyerhoff & White, 1986; Moles, 1987, 1996a, 1996b; National Association of State Boards of Education, 1988, 1991; Warner, 1991). This chapter focuses on the goal of good center–school–home–community relationships with suggestions for procedures and methods to start the process.

SCHOOL CLIMATE AND PARENTAL ATTITUDES

When you walk into a school, preschool, or child-care center, are you able to sense its spirit? Does it seem to invite you to visit? Or does it make you feel unwelcome? Can you pinpoint the reasons for your feelings? Each school differs in its character (usually set by the administrators) and reflects the morale and attitudes of the personnel. Some say, "Come, enjoy with us this exciting business of education." Others say, "You are infringing on my territory. Schools and child-care centers are the professional's business. Send us your children. We will return them to you each evening, but in the meantime, let's each keep to our own responsibilities." In the first instance, there is joy in the educational spirit. In the second, fear and avoidance are dominant.

Parents bring different attitudes into the home–school relationship. One parent may feel excitement and anticipation about a forthcoming visit to the school or center, whereas another may be struck with dread over a required conference. Parents come from diverse backgrounds. If their past school experiences were pleasant and successful, they are likely to enjoy visiting schools again. If their experiences were filled with failures and disappointments, whether real or imagined, the thought of school is depressing; if they do approach the school, it is with trepidation. When you recognize, understand, and respect parents' cultural and social backgrounds, you are more likely to succeed at bringing those parents into a partnership with the school.

Coupled with the parents' past experiences are current pressures. In some districts the burden of poverty will consume the parents. Parents concerned with mere subsistence have little energy left for self-fulfillment or for meeting their children's emotional and educational needs. Maslow's (1968)

Box 5.1

OVERHEARD IN THE TEACHER'S LOUNGE: WHICH SCHOOL WOULD YOU CHOOSE?

"It happened again today," Gloria complained in ever-increasing disgust. "Sara came to school late, obviously tired, without a coat, and when I asked her where her coat was, she burst into tears. Her parents just don't care. What am I supposed to do? I wrote her mother a note last week, but she hasn't responded."

"Did you really expect an answer?" Melody asked. "I thought when I moved to suburbia my problems would be over, but the parents of the children in my room don't volunteer, and only half of them show up for conferences. I've thought about calling them, but I'm just too busy."

"Don't complain," Susan responded. "I'd rather have parents who stay away from my classroom than those who are so involved that they pester you and even try to tell you how to work with their child. A good parent is a quiet parent. Just teach to the exams and make sure the students' scores are above average. I was at one school where parents were so involved that they had a fit when we scored below the 50th percentile. Have you heard about . . . ?"

Or

"The programs at school and outside resources really helped me this fall. One child, Sara, came from a family who seemed uninterested in the welfare of their child. She came to school obviously tired, without a coat, and when I asked her where her coat was, she burst into tears," Gloria shared one day.

"The social worker shared with me what she knew about Sara's circumstances," she continued. "It seems that her father was in a terrible automobile wreck, and has been hospitalized and out of work for the last 6 months. The mother is overwhelmed with the lack of finances, caring for her children, and fear for her husband's condition.

"I called Sara's mother and let her know that we would be supportive of Sara and help her be successful in her schoolwork. We also discussed the resources available at the school as well as social services and nonprofit organizations. She had not known about most of the resources available to her. Then we used the exchange room to find some new clothes for Sara.

"Guess what? She came to back-to-school night. Other parents offered to baby-sit her children so she can get out, visit her husband, and take a part-time job. She was so appreciative. It will be a long struggle, but this family will make it. It really makes me feel good to know that we were able to help."

And

"Ann, do you think you could help me with the workshop on family math? Eighteen families showed up last night for the first session. They got so involved and were so appreciative that we're planning another the week after next. We're going to make manipulatives that they can use at home with their children."

"Sounds great," Ann said. "I've been thinking of developing a workshop on inventive spelling and writing. I also want to involve the parents in developing an authors' library. My students are so excited about writing their own books. Let's brainstorm together and plan both of the workshops. It will be more exciting if we work together, and don't forget that I have four parents who are fantastic volunteers. I'm sure they will want to help. We need to check on child care, too. I know some parents have difficulty finding someone to take care of their children. If we get Nadine to plan for the children, we can let the parents observe her interaction with them. She's wonderful, sensitive, and has so many enriching ideas."

Observed in the Child-Care Center

Agnes, mother of 2 preschoolers, rushes into the center. Jeff, the 2-year-old, crying that he lost his doggy on the bus, continues crying as Agnes pulls him into the Goldenrod toddler room. With Susan pulling her mother's arm, Agnes leaves Jeff, alone and still crying, as she rushes to the Sunflower room, where Susan joins the other 4-year-olds. Agnes glances into the Goldenrod room, does not see her son or the lead teacher, so she hurries out of the center and goes to the bus stop. As she stands there waiting for the bus, she worries about Jeff. She glances at her watch and wonders if she will be late for work again.

Or

Agnes, mother of 2 preschoolers, rushes into the child-care center. As she turns into the family room, she talks with Jeff, her 2-year-old, and Susan, her 4-year-old, about the morning treats in the room. What would you like, orange juice, milk, or chocolate milk? After giving the children their drinks, she pours a cup of coffee for herself. They join another family who also arrived a little early. After the children eat a nutritious treat they turn to the children's area while the mothers

(Continued)

Box 5.1 Continued

interact with their children or relax and talk with each other. The handout on the table gives suggestions for activities to do during the next holiday. Agnes glances at the books on the library shelf to see if a book on nutrition is available. After chatting and talking with center staff, they glance at the clock. It's time to go to the children's rooms. As they leave the family room they greet other parents and children just arriving at the center.

hierarchy of needs stresses that basic needs must be met before a person can climb higher rungs of the ladder toward self-actualization. Parents contending with unemployment, inflation, and social change will need special understanding. "Humans of all ages get caught in a powerful web spun of two strong threads; the way they were treated in the past, and the way the present bears down on them" (Hymes, 1974, p. 16). Schools and centers must be support systems working cooperatively with the home rather than another agency viewing the parents as failures. Add the parents' concerns for their children's welfare and you will recognize why school–home relationships can be either negative encounters or effective partnerships.

The importance of parent involvement in their child's growth and education has been recognized for many years. Hymes (1974) eloquently described the parent–child–teacher relationship when he said that parents love their children, and if the teacher "feels this same love, then parents are your friends. Show your interest in a child and parents are on your side. Be casual, be off-handed, be cold toward the child and parents can never work closely with you. . . . To touch the child is to touch the parent. To praise the child is to praise the parent. To criticize the child is to hit at the parent. The two are two, but the two are one" (pp. 8–9).

Debilitating experiences with schools or centers, feelings of inadequacy, poor achievement by children, and current pressures can cause some parents to stay away from the school. On the other hand, some parents tend to dominate and are compulsively involved with the schools. Between these two extremes are (a) parents who need encouragement to come to visit, (b) parents who readily respond when invited, and (c) parents who are comfortable about coming to school and enjoy some involvement in the educational process (see Figure 5.1).

Each group requires a different response from the professional staff. The parents who tend to stay away will need time to overcome negative experiences and learn to appreciate that the school or center can be trusted to help their children. If the school has an inviting and responsive climate, the three groups of parents in the middle ground will feel welcome. These groups, which encompass the largest portion of parents, will soon begin contributing to the school's activities. They can also form a supportive advocacy for school plans.

Parents in the domineering group can also become positive assets. Let them lead by taking on a responsibility, such as fund-raising or organizing a social get-together. Offering a variety of tasks and different degrees of involvement assures parents that they may contribute according to their talents and available time and allows all of them to be comfortable about coming to school and enjoying involvement in the educational process.

It is up to the teachers and administrators to develop a school or center that welcomes parents. They must be aware of their own feelings, ability to work with and support parents as they develop their plans for the upcoming year.

THE CASE FOR IMPROVED RELATIONSHIPS

Schools and centers have more contact with families than any other public agency. Almost every child from the age of 5 spends 9 months a year, 5 days a week, 5 or 6 hours a day in school. Children in centers often spend the entire year while their parents are employed outside the home. With child-care centers and preschools, the school–home–community relationship begins very early. Locally controlled schools can respond to the needs of the community. If schools and community join forces in a coordinated effort to support families and children, they can have an enormous effect. The school and home also have a natural opportunity to work together. With the community, they can achieve their goals for children.

FIGURE 5.1 Parents respond to schools based on their past experiences and their current situations.

Research

The 2005 Phi Delta Kappa/Gallup poll found that 48 percent of the respondents graded their own schools with either As or Bs. Those closest to the schools, the parents, graded the public schools even higher with 20 percent As and 37 percent Bs for a total of 57 percent A and B responses. There was no corresponding questionnaire for parents with preschool children.

It seems that those who are most knowledgeable about their particular school district grade their schools higher than they grade schools in the nation as a whole. Only 24 percent gave grades of A and B in the national total.

The respondents also showed support of their schools by 68 percent choosing to reform the system rather than changing to an alternative. Fifty-seven percent of respondents do not feel that students should have the opportunity to attend private schools at public expense, while 38 percent agree with the support that enables students to attend private schools.

Although 49 percent of the public approve charter schools, 80 percent believe that they should be accountable to the state the same as regular public schools, and 65 percent are opposed to charter schools if having them reduces the public school support (Rose & Gallup, 2005).

In an extensive research project, Williams (1992) found both school personnel and parents concerned about the necessity of parent involvement in schools. He found that 86.8 percent of teachers and 92.1 percent of 2,300 principals believed teachers needed parent-involvement training.

What do beginning teachers feel about parent involvement? In a survey conducted for MetLife by Harris Interactive in 2005, 88 percent of 800 representative new elementary school teachers strongly agreed and 11 percent somewhat agreed that "effective teachers need to be able to work well with student's parents" (p. 31). New elementary school teachers report that they encourage parents to become involved in a variety of ways. Representative activities for parent participation included (a) attend parent teacher conferences, 99 percent of new teachers support this activity; (b) support homework, 97 percent; (c) participate in fund raising, 95 percent; (d) be involved in learning activities at home, 98 percent; and (e) volunteer to go on field trips, 95 percent. The teachers in the research reported that slightly more than half of the parents participated in these activities (Markow & Martin, 2005).

Epstein found that teachers who were leaders in parent-involvement practices enabled all parents, regardless of the parent's educational level, to be involved. These teachers asked parents to conduct learning activities at home, such as reading aloud, asking their children about the school day, playing games, visiting the classroom, going to the library, and helping children with their homework. Teachers who did not involve parents had attitudes that stereotyped less-educated single parents and low-socioeconomic parents (Epstein 2001, 2002; Epstein & Dauber, 1991).

Family Involvement

Six types of involvement were suggested by Epstein as a result of research in the Baltimore schools (Epstein, 1996, 2001, 2005a; Epstein & Dauber, 1991). They concluded that the schools have a basic responsibility to do the following:

1. Enable families to provide the skills and knowledge needed to help their children at each age level.
2. Communicate with families through notes, telephone calls, conferences, and other types of communication. Communication was also studied by Loucks (1992), and parents responded that parent–school communication could be strengthened by more opportunities in (a) one-on-one contact with school personnel, (b) participation in the curricula that their children experience, (c) joint problem solving between the school and home rather than by the school alone, (d) precise suggestions on how parents can help their children, and (e) more observations of children as they are involved in school activities. Students indicated that their parents were discouraged from being involved positively with the schools. Instead, they were contacted when there were discipline concerns or problems in the academic area. The students said they would feel better if their parents attended school functions, were used as volunteers, served on committees, and participated with the ongoing activities of the school.
3. Include parents as volunteers and assistants in the classrooms and other areas of school. Make it possible for parents to attend school functions (Epstein, 2001, Epstein & Dauber, 1991). In 1997, 69 percent (73 percent of women, and 64 percent of men) of respondents to a Gallup poll said they would be willing to work as a volunteer. The highest percentages were those with college degrees (73 percent) and those who were public school parents (78 percent) (Rose, Gallup, & Elam, 1997).
4. Guide parents so they can help their own children through monitoring, discussing, and helping with homework.
5. Involve parents in decision making. Provide training for them to communicate with other parents. Include parents in governance and advocacy. Encourage participation in PTO/PTA and advisory councils.
6. Resources and services available in the community may be integrated with the school's programs. For each of these guidelines, child-care centers and preschools should be included.

For more discussion on types of parent involvement, see chapter 7.

Parent–School Collaboration

Of course, most teachers are also parents. Their role confusion was dramatically illustrated at a workshop involving parents, teachers, and administrators. The participants were asked to raise their hands if they were parents. Almost every person in the room raised a hand. Suddenly the teachers and administrators were in their parental rather than professional roles. Teachers described how different their feelings were when their roles switched.

The emotional change between being a parent receiving services or being a professional responsible for the education of someone else's child was felt immediately. Before coming to the workshop, participants held varying views on parent involvement. Some believed in working with parents, some were already highly successful at parent involvement, and some wanted to keep parents at a respectable distance. As they experienced the change of roles, they recognized how trying to understand parents' feelings and concerns is a giant step toward creating effective home–school relationships.

Picturing parents as a group separated from the school sets up an artificial barrier. Parents are no special breed. We are the parents of the current generation of young people. To understand ourselves as parents is to begin to understand others. What makes us effective participants in home–school–community relationships are those same qualities that make others productive members of the home–school–community team.

ROLES OF ADMINISTRATORS, CHILD-CARE DIRECTORS, TEACHERS, AND PARENTS

School, Child-Care Center, or Preschool Atmosphere and Acceptance of Parents

Schools and preschools let parents know how welcome they are. The attitude of the personnel is reflected in the way parents are met in the principal's or director's office, the friendly or unfriendly greetings in the hall, and the offerings in the school. If visitors walk into the school and the secretaries ignore them for a time, the body language and the attitudes reflect that the school would prefer that they not visit. If schools want to collaborate with parents, they must make sure the office is staffed by people who can make a visitor feel welcome. This, along with positive school policies and services, indicates whether the school recognizes families as important.

Teachers and caregivers who are leaders in parent-involvement practices enable the parent to be involved.

The Administrator's or Center Director's Role in Parent Involvement

School climate—the atmosphere in school or center— reflects the principal's or director's leadership style. Five aspects of school–parent interaction are affected by this leadership. First, the *spirit* of the school or center and the enthusiasm of its staff reflect the administrator's role as morale builder. Supportive guidance, with freedom to develop plans based on individual school or center needs, allows the principal or director to function with productive autonomy. The principal or director builds staff morale by enabling staff members to feel positive, enthusiastic, and secure in their work with children and parents.

With the increase in violence in the schools and the recognition of bullying in its many forms (see chapter 11), it is imperative for administrators to recognize the signs of bullying and the lack of a caring environment in their schools. It is necessary to provide an environment for children in which they feel safe and an accepted member of the school.

A second leadership role, *program designer,* involves implementing the educational program. The principal or director needs to recognize the importance of home–school–community relationships in the success of the educational program and strive toward implementation of such a working relationship. If the principal or director allows teachers the autonomy to work with parents, using volunteers and aides in the development of individualized curricula, the school is on its way to an effective program of parent involvement.

The administrator's third role requires the development of an effective *principal–parent relationship* or *director–parent relationship.* The principal or director determines whether the school atmosphere makes parents feel welcome. Besides influencing the general spirit and morale of the school, the principal or director is responsible for maintaining an open-door policy, scheduling open houses, providing and equipping resource areas for parents, arranging parent education meetings, developing parent workshops and in-service meetings, and supporting the PTA, PTO, or family organization.

Fourth, the principal serves as a *program coordinator.* Individual teachers may develop unique programs using the talents of parents, but the achievement of continuity requires the principal's or director's knowledge and coordination of parent-involvement programs.

Finally, the principal or director has a *leadership* role in developing site-based management and leading advisory councils and decision-making committees. This new role needs strong leadership ability to encourage and enable teachers, staff, and parents to work together and develop an educational program specific to their community's needs. Child-care center directors can develop a program that fits the center's individual needs.

In order to achieve the roles, an administrator who uses collaborative or shared decision making with other members of the staff and with the community, including parents, has others who have come to the same decisions and who will be comfortable with and supportive of the decisions.

Administrators need to be able to diffuse anger by listening, treating others with respect, paraphrasing the issues, and responding with plans for what will be done (Meadows & Saltzman, 2000).

The Teacher's Role in Parent Involvement

The teacher is central to parent involvement in the educational process. Teacher roles include facilitator, teacher, counselor, communicator, program director, interpreter, resource developer, and friend. These roles are illustrated through the activities described later in this chapter and in chapter 6—for example, parent–teacher conferences, volunteer programs, and program development.

Teacher Attitudes and Feeling

The school needs personnel who accept parents, but sometimes teachers and administrators are unaware of how they feel toward parents. The questions in Figure 5.2 were developed to help teachers assess their attitudes toward parents.

It is also helpful for teachers to discuss their work with another person. Teachers can talk to a close colleague about what they value in their work with students and parents. They can then reflect on how their own ideal values compared to the values that act on in their daily work. They should ask a close colleague to evaluate apparent values, and compare their real with their ideal values. This will help teachers focus on their attitudes about working with parents. There are no right or wrong answers; the purpose is to recognize attitudes and perhaps anxiety about having parents in the classroom. An answer to anxiety about parents in the classroom is to organize activities in the classroom that allow parents to be involved and helpful. An example would be the parent who could go to a quiet spot with an individual child and let the child read to the parent or discuss their plans for an assignment or activity.

Roles of Parents

Within each school, parents may assume a variety of roles (see Figure 5.3). Most commonly, parents observe what the school does with their children in the educational process. But parents may also assume other roles simultaneously.

The room parent, for example, who provides treats and creates parties, is an accessory or temporary volunteer. Volunteers can provide needed services, but their involvement is geared only to a specific time and task. Figure 5.4, the parent questionnaire, asks the parent what they want to know about the school or centers well as how they would like to be involved. Each classroom can develop an appropriate questionnaire that would be based on the plans in the classroom and the opportunities available for parents as they volunteer in the school.

Increasingly, parents are serving as more regularly scheduled resources to the schools. Some parents spend a morning or a full day each week working in the resource center, developing materials, and sharing with other parents. You may find others making books with children's stories or listening to children read and discussing ideas with them. Still others work as unpaid aides in the classroom. Since many employed parents use a child-care center, their contributions will need to be geared to their availability. Some centers have an occasional activity on Saturday with those parents in mind.

Parents may also help make policies. School boards have been composed of community leaders charged with making educational policy for many years. Early control of schools was accomplished by community leaders who were generally the elite of the area. At least 50 percent of the Parent Advisory Councils in Head Start must be composed of parents served by the program. Parent involvement, including input into the program is recommended. With this representative membership, policy control has reached down to the grass roots of the constituency being served. The decisions of policy-making parents directly affect the schools their own children attend.

Collaborative decision making brings parents of children in the schools into the decision-making process. Also called site-based management, the process involves teachers and parents as well as the traditional mix of administrators, principals, and superintendent. Together they determine the needs of individual schools and make decisions and plans that will make their school more effective. Clearly, parents are teachers of their own children. There is now emerging an increasing awareness of the link between informal and formal instruction. Parents can enhance the informal education of their children by understanding the formal education process, although they are encouraged to teach in an informal manner. Daily incidental teaching of language and problem solving, for example, encourages development of intelligence in the young child. Infants learn as they listen, look, touch, and are touched. As the parent lets the child select socks that match the color of the child's shirt, the preschooler is learning color discrimination and matching. Setting the table and putting away the dishes involve classification of articles. Programs to help parents in their role as the child's early educator have been successful.

As a Teacher I . . .	How You See Yourself		How You Wish You Were	
	Yes	No	Yes	No
1. Feel that parents are more work than help.	❑	❑	❑	❑
2. Feel tense when parents enter my room.	❑	❑	❑	❑
3. Prefer to work alone.	❑	❑	❑	❑
4. Compare brothers and sisters from the same family.	❑	❑	❑	❑
5. Feel threatened by parents.	❑	❑	❑	❑
6. View parents as a great resource.	❑	❑	❑	❑
7. Believe that low-income children have parents who do not care.	❑	❑	❑	❑
8. Enjoy working with several outside persons in the classroom.	❑	❑	❑	❑
9. Have prejudiced feelings about certain groups.	❑	❑	❑	❑
10. Feel that parents let children watch too much television.	❑	❑	❑	❑
11. Feel that parents are not interested in their children.	❑	❑	❑	❑
12. Work better with social distance between the parent and myself.	❑	❑	❑	❑
13. Believe parents who let their children come to school in inappropriate clothing are irresponsible.	❑	❑	❑	❑
14. Feel that a close working relationship with parents is necessary for optimal student growth.	❑	❑	❑	❑
15. Am pleased when all the parents are gone.	❑	❑	❑	❑
16. Anticipate parent conferences with pleasure.	❑	❑	❑	❑
17. Feel that parents have abdicated the parental role.	❑	❑	❑	❑
18. Enjoy working with parents.	❑	❑	❑	❑

FIGURE 5.2 Teachers can assess how they feel about collaboration with parents by answering these questions.

(*Continued*)

	As a Teacher I . . .			As a Teacher I Believe That I Should . . .	
	Always	Sometimes	Never	Essential	Not Important
1. Listen to what parents are saying.	❑	❑	❑	❑	❑
2. Encourage parents to drop in.	❑	❑	❑	❑	❑
3. Give parents an opportunity to contribute to my class.	❑	❑	❑	❑	❑
4. Have written handouts that enable parents to participate in the classroom.	❑	❑	❑	❑	❑
5. Send newsletters home to parents.	❑	❑	❑	❑	❑
6. Contact parents before school begins in the fall.	❑	❑	❑	❑	❑
7. Listen to parents 50% of the time during conferences.	❑	❑	❑	❑	❑
8. Contact parents when a child does well.	❑	❑	❑	❑	❑
9. Allow for differences among parents.	❑	❑	❑	❑	❑
10. Learn what objectives parents have for their children.	❑	❑	❑	❑	❑
11. Learn about interests and special abilities of students.	❑	❑	❑	❑	❑
12. Visit students in their home.	❑	❑	❑	❑	❑
13. Show parents examples of the student's work.	❑	❑	❑	❑	❑
14. Enlist parent volunteers for my classroom.	❑	❑	❑	❑	❑
15. Ensure a caring environment.	❑	❑	❑	❑	❑
16. Encourage both mother and father to attend conferences.	❑	❑	❑	❑	❑
17. Make parents feel comfortable coming to school.	❑	❑	❑	❑	❑
18. Include parents in educational plans for their children.	❑	❑	❑	❑	❑
19. Try to be open and honest with parents.	❑	❑	❑	❑	❑
20. Send notes home with children.	❑	❑	❑	❑	❑
21. Include students along with parents during conferences.	❑	❑	❑	❑	❑
22. Let parents sit at their child's desk during back-to-school night.	❑	❑	❑	❑	❑
23. Keep both parents informed if parents are separated.	❑	❑	❑	❑	❑
24. Consider parents as partners in the educational process.	❑	❑	❑	❑	❑

FIGURE 5.2 Continued

Parents who are aware of their roles in the educational development of their adolescent children promote the successful completion of their formal education. Parents are the one continuous force in the education of their children from birth to adulthood.

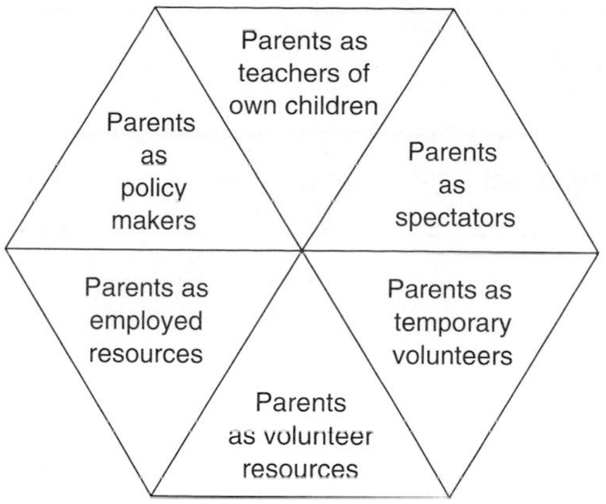

FIGURE 5.3 Possible roles for parents in schools.

Note: These roles for parents in schools are typical of those that emerge in the interaction of parents and schools. It is important to have parents involved as more than spectators.

Ways to Enhance Center–School–Home–Community Relations

Why does one school or center have superb relationships with parents and community, whereas one nearby does not? Most often the leadership of the administration and individual teachers makes the difference. Their leadership has made the school responsive to the parents and the parents supportive of the school. Schools or centers usually do not change overnight, but gradually the school, home, and community can become united in a joint effort.

Many of the techniques geared to improve center–home–school–community relationships are already in place. This chapter is a reminder to keep doing the positive activities that have helped, increase attention to making a partnership, and change negative attitudes. It focuses on five areas: (a) center–school atmosphere and involvement of parents, (b) activities and resources for parents, (c) contact early in the school year, (d) meeting the needs of the school or center area, and (e) volunteers.

Chapter 6 focuses on communication and the need for positive communication with parents. One-way and two-way communications can increase contact between family, center, and school. Communication ranges from the simplest note sent home by the teacher to a complicated news report in the media. Parents want to know what is happening at school or center and are interested in program development and curriculum decisions. The use of the strategies mentioned in this chapter along with effective communication discussed in chapter 6, can turn a school or center around.

Welcoming is only one aspect of restructuring needs. Employment, elimination of discrimination, inclusion of minority groups and new immigrants set the stage for all to participate meaningfully in a democratic society. Supporting and recognizing all families and children will be necessary before schools or centers can meet their challenge.

Situation

"I thought when we moved to this school district that Josi would receive an excellent education, but she is so upset over the way the children in her room are treating her that she cries when she comes home from school. I have to force her to go to school in the mornings. I wish we hadn't moved. Having a larger house just isn't worth the pain," Susan mournfully told her friend, Elizabeth.

"What's going on?" Elizabeth asked.

"The school just doesn't care about my child," Susan said. "I've talked with the principal several times, and I go visit every week and talk with the teacher, but she doesn't respond to my concerns at all. Miss Block, her homeroom teacher, thinks it is just natural for children to have a hard time in a new school. I think the children pick on Josi because she is small and defenseless, but Miss Block insists that Josi stands up for herself and just complains because she wants attention. She thinks Josi enjoys this attention. Oh, she also says that her self-esteem in the new school is not strong yet and that she doesn't have any friends, but that will come if we just let the children work it out for themselves."

"That attitude must really be hard on you and Josi," Elizabeth replied.

"It makes me angry! I think that the principal and teacher hate me and my child," Susan said, her voice trembling.

1. Could this situation have been avoided? How?
2. What can the teacher and parent do to turn Susan's concerns into a collaborative effort rather than a confrontation?
3. What could Susan do to help Josi?
4. What could be done in the classroom to eliminate the concern?

PARENT QUESTIONNAIRE

1. What I want to know about the school:

	Very important	Somewhat	Not at all
1. What curriculum will my child have?			
2. How is the school organized?			
3. What is the procedure for seeing school personnel?			
4. If I have a problem with the school, not the class, whom do I see?			
5. How is reading taught?			
6. What books are used in the school?			
7. What books should I use with my child?			
8. How is mathematics taught?			
9. How should I help my child with math?			
10. Other			

2. How I would like to be involved with the school:

	Very interested	Somewhat	Not at all
1. Be a classroom volunteer			
2. Serve on policy committees			
3. Make games for the classroom			
4. Help with money-raising events			
5. Collect resources for the classroom			
6. Be a room parent			
7. Organize a volunteer program			
8. Share expertise or experiences			
9. Work in family resource room			
10. Other			

Comments: ______________________

FIGURE 5.4 This questionnaire is a simplified needs assessment of what parents want to know about the school and how they would like to be involved. Asking these questions at the beginning the year shows interest in the parents and can help the school plan meetings and activities.

Open-Door Policy

An open-door policy is more an attitude of the school than a series of activities, although periodic open houses, forums, coffee hours, and interactive seminars can add to the receptive climate of the school. Parents are welcome at any time in schools with an open-door policy. Schools that have unpleasant announcements rather than welcome signs on their doors or that require appointments to visit the principal, teachers, or classrooms are saying, "Come only by request or when you want to discuss a problem." Schools and parents need to avoid the problem-conference syndrome. Dialogue between parents and schools should occur before a problem develops. This can be done through coffee klatches and seminars. Parents can give suggestions and get answers; school personnel can ask questions and clarify school procedures and curriculum long before an issue develops into a problem. By establishing two-way communication early, the climate is set for parents and school to work together on behalf of, rather than suffer a confrontation over, a child.

Parent Advisory Councils and Site-Based Management

Title I of the Elementary and Secondary Education Act was developed to improve the academic achievement of disadvantaged children and to "ensure that all children have a fair, equal, and significant opportunity to achieve a high quality education and reach, at a minimum, proficiency on challenging State academic achievement standards and State academic assessments (U.S. Department of Education, 2002, p. 1). All schools can establish parent advisory councils. Title I components establish two parent advisory councils, a districtwide council, and a local council for each involved school. The councils give input on the planning, implementation, and evaluation of the Title I program. Head Start and Home Start have had participatory advisory councils since the 1960s, but public schools were not required to have such parent participation until 1974. Fifty percent of council members should be selected from among parents of students receiving Title I services.

The success of parent advisory councils in Head Start, Home Start, and Title I programs has demonstrated that parents can be involved in policy and decision making in a meaningful and constructive way. Although schools can implement a parent advisory council related to their own situation, they can also learn from the Title I experience, in which schools actively solicit parents' participation and give them the information and training needed to become effective policy and decision makers.

Site-based management has been established in schools across the nation. Still in its infancy, the site-based management theory lies in the belief that those closest to an issue are the ones who can make decisions and find the most appropriate answer. Parents are on the team, which also includes teachers, school personnel, and community representatives. Usually led by the principal, the team determines the best way to administer the school, develop curriculum, and respond to the needs of the students and community.

Strategies for Supporting and Involving Families

Kaufman (2001) describes a process to involve and support families. Start out by establishing "strong relationships between the center and the home,"

Eugenia Hepworth Berger

Schools should let parents know how welcome they are. Parents can enable teachers to expand their activities and offerings.

using empathy and patience to forge relationships. Families need to know that they and their ideas are respected (p. 83). Second, the family's concerns need to be validated without being judged. The discussion between the family and center professional helps evaluate the options and possible appropriateness of action and assistance. Third, know the resources available and be able to recommend them and offer addresses and telephone numbers. If the parents have limited English skills, try to locate volunteers who can translate for them. Fourth, adapt communication to the parents. Recognize that some parents may have limited reading ability; others may not speak English well. Discuss issues in languages that are easily understood. Kaufman also recommends methods of communication with parents including newsletters, open-door policy, greeting and seeing parents at drop-off and pick-up times. The final recommendation is the collaboration with other agencies such as Head Start, English Speakers of Other Languages (ESOL), General Education Diploma (GED) programs, advocacy programs, and public schools (Kaufman, 2001).

Public Response

In the 1992 Gallup Phi Delta Kappa poll, respondents showed recognition of society's needs and evidence of restructuring community responsibilities. It showed that most people (77 percent) favor using public school buildings for extended services in the community. Eighty-seven percent favored keeping the buildings open after hours on school days, 67 percent were in favor of keeping them open during weekends, and 72 percent wanted use of the buildings during vacations (Elam, Rose, & Gallup, 1992). This would make it possible for health and social services to use public school buildings as support centers for youth services.

In the same survey, respondents also believed that preschool programs would help low-socioeconomic children do better in schools. Seventy-four percent said that providing preschool programs would help either quite a lot or a great deal. Only 21 percent thought these programs would not help much or not help at all. Forty-nine percent were willing to pay more taxes to make this possible, and 64 percent were in favor of federally subsidized child care (Elam et al., 1992).

Private schools, and virtually all colleges and universities, plan many occasions to bring their alumni back to their campuses to keep them interested in the school. The public schools could adopt the same policy to their advantage, inviting not only alumni to attend such events but also members of the community who have attended schools in other areas.

Home–School Continuity

Continuity between home and school is a necessary and important support system for families today. One in five families has a single-parent mother; one in two children has both parents working outside the home. This was not the case 40 years ago. More than half of school-age children go home to empty homes or alternative child care. Families cannot afford to be caught in an adversarial position with the school. They need cooperation, support, and facilities that make it possible to supply their children with a stable environment. If you do not know their needs, you will not be able to respond to them.

A good way to improve relationships between school and home is to do a needs assessment or survey to determine what the families in the school area desire. The questionnaire in Figure 5.4 is just an example. If you know several of the parents or have access to the parents' addresses, asking them what topics they want or need included on the questionnaire would make the assessment more meaningful.

School schedules that involve split sessions or classes finishing at 2:30 P.M. and a lack of after-school programs are indicators that our society has little concern for the family. Tradition controls the time school is in session, as well as how school buildings are used.

The public is apparently in favor of having after-school programs. In a 1997 National Opinion Research Center poll, 77 percent of parents of primary-age children and 82 percent of parents of middle school students favored after-school programs (U.S. Department of Education, 1998b).

Continuity needs to be a cooperative effort. Community outreach that continues to help families even when school is not in session is a positive step toward achieving continuity. Groups such as recreation program leaders, library services personnel, special after-school teachers, and artists in residence should be enlisted to help extend the school day to accommodate parents' schedules. Parents who are not employed outside the home could volunteer or be paid to help with before- and after-school programs. Enrichment activities, physical development, and social opportunities should be provided for children who have working parents and for others who wish to partake of the opportunities. The coordination of school programs with social agencies, recreation departments, and other community resources will greatly enhance the chance of successful continuity.

Family Center

Parents need a place within the school where they can meet, share information, work, and relax. Ideally, parents will have a room similar to that traditional haven, the teachers' lounge, as well as a space within each classroom.

The family room can be equipped and stocked by the parents. Typical items include a sofa, comfortable chairs, table, coffeepot, microwave, telephone, typewriter, computer, bulletin board, storage area, supplies, and reading materials. If a room is not available, a small area shared in a workroom, an area in an unused hall, or a large closet would give minimal space. In each, both storage space and a bulletin board for notices should be available.

Teachers can help parents develop a base in each classroom. An extra desk, a corner, or a bulletin board lets parents claim a spot within their child's classroom. If the area contains information on current assignments, new curriculum ideas, activities to be used at home, taped messages from the teacher, or a display of children's work, parents will make a point to stop by. Parents of preschool, kindergarten, and elementary children can use the corner to find activities that will continue the educational experience in the home or to talk or work with individual children or small groups. Teachers can use the corner for short conferences with parents. The parents' room implies that parents are expected to be in the building. There is a place for them to stop and a base from which they can reach out in their involvement.

SCHOOL ACTIVITIES AND RESOURCES

The following school activities and resources encourage parent participation. Parent involvement fosters interest and support of children's education.

Back-to-School Nights

A time-tested school event, the back-to-school night has proved very successful. Teachers often complain that the parents who need to learn about the educational program are the very ones who do not show up, but this type of evening program nevertheless has improved home–school relationships from preschool through secondary schools. Parents enjoy sitting in the desk normally occupied by their child, viewing the curriculum materials, observing the displays in the room, and listening to the teacher. Parents expect the teacher to tell them about school programs. Following a presentation of the course objectives, there is usually a period for questions and answers. Back-to-school night is not a time for talking extensively about individual children, although the teacher should identify which parents belong to which students. It is a good time to set up a special conference if you have concern about the progress of a student.

A variation on the back-to-school night is the Saturday morning session. Some working parents have difficulty attending evening programs, and offering an alternative time can increase parental participation. The Saturday morning activity can be a workshop with parents participating in their children's normal activities, or it can be a presentation-discussion similar to the evening session. Saturday morning programs work well for child care and preschools as well as schools. The programs can become a meaningful educational experience for both children and families by involving a series of parent–child programs.

Alumni Events

Private schools have long used alumni activities and events to keep their graduates as members of a cohesive group. Public schools that encourage alumni to come back for special events also develop alumni support for the school. Alumni can help with school morale, as well as with developing programs that tie the school with business, industry, or social services. Strong alumni can rise to the occasion and support the school in many areas.

Sharing Reading

A practice that has had promising results is inviting parents, community celebrities, and school personnel to share a book they enjoy with the children in the class. The book, of course, needs to be one that fits the developmental level of the children and short enough to be read in one session. Parents enjoy the opportunity of coming to the class to read a story to the children during sharing time. Principals can use this as an opportunity to get to know children better. Afterward children will be able to relate to the principal as someone who spent time reading with them. Children are excited to meet a celebrity who comes to share with them. Following the visits, letters may be written to thank the contributor.

Parent Education Groups

Parent education groups are discussed in detail in chapter 7. Meetings can range from a one-day workshop to an organized series of workshops throughout the year. Individual teachers use the parent group meetings for in-service training of volunteers in their rooms, dissemination of information to parents, or presentation of programs that answer parents' needs. Parents become real resources for the school through parent education meetings, which teach them to become effective tutors and school volunteers.

Parent education may be offered whenever the need arises. The school can have a list of workshops available or determine the needs of the community. If a telephone answering machine is available, parents could call any time for school-related information. Besides workshops, articles or individual conferences can be arranged to help the parents.

Parent education meetings offered by schools are viable for those with children at any age level. The parent of a young child may be interested in child development, enrichment activities, and promotion of creativity. Parents of children of all ages are concerned about drugs and alcohol. Parent education groups, allowing parents to meet and discuss common concerns, are an essential part of the educational program. Interestingly, middle and high schools have very few parent education groups, but the parents of these students are vitally concerned about their children's futures.

Parents of adolescents need information but, just as important, they need the support system that a parent education group offers. If parents of adolescents can discuss problems and understand that other parents have the same concerns, they can cope with pressures better. An advocacy group for children and parents can be formed. Responsibilities and guidelines for students, determined by parents and students in a specific community, can support parents in the rearing of their children. Schools need to offer parent education. In doing so, they strengthen parent–school–community relationships.

Parent Networks

Parent networks may form naturally out of parent education groups, but many parents with no interest in parent education might want to join a network group of parents. Now, more than ever, parents need to cooperate with one another to handle the pressures of the social world. Drugs, alcohol, and teenage pregnancies hurt many school children. Parents in a network can cooperate to approach a problem from two vantage points. First, they can advocate for better facilities for students. Young people need places to gather, socialize, and have fun. They need programs after school that enrich their lives and give them an opportunity to belong to a group. Second, parents can develop guidelines for dress, participation in activities, at school or in the community, that all families can support. In this way, the students may not feel as if they are the only ones who have to follow rules. The community will be united in its support of children.

School–Home Activity Packets

Parents appreciate knowing activities and enrichment ideas that support the school curricula. Many teachers make calendars that describe what the child will be learning at school. Sending home packets with activities that support the curriculum enhances parents' involvement in their children's education. The activities need to be relevant to the curriculum within each class and each school.

These packets may be supported by workshops in which parents learn about the activities, or they may be ongoing informational packets related to what the child is learning at school.

One workshop could be developed in which parents make tote bags their children can use to bring ideas and materials for the activities to be done at home. At this workshop the ideas behind the take-home activity kits could be explained and discussed. Research that supports family involvement can be shared (Binkley, 1988; Boyer, 1991; Epstein, 2001, 2005; Epstein & Dauber, 1991). Some families have difficulty completing home-school activities. Communicate with them; develop quick activities for parents who do not have a lot of time, and try to encourage interactions between parent and child that are positive and fun. Some early childhood classrooms send home a stuffed teddy bear, asking the family to include the bear in their weekend and then write a story about the bear's adventures. Other schools send home fish, gerbils, or other live animals to be cared for during break. These activities are similar to those in school–home activity packets, but the kits usually include many educational activities, with some, but not all, related to the family. For example, children might measure their parents' height, design the week's menu, plan a garden, calculate the number of times each person can jump while playing jump rope, or write a story about their family. Think about the children and families with whom you work. Recognize their interests and their needs, and plan how to organize the school–home activities.

1. School–home activity packets should relate to the curricula.
2. Activities should be interesting and enjoyable for the parent and child.
3. The packets should include any special materials needed to complete the activity, unless the materials are common to the homes in your area.
4. Send home clear instructions; be available to answer questions by telephone.
5. Stress that the activities are to be enjoyed; if they cause stress rather than a positive interaction, do not insist that they be completed.
6. Ask parents to complete an evaluation form that is included with the instructions.
7. If the activity kit has permanent equipment, make sure that it is returned the following day.

School Programs and Workshops

Remember when the introduction of "modern math" made it impossible for some parents to help their children with homework? Parents in that predicament appreciated workshops that explained the new terminology and processes. Schools can offer programs and workshops to the community with the same success. Parents from the community can plan and implement some of the workshops; speakers can be obtained; projects can be started.

A project in which parents make books of their children's work can be a great success and also create remembrances to be kept for years. Simple construction-paper books, as well as hardback books, can be developed. Books containing stories and poems composed by parents or children can be placed in the library and classroom for all students to use.

Try to arrange alternate times to offer workshops. If you offer meetings during the day, in the evening, and on Saturdays, parents will be able to come to the ones that fit their schedules.

District or School Conferences

Professionals go to conferences to gain information and be stimulated to try something new. Why not have the same kind of conference for parents? Instead of a workshop, plan a half-day or full-day conference where teachers and other professionals hold sessions for parents and community personnel to attend. These sessions could include such subjects as phonics, family math, whole language, music and movement, art, language arts, social studies, science, and computers.

School Projects

Enlist parent help if you plan to add to the playground or build a reading loft in your classroom. Most parents enjoy contributing their time for something permanent. Children will be proud that their parents helped build the jungle gym or plant the elm tree in the school yard. Saturday sessions give ample time to develop, plan, and build. Many fathers find this the most comfortable way to contribute to the school. Working on a project can start a relationship that brings them into a partnership with the school.

PTO or PTA

The tradition of parent–teacher associations (PTAs) extends back to the 1890s. Their influence on parent–school relationships has been demonstrated over the years. The PTA publishes material for parents and strives for parent-school cooperation. Many parent-teacher groups, generally called parent–teacher organizations (PTOs), do not join the national PTA but have similar structure and interaction with the schools. Both PTAs and PTOs can serve as avenues toward greater parent–school interaction.

Fairs, Carnivals, and Suppers

Traditionally the PTO or PTA sponsors spaghetti suppers, potluck dinners, dinner theaters, or similar activities that promote a community spirit, give families a night of fun together, and usually increase the treasury. Parents and children flock to school to attend a carnival produced by parents and school staff. Money earned is generally spent on materials or equipment for the school program.

Exchanges

Children grow; toys get tiresome; books are read. Why not have an exchange? A popular exchange is to have children bring boots, heavy jackets, and raincoats to school to be traded or sold. Boots seldom wear out before they're outgrown, so a boot exchange works very well. Toys can also be exchanged. How often have you seen toys sit for months without being used? Some schools have children bring two toys, one for exchange and one to give to another child. Children swap the toy they brought for a different one.

Children also tire of some books and can exchange their old ones for books they have not read. A parent volunteer checks in the books and issues tickets to be used to "buy" another one. Children look through the books until they find a book they want and then use the tickets to buy it.

Learning Centers

Parents or volunteers from the community can be put in charge of learning centers. Use the resource room to furnish ideas and supplies for parents, or have a workshop to demonstrate how to plan and prepare a learning center. Learning centers can include, for example:

- A place for games
- A reading center
- A center for writing and making books
- A puzzle center
- A center for problem-solving activities
- A science area
- A talk-and-listen center
- A place for music and tapes
- A weaving center
- An art project center

Rules and regulations for using the center should be posted.

Telephone Tutor

With call forwarding, which is available in most communities, the school can set up a tutor aid program through telephone calls in the evening. Volunteers or teachers can answer the telephone in the afternoon at the school. Later calls can be forwarded to the homes of a volunteer or paid aide working with the children that night. In a well-coordinated program the volunteer could know what curriculum is being covered in the class. If the entire district uses the telephone tutor, special numbers could be assigned for mathematics and language arts.

If call forwarding is not available, a telephone answering machine could direct students to help by listing the names and phone numbers of tutors on call for that night. An excellent way to draw attention to the needs of the school district is to enlist important people in the community to serve as volunteer tutors. Their leadership will provide publicity and credibility to the volunteer program.

Internet

Many families have access to the Internet. E-mails may be sent to each child in each classroom or to all

Eugenia Hepworth Berger

Children learn when they are involved in their activities and work.

the children in the school if their families are willing to share their e-mail addresses. In addition, the school could have its own Web page with descriptions of upcoming school events or information about achievements and activities in the school and individual classrooms.

Resource Room

When parents see they can contribute to a project that has obvious benefits for their children, some will become actively involved. A resource room can be beneficial to both school and parents. Resource materials located in an empty room, a storage closet, the corner of a room, or a metal cabinet can be a great help to teachers. Involve parents in developing a resource center by holding a workshop to describe and discuss the idea. Brainstorm with parents and other teachers on ideas that might be significant for your school. Parents can take over after the workshop to design, stock, and run the center. Later, as assistants in the classroom, they will use it. They can help supply the center with articles on teaching, ideas and materials for games, and recycled materials to use in activities.

Articles on Teaching

Parents and community volunteers check old magazines related to teaching and classify useful articles according to subject and student age level. These are filed for use by teachers and aides. In searching for and classifying the articles, parents learn a great deal about teaching activities for home and school so the exercise is beneficial for the parent and the school.

Games

Parents check books, magazines, and commercial catalogs for ideas for games and adapt them to the school's needs. Volunteers make universal game boards for reading, spelling, and math from poster board or tag board. Felt markers are used to make lines and note directions; games are decorated with artwork, magazine cutouts, or stickers. Game materials should be laminated or covered with clear plastic.

Recycled Materials

Volunteers collect, sort, and store materials for classroom teachers. Items such as egg cartons, wood scraps, wallpaper books, cardboard tubes, felt, fabric remnants, and plastic food holders are used for many activities. Egg cartons, for example, can be used to cover a dragon, make a caterpillar, hold buttons for classification activities, and hold tempera paint for dry mixing. Milk cartons are used for making items from simple computers to building blocks. Science activities are enriched by a collection of machines, for example, motors, radios, computers, clocks, and typewriters. The articles can be used as they are or taken apart and rebuilt. Recycling is limited only by lack of imagination.

Libraries

A collection of magazines and books can be useful to parents or teachers in the development of teaching aids—such as games and learning activities—or for information on how children learn. From ideas therein, a toy lending library, an activity lending library, a book and magazine library, or a video lending library can be developed. Items can be checked out for a week or two. Checkout and return are supervised by parent volunteers.

Toy Lending Library

The toy lending library was developed with educational toys for young children (Nimnicht & Brown, 1972) or with a collection of toys for older children. The toys for young children can be built and collected by parents. Toys for older children can be collected from discarded toys left over after the toy exchange, or they can be built by parents and children.

Activity Lending Library

Games and activities developed by parents and children can be checked out for a week or two.

Book and Magazine Library

Discarded magazines and books can be collected and used to build a comprehensive lending library. Professional magazines have many articles on child development, education, and learning activities. Booklets distributed by numerous organizations can also be lent. Pamphlets and articles cut from magazines can be stapled to file folders and loaned to parents. To keep track of the publications, glue a library card pocket in each book or on each folder. Make a card that states the author and title of the publication, with lines for borrowers to sign their names. As each is taken, have the borrower sign the card and leave it in the card file. When the publication is returned, the name is crossed out, and the card is returned to the pocket.

Video Lending Library

Videotapes or CDs made by teachers to illustrate their lessons on math, social studies, language arts, art, physical education, music, and other subjects or activities can be very helpful to parents. Homework or "homefun" assignments can be explained on the videos. Teachers can also share creative activities that families would enjoy together. This would be especially beneficial during breaks or weekends.

Actual classes can also be the subject of videos so that parents can see their child at work or play during the school hours. This type of video is often used to accompany parent–teacher conferences, but could also be available in the family resource room. Selected videos and videos of student activities would offer a look at students at school; homefun or homework assignments; educational movies; videos on educational programs such as language, a writer's workshop, mathematics, geography, or science; and age-appropriate movies for entertainment.

Summer Vacation Activities

Parents can keep students, particularly elementary-age children, from losing academic gains during the summer. Research shows that the parents who are involved by teachers and child-care leaders become more positive about them and rate them higher in interpersonal skills and teaching ability. The most significant feature of parent–school involvement is providing activities for the parent to use with the child (Epstein, 1986, 2001; Epstein & Dauber, 1991). Activities differ depending on the age of the child. Let the parent of an infant child know how important it is to have eye and voice contact with their infant. Hold one way conversations and let the infant respond; read and sing with the infant; move to music.

Parents as Resources

Parents should be asked early in the year if they have any talents or experiences they would like to share with classes. Parents might share information about their careers, or they might have a hobby that would spark student interest or supplement learning programs. Storytelling is an art that is often overlooked. Invite some senior citizens to tell about their childhoods. The resources in the community are unlimited.

Book Publishing

One of the most beneficial activities that has developed from the emphasis on reading, writing, and writing workshops is the opportunity for parents to be involved in helping children publish their own books. The activity may be done at home or at school. Some schools have the equipment that allows the parent to volunteer to be a book publisher. The child may develop a story during a writing workshop period, a session on whole language, or traditional reading and writing sessions. After the story is completed, it can be published with or without editing, although editing helps the child learn conventional spelling and grammar in a positive situation. If parents are available, they can help with the process. The following steps are usually taken:

1. The story is written during a writing workshop or (for the younger child) the story is dictated to the parent.
2. The story is edited by the student, by the student and the parent, or by the parent alone. In some classes an editing panel is established and students edit together.
3. The story is typed on a computer or typewriter by the student or parent. If the story is to be published in handwritten form, this step is eliminated. Copies of the stories may be made on a copy machine.
4. If the book is going to be handled and read by many students, the pages should be laminated. A laminating machine or clear contact paper can help make the book permanent.
5. The book is bound. Many schools have spiral binding equipment available for the parent to use. In other schools, binding may be done by simply stapling the pages together and covering the book with heavy paper. Traditional bookbinding can also be accomplished by parents. A bookbinding workshop would show parents how to sew the pages together and make the outside cover. The outside sheet between the cover and the inside pages is a plain sheet of construction paper. The construction paper is glued to the outside cover. Depending on the material used, the outside cover can also be laminated.
6. The completed works should then be recognized and shared. Some schools have complete libraries of children's books displayed in the front halls or rooms. Others have classes that keep their published books in their own rooms. One school has the books circulate from room to room with an insert that allows children to write that they have read the book and to add a complimentary comment. The young writer receives recognition for the work!

Career Day

Plan a day or a series of days when parents and community volunteers come in and explain their careers. Rather than have parents talk to the whole class, let them work at a center. Have them explain their careers, the pros and cons, the necessary skills, and the satisfaction obtained from their work. If feasible, the parents can provide some activities the children could do related to the career. For example, a carpenter could bring in tools, demonstrate their use, and let the children make a small project, supervised by the carpenter and an aide or another parent.

Talent Sharing

Let parents tell stories, sing folk songs, lead a creative dramatics project, or share another talent. You might persuade some to perform before the class; some may wish to work with a few childre t a time and let the children be involved. Some parents may have a collection or a hobby to share. Quilting is popular and could be followed by a lesson in stitchery. Basket making, growing orchids, stamp collecting—all provide opportunities for enriching the classroom learning experiences. Bring those educational and fun lessons out to enjoy.

PARENTS AS PARTNERS IN EDUCATION AT HOME

Reading at home throughout the year should be encouraged. Figures 5.5 and 5.6 illustrate a way to get parents involved in a home reading program. First, a letter is sent to parents describing the program (Figure 5.5). An explanation could also be given at back-to-school night or during a workshop. After the children read a book, they color in a book on the sheet sent home with the letter. When all the books on the sheet are colored in, a certificate is awarded (Figure 5.6). Each teacher sends home a list of books that are appropriate for the child to read. Bookmarks with the titles of books related to

[School Letterhead]

Dear Parents,

I would like to invite you and your child to participate in Read-Aloud Month during October. This statewide project is sponsored by the Colorado Council of the International Reading Association. The purpose is to encourage parents and children to read aloud together. Children who are read to become better readers—it's a fact!

Each student who participates in Read-Aloud Month will be given a time sheet to take home. This will be used to record time you or other adults spend reading aloud to your child. For every 15 minutes of read-aloud time, your child may color one book on the time sheet.

To successfully complete this project, all the characters on the time sheet must be colored in by the end of October. Each child who completes the time sheet will receive a certificate rewarding participation in the project.

Setting aside time to read with your child helps your child learn and develop an interest in reading. Take a few minutes each day to share the joy of reading with your child!

Sincerely,

P.S. I'm also sending home a bookmark, an annotated bibliography with suggestions for good books to read aloud, and a Join the Read-Aloud Crowd poster for your refrigerator door or family bulletin board. Be sure to read the suggestions on the back of the poster.

FIGURE 5.5 Encouraging parents to be involved in their child's reading is a positive way to accomplish good reading habits and communicate with parents.

Source: Printed with permission. Colorado Council International Reading Association.

Certificate of Participation

STUDENT'S NAME

has participated in

Read-Aloud Month.

In recognition of your success,
this award is presented
this ________ day of ________________

TEACHER'S NAME

Colorado Council International Reading Association

FIGURE 5.6 Attractive certificates, suggested books, and posters highlight the importance of reading.

Source: Art by Richard Florence.

the age of the child are a good idea. In addition, books from the school library can be checked out and taken home.

CONTACTS EARLY IN THE SCHOOL YEAR

Many teachers have found that early communication is well worth the time it takes, even during summer vacation. It is quite common for kindergarten teachers to invite the new kindergarten class and their parents to a spring orientation meeting. Generally, these functions are scheduled in the hope that the strangeness of school will diminish and that, as a result, subsequent entry into kindergarten will be more pleasant. Just as important is the message to the parents that the school cares. This idea can be carried over into other levels of education with results that are just as gratifying.

Letters in August

Some teachers send letters, with pictures of themselves enclosed, to each new student coming to their classes. The student and parents learn the teacher's identity and know that the teacher cares enough to write. A good rapport between teacher and home is established before school begins.

Neighborhood Visits

Rather than waiting until the regular conference period arrives or a problem arises, teachers should contact each parent early in the year. Visits to the neighborhood are excellent ways to meet parents.

Block Walks

Try a block walk while the weather is warm and sunny. Map the location of all your students' homes (this may be a class project) and divide the area into blocks. Schedule a series of block walks, and escort the children living in each block area to their homes on a selected day. Have the students write letters or notes in advance indicating that you will visit a particular block. Choose an alternate day in case of rain. On the appointed day, walk or ride the bus to the chosen block. Meet the parents outside and chat with them about school. You may also accumulate some curriculum materials such as leaves, sidewalk rubbings, or bits of neighborhood history to be used later by the children in the classroom. This initial contact with parents will be positive, and possibly make a second meeting even more productive. You can reinforce the positive aspect of an early meeting by making an interim telephone call to inform the parents of an activity or an interesting comment made by their child.

Bus Trips and Coffees

An all-school project, with teachers riding a bus to tour the school's enrollment area, allows parents and teachers to meet before the opening of school. If prior arrangements are made for coffees at parents' homes, other parents may be invited (Rich & Mattox, 1977).

Picnics

A picnic during the lunch hour or while on a field trip during the early part of the year will afford teachers the opportunity to meet some parents. Plan a field trip to a park or zoo and invite the parents to a bring-your-own-lunch gathering. Have another picnic after school for those who could not come at lunchtime. After the lunch or picnic, call to thank those who came. Because some parents work and will be unable to attend either picnic, you might wish to phone them for a pleasant conversation about their child.

WHAT WORKS

The What Works Clearinghouse, administered by the U.S. Department of Education, established contracts in 2002 with the American Institutes for Research and the Campbell Collaboration, both leaders in education research to provide current research in education. "The What Works Clearinghouse is intended to help states, educators, and parents gain access to the available scientifically valid research concerning education programs, products, and services" (What Works Clearinghouse, 2006, p. 1).

Earlier research has revealed it works for parents to provide active support of their children. This contributes more to their child's success in school than those who provide passive support. The least effective parents—in terms of the child's ability to succeed—are those who are nonsupportive. Parents must actively help their children as well as encourage them to attend school and achieve (Epstein, 1996, 2001, 2002, 2005a; Liontos, 1992). Parent behaviors that support the child's cognitive development include:

1. Talk with children and listen to their concerns.
2. Read to children and listen to them read.
3. Establish daily routines that include study time for homework in an area conducive to study (if the child is old enough to have homework).
4. Provide opportunities for exploring and play.
5. Eat meals together.
6. Have appropriate bedtime schedules.
7. Guide and monitor out-of-school time.
8. Model good values and positive behavior.
9. Have high expectations of achievement.
10. Gain knowledge of child development and parenting skills.
11. Use authoritative rather than authoritarian control.
12. Take a strong interest in the schools.
13. Communicate with the teacher.
14. Collaborate with and support the school (Berger, 1996a, 1996b; Epstein, 1996, 2001; Hess & Holloway, 1984; Liontos, 1992; Rutter, 1985).

Research from the U.S. Department of Education on Follow Through, Title I, Title VII Bilingual, and the Emergency School Aid Act and from Epstein's work at the Center for Families, Schools, Community, and Children's Learning found that:

- Children do better in school if their parents help them. The children also behave better and are more diligent than children whose parents do not involve themselves.
- Teachers and principals show greater respect to parents who participate in school activities and also have better attitudes toward the children of these parents.
- School personnel find out about how parents feel and what they need and are better able to respond to them when there is caring and parent involvement (Lyons, Robbins, & Smith, 1983; Swick, Da Ros, & Kovach, 2001).
- When teachers involve families, they rate the parents more positively and do not stereotype single parents and those with less education. The teachers recognize that parents are equally willing to help and follow through at home. When they do not work with single parents or parents

with less education, they rate these parents as less willing to help and follow through at home.

- Work at home with one subject—for example, reading—resulted in increased scores in that subject, but did not transfer to other subjects—for example, math.
- Parents are able to influence and make a contribution to the education of their children.
- Students, parents, and school personnel all agree that parent involvement is important.
- The way teachers work with parents is more important than the family background, including class, race, marital status, and whether both parents work (Epstein, 1996). Socioeconomic status is not the primary causal factor in school success or lack of success; it is parental interest and support of the child.

Parents can do many things at home to help their children succeed in school. They do this through their daily conversations, household routines, attention to school matters, and affectionate concern for their children's progress. Conversation is important. Children learn to read, reason, and understand things better when their parents:

- Read, talk, and listen to them.
- Tell them stories, play games, and share hobbies.
- Discuss the news, TV programs, and special events.

To enrich the "curriculum of the home," some parents:

- Provide books, supplies, and a special place for studying.
- Observe routine for meals, bedtime, and homework.
- Monitor the amount of time spent watching TV and doing after-school jobs.

Parents stay aware of their children's lives at school when they:

- Discuss school events.
- Help children meet deadlines.
- Talk with their children about school problems and successes.

Booklets covering educational issues are available to help the No Child Left Behind concept succeed. One booklet, "Helping Your Child Become a Reader," cited simple strategies from "Reading Tips for Parents" (U.S. Department of Education, 2002). The suggestions include:

- Invite your child to read with you every day.
- When reading a book where the print is large, point word by word as you read. This will help your child learn that reading goes from left to right and understand that the word said is the word seen.
- Read your child's favorite book over and over.
- Read many stories with rhyming words and repeated lines. Invite your child to join in on these parts. Point, word by word, as your child reads along with you.
- Discuss new words. For example, "This big house is called a palace. Who do you think lives in a palace?"
- Stop and ask about the pictures and about what is happening in the story.
- Read from a variety of children's books, including fairy tales, song books, poems, and information books.

Information on these government publications may be obtained by calling 1–800-USA-LEARN.

MEETING THE NEEDS OF YOUR SCHOOL AREA

Schools can make a special effort to help families function more effectively. Some parents travel constantly; the stay-at-home partners in those families have many of the same problems that a single parent has (see chapter 2). A parent with a disability may need help with transportation or child care. An early survey of families will disclose what parents need and suggest ways the school can encourage participation.

Worksite Seminars

Meet the needs of parents by offering seminars and parent education at companies and businesses during the lunch hour. Some corporations hire a parent educator to set up a program for their employees. School personnel could coordinate with them and be a resource for the parent educator. Topics for seminars range from school activities and parent–child communication to child development. If the company does not have an employee to set up the program, the school could offer seminars on an ongoing basis.

Telephone Tree or E-mail

A telephone tree set up by the PTO or PTA can alert parents quickly to needs in the community. One caller begins by calling four or five people, who each call four or five more. Soon the entire community is alerted. Depending on the availability of the Internet, e-mail can be used to send information to parents and children.

Transportation

If a parent group is active, it can offer transportation to those who need help getting to the school or to the doctor's office. Those in need might include people with disabilities and families with small children or a child who is ill.

Parent-to-Parent Support

Parents without an extended family living nearby can team up with other parents. The parent organization can set up a file on parents that includes their needs, interests, children's ages, and location, with cross-references for parents to use. Parent education group meetings tend to promote friendships within the group. Isolated parents are often the ones who need the help of another parent the most. One parent may be able to manage the home efficiently, whereas another needs tips and help. Some parents were not exposed to a stable home environment and need a capable parent as a model. Although educators may not want to interfere in the lives of parents, they must remember that they meet and work with all parents and thus have the greatest access to the most parents of any community agency.

Child Care

Child care during conferences can be offered to families with young children. Older children can participate in activities in the gymnasium, while young children can be cared for in a separate room. It is difficult for some parents to arrange for child care, and a cooperative child-care arrangement with parent volunteers would allow greater participation at conferences.

Crisis Nursery

A worthwhile project for a parent organization is the development of a crisis nursery. Schools would have to meet state regulations for child care to have a nursery within the school, but it provides a great service and a chance to meet parents and children before school starts. An assessment program, similar to Child Find, might alert parents and schools to developmental problems, such as hearing loss or poor sight.

A neighborhood home can also be used as a crisis base. If a parent with several children must take one child to the doctor, the crisis center can care for the other children during the parent's absence. Abusive parents can use the crisis center as a refuge for their children until they regain control of their emotions.

After-School Activities

Schools can become centers for the community. One step toward greater community involvement is an after-school program. With so many working parents, many children become latchkey kids, going home to an empty house. If schools, perhaps working with other agencies, provide an after-school program for children of all ages, a great service is accomplished. Teachers should not be expected to be involved in after-school programs. However, recreation workers, trained child-care workers, and volunteers can implement a program that supplements the school program. Children can be taught how to spend leisure time through participation in crafts, sports, and cultural programs.

Although it is generally recognized that young children need supervision, the needs of secondary students are often ignored. Older students may have three to four unsupervised hours between the time they are out of school and the time their parents arrive home. School dropouts are rarely involved in school activities. If you look at community structure, it becomes clear that schools are the major link between the family and the community.

Family Literacy Programs

Parents who can read with their children are better able to help and encourage the children in their reading and learning. Family literacy programs are needed by families new to the United States for whom English is a second language, as well as the many parents who went through school without learning to read. (See chapter 8.) Join with a family literacy program and offer space and help in providing literacy development, or develop the school's literacy program. This program could be enhanced by including programs for those who are able to read. Expand by offering family literacy, workshops on great books for children, Great Books, and Great Decision programs. Solicit volunteers from the community, including retired teachers who might enjoy the challenge.

Skill Training

Offer workshops that provide skill training for the amateur as well as for the person who needs a skill to get a job. Courses in computer training, carpentry, typing, financial management, and organizational skills would all be appropriate workshops to help the parents in the community.

Underemployed parents may need to develop more skills to become self-sufficient. Offer life-skills training. Teach classes on parenting, relationships, anger management, and leadership.

Help identify the abilities and needs of fathers. Provide literacy, job training, and employment opportunities, information, and referrals (Governor Romer's Responsible Fatherhood Initiative, 1997).

Emotional and Educational Support for Parents Experiencing Homelessness

1. Attitude counts. Be sure the classroom accepts and values all children—all ethnic groups, diversity, and conditions including homelessness.
2. Make it easy for a family to enroll in the school with friendly, immediate, and trouble-free registration procedures.
3. Provide breakfasts, snacks, and lunch, without stereotyping people who receive these meals, at reduced prices or free.
4. Provide child-development centers for infants and toddlers.
5. Offer early childhood classes for preschoolers.
6. Provide parent education and parent participation programs.
7. Provide English Speakers of Other Language (ESOL) courses as well as family literacy programs.
8. Offer classes or find classes that can help the parent become ready for employment.
9. Provide support meetings that help parents deal with depression and anxiety.

Advocacy

1. Assign a teacher, staff member, or liaison to help the child and family during crisis.
2. Advocate for the family, if necessary, to get needed services.
3. Help with job search and placement.
4. Mentor the family. (Adapted from Eddowes, 1992; Klein et al., 1993; McCormick & Holden, 1992; Nuñez, 1996; Swick et al., 2001; Stronge, 1992)

BUILDING FAMILY STRENGTHS

All families have strengths. They are expressed in a variety of ways, but the approach that schools and agencies must take when working with families is to focus on their strengths and, through this focus, eliminate their problems. Research shows that parents respond positively to schools that set out to collaborate with them. During 2001–2008 many families have had breadwinners who were out of work or had difficulty finding work that allows them to provide for their families. Other families have both parents working, so time becomes a scarce commodity. If projections hold true, three fourths of parents with school-age children and two thirds of parents with preschoolers will be working outside the home as well as providing caregiver roles in the home after work hours. Schools can help make this dual role easier for parents by providing or allowing other agencies to use the school building to provide before- and after-school care.

We tend to look at the half-full glass as half empty. Even if a majority of both parents will be working outside the home, there are still many families who have one parent as caregiver at home with the children. Many of these parents sacrifice to have one parent remain home, and they are willing to be partners with the school. Others can provide the needed security and support their children need to make the school's responsibility of educating easier. Programs such as the Building Family Strengths program, designed at the University of Nebraska, focus on areas that parents need to address to keep their families strong. These include the following:

- *Communication.* Effective communication in strong families involves clear, direct channels between the speaker and listener. Families develop complicated ways of communicating. Strong families have learned to communicate directly and use consistent verbal and nonverbal behaviors (see chapter 6).
- *Appreciation.* Appreciation involves being able to recognize the beautiful, positive aspects of others and letting them know you value these qualities. It also means being able to receive compliments yourself.

> South African diamond miners spend their working lives sifting through thousands of tons of rock and dirt looking for a few tiny diamonds. . . . We sift through diamonds, eagerly searching for dirt. (Stinnett & DeFrain, 1985, p. 49)

Appreciative family members look for the diamonds.

- *Commitment.* Commitment in strong families means that the family as a whole is committed to seeing that all members reach their potential.
- *Wellness.* Family wellness is the belief in positive human interaction. This belief helps family members trust others and learn to give and receive love. Family wellness is not the absence of problems. Strong families have their share of troubles, but their trust and love enable them to deal with their problems effectively.
- *Time together.* Spending time together as a family can be the most rewarding experience for humans. Two important aspects of time together are quality and quantity. Members of a strong family spend a lot of meaningful time with each other. This gives a family an identity that can be had in no other way.
- *The ability to deal with stress, conflict, and crisis.* All the previous strengths combine to make an inner core of power for families. This core serves as a resource for those times when conflict and crisis come. Strong families are able to survive and even grow in the face of hard times (Achord et al., 1986).

Developing these strengths takes time and energy, but realizing their significance can help a family focus on the important interactions within the family. Many families do not realize the importance of spending time together, communicating clearly with one another, and showing appreciation. These last two strengths take no extra time; they may take practice, but clear communication and showing appreciation can become a natural part of family life.

Families benefit from programs offered at the school or from home visits by school personnel who are able to share ideas about developing family strengths, discipline, school activities, and "homefun." Chapter 6 has more discussion on communication and parent programs.

VOLUNTEERS

Have you ever wondered why some teachers have extra help? One answer lies in the recruitment of volunteers and the subsequent interaction with them.

Parents want the best for their children; most will respond to an opportunity to volunteer if the options for working are varied and their contributions are meaningful. When both parents work, short-term commitments geared to their working hours will allow and encourage participation from this group. Although the world is a busy place, time spent at school can bring satisfaction and variety to a parent's life.

Volunteers: Used or Users?

Volunteerism has been criticized by some as inequitable and an exploitation of "woman power." To avoid such accusations, try to choose volunteers who can afford the time, or allow busy parents to contribute in such a way that they enjoy the time away from their other obligations. If education and training are included in your volunteer program, the participants can gain personally from the experience.

Eugenia Hepworth Berger

Enlist volunteers to work in the schools. They can help with programs that are impossible to offer without their help.

For many, volunteering in school may be the first step toward a career.

If you are alert to the needs of parents, using them as volunteers can become a means of helping their families. If you work with them over a period of time, listen and use your knowledge of community resources to support the families in solving their problems. Volunteerism should serve the volunteer as well as contribute to the school.

Who Should Ask for Volunteers?

All teachers can benefit from the services of volunteers, but they should first determine the extent to which they are ready to use the assistance. Volunteer programs vary in their scope and design. Individual teachers may solicit volunteers from parents; individual schools can support a volunteer program; or school districts can implement a volunteer program for the total system.

A teacher who has not used aides, assistants, or volunteers should probably start with help in one area before expanding and recruiting volunteers for each hour in the week. In preschools, the free-choice period is a natural time to have added assistance. In elementary schools, assistance during art projects is often a necessity. Add to this initial use of volunteer help by securing extra tutors for reading class. In secondary schools, recruitment for a special project provides an excellent initial contact.

Easing into use of volunteers may not be necessary in your school. Because most preschools and primary grades have used assistance for many years, their teachers are ready for more continuous support from volunteers. Yet involving other people in the classroom program is an art, based on good planning and the ability to work with and supervise others. Successful involvement of a few may lay the groundwork for greater involvement of others at a later time.

Recruitment of Volunteers by Individual Teachers

Many teachers have been successful in implementing their own volunteer programs from among the parents of their students. If you have used volunteers previously and parents in the community have heard about your program from other parents, recruitment may be easy. Early in the year, an evening program, during which the curriculum is explained and parents get acquainted, is an effective time to recruit parents into the program. If parents have not been exposed to volunteerism, encourage them to visit the room and give them opportunities to participate in an easy activity, such as reading a story to a child or playing a game with a group. Ask them back for an enjoyable program so they begin to feel comfortable in the room. Sharing their hobbies with the children introduces many parents to the joys of teaching.

Gradually the fear of classroom involvement will disappear, and parents may be willing to spend several hours each week in the classroom.

Invitations That Work

Suppose you write notes or publish an invitation in the newsletter inviting parents to visit the school or child-care center, but nobody comes. If you have had this experience, you need a "parent-getter." Judge your activity and invitation by the following questions:

- Does the event sound enjoyable?
- Is there something in it for the parents?
- Are the parents' children involved in the program?
- Does the program have alternate times for attendance?

The first criterion, making the event sound enjoyable, can be met by the wording of the invitation. The second and third vary in importance; one or the other should be addressed in each bid for parent attendance. Scheduling alternate times depends on your parents' needs.

One teacher complained that the parents at her school were just not interested in helping. Only three had volunteered when they were asked to clean up the playground. When asked if there were any other enticements for the parents to volunteer to help, the teacher said no. "Would you have wanted to spend your Saturday morning cleaning up the playground?" she was asked. The teacher realized she would not have participated, either, if she had been one of the parents. An excellent means of determining the drawing power of a program or activity is your own reaction to the project. Would you want to come? Had the Saturday cleanup project included the children, furnished refreshments, and allowed time for a get-together after the work was completed, the turnout would have been much better. Make it worth the parents' time to volunteer.

Performances

Many schools have children perform to get parents to turn out. The ploy works; parents attend! Some professionals discourage this method because they believe that children are being exploited to attract parents. However, it is probably the manner in which the production is conceived and readied rather than the child's involvement that is unworthy. What are your memories of your childhood performances? If the experiences were devastating, was it the programs themselves or the way they were handled that led to disappointment? If the performance is a creative, worthwhile experience for the child and does not cause embarrassment, heartache, or a sense of rejection for the child who does not perform well and if all children are included, this method of enticing parents can be valuable for both child and parents. Experience in front of an audience can develop poise and heightened self-concept—and be fun for the child. Parents invited to unpolished programs enjoy the visit just as much as if they had attended refined productions. Small, simple classroom functions, scheduled often enough that every child has a moment in the limelight, are sure to have high parent turnout. The more parents come to school and get involved with the activities, the better chance you have of recruiting assistance.

Field Trips

Use a field trip to talk with parents about volunteering in the classroom. Parents will often volunteer for field trips, during which teacher and parent can find time to chat. See if the parents' interests include hobbies that can be shared with the class. Be receptive to any ideas or needs that parents reveal. The informal atmosphere of a field trip encourages parents to volunteer.

Want Ads to Encourage Sharing Experiences and Expertise

Parents have many experiences and talents that they can share. Who lived on a farm? Who just traveled to Japan? Who knows how to cook spaghetti? Who can knit? Who has a collection of baseball cards? Who can speak a different language? Who has some stories to tell? Who is a geologist? Who is a food server? Ask parents to share their talents, hobbies, and experiences with your class. Send home a want ad to parents (see Figure 5.7) and ask them to return a tear-off

Help Wanted
Positions Available

Tutor for Reading
Do you have an interest in children learning to read? Come tutor! We will train you in techniques to use.

Good Listener
Are you willing to listen to children share their experiences and stories? Come to the listening area and let a child share with you.

Costume Designer
There will be a class presentation next month. Is anyone willing to help with simple costumes?

Tour Guide
Do you have memories, slides, or tales about other states or countries? Come share.

Talent Scout
Some talented people never volunteer. We need a talent scout to help us find these people in our community.

Good-will Ambassador
Help us make everyone feel an important part of this school or center. Be in charge of sending get-well cards or congratulatory messages.

Reader of Books
Read to the children.Choose a favorite book or read one chosen by the teacher.

Photographer
Anyone want to help chronicle our year? Photographer needed.

Collector
Do you hate to throw good things away? Help us in our scrounge department. Collect and organize.

Game Player
We need someone who enjoys games to spend several hours a week at the game table.

News Editor
Be a news hound. Help us develop and publish a newsletter. The children will help furnish news.

Book Designer
The class needs books written by children for our reading center. Turn children's work into books.

Volunteer Coordinator
The class needs volunteers, but we also need to know who, when, and how. Coordinate the volunteer time sheet.

Construction Worker
Are you good at building and putting things together? Volunteer!

Computer Programmer
Share your expertise with the class.

SIGN UP IN YOUR CHILD'S CLASSROOM OR RETURN THIS FORM WITH YOUR INTERESTS CHECKED.

Tutor____ Listener____ Costume Designer____ Tour Guide____ Talent Scout____ Ambassador____
Reader____ Photographer____ Collector____ Game Player____ News Editor____ Book Designer____
Volunteer Coordinator____ Construction Worker____ Computer Programmer____ Other____________

Name ____________ Address ____________ Telephone ____________ E-mail ____________

FIGURE 5.7 One way to solicit school volunteers is through a want ad.

portion, or call them and ask them personally to come to the school. Schedule each parent at a time that is convenient for parent and teacher. If possible, a follow-up in class of the ideas presented will make the visit even more meaningful. After the presentations, write thank-you notes with suggestions that parents might come to class again, providing another means of recruiting potential volunteers.

Invitations to Share

Sending home invitations with the children asking parents if they are interested in volunteering is a direct way to recruit. Each teacher should design the invitation to fit the needs of the class. A letter that accompanies the form should stress to parents how important they are to the program. Let them know the following:

- Teachers and children need their help.
- Each parent is already experienced in working with children.
- Their child will be proud of the parents' involvement and will gain through their contributions.

Friendly requests along with suggestions enable parents to respond easily. Be sure to ask parents for their ideas and contributions. You have no way of knowing what useful treasures you may find! Let parents complete a questionnaire, such as the one in Figure 5.8, to indicate their interests and schedules. Perhaps a parent cannot visit school but is willing to make calls and coordinate the volunteer program. This parent can find substitutes when regular parent volunteers call in to say they must be absent. Others who are homebound can aid the class by sharing child care, making games and activities at home, designing and making costumes, writing newsletters, and making phone calls.

Parents who are able to work at school can perform both teaching and nonteaching tasks. Relate the task to the parents' interests. Nothing discourages some volunteers as much as being forced to do housekeeping tasks continually, with no opportunity for interaction with the children. The choice of tasks should not be difficult, however, because the opportunities are numerous and diversified, as the following lists indicate:

Teaching Tasks

School, Preschool or Child-care Center

Supervise learning centers.

Listen to children.

Play games with students.

Tell stories.

Play instructional games.

Work with underachievers or children with learning disabilities.

Help select library books for children.

Read to children.

Take children to the resource center.

Assist in learning center.

Share a hobby.

Speak on travel and customs around the world.

Demonstrate sewing or weaving.

Demonstrate food preparation.

Show filmstrips.

School

Teach children to type.

Help children prepare and practice speeches.

Supervise the making of books.

Supervise the production of a newsletter or newspaper.

Nonteaching Tasks

Make games.

Prepare a parent bulletin board.

Repair equipment.

Select and reproduce articles for the resource room.

Record grades.

Take attendance.

Collect lunch money.

Plan a workshop for parents.

Grade and correct papers or write comments.

Organize cupboards.

Help with book publishing.

Contributions from Home

Serve as telephone chairperson.

Collect recycling materials.

Furnish refreshments.

Furnish dress-up clothes and costumes.

Wash aprons.

Make art aprons.

Design and/or make costumes.

Repair equipment.

Make games.

Care for another volunteer's children.

Write newsletters.

Coordinate volunteers.

Please Share With the School or Center

Dear Parents:

We need volunteers to help us with our school. You can share your time by helping while you are at home or at school. If you want to share in any way, please let us know.

Are you interested in volunteering this year? ____ Yes ____ No

Check the ways you want to help.

____ In the classroom

____ In the resource center

____ At home

WHAT WOULD YOU LIKE TO DO?

____ Share your hobby or travel experience

____ Help children in learning centers

____ Be a room parent

____ Work in a resource room

____ Supervise a puppet show

____ Go on field trips

____ Care for another volunteer's children

____ Substitute for others

____ Develop a learning center

____ Tutor reading

____ Tell stories

____ Check papers

____ Check spelling

____ Help with math

____ Read to children

____ Make games

____ Listen to children read

____ Play games with children

____ Make books

____ Share your recipes

Any other suggestions? ____

____

Comments ____

When can you come?

Monday	Tuesday	Wednesday	Thursday	Friday
AM PM	AM PM	AM PM	AM PM	AM PM

Can you come each week? ____ Other ____

What time can you come? ____

How long can you stay? ____

________________ ________________ ________________

Name E-mail Telephone

FIGURE 5.8 Questionnaires are another way to obtain parents' interests and schedules.

Teaching embraces creative ideas and methods; volunteers, responding to the challenge, can provide a vast reservoir of talent and support. Book publishing is an excellent example of an effective volunteer activity that is both a teaching and a nonteaching role.

Management Techniques

Use management skills in organizing and implementing your volunteer program. A parent coordinator can be very helpful in developing effective communication between teacher and parent. Two types of charts—schedules and volunteer action sheets—can clarify the program and help it run more smoothly.

Schedules

Schedules can be adjusted if weekly charts are posted at school and sent home to parents. When parents can visualize the coverage, the class will not be inundated by help in one session and suffer from lack of help in another.

Volunteer Sheet

Because volunteers are used in many ways, developing an action sheet that describes each person's contribution is helpful. Figure 5.9 illustrates the scope of involvement within one classroom. With this list the parent coordinator can secure an effective substitute for someone who must be absent. If the teacher needs games constructed, the parent coordinator can call on parents who have volunteered for that activity. Special help in the resource center or with a student project may be found quickly by calling a parent who has already indicated an interest in helping this way. The responsibility for the volunteer program does not need to rest solely on the teacher's shoulders. Parents and teachers become partners in developing a smoothly working system.

Increasing Volunteer Usage

Although permanent volunteers are more effective in establishing continuity in a program than periodic contributions by occasional volunteers, both are needed. As the year progresses, some parents may find they enjoy teaching immensely. These parents may extend their time obligation and in doing so, bring more continuity to the program. Ideally, an assistant should tutor a reading group or a child for several sessions each week rather than just one. When initiating a program, it is best to start out with easily handled time slots and then expand the responsibilities of parents after they become secure and familiar with the class, the objectives, and the material.

Volunteer Training

Suppose that several parents have indicated interest in being permanent volunteers in your classroom. What is your next step? The time spent explaining your routine, expectations, and preferences for teaching will be well worth the effort in the parents' abilities to coordinate with you in your classroom. Most teachers have specific preferences for teaching that they will want to share with the volunteers helping them. These, in addition to some general guidelines, will help prepare the volunteer. The following humanistic guidelines for working with children are appropriate for all volunteers:

- A healthy, positive self-concept is a prerequisite to learning.
- The act of listening to a child implies that you accept the child as a worthwhile person.
- The child will develop a better sense of self-worth if you praise specific efforts rather than deride failures.
- Provide tasks at which the children can succeed. As they master these, move on to the next level.
- Take time to know the student as a person. Your interest bolsters confidence in your relationship. (Adapted from DaSilva & Lucas, 1974)

Many children who need extra help with their work also need their self-concepts strengthened. Volunteers can provide an extra touch through kindness, interest, and support.

The Teacher's Responsibilities to the Volunteer

As teachers enlist the help of volunteers, certain responsibilities emerge. The teacher's responsibilities follow:

- Make volunteers feel welcome. Smile and reassure them.
- Explain class rules and regulations.
- Introduce volunteers to the resources within the school.
- Explain the routine of the class.

Name	Telephone	Classroom Regularly	Classroom Substitute	Special Presentation	Child Care	Make Games at Home	Work in Resource Center: Help Students	Work in Resource Center: Develop Resources	
								Type	Make games
Names of volunteers	555-5555								
" "	x							x	
" "		x	x						
" "		x	x						
" "	x		x						
" "		x	x		x				
" "	x				x				
" "				x	x				
" "						x	x		
" "	x								
" "	x								
" "	x		x						
" "						x	x	x	
" "	x								
" "			x		x		x	x	
" "				x					
" "		x							
" "		x							
" "		x			x				
" "		x							
" "		x			x				
" "				x					
" "				x					
" "			x	x					
" "					x				
" "		x				x	x	x	
" "		x							
" "		x		x					
" "			x	x					

FIGURE 5.9 Volunteer action sheets help organize an orderly volunteer program.

- Describe your expectations for their participation.
- Remember that volunteers are contributing and sharing time because of satisfaction they receive and to help the child.
- Give volunteers reinforcement and recognition.
- Meet with volunteers when class is not in session to clarify, answer questions, and, if needed, give instruction and training.
- Appreciate, respect, and encourage volunteers.

Awareness of these points will make the cooperative effort of teacher and volunteer more fulfilling for both.

The Volunteer's Responsibilities to the Teacher

If parents or others in the community volunteer to help in the school, they accept certain responsibilities, which include the following:

- Be dependable and punctual. If an emergency requires that you miss a session, obtain a substitute or contact the volunteer coordinator.
- Keep privileged information concerning children or events confidential. Do not discuss children with people other than school personnel.
- Plan responsibilities in the classroom with the teacher.
- Cooperate with the staff. Welcome supervision.
- Be ready to learn and grow in your work.
- Enjoy yourself, but do not let your charges get out of control.
- Be fair, consistent, and organized.

Volunteer aides are not helpful if they continually cancel at the last moment, disrupt the room rather than help it run smoothly, or upset the students. They are immensely helpful if they work with the teacher to strengthen and individualize the school program.

Recruitment by Schools and School Systems

Many schools and school districts assist teachers by recruiting volunteers for their classes. The first step in initiating a volunteer program for a school or school system is the development of a questionnaire to ascertain the teachers' needs. The teachers complete a form, based on the curriculum for each age level of students. After the forms are completed, the coordinators can determine the requirements of each room.

After teachers have indicated their needs, the coordinator begins recruitment. Many avenues are open for the recruiter. A flyer geared to the appropriate age or level of children, asking people to share their time with the schools, can bring about the desired results. Organizations can also be contacted. The PTA or PTO, senior citizen groups, and other clubs have members who may want to get involved as volunteers in the school.

The points discussed earlier for obtaining volunteers for the individual classroom are also appropriate for volunteers who are solicited on a larger scale. The major differences are organizational and include the following:

- Teachers should contact the volunteer coordinator or reply to the coordinator's questionnaire if they want a volunteer.
- Districts usually require volunteers to fill out an application stating their background, giving references, and listing the hours they are available.
- Many school districts have an extensive compilation of resource people who have agreed to volunteer in the schools. An alliance with businesses encourages companies to allow their employees to visit schools and tell students about their careers. These resource people and experts can share their knowledge with classes throughout the school district. Lists of topics with resource people available to share expertise can be distributed throughout the district. Teachers can request the subject and time they want a presentation.
- Outreach such as a community study hall can be initiated and staffed by the volunteer program. Volunteers can tutor and work with children after school hours in libraries, schools, or other public facilities (Denver Public Schools, n.d.).
- Certificates or awards distributed by the district offer a way to thank the volunteers for effort and time shared with the schools.

Individual teachers tend to use parents as aides and resource people in the room. The district most often furnishes resource people, drawn from the total population, in schools throughout the district. The school's volunteer coordinator uses both approaches, enlisting volunteers to tutor and aid in the classroom and recruiting resource people from residents of the school's population area to enrich the curriculum.

SUMMARY

Understanding parents' feelings and concerns provides the basis for creating effective home–school relationships. Schools have character; some invite parents to participate; others suggest they stay away. Parents have feelings about schools that range from a desire to avoid the school to such a high interest that they are overly active. Parents participate in schools as spectators, accessory volunteers, volunteer resources, paid resources, policy makers, and teachers of their children.

Schools can develop attitudes that welcome parents and conduct activities that invite them into the school. Personnel in the school need to understand and examine their own attitudes toward parents. The use of questionnaires helps in the recognition of these attitudes.

An open-door policy with open forums, coffees, and seminars invites comments from parents. Initial contact should be made early in the year or even during the summer before the school year begins. Suggestions for early contact include neighborhood visits, telephone calls, home visits, and breakfasts.

A resource room, established and staffed by parent volunteers, makes parents significant educational resources. The resource room includes articles on teaching, games, recycled materials, and a lending library for toys, books, and games. A family center gives parents a place to stop and a base from which they can reach out to help children.

Parents today are more involved as policy makers than in the past. Parent advisory councils are part of Title I, and parents confer with school administrators on program planning, implementation, and evaluation.

Schools can become community centers and meet the needs of families in the area by organizing parent volunteers for parent-to-parent groups, child-care centers, crisis centers, and after-school programs. If schools focus on family strengths they will help families develop and keep these strengths, which are effective communication, commitment, wellness, time together, and the ability to deal with stress, conflict, and crises. Parents and others from the community can also be included in the schools as volunteers. Teachers need to develop skills to recruit, train, and work with volunteers as part of an educational team.

SUGGESTED CLASS ACTIVITIES AND DISCUSSIONS

1. Make a list of suggestions from this chapter. Use it as a checklist to test your school's response to parents.
2. Contact the president of the PTA or PTO in a neighborhood school. What are his or her goals for parent involvement in the school? Which programs have been planned for the year? Which direction would he or she like the PTO or PTA to take?
3. Discuss why some parents may feel intimidated by schools and why some teachers may be reluctant to have parents involved. Role play the teacher and parent roles and share your feelings.
4. Describe an ideal parent–teacher relationship. List five things a teacher can do to encourage such a relationship. List five ways a parent can work with the school.
5. List what makes you feel comfortable or uncomfortable when you visit a center or school.
6. Visit a school and look at bulletin boards, notices, and family centers that might welcome parents. Make a list of things that might invite parents as well as things that might intimidate parents.
7. Examine the offerings of a school system or an individual school. What programs or activities does the school offer? List and describe the offerings such as Head Start, family literacy, telephone tutoring, resource rooms, exchanges, prekindergarten programs, and parent advisory council.
8. Describe the different families you might find in the school in your neighborhood and in a different neighborhood. What are their living arrangements, their values, their ambitions, their hopes for the future?
9. Write guidelines for parents to use when they visit or work in the classroom. Describe the guidelines on a poster or handout.
10. Examine your community and develop a list of field trips and home-learning activities. Plan a packet for parents to use with their children during spring break.
11. Design a want ad or letter that invites parents to become volunteers in the classroom.
12. Search the community for resources that can be used in the school. Include specialists, materials, and places to visit.
13. List the strengths that help families. What other strengths might you add? How would you help families build their strengths?

WEB SITES

Clearinghouse on Early Education and Parenting (CEEP): ERIC/EECE Archive of Publications and Resources
http://ceep.crc.uiuc.edu/eecearchive

CEEP maintains the ERIC/EECE elementary and early childhood archive. Many useful publications are available.

Parents as Teachers National Center (PATNC)
www.patnc.org

PATNC and MELD have joined resources and both have literature and many positive programs helpful to parents and those working with parents.

Reading Is Fundamental
www.rif.org

The site offers a monthly calendar with activities that enhance reading.

Zero to Three
www.zerotothree.org

Zero to Three focuses on the very young child and has an excellent program and information on children aged 0 to 3.

6 Communication and Parent Programs

To really communicate one must listen, one must share true meaning, and one must reflect upon the message being shared.

E. H. Berger

"The time has come," the walrus said,
"To talk of many things:
Of shoes—and ships—and sealing wax—
Of cabbages and kings
And why the sea is boiling hot—
And whether pigs have wings."

Carroll, 1968, p. 78

In this chapter on communication you will find methods for effective communication that will enable you to do the following:

- Discuss effective communication.
- Identify and use one-way communication.
- Identify and use two-way communication.
- Describe roadblocks to communication.
- List elements of effective communication with parents.
- List steps to improving listening skills.
- Define *rephrasing, reframing, open responses, problem ownership,* and *reflective listening.*
- List and describe parent education programs.
- Work on concerns that emerge in relationships with students and parents.
- Develop a plan for an effective parent–teacher conference.

COMMUNICATION

What do you have in mind when you think of effective communication? Is it the transmission of feelings, information, and signals? Is it the sending and receiving of messages? Is it a verbal exchange between people—for example, parents and teachers?

Definition of Communication

Most definitions of *communication* encompass more than mere interchange of information. They range from the definition given in *Webster's Encyclopedic Unabridged Dictionary of the English Language* (1989)—"the imparting or interchange of thoughts, opinions, or information by speech, writing, or

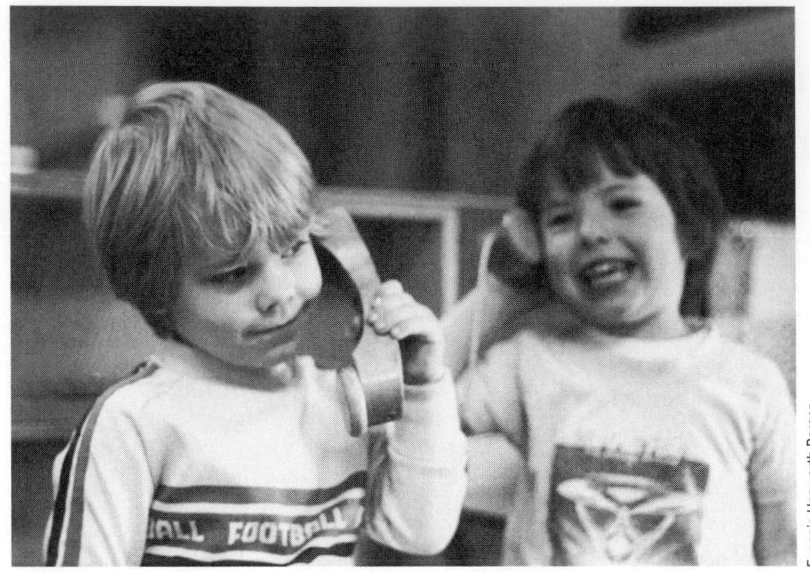

Eugenia Hepworth Berger

If the intent of the message sent is accurately received by the listener, good communication has occurred.

signs"—to definitions that focus on the effect a message has on the receiver. Is the message received with the meaning that the sender intended to convey? In working with parents, it is essential that messages are sent and received as intended.

Messages

Each message has at least three components: (a) the words or verbal stimuli—what a person says; (b) the body language or physical stimuli—the gestures; and (c) the vocal characteristics or vocal stimuli—the pitch, loudness or softness, and speed (Gamble & Gamble, 1982).

The sender gives a message; it is received and interpreted by the receiver. If the intent of the message is accurately received, effective communication has occurred. For this to happen, the listener must be an active participant. The listener must be able to hear the message, the feeling, and the meaning of the message.

Communication includes (a) speaking, (b) listening, (c) reflection of feeling, and (d) interpretation of the message. It is a complicated process because so many variables come into play. The sender's voice and body language, the message itself, the receiver's reaction to the sender, and the receiver's expectations all affect the message. To be effective in communication, speakers need to understand their own reactions and the reaction of others to them, and they must listen to the meaning of the message.

The receiver must correctly interpret the meaning of the message and the sender's intent. If the message— or the receiver's response—is misinterpreted, miscommunication occurs. Miscommunication can be overcome. The receiver may check out understanding by rephrasing and recycling the conversation or by further questioning within the context of the subsequent discussion.

Miscommunication

Interpersonal communication may be visualized as messages within an ongoing circle or oval configuration. As pictured in Figure 6.1, the message (filtered through values and past experiences) goes to the receiver (where it also is filtered through values and past experiences), is decoded, responded to, and sent back to begin the cycle again. Communication is a dynamic, continuous process that changes and evolves.

Visual Messages

When talking with one another it is easy to assume that what one says is the most important element in the conversation. However, research shows that oral, verbal messages (the spoken words) account for only 7 percent of the input;

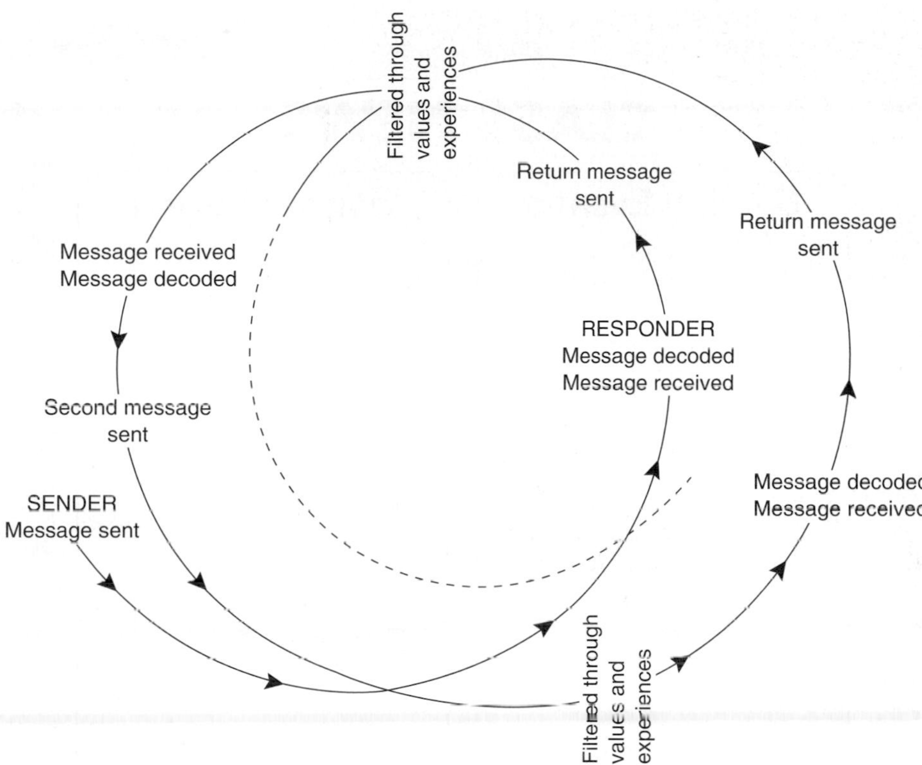

FIGURE 6.1 Messages are filtered through the receiver's value system and experiences before they are decoded and responded to. Communication is a dynamic, continuous process.

vocal and tonal messages (the way in which the words are spoken) account for 38 percent; and visual messages (body language) account for 55 percent (Miller, Wackman, Nunnally, & Miller, 1988). If this is the case, teachers, principals, and child-care professionals need to focus on their total communication system and be aware of their body language and tone of voice, as well as their verbal messages.

One- and Two-Way Communication

One-way communication from the school merely informs parents about the school's plans and happenings. Two-way communication, which requires interaction among participants, allows parents to give feedback to the school on their knowledge, concerns, and desires. Both the school and parents gain. The steps to achieve effective communication among school, home, and community are easy to implement once the importance of effective communication is acknowledged. A number of strategies for establishing improved communication are described on the following pages. Choose the ones that fit your individual needs, and add others that work for you.

ONE-WAY COMMUNICATION

A newsletter may be sent by the school as a message from the principal, or it may be sent home by each teacher. It is a simple form of one-way communication, and the format varies with the goals and objectives of each newsletter. Design ranges from a very simple notice to an elaborate and professionally written letter.

Simple Newsletters

The more newsletters you write, the easier they become. The design may vary from a simple notice that is hand-printed and photocopied (see Figure 6.2) to a letter created through a desktop publishing program on the school computer (see Figure 6.3). Items

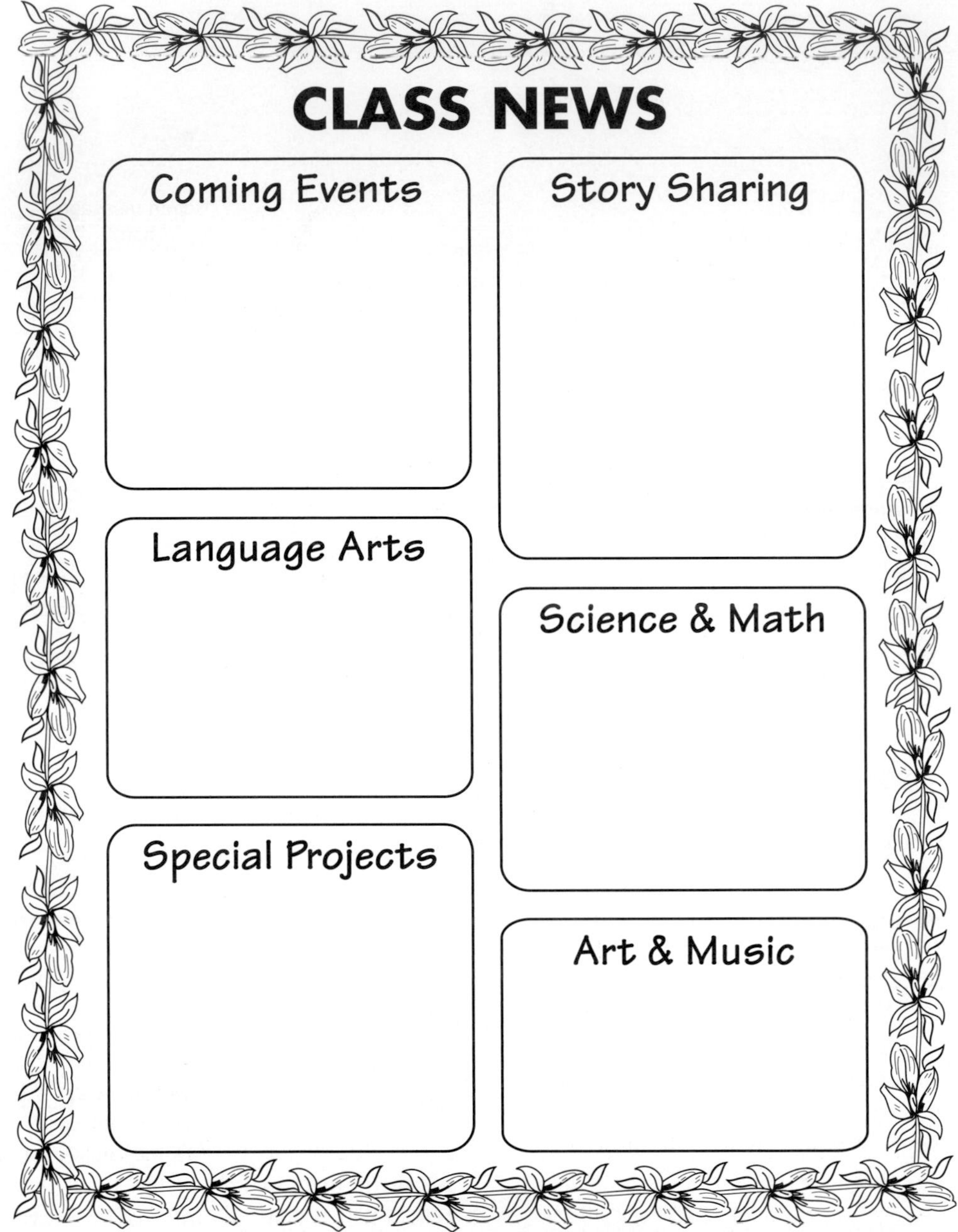

CLASS NEWS
Coming Events
Story Sharing
Language Arts
Science & Math
Special Projects
Art & Music

FIGURE 6.2 Newsletters may take many forms, ranging from this informal design to very sophisticated publications.

may include the children's activities in curriculum areas such as math contracts or contests, reading projects, group presentations in social studies, hands-on work in science, practice in music skills, art experiences, field trips, care of classroom pets, contributions by resource people, creative drama experiences, and accomplishments or remarks by individual children. In addition, items may include information important to parents such as parent–teacher conferences, back-to-school nights, and parent breakfasts. Not every newsletter contains all the information, for it is an ongoing communication.

Newsletters may also be used at the secondary level with sections blocked for each course of study. Newsletters at the secondary level also provide parents with information regarding deadlines, such

PARENT NEWSLETTER

YOUR SCHOOL **SEPTEMBER**

2000 CENTURY STREET
SOMEWHERE, UNITED STATES

ANNOUNCEMENTS **Dates to Remember**

BACK TO SCHOOL NIGHT **Thursday, September 12**
Go to your child's classroom at 7:00 P.M.
Refreshments at 8:30 p.m.

Workshop on Conferences **Tuesday, September 17**
Auditorium at 7:00 P.M.

Conferences **Thursday, September 19**

Sign your forms and return them
To your child's teacher

The Adventurer Room

Our class had an adventure by visiting a historical 1890 farm. We saw a home that was furnished with all the furniture that a farm family would have. We were able to pet the animals. There were horses, sheep, pigs and chickens. We had a great time!!! Our class will write a book about farms at the turn of the century.

Space Adventurers

To start the year we decided to have a space adventure. The class was divided into four groups, and each group made plans for their space shuttle. We planned the food, the equipment, and the lift off. Parents have volunteered to come in and help with our book publishing. Each group will write about their space adventure.

FIGURE 6.3 If you regularly collect anecdotes and children's work, you will easily have enough material for a four-page newsletter for parents.

as those related to testing dates, scheduling, and financial-aid submission dates.

For both elementary and secondary schools newsletters can also provide parents with a means of staying in touch with each other. Selected parents can be identified as liaisons for particular school events or just as resources when parents have questions. This is particularly helpful when many parents speak languages other than English and need assistance with translations more quickly than the school can provide. Communication between home and school is essential.

Students who are old enough can be given the responsibility of writing the periodic newsletter. This way, the newsletter serves two purposes: curriculum and communication. The students are challenged to write neatly, spell correctly, and construct a readable newsletter. Younger children can make individual contributions by painting a picture or making a comment that can be shared.

Consider using the following in your newsletter:

- Clear headlines that identify the topic
- Colorful paper

- Calendar of the week or month
- Book suggestions
- Recognition of birthdays
- Children's or students' work
- Quotes of children
- Artwork

Preschool

Publication of newsletters at this stage is the teacher's responsibility, although children can contribute drawings and stories.

Try collecting newsletter ideas throughout the year. State Cooperative Extension agencies, family and consumer sciences, will probably have some excellent ideas to contribute. Commercial newsletters are available that can be used with inserts from your own center to reflect your concerns and news. As you collect interesting comments by the children or complete special projects, make a short note for the newsletter. If you choose a "very important person" each week, include information about that child in the newsletter. If you include articles about individual children, be sure to include each child before the end of the term. When time comes for publication, you will have more than enough news. It is more important to have a newsletter than to worry about its design. If a computer isn't available and typing isn't practical, write in your neatest script. Subjects that parents will find interesting include nutrition, child development, communication, and activities for rainy days, as well as events specific to your center or class. A picture drawn by a child to accompany the news is an attractive addition.

Elementary

A newsletter is an excellent curriculum tool in elementary school. Although children in the first grade may not be able to produce their own newsletter, you will be surprised at how well young children can write and edit their news. Make the newsletter an ongoing project, with a center set up to handle the papers and equipment. Assign a group in each subject area to be responsible for the newsletter. Let them collect the news and determine the content and design of the letter. You can have the children develop the newsletter on the computer. Different children could add messages or articles. If you cut and paste, the children can be allowed to type their own copy. Photocopy the master and print it by the most convenient method of duplication.

Middle and Secondary

Although seldom used at this level, the newsletter is an excellent mechanism for secondary students to gain experience in writing, composition, and

Eugenia Hepworth Berger

Let the children help with the notes, letters, or newsletters.

making page layouts. You receive dual benefits—students learn through the process of doing, and a communication system between school and home is established.

A sophisticated newsletter may be the goal for upper-level students, but the importance of the newsletter as a communication tool should not be overlooked. If producing a sophisticated newsletter is too time consuming, write the newsletter in a simple, informative style (see Figure 6.3). The major objective is communication between the teacher and home. What is the class studying? What assignments are the students expected to complete? Is there any problem solving being done in class? Which problems seem the most difficult? Are there any parents who would like to contribute to the subject being covered?

The newsletter is a short, practical form of newspaper. It is easily produced on a computer or by a cut-and-paste method and can relate to a smaller and, therefore, more specific group of students. It can address current concerns and interests and can inform a select group of parents of the happenings that affect their children.

Notes and Letters

When a child is doing well, send home an "upslip" to let the parents know (see Figure 6.4). It is a good idea to buy small sheets of paper with space enough for a one- or two-line note. If you write too much, you may be forced by time limitation to postpone the incidental note, and the positive effect of timeliness is lost.

Letters sent prior to the beginning of school also help establish good communication. They should include significant dates, reminders, and school events (see Figure 6.5).

Many teachers like to use "good news notes," happy faces, "happy grams," or similar forms periodically to report something positive about each child. The concept behind each of these formats is the same—to communicate with parents in a positive manner, thereby improving both parent–teacher relations and the child's self-concept. Make a concerted effort to send these notes in a spirit of spontaneous sincerity. A contrived, meaningless comment, sent because you are required to do so, will probably be received as it was sent. Preserving good relations requires that the message have meaning.

Newspapers

Most school districts have newspapers, yearbooks, and other school-sponsored publications. These, along with the district newsletter, are important school traditions and effectively disseminate information. Don't stop publishing them, but always remember that the newsletters that touch on their children are of greater importance to parents. Those most affected by yearbooks are those whose children are pictured in them. Parents most affected by newspapers are those who find articles in them concerning activities in which their children are involved.

Relying solely on newspapers and yearbooks for communicating with parents may promote complacency; some administrators and teachers assume communication is complete because a newspaper comes out periodically and a yearbook is published when seniors graduate. Yearbooks have very little effect on school–home relationships. They arrive after the student's school career ends, they often picture a small segment of the school population, and they are generally the product of a small, select group of students. The majority of students may be omitted or ignored. The school newspaper cannot take the place of individual class newsletters. Parents are more interested in their own children than in school leaders and star athletes. Newspapers and yearbooks meet different needs and are significant in their own way, but to establish a real, working relationship between parents and schools, the school's publication must concern the parents' number one interest—their own children.

District Newsletter

Many school districts use newsletters to keep the community up-to-date on school events. Often produced by professional public relations firms, they may display excellent style and format and contain precise information, but they may also lack the personal touch and tend to be viewed as a communiqué from the administration. District newsletters do have a place in building effective home-school-community relations, and some districts want all press releases to originate from administration;

FIGURE 6.4 Happy grams, "upslips," and short notes are appreciated by parents and child.

however, these may be supplemented by individual class reports (newsletters). In this way, parents receive both formal and personalized communication about their children's schooling.

Media

A formal and effective means of reaching parents is through the community newspaper and television and radio stations. Television and radio often make public service announcements. Use the format of "who, what, when, where, why, and how" information to send to television and radio stations. Be brief but include a contact name and phone number. Send the communication several weeks before it needs to be aired or published. Use these opportunities to inform the community about events at school. Many communities have access to a cable information line that alerts the community to upcoming events. These may include conferences, sports events, musical performances, debates, theater, school board meetings, community meetings, back-to-school nights, and carnivals.

Suggestion Box

A suggestion box placed in the hallway encourages parents to share their concerns and pleasures with the school anonymously. Although this is really a one-way communication system, it effectively tells

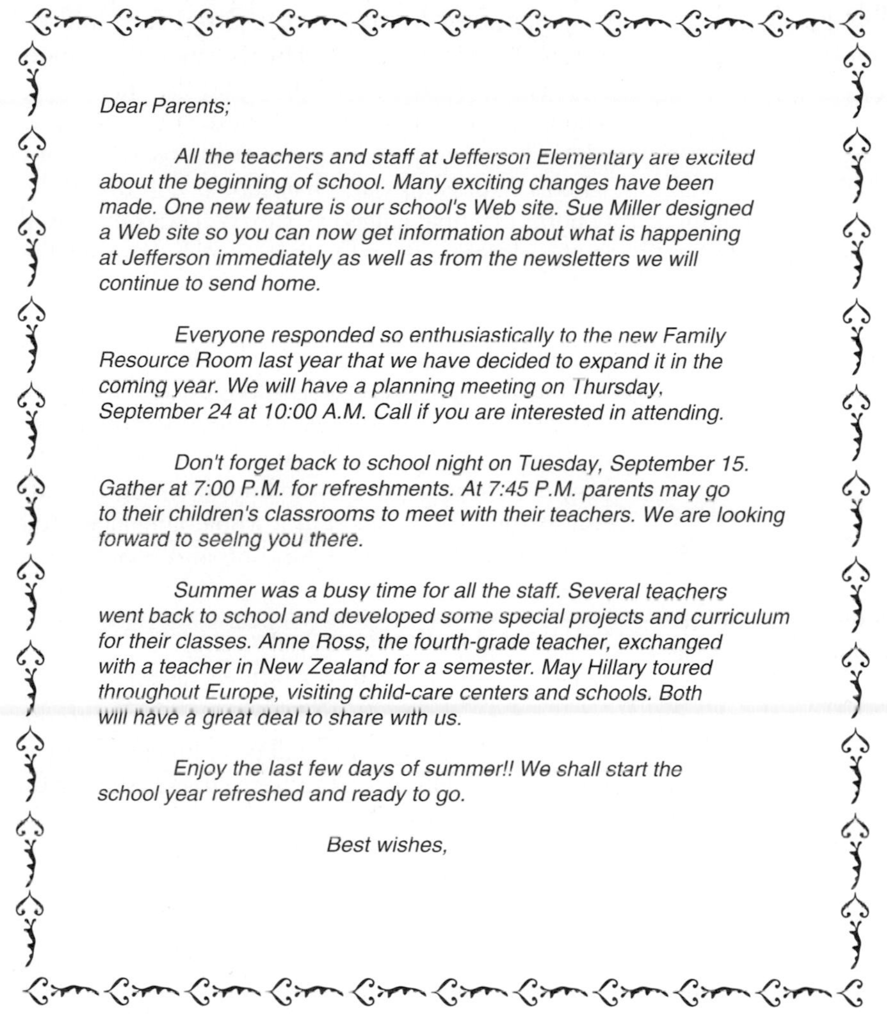

Dear Parents;

All the teachers and staff at Jefferson Elementary are excited about the beginning of school. Many exciting changes have been made. One new feature is our school's Web site. Sue Miller designed a Web site so you can now get information about what is happening at Jefferson immediately as well as from the newsletters we will continue to send home.

Everyone responded so enthusiastically to the new Family Resource Room last year that we have decided to expand it in the coming year. We will have a planning meeting on Thursday, September 24 at 10:00 A.M. Call if you are interested in attending.

Don't forget back to school night on Tuesday, September 15. Gather at 7:00 P.M. for refreshments. At 7:45 P.M. parents may go to their children's classrooms to meet with their teachers. We are looking forward to seeing you there.

Summer was a busy time for all the staff. Several teachers went back to school and developed some special projects and curriculum for their classes. Anne Ross, the fourth-grade teacher, exchanged with a teacher in New Zealand for a semester. May Hillary toured throughout Europe, visiting child-care centers and schools. Both will have a great deal to share with us.

Enjoy the last few days of summer!! We shall start the school year refreshed and ready to go.

Best wishes,

FIGURE 6.5 Friendly letters sent prior to the opening of school can set the stage for a cooperative and pleasant school year.

parents, "We want your suggestions. Let us know what you feel," and encourages them to respond.

Handbooks

Handbooks sent home before the child enters school are greatly appreciated by parents. If sent while the child is a preschooler, the school's expectations for the child can be met early. If given to parents at an open house during the spring term, they can reinforce the directions given by the teacher at that time. Handbooks can help parents new to the area by including information on community activities and associations for families. A district handbook designed to introduce parents to the resources in the area—with special pages geared to each level of student—can be developed and used by all teachers in the district. Moles (1996a) suggests the following handbook inclusions:

- Statement of school goals and philosophy.
- Discipline policy and code.
- Operations and procedures regarding:
  a. grades and pupil progress reports
  b. absence and tardiness
  c. how to inquire about student difficulties
  d. emergency procedures for weather and other events
  e. transportation schedules and provisions for after-school activities
- Special programs at the school such as after-school enrichment or child-care programs.

- Parent involvement policies and practices at the school, with items that describe:
  - a. "Bill of Rights" for parents
  - b. "Code of Responsibilities" for parents
  - c. open house and parent–teacher conferences
  - d. involvement opportunities, such as volunteer programs, advisory councils, and PTAs
- A calendar of major school events throughout the year: holidays, vacations, regular PTA meetings, report card periods, open houses, other regularly scheduled school–home contacts.
- Names and phone numbers of key school contact people.
- Names and phone numbers of parent leaders (e.g., members of advisory councils, key people in parent organizations, and room parents).
- A tear-off response form allowing parents to ask questions, voice concerns, and volunteer at the school. (p. 9)

In addition, consider the following items when you compile your handbook:

- Procedures for registration
- Invitations to visit the school
- Conferences and progress reports
- Testing and evaluation programs
- Decision-making process, advisory committees, site-based management
- Facilities at the school (cafeteria, clinic, library)
- Special programs offered by the school (band, chorus, gymnastics)
- Summer programs
- Recreation programs
- Associations related to families and children
- Community center

Specialized Handbook

A special handbook related to the child's grade level and academic program can be an effective way to gain parents' cooperation. If it is sent out early in the school term, include the teacher's name and a short autobiography.

A special section related to the curriculum in the child's grade level can be developed by classroom teachers at each level and inserted for children assigned to their classes. This is especially important when the school is changing the manner in which the curriculum is taught. For example, whole-language programs are being used in many schools. Workshops and handbooks describing the benefits of whole language, the methods being used in the classroom, and activities at home that the children can use will help the parents support the program. This is especially important with the writing portion of the program. The development of writing and spelling, from prephonic and invented spelling to conventional spelling, needs to be explained to parents. A handbook that describes the process, along with a workshop at which parents can see and be involved in a whole-language project, will increase understanding and cooperation between home and school.

Summer Handbook or Note

If a handbook does not give individualized, personal information, a note from the teacher mailed to the home during the summer will be appreciated by the family and will set the tone for a successful home–school relationship.

TWO-WAY COMMUNICATION

Although one-way communication is important, two-way communication is essential. It is possible only when school personnel meet the children and their parents. The school principals or center directors set the climate of acceptance within their institutions. Their perceptions of the role of the school in communicating with parents permeate the atmosphere, making parents feel either welcome or unwanted.

Increased involvement is necessary for a true partnership. Telephone calls, home visits, parent visits at the school, parent–teacher conferences, and school activities encourage continued parental involvement. Use of the Internet capabilities on computers allows schools and parents to have immediate opportunities for information exchanges. Sharing e-mail addresses makes this possible.

Visits to the classroom allow parents to become acquainted with their child's educational environment, the other children in the room, and the teacher. Periodic conferences continue the dialogue on the educational progress of the child. Participation in school activities allows parents to become working members of the education team.

Homework Hot Line

The telephone system allows for many inventive ways to serve the student. This includes such services as call forwarding, taped responses, answering machines, and having people available at the school's telephone number. The traditional use of the telephone requires volunteers or paid professionals to answer the phone at school. Some schools have a hot line open each day after school for students to call when they have questions about homework. If specialists in each academic field are available, the hot-line call may be transferred to the appropriate specialist to answer questions about homework. In individual schools, teachers can leave their assignments with the hot-line specialists so they have the information available for each class. Using call forwarding, people responding to homework hot-line calls can work out of their homes.

Some communities have the homework hot line connected to local celebrities and others who volunteer for a set number of hours at a special telephone number. Details of individual assignments are more difficult to handle in this type of setup, but it serves well as a public relations format and general questions about homework may be answered.

Enlist a TV station as a partner in education. Some stations sponsor tutoring programs. Students are encouraged to call designated numbers—such as 555-HELP, 555-PASS, or 555-AIDE—to talk to someone about homework. The station commits funds to hire tutors to answer questions children or parents might have about homework. It also works to have recognizable personalities take turns on the telephone. Watch the tutor service take off if parents and children know that local celebrities are willing to help.

Computer Information Line

Computers can be used in a variety of ways. Each school would have to determine if computers were available to the families in its area. Families would either own their own online computer or community libraries can provide them. A questionnaire could be used to determine if the family has accessibility and if they want to use computers for information access with the school.

E-mail

Individual messages can be used for specific correspondence between the school and the student or the student's family.

E-mails to families whose children have been ill and unable to attend school would help the children keep up with schoolwork. When children are ill it is often difficult for parents to get to the school to get assignments. A teacher could e-mail an assignment that would be printed and used by the child.

Background Material and Assignment Explanations

Permanent explanations and discussions of academic assignments could be available on the computer. This would be similar to course work that is done via the computer by many institutions of higher education. Although it would be time consuming to set up the programs, they could be easily revised and used again.

Telephone Calls

If it is impossible to visit a parent in person, rely on a telephone call. A telephone call early in the school year produces many benefits from appreciative parents. Beware, however, that most parents will wonder what is wrong when their child's teacher calls. This is quite an indictment of our communication methods; parents are generally contacted only when something is amiss. Change that practice by setting aside a short period each day for making telephone calls to parents. Begin the dialogue on a positive note. Early in the year, calls can include information about who you are, why you are calling, and a short anecdote about the child. If each call takes 5 minutes and you have 30 children in your class, the calls will consume 2 ½ hours—a small amount of time for the results you will see. Divide the time into segments of 20 to 30 minutes each evening. Parents also appreciate a note sent home saying you hope to call and asking for a convenient time. A sample letter is shown in Figure 6.6.

Dear ______________________________:

During the school year, I will be making periodic telephone calls to parents of my students. I am able to call on Tuesday evening from 7:00 P.M. to 9:30 P.M. or on Wednesday afternoon from 3:30 P.M. to 5:00 P.M. Could you mark the time that would be most convenient for you?

Should you want to call me, you will find me available on Thursday evenings from 7:00 P.M. to 9:00 P.M. Feel free to call my home at ______________ if you have questions or would like to talk.

I am looking forward to visiting with you this year.

Best wishes,

____

Telephone call preference
Tuesday: ❑ 7:00 to 8:00 P.M. Wednesday: ❑ 3:30 to 4:00 P.M.
❑ 8:00 to 9:30 P.M. ❑ 4:00 to 5:00 P.M.
If none of these times are convenient, please let me know.

FIGURE 6.6 Asking parents when they are available for telephone calls and letting them know when they can call you encourages communication.

Home Visits

Some teachers make the effort to visit their students' homes early in the fall. This may be the only way to reach parents who have no telephone. It is also a rewarding experience for any teacher who can devote the time required. Not all parents are receptive to home visits, however, and some are afraid that the teacher is judging the home rather than coming as a friendly advocate of their child. Take precautions to avoid making the family feel ill at ease. Always let the family know you are coming. It is a good idea to write a note in which you request a time to visit or, possibly, give parents the option of meeting at another place. Once home visits become an accepted part of the parent-involvement program, they become less threatening, and both parents and children look forward to them. Chapter 9 gives suggestions for making home visits successful.

Visits to the Classroom

The traditional visit with parents invited for a specific event works very well in some school systems. In other schools, special events are complemented by an open invitation to parents to participate in ongoing educational programs.

Outside the classroom or just inside the door, hang a special bulletin board with messages for parents. It might display assignments for the week, plans for a party, good work children have done, requests for everyday items to complete an art project, requests for special volunteer time, or just about anything that promotes the welfare of the room. Parents can plan and develop the bulletin board with the teacher's guidance.

Participation Visits

Directions for classroom participation are necessary if the experience is to be successful. Parents or other visitors feel more comfortable, teachers are more relaxed, and children benefit more if parents or visitors are given pointers for classroom visits. They can be in the form of a handout or a poster displayed prominently in the room, but a brief parent–teacher dialogue will make the welcome more personal and encourage specific participation.

The best welcome encourages the visitor to be active in the room's activities. Select activities that are easily described, require no advance training, and contribute rather than disrupt. You may want to give explicit directions on voice quality and noise control. If you do not want the parent to make any noise, request that a soft tone be used when talking with students in the room. Or you might want to ask the parent to work in a specific area of the room. Most visitors are happiest when they know what you want.

If it bothers you that some parents tend to give answers to students rather than help the students work out their own problems, suggest the method of instruction you prefer. You might give them a tip sheet for working with students that describes your favorite practices. Making activities simple for "drop-in" participants will keep problems to a minimum. If some parents prefer to sit and observe, don't force participation. As they become more comfortable in your room, they may try some activities. Selecting and reading a story to a child or group, listening to a child read, supervising the newsletter center, playing a game chosen from the game center with a student, supervising the puzzle table, or talking with students about their work are appropriate activities for new volunteers.

Visits by Invitation

A special invitation is sent to parents of a different child each week asking them to visit as "Parents of the Week" or VIPs—very important parents. The invitation, written by the child or teacher, is accompanied by a memo from the administration that explains the objective of the visit. Have the child bring in information about brothers and sisters, favorite activities, and other interesting or important facts about the family. Place a picture of the family on the bulletin board that week. The family could include parents, grandparents, special friends (young or old), and younger siblings. Parents and guests are asked to let the teacher know when they plan to visit.

You could also improve a child's self-concept by making the child "Student of the Week." Not only do the children have a chance to feel good about themselves on their special day, but it also helps children get to know one another better. Feedback from parents after a visit is important. A reaction sheet is given to parents asking them to write their impressions and return it to the school. Comments range from compliments to questions about the school. This process encourages two-way communication.

Student–Parent Exchange Day

An idea similar to the student visiting the parent's place of employment is to have the parent take the place of the student at school. This can be done in several ways. The parent may accompany the student to class and spend the day with the child, or the parent and child may exchange places for the day. Exchanging places for the day works best for an older student who can fulfill some obligation at home or go on a field trip while the parent goes through the student's exact schedule. The parent is responsible for listening to the lecture or participating in the class and doing the homework. The parent learns about the school program, becomes acquainted with the teacher, and is better able to relate to the child's school experience. If the child is young and the school and parent prefer to participate in the school day without the child, the process is possible if the parent hires a baby-sitter or if the school provides a field trip for the children in the class.

Student–Parent–School Exchange

When concerns arise about drugs, alcohol, vandalism, or premarital sex, an enlightening way of having parents interact with students and school personnel is to have the parents visit a school nearby with similar concerns. Parents talk with children they don't know and find out how the students feel about the social issues they face. With the anonymity of parents and students, the discussion becomes more open. This arena can help bring about problem solving and answer some of the students' concerns. Perhaps the students need better after-school facilities to eliminate the attractiveness of misuse of time. Perhaps they want more guidance for their friends so that peer pressure is not so demanding.

Breakfasts

If you have a cooperative cafeteria staff or volunteers who are willing to make a simple breakfast, you can invite parents to an early breakfast. Many parents can stop for breakfast on their way to work. Plan a breakfast meeting early in the fall to meet parents and answer questions. Breakfast meetings tend to be rushed because parents need to get to work, so schedule a series of breakfasts and restrict the number of parents invited to each. In this way, real dialogue can be started. If a group is too large, the personal contact that is the prime requisite of two-way communication between school and home is prevented. Breakfasts also support parent-to-parent communication. It is important that parents get an opportunity to meet the parents of their children's friends. It should be made clear to parents the potential advantage of attending the breakfasts.

ROADBLOCKS TO COMMUNICATION

The goals of those who work with young children are to meet the needs of the children, educate them, and help them reach their potential as children and develop into productive adults. What is the challenge to parents? They have the same goals! Because parents and school personnel have the same goals in mind, it would seem that communication would be quite easy. Such is not the case. There are many roadblocks to good communication between school personnel and parents. Both school personnel and parents set up roadblocks. Some roadblocks are used to protect positions, and others occur because the participants are unable to understand one another's positions.

The roadblocks that hinder communication between parents and school personnel are similar to those that affect any communication, but different concerns emerge. Some of the most common parent-and-school roadblocks will be described so we can work to overcome them.

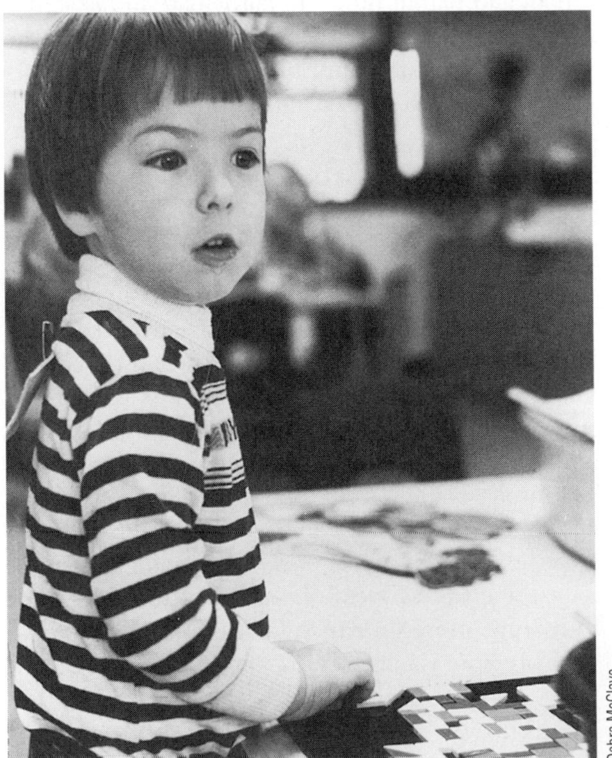

Debra McClave

A parent's vested interest in the child can be channeled in a positive direction. Effective communication with positive suggestions for encouraging the child can help the parent become a partner with the school.

Parent Roadblocks

Parents may exhibit roles, ranging from inadequacy to abrasive domineering, that inhibit their ability to communicate effectively with the schools. Descriptions of some roles follow.

Protector Role

Parents protect their own egos when they overprotect their children. Many parents, often subconsciously, view their children as extensions of themselves. "Criticize my child and you criticize me" is their message. "Are you saying that I did not rear my children correctly?" "Is my child slow in school because I am the parent?" "Is there something that I should have done differently in my childrearing?"

When a parent puts up a shield against perceived criticism and attack, it becomes very difficult to communicate. When parents are hurt by a child's inability to progress satisfactorily in school, they may withdraw from open, honest communication in an effort to protect their child and their own self-esteem.

A parent's vested interest in the child can be channeled in a positive direction. Effective communication, with positive suggestions for encouraging the child, can help the parent become a partner with the school.

Inadequate-Me Role

Many parents do not feel comfortable talking with school personnel. These parents avoid going to civic events—including events that take place at schools—because they do not feel as if they belong. If parents feel inadequate, they avoid coming in contact with the schools. If they do come, they find it difficult to communicate their desires or feelings to the staff. These parents can benefit from encouragement so that they can contribute and be involved.

Avoidance Role

The avoidance role may include self-assured parents who do not respect the school or the way it treats parents and students. It also includes parents who had a difficult time in school when they were growing up. Perhaps they dropped out of school—the building might bring back bad memories. Schools must reach out to these parents by caring and offering activities and services that the parents need and desire.

Indifferent-Parent Role

It seems more difficult today to be a concerned, involved parent because of financial and time pressures. Although most parents want what is best for their children, some are willing to shift their parental responsibilities to others. The institution where children spend most of their working hours is the school. When children are reared by indifferent parents, their futures can be devastated. If no one cares, why should the children care? Drug abuse, teenage pregnancies, alcohol abuse, truancy, and criminal behavior may be evidence that children have indifferent, dysfunctional, or too-busy parents. Early communication with parents can help reverse the trend.

Don't-Make-Waves Role

Many parents are unwilling to be honest in their concerns because they do not want school personnel to take it out on their child. They believe that the teacher or principal might be negative toward their children if they make suggestions or express concerns. This represses communication.

Club-Waving-Advocate Role

Sometimes parents get carried away with their devotion to their children, and they exhibit this through a power play. These advocates often become abrasive in their desire to protect their children or change school policy. These parents are the opposite of the "inadequate-me" or the "don't-make-waves" parents. "Club-waving" parents express their concerns through confrontation. Schools must acknowledge these concerns and change the situation when it is sensible to do so. In addition, give the parents opportunities to be leaders in areas where they can contribute.

School Roadblocks

Many times schools install roadblocks to effective communication without even realizing it. Sometimes they do so intentionally. The stress of educating and working with many children and families, the pressure to accomplish many tasks, and the desire to be seen as efficient all get in the way of unhurried, effective communication. The following roles describe some of the roadblocks that hamper communication between home and school.

Authority-Figure Role

School personnel who act as chief executive officers all too often hinder communication. These teachers and administrators claim to be the authorities, ready to impart information to the parent. They neglect to set the stage for the parent to be a partner in the discussion. If staff members take all the responsibility of running the school without considering the parents' backgrounds and knowledge, there seems to be no reason to communicate. Parents are locked out of the decision-making process. Schools that ignore parents destroy communication between parents and schools.

Sympathizing-Counselor Role

School personnel who focus on the inadequacy of the child in a vain attempt to console the parent miss a great opportunity for communication. Parents want to solve their concerns through constructive remediation or support. Parents and schools both need to focus on the achievements that can be attained through cooperation and collaboration.

Pass-the-Buck Role

Communication stops when school personnel refer the concerns of the parent to another department. "Sara may need help, but we cannot schedule her for tests for 5 months." "It is too bad that Richard had such a bad experience last year. I wish I could help, but he needs special services." Sometimes parents think the school is deliberately stalling while their child falls further and further behind.

Protect-the-Empire Role

A united, invincible staff can cause parents to think no one cares about their needs. School personnel need to work together and support one another, but they also need to listen to the parent and should advocate for the parent as they formulate an educational plan for the student.

Busy-Teacher Role

Perhaps the greatest roadblock to good communication between parent and teacher is time. If you are harried, you do not have time to communicate with your students or their parents. Both teachers and parents need to reduce stress and set aside time for communication. Reorganize schedules to include on-the-run conferences, telephone calls, and short personal notes to parents and children. Principals and directors might take over the classroom occasionally so teachers could make telephone calls to parents. The principals and directors would get to know the children in the classes and the importance of teacher–parent interaction would be emphasized. Roadblocks can be overcome.

EFFECTIVE COMMUNICATION WITH PARENTS

To achieve effective communication, parents and teachers need to recognize roadblocks to their success. At the same time, they can increase their communication skills by practicing positive speaking, rephrasing, and attentive listening.

When teachers talk with parents, they communicate in many ways—through their words, their body actions, and their manner of speaking. Every contact communicates whether the speaker respects the other person, values that person's input, and is willing to collaborate. The self-fulfilling prophecy works with parents as well as with students. If teachers treat parents as if they are incapable of being partners, the parents will fulfill that prophecy. They will not work with teachers effectively.

Cooley's Looking-Glass-Self

Cooley's (1964) Looking-Glass-Self concept reveals that how you view yourself depends on your perceptions about how others see you. The Looking-Glass-Self contains three phases: (a) *reflection* (parents looking into the mirror), (b) *interpretation* of the reflection (how the parents interpret what they see), and (c) *feeling of pride or mortification.* If, in the second step, parents interpret the reflection as positive, they will, in the third step, feel pride in being able to work with the school to the benefit of their children. If they see disregard and no respect, they will find it difficult to work as partners.

A teacher views parents as either partners or subordinates. The teacher can either help parents feel that they are enablers, empowering them to help their children, or reject the parents.

Effective Communication Skills

Teachers can establish rapport with parents by using effective communication skills. A good partnership, however, takes two partners, so parents also need to work on their skills. Effective communication takes time, is honest, and is open. Good communicators listen, rephrase and check out, and avoid criticizing and acting superior.

Teachers are good communicators when they:

1. Give their total attention to the speaker. They establish eye contact and clearly demonstrate through body language that their interest is focused on what is being said.
2. Restate the parents' concerns. They clarify what has been said and try to discern the speaker's meaning and feeling. They avoid closed responses or answering as a critic, judge, or moralist.
3. Show respect for the other person. They recognize that their concerns, opinions, and questions are significant factors in mutual understanding and communication.

4. Recognize the parents' feelings. How much can they discuss with parents?Perhaps they need to establish a better parent–teacher relationship before they can completely share their concerns for the child.
5. Tailor discussions to fit the parents' ability to handle the situation.
6. Do not touch off the fuse of a parent who might not be able to handle a child's difficulties. They don't accuse; they spend more time with the parent in other communication and conferences.
7. Emphasize that concerns are no one's fault. Teacher and parents have to work on problems together to help the child. They use concerns as forums for understanding one another.
8. Remember that no one ever wins an argument. Calmly, quietly, and enthusiastically they discuss the *good* points of the child before bringing up any concerns.
9. Protect the parents' egos. Teachers don't place blame or make parents believe they are to blame for their child's deficiencies. They focus on the future. On the other hand, they give parents credit for their child's achievements.
10. Focus on one issue at a time. They are specific about the child's progress or concerns.
11. Listen. They hear the feeling and meaning of the message, and rephrase and check out the message to be sure that they received it correctly.
12. Become allies with parents.

Parents become partners in the educational process when they:

1. View the teacher as a source of support for their child and themselves.
2. Listen carefully and give total commitment to the speaker.
3. Show respect for the teacher—recognize that the teacher's concerns, opinions, and questions are significant to mutual understanding and communication.
4. Recognize that the teacher has a difficult challenge to meet the needs of all students. They help the teacher succeed.
5. Rephrase and check out understanding of messages during conversations or conferences.
6. Speak openly and honestly about the child.
7. Use concerns as forums for understanding the school and teacher.
8. Become allies with the teacher.

The following sections on positive speaking, listening, reflective listening, rephrasing, and reframing elaborate on each of these communication skills.

Positive Speaking

If your message is positive, the parent is more likely to want to listen. The relationship between teacher and parent is enhanced. A positive statement needs to be accompanied by attentive behavior, good body language, and a warm tone of voice. Add clear articulation, and you have the recipe for effective communication between parent and teacher.

Listening

Listening is the heart of effective communication. Listening is more than hearing sounds. Smith (1986) describes listening as the "basis for human interaction" (p. 246). It is the active process of interpreting, understanding, and evaluating the spoken and nonverbal speech as a meaningful message. Listening, not speaking, is the most-used form of communication. Forty-five percent of verbal communication is spent listening; 30 percent, speaking; 16 percent, reading; and 9 percent writing.

In education, much attention is given to the ability to write, yet there is very little training for listening. Greater understanding and retention of information would occur if an appropriate amount of time were spent on helping people listen effectively. Smith (1986) recommends these steps to improve listening skills:

1. *Be receptive.* Listeners encourage the speaker by being receptive and providing an environment where the speaker feels free to express ideas and feelings.
2. *Pay attention.* Make an effort to concentrate on what is being said.
3. *Use silence.* Communicate that you are listening through attentive behaviors while remaining silent.

4. *Seek agreement.* Look for the broader meaning of the message rather than focusing on isolated facts.
5. *Avoid ambiguity.* Ask questions to clarify, look for main ideas, and focus on intent as well as content.
6. *Remove distractions.* Eliminate daydreaming, remove physical barriers, and delay other important messages to make the climate clear for listening.
7. *Be patient.* Don't rush the speaker. Allow time for the message to be completed.

Teachers and parents communicate when they:

- Listen carefully to the other person.
- Have good eye contact.
- Encourage the speaker using body language and verbal expressions such as "yes."
- Observe the speaker and have a facial expression that shows interest.
- Respond with attentive body language such as leaning forward or touching.
- Can rephrase the substance and meaning of the message they receive from the speaker.

Poor listening is evident if the receiver:

- Has little eye contact.
- Displays a stiff appearance.
- Changes subjects.
- Looks uninterested.
- Is unable to rephrase or interpret the communication properly.

Communicating with Parents Without English Proficiency

Teachers will need to make special efforts to communicate with parents who have difficulty expressing themselves in English. For example, parents whose first language is not English may have difficulty being articulate in English. Parents who are emotionally distraught may not be able to receive the intended message. In these cases it is of even greater importance that teachers have excellent listening skills. They can recognize any miscommunication and strive for clearer understanding.

When parents or teachers listen, they not only increase knowledge and understanding of the message, but they also demonstrate a caring attitude. Listening reduces tension and stress and encourages trust (Center for Family Strengths, 1986).

Open Responses—Closed Responses

An open response encourages communication to continue. Open responses can vary from positive body language demonstrated by a nod of the head or a smile indicating that you wish the speaker to continue, to a verbal response in which you indicate your interest. If a child comes into a home or classroom with a caterpillar in hand ready to display the treasure to mother or teacher, an open response would be a smile, a nod, or a question such as, "Where did you find such a marvelous caterpillar?"

A closed response would be a frown or a comment such as, "Take that caterpillar away this very minute." What child would dare to explain that the caterpillar was a treasure?

Should a child be a problem to a teacher, the easy response to a question by the parent would be a closed response. "Why does John have trouble with arithmetic?" the parent asks. "If you would help him with his homework, he wouldn't have so much trouble," the teacher responds. The conversation is ended. No one has sought to communicate and find out the best way to handle the situation.

Reflective Listening

Reflective listening is the ability to reflect the speaker's feelings. The listener's response identifies the basic feelings being expressed and reflects the essence of those feelings back to the speaker. Reflective or active listening is used in several parent programs such as the Parent Effectiveness Training (PET) (Gordon, 1975, 2000), Active Parenting (Popkin, 2002), Parent's Handbook. Systematic Teaching of Effective Parenting (STEP) (Dinkmeyer, McKay & Dinkmeyer, 1997), and Teaching and Leading Children (Dinkmeyer, McKay, Dinkmeyer, & Dinkmeyer, 1992). These programs are described in the next section. The examples illustrate the use of active or reflective listening.

Reflective Listening and Reflective Responses

Reflective listening encourages open responses. A reflective response is effective if the listener recognizes the feelings of the speaker and is able to respond accordingly. The parent asks, "Why does John have trouble with arithmetic?" A reflective response would be, "You are concerned about John's ability to do his arithmetic?" The parent at that point probably would say "Yes."

To practice reflective listening think of the following three steps:

1. Use attending behavior. Make eye contact. Lean forward and be interested.
2. Listen for the feeling behind the message.
3. Respond with a statement of that feeling.

I–You–We Messages

One useful communication skill relies on "I" messages instead of "you" messages. A "you" message places the responsibility on the person receiving the message, and it is often a negative message. With a parent, it might be used in the following way. "If you would just help John with his homework, he would be more successful at school." To change that statement to a more positive "I" message, use words like those described in the following three steps:

1. "When [describe the behavior that is bothering you]."
2. "I feel [state how you feel about the concern]."
3. "Because [describe what you think might happen]."

For example, "*When* John does not finish his homework, *I feel* worried *because* I am afraid he will fall behind and not be able to catch up." Gordon (1975, 2000) introduced the "I" message and Dinkmeyer and McKay (1983, 1997) and Popkin (2002) use "I" messages in their parenting programs. There are times when a "we" message is more appropriate than an "I" message (Burr, 1990). "When Mary does not finish her homework, we have real concerns because she may fall behind her classmates." By using a "we" message the teacher acknowledges that the parent is also concerned.

Rephrasing

Rephrasing is restating the intent of the message in a condensed version. There are three steps in rephrasing. First, the listener must determine the basic message and the intent of the message. Second, the listener restates the intent of the message. Third, the listener checks out the accuracy of the rephrasing.

When listeners seek to check out or clarify a statement by saying something like, "It sounds as if you feel . . . " or "I'm hearing you say . . . " they are rephrasing the statement. With rephrasing, communicators can avoid misunderstanding the message by checking the accuracy. Confusion and ambiguity in communication are avoided. The interest displayed by rephrasing also shows caring and builds trust (Center for Family Strengths, 1986).

Reframing

Reframing involves taking the sting out of the negative description of a child. When communicating with parents, if your answer reflects your understanding of parents' concerns, the conversation will remain open, but the words you choose can bring either desirable or disastrous results.

A teacher with good intentions and great concern for a child once opened a conference with a parent by referring to the child's "problem" of not staying on task. The antagonized parent struck back: "I think you're obnoxious!" The family was already overwrought by strain and worry over the child. The rest of the conference time had to be devoted to rebuilding a working relationship, allowing no time for productive dialogue about the child and leaving both teacher and parent with emotional scars.

Instead of focusing on the negative aspects of an individual, start with positive comments. Then reframe the child's troublesome quality into an acceptable or even positive trait. Had the teacher started the conference with some friendly remarks and then stated, "I have some concerns about John that we should work on together," the parent might not have responded with such anger.

Examples of phrases that reframe a "problem" as a concern about the child include the following:

Problem	Concern
loud and boisterous	very active
gives others answers	can't help sharing
steals	takes without asking
won't follow rules	has own agenda, or is determined
shy	self-contained
talks too much	likes to share with others
does not pay attention	is preoccupied

It is particularly important in parent–teacher conferences and other communication between parent and teacher to couch the annoying behavior in terms that allow for dealing with it. There may be times, however, when the teacher's concern has reached such proportions that it must be faced squarely and openly. After several fruitless attempts at communicating, it may become obvious that the parent does not recognize that the behavior is hurting the child's progress. In such cases you may have to use more forthright terms. Just beware of the terminology you use. Harsh terms may completely cut off communication.

PARENT EDUCATION PROGRAMS—PET, ACTIVE PARENTING, STEP

Many parent education programs incorporate the resources of child-rearing suggestions in Parent Effectiveness Training (PET), Systematic Training for Effective Parenting (STEP), or Active Parenting. Excerpts from these programs illustrate the materials and communication techniques each uses.

Parent Effectiveness Training: The Proven Program for Raising Responsible Children

In PET, Gordon (1975, 2000) discusses many topics, including active listening, "I messages," changing behavior by changing the environment, parent–child conflicts, parental power, and "no-lose" methods for resolving conflicts. The following excerpt relates to problem ownership and active listening. Published originally in 1975, the Parent Effectiveness Training was followed by Teacher Effectiveness Training (TET) and later by Leader Effectiveness Training (LET). Parent Effectivness Training was revised in 2000, with current examples clarifying the methods of resolving conflicts and communicating effectively with children.

In the parent–child relationship, three situations occur that we will illustrate with brief case histories:

1. The child has a problem because he is thwarted in satisfying a need. It is not a problem for the parent because the child's behavior in no tangible way interferes with the parent's satisfying his own needs. Therefore, *the child owns the problem.*
2. The child is satisfying his own needs (he is not thwarted) and his behavior is not interfering with the parent's own needs. Therefore, *there is no problem in the relationship.*
3. The child is satisfying his own needs (he is not thwarted). But his behavior is a problem to the parent because it is interfering in some tangible way with the parent's satisfying a need of his own. *Now the parent owns the problem.*

It is critical that parents always classify each situation that occurs in a relationship. Which of these three categories does the following situation fall into? It helps to remember this diagram [see Figure 6.7].

When parents accept the fact that problems are owned by the child, this in no way means that the parents cannot be concerned, care, or offer help. Professional counselors have real concern for, and genuinely care about, each child they are trying to help. But, unlike most parents, the counselors leave the responsibility for solving the child's problem with the child. They allow the child to own the problem. They accept the child's having the problem. They accept the child as a person separate from herself or himself. And they rely heavily upon and basically trusts the child's own inner resources for solving the problem. Only because they let the child own the problem areas, the professional counselors are able to employ active listening.

Active listening is a powerful method for helping another person solve a problem that that person owns, provided the listener can accept the other's ownership and consistently allow the person to find the solutions. Active listening can greatly increase the effectiveness of parents as helping agents for their children, but it is a different kind of help from that which parents usually try to give.

Paradoxically, this method will increase the parent's influence on the child, but it is an influence that differs from the kind that most parents try to exert over their children. Active listening is a method of

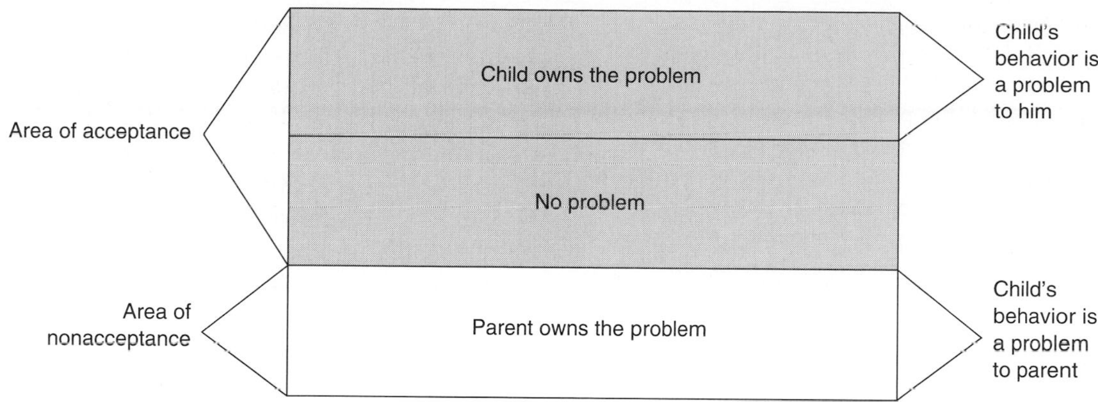

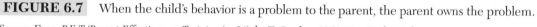

FIGURE 6.7 When the child's behavior is a problem to the parent, the parent owns the problem.

Source: From *P.E.T./Parent Effectiveness Training* (p. 64), by T. Gordon, 1975, New York: Wyden.

influencing children to find their own solutions to their own problems. Most parents, however, are tempted to take ownership of their children's problems, as in the following case:

Johnny: Tommy won't play with me today. He won't ever do what I want to do.
Mother: Well, why don't you offer to do what he wants to do? You've got to learn to get along with your little friends. *(advising; moralizing)*
Johnny: I don't like to do things he wants to do, and besides I don't want to get along with that dope.
Mother: Well, go find someone else to play with, then, if you're going to be a spoilsport. *(offering a solution; name-calling)*
Johnny: He's the spoilsport, not me. And there isn't anyone else to play with.
Mother: You're just upset because you're tired. You'll feel better about this tomorrow. *(interpreting; reassuring)*
Johnny: I'm not tired, and I won't feel different tomorrow. You just don't understand how much I hate the little squirt.
Mother: Now stop talking like that! If I ever hear you talk about one of your friends like that again, you'll be sorry. *(ordering; threatening)*
Johnny: (walking away and sulking) I hate this neighborhood. I wish we would move.

Here is how the parent can help the same boy with active listening.

Johnny: Tommy won't play with me today. He won't ever do what I want to do.
Mother: You're kinda angry with Tommy. *(active listening)*
Johnny: I sure am. I never want to play with him again. I don't want him for a friend.
Mother: You're so angry you feel like never seeing him again. *(active listening)*
Johnny: That's right. But if I don't have him for a friend, I won't have anyone to play with, then.
Mother: You would hate to be left with no one. *(active listening)*
Johnny: Yeah. I guess I just have to get along with him someway. But it's so hard for me to stop getting mad at him.
Mother: You want to get along better, but it's hard for you to keep from getting mad at Tommy. *(active listening)*
Johnny: I never used to, but that's when he was always willing to do what I wanted to do. He won't let me boss him anymore.
Mother: Tommy's not so easy to influence now. *(active listening)*
Johnny: He sure isn't. He's not such a baby now. He's more fun, though.
Mother: You really like him better this way. *(active listening)*
Johnny: Yeah. But it's hard to stop bossing him—I'm so used to it. Maybe we wouldn't fight so much if I let him have his way once in a while. Think that would work?
Mother: You're thinking that if you might give in occasionally, it might help. *(active listening)*
Johnny: Yeah, maybe it would. I'll try it.

In the first version, the mother used eight of the "Typical Twelve" categories of responding. In the second, the mother consistently used active listening. In the first, the mother "took over the problem"; in the

> second, her active listening left ownership of the problem with Johnny. In the first, Johnny resisted his mother's suggestions, his anger and frustration were never dissipated, the problem remained unresolved, and there was no growth on Johnny's part. In the second, his anger left, he initiated problem solving, and he took a deeper look at himself. He arrived at his own solution and obviously grew a notch toward becoming a responsible, self-directing problem solver.[1]

Gordon clarifies active listening and problem ownership through examples such as these. Parent groups follow up with a parent notebook and discussion within the group. Open discussion, led by a person knowledgeable about PET, allows parents to apply the methods to their own experiences in childrearing.

Systematic Training for Effective Parenting (STEP)

The STEP program offers a variety of training programs. The first, Systematic Training for Effective Parenting, which focused on children 6 to 12 years of age, was followed by Parenting Young Children: Systematic Training for Effective Parenting of Children Under Six, and Systematic Training for Effective Parenting of Teens. The *Parent's Handbook: Systematic Training for Effective Parenting* was written by Don Dinkmeyer Sr., Gary D. McKay, and Don Dinkmeyer Jr. (1997). STEP programs, offered in English and Spanish, furnish videos, a parent's manual, and a leadership and resource guide used to facilitate parent meetings. The child's goals in behavior, which include attention, power, revenge, and displays of inadequacy, are examined. Parents learn to understand their child and themselves through engaging in topics that include listening, encouraging, learning to cooperate, and understanding emotions and beliefs.

Active Parenting

The Active Parenting program is similar to both PET and STEP in that it is also based on the theories of Alfred Adler and Rudolf Dreikurs. Goals of misbehavior, logical consequences, active communication, exploring alternatives, and family council meetings are described. A handbook and workbook supplement the group meetings, and a leader's handbook gives detailed instruction on how the class should be conducted. Each session has a corresponding portion of a video that illustrates the child and family issues under discussion.

In the 21st century the founder, Michael Popkin (2002) added another method of delivery and offers online parenting classes. Enrollment in the course, Active Parenting Today Online Group, is limited to 25 persons for each 6-week session. The process includes two CDs, which contain course material with 159 minutes of video and instruction as well as the 164-page manual, *Active Parenting Today's Parents' Guide.*

PARENT–TEACHER CONFERENCES

A parent–teacher conference is a collaborative effort to coordinate the best possible effort for the education of the child in the classroom. It is a time

Eugenia Hepworth Berger

Keep records, paper, and anecdotal notes to share during parent–teacher conferences.

[1]From *P.E.T./ Parent Effectiveness Training* (pp. 64, 66–68), by T. Gordon, 1975, New York: Wyden.

for listening and sharing on the part of the school staff and the parents (Manning, 1985; Moles, 1996a). To accomplish the greatest cooperation between home and school and the greatest benefit for the student, the conference needs to continue the communication between the parent and school, based on agreed-upon goals for the child throughout the year.

Start the school year with a positive interchange between teacher and parent by an early telephone call or a block walk—to initiate the parent–school partnership. A preconference discussion can then be used to set goals and direction for the child during the school year. The goals should reflect that teacher and parent want what is best for the child. The first conference can be a progress and planning session based on those goals.

It is possible to get 100 percent attendance at conferences. In the National Association of Elementary School Principals (1994) discussion of exemplary programs, the Klondike Elementary School in West Lafayette, Indiana, reported a tradition of 100 percent participation at conferences. Rides are provided for parents without transportation. For parents who cannot come to the school, school personnel go to the home or workplace to have the conference. They feel it is worth the extra effort to have high-priority conferences.

Parent–teacher conferences are personal opportunities for two-way communication between parent and teacher or three-way communication among parent, teacher, and student. Parents, as well as teachers, recognize the conference as an excellent opportunity for clarifying issues, searching for answers, deciding on goals, determining mutual strategies, and forming a team in the education of the student. Most schools schedule conferences two or three times a year. How can conferences be as productive as possible and yet nonthreatening to parents, teachers, and students?

Collaborative Conversations

Collaborative conversations can help develop cooperation and resolution of issues. Koch and McDonough (1999), using an example of a young child who hit and bit other children, describe five stages to improve parent–teacher conferences through collaboration, with all parties part of the team.

Stage 1. *Development of trust.* It is essential that a trusting relationship be developed. This can be enhanced prior to the conference at back-to-school nights, home visits, and informal interactions at school.

Stage 2. *Invite.* Extend an invitation that promotes cooperation and involvement. For example: "When would be a good time for us to talk together about Mary? Would you prefer to talk at school or at your home? Is there anyone else involved with Mary who could join us? Between now and the time we meet, let's all notice when Mary expresses her feelings safely" (p. 12).

Stage 3. *Set a mutual goal.* Facilitate or have a facilitator establish a cooperative atmosphere. Focus on the positive actions of the child when she appropriately handled the situation. Come to an understanding of your goal to enhance the positive.

Stage 4. *Listen to all viewpoints and expand understanding.* Allow all participants to express their feelings and ideas. The discussion moves from "identification of and observations about the effects of the problem to a dialogue about the unique outcomes/exceptions and the significance of these for all persons concerned" (p. 14).

Stage 5. *Restate the goal, measure it, and decide what to do about it.* "Collaborative conversations create an atmosphere filled with possibilities and ideas that enhance the lives of children and the adults that care for them" (p. 14).

Invitations and Schedules

The invitation to attend a conference sets the tone. If it is cordial, shows an awareness of parents' busy lives and obligations, and gives the parents time options for scheduling the conference, the teacher has shown consideration of the parents and a desire to meet with them. Most school systems have worked out procedures for scheduling conference periods. Release time is usually granted teachers. Originally, most conferences took place in the afternoons. Children attended school in the mornings, and classes were dismissed at noon, with conferences between school personnel and parents—usually mothers only—occurring in the afternoon. With the increase in the number of working parents and single-parent families, plus the growing number of fathers becoming more directly involved in their children's education, many schools are scheduling more evening conferences, while retaining some afternoon conferences.

To prepare the schedule, notes are sent to parents asking for their time preference. The formal note should be direct and list specific options for the time and place of the conference. A sample note is found in Figure 6.8. After the responses have been returned, staff members, including teachers in special areas of education, meet to schedule back-to-back conferences for parents with more than one child attending the school.

A telephone call from the teacher to each parent adds a personal touch. These calls, made either before or after the invitation has been sent, may clarify questions and let the parents know they are really welcome.

Notes confirming the exact time and date of the conference should be sent home, whether the parent has been contacted or not. This ensures that both teacher and parent have the same understanding of the conference time. This confirmation note from the teacher to each parent could be personal, or a form could be used (see Figure 6.9).

A personal note might read:

> I am looking forward to meeting ______ 's parents. I enjoy her contribution to the class through her great interest in ______. The time and date of the conference are ______.

Private and Comfortable Meeting Place

How often have you gone into a school, walked down the halls, and seen parents and teachers trying to have a private conversation in the midst of children and other adults? To achieve open, two-way communication, parent and teacher need to talk in confidence. Select a room designed for conferences or use an empty classroom, and attach a note to the door so people won't interrupt. Give the parents adult-size chairs so they can be comfortable and on the same level as the teacher. Place a table in front of the chairs so materials, class projects, and the student's work can be exhibited. The parent, teacher, and student (if it is a three-way conference) can sit around the table and talk and exchange

Dear ______________________:

We are looking forward to meeting with you and discussing ______________ experiences and progress at school. Will you please let us know when a conference would be most convenient for you? Please check the date and time of day you could come.

Thank you,

____

Teacher or principal s name

Could you give a first and second choice? Please write "1" for your first preference and "2" for your second.

	Afternoon 1 to 4 P.M.	Evening 6 to 9 P.M.
Tuesday, November 12	______	______
Wednesday, November 13	______	______
Thursday, November 14	______	______

Please return by ______________________

FIGURE 6.8 Send a note home to schedule a conference.

Dear ______________________________:

Thank you for your response to our request for a conference time about your child's progress. Your appointment has been set for ________________ (time) on ________________ (day, month, and date) in room ________________ .

We have set aside ________________ minutes for our chance to talk together. If the above time is not convenient, please contact the office, and we can schedule another time for you.

We are looking forward to meeting with you.

Best wishes,

____

Teacher

FIGURE 6.9 This note confirms and reminds of conference times.

information. The room should be well ventilated and neither too warm nor too cold.

Teachers also should be alert to psychological and physical barriers. People conducting interviews often set up such barriers to maintain social distance or imply a status relationship; an executive may sit behind a desk to talk with a subordinate. When teachers set themselves apart from the parents, a barrier is created.

Two-Way Communication in Conferences

"At the heart of effective parent-teacher conferences specifically and the parent-teacher relationship in general are interpersonal communication skills" (Rotter & Robinson, 1986, p. 9). Conditions necessary for effective communication during conferences include warmth—an attitude of caring—shown through attentive behaviors, smiling, touching, and body language. Along with warmth is empathy, the ability to listen and respond in such a way that the parent knows you understand. Respect is key to the success of building a collaborative connection between parent and teacher. If teachers and parents respect each other and enter the conference with a warm, caring attitude, able to listen effectively and understand the other's meanings and feelings, the stage is set for a successful conference (Rotter & Robinson, 1986).

Some school administrators and teachers make the mistake of seeing parent–school communication as the school informing the parent about the educational process, rather than as a two-way system. During a conference the teacher should spend only about half the time speaking. If teachers recognize the conference as a sharing time, half the burden has been lifted from their shoulders. They can use half the time to get to know the parent and child better.

Have you ever had a conversation with a friend who seemed miles away in thought? During conferences, communicators need to believe that what they have to say is important to the listener. Body language can reflect feelings contrary to the spoken word, causing the verbal message to be misunderstood or missed altogether. It is important to be aware of what you are communicating. If you are rushed, pressured, or concerned about your own family, you will have to take a deep breath, relax, and concentrate on the conference.

Just as some physical gestures communicate distraction or lack of interest, so does some body language convey your interest and attention to parents' concerns. Use appropriate, attentive behavior to signal your interest.

1. *Eye contact.* Make sure you look at the person as you communicate. Failure to do so could imply evasion, deception, or lack of commitment.
2. *Forward posture.* Leaning forward creates the image of interest in what is being said. Be comfortable but do not slouch, which can indicate that the whole process is boring or unimportant.

3. *Body response.* A nod in agreement, a smile, and use of the body to create an appearance of interest promote empathy. If you act aware and interested, you will probably become interested. If you do not, perhaps you are in the wrong profession.

Listening has been known to be an effective tool of communication since the early 1960s, when Rogers affected methods of psychological counseling with his concept of reflective listening.

Earlier in this chapter we saw how the concept has been extended and reinterpreted in the day-to-day world of teaching parents and children. Gordon (1975) talked about the language of acceptance and the use of active listening as essential for improved parent–child relationships. Whether called "active" (Gordon, (1975, 2000) "effective" (Dinkmeyer & McKay, 1989), "responsive" (Chinn, Winn, & Walters, 1978), or "reflective" (Rogers, 1983), this kind of listening works. It helps open up the communication process.

Understandable Language

Specialized language gets in the way of communication. Although medical terminology is familiar and efficient for a doctor, it often sounds like a foreign tongue to a patient asking for an explanation of a diagnosis. Each year new terms and acronyms become common language in the schools, but they freeze communication when used with people not familiar with the terms. Imagine a teacher explaining to a parent that the school has decided to use the SRA program this year in second grade, but the first grade is trying whole language. Or one who says, "I've been using behavior modification with Johnny this year, and it has been very effective, but with Janet I find TA more helpful." Jargon can create misunderstanding and stop communication.

Sometimes terms have meaning for both communicators, but the meanings are not the same. Hymes (1974) declared that lack of communication, superficial communication, and "words and vocabulary, without friendship and trust and knowledge, get in the way of understanding" (p. 33).

> Look, for example, at "progressive education." Use those words and you have a fight on your hands. People get emotional, and wild charges fly. Yet parents will be the first to say, "Experience is the best teacher"—and there you have it! Different words, but a good definition of what progressive education stands for. (Hymes, 1974, p. 33)

Practice

To achieve the ability to listen reflectively and respond in a positive manner, practice until it becomes natural. You can practice alone, but it is more effective if you can role play the conference. Having an observer present provides both practice and feedback. Teachers can choose a typical case from among their records or invent a hypothetical one. For example:

> Andy, a precocious third-grade child, spends most of the class period doodling ideas in a notebook. Although he completes his assignments, Andy takes no pride in his work and turns in messy papers. Special enrichment centers in the classroom do not attract him. Andy participates positively during recess and in physical education and music.

Each participant in the role play has basic information: the child's sex, grade assigned, and background. Assign one participant to act as the parent, another as the teacher. The third member of the team observes the interaction between the parent and teacher to check on the following:

1. Reflective listening
2. Attentive behavior (eye contact, forward posture, etc.)
3. Sensitivity to parents' feelings
4. Positive language
5. Cooperative decision making

Because no two teachers or parents are identical, there is no prescribed way to have a conference. The dialogue will be a constant flow, filled with emotions as well as objective analysis. You can prepare yourself, however, by practicing good reflective listening and positive communication. Look forward to sharing together.

Preparation for the Conference

Two types of preparation will set the stage for a successful conference. The first, an optional program, involves training teachers and parents for an effective conference. The second is essential—analyzing the child's records, current performance and attitude, and relationship with peers, and gathering examples of work along with recent standardized test results.

Preconference Workshops and Guides

Workshops for parents, teachers, or a combination of both are fruitful. A discussion of what makes a conference a success or a calamity can bring forth an enormous number of tips for both parents and teachers. If parents and teachers form small groups, many ideas will emerge that can be recorded on the board for discussion later by the total group. Encourage parents to ask questions about their part in conferences. Clarifying objectives and expectations will help parents understand their responsibilities. Parents and teachers attending a workshop together can learn the art of reflective listening and communication. Role playing during conferences can elicit discussion. Many participants will see themselves in the roles portrayed and will attempt to find alternative methods of handling conference discussions. Films that illustrate common communication problems can also be used as starters for discussion.

At the close of the workshop, handouts or conference guides may be distributed to the participants. The guide should be designed with the school's objectives in mind. Parents can be told what to expect in the school's report and what the school expects from them. If your school does not schedule preconference workshops, put the handout in a newsletter and send it home to the parents before the conference. Questions in the conference guide should be those the school would like answered and also ones the parents might be interested in knowing. Typical questions include the following:

1. How does your child seem to feel about school?
2. Which activities does your child talk about at home?
3. Which activities seem to stimulate your child's intellectual growth?
4. How does your child spend free time?
5. Is there anything that your child dreads?
6. What are your child's interests and hobbies?

Some schools might also include questions about current concerns:

7. What concerns do you have about drugs and alcohol?
8. What kinds of support or collaboration would you like from the school to help your family?

A similar memo suggests questions the parents might want to ask:

1. How well does my child get along with other children? Who seem to be my child's best friends?
2. How does my child react to discipline? What methods do you use to promote self-discipline and cooperation?
3. Does my child select books at the proper reading level from the library?
4. Does my child use study periods effectively?
5. Are there any skills you are working on at school that we might reinforce at home?
6. Do you expect me to help my child with homework?
7. Are there any areas in which my child needs special help?
8. Does my child display any special interests or talents at school that we might support at home?
9. Does my child seem to be self-confident, happy, and secure? If not, what do you think the home or school can do to increase my child's feelings of self-worth?

Supplying questions before the conference is helpful in preparing parents, but it can also limit questions that develop naturally. In addition, if these questions are strictly adhered to during conferences, they can limit the scope, direction, and outcome of the conference. A checklist (Figure 6.10) can help ensure everything is covered.

Teacher Preparation

Throughout the school year teachers should make a practice of accumulating anecdotal records, tests, workbooks, art projects, and papers that represent both academic and extracurricular areas. Folders created by students, an accordion file, or a file box or cabinet can store the papers until conference

Conference Checklist

Yes	No	Did You
❑	❑	1. Review information about the child's family? Did you know the parents' last names? Were you aware of the child's educational experience?
❑	❑	2. Prepare ahead by collecting anecdotal records, tests, papers, notebooks, workbooks, and art materials from the beginning to the end of the reporting period?
❑	❑	3. Provide book exhibits, displays, or interesting reading for parents as they waited for their conferences?
❑	❑	4. Make arrangements for coffee or tea for parents as they waited for their conferences?
❑	❑	5. Prepare your room with an attractive display of children's work?
❑	❑	6. Welcome the parents with a friendly greeting?
❑	❑	7. Start on a positive note?
❑	❑	8. Adjust your conference to the parents' needs and levels of understanding?
❑	❑	9. Have clear objectives for the conference?
❑	❑	10. Say in descriptive terms what you meant? Did you avoid educational jargon and use of initials?
❑	❑	11. Listen reflectively?
❑	❑	12. Keep the communication lines open? Were you objective and honest?
❑	❑	13. Avoid comparing students or parents? Did you discuss other teachers only if it was complimentary?
❑	❑	14. Check your body language? Were you alert to the parents' body language?
❑	❑	15. Plan the child's educational program together?
❑	❑	16. Summarize your decisions? Did you make a record of your agreements and plans?
❑	❑	17. Begin and end on time? If you needed more time, did you set up another appointment?
❑	❑	18. Follow up with a note and a telephone call?

If you had the student lead the conference, in addition to the above

Yes	No	Did You
❑	❑	1. Work with the student to develop goals and objectives?
❑	❑	2. Encourage the student to achieve his/her goals and objectives?
❑	❑	3. Have the student prepare a portfolio with projects, papers, research, tests, and other achievements?
❑	❑	4. Have practice sessions in which the student developed the ability to explain objectives and progress? (Students may work with partners and/or other peers.)
❑	❑	5. Make yourself available to discuss the student's progress with the family during the conference period?

FIGURE 6.10 A checklist reviews important conference practices.

time. Students may then compile a notebook or folder of samples of their work to share with their parents during conferences. If the file is worked on periodically throughout the term, papers can be placed in chronological order, thus illustrating the progress in each subject. The child's work is an essential assessment tool.

Standardized tests that reveal the child's potential compared with actual performance level are useful in tailoring an education program to fit the student. With this information, parents and teachers can discuss whether the student is performing above or below potential. Parents and teachers can use the information to plan for the future.

One word of caution on the use of standardized tests: These tests are not infallible. One child might not feel well on the day of testing; another might freeze when taking tests. Standardized test results should be used to supplement informal assessment tools such as class papers, notebooks, class observation, and informal tests, but not to replace those tools. With the increasing number of tests children are now mandated to take at every grade level, it is very possible that children will "burn out" or simply refuse to complete the standardized tests. Therefore, it is important to be selective in administering tests.

If standardized test results and your informal assessment are congruent and the child scores high on aptitude tests and shows moments of brilliance in class but consistently falls short on work, you can be fairly certain that the child is not working up to ability. If the child scores low but does excellent work in class, observe closely before deciding that the child is under too much pressure to achieve. In that case, the test may not indicate the child's true potential. Should the child score low on the test and also show a high level of frustration when working, you may want to make plans to gear the work closer to the child's ability. The standardized test, used as a backup to the informal assessment, can help teachers and parents plan the child's educational program.

Congruent Beliefs About the Child

Have you ever had a disruptive child in a class only to discover that the child was retiring and well behaved during Scouts? Sometimes the disparity makes one wonder if it is the same child. It is difficult to discuss a child on common ground if the parents' and teacher's perceptions of the child are completely different. Teachers and parents may need to compare their perceptions of the child. It is often meaningful to have students sort their own views so the perceptions of teacher, parents, and student can be compared.

Conference Membership

When children are taught by more than one teacher or have contact with numerous specialists (such as a speech teacher or physical therapist), including all professionals involved with the child is appropriate and requires cooperative planning. Beware of the effect on the parent, however, because a ratio of four professionals to one parent may be awesome and foreboding. If special care is taken to assure parents that all specialists are there to clarify and work with the teacher and parent as a team, the cooperative discussion and planning can have worthwhile results.

An alternative plan allows the parent to talk individually with each involved specialist. In some schools the homeroom teacher reports for all the specialists, but personal contact with each person involved with the child's education is more satisfying to the parents. If time is short, the entire group could meet with the parents once in the fall and assure the parents they will be available whenever the parents have a concern.

Consider including the child in the conference. Who is better equipped to clarify why the child is doing well or needs extra help? Who has more at stake? Preschoolers make less sustained conference members, but as soon as the child becomes interested in assessment and evaluations and recognizes the goal of parent–teacher conferences, the teacher should consider including the child in the process. Initially, the child may attend for a short portion of the conference, but as interest and attention span increase, the child might be present for the entire conference. If portions of the conference need to be conducted without the child present, have a supervised play area available. If older students are included as members of the team, issues can be clarified and goals set. The student is part of the discussion and helps in setting realistic goals.

Bjorklund and Burger (1987) describe a four-phase process for collaboration with parents. *Phase 1*, scheduled early in the year, sets the stage with an overview of when conferences will take place, techniques for observation of the children, and a detailed account of the curriculum based on developmental goals. During this phase, both the teachers and parents are encouraged to consider the developmental goals of the program. *Phase 2* is based on the goals. Parents, teachers, and administrators meet and set priorities using observation, testing, anecdotal records, and work samples. Two to four goals are given priority for each child.

In *Phase 3*, observations, anecdotal records, checklists, and rating scales are collected for review.

Phase 4 involves the child. The teacher sends a progress report home in which all the developmental areas are reviewed. A guide for the conference is also sent, with three questions that parents should discuss with the child before the meeting. These are: (a) What do you like best about school? (b) Who are some of the special friends you like to play with at school? (c) Are there any things at school you would like to do more often? "The teacher begins the progress conference by sharing examples of the child's growth through anecdotes which describe some of the child's best skills or characteristics. This leads into a discussion of the three questions with the child" (Bjorklund & Burger, 1987, p. 31). The conference promotes a good self-image for the child by emphasizing the child's positive growth.

Student–Teacher–Parent Conferences

Many schools have conferences that give the task of deciding about objectives and goals to students. The advantage of this approach is that it empowers students to be responsible for their own learning. The conference planning involves the teacher, any special professionals, and the student. In a private setting, the teacher and student decide what the student is going to accomplish.

When conference time arrives, the student and teachers meet in advance to decide what they will talk about at conference time and what they will put in the portfolio to share with the parents. These conferences involve more planning with the student than the traditional conference. At conference time, the student leads the discussion of what has been accomplished, what needs to be worked on, and what the future goals are. The concept behind this conference is similar to the Individualized Education Plan in that plans are made for individual students, but the pupil is more responsible for determining the objectives and goals.

Some schools organize student–teacher–parent conferences into a participatory situation with four sets of parents and children meeting at the same time. Each set discusses the child's achievements and goals. The teacher enters the discussion whenever a parent or child has questions or comments, or when the teacher has a reason for participating in their conference. At some point during the session, each set of parents and students include the teacher in their discussion.

Different issues arise with this change in the format of the conference. With this type of conference, the child and parents are responsible for its success. Teachers must have good organizational and leadership skills so that the student has established goals and direction before the conference. During the conference the teacher will not have the opportunity to monopolize the discussion, but the student and parents must take the teacher's responsibility seriously if the conference is to be successful.

Congruent Conferences

Conferences go more smoothly when the teacher and parents have congruent expectations about the performance of the child. If the child is an excellent student and both teacher and parents are pleased with the evaluation, it is easy to accept the report.

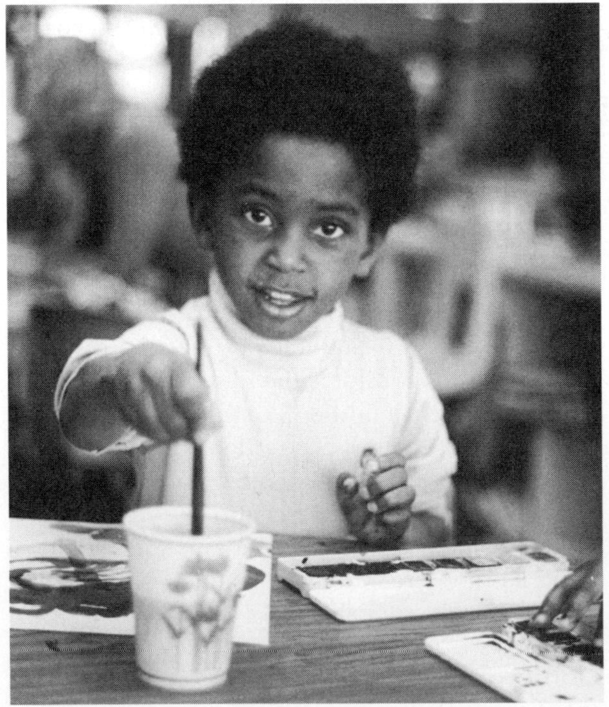

Eugenia Hepworth Berger

To promote the well being of this child, conferences need to be cooperative with the teacher sensitive to the parent's feelings.

If the child has a disability and both teacher and parents recognize the disabling condition, they can work together to plan an appropriate program for the child.

Too often the outward signs of good marks and pleasant personality and behavior fail to uncover how the child feels and whether the teacher can make the educational experience more satisfying and challenging. In working with a successful student, parents and teachers may fail to communicate about the child's potential and the need to have a good self-concept. Special interests of the child, friends, reading preferences, experiences, and needs are important for the teacher to know. Bring the child into the decision-making process. Together, the parents, teacher, and child can plan activities that will encourage growth and improve self-concept. Let these parents and children communicate, too.

Situation

Julie is one of those students every teacher loves to have in class. She is enthusiastic, stays on task, completes her work, and never causes a disturbance. A quiet, attractive girl with her long brown hair pulled back in a ponytail, Julie always does the correct thing. She is polite to everyone and avoids fighting or taking sides when others are arguing.

Mrs. Collins relaxed in her chair as she prepared for the conference with Julie's parents. What an easy conference, she thought. I really don't have to talk with Julie's parents because she fits into the routine, is well adjusted, and is progressing nicely. As she looked up, she saw Mrs. Rivers, Julie's mother, standing outside the door. She rose to greet her and led her into the room, offering her a chair. As they sat side by side, Mrs. Collins remarked, "It is really good to see you, Mrs. Rivers. I enjoy Julie in class, and she is having no problems. Here are some of the papers I have collected. You can see that she completes her work and does a good job. I wish all my students were like Julie."

After looking over the papers, Mrs. Rivers looked up and said, "It is nice not to have to worry about Julie. I wish that Anne were as conscientious. I'm dreading that conference. I've really enjoyed having you be Julie's teacher."

Mrs. Rivers and Mrs. Collins glanced at Julie's papers and leaned back, satisfied.

"Look at the time; we finished in 10 minutes," Mrs. Rivers said. "You have five minutes to spare. Have a good day."

"You have a good day, too," the teacher said as she escorted Julie's mother to the door.

1. What did the conference accomplish?
2. Could there be a problem? How does Julie feel?
3. What should Mrs. Rivers and Mrs. Collins consider as they think about Julie? Does Julie feel good about herself? Is she a class leader? Does she get along well with the other children?
4. What does she enjoy doing the most? Is there anything that might make her school career even better?

Situation

"Welcome, Mrs. Alene. We are so pleased to have Joel with us this year," said Joel's preschool teacher, Mr. Better, greeting the boy's mother.

"He's just so happy to be here," Mrs. Alene said. "He was a little anxious at first, but you have made him feel welcome."

"I'm pleased Joel is beginning to feel comfortable. I noticed that he is interacting with the other children more—he played on the jungle gym today. His coordination is improving, and he is much more outgoing than he was 3 weeks ago when he first started. Let me share some of his paintings and some stories we have recorded. He illustrated this story. Look at the detail. What a great imagination!"

Mr. Better and Mrs. Alene looked at the papers together.

"What does Joel enjoy doing at home?" Mr. Better asked.

"He becomes very involved in building with his Lego set," Mrs. Alene said. "He loves to have us read him stories. We share stories together each afternoon and in the evening before he goes to bed. I try to limit his television viewing, though he does get to watch *Sesame Street* and *Mister Rogers* occasionally."

"Does he have any children to play with in his neighborhood?"

"There are no 4-year-old children, but Bobby, who lives down the street, is in kindergarten, and he plays with Joel about 3 times a week."

"I'll bet they play hard, too!" Mr. Better said, and then turned to the current class activities.

"Our theme for this month is the sun," he said. "We're studying about shadows, reflections, and how the sun helps flowers to grow. These are some of the collages we have made. As you can tell, a lot of the pictures were made by tearing the paper, but we are also working on cutting. Let me show you how we are having him hold his scissors. Do you think you can help him with this at home? I'll be sending home activity suggestions and notes that let you know what we are doing at school."

"Thank you," Mrs. Alene said. "That way, I'll be more able to help Joel at home if he needs it."

"Why don't you go into the observation room and watch him for a while before you leave," Mr. Better said. "Don't forget that you can observe anytime, and you might want to volunteer to help in the preschool."

Joel's mother looked surprised and answered, "I hadn't thought about that, but it might be enjoyable."

"What haven't we covered? Do you have any questions that we neglected to discuss?" Mr. Better asked. After a pause, he added, "It was nice to be able to share with you about Joel's experiences here. Be sure to call if you have any concerns or if something is happening at home that we should know about. We want to keep in touch."

"I enjoyed talking with you. I can see why Joel enjoys school so much. Goodbye," Joel's mother said as she walked toward the observation room.

1. What was effective in this conference?
2. Did the mother get to share enough?
3. What would you suggest to make it better?

Situation

Benny, a charming 7-year-old with big brown eyes, curly black hair, and a sparkling smile, seemed older and larger than most children his age. When he came into the classroom before school started, he always went up to Miss Allen and told her about what was going on in his neighborhood. The stories were usually about fights, guns, holdups, gangs, and anger. There was reason to believe that he was relating what he had actually witnessed or heard. Benny lived with his father; his mother had disappeared several years earlier and, although Benny knew she was still alive, he had no contact with her. At one period in Benny's life, he lived in a cardboard box. Life had not been easy for this child, who had experienced much change and abuse.

When school starts, Benny is unable to stay on task. He seems to crave attention, whether it be from sharing, describing a story in the author's chair, or acting out. His primary method of obtaining attention is through acting out. He speaks out of turn, takes pencils from other children, and shoves and pushes. Because he is large for his age, he can hurt another child with a shove.

One day, Benny threatened an aide working in the classroom by suggesting that his older sister would beat her up. Timeout does not help because he does not oblige, but he does seem to be threatened by a trip to the office. The school year is in its fourth week and there have been no parent–teacher conferences.

1. What would you suggest the teacher do to obtain parent collaboration?
2. Do you believe that parent–school cooperation is feasible? Why or why not?
3. What could you do as a teacher to help Benny become a productive child?
4. Would a conference that included Benny and his father be a good idea? Why or why not?
5. If you believed that Benny comes from an abusive home, would you change your approach? Why or why not?

Preconference Preparation

Before the day of the conference and throughout the reporting period, you, as the teacher, prepare by getting to know the student, conducting ongoing assessment, and developing a portfolio. Before the conference, review the child's history, family situation, successes, and concerns. Depending on which records are kept by the school, try to learn about the student's educational experience. Review the papers in the current portfolio so that you can know the student's growth or delay that has occurred under your guidance.

Try to have 3- to 5-minute individual conferences with each child to talk about what you are going to cover in the conference. Determine if there is anything that the child would like to see included, thus providing you insight into the child's thoughts. If you recognize the child's thoughts as important you increase the child's respect for self and belief in the teacher or a caring ally.

The Day of the Conference

During the conference, review your objectives, use effective communication skills, discuss concrete examples of work, and plan together.

Clear Statement of Objectives

Some objectives may be universal; others will be specific for the individual conference. Use the following objectives as a guide:

1. To gain a team member (the parent) in the education of the child
2. To document the child's progress for the parent
3. To explain the educational program you are using as it relates to the individual child
4. To learn about the environment in which the child lives
5. To allow the parents to express feelings, questions, and concerns
6. To get a better understanding of the expectations the parent holds for the child
7. To set up a lasting network of communication among parent, teacher, and child
8. To establish cooperative goals for the education of the child

Recognition of the Parent as Part of the Team

After you have made sure the room is comfortable, two-way communication will be uninterrupted, and you are ready to listen and be responsive to the parent, it is easy to recognize the parent as a part of the educational team. Parents arrive at conferences as experts on their children's history, hobbies, interests, likes and dislikes, friends, and experiences. You, as the teacher, can gain a great deal of knowledge and understanding of the child from the parents.

The Conference

Begin the conference in a relaxed, positive manner. Besides being adept at reflective listening, you need to listen intuitively to determine if parents have problems within their homes or are themselves emotionally immature. Such problems make it difficult for the child to have the home support needed for educational success. When indicated, invite other professionals, such as the school's social worker or principal, to the conference to support and help the family and child. You can be more understanding of the child's needs if you understand the child's home (Grissom, 1971).

Why do parents enter into parent–teacher conferences with apprehension? Some are worried because they want the best for their child but do not know how to achieve it. They are unsure of themselves in the discussion and might be threatened by jargon. If parent and teacher can throw away their usual roles during the conference and view it as a meeting place for the exchange of ideas and information and a chance to support each other, both can enter into the conference with enthusiasm and confidence.

Relax before conference time. It is important to establish a cooperative climate. If the teacher is relaxed and poised, parents will be able to relax, too, and the climate for communication will be improved. Meyers and Pawlas (1989) recommend developing a form to use for record keeping for planning as well as keeping records for future conferences. The teacher is able to focus on one or two predetermined issues and keep records of the collaboration. Multiple concerns can be overwhelming; time does not allow all issues to be resolved. When determining the issues to be discussed, however, parents should have the option of helping determine the agenda. Perhaps they have a concern that is not known by the teacher. They can either share their concerns by sending back an information sheet suggesting what they would like to discuss, or during the conference the teacher can encourage them to bring up their concerns or comments.

Sandwich Approach

Use the sandwich approach when you plan a conference (Manning, 1985). Start the conference with pleasant and positive items. If you have negative comments or concerns to be discussed, bring them up during the middle of the conference. Always end with a positive summary, spend time planning with parents, and make a pleasant comment about the child.

Team Membership

Explain to the parents that all participants in the conference are members of a team looking at the progress of the child and working together to benefit the child. How can *we* help the child who is having a difficult time? How can *we* enrich the program for the child who is accelerated? How can *we* get the child to do the task at hand? How can *we* promote self-esteem? If the teacher and parents work as a team to answer these questions, the conference will be far more productive than if the teacher simply dictates answers to the parents. Here are some tips that will help parents feel they are part of the team:

- Know the parent's name. Do not assume that the child and parent have the same last name. Look in the record for the correct name.
- Ensure the privacy of the conference.
- Know the time limitations.
- Do not use terminology that may have meaning for you but not the parent.
- Do not refer to organizations, forms, tests, materials, or ideas by their initials or acronyms. Do not assume that everyone knows what the initials or acronyms mean.
- Have some questions about and show interest in the child.
- Remind parents that they may ask questions at any time and you will be pleased to explain anything that is not clear.
- Begin on a positive note. Start by praising an accomplishment of the child or a contribution the child has made to the class.
- Review your file and know enough about the child before the parent arrives that the parent can tell you have taken a personal interest in the child's welfare.
- Keep on the subject: the child's schooling and development.
- Encourage the parents to contribute. Allow parents to talk for at least 50 percent of the time.
- Show that you understand the parent by checking periodically during the conference. For example, you might ask, "Would you agree with this?" or "Do you have suggestions to add about this?"
- Make note of an idea suggested by a parent, but do not get so involved in writing that you lose the flow of the conversation.
- Maintain eye contact.
- Use attentive behaviors—that is, lean forward, look interested, and nod when in agreement.
- Do not ignore a parent's question.
- Be honest, yet tactful and sensitive, to the parent's feelings.
- Base your discussion on objective observation and concrete examples of work.
- Deal in specifics rather than generalities whenever possible.
- Evaluate needs and select methods of remediating deficiencies.
- Evaluate strengths and select methods of enriching those strengths.
- Plan educational goals together.
- Clarify and summarize the discussion.
- Make plans to continue the dialogue.

Concrete Examples of Child's Work and Behavior

Both parent and teacher are interested in the child's accomplishments. By making objective observations of the child's classroom behavior, with anecdotal notes collected in a loose-leaf notebook, throughout the reporting periods, the teacher documents the child's social as well as intellectual achievements. Anecdotal records of significant behaviors are especially valuable for conferences with parents of young children. Papers and tests may not be available, so the anecdotal records become tools for evaluating the child's social, intellectual, and physical progress. In the case of children with behavioral problems, it is also important to be able to cite specific incidents rather than vague generalizations about disturbances.

The accumulated examples of the child's work with a few words from the teacher also illustrate to parents what their child is doing. It is not necessary to state when a child has not progressed, for that will be obvious. If another child has made great progress, that too will be evident from the samples collected. Consider asking parents if they have come to the same conclusion as you when comparing early and subsequent papers.

Some teachers supplement papers and anecdotal records with videotapes of children in the classroom. Although time consuming, a film or video report is enjoyable for parents and encourages interaction between parent and teacher on the child's classroom participation.

Bringing concrete examples to the conference illustrating the child's work may prevent a confrontation and allows parent and teacher to analyze the work together. Include anecdotal records and samples of the child's work in comparison with expected behavior at that age level. In preschool this may include fine-motor control, large-muscle activities, art, and problem solving. For school-age children, examples may include papers, artwork, projects, work in academic subjects, tests, notebooks, workbooks, and anecdotal records. It is also helpful to parents for the teacher to collect a set of unidentified "average" papers. If parents want to compare their child's work with that of the "average" child, they have a basis for this comparison.

Whatever the level of the child's performance, the parent and teacher need to form a team as they evaluate the child's educational progress and work together for the good of the child.

Use the conference form recommended by Meyers and Pawlas to keep a record. Parents and teacher—and student, if in attendance—decide on goals, highlights or accomplishments, and plans for the future. All attendees should read and sign the conference form and retain a copy.

Postconference Plans

After the conference, write a note thanking the parents for their participation. Later, in a follow up telephone call, let the parents know how the conference plans are being implemented and how the student is participating. Each contact increases the parent-school collaboration.

A checklist may be used for self-evaluation, as shown in Figure 6.10. If you are able to answer yes to these questions, you are ready to have productive parent-teacher conferences.

Dealing with Angry Parents

What do you do when an upset and angry parent confronts you? Most professionals face such a situation at one time or another. Margolis and Brannigan (1986) list seven steps to help you control the volatile situation and allow the parent to regain composure. If you understand the dynamics of anger, you can engage in reflective listening. As a result, you can redirect the wrath and empathize with the parent. The steps include the following:

1. Remain calm and courteous, and maintain natural eye contact through the barrage. After the parents have expressed their anger, usually dominated by emotion, ask them to repeat their concerns so you can understand the situation better. The second time around, the statements are usually more comprehensible and rational.
2. Use reflective listening and give reflective summaries of their statements. You can explore the content of their messages later, but during this stage attempt to establish a more relaxed and trusting atmosphere.
3. Continue with reflective listening, and ask some open-ended questions that allow them to talk more as you gain greater understanding.
4. Keep exploring until you have determined what the underlying critical issues are. Do not evaluate, and do not be defensive.
5. After the issues have been fully explored, rephrase and summarize, including points of agreement. Check to see if your summary of their concerns is correct. Offer to let them add to what you have summarized. When you clearly define the concerns, they often seem more manageable.
6. Margolis and Brannigan (1986) point out that by now, listening has been used to build trust and defuse the anger. You are more likely to understand the problem from the parent's perspective. "When steps one through five are followed in an open, sincere, and empathetic manner, disagreements frequently dissolve and respect emerges" (p. 345). If such is not the case, go back and allow free exploration again.
7. Use a systematic problem-solving approach to any issues that remain unresolved. The steps in collaborative problem solving include: (a) understand each other's needs and the resources available to help satisfy those needs, (b) formulate a hypothesis that might solve the problem, (c) brainstorm other solutions, (d) combine ideas and solutions to create new solutions, (e) together, develop criteria to judge the solutions, (f) clarify and evaluate solutions, and (g) select the most likely solution. At the end of the confrontation, the result should satisfy both educator and parent.

Situation

"I've never come to a school conference without having to wait 45 minutes to talk with you. Then, when I get in, you rush me, never let me ask questions, and just tell me how poorly Mary is doing. I know that Mary is doing poorly! I have my hands full just trying to go to work and feed my four children. Can't you do something to help Mary? Do you care?" Mary's father breathlessly expressed his anger and frustration.

"Hold on, Mr. Wimble," Mr. Bush said. "You're responsible for Mary, not me. She does poorly because she doesn't pay attention; she's more interested in her friends than in school, and she cuts class. I can work with students who come to school ready to learn. I just don't have the strength or the patience to take on your daughter until she changes her attitude."

"I waited 45 minutes to hear that?" Mr. Wimble asked. "What's going on here? No wonder Mary skips school. Where's the superintendent's office? I need to talk with your supervisor." Mr. Wimble stalked out of the room.

1. How could Mr. Bush respond in a manner to reduce Mr. Wimble's anger?
2. What kind of interaction should take place to promote problem solving?
3. Is there anything Mr. Bush can do to help this situation?
4. What can Mr. Wimble do to help resolve his daughter's problems?
5. What responsibility does Mary have?

Making a Contract—Parent–Teacher Communication

Most teachers have experienced working with children who do not stay on task, daydream, act out in class, or seem to be wasting their potential. Parents of these children are usually just as concerned as the teacher. In a contract arrangement, the parents are empowered to get involved in the child's school behavior. In an effort to increase the student's positive participation in school, teachers and parents have an ongoing communication system that acknowledges how the child does in school. Parents and teachers work together to establish the goals and parameters of the contract. Usually a note is sent home each day detailing how the student performed at school. This includes schoolwork as well as classroom behavior. The parents reinforce the positive behavior and help diminish the negative. By communicating each day, parents and teachers form a team to help the child become successful in school, by focusing on the goals of the contract—which includes schoolwork as well as behavior.

Kelley (1990) describes a home-based reinforcement method in her book on school–home notes. It is based on behavioral theory and is similar to the contract method. This approach is beneficial for children who are disruptive, do not stay on task, or are not performing up to their abilities. The school–home note or daily report card is an intervention method that requires the participation of parents as well as teachers. Together they collaborate on problem solving and determine their approach. Each day the teacher completes a simple form and sends it home, letting the parents know how the child behaved and participated in class that day. The parent follows up with consequences. It is important that the consequences fit and that they have the desired result. "The goals in any contingency management system are to reinforce appropriate behavior (so as to increase its frequency) and to ignore or punish inappropriate or unacceptable behavior (so as to decrease its frequency)" (p. 16).

If the school–home contract or notes are not working, the teachers and parents should meet again and revise their plan.

DEALING WITH CONCERNS THROUGHOUT THE YEAR

The following principles (Franklin, 1993) will help facilitate good home-school communication as issues emerge throughout the year.

1. Approach the parents at every meeting with the assumption that you have a common goal—a good environment in which the child can learn and develop.
2. Try to facilitate the best in the parent, just as you support and try to develop the best potential in the child.

3. Avoid confrontation and defensive responses. Model working together as partners.
4. Assess your motives before giving negative feedback to parents. Why are you telling this to the parent? What do you hope will come out of the exchange? Will it help the child's learning? Do you expect a positive outcome?
5. Avoid setting yourself up as an authority figure with parents. Work toward establishing a partnership with the parents. Respect the parents' knowledge of their child and ask them to share information with you. Parents and teachers can learn from each other and provide different perspectives.
6. Try to avoid judging the parent, just as you hope they are not focused on evaluating you.
7. Give a careful and thoughtful response to parent concerns. Be available and unhurried in your interaction.
8. There are no typical responses from parents. They are as different from one another as teachers are from one another. Be an active listener, and remain open to different perspectives.

SUMMARY

Effective communication between parents and schools allows parents to become partners in education. Communication includes speaking, listening, reflection of feelings, and interpretation of the meaning of the message. If the message sent is not correctly interpreted by the receiver, then miscommunication has occurred. It can be overcome by rephrasing and checking out meanings. Talking is not the most important element in communication. The way a message is spoken and the speaker's body language account for 93 percent of the message.

It is essential for schools to have good communication with families. One-way communication describes the method that schools use when they offer parents information through newsletters, newspapers, media, and handbooks. Two-way communication allows parents to communicate with school personnel through telephone calls, home visits, classroom visits, and school functions. It continues through the year with classroom visits and participation, back-to-school nights, parent education groups, school programs, projects, workshops, PTA carnivals, exchanges, and a suggestion box.

Parents and schools both put up roadblocks to communication. Parent roadblocks include the following roles: protector, inadequate-me, avoidance, indifferent-parent, don't-make-waves, and club-waving advocate. Roadblocks put up by schools include the following roles: authority-figure, sympathizing-counselor, pass-the-buck, protect-the-empire, and busy-teacher.

Effective communication and trust building between parent and educator are important. The areas of communication that can be developed include positive speaking, listening, reflective listening, rephrasing, reframing, and attentive behavior. PET, STEP, and Active Parenting all include communication with an emphasis on reflective or active listening in their parent education format.

Parent–teacher conferences are the most common of two-way exchanges. Conferences can be effective if educators and parents prepare for them in advance. Teachers need to make parents feel welcome; materials and displays should be available. Two-way conversations will build cooperation and trust. Teachers can develop expertise in conducting conferences by relating to the parents, developing trust, and learning from them about the child. A checklist is included to analyze the effectiveness of the conference.

The chapter includes suggestions for dealing with angry parents and how to deal with concerns parents may have throughout the year.

SUGGESTED CLASS ACTIVITIES AND DISCUSSIONS

1. Develop a simple newsletter, a note to parents, and a detailed newsletter.
2. Practice speaking positively. Develop situations in which a child has average ability, has a learning disability, or is gifted. Role play the parent and the teacher. Make the interaction focus on positive speaking. Then reverse your approach and become negative in your analysis of the child. How did you feel during each interchange? You can videotape the role playing, so you can analyze the results objectively.
3. Practice listening. Divide the class into groups of three. One person is the speaker, another is the listener, and the third is the observer. Exchange roles so each person in the group gets to play each role. Have each person select a topic of interest, from something as simple as "my favorite hideaway" to something as serious as "coping with death in my family." Each person tells a story; the listener listens and then repeats or rephrases the story. The observer watches for body language, attentive behavior, interest, and correct rephrasing. A checklist is an excellent way to make sure the observer watches for all elements of listening.

4. Visit a school and obtain a copy of the school's newsletter. Analyze it. Does it communicate with parents effectively? How would you improve it?
5. Consider your beliefs and value system. What beliefs might be blocks to communication with parents, particularly those with a different value system?
6. Brainstorm in class for words to use in rephrasing. For example, what words could you use to describe a child who hands in sloppy work?
7. Role-play the parent putting up roadblocks to communication.
8. Role-play the roadblocks that schools put up that hinder communication.
9. Sit in on a staffing or a parent-teacher conference. Observe the parents' and the educators' interaction.
10. Compose situations that need constructive, positive answers. Make up several answers that would be appropriate for each situation.

WEB SITES

Association for Childhood Education International (ACEI)
www.acei.org
ACEI publishes the journals *Childhood Education* and *Journal of Research in Childhood Education.* A series of documents is available on the Web site.

Frank Porter Graham Child Development Institute
www.fpg.unc.edu
The institute, housed at the University of North Carolina, Chapel Hill, offers a wide range of information and knowledge on a child's development.

National Association for the Education of Young Children
www.naeyc.org
NAEYC publishes a journal, *Young Children,* which includes articles about child growth, development, and literacy. Its Web site suggests books for children and families.

Reading Is Fundamental
www.rif.org
Reading is fundamental to communication.

Teaching Strategies
www.teachingstrategies.com
Teaching Strategies offers information, training materials, and parenting resources to help children birth through 8 years of age.

Zero to Three
www.zerotothree.org
Zero to Three provides support and information for parents of infants through age 3. Included is BrainWonders, which has information about brain development.

7 Collaborative Leadership—Working with Parents

A leader is best
When people barely know that he exists
Not so good when people obey and acclaim him
Worst when they despise him
Fail to honor people,
They fail to honor you,
But of a good leader, who talks little
When work is done, his aim fulfilled
They will all say, "we did this ourselves."

Lao-tze, ancient Chinese philosopher

Education makes a people easy to lead, but difficult to drive; easy to govern, but impossible to enslave.

Brougham, 1828

In this chapter on collaborative leadership you will find procedures that will enable you to do the following:

- Use collaborative leadership skills as you work in site-based or community management, charter schools, classroom management, cooperative education, or parent involvement and parent education.
- Describe types of leadership.
- Cite research that supports parent involvement and parent education.
- Plan and develop a needs assessment.
- Organize the format of a meeting.
- Recognize roles that develop in participation in meetings.
- Select the meeting format that meets the needs of the participants.
- Select appropriate topics for meetings.
- Evaluate meetings.

Have you ever attended a meeting where everyone was accepted and encouraged to participate and the objectives of the meeting were accomplished? Each person participated and, as a result, developed higher self-esteem and had the opportunity to be a part of a productive group. A well-led parent group or school team is representative of such a meeting and accomplishes its goals by including parents and, in the process, educating all and clarifying and responding to questions and concerns.

Leadership ability is a skill that helps in all facets of human interactions. School professionals find it essential whether they are parent educators, principals, or teachers. Principals, always the educational leaders in their buildings, are being asked to provide more leadership in community or collective collaboration in site-based management of schools. Teachers need leadership skills to encourage problem solving and critical thinking, and to set the stage for learning. In addition, teachers are being asked to serve on site-based or community-based committees. In group decision making, leadership skills are essential to accomplish the goals or objectives of the group. As you read this chapter, which focuses on parent education, expand your thinking to visualize how good collaborative involvement and leadership can be used in classrooms, family meetings, professional meeting, and group activities.

FAMILY INVOLVEMENT

Family involvement offers the professional an exciting opportunity to work with highly motivated, interested adults. Whether involved in a site-based, collaborative decision-making team, as a participant in their child's education, or in a parent education program, parents usually are highly motivated. Most parents are concerned and committed to their children, and are eager and ready to gain information that will help them in the first months of the baby's life. If educators work with other caregivers (substitute parents), such as relatives, foster parents, adoptive parents, grandparents, and nonrelated caregivers, they will also find caregivers who are eager to provide the best environment for their young child. If educators work with parents or caregivers who have preschool children, they will find caregivers who have several years of on-the-job training—experience that will help them build their knowledge base. In either case the parents will have concern for the well-being of their children and family. Two elements necessary for effective learning—interest and need—will be present.

Parents, as adult learners, bring with them many of the ingredients of a stimulating, productive learning environment. Their interest and need make it easy to develop topics that are important to the membership. The background and experience of the parents provide rich educational material, an opportunity for sharing expertise and knowledge, and an impetus for self-directed learning. Parent involvement groups should be carefully monitored to make sure that all levels of expertise are allowed to flourish. It is up to the leaders to provide an accepting, risk-free environment, involve the parents in planning, provide relevant materials and knowledge, and devise appropriate delivery systems (such as group discussions, simulations, role playing, and experts).

DEVELOP COLLABORATIVE LEADERSHIP SKILLS

Good collaborative leadership skills are beneficial in many areas of life. Whether it be the home, school, or the wider arena of the community, information on group leadership and processes is very useful. Students of all ages can participate in a family meeting, and those in intermediate middle school and high school often have presentations about a project they have developed. They learn from the organization and design of the presentation, the research and background information needed to prepare, and from the presentation.

Professionals and/or classroom teachers who can support and motivate the group can accomplish the goals of the group without undermining the responsibilities of the participants. The style of the leader will be determined by the individual's training and personality as well as the makeup of the group. Group management can be enhanced by collaborative leadership training sessions where members of the group can be introduced to group methods, curriculum, and resources. It helps if participants have a basic understanding of group processes and communication, whether the group is being led by students, parents, principals, or professionals.

In collaborative decision making for the school and child-care center, the principal or director are usually the leaders. Because the approach is collaborative, the designated leader should be a facilitator, one with information and background material that can be used by the entire group. The leader also should be aware that those on the committee have much to share and must be willing to encourage interaction. Leadership skills go beyond administrators to those with whom they work. These leaders, along with teachers, must collaborate with parents and other community members to establish the management and objectives of the school. In site-based management, members of organizing committees who understand group

Eugenia Hepworth Berger

The background and experience of the parents provide an opportunity for sharing expertise and knowledge and an impetus for self-directed learning.

dynamics, growth, and leadership responsibilities will be more effective than those who flounder trying to develop meaningful and effective group decision making. Using a collaborative approach proves to be very effective.

PARENT EDUCATION

Leadership in parent education may be viewed along a continuum (Figure 7.1) that ranges from a lay leader, a nonprofessional with little training, to a knowledgeable expert trained to expedite group processes, a professional who lectures as an authority. As you begin a parent education program, keep in mind that groups can be organized in different fashions. A trained professional should not dominate the group with specific, didactic teaching, nor should the lay group be left without direction.

The use of lay leaders—parents leading their own groups—encourages parents to be actively involved. Because educational growth and positive change are what is wanted in parent education groups, active involvement is highly desired. More change will occur if the parent formulates some of the educational suggestions and acts upon the information. Parents are more able to develop ways of handling parent–child relationships if they develop their expertise from their own research and interact with other members of the group. This does not mean excluding experts in the field. At times it is necessary to have an authority give background material. After the information is received, however, parents need to discuss and act upon it themselves.

This chapter describes various types of meetings and group processes as a guide in the development of new parent-group programs. The programs discussed here range from those led by the unskilled person without curriculum guides, on the left of the continuum in Figure 7.1, to the authoritative meeting on the right. At the center of the continuum is the parent education group that is most appropriate for achieving parental

Parent leader with no training	Parent leader with leadership training	Parent leader with a structured curriculum	Parent leader with professional support	Professional leader with parent support	Professional teacher

FIGURE 7.1 Continuum of leaders in parent education.

self-determination, attitudinal change, competence, and educational gains—that of parent leadership with professional support. Descriptions of programs that illustrate each of the types include:

1. Unstructured meetings with no goals, curriculum, or trained leader.
2. Meetings led by lay leaders to get comments, solve a problem, study an issue, or become better acquainted.
3. Meetings led by lay leaders who follow a curriculum devised by professionals, such as Active Parenting, Parent Effectiveness Training (PET), and Systematic Training for Effective Parenting (STEP).
4. Meetings called by a parent or a professional that involve members and respond to their concerns with professional support. In the case of site-based management, the professional (principal) involves members of the committee and leads them to a consensus or a decision by majority vote.
5. Meetings called and led by a professional, with participation by lay members.
6. Meetings called, led, directed, and controlled by the professional, with members of the audience as observers only.

The aims of traditional parent education are furthered in the recent restructuring trend and collaborative decision making in public education. Parent involvement includes shared goal setting and decision making (Comer, 1988; Seeley, 1989; Swick, 2001). Encouraging parents to be involved calls for active parent collaboration that includes the parents in "mutual accountability. . . . This brings a power into the relationship that supersedes the power of bureaucratic control" (Seeley, p. 48). Belief in the autonomy of parents inspires the promotion of their decision-making abilities and allows them to be full partners in the education process.

Although parent involvement programs differ in their underlying structure—some are led by professionals, others by lay leaders—they are similar in their goal of developing parent participation in their children's education and development (Moles, 1996a, 1996b; Swick, 1983, 2001; U.S. Department of Education, 1994).

Effectiveness of Parent Involvement

Swick, Varner, and McClellan (1991) describe a statewide evaluation framework that can be used for parent education. An example of a controlled design is the research by Tebes, Grady, and Snow (1989), who had parents of 630 children selected randomly and assigned to experimental and control groups. Four skills were studied: (a) empathic responding level I, or the ability of the parent to respond to the child's feelings with understanding; (b) empathic responding level II, or the ability to respond empathetically to the child when the parent is disturbed by the behavior of the child; (c) facilitation of alternatives in decision making; and (d) facilitation of consequences, or being able to develop appropriate consequences. The findings supported the premise that education could help parents respond empathetically and develop decision-making behavior for parents of adolescents.

NEEDS ASSESSMENT

Before you begin a parent education program—and periodically during the program—you should determine the interests and needs of the community. First, meet with a group of parents representative of the diverse ethnic and socioeconomic levels within the community. Jot down the ideas or questions that concern and interest them. A brainstorming session is an ideal mechanism for eliciting many ideas. To facilitate the session, distribute a handout of the problems from Gallup polls and other surveys.

Once you have developed your basic list of interests and concerns, give it to a trial group and ask the members to add new ideas and concerns. Next, construct a needs-assessment tool listing possible topics or formats for parents. Disseminate the questionnaire to adults in the school or center community. Finally, choose from the questionnaire those items that received the most requests and develop a program to meet the needs of the community. Be sensitive to minorities and single parents and incorporate their responses to such needs and desires into the parent program.

Developing Items for a Needs Assessment

According to a 2001 Phi Delta Kappa/Gallup poll, respondents were asked to choose the biggest problems that schools and communities face. Fifteen percent of the respondents felt the lack of discipline and 15 percent saw the lack of financial support and funding as two of the biggest problems. Other choices recognized as problems included fighting, violence, and gangs (10 percent), overcrowded schools (10 percent), and the use of drugs and dope (9 percent). The difficulty in obtaining high-quality teachers rounded out the list with 6 percent (Rose & Gallup, 2001). In 2000, the Phi Delta Kappa/Gallup poll also included overcrowded schools, concern about standards, and crime and vandalism. Current issues such as bullying and peer pressure could be added. After a few suggestions, lists can be generated by parents for use in developing their own needs assessment. Suggestions are meant to help generate ideas and should not restrict the needs recognized by the parents, however. Concerns are selected on the basis of what the current group of parents indicates as their greatest needs, with the final selection of interests and concerns based on individual needs of each group.

Needs assessments at the individual small-group level can be less formal:

1. Brainstorm ideas for concerns and interests.
2. Collect as many ideas as your group can generate.
3. Show the group a similar list that might provide inspiration for other ideas to add to their list.
4. Form buzz groups, and let the participants discuss the lists.
5. Let the members list their choices in order of importance.
6. Generate your programs for the year from the group responses.
7. If a new issue arises that concerns most of the group, find a space or add a session to cover the important topic.

Needs assessments are necessary when new programs are developed, as well as when established parent groups reassess their needs. Less formal assessments are used frequently by ongoing groups.

Interest Finders

If a parent group is already established, members may use a number of informal methods to indicate their interests. These range from brainstorming among the members to soliciting suggestions in a question box.

Brainstorming

For a brainstorming session, choose a recorder and encourage all members to contribute ideas for programs. A list of past successful programs may be distributed. Write ideas on a chalkboard or white board, or on a transparency on an overhead projector. Caution members not to judge any suggestions good or bad—all suggestions are valid at this point. After all suggestions are listed, have members choose in writing three to six ideas that interest them most. Develop your program from the interests that receive the most votes (or are most frequently mentioned). If the group has difficulty thinking of items, you may be able to generate responses by having participants complete statements such as these:

My greatest concerns are . . .

My greatest happiness comes from . . .

If I had three wishes, I would . . .

If I could eliminate one problem from my home, it would be . . .

Questions that concern me about my child's education are . . .

Questions that concern me about my child's development are . . .

As a parent I hope to be . . .

Annoyance Test

An annoyance test is relevant for parents. The leader writes the following on a chart, blackboard, or white board:

My children annoy me when they . . .

I annoy my children when I . . .

The parents then list points under each, and the results are tabulated. The four or five most popular topics may then be discussed in subsequent meetings (Denver Public Schools, n.d.).

Open-Ended Questions

Parent groups can solicit requests for a wider knowledge of the community and possible ways for parents to become more involved in schools and the community. The leader asks parents to respond to such topics as:

- What do I want to know about my school?
- What do I want to know about my community?
- What would I like to do about my school and/or community?

Questionnaires

Develop a questionnaire, such as *Test Your Know-How as a Parent,* that will bring out differences in opinions in the group and show where interests and room for learning occur.

Question Box

Some parents are hesitant to make suggestions in an open meeting. They might feel more comfortable dropping questions and comments into a box that is available throughout the year.

During early planning it may also be advisable to let the members anonymously write their ideas on a small sheet of paper. Parents may be concerned about alcohol and other drugs, for example, but hesitate to mention that lest they reveal they have that problem in their homes.

Development of Objectives

After the group's interests have been assessed, the program is developed. Within most programs, at least two aspects should receive attention: the content of the meeting and the changes in behavior and attitudes of the participants.

Most parents know when they want help with parenting skills, although reticent parents may need special encouragement. When a new family is formed and the first baby comes home to live, parents are intensely interested in knowing how to care for the baby. An opportune time for parent education is before the birth and during the child's first 3 years of life.

Parents are also ready for sharing information during the child's preschool years. Parent education and preschool programs bring the professional and the parents together to share concerns and experiences.

During the child's school-age years, parent education programs that focus on learning activities, building family strengths, and concerns specific to the group are beneficial. There is also growing interest in parent education at the secondary level. Worries about drugs, alcohol, misbehavior, and suicide cause parents to look for help. At parent education meetings they may share issues, talk about common problems, become united in their efforts, and become aware of resources available to help them. Parents want parent education when they feel the need for it. It is important at that time to offer programs that speak to their concerns and allow them to have input into the agenda. Parents need to share, ask questions, and be a part of the decision-making process.

HOW PARENTS LEARN BEST

Parent educators facilitate the learning experience for parents. They design the program and the environment so that the parent is an active participant in the delivery of knowledge. Parents and parent-substitutes will be more apt to become involved in the learning process and thereby change their attitudes more easily if:

- A positive climate is established.
- Risk is eliminated.
- Parents are recognized as having something worthwhile to contribute.
- Parents are actively involved in their own education.
- The curriculum addresses their concerns and needs.
- Parents discover the need for change on their own.
- Respect and encouragement are present.
- Real situations and analogies are used to bring theories to life.
- Positive feedback is used.
- Different approaches (role playing, short lectures, open discussion, debates, brainstorming, workshops) allow them to learn to use a variety of techniques.
- Different approaches use a variety of sensory experiences (sight, sound, touch, taste, and smell).
- Problem solving and analysis enable the learner to continue learning beyond the personal contact.

- The topic is relevant.
- Parents are considered part of the learning-teaching team.

You may have noted that the way parents learn best can apply to students, professionals, or even young children. Most everyone learns better when it is a positive environment with relevant material.

In addition, it is important to note that parents will have difficulty focusing on their children if their own immediate needs are not met. Therefore, it is important to provide support, resource, and referral information to parents to help them meet their own needs. Once this has been accomplished, they will be able to focus their energy on the children. And the impact will have long-lasting effects.

GROUP DISCUSSIONS

Most meetings involve group discussion, which can range from the use of open discussion as the total meeting format to a short discussion after a formal presentation.

The following examples, an informal discussion plan and a problem-solving format, illustrate two uses of group discussions. The first focuses on the informality of the process, and the second requires prior development of expertise and a resolution of the issue.

Informal Discussion Plan

A. Stems from interest or needs of group.

Example: How can parents be more involved in their child's school?

B. Establishes goals and objectives.
   1. Goal—parental involvement.
   2. Objectives
      a. To determine why parents do not feel comfortable coming to school.
      b. To encourage parents to participate in schools.
      c. To initiate a plan for getting parents involved.
      d. To suggest activities in which parents can be involved.

C. Provides for informal group meetings.
   1. Allows parents to speak freely.
   2. Emphasizes the clarification of feelings and acceptance of ideas.
   3. Encourages participation.
   4. Includes keeping a record of suggestions.

D. Selects and analyzes relevant information that emerges during the discussion.

E. Outlines a plan for action, if the group desires.

Problem-Solving Format

A. Recognition of the problem—state the hypothesis.
   1. The problem should be selected by the group and reflect its needs and interests.

Example: Does violence on television impact our children and cause more violence in the country?

   2. The leader writes the question or problem for discussion on a chart, chalkboard, or white board.

B. Understanding the problem—discuss the nature of the problem.

Example: Is television viewing a problem and, if so, why?

C. Data collection—gather a wide range of ideas and determine which are relevant.
   1. Prior development of expertise—identify resources and read before meeting.
   2. Nonjudgmental acceptance—accept and record comments and ideas from participants.

D. Analysis of the problem.
   1. Focus on the subject so that it can be discussed thoroughly by participants.
   2. Establish criteria for evaluation of a solution.
   3. Keep participants focused on problems.

E. Conclusion and summary.
   1. Suggest solutions.
   2. List possible conclusions.
   3. Seek an integrative conclusion that reflects the group's goals and thinking.

CRITERIA FOR GROUP COMMUNICATION

1. Come to the meeting ready to ask questions and share your ideas.
2. Once your ideas and thoughts are given to the group, do not feel compelled to defend them. Once shared, they become the group's property to discuss and consider. Clarify meaning if it would help the group proceed, but don't feel responsible for the idea just because you suggested it.
3. Speak freely and communicate feelings. Listen to others with consideration and understanding for their feelings.
4. Accept others in the interchange of ideas. Allow them to have opinions that differ from yours. Do not ignore or reject members of the group.
5. Engage in friendly disagreements. Listen critically and carefully to suggestions others have to offer. Differences of opinion bring forth a variety of ideas.
6. Be sincere. Reveal your true self. Communicate in an atmosphere of mutual trust.
7. Allow and promote individual freedom. Do not manipulate, suppress, or ridicule other group members. Encourage their creativity and individuality.
8. Work hard, acknowledge the contributions of others, and focus on the objectives of the group's task.

FIGURE 7.2 Criteria for group communication.

F. Appropriate action.
   1. Develop a timetable.
   2. Determine a method of accomplishing tasks.
   3. Delegate tasks.

LEADERSHIP TRAINING

Lay leaders benefit from having guidelines to follow in developing their leadership skills. The leader's goal is to establish an environment that facilitates and guides members in achieving the objectives.

Group members can participate more effectively if they are aware of their rights and responsibilities within the group. A handout on communication skills, given to members early in the school term, helps eliminate problems and encourages a relaxed, productive group (Figure 7.2). Use the handout as a guide. This handout, along with a description of group roles (Table 7.1), will enable group members to grow into productive participants in group interaction. As a leader, it is your responsibility to share these communication tips with the group membership.

TABLE 7.1 Role interaction. Both task and maintenance roles are necessary for effective group participation.

Task Roles	Group Building or Maintenance Roles	Dysfunctional Roles
Initiator-leader	Encourager	Dominator
Facilitator	Harmonizer	Aggressor
Information giver/seeker	Listener	Negativist
Clarifier	Follower	Playboy
Questioner	Tension breaker	Blocker
Asserter	Compromiser	Competitor
Energizer	Standard setter	Recognition seeker
Elaborator	Observer	Deserter
Orientator	Recorder	Challenger
Opinion giver	Gatekeeper	
Opinion seeker		
Summarizer		

General Qualifications

The following pointers emphasize the leader's personality, interpersonal relationships, and skill in handling group discussions:

A. Leader's personality

1. Ability to think and act quickly. The leader may need to change plans on the spur of the moment.
2. Ability to get along with others, be well liked, and not have a tendency to "fly off the handle."
3. Respect for the opinions of others. The leader should be a good listener and avoid telling others what to think.
4. Willingness to remain in the background. Instead of voicing opinions, ask questions and guide but do not dominate.
5. Freedom from prejudice.

B. Leader's knowledge and skills

1. Knowledge of the discussion method. The leader must know the purpose and the procedure agreed upon if the meeting is to be successful.
2. Knowledge of the opinions of authorities on the subject so that conclusions will be based on evidence rather than on the leader's opinion.
3. Skill in asking questions. The leader should present questions that bring out the opinions of others. Use questions to avoid hasty decisions or the acceptance of conclusions not based on good evidence. Throwing out a question to the group can help the leader avoid expressing personal opinions. The following suggestions give examples of how to handle certain situations that may arise in a discussion:

   a. To call attention to a point that has not been considered: "Has anyone thought about this phase of the problem—or about this possible solution?"

   b. To evaluate the strengths of an argument: "What reasons do we have for accepting this statement?"

   c. To get back to causes: "Why do you suppose a child—or a parent—feels or acts this way?"

   d. To question the source of information or argument: "Who gathered these statistics that you spoke of?" or "Would you care to identify the authority you are quoting?"

   e. To suggest that new information has not been added: "Can anyone add a new idea to the information already given on this point?"

   f. To register steps of agreement or disagreement: "Am I correct in assuming that all of us agree [or disagree] with this point?"

   g. To bring a generalizing speaker down to earth: "Can you give us a specific example?" or "Your general idea is good, but I wonder if we can't make it more concrete. Does anyone know of a case . . . ?"

   h. To handle the member who has "all the answers": "Would your idea work in all cases?" or "Let's get a variety of opinions on this point."

   i. To bring an individual back to the subject: "I wonder if you can relate your ideas to the subject we are discussing?"

   j. To handle a question directed to the leader:

      (1) If the leader knows the answer but does not wish to be set up as an authority, the question can be redirected to the group.

      (2) The leader can quote from resource material and ask for additional opinions.

      (3) If the leader is a specialist in the area, occasional questions may be answered.

      (4) The leader can say, "I don't know. Who does? Shall we research this?"

   k. To cut off a long-winded speaker: "While we're on this point, let's hear from the others" or "Shall we save your next point until later?"

l. To help the members who may have difficulty expressing themselves: "I wonder if I am interpreting you correctly—were you saying . . . ?" or "Can we tie in what you are saying with our subject something like this . . . ?"

m. To encourage further questions: "I'm glad you raised that question. Can anyone answer?"

n. To break up a heated argument: "I'm sure all of us feel strongly about this. Would some of the rest of you care to express opinions?"

o. To be sensitive to body language of the group, watch for people who want to speak and bring out their contributions.[1]

Leaders do not have to be superhuman, charming, physically attractive people. Leaders initiate, plan, guide, and build group norms; give support; challenge; and encourage group growth. In building the group norms, special attention should be paid to the feelings of people in the group.

1. Each person is respected, listened to, and recognized.
2. The meeting is a safe place to be; no one will be ridiculed or put down.
3. Feelings are important, and the expression of feelings helps the group solve problems.
4. Feelings may be discussed.
5. The participants and leader are encouraged to be objective. (Adapted from Denver Public Schools, n.d.)

Leaders who show a caring attitude are most effective. They offer protection, affection, praise, and encouragement as well as friendship. But caring is not enough. The effective leader is there to give support, explain, and clarify if needed.

[1] From "Pointers for Discussion Group Leaders" in *Parent Education and Preschool Department Leadership Handbook*, by Denver Public Schools (n.d.), Denver, CO: Author.

USING TECHNOLOGY

The increased use of communication through the Internet allows parents, leaders, teachers, and students to interact online. The process allows participants to respond to one another. Currently, body language is not available to increase understanding of the messages sent to and fro; however, the availability and the convenience of flexible schedules and immediate discussion makes Internet communication a viable option. This is especially true for those parents who live a distance from the school or meeting place and for those whose work schedule or children at home make it impossible for them to attend meetings.

E-mail

E-mail may be used to communicate and provides an opportunity for an immediate response. It can be used to give information and to receive parent responses and questions.

Web Sites

Schools can develop Web sites that communicate with parents about the happenings at school. Emergencies can be explained; assignments may be posted and explained; and extensions that include articles about educational ideas and procedures for improving academic achievement may be available. Articles that concern education and child development can be placed on the Web site for the parents or students to read. If the school has had some difficulty with bullying and rejection of some students by others, information from the school can help set up programs and encourage both parents and the school to work on the concerns.

For parents who have been excluded from meetings because of their schedules, the Internet expands their opportunities to be involved with the school.

ESTABLISHING A POSITIVE ATMOSPHERE

Icebreakers

To create an accepting, warm atmosphere, get-acquainted activities help people relax and become involved in the group. These icebreakers range from introductions of the person to mixers during breaks.

While Members Gather

Signature Sheets

Make a form before the meeting that includes statements about people. Following each statement is a signature blank. These sheets can be made specifically for the group or can be broad enough to be used in any group. The kinds of signature sheets are not limited—create original ones. As the group arrives, give one to each participant. Encourage mixing and meeting new people. By the time the period is completed, the members will have an opportunity to meet and talk with a large number of people. A typical signature sheet is shown in Figure 7.3A. Figure 7.3B illustrates another design for a signature sheet.

Bingo Card

Give each member a card that contains 12 to 25 squares, as shown in Figure 7.4. Ask members to fill each blank with a signature. Signatures may not be repeated. This encourages interaction with all members.

A variation of the bingo card includes a letter within each square. Find someone whose name begins with that letter. Check the roster ahead of time and use the members' initials in the squares. Another variation is similar to the signature sheet but asks for the signature of someone who fulfills the attribute.

Who Am I?

Attach a piece of paper with the name of a famous person to the back of each person. Members go from person to person asking questions until they determine who they are. Questions must be phrased so that a yes or no answer is adequate. Variations include changing the famous person to an event, an animal, or an educational statement.

Scrambled Name Tags

Make up name tags with letters out of order, for example, *Ilaehs* (Sheila). Have the members try to figure out each name as they talk with each person. Obviously, this has to be done at the first or second meeting, before the group becomes acquainted.

After Members Are Seated

Dyad Introductions

Have members talk to each other in pairs with the idea that they will introduce each other. You may give specific instructions, for example, to ask the number of children in the family and what the member expects from parent education, or you may leave the discussion completely up to the two individuals. Following the discussion, go around the room and have members introduce their partners.

Find people who meet the qualifications listed below and have them sign their names.

1. Find someone who is wearing the same color clothes as you. ____________
2. Find someone who has the same color eyes as you. ____________
3. Find someone who has the same number of children as you. ____________
4. Find someone who lives in the same area as you. ____________
5. Find someone who has a child the same age as yours. ____________
6. Find someone who likes to go hiking. ____________
7. Find someone who plays the piano. ____________
8. Find someone who has the same hobby as you. ____________
9. Find someone who has lived in this state as long as you have. ____________
10. Find someone who was brought up in the same area you were. ____________

FIGURE 7.3A Use a get-acquainted activity such as a signature sheet at the beginning of a meeting.

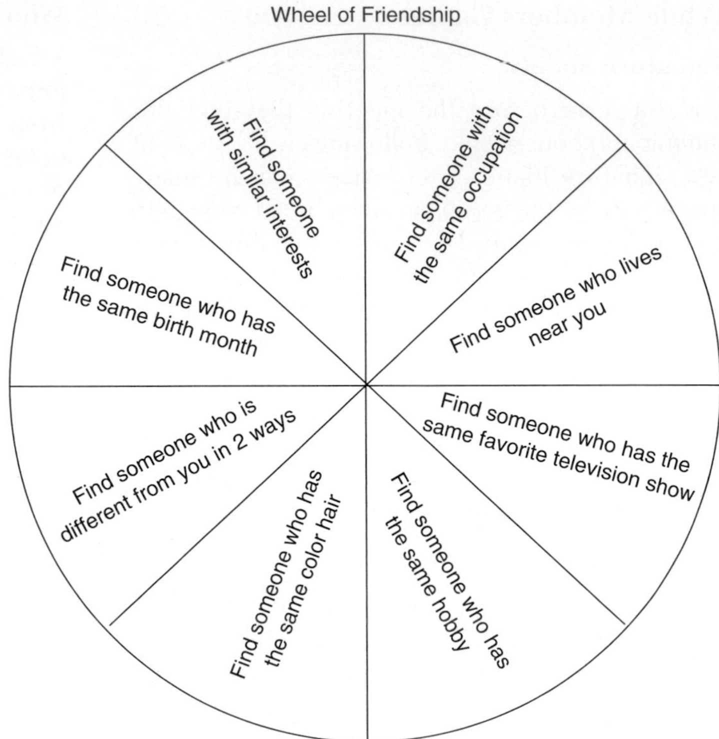
Wheel of Friendship
Find someone with similar interests
Find someone with the same occupation
Find someone who lives near you
Find someone who has the same favorite television show
Find someone who has the same hobby
Find someone who has the same color hair
Find someone who is different from you in 2 ways
Find someone who has the same birth month

FIGURE 7.3B During the next few minutes you are to find people who have the same attributes as you. Have them sign their names in the wheel of friendship between the wheel spokes.

I watch television regularly.	I enjoy reading.	I have more than two children.	I like to dance.	My favorite color is orange.
I have dark hair.	I like to go shopping.	I enjoy skiing.	I enjoy hiking.	I enjoy biking.
I have red hair.	I have blonde hair.	I have brown eyes.	I have blue eyes.	I have a son.
I have two children.	I live near here.	I have lived in this area for more than one year.	I enjoy music.	I enjoy helping in school.
I exercise regularly.	I have a daughter.	I have a brother.	I have a sister.	I work outside the home.

FIGURE 7.4 Find a person who can sign the squares. When you have completed an entire line, you can call "Bingo!" Bingo games can use initials or attributes of the members of the group.

It is interesting to have the dyad discuss memory questions such as something the partner remembers that happened before the age of 5 or the person's happiest experience. This activity can be used later in the year as well as at the beginning. Allow members to introduce themselves. Topics they might use include the following:

My secret hiding place was . . .

As a child I liked to . . . best.

Summertime was . . .

If I had my wish, I would be . . .

What I liked most about school was . . .

What I remember about walking or riding the bus home from school was . . .

I've Got a Secret. After people have become acquainted, ask each participant to write a secret on a piece of paper. (Be sure that the person does not mind having the secret revealed.) Place the pieces of paper in a bag, and as they are drawn and read, group members try to guess who has that secret.

Activities that promote good relations and allow members to get acquainted are limited only by the planner's imagination. The chairperson or leader may be in charge of this part of the program or may delegate the responsibility to a number of persons charged with the task of discovering new means of interaction.

GROUP ROLES

Within each group, roles emerge that are functional and task-oriented, that move the group forward; others that are group-sustaining, expressive, and maintain the group; and still others that are negative and dysfunctional and reduce the effectiveness of the group. Group members should be given descriptions of group roles to help them identify their participatory roles or roles that they would like to develop (see Table 7.1).

Roles emerge within groups and influence the interactive process. A *role,* defined as the behavior characteristic of a person occupying a particular position in the social system, influences the actions of the person and the expectations of others toward that person. Parent groups (in this text) are the "social system"; members of the group expect certain norms or standards of behavior from the perceived leader of the group. These role expectations are projected in members' role behavior toward the leader. Likewise, the leader's own interpretation of the role influences the resulting role behavior or role performance. Should members of the group hold different expectations of behavior for the leadership role from those held by the occupant of that role, interrole conflicts may arise (Applbaum, Bodaken, Sereno, & Anatol, 1979; Berger, 1968; Biddle & Thomas, 1979; Borchers, 1999). For these reasons, it is beneficial to discuss or clarify standards and duties of roles within a group.

Role continuity is easier to obtain in parent education groups with ongoing memberships. Parents are encouraged to participate for at least 2 years. New officers and leaders, already familiar with the standards of the group, may be elected in the spring and be ready to take over leadership in the fall. Although this system ensures greater continuity than the establishment of a new group each year, the returning members must be careful to be flexible, open to new ideas, and sensitive to the desires of new members.

Early in the year, a session may include a discussion of roles and group dynamics. Role playing is an excellent mechanism for clarifying role behavior. If group members are aware of the effects that roles have on the functioning of a group, they will not fall into dysfunctional roles so readily. By discussing group dynamics with the group before establishment of role patterns, group production is often increased (Beal, Bohlen, & Raudabaugh, 1962).

A leader can deter or eliminate the problem of domination or withdrawal by group members if members are aware of roles and how each member of the group can influence the group's functioning, either positively or negatively. Most people do not want to be viewed as dysfunctional members and will, therefore, refrain from acting in ways that are detrimental to group interaction. I have used this technique of discussing roles in parent groups and classes for many years and have found that the group discussion and the role-playing of group roles greatly enhance the productivity of the group.

This knowledge will encourage some members, but it can also inhibit others who worry about which role theory they are enacting. Although this is a possible negative result of a discussion of group roles, role definition can benefit the total group in the elimination of one common problem in groups—domination of the discussion by a few participants. It is also beneficial to reticent communicators to learn that they can become productive group members despite the inability to express themselves. Asking questions, being an active listener, and being a positive member of the group are shown to be valuable contributions to a well-functioning discussion group. When balanced out, the positive aspects of discussing group roles overshadow the negative ones. One word of caution, however—do not wait until a problem has become obvious before discussing dysfunctional roles. That would embarrass and alienate the person who has been a negative contributor. It is best to handle such a problem through the leadership techniques discussed on pp. 212–214.

DYNAMICS OF ROLES WITHIN GROUPS

Observation of interaction within groups shows that role behavior influences the cohesiveness and productivity of the group. Observation will be facilitated if analysis of the group is based on role interaction (Table 7.1), wherein behaviors within a group are divided into task, group building and maintenance, and dysfunctional roles.

Task Roles

The roles related to the task area in Table 7.1 are attributed to members of the group who initiate, question, and facilitate reaching the group's goals or objectives.

Group Building and Maintenance Roles

The roles related to group building or maintenance are attributed to members of the group who support and maintain the cohesiveness, solidarity, and productivity of the group.

Dysfunctional or Individual Roles

The roles in this area are attributed to members who place their own individual needs, which are not relevant to group goals, above group needs. These individual goals are not functional or productive to group achievement, but if such members are brought into the group process, they can become contributing participants.

Members of groups generally do not fit into only one role category. Members may participate in a

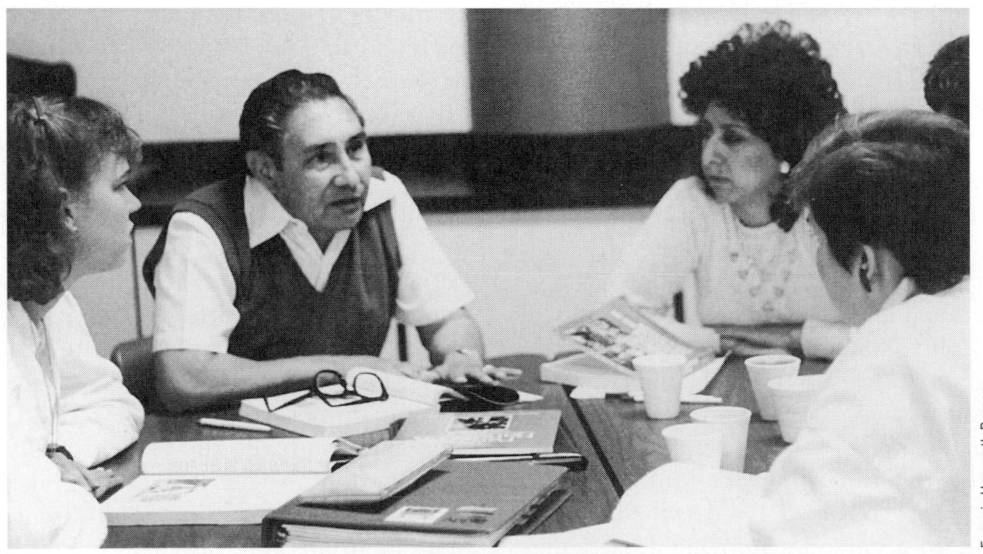
Eugenia Hepworth Berger

Whether in a site-based, collaborative decision-making team, as a participant in their child's education, or in a parent education program, parents bring their interest and desire to be involved.

task role and switch to a maintenance role with the next action or comment. For example, Helen is anxious about absenteeism and suggests that the group might improve attendance by organizing a car pool. May responds by suggesting a telephone network to contact members. Helen welcomes the idea, "Good thought, May. We might be able to start right away." Helen, within the space of 2 minutes, has initiated an idea, acting in a task-oriented role, and has then supported May's contribution with a group building or maintenance statement. There may be moments when members lapse into a dysfunctional role, but as long as the mix of interaction remains primarily positive and productive, the group will be effective.

ROLE DESCRIPTIONS

The following role descriptions are based on Beal and colleagues (1962); Benne and Sheets (1948); Borchers, (1999); King (1962); and MSU Extension, (1999).

Task-Oriented

Task roles are the roles that initiate and keep the group discussion meaningful and ongoing.

Initiator-leader: Initiates the discussion, guides but does not dominate, contributes ideas or suggestions that help move the group forward.

Facilitator: Helps the group stay on track and encourages member participation.

Information giver: Contributes information and facts that are from authoritative sources and are relevant to the ongoing discussion.

Information seeker: Asks for clarification or expansion of an issue from additional relevant, authoritative information.

Clarifier: Restates the discussion of an issue so that points are made clear to the group and relationships between ideas are clear.

Orientator: Takes a look at the group's position in relation to the objectives of the meetings and where the discussion is going and as a result may refocus the group discussion.

Questioner: Asks questions about issues, requests clarification, or offers constructive criticism.

Asserter: States a position in a positive manner; may take a different point of view and disagree with opinions or suggestions without attacking them.

Energizer: Stimulates and facilitates the group to action and increased output and problem solving.

Elaborator: Expands an idea or concept; brings out details, points, and alternatives that may have been overlooked.

Opinion giver: States own opinion on the situation, basing the contribution on personal experiences.

Opinion seeker: Requests suggestions from others according to their life experiences and value orientation.

Summarizer: Brings out facts, ideas, and suggestions made by the group in an attempt to clarify the group's position during the meeting and at the conclusion.

Group Building and Maintenance Roles

Group building or maintenance roles help the group develop and maintain the existence and quality of the group. The first six roles will emerge within the group; the last four are appointed or elected maintenance roles.

Encourager: Supports, praises, and recognizes other members of the group; builds self-confidence and self-concept of others.

Harmonizer: Mediates misunderstandings and clarifies conflicting statements and disagreements; adds to the discussion in a calming and tension-reducing manner.

Listener: Is involved in the discussion through quiet attention to the group process; gives support through body language and eye contact.

Follower: Serves as a supportive member of the discussion by accepting the ideas and suggestions of others.

Tension breaker: Uses humor or clarifying statements to relieve tension within the group.

Compromiser: View both sides of the question and offer solutions or suggestions that move group to a position which fits conflicting viewpoints.

The following four roles are appointed or elected positions:

Standard setter: Sets standards for group performance; may apply standards as an evaluative technique for the meeting.

Observer: Charts the group process throughout the meeting and uses the data for evaluation of group interaction.

Recorder: Records decisions and ideas for group use throughout the meeting.

Gatekeeper: Regulates time spent and membership participation during various parts of the program; keeps communication open and the meeting on schedule.

Dysfunctional Roles

Dysfunctional roles interfere with achievement of the goals of the group.

Dominator: Monopolizes the meeting and asserts superiority by attempting to manipulate the group.

Aggressor: Shows aggression toward the group in a variety of forms; for example, attacks ideas, criticizes others, denigrates others' contributions, and disapproves of solutions.

Challenger: Challenges other group member's ideas and suggestions.

Negativist: Demonstrates pessimism and disapproval of suggestions that emerge within the group; sees the negative side of the issue and rejects new insights.

Playboy/Playgirl: Refuses to be involved in the discussion and spends time showing this indifference to the members by distracting behavior; for example, talks to others, shows cynicism, makes side comments.

Blocker: Opposes decision making and attempts to block actions by introducing alternatives that have already been rejected.

Competitor: Competes with other members of the discussion group by challenging their ideas and expressing and defending his or her own suggestions.

Recognition seeker: Needs recognition and focus on himself or herself.

Deserter: Leaves the group in spirit and mind but not in body; doodles, looks around the room, appears uninterested, and stays aloof and indifferent to the group process.

PRODUCTIVE GROUPS

In productive groups, members of the group are both active and productive.

1. Members listen and pay attention to one another.
2. Members discuss the subject at hand.
3. Everyone's ideas and suggestions are welcomed.
4. Everyone has a chance to state his or her views.
5. The group uses its agenda as a guide for discussion.
6. One or two members are appointed to summarize the discussion and to see that everyone has had a chance to speak.
7. Members know and use problem-solving steps.
8. Members are clear about group decisions and committed to them (MSU Extension, 1999, p. 5).

Less productive groups often do the following:

1. Members do not listen and everyone tends to talk at the same time.
2. The discussion jumps from one idea to another.
3. Some members' ideas don't seem to count, so they feel that they don't belong.
4. One or two members do all the talking.
5. The agenda is not clear and there is no written guide for discussion.
6. No one summarizes or checks to see if everyone who wants to speak has actually spoken. Discussions go on and on until people get tired.
7. No order is followed for identifying and solving problems.
8. Decision making is muddy and people are not committed to the plan (MSU Extension, 1999, p. 5).

Role-Playing Group Roles

Early in the formation of a group, members can benefit from a session in which they role play task, maintenance, and dysfunctional roles while discussing an issue of high interest. This exercise will illustrate to members how role performance can support or destroy a group. It is practical to arrange seating in two concentric circles, allowing the inner circle to discuss an issue in light of the roles assigned, whereas the outer circle observes and analyzes the roles being demonstrated. The session will be humorous, with members enthusiastically playing dysfunctional roles, but it should end with the understanding that each member is important to the effectiveness of the group process. It is also important to observe the course of the session. If there is any indication that a participant is having difficulty functioning within the group, the leader needs to provide support and redirect the activity.

Observer

Analytical observation of group interaction reveals patterns that are not always obvious to the casual observer. A systematic observation can pinpoint problems and illustrate strengths to the members. One simple technique for analytical observation is the construction of a discussion wheel. A diagram of the participants is made, with names or numbers reflecting individual members. If the participants are sitting in a circle, the diagram would be similar to the one in Figure 7.5.

As members speak, the observer uses arrows to record the direction of each interaction. An arrow pointed toward the center indicates that the communicator is speaking to the group; an arrow pointed from one member to another represents a statement made to an individual rather than to the group (Beal et al., 1962). A glance at Figure 7.5 shows that Ralph did not make any suggestions; he had either withdrawn from the group or lacked its supportive encouragement. Most members contributed to the group process, rather than making side comments to individual communicators. As interaction continues throughout the meeting, the observer can make cross marks on the arrows to reflect duplication of communication, eliminating an overabundance of lines in the observation circle (Figure 7.6).

End-of-Meeting Evaluations

Evaluations are used effectively by many groups to see if the needs of the group are being met. Because every group is somewhat different, evaluations should be constructed to meet the needs of the group and should be based on the goals and objectives of the meeting. Sample evaluations are helpful, however, to guide the group in its development of evaluative methods that work for that particular group. The example in Figure 7.7 may be adapted to any group's needs.

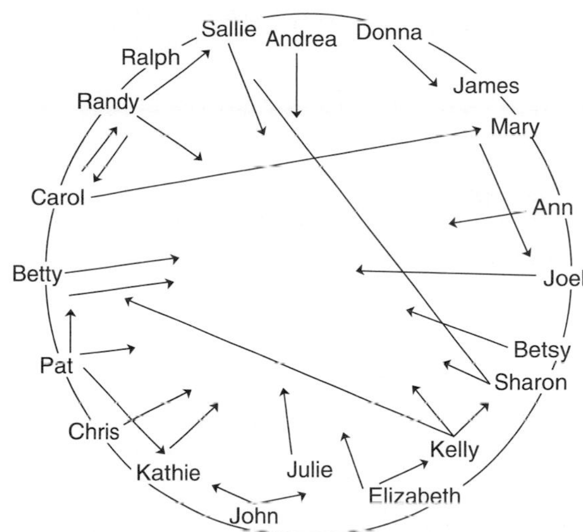

FIGURE 7.5 Group interaction recorded on an observation wheel.

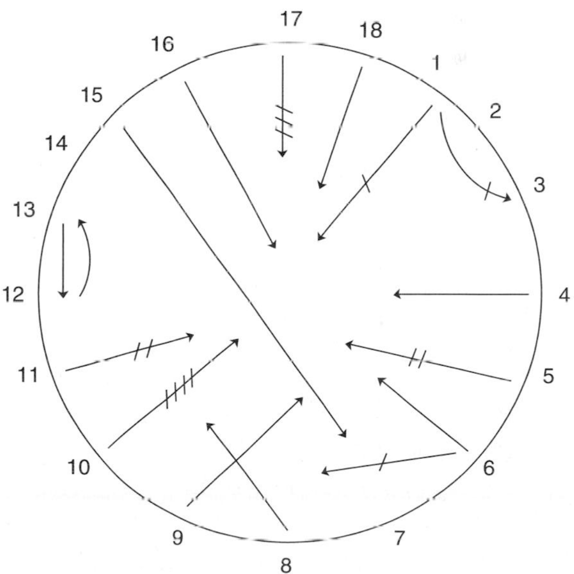

FIGURE 7.6 Group interaction is anonymously recorded on an observation wheel. Each time a person speaks, a mark is added to the interaction line. In this manner, one can see how often and to whom each participant communicates.

Topic: ______________________ Date: ______________

Group: ______________________

Check along the continuum.

1. Was the meeting of interest to you?	Very much	Some	Very little
2. Did you receive any pertinent ideas that will be helpful to you?	Many ideas	Some	No ideas
3. Did the group participate and seem involved in the meeting?	Very involved	Some	No involvement
4. Did the meeting give you any new insights, or did you change any of your attitudes as a result of the meeting?	New insights	Some	No effect
5. Were you encouraged to contribute as much as you wanted?	Participation encouraged	Neutral	Left out
6. Did the leader respond to the needs of the group?	Good leadership	Neutral	No leadership
7. Was there adequate preparation by the members?	Excellent preparation	Some	Poor preparation
8. Were group members encouraged to participate?	Strong	Average	Poor
9. Was there enough time for discussion?	Too much	Just right	No time
10. Was the atmosphere conducive to freedom of expression?	Safe environment	Neutral	Felt threatened

11. Do you have any suggestions for improvement?

12. What were the strong points of the meeting?

13. Comments:

You do not need to sign this sheet.

FIGURE 7.7 A meeting evaluation form lets you know exactly how the participants viewed the program.

TYPES OF MEETINGS

Meetings can range from formal lectures to informal buzz sessions. In parent groups, informal meetings are used most often to reinforce the active involvement that proves so critical to understanding concepts and changing attitudes. The formal meeting has its place, however, if the group needs a specialist to give an organized background lecture on a specific topic. Figure 7.8 illustrates types of meetings that can be used as needs, time, space, subject, and resources dictate. On the right are meetings that are the most informal and require active involvement by the participants; in the center is the panel meeting; on the left is the most formal lecture where the only audience participation is listening to the speaker. Although each type of meeting has its place in parent group meetings, the informal meeting elicits more participation by group members—a necessary ingredient for attitude clarification, learning, and change.

ARRANGEMENTS FOR MEETINGS

All parent group meetings require certain procedures, regardless of the meeting format. Parents need to feel physically and emotionally comfortable at every meeting, whether formal or informal. To ensure this, the person in charge of the meeting should do the following for all meetings:

1. Check the meeting room to be sure the temperature is appropriate, the ventilation and lighting are adequate, and the room is large enough to accommodate the group.
2. As members or guests arrive, make them feel welcome. Greet them, offer name tags, and suggest that they have refreshments, look at a book display, or participate in an icebreaker activity before the meeting begins. Call members or guests by name as soon as possible.
3. Have refreshments available before the meeting, during the break, or at both times. A 15-minute refreshment period before the meeting gives latecomers an opportunity to arrive before discussion commences. It also sets a relaxed tone and gives members a forum for informal interaction.
4. As participants arrive, involve them in an informal discussion through an icebreaker activity. Get-acquainted activities are important, but choose an appropriate one. For meetings at which few people know one another, it may prove beneficial to use a signature sheet or the dyad-introductions technique of asking the entire group to form into pairs, with each partner introducing the other one to the group.

Formal	Informal
Lecture	Brainstorming
Lecture forum	Roundtable
Symposium	Concentric circles
Audio	Buzz sessions
Audiovisual	Workshop
Book review	Dyad interaction and feedback
Debate	Role playing
Colloquy	Dramatization
Panel	

FIGURE 7.8 Types of meetings range from the informal on the right to very formal on the left.

5. In large groups where icebreakers are not appropriate, the participants can respond to group questions—where they live, what they do, how many children they have, what their interests are, and so on. Responses to the questions (by a show of hands or verbal answers) help the speaker know more about the audience to be addressed, and audience members feel they have been recognized.
6. After the group feels comfortable, the meeting can commence. Open discussion is part of all but the most formal or informal meetings, so it is important that all group leaders are able to conduct discussion sessions. Debates, panels, audiovisual aids, buzz sessions, workshops, role playing, book reviews, dramatizations, and observations can precede open discussion. The leader should gauge the time and conclude the meeting.
7. After the presentation and discussion (or question-and-answer session), thank the presenters and give appropriate recognition for their contributions.
8. Announce any specific instructions necessary for the next meeting before the group disperses.

The descriptions of the types of meetings that follow are compiled from my experiences with parent education (I directed a parent education and preschool program for nearly 4 years) and information found in Applbaum et al. (1979), Denver Public Schools (n.d.), and Kawin (1970).

Roundtables (Open Discussions)

Although not the most informal meeting available, the roundtable is a true open discussion, the mainstay of group interaction (see Figure 7.9). It is used to complement most meetings, such as, panels, symposiums, role-playing sessions, or buzz sessions. The roundtable discussion is also used for decision-making meetings and parent councils.

In a roundtable discussion all members are encouraged to participate throughout the meeting. Care must be taken to promote good communication among all members of the group. To facilitate

FIGURE 7.9 The roundtable is the basic open discussion group.

good group interaction, leaders should keep in mind the following suggestions from the Denver Public Schools:[2]

1. Have a clear understanding of the topic as defined by the group.
2. Obtain materials.
3. Get a general knowledge, through reading, to be able to direct and add to the contributions from the group.
4. Be sure to plan an introduction that will stimulate interest of the group.
5. Prepare a logical, progressive list of questions to start the ball rolling and keep it moving.
6. Keep the discussion on track; keep it always directed, but let the group lay its own track to a large extent. Don't groove it narrowly yourself.
7. Be alert to adjust questions to needs of group—omit, change, reword.
8. Remember—the leader's opinion doesn't count in the discussion. Keep your own view out of it. Your job is to get the ideas of others out for airing.
9. If you see that some important angle is being neglected, point it out; "Bill Jones was telling me last week that he thinks. . . . What do you think of that?"
10. Keep spirits high. Encourage ease, informality, good humor. Let everybody have a good time. Foster friendly disagreement. Listen to all ideas with respect and appreciation, but stress what is important and turn discussion away from what is not.
11. Take time every 10 minutes or so to draw loose ends together: "Let's see where we've been going." Be as fair and accurate in summary as possible. Close the discussion with a summary—your own or the secretary's.
12. Call attention to unanswered questions for future study or for your reference back to speakers. Nourish a desire in group members for continuing study and discussion through a skillful closing summary.

Problems that could emerge in a roundtable meeting include domination of the discussion by one or two members, withdrawal from the group and side discussions by two or three people, or lack of preparation by the membership. Good leadership makes it possible to avoid these pitfalls. If the leader is prepared for the meeting and if members come to the meeting prepared, have relevant experiences, or have background expertise on the subject, the meeting can be a most effective means of changing attitudes and educating members. It allows all members to contribute and become involved in discussion, clarification of issues, and decision making.

Arrangements Before the Meeting

1. Select a topic for open discussion and announce it to the membership.
2. Provide members with materials and bibliography.
   a. Duplicate and distribute background information on the topic through a distribution system or at a meeting before the roundtable.
   b. Select members to read relevant material before the meeting.
   c. Come to the meeting well prepared and ready to guide but not dominate.
3. Review the "Arrangements for Meetings" section (pp. 223–224) and make appropriate preparations.

Setup

1. Arrange chairs in a circle or semicircle or around tables so that all participants can see each other and eye contact is possible.
2. Check the room for comfort—ventilation, lighting, and heat.

Procedure

1. The leader starts the meeting with a thought-provoking question or statement of fact. Throughout the discussion, the leader tries to keep the meeting from wandering. Before the meeting, the leader has prepared a list of questions or statements that may keep the discussion moving forward.

[2] From *Parent Education and Preschool Department Leadership Handbook*, by Denver Public Schools (n.d.), Denver, CO: Author.

2. During the meeting the leader avoids dominating the discussion. Instead, the leadership role brings others into the discussion, helps clarify, and keeps the meeting on the topic.
3. The leader summarizes at the conclusion.
4. If the members want to take action on the conclusions, the leader should call for appropriate action, help the group make plans, and assign tasks.

Appropriate Topics

1. Learning activities that work
2. Behavior and misbehavior
3. Influence of television on children
4. Rivalry between brothers and sisters
5. Problem solving
6. Bullying in the schools
7. Helping children cope with terrorism

Concentric Circles

The concentric-circle arrangement is a variation of the open discussion or roundtable meeting. Instead of one circle, there are two, one inside the other, with everyone facing the center. The dialogue among members is similar to that of the open discussion, only the smaller circle within the larger circle contains the communicators at first (Figure 7.10). Divide the group so that the smaller group has 6 to 12 people. The members of the smaller group discuss the issue; those in the larger group listen to the discussion. After a designated time of 5 to 10 minutes, the meeting is opened to the entire group. If you have 24 to 30 people, with people who are reticent in a large group, the concentric circle will help solve the problem. Those within the inner circle form a small group with which to interact. This arrangement precipitates more discussion from them and succeeds in getting the total group interested in the discussion. Those sitting in the outer circle are required to listen, but the statements, questions, and ideas offered usually promote their interest as they listen. This method is surprisingly effective in getting groups to discuss. By the time the discussion is opened up to the entire group, many ideas have emerged.

Setup

1. Arrange chairs with one large circle on the outside and a smaller circle within the larger circle.
2. Review the "Arrangement for Meetings" section (pp. 223–224) and make appropriate preparations.

Procedure

1. The leader of the total group may request a volunteer leader for the inner circle, or the leader may take that role.
2. The session is started with a statement or question to promote interest and dialogue.
3. The inner circle discusses the topic, using a small-group, open-discussion format. The outer circle listens. At the end of a designated period, for example, 6 minutes, the discussion may be opened to all in the room. At that time the leader continues to control the meeting but does not dominate it.
4. For variation, reverse the roles. Those now is in the outer circle move to the inner circle and have the opportunity for more-involved discussion, while those from the outer circle listen to this discussion. A separate issue or different questions concerning one issue may be used for each group in its discussion.

Appropriate Topics

1. How to build self-esteem in children
2. What to expect of 2-, 3-, 4-, or 5-year-olds
3. Problem solving
4. Living with change
5. Positive uses of television
6. Courses and workshops that could be offered at school
7. Issues and concerns of children

Buzz Sessions

Buzz sessions are an excellent means of eliciting participation from all members of the group. They must be small enough to allow interaction among all participants. The smallest session consists of two people, and the maximum size should be 6 to 8. This makes it possible for all members to have the chance to express their opinions easily. Even in a

FIGURE 7.10 Concentric circles encourage those who might not participate freely to get involved.

large group, the audience can divide into smaller groups and discuss. The latter is called a 6–6 discussion, with 6 people discussing for 6 minutes. Because the session time is limited, it does not allow thorough examination of issues, but it does bring forth ideas from all involved in a very short period of time—an objective that is not accomplished in an open discussion with a large group.

Setup

1. Up to 24 people.
   a. Arrange chairs in a circle or semicircle.
   b. When the smaller group session is to begin, six people turn their chairs together to form their group. It is also possible for a group to move to another area for a quieter meeting.
2. Large auditorium.
   a. If people are seated in rows, three people turn around and discuss with three people behind them.
   b. Use some other technique to form groups of six throughout the auditorium.

Procedure

1. Buzz sessions may be formed at the beginning of the meeting, or they may be initiated later. The leader announces the formation of buzz groups either by proximity of chairs, a common interest in specific discussion areas, or by a mechanism to distribute members, such as counting off one through six and having those with common numbers form a group.
2. Each group chooses a leader and a recorder.
3. The topic is introduced to the group for discussion, and people are encouraged to participate much as they would in any other small-group discussion.
4. The recorder keeps relevant thoughts ready to report back to the larger group. In the smaller meeting (24 people), each group might have the time to give a short report to the total group. In an auditorium 6–6 meeting, it might not be possible to have everyone report back. Allow a specific number of groups that indicate interest in doing so to report back to the total audience.

Appropriate Topics

1. Home-management tips
2. Feelings about childrearing
3. Discipline
4. Moral values
5. Vacation ideas
6. Solving problems around home
7. Issues concerning school
8. Decisions that should be made concerning education

Brainstorming Sessions

Brainstorming is a unique method of active interaction by all members of the group. It promotes interchange, encourages lateral thinking, and facilitates expansion of thought. In brainstorming sessions, all contributions are accepted. Everyone is encouraged to suggest ideas and solutions. The participants may add to, combine, or modify other ideas, or they may introduce something new. There are no value judgments on the quality of suggestions. Osborn (1957) suggested that the "average person can think of twice as many ideas when working with a group than when working alone" (pp. 228–229).

The free and open brainstorming session provides an environment that facilitates the production of a variety of ideas from the participants. Members who are reluctant to contribute during an open discussion because they are not sure their ideas are worthy have a guaranteed safe environment in which to contribute during brainstorming. Quantity of ideas is the object. Later, the ideas may be analyzed, judged as to quality, and reduced to selected items. The brainstorming technique, therefore, is excellent for stimulation of diversified thought and solutions to issues and problems. It also reinforces the socioemotional aspects of a group by accepting the contributions of all people freely.

Setup

1. Arrange chairs in a circle if the group has fewer than 30 members. A small group allows for more interaction.
2. Brainstorming may be used in a larger group with an auditorium arrangement of chairs. In that case, the entire group has difficulty participating, but the mechanism is effective for bringing forth a quantity of ideas and thoughts.

Procedure

1. The brainstorming session requires a leader and a recorder.
   a. Appoint a recorder or ask for a volunteer.
   b. Appoint a leader or assume the leadership role.
2. The leader begins the brainstorming session by explaining the rules and emphasizing that all contributions are wanted and accepted. Even if ideas seem unusual, all members should contribute. Ideas should be interjected as they occur.
3. The topic or issue is explained to the group.
4. The session is opened to contributions from the group.

5. The recorder writes on a board or piece of paper all the ideas that come from the group.
6. After a selected amount of time—4, 6, or 10 minutes, depending on the issue and the flow of ideas—the group may turn to analyzing all the suggestions and pulling out the ones that seem to answer the issue or problem best.
7. A summary of the solutions and ideas gained from brainstorming is reported by the leader.
8. If this is an action meeting, plans for action should be identified at this time.

Appropriate Topics

1. Ideas to solve problems—for example, subjects for meetings, summer activities
2. How to get your child to study (or eat or go to bed)
3. Creative activities
4. Exploring your environment
5. Nutrition
6. Ways to improve relations at the school
7. Summer offerings for families

Workshops and Centers

Workshops are a superb means of achieving involvement by members. Most useful for demonstrating programs and curricula, they can also be used as an effective means of explaining procedures, illustrating the learning process, and developing understanding. The major ingredient in a workshop is active participation by members, whether through making puzzles and toys, working on mathematics, painting, modeling with clay, editing a newspaper, composing music, writing poetry, or planning an action.

Although often confused with workshops, centers are different in that they do not require participants to be actively involved in the project. Centers allow subgroups of the membership to gather simultaneously in various areas of the room, where they might see a demonstration, hear an explanation of an issue or program, or watch a media presentation. If time allows, more than one center may be visited. The variety of centers is limited only by the imagination and productivity of the planning group. The advantages of this diversified meeting are that (a) it reduces group size and thus promotes more interaction and allows individual questions; (b) participants are able to select topics of interest to them; and (c) tension and anxiety of the presenters are reduced because of the informal format.

Setup

1. Depending on available space, workshops and centers may take place in separate rooms or in one large room with designated areas.
2. Each presenter might have different requirements. The amount of space and number of tables and chairs requested should be set up according to those requirements.

Procedure

1. The chairperson explains the variety of workshops or centers available and procedures to be used.
2. Participants choose a workshop or center. These may be assigned according to several procedures: free choice, numbers on name tags, or preregistration.
3. Participants attend one or more workshops depending on time available. If plans include a time limit for each, the groups proceed from one to the next at a signal.
4. Members may gather together at the close of the meeting, or it may conclude with the final workshop or center.

Appropriate Topics

1. Learning activities
2. Art activities
3. Bookmaking
4. Games and toys
5. Math activities to do at home
6. Science activities to do at home
7. Rainy-day activities
8. Leadership training session

9. Writer's workshop
10. Learning to read

Observations and Field Trips

Although observations and field trips can be quite different in their objectives, they are similar in theory and procedure. The active viewing of a classroom, like a visit in the community, encourages the participant to be involved in observing activities. The opportunity to see an activity in process clarifies that process as no written or spoken word can. It is imperative, however, to discuss objectives and points to consider before the field trip or observation. It is also essential to analyze and discuss observations after the visits, to clarify the experience and bring it into focus. Many times the end of a field trip can be the beginning of a new, expanded project for the individual or group.

Arrangements Before Observations or Field Trips

1. Select the time and place for the observation or field trip.
   a. Plan classroom visits in advance. Specific objectives may be discussed prior to the observation.
   b. If the classroom has an observation area, observers can easily watch without disturbing the class. If there is no observation area, those going into the classroom should know the teacher's preferred procedure.
   c. Field trips must be planned and permission for visiting obtained.
2. Participants learn more and receive more satisfaction from field trips if background information and items to be aware of are discussed before the visit.
3. If the members are going to a place different from their regular meeting area, group travel arrangements should be made.

Procedure

1. The leader plans and conducts a previsit orientation.
2. The observation or field trip is completed.
3. Discussion of the experience clarifies the issues and focuses on the learning that has taken place. Many field trips tend to be an end in themselves, but that omits the most important followup, where new ideas and greater understanding are generated.

Appropriate Observations and Field Trips

1. In classroom observations, look for the following:
   a. How children learn
   b. Play—child's work
   c. Interpersonal relations
   d. Aggression
   e. Fine- and gross-motor control
   f. Hand–eye coordination
   g. Stages and ages
2. Field trip options include the following:
   a. Children's museums
   b. Art museums
   c. Parks
   d. Special schools
   e. Newspapers
   f. Hospitals
   g. Businesses
   h. Farms
   i. State legislature

Dyad or Triad Interaction and Feedback

During structured programs such as STEP and PET, interludes that allow the audience or participants to clarify, practice, and receive feedback on their interaction with others are beneficial. For example, if parents and teachers were working to improve interaction during a conference, sample statements would allow them to practice listening and other communication skills. If the topic were reflective listening, one member of the dyad or triad would share with the others an aspect or concern. The second person would answer with a reflective listening response. The third then would critique the response. Each member of a triad would have an opportunity to play each role: the speaker, listener, and observer.

Setup

1. Small group (up to 24).
   a. Arrange chairs in a circle, semicircle, or around tables.
   b. Have participants arrange their chairs so that two or three can communicate with each other.
2. Large auditorium.
   a. Start at the beginning of the row and have the aisle person turn and discuss with the person to the right. Dyads or triads can be formed all along each row.

Procedure

1. After a topic has been described or a video shown, stop the program and have the participants form dyads or triads.
2. Have the dyad or triad decide who will be the speaker, the listener, and the observer.
3. Describe a situation or problem that needs to be clarified or solved. Handouts describing situations are effective in large meetings.
4. Have the participants play out their parts.
5. The observer then critiques the statement and response using positive reinforcement as well as suggestions.

Appropriate Topics

1. Communication
2. Behavior and misbehavior
3. Determination of problem ownership
4. Reflective and active listening
5. Natural and logical consequences

Role Playing

Role playing is the dramatization of a situation where group members put themselves into designated roles. Role playing is a very informal type of meeting, similar to presenting a drama, so it can be adapted to a variety of situations. The roles that people play can be initiated by the players, or players can follow a set format or enact a specific situation. In either situation, the people playing the roles are to put themselves into those roles. They are to feel that they are the character in the role and respond with appropriate reactions and emotions. For this reason, spontaneous role playing is advantageous over the planned drama.

Role playing can be used to demonstrate a problem or develop participants' sensitivities to a situation. In demonstrating a situation, the group members discuss their feelings and reactions and offer solutions. It is an excellent means for getting many people involved in a situation and is easily used to illustrate parent–child interaction.

In development of sensitivity, role reversal is often used. For example, a teacher plays the role of principal while a principal plays the role of teacher. Not only do participants begin to understand the obligations of the other role, but through their playing of the role they also are able to demonstrate their feelings. This clarifies feelings for both parties. Another role-reversal situation that can be used is the parent–child relationship, with one participant playing the child's role and another playing the parent's role. The parent in the child's role develops sensitivity to the child's position.

Participants in role playing feel free to communicate their feelings and attitudes because they are not portraying themselves. This encourages greater openness and involvement. When group members begin role playing, they tend to be hesitant to get involved emotionally with the part. After using role playing for a time, hesitancy and reluctance to be involved disappear and people enjoy the opportunity to participate. If the group progresses to a therapeutic enactment, professional counselors should be included and consulted.

Setup

1. Role playing can be used in a variety of formats: (a) within the circle of participants—the center of the circle is the stage; (b) with chairs arranged in semicircles and the stage at the front—this is appropriate for larger groups; (c) in a large group meeting with an auditorium stage for the actors.
2. If the role playing is planned for participation by the entire group, allow members to meet first in a circle arrangement and then break into smaller groups after an introduction.

Procedure

1. A short discussion of the topic or situation is introduced by the leader or panel.
2. The situation that will be role played is introduced. This may be done by (a) volunteers, (b) people selected before the meeting to start the initial role play, or (c) breaking up the total group into groups of four or five, giving each group a topic with an outline of the role situation or a challenge to develop its own role situations.
3. The role can be played in two ways:
    a. It can be done in front of the entire group with members watching and listening to the dramatization and interaction. After the role play, the members use the open discussion method to clarify issues, study the problem, and make decisions.
    b. If the members are divided into smaller groups, it is beneficial to let each group play its roles simultaneously and have each small group discuss the feelings and attitudes that arose while they were playing their roles. After this, the small groups may discuss alternative means, ideas, and solutions.
4. If the small groups have all met and developed specific situations, it is also meaningful to have each group perform its role playing in front of the full group. Afterward, the larger group may discuss the role playing openly. Clarification, questions, and solutions are brought forth at this time.
5. The leader thanks those who participated in role playing.

Appropriate Topics

1. Parent-teacher conferences
2. Behavioral problems
3. Building self-esteem
4. Reflective listening
5. Roles within groups

Dramatizations

Short plays, written by group members or selected from those available from commercial companies, mental health organizations, or social agencies, can be used as springboards to discussions. There is an advantage to using skits composed by members. First, the skit can be kept short with parts that are easy to learn. Second, the action may be specifically related to the group's needs. Third, the preparation of the skit encourages group participants to become actively involved in the process and in the material that is presented.

A variation of the drama can be the use of puppets. Many participants like to use a puppet because it takes away the threat of performing.

Setup

1. Depending on the number of people at the meeting, the room can be arranged as follows:
    a. Use a circle for a small group, with the dramatization performed as a play in the round.
    b. If the group is small, chairs may be arranged in a semicircle with the "stage" at the opening. The stage may be raised or on the same level as the group members.
    c. If the group is large, an auditorium arrangement is appropriate. The dramatization can be performed on a stage.

Procedure

1. The leader convenes the meeting and introduces the drama and the cast of characters.
2. The dramatization is presented.
3. Open discussion ensues, which clarifies feelings, emotions, and information presented.
4. The leader thanks the performers.

Appropriate Topics

1. Family violence
2. Handling the stubborn child
3. Rivalry between children
4. Family rivalry
5. Family conferences
6. Communication among family members

Panels

A panel is an informal presentation by four to six presenters who discuss an issue or idea. Panel members come prepared with background material on a selected subject and, seated behind a table or in a semicircle, discuss the subject among themselves. The presentation allows informal interaction and conversation among the members.

The chairperson, although a member of the panel, has different responsibilities from the other members. The chairperson introduces members, presents the topic, and then encourages participation by the other members. Like a leader, the chairperson can clarify, keep the panel focused on the topic, and summarize the closing.

Setup

1. Place a table, or two tables slightly turned toward each other, in front of the audience. Set chairs for the panelists behind the table, allowing members to see and converse with one another easily.
2. Seat the audience or remaining members of the group in a semicircle, with the panel facing them. If the audience is large, auditorium-style seating may be used with a panel presentation.

Procedure

1. The chairperson does the following:
   a. Clarifies the panel procedure to the audience.
   b. Presents the topic for discussion and the relevance of the topic to the group's concerns.
   c. Introduces the panel members.
   d. Starts the discussion with a question or statement. The panelists begin a discussion, freely interacting and conversing with one another.
   e. Asks for questions from the audience. Questions are discussed among panelists.
   f. Summarizes the major points and the conclusions of the panel.
   g. Thanks the panel members for their contributions.

Appropriate Topics

1. Child development–social, intellectual, emotional, and physical
2. New methods of classroom teaching
3. Bias-free education
4. Exceptional children
5. Influence of drugs and alcohol on children
6. Discipline
7. Emotions in children
8. Managing a home with both parents working
9. Nutrition

Colloquies

The colloquy is a panel discussion by an informed or expert panel where members of the audience are encouraged by the chairperson to interject questions or comments during the presentation. This allows information pertinent to the audience's interests to be discussed during the main part of the presentation instead of waiting for a question-and-answer period after the presentation.

A second form of the colloquy includes two sets of panels, an expert panel and a lay panel. The lay panel uses the procedures for a panel discussion. The expert panel gives advice when called upon by the lay panel or when it thinks pertinent information is being overlooked.

Setup

1. For a single panel, place chairs behind tables that are turned so the members of the panel can make eye contact with one another.
2. For two panels—lay and expert—seat the chairperson in the center with one panel on the left and one on the right. Both sets of panel members should be facing slightly toward the center so they can see each other and the audience.

Procedure

1. Single-panel colloquy:
   a. The leader or chairperson explains and clarifies the colloquy procedure to the audience.
   b. The topic for discussion is introduced.
   c. Panel members are introduced.
   d. The chairperson offers a stimulating comment or question to start the discussion.
   e. The chairperson encourages free interaction among panel members and takes questions and comments from the audience.

f. An open forum follows the conclusion of the panel discussion.

g. The leader summarizes and concludes the meeting.

2. Dual-panel colloquy:
   a. The chairperson explains and clarifies the two-panel colloquy to the audience.
   b. The chairperson introduces the subject for discussion.
   c. The expert and lay panels are presented to the audience.
   d. The leader starts the discussion with a stimulating remark or question.
   e. As expert advice is needed, the second panel is called upon to contribute.
   f. A question-and-answer period follows the presentation, with comments and questions from the audience answered and discussed by both the lay and expert panels.
   g. The chairperson summarizes, thanks the participants, and concludes the colloquy.

Appropriate Topics

1. Dealing with your child's fears
2. Handling stress
3. Drug addiction and alcoholism
4. Helping exceptional children
5. Nutrition

Debates

When an issue is of a pro-and-con nature, a debate is an effective means of presenting both sides. The debate team presents opposing views of a controversial issue.

Setup

1. Place enough chairs for the members of each debate team on either side of a podium or table.
2. Place chairs in a circle for a small audience; if the group is large, use an auditorium formation.

Procedure

1. The question to be debated is announced by the chairperson, and the issue is turned over to the speakers for each side.
2. One speaker for the affirmative begins with a 2- to 4-minute speech. The next speaker is from the opposing position. The teams alternate until each member has spoken.
3. Rebuttal following each speech is optional, or leaders of both debate teams may conclude the debate section with rebuttals.
4. The chairperson entertains questions from the audience, and the debate teams answer and discuss the issue.

Appropriate Topics

1. Sex education—home or school?
2. Behavior modification versus logical consequences
3. Open education versus traditional education
4. Encouragement toward achievement versus "Don't push my child"
5. Back to basics versus inquiry and/or literacy-based education

Book Review Discussions

Book reviews by group members or experts provide a format that brings out stimulating new ideas or acknowledges expertise. The review may be given by one presenter or several members. An open discussion by the entire group follows.

Setup

1. Place chairs for book reviewers behind a table in front of the group.
2. Arrange chairs for the audience in a circle or semicircle.

Procedure

1. The chairperson tells a little about the book to be reviewed and introduces the book reviewer or book review panel.
2. The book reviewer discusses the author of the book.
3. The book review is given.
   a. If the book is to be reviewed by panel discussion, the group discusses issues and ideas in a conversational format.
   b. One person may give the book review.

c. Two or three people may each review a portion of the book.

4. After the review, the entire group joins in an open discussion of the book.

Appropriate Topics

1. Values
2. Decision making
3. Building self-concept
4. Communication
5. Divorce
6. Role identification
7. Single parents

Audiovisual Presentations

Visual stimuli, programmed material, and film presentations can be catalysts for a good open discussion. The audiovisual format is directed toward two senses—hearing and sight—whereas an audio presentation relies solely on hearing. The addition of visual stimuli is beneficial to those who learn better through sight than sound. Accompanying charts, posters, or pictures always help clarify ideas. Films, filmstrips, and video presentations can present information in an interesting and succinct manner.

Techniques

1. Audiotapes and records.
2. Audiovisual:
   a. Filmstrips with records or tapes
   b. Sound films
   c. Videotapes
   d. Slides with running commentary
3. Visual:
   a. Charts
   b. Posters
   c. Chalk drawings
   d. Filmstrips with printed information
   e. Opaque projector images
   f. Overhead projector transparencies
   g. Computers

Arrangements Before the Meeting

1. The teacher or group decides on information needed by members through interest finders.
2. Review and select films, slides, or tapes. (Choose only programs that are relevant, interesting, and presented well.)
3. Choose a member to give a presentation.
4. Reserve films, videos, or tapes, and order equipment—tape or record players, projectors, chart stands, projection carts, extension cords, outlet adapters, screen, and so on.
5. Preview audiovisual and audio materials to be sure of quality and develop questions and comments relevant to the presentation. Do not use audiovisual materials as fillers; use them only as relevant additions to the curriculum.
6. Review the "Arrangements for Meetings" section (pp. 223–224) and make appropriate preparations.

Setup

1. Check and prepare equipment before the meeting. Have film, slides, or filmstrips ready to begin and have charts and posters set up.
2. Arrange chairs so everyone can see the presentation.

Procedure

1. The chairperson introduces the topic and the presenter.
2. The presenter gives background information on audiovisual material and points out important aspects of the showing.
3. After the presentation, the presenter leads an open discussion and question-and-answer period.

Appropriate Topics

1. Foundations of reading and writing
2. Emotional growth
3. Dealing with fears
4. Exceptional children, for example, those with learning disabilities, autistic, and gifted
5. AIDS

6. Attention deficit disorder
7. Drugs and alcohol
8. Drop-out problems
9. Teenage pregnancies

Symposiums

A symposium is a formal presentation by several speakers on various aspects of a topic. Each symposium presenter develops a specific talk of 5 to 15 minutes in length. The symposium is similar to a lecture, but information is given by several lecturers rather than just one. Its value, to share expert information, is the same.

Setup

1. Place chairs for the presenters behind a table in front of the audience.
2. Chairs for the audience may be in a circle or semicircle for a small group, or auditorium arrangements can be made for a large group.

Procedure

1. The chairperson or leader introduces the symposium speakers.
2. Each presenter gives a talk.
3. The chairperson or leader provides transitional statements between each speaker's presentation.
4. At the end of the presentations, questions directed to a specific speaker or to the entire symposium are entertained by the chairperson. A discussion of questions follows.
5. The chairperson summarizes the main points of the meeting.
6. Symposium presenters are thanked for their contributions.

Appropriate Topics

1. Nonsexist education
2. Single parenthood
3. Gender-role identification
4. Multicultural understanding
5. Consumer education
6. Death and dying
7. Safety in the home (e.g., toys, poison, home arrangement)
8. AIDS
9. Drugs, alcohol
10. Suicide
11. Restructuring schools

Lectures

A lecture is a talk prepared by an expert or lay presenter. No interruptions or questions are allowed during the presentation, but there may be a question-and-answer period afterward. The lecture without a forum following it results in a formal presentation with no interaction between speaker and audience. A lecture forum that includes a period for questions and answers at the end of the address permits some interaction and allows the audience an opportunity to ask questions, clarify points, and make comments.

The lecture is an excellent vehicle for dissemination of specific information. As a result, care must be taken to choose a speaker who not only knows the subject but who also presents unbiased material.

Arrangements Before the Meeting

1. Select a topic and obtain a speaker who is recognized as an unbiased authority.
2. Communicate with the speaker on group interests and needs, time limit for speech, and forum period.
3. Prepare an introduction that is based on the speaker's background and expertise.
4. Review the "Arrangements for Meetings" section (pp. 223–224) and make appropriate preparations.

Setup

1. Place a podium or table at the center of the stage if the audience is large. Place chairs in a circle with a small table in front of the speaker if the audience is small.
2. Check the sound system if the area is large.
3. Obtain a glass and a pitcher of water for the speaker.

Procedure

1. The chairperson introduces the speaker and topic.
2. The speaker gives a talk for a specific period of time.
3. The chairperson conducts a forum for questions with the guest speaker responding to comments and answering questions.
4. The chairperson thanks the speaker, and the meeting is concluded.

Appropriate Topics

1. Money management
2. Specialists, for example, psychiatrist, pediatrician, dentist, nutritionist, obstetrician, special educator, speech therapist, physical therapist
3. How to manage stress
4. Dealing with illness and death
5. Preventive health measures
6. Childhood diseases
7. School finances
8. Preventing violence

Select the meeting format that fulfills your needs and is most appropriate for the topic. Members of the group have responsibilities to themselves and to the group. After a positive group meeting, the participants should feel supportive and supported as well as fulfilled and productive.

SUMMARY

Parent group meetings are among the most efficient and viable forms of parent education. Positive leadership skills are essential to facilitate productive parent groups. Included in this chapter are a description of a needs assessment and a discussion of the formation of parent groups.

Leadership skills and good group interaction can be developed if groups are aware of leadership and group roles. Roles that emerge within groups affect the interaction among participants. A knowledge of task, maintenance, and dysfunctional roles improves the productivity of group interaction through the concerted elimination of dysfunctional roles. An analysis of group discussion illustrates the interaction in process.

Group meetings use a variety of meeting formats, either individually or in combination. The formats include roundtables, concentric circles, buzz sessions, brainstorming sessions, workshops, field trips, dyad or triad interaction and feedback, role playing, dramatizations, panels, colloquies, debates, book reviews, audiovisual presentations, symposiums, and lectures. Choice of topics for the meetings should fit the interests and needs of the groups.

Evaluations are necessary in ongoing parent groups because they provide a basis for improvement of group interaction and suggestions for the continuing program.

SUGGESTED CLASS ACTIVITIES AND DISCUSSIONS

1. Generate some innovative icebreakers. Try them out on your classmates.
2. Conduct an opening period of a parent meeting. Include icebreakers and interest finders.
3. Make an interaction pattern on an observation wheel. Discuss the interaction pattern.
4. Conduct a needs assessment within the entire class or group. From the results, pick one topic for each of the formats, that is, panel, debate, symposium, workshop, buzz session, and so on. Let each group be responsible for conducting a meeting using these topics and formats.
5. Attend a parent education meeting in your community. Visit with the members. Note how the meeting is conducted, the involvement of the parents, and the feelings of the members. Talk with the director about the goals and objectives of the group. Talk with parents about their desires for the group.
6. Develop a workshop or meeting for parents. Include the objectives of the meeting, questions to be answered, background material on the questions, and a list of additional resources.
7. Attend a board meeting of your district.
8. Attend a parent advisory council meeting.
9. Attend or participate in a site-based or community management meeting.
10. Develop a format for team building in your school.

WEB SITES

Web sites for this chapter include issues and concerns that might be important to members of the class. Many topics chosen by the group for study and discussion may be found on Web sites.

National Center for Educational Statistics
http://nces.ed.gov

This is the primary federal center for analyzing data which includes early childhood education. It is located in the U.S. Department of Education and the Institute of Education Sciences.

Council for Exceptional Children
www.cec.sped.org

The CEC has information on special needs children including those with autism.

National Dropout Prevention Center
www.dropoutprevention.org

This network provided by the U.S. Department of Education Office of Special Education Programs promotes networking for parents, policymakers, and researchers to help at risk children find and receive the programs they need.

Center on School, Family & Community Partnership, Johns Hopkins University
www.csos.jhu.edu

The center's site has many articles and programs concerning family and school partnerships.

8 School-Based Programs

Education is the great equalizer. All children deserve the opportunity to an education that will allow them to achieve their hopes and visions.

E. H. Berger

It takes an entire village to educate a child.

African proverb

When schools work together with families to support children's learning, children tend to succeed in both school and later life. Many people are surprised that the most accurate predictor of a student's achievement is not income or social status, it is how involved the student's parents are in their children's education.

Comeau (2006, p. 1)

In this chapter on school-based education you will read about effective parent–school programs. After completing the chapter you should be able to do the following:

- Describe the roles that parents have in school involvement.
- List and describe successful programs related to early childhood and parent involvement.
- Describe how parents can have an active involvement in schools.
- Help reticent parents become involved.
- Describe a school where parents are active partners.
- Describe the Head Start program and its parent involvement.
- Describe Comer's School Development Program.
- Recognize the importance of parent involvement as illustrated by Reggio Emilia.
- Identify resources such as the Center on Families, Communities, Schools, and Children's Learning; National Center for Family Literacy; Family Resource Center of America; the Institute for Responsive Education; and the U.S. Department of Education.
- Develop activities that strengthen families and parent–school collaboration.
- Describe how Family Support America support families.
- Identify the importance of literacy and the development of literacy programs to help overcome illiteracy.

Eugenia Hepworth Berger

Teachers, reaching out to children in a caring, supportive way, let children know that they matter and that they belong. Teachers and parents want to provide an environment that facilitates children as they become educated.

Parents, schools, and society have extremely strong vested interests in the success of students in the schools. Parents want their children to develop into productive, intelligent, mentally healthy young adults. Schools want to provide an environment that facilitates and teaches children as they become educated and successful, fully functioning young adults. Society requires an educated citizenry. These desires have been expressed many times during the past decade. Scores of schools, recognizing the importance of home–school collaboration, have developed special programs that brought about a greater sense of cooperation.

When the first edition of this book was published, although programs for early childhood were evident, it was difficult to find descriptions of schools that were committed to involving parents. Today, a surge toward parent involvement is expressed by many schools and described in a voluminous number of articles. Involvement ranges from offering breakfasts for fathers to recognizing the school as one part of the community that must meet the needs of the family. This would include the following:

1. Implementation of strategies based on the strengths of families and their knowledge of their children.
2. Identification and implementation of preventive strategies that recognize the stresses affecting many families today—financial, emotional, social, and personal—to make the school family-friendly and supportive.
3. Collaboration with community agencies that offer resources for students and families.
4. Exploration of different models that will help schools reach out to families; replication of models that meet the needs of the community and school or development of programs based on community and family needs.
5. Inclusion of parent–school support in preservice classes, and knowledge of resources and parent involvement programs by teachers and administrators (Edwards & Young, 1992).

The forces toward involving parents came from many directions. Parent involvement, however, is not new (see chapter 4). Head Start included a parent commitment when it was implemented in 1965. Special education programs involved parents in the development of Individualized Education Plans after Public Law 94–142 was enacted in 1975 (see chapter 10). Hospitals and social agencies developed programs to work with schools to provide children and families with health and diagnostic provisions. Public schools looked toward parent involvement as one method of ensuring student success. The increasing number of child care facilities evoked concern for the child and the need for child care to reinforce the family, not replace it.

NINE LEVELS OF PARENT COLLABORATION

Parents may be involved with schools on nine different levels, ranging from those who are active educational partners at home and school to those who participate only as recipients of education and support. (See Figure 8.1.)

1. *Parent as an active partner and educational leader at home and at school.* The parent who is actively involved both at home and at school is highly committed. These families want to support their children through active involvement at home as well as in the school. Their roles may end with their commitment to their children or they may also be involved in the second level.
2. *Parent as a decision maker.* The second role goes beyond active involvement to include decision making. These parents may serve on the school board, on a site-based management team, or on an advisory council. With decision making comes the power to affect the offerings and climate of the school. Power and decision making are seen in the use of policy committees, site-based collaborative decision making, advisory task forces, and school boards. The trend toward site-based management, collaborative decision making, and charter schools shows an emerging shift in position. If this trend continues, decision making in public schools will include parents. Charter schools, financed by the public school systems, will continue to increase in numbers with parents acting as the decision makers.
3. *Parent as an advocate to help schools achieve excellent educational offerings.* Some parents are primarily involved with the schools as advocates for the school and as fund-raisers. Think of the parent who spends hours setting up the booths for a school fair to earn money to buy computers or some other equipment the school needs. Think of the parent who writes letters to newspapers or administrators supporting school programs or advocates forcefully for educational principles. Advocacy has spurred the development of programs for special education students. Case advocacy, in the hands of individual parents, can give parents the opportunity to state their case and get it resolved to their satisfaction. There are many levels of advocacy and a variety of ways parents can advocate for their children and the concerns they have.
4. *Parent actively involved with the school as a volunteer or paid employee.* Parents who work in the school enjoy a special position there.

Parent Collaboration with Schools

Parent as an active partner and educational leader at home and at school

Parent as a decision maker

Parent as an advocate for the school

Parent actively Involved as volunteer or paid employee

Parent as a liaison between school and home to support homework

Parent as supporter of the educational goals of the school

Parent as a recipient of education and support

Parent as member of parent educational classes

Parent as representative and activist in the community

FIGURE 8.1 Parents relate to the schools in ways ranging from support of their children's education to decision making.

Through their work they can view the operations of the school, learn about the curricula, and become acquainted with teachers and administrators as friends and colleagues. It is important for the school and parent to have specific guidelines on duties and responsibilities. They can help as advocates for the school in the community.

5. *Parent as a liaison between school and home to support homework and to be aware of school activities.* Parents who act as liaisons between school and home do not become involved in power or advocacy and are most interested in the school as the agency that educates their children.
6. *Parent, though not active, supporting the educational goals of the school and encouraging the child to study.* These parents, similar to those who serve as liaisons, are supportive of the schools. Perhaps they are too busy to be involved, or perhaps they do not remember schools with fondness and prefer to keep their distance, but they do not undermine the school's objective to educate their children. Schools should reach out to these parents and make them feel welcome.
7. *Parent as recipient of support from the school.* Schools reach more families than any other agency, and so it becomes expedient to look to schools for support. Parent involvement and family education can help mothers and fathers become better informed and offer support that enables them to strengthen their families. Offerings in the school may include family literacy classes, a crisis nursery, before- and after-school programs for children, a family resource room, clothes and boot exchanges, free breakfasts and lunches for children, as well as parent education. Schools can also serve as referral agencies for community services if families are in need.
8. *Parent as member of parent education classes.* If parents can be encouraged to attend classes, knowledge of child development and literacy education may help with their raising their children. For example, knowledge of the importance of language development, based in the first 4 years of life, is essential for later school success. During parent education classes it has come as a surprise to many parents that talking and reading with their young child are important. This small amount of parent education can help turn a child into a capable student.
9. *Parent as a representative and activist in community.* Parents with knowledge of community offerings, and active membership in community endeavors, may have the ability to solicit information and help from organizations in the community. For example, these community offerings may be able to help the family who is homeless, the child whose parents are on drugs, the family who needs help in obtaining employment, the child who needs protection, or the child who needs extra help with lessons. Parents who know the community strengthen the school's ability to use community offerings.

Society today needs agencies to collaborate and help families grow in strength and ability to survive. With the large number of parents working, all agencies involved with the family (recreation, health, social agencies, businesses, schools, and churches) will need to collaborate to ensure continuity. Employers must reevaluate their structure to allow more part-time, shared, and flexible hours and release time for parents to visit and volunteer in the schools; and they must collaborate with high schools to provide occupational internships. Health agencies also must collaborate with schools. Social agencies can provide support for parents that are unable to provide adequately for their families or that might be neglectful or abusive if they do not have support. Schools cannot be expected to solve all of society's problems and answer all the questions involved in change, but they should work with other agencies and provide education and facilities to help strengthen families.

The emerging family resource centers and the increasing number of schools offering family literacy classes are steps in the right direction. Parents are more able to care for and teach their children if they can read and write themselves. Parents can be more supportive of their children if they can participate in society successfully, earn a living, and provide a home.

SIX TYPES OF INVOLVEMENT

Epstein (1995, 1996, 2001) shares a framework of six types of involvement that schools may implement to increase collaboration among schools, families, and community. They are:

1. *Parenting* —Help parents with skills and an understanding of child and adolescent development that enables them to have a home environment that supports learning and school success.
2. *Communicating* —Communicate effectively, school to home and home to school, about children's progress and school programs.
3. *Volunteering* —Involve parents as volunteers with recruitment, training, and flexible schedules available so that parents can be involved.
4. *Learning at Home* —Provide information and activities that parents can use in learning at home, connecting the family and school.
5. *Decision Making* —Include parents in school decisions and governance and strengthen the parents' leadership skills.
6. *Collaborating with the Community* —Integrate services and resources of the community with the schools to strengthen families, school programs, and children's development and learning (Epstein, 1996, 2001).

Studies on Involvement

Epstein suggests that the six-component framework be used to extend research and knowledge about parent involvement. Studies by her and others revealed there are questions to be answered. One shows that teachers' views of parents are different from parents' views of themselves. The common belief that students want their parents to be uninvolved in middle and secondary schools was challenged when students indicated that they wanted their parents to be more involved and be available for guidance and knowledge about the schools (Epstein, 1996, 2001).

Teachers who reach out to parents are more accepting of and more knowledgeable about the families than those who hesitate to be involved with parents. Studies found that teacher practices in their involvement with families were more critical than family background in determining how students progress. "At the elementary, middle, and high school levels, surveys of parents, teachers, principals, and students reveal that if schools invest in practices that involve families, then parents respond by conducting those practices, including many parents who might not have otherwise become involved on their own" (Epstein, 1996, p. 217).

Teachers who involve and work well with parents tend to evaluate the parents without stereotyping them, whether the parents are single or married, educated or lacking in education. When teachers involve parents, they find that the parents are helpful. When teachers do not involve parents, they often stereotype single parents and those with less education as not being helpful (Epstein, 1996).

The Center on School, Family, and Community Partnership focuses on elementary, middle, and secondary schools in their research and publications. They have guidelines to assist schools in building school–family–community partnerships (Epstein, 2001).

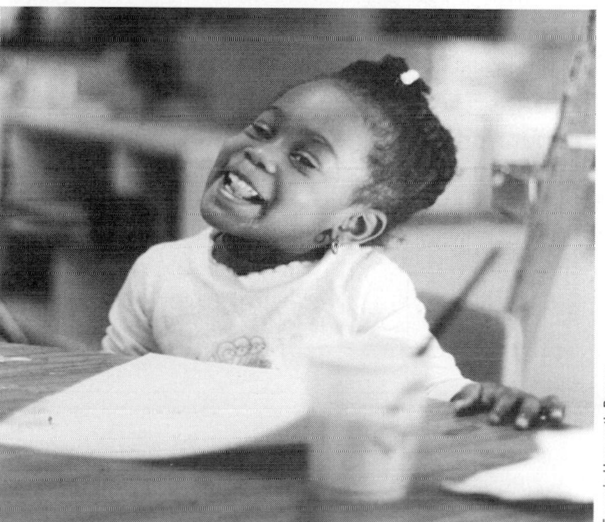

Eugenia Hepworth Berger

Three principles, consensus, collaboration, and no-fault are needed to develop a climate that allows schools, children and parents to thrive (Comer, 1996).

COMER PROCESS

Over 30 years ago in New Haven, Connecticut, the Yale Child Study Center and New Haven Public Schools collaborated to bring change to two public schools. Comer analyzed issues and problems in the schools drawing on his own childhood experiences and his professional background in medicine and psychology. The process Comer used to develop nurturing and successful schools has

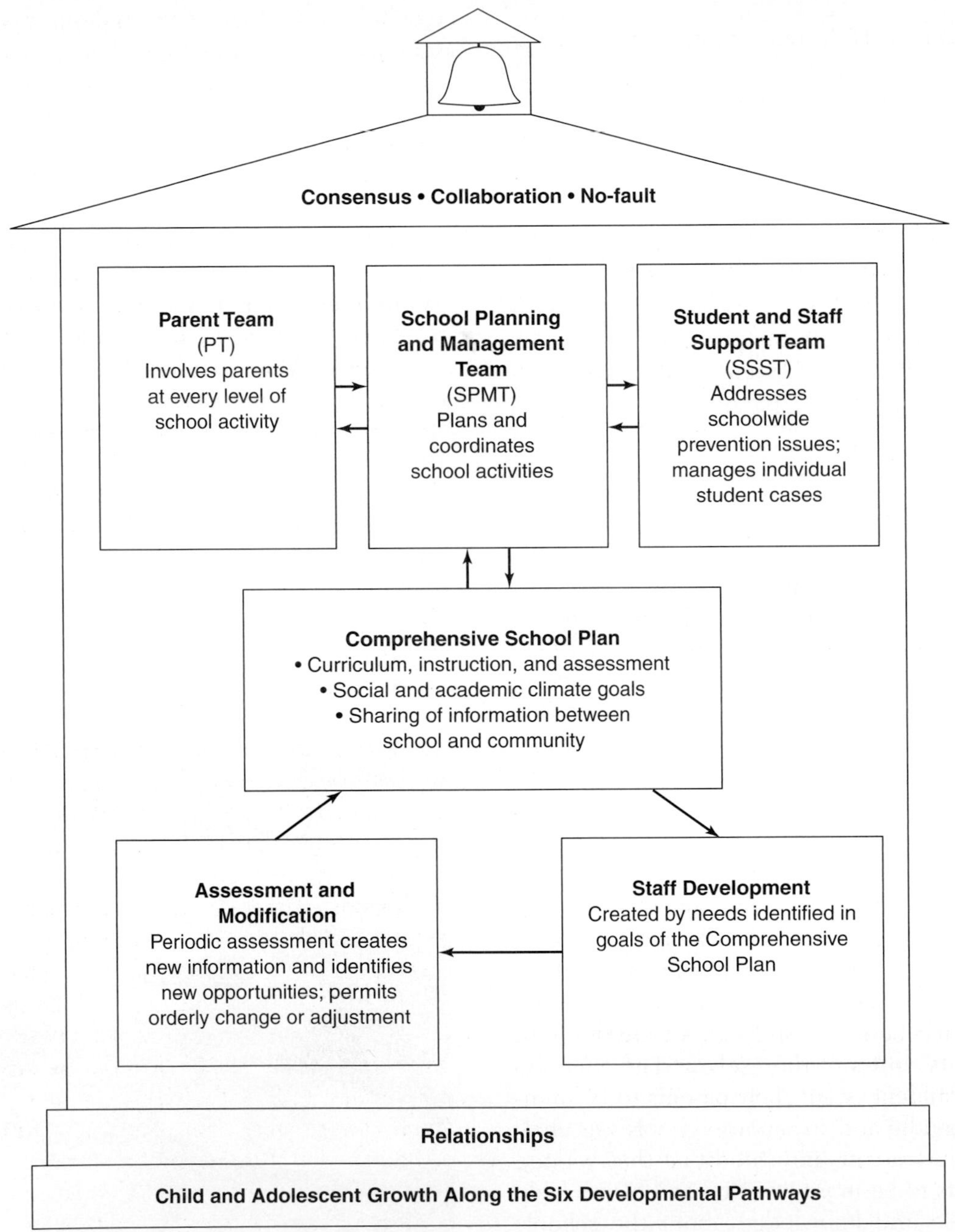

FIGURE 8.2 The foundations of Comer's theoretical framework of school reform.

Source: Reprinted by permission of the publisher from Comer, J. P., Haynes, N. M., Joyner, E. T., & Ben-Avie, M. (Eds.). *Rallying the Whole Village: The Comer Process for Reforming Education*. (New York: Teachers College Press © 1996 by Teachers College, Columbia University. All rights reserved.), Figures 1.1 & 2.1.

succeeded and been copied throughout the United States.

Comer's School Development Program (SDP) is based on three principles—consensus, collaboration, and no-fault—needed to develop a climate that allows schools, children, and parents to thrive (see Figure 8.2). In using these principles, school personnel and parents can review aims and concerns without fault being assigned to anyone. Consensus allows discussion, brainstorming for ideas, and decision making without requiring a vote that might cause divisiveness. Collaboration allows the schools, families, and community to move forward to develop a viable, responsive environment for children (Comer, 1997, 2004; Comer, Haynes, Joyner, & Ben-Avie, 1996).

The SDP schools focus on child development and positive relationships. The school is empowered to meet the needs of the students through the curriculum, social activities, and teaching methods, while it reinforces the positive aspects of home and builds social networks.

Each school is an ecological system. In order to change children's perceptions and feelings, the interactions in the system must change. How does this change come about? SDP schools are developed through an ongoing process that places the child at the center.

Comer based the framework for school change on Field Theory, Human Ecological Systems Theory, the Population Adjustment Model, and the Social Action Model. The foundation of Comer's framework is illustrated in Figure 8.3, with brief descriptions of the theories behind the school reform. Comer saw that children's behaviors were determined by their environment. Children need to have positive interactions in order to develop physically, socially, and emotionally.

The child-centered environment is facilitated by planning and collaboration between professional and community. To do this, three teams guided by the three guiding principles plan and work to develop a school climate that nurtures the children. The three teams, as shown in Figure 8.2, are:

1. *School Planning and Management Team (SPMT).* The School Planning and Management Team plans and coordinates school endeavors such as curriculum, assessment, and instruction.
2. *Student and Staff Support Team (SSST),* which was first called the Mental Health Team. The Student and Staff Support Team works to prevent concerns from becoming problems and responds to the issues and needs of individual students.
3. *Parent Team (PT).* The Parent Team involves parents at all levels of the school and integrates the school with the community. (Comer, 2004; Comer, Haynes, & Joyner, 1996; Emmons, Comer, & Haynes, 1996; Haynes, Ben-Avie, Squires, Howley, Negron, & Corbin, 1996)

To develop an SDP school participants must build trust, plan well, empower parents, and continually monitor, assess, and modify as necessary (Haynes et al., 1996, pp. 50–51). For more information, refer to the following books by Comer, Haynes, Joyner, and Ben-Avie (1996), *Rallying the Whole Village: The Comer Process for Reforming Education*, and Comer (2004) *Leave No Child Behind: Preparing today's youth for Tomorrow's World*, or contact the School Development Program in New Haven, Connecticut.

EARLY CHILDHOOD LONGITUDINAL STUDY

Although the Early Childhood Longitudinal Study, Kindergarten Class of 1998–99 (ECLS-K), about early childhood does not specify the contributions of parent involvement versus instruction at school, it does consider the following: age at school entry, health status, home educational experiences, child care histories, and race/ethnicity. The study included more than 1,000 kindergarten classes with over 22,000 children who began kindergarten in the fall of 1998. The 2002 report includes three studies, and further studies will follow the children until the end of their fifth grade. The first two grade reports, *American Kindergartners* and *The Kindergarten Year*, revealed that the children's skills and knowledge differ in health status, education in the home, child care, race/ethnicity, and age when they began kindergarten. These first two reports were concerned about the children's kindergarten years. The third report looked at mathematical and reading achievement and skills as they relate to child,

Field Theory
Lewin (1936)

- Everything an individual knows, feels, and perceives is done in a subjective reality.
- This subjective reality is known as a person's psychological field or life space; only those things present in the life space influence behavior.

Human Ecological Systems Theory
Kelly (1966)

- Behavior is an interaction of human beings with the physical, social, and psychological environments, making behavior adaptive.
- The theory's four principles are:
  - — The community is the client.
  - — Reduce those community services that maintain the status quo.
  - — Strengthen community resources.
  - — Plan for change.

Comer's Theoretical Framework of Child Development

- A child's behavior is determined by his or her interaction with the physical, social, and psychological environments.
- Children need positive interactions with adults in order to develop adequately.
- Child-centered planning and collaboration among adults facilitate positive interaction.
- All planning for child development should be a collaborative effort between professionals and community members.

Comer's Framework Applied
The School Development Program

- Three Guiding Principles
- Three Mechanisms (Teams)
- Three Operations

Population Adjustment Model
Becker, Wylan, and McCourt (1971)
Hartman (1979)

- Identify populations at risk for developing mental illness.
- Intervene through modifying the environment to promote mental health.

Social Action Model
Reiff (1966)

- Program planning should be a collaborative effort between professionals and community members.
- Professionals should have an integral knowledge of the community in which they are working.

FIGURE 8.3 Model of the SDP process.

Source: Reprinted by permission of the publisher from Comer, J. P., Haynes, N. M., Joyner, E. T., & Ben-Avie, M. (Eds.), *Rallying the Whole Village: The Comer Process for Reforming Education*. (New York: Teachers College Press, ©1996 by Teachers College, Columbia University. All rights reserved.), Figures 1.1 & 2.1.

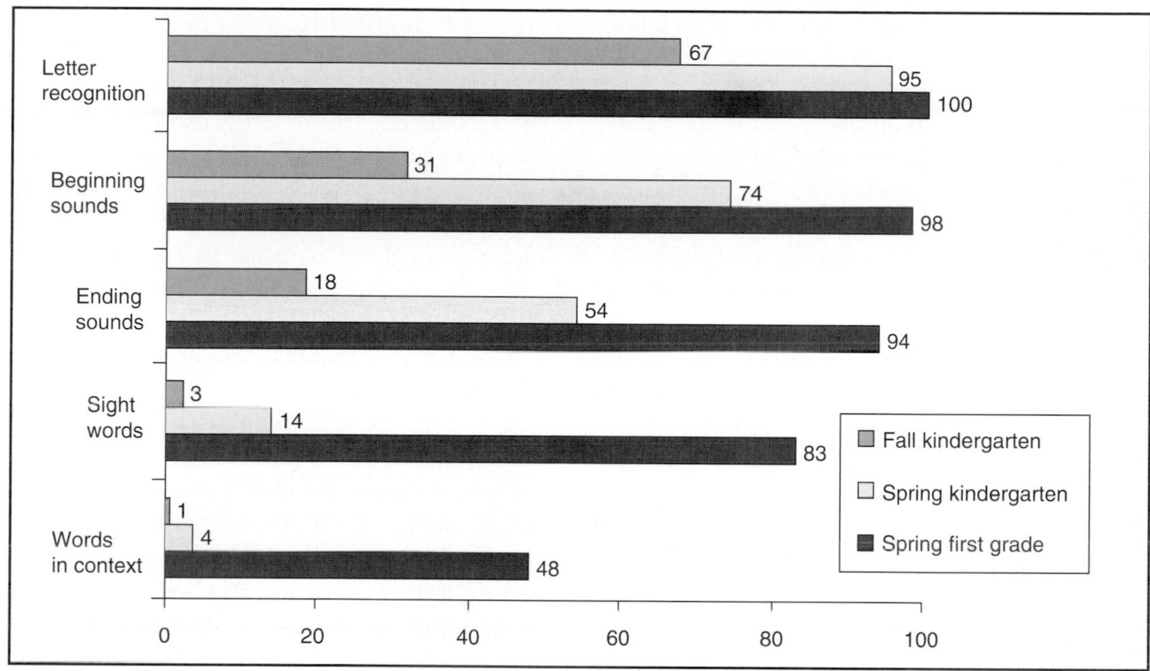

FIGURE 8.4 Percentage of children demonstrating specific reading knowledge and skills for fall kindergarten, spring kindergarten, and spring first grade: 1998–99 and 2000.

Note: Estimates reflect children assessed in English in all three rounds of data collection and who entered kindergarten for the first time in the fall of 1998 and were promoted to first grade in the fall of 1999. The estimates in this report do not exactly match those found in previous reports based on the same data. This report uses a different weight in making the estimates, which is stricter in its response requirements and utilizes a slightly smaller sample of children. For more information, see the Analytic Sample section of this report.

Source: From *Early Childhood Longitudinal Study, Kindergarten Class of 1998–99*, Base Year Public-Use and First Grade Restricted-Use data files, by the U.S. Department of Education, National Center for Education Statistics.

family, and school characteristics at the end of first grade. The report also considered how the children's abilities and health when they entered kindergarten related to their approaches to learning, literary, and health at the end of kindergarten and first grade. Both recognition of numbers and recognition of letters were used in the study because they both represent the child's understanding that symbols have meaning.

Are there differences in reading and mathematics abilities between kindergarten and first grade and do they differ in relation to family, child, and school? The relationships examined were (a) proficiency in recognizing letters; (b) being read to at least three times a week; (c) proficiency in recognizing numbers and basic shapes; (d) proficiency in the mathematical concept of relative size; (e) demonstration of a positive approach to learning often or very often; and (f) being in very good to excellent general health.

Figure 8.4 illustrates the levels of achievement at the beginning of kindergarten, in the spring after a school year of kindergarten, and in the spring of the children's first-grade year. When first entering kindergarten, 67 percent had letter recognition; by the end of the year 95 percent knew the letters in the alphabet; and by the end of first grade almost 100 percent were able to recognize letters. Thirty-one percent of the students knew beginning sounds at the beginning of kindergarten and 74 percent were able to recognize beginning sounds by the end of the year. By the end of first grade 98 percent were able to identify beginning sounds. Sight words improved considerably between the beginning of kindergarten, when only 3 percent recognized words and the end of first grade when 83 percent identified words, by sight. Words in context improved to 48 percent by the end of first grade, up from 1 percent in the fall of kindergarten and 4 percent in the spring.

According to the National Center for Education Statistics (2002): Children who recognize their letters, who are read to at least three times a week, who recognize their basic numbers and shapes, and who demonstrate an understanding of the mathematical concept of relative size as they enter kindergarten demonstrate significantly higher overall reading and mathematics knowledge and skills (in terms of an overall scale score) in the spring of kindergarten and the spring of first grade than children who do not have these resources. The same pattern is true for children who frequently demonstrate a positive approach to learning and who are in very good to excellent health as they enter kindergarten (p. 2).

> Differences in children's achievement (as represented by their overall achievement score) by their family's poverty status, race/ethnicity, and school type persist from kindergarten through the spring of first grade. However, children's overall reading and mathematics achievement does not vary by their sex. (p.1)
>
> By the spring of first grade, females are more likely to be reading and males are more likely to be successful at advance mathematical operations (i.e., multiplication and division). When considering the poverty status of children's families from the kindergarten year, first graders from economically stable families are more likely to recognize words by sight than first graders from poor families. The same is true for addition and subtraction. Moreover, about twice as many first graders from economically stable families are proficient at understanding words in context and performing multiplication and division as first graders from poor families. (pp. 1, 2)

A WALK THROUGH AN ELEMENTARY SCHOOL

Assume the role of a parent who visits a school committed to the involvement of parents. As you open the school door, you notice a sign that welcomes you. The staff greets you with smiles when you check in at the office. If you want to have a cup of tea or coffee, look through the school's curricula, or read an article, you can visit the family center. There, several parents are developing curriculum material for the school's resource room. One parent is making a game for the third- and fourth-grade classes. Another is clipping curriculum-related articles to be filed for reference. As you sip your coffee, the sounds of young children echo down the hall from the west wing of the building. Parents and their children are arriving for parent education classes or parent–child meetings. The school offers programs for parents of infants, toddlers, and preschool children. Both parents are invited and included in the programs. For those who cannot come during the week, a Saturday session is available. On the fourth Tuesday of every month, the school has a breakfast for students' fathers or friends.

You came to school today to visit your child's classroom, so, after a brief visit in the family center, you walk to your child's room. On the bulletin board outside the door is a welcome notice that shows in detail what the children have been accomplishing. Here the teacher has described the happenings for the week, listed volunteer times for parents, and asked for contributions of plastic containers to be used in making tempera paint prints.

Immediately aware of what is happening in the room, you make a note to start collecting "scrounge materials" for recycling in the classroom. An invitation to an evening workshop reminds you that you have saved next Tuesday evening for that very event. In the space for notes to and from parents, you write a short response to the message you received from the teacher last week.

Also attached to the bulletin board are "Tips for Visiting." These let you know that you can become involved in a classroom activity rather than spend your time passively observing. The teacher smiles and acknowledges your presence but, being involved with the class, continues teaching. The class greeter, a child chosen as a "very important person" this week, comes up and welcomes you. Later, during a center session or break, you have an opportunity to talk with the teacher and your child. Recruitment of volunteers is under way so you are encouraged—but not forced—to contribute. Flexible hours, designated times, child care services, and a variety of tasks make it easy to share some time in this classroom.

Knowing that the principal holds an open forum each week at this time, you stop by and join a discussion on school policy. Parents are being encouraged to evaluate the "tote bag" home learning activities that have been sent home with children. In addition, plans are under way for an after-school recreation program. The principal will take the comments to the Parent Advisory Board meeting later this week. As you leave the school, you feel satisfied that this school responds to the needs of both you and your child.

See Figure 8.5 for an illustration of schools reaching out and collaborating with families and communities.

CHARACTERISTICS OF EFFECTIVE COLLABORATION

The characteristics of effective parent–school collaboration include the following:

1. Principals, teachers, child-care providers, staff, and parents who believe in parent involvement.
2. Schools and child-care centers that encourage parent collaboration by encouraging parents to

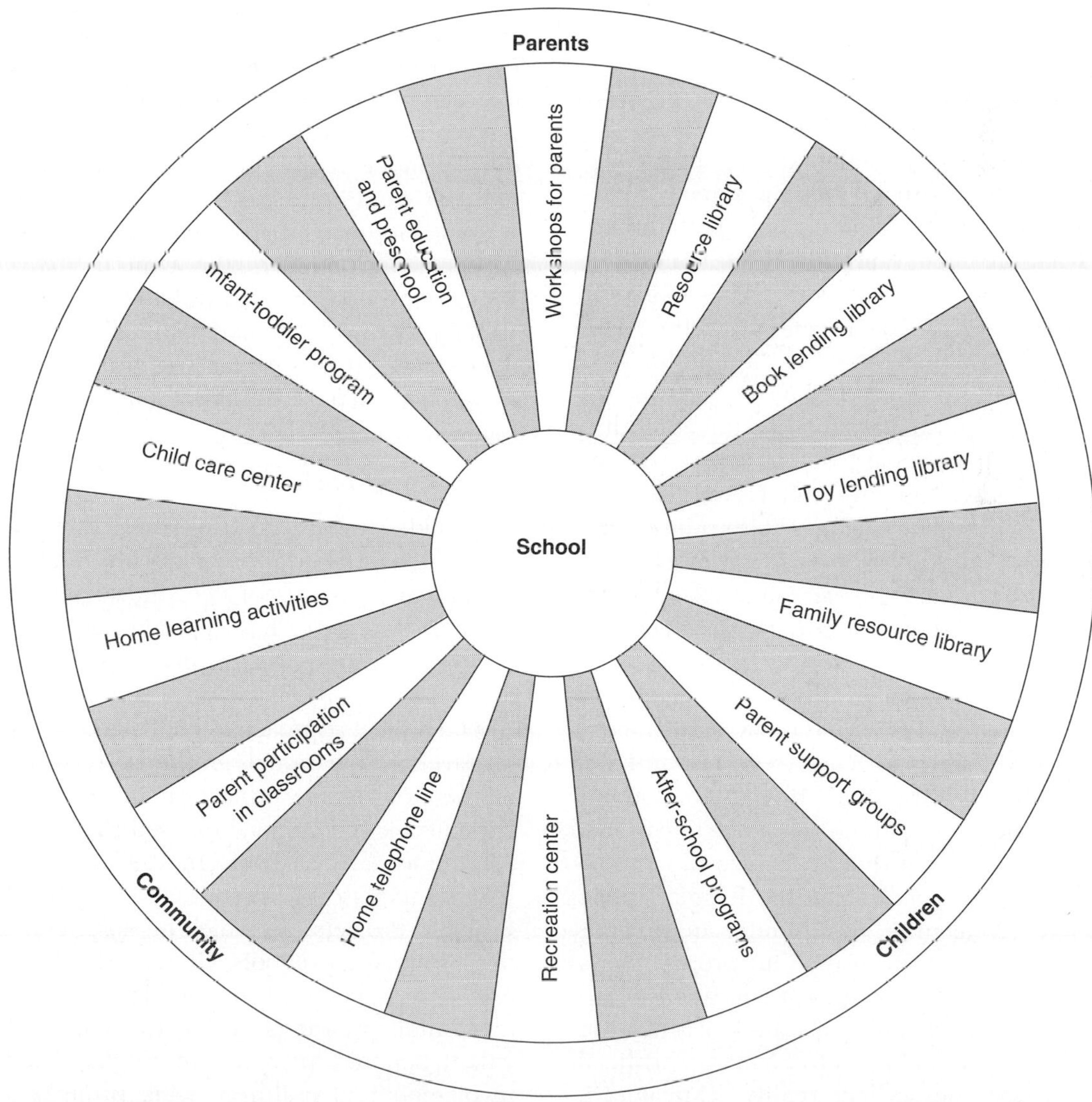

FIGURE 8.5 The spokes of the wheel radiate from the school and reveal opportunities for involving parents, childern, and the community.

participate at the level that best fits their interests and time (see Figure 8.1).

3. An open-door policy and climate that respond to parent concerns with effective communication.
4. Children, new to the school or center, are paired with a classmate to help the new child become a class member more easily.
5. Conferences, with child care available, are held at times that make it possible and convenient for parents to attend.
6. A feeling of family, schools, center, and community joined together in a cooperative effort to support children's health and educational growth.

Visiting Reggio Emilia

Reggio Emilia, an early childhood program located in northern Italy, illustrates the importance of parent involvement in education. In Italy, both municipal and national programs share the belief that young children, infants, toddlers and 3- to 5-year olds deserve the right to care and education. The 1968 national law that required funding for free public preschool for the 3- to 5-year olds was followed by one in 1971 that established infant/toddler centers with both national financing and contributions from parents (Gandini, 1993; Hewett, 2001).

The story of parent involvement starts even earlier. After the end of World War II, the first preschool was established by parents who were able to sell a war tank, six horses, and three trucks that were left behind when the Germans retreated (Hewett, 2001). "The essential role and intimate involvement of parents in their children's education is, to this day, a fundamental element of the Reggio Emilia Approach" (p. 4).

When authors write about Reggio Emilia and describe the program with no reference to parents, it makes one wonder if they recognize the importance and essential quality that the Reggio Emilia schools have. Malaguzzi, the founder and former director, described it this way: "Our proposition is to consider a triad at the center of education—children, teachers, and families. To think of a dyad of only a teacher and a child is to create an artificial world that does not reflect reality" (Malaguzzi, 1993, p. 9). The inclusive nature of the Reggio Emilia program shows the child as forceful, capable, with strong potential connected to parents and teachers as a participating member of their education. The interaction of children with adults and other children is essential for their development. "Interaction among children affects social, emotional, communicative, and cognitive behavior and development . . . different from those usually reached by children working in isolation" (p. 12).

Hewett (2001) describes the role and image of the learner and the role of the teacher. The child has rights; the child is an active constructor of knowledge; the child is a researcher, and the child is a social being. The teacher is a collaborator and co-learner; the teacher is a guide and facilitator, the teacher is a researcher, and the teacher is a reflective practitioner (pp. 96–98). If you add parent to the roles of the teacher, you will be able to visualize the triad of child, teacher, and parent in the total development of the child. Review chapter 1 for more discussion of the Reggio Emilia approach. A similar approach that strengthens the child's educational experience in the United States is the Project Approach, which involves the child as a constructor of knowledge and research. The similarity does not end there; the teacher is also a co-learner, researcher, guide, and facilitator as described in the following section.

Project Approach

The child as a constructor of knowledge is a central part of the project approach. This concept is not new. It has been present since the beginning of civilization. Mankind has learned and developed through finding ways to answer challenges and questions.

The project approach as known today has it roots in earlier educational methods. It was evident in the progressive education movement. W. H. Kirkpatrick and colleagues used the term *project method* as early as 1918. In 1925, an elementary school supervisor, F. W. Rawcliffe, wrote "Practical Problem Projects," in which he described projects in Chicago-area schools, (Katz, n.d,). Both Piaget and Vgotsky believed that children construct their own understandings (refer to chapter 1). The Infant Schools (primary) in England had active involvement of children using projects as early as the 1970s. More recently the constructivist approach in the United States and Reggio Emilia in Italy have revived the interest in education revolving around projects. When a project is chosen that sparks the children's interest, the resulting work, development, discovery, documentation, and recording make education and learning come alive.

The term *project approach* describes the focus of the lesson without any need for other descriptive terms. It does not, however, describe the in-depth construction of learning that can be achieved by being involved in the planning, discovery, conducting of research, or the describing and writing the results of the project. The levels of involvement can be from simple for very young children (it would not seem simple to them) to the very complex work of older children. Children grow socially when they can work cooperatively and share both the excitement and challenge of learning about their chosen project. Whether the idea for a project comes from the teacher, child-care provider or from a child, it is essential that there be an opportunity to succeed in its development.

A good example of a project appeared in *Young Children* in an article by Helm, Hebner, and Long (2000) titled "Quiltmaking: A Perfect Project for Preschool and Primary." In most project approaches there are three phases: (a) planning, researching, and organizing; (b) investigating, discovering, constructing and working; and (c) completing the project and celebrating its success. The authors showed how both preschool classrooms and primary classrooms could use the same project theme, quilting. Using quilts also provided a bridge to home and parent involvement. Children made class quilts of paper, fabric, Velcro, tie-dye, and panels made into a banner. The curriculum was enhanced. The preschool room had language, art/music, drama, science, and math, all based on quilts. The primary room had reading enrichment, math, social studies, and art/music. Throughout the project children were communicating, cooperating, and constructing a knowledge base.

SCHOOL AND CENTER PROGRAMS

As an early childhood educator one might question why parent involvement has suddenly been recognized as important. The tradition of involving parents has been strong in the early childhood profession for years, as exemplified in the parent cooperative movement and carried forth by many child care providers and educators. The following describe programs for early childhood-age children.

Eugenia Hepworth Berger

When a project sparks the children's interest, the resulting work, development, discovery, documentation, and recording make education and learning come alive.

Effective Programs—Research Briefs

Effective programs, according to research reported by Koraly, Kilburn, & Cannon (2005) and Rand Corporation, included the following early childhood education programs, which were combined with parent education and/or home visitations. All of the following programs were found to be effective.

Head Start, High/Scope Perry Preschool Project, Carolina Abecedarian Project, Project CARE, Syracuse Family Development Research, Houston Parent–Child Development Center, Early Training Project, Chicago Child Parent Center, and Oklahoma Pre-K

The key findings concluded that early intervention have more favorable results if the caregivers are well trained. There is also evidence to suggest that center-based programs with smaller child-to-staff ratios are more successful. Early childhood programs benefit education progress and academic achievement, reduction of delinquency and crime, and improved ability in the labor market. For every dollar spent on programs, there is a return ranging from $l.80 to $17.07. Descriptions of Head Start, High/Scope Perry Preschool Project, Carolina Abecedarian Project, Project CARE, Syracuse Family Development, and Houston Parent–Child Development Center, Early Training Project, Chicago Child Parent Center, and Oklahoma Pre-K follow.

Head Start

Head Start, a federal program with such credibility that funding has continued since 1965, is a comprehensive early childhood program that provides child development programs for low-income, preschool children in the United States, District of Columbia, Puerto Rico, and the U.S. territories (U.S. Department of Health and Human Services, 2002). From its inception, Head Start involved the family in its outreach, with spokes of the wheel including education; health care, including medical, dental, and mental health; nutrition; social services; staff development; and parent involvement. Head Start makes a significant difference in the lives of children and their parents through these services.

Funding for Head Start increased to $6.8 billion in 2006. This has enabled Head Start to fund 1,604 local programs, and it has served more than 900,000 children (U.S. Department of Health and Human Services Research, 2006). Research indicates that the services of Head Start improve vocabulary, math, and social skills. In addition, Head Start parents are more involved with their children's education. Two thirds read to their children three times a week or more, three fourths attend parent–teacher conferences, and most volunteer in the classroom (U.S. Department of Health and Human Services Fact Sheet, 2002).

Parent Involvement In 2004, revised Head Start Performance Standards (HSPS) were implemented. The standards reinforce previous practices of family partnerships. Parent involvement policies HSPS 1304.40 Family Partnerships include:

a. Family goal setting

1. Grantee and delegate agencies must engage in a process of collaborative partnership-building with parents to establish mutual trust and to identify family goals, strengths, and necessary services and other supports. This process must be initiated as early after enrollment as possible and it must take into consideration each family's readiness and willingness to participate in the process.

b. Parent involvement—general

1. Grantee and delegate agencies must provide parent involvement and education activities that are responsive to the ongoing and expressed needs of the parents, both as individuals and as members of a group. Other community agencies should be encouraged to assist in the planning and implementation of such programs opportunities in policy making, parent involvement, and education.
2. Early Head Start and Head Start settings must be open to parents during all program hours. Parents must be welcomed as visitors and encouraged to observe children as often as possible and to participate with children in group activities. The participation of parents in any program

activity must be voluntary, and must not be required as a condition of the child's enrollment.

3. Grantee and delegate agencies must provide parents with opportunities to participate in the program as employees or volunteers.

c. Parent involvement in child development and education

1. Grantee and delegate agencies must provide opportunities to include parents in the development of the program's curriculum and approach to child development and education.
2. Grantee and delegate agencies must provide opportunities for parents to enhance their parenting skills, knowledge, and understanding of the educational and developmental needs and activities of their children and to share concerns about their children with program staff.
3. In addition to the two home visits, teachers in center-based programs must conduct staff–parent conferences, as needed, but no less than two per program year, to enhance the knowledge and understanding of both staff and parents of the educational developmental progress and activities of children in the program.

In 1304.51 Management Systems and Procedures, the HSPS include:

a. Communication with families

1. Grantee and delegate agencies must ensure that effective two-way comprehensive communications between staff and parents are carried out on a regular basis throughout the program year.

The thrust of the message is to enable parents to help themselves. Parents can do this only with more education, more options, more knowledge, greater self-esteem, and more empowerment. Although Head Start parents have had more access to parent involvement than parents in most early childhood programs (with perhaps the exception of parent cooperatives), the task force and standards encourage a more active commitment to ensuring true parent involvement.

Before initiating any parent program, it is wise to ask parents how they perceive their needs. Although needs will change throughout the life of any program, early assessment with periodic review will show the initial needs and the progression of later needs. Develop a needs assessment specific to the population.

After Head Start parents complete a needs assessment, plans for parent participation can be devised with better understanding. As parents become more familiar with the program and more sophisticated in their learning, their needs and requests will vary, so provide ongoing assessment by continued use of questionnaires.

In the area of decision making, Head Start programs involve parents at two or three levels: the Head Start Center Committee, the Head Start Policy Committee for the delegate agency, and the Head Start Policy Council (for the grantee funded by the federal government). The first is initiated by each center, which should have a committee composed of parents whose children are enrolled.

Head Start, initially conceived with a parent component, has integrated parents into every aspect of its program. Visualize the degree of parent involvement in the Head Start program. On a visit to a typical Head Start class, you will find a teacher and aide surrounded by 12 eager 3- and 4-year-olds, working, singing, playing, and laughing. Because the center is located in the community it serves, parents usually drop off and pick up their children. As they enter the school, teachers and parents exchange pleasant greetings. On some days the parents stay and help.

The teacher may be a college graduate from another neighborhood, but, just as often, the teacher is a local parent who had children enrolled in the Head Start program or who has a college degree and who has earned Child Development Associate (CDA) credentials. The aide chats with the parent about something exciting the child did yesterday. The aide, who lives in the neighborhood and also has children, knows the child well. The person responsible for lunch is another community parent. Through a Head Start career ladder, many low-income parents are hired to assist in the program. After lunch, the parent coordinator drops in to check on a child who has been ill. The parent coordinator was chosen by the policy committee because the parents respected and liked this neighbor. This person has succeeded in establishing rapport with and support for the neighbors. Two of the most essential and greatest strengths of the Head Start philosophy are the involvement of parents and the belief that parents can achieve.

Early Head Start. Early Head Start, a program that serves low income families who have infants and toddlers, was created with the reauthorization of the Head Start Act in 1994. From 68 programs in 1995, it grew to 635 programs in 2001 that serve 45,000 children. In 2002 and 2003, Early Head Start (EHS) received 10 percent of the Head Start appropriation. In January 2001, a national evaluation that covered the first 2 years of 3,000 children showed that EHS children performed significantly better on cognitive, social–emotional development, and language. In addition, the parents scored higher than the control group on knowledge of infant–toddler development, parenting, and home environment. It was also found that parents of children were more likely to go into job training or attend school, and that family conflict declined (Fenichel & Mann, 2001).

Families may be served in center-based or home-based environments, or a combination of the two. Programs need to meet or exceed federal Head Start performance standards (Buell, Hallam, & Beck, 2001). For children from birth to 36 months who are enrolled in out-of-home programs, the EHS standard is a maximum of eight children and a child ratio of 1:4. This standard helps ensure the high-quality care and nurturing environment that infants and toddlers need.

High/Scope Perry Preschool Program

In November 2004, High/Scope reported a long-term study of adults at age 40 who, as low-income 3- and 4- year old children, had participated in a 2-year early education and care program provided by High/Scope. From 1962 through 1967, High/Scope operated the High/Scope Perry Preschool program with a limit of eight children per teacher. A sample of 123 low-income African American boys and girls were randomly assigned to five preschools or to a group who received no preschool program. Classes were held five days a week for $2\frac{1}{2}$ hours. Teachers were college graduates, certified in early childhood, special education, or elementary education. "The early childhood education was most relevant to their classroom practices" (Schweinhart, 2005, p. 8).

Research Results. High/Scope Educational Research Foundation staff studied these children every year from the age of 3 until they were 11 and then at ages 14, 15, 19, 27, and 40. They found that more students who had preschool graduated from high school than did those in the no-program group (65 percent vs. 45 percent), with women significantly higher than men (84 percent vs. 32 percent). Sample comparisons of the High/Scope program versus no program at age 40 showed that 70 percent program versus 50 percent no program were employed; 37 percent program versus. 28 percent no program owned their own home; 76 percent program versus 50 percent no program had savings accounts; 2 percent program versus 12 percent no program committed violent felonies; and 3 percent program versus 20 percent no program were cited for having dangerous drugs.

Curriculum Research. High/Scope conducted a High/Scope Preschool Curriculum Comparison study after the High/Scope Perry Preschool study and found that the High/Scope model was successful. The researchers studied the direct instructional model, in which teachers taught the children academic skills and rewarded them for correct answers. They also examined the traditional Nursery School Model in which teachers responded to the children's self-initiated activities in a supportive and loosely structured environment. In the High/Scope model, teachers design their classrooms with both large-and small-group activities, emphasizing self-initiated learning. The children, with help from the teacher, plan their own activities and review these activities after they have carried out their plans (Schweinhart, 2005). When research was conducted of the participants of Nursery School and High/Scope at 23 years of age, it showed that the Nursery School and High/Scope had similar outcomes (Schweinart & Weikart, 1997). Although the direct instructional model shows early improvement in academics, it is temporary, and it loses the opportunity for improvement in long term social behavior improvement

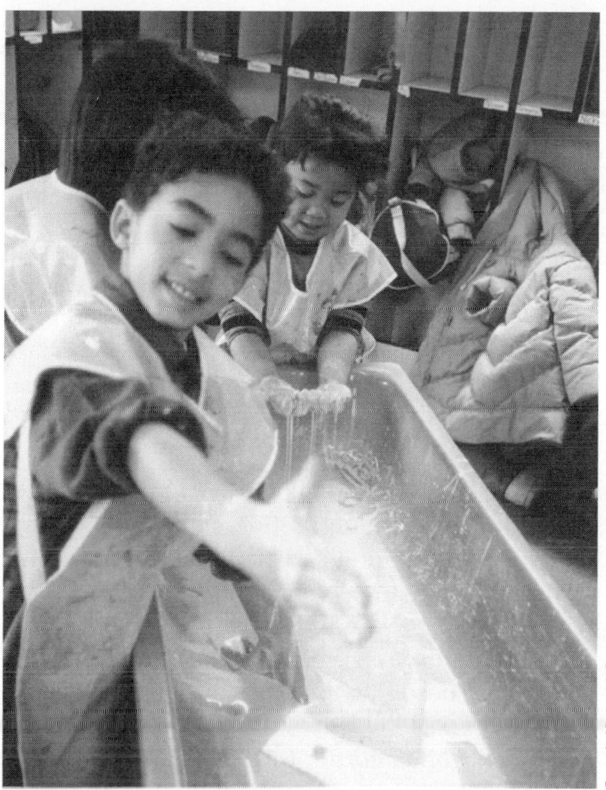

Programs ranging from Head Start, High/Scope, Carolina Abecedarian Project, Project CARE, Syracuse Family Development Research, Houston Parent–Child Development Center, Early Training Project, Chicago Child Parent Center, and Oklahoma Pre-K proved to be effective for early intervention.

(Schweinhart, 2005). These two programs, Head Start and High/Scope, illustrate successful programs that continue to be actively effective.

Parent Involvement. The spring issue 2006 of *Resource; A Magazine for Educators* highlights the Head Start Performance Standards as it relates to High/Scope and points out the ways in which it has involved parents in its program. Suggestions include:

1. Include parents through conversations during arrival and departure time. Ask the parent to leave a note if special instructions are needed.
2. Provide parents with copies of the daily routine and furnish a bulletin board for messages. A welcome packet lets parents know that the caregivers want to keep parents informed.
3. Write daily notes, share observations through phone calls, keep pass-down logs, have daily news sheets and newsletters, make and give digital photos of the child participating in preschool, and use e-mail for parents who have Internet capability.
4. Hold open house at a time when parents can participate, learn more about the setting, and talk with staff.
5. Include parents in the program if they are able to volunteer.
6. Supply an information sheet that includes suggestions for learning experiences at home. (Kruse, 2006)

The Carolina Abercedarian Poject.

The North Carolina Abercedarian Project was a program in which children from low-income families had high-quality full-time educational intervention, infancy through age 5. The development was achieved through individualized education with the activities consisting of "games" included in their regular day. The activities had an emphasis on language development with social, intellectual, and emotional development also included. The recruited children were born between 1972 and 1977.

The Woodcock-Johnson Achievement Test was given children in the Abecedarian Project in the fall and spring of their third year of school. The children were monitored and had follow-up studies during the summer following their seventh-grade year (age 12),tenth-grade year (age l5), and at 21 years of age. It was found that high-quality intervention and education during early childhood can carry over academically as the child progresses through school. The children had higher cognitive test scores beginning as toddlers and the scores continued through until the last study at age 21. Improved language development seems to have enhanced the resulting cognitive test scores. Other major findings included: intervention children on the average were older when they had their first child; academic achievement in both reading and math was higher from early grades to young adulthood, and the children were more likely to attend a 4-year college (University of North Carolina, FPG Child Development Institute, n.d.).

Carolina Approach to Responsive Education (Project CARE)

A related study to the Abecedarian Project was the Carolina Approach to Responsive Education (Project CARE). Recruited children who were born between 1978 and 1980 were randomly assigned to one of three groups: educational child care plus home visits from 6 weeks until school entry, home visits from 6 weeks until school entry, and the control group. The first two groups received home school resource services during the first 3 years of school. Extensive testing was done during the period in school as children were tested on the quality of family environment, maternal measures, cognitive, and academic achievement. The Woodcock-Johnson was administered fall and spring, during the first 3 years of school, and in the summer after their seventh year of school. Project CARE was identified as a successful program by the Rand Corporation (Karoly, Kilburn, & Cannon, 2005).

Syracuse Family Development Research Program

The Syracuse Family Development Research Program (FDRP) was a comprehensive early childhood program that included home visits, parent training, and a Children's Center with a program of education, health, nutrition, and other human services, prenatal to the beginning of elementary school. The targeted program participants were low-income families of young African American single parents. Honig, Lally, and Mathieson assessed the program in 1982, finding that the FDRP kindergarten children had emotional functioning superior to those in the control group and were more flexible, purposeful, energetic, social, relaxed, and affectionate to others than the children in the control group. In addition, those in the FDRP groups had more children who attained an IQ score above 89. The first-grade group continued to have positive behavior toward other children, but they had more negative and positive behavior toward adults than the control group (Promising Practices Network, n.d., p. 3). In 1988 the research found that by eighth grade none of the FDRP girls had failing averages, whereas 16 percent of the control group did. Seventy-two percent of the FDRP girls maintained a C average or better, compared to only 47 percent of the comparison group. There were no significant differences in achievement between FDRP boys and the comparison group. Research on delinquency reported by Lally, Mangione, and Honig in 1988 found that three of the comparison group compared to none of the FDRP had committed violent crimes. An analysis reported in 2001 by Aos, Barnoski, and Lieb found that the FDRP children committed fewer crimes than the comparison, but of those who committed crimes there was no difference in the number of offenses that had been committed (Promising Practices Network, n.d.).

Houston Parent–Child Development Center Infant Health Development Program

The Houston Parent–Child Development Center focused on very young Latino children. The first year included 25 home visits. Each $1\frac{1}{2}$-hour visit focused on infant development. Small groups met together on weekends for family workshops in which they discussed communication, decisions, and issues chosen by the participants. English as a second language classes were also offered to the mothers of the children. Information on child and public health was furnished by a visiting nurse. Transportation and information on ways to obtain resources were provided.

During the second year there were center-based classes for mothers and their 2-year-old for 4 hours, 4 mornings a week. Transportation and lunch were provided and the group discussion and information of home management and child care continued. Fathers attended monthly meetings, which strengthened their paternal roles. Information and manuals on the program can be obtained from the Department of Psychology, University of Houston, Houston, TX 77204, Attn: Dale L. Johnson, Ph.D.

The Early Training Project

The Early Training Project was an early (1962–1965) research project in which 65 Black children who were 4 to 5 years old were chosen to participate in a study to improve educational achievement. The children were chosen from low-income families based on education, occupation, housing, and income. The children were randomly assigned to a 10-week summer program for either (a) 2-summers program, (b) 3-summers program, or (c) a control group. Those in the intervention programs also received weekly home visits throughout the school year. Assessments of the program were conducted during the intervention period and in 1965, 1966, 1968, 1975, and 1978. In 1965, at the end of first grade the children scored high on three of the four subtests of the Metropolitan Achievement (Karoly, Kilburn, & Cannon, 2005). Significant differences were found, but they faded as the children matured. Participants were less likely to be placed in special education, be retained in grade, or drop out of high school (Karoly et al., 2005). The reduction of special education at age 12 showed that only 5 percent of Early Training Project students were in special education compared to 29 percent of the control group and that 8 percent graduated compared to 52 percent of the control group (Currie, 2000).

Chicago Child–Parent Center

Chicago Child–Parent Centers are centers integrated in 1967 with primary schools in Chicago. Initially, the program was a half day preschool program for 3- to 4-year-old children. Using federal Title 1 Funds the center provided health, social services, a preschool, and encouraged *parent participation and involvement*. The preschool program was designed to prepare children for school with a focus on language skills and preparation for reading.

In 1978, with the addition of state funding, the kindergarten was increased to full day and the program was extended through third grade. The adult to child ratio in preschool was 1 to 8 in a class of 17; in kindergarten, the ratio was 1 to 12 in a class of 25. The primary program had coordinated instruction and parent involvement. The class size was reduced and children received free breakfasts, lunches, and health screening.

Findings based on children at 9 years of age showed that CPC children had significantly higher math and reading achievement scores, less retention, and more *significant parent involvement*. There was no difference in special education placement, but the number of years spent in special education was significantly lower (Karoly, Kilburn, & Cannon, 2005).

The *parent involvement* dimension was strong. Activities included *parenting classes*, clerical assistance by parents, and involvement in school activities such as developing resources, and coordinating school projects (Chicago Longitudinal Study, 2004).

Oklahoma Pre-K

Oklahoma has been a leader in providing public school prekindergarten offerings. As early as 1980 Oklahoma was considering standards for a program for 4-year-old children. In 1990, Head Start eligible students could attend prekindergarten without cost and, if space was available, others could pay tuition and attend. The standards for a pre-K program include early childhood certified teachers who have a bachelor's degree and who pass an early childhood education subject area competency test. The pre-K teachers are also paid on the same salary scale as the K–12 teachers. Pre-K has small class size of 20 students and an adult-to-child ratio of 1:10. Family involvement is also encouraged. Developmentally appropriate curriculum and continued professional development of certified personnel is required (Garrett, 2004; Gormley, Gayer, Phillips, & Dawson, 2004).

In September 2003, the Woodstock-Johnson Achievement Test was given to 1,567 pre-K children and 3,148 kindergarteners in Tulsa, Oklahoma. The pre-K students were ready to begin their pre-K program for the year, and nearly half of the kindergarten students had participated in the pre-K program the year before. Key findings included a 52 percent gain in letter word identification, a 27 percent gain in spelling test scores, and a 21 percent gain in applied problems. These are percentages above the average gain that occurs over one year. Gains for minority students were even more impressive. Hispanic students showed a 79 percent gain in letter word identification. There was also a 39 percent gain in spelling, and a 54 percent gain in applied programs (Gormley et al., 2004).

The programs show a wide variety of means and methods of reaching families and their children. Each can be studied to find the successes and the challenges.

Other Examples of Successful Programs—School on Saturday

In the Ferguson-Florissant School District in St. Louis, Missouri, home and school joined hands to offer a Saturday School. This included two 3-hour preschool sessions for 4-year-olds on Saturdays throughout the school year. Although the program is no longer available in the school district, the concept behind it is appropriate for districts that could have a Saturday program, especially if they were unable to furnish full-time preschools. The program had three major objectives:

- To provide an education program that will help 4-year-old children succeed in school
- To involve parents in the education of their children
- To provide support for families

These objectives were accomplished by providing the following:

1. Diagnostic screening at the beginning of the school year to establish appropriate goals.
2. Half-day preschool each Saturday in a public kindergarten.
3. Opportunities for participation by parents in the preschool. (Parents had to participate every 4 to 6 weeks as a parent helper in the preschool.)
4. Home visits, one hour each week, with a group of two or three children and their parents.
5. Home activity guides that provided ideas for projects and other activities for the 4-year old child—and younger siblings, if any—to do at home; these activities fostered skills needed for success in school.
6. Consultants in child development, who were available to consider specific concerns as well as provide parent meetings.

Although the program was ended in Ferguson-Florissant, Saturday School worked! Children gained in intellectual, language, and eye–hand coordination. Parents gained in their ability to communicate with their children, use appropriate reinforcement techniques, and sense a child's learning readiness. The program reached out to fathers as well as mothers. The curriculum, dealing with motor coordination development, goes hand in hand with positive interaction between child and father. See Figure 8.6 for an example of activities for father and child.

What can other programs gain from the Saturday School? These aspects seem especially important:

1. Active participation by both parents in teaching their own children
2. Diagnostic and prescriptive activities for children with disabilities
3. Observation and participation by parents in a school setting
4. Guidance and activities that support the parents' efforts
5. Teacher visits to the home, which establish a team rapport between teachers and parents
6. Opportunities for the child to experience routine school activities and an enriched curriculum each week
7. Home-learning activity booklets to be used by parents of children from birth through age 3

The varied approaches of the Saturday School met many more needs than a program with only one dimension—for example, preschool without the parent component.

Brookline Early Education Project

An excellent example of how the public school system can collaborate with a health organization was the Brookline Early Education Project (BEEP). In 1972, Brookline Public Schools and Children's Hospital Medical Center and researchers from the Boston-area universities joined to develop a coordinated plan for physical checkups and educational programs for young children up to kindergarten age (Figure 8.7). Together, the hospital and school supplied a reassuring support system.

Based on the theory that parents are the child's most influential teachers, BEEP had three interrelated components:

1. *Parent education and support.* Three levels of support were provided, ranging from frequent home visits and meetings to parent-initiated support. Home visits, parent groups, and center visits were available.
2. *Diagnostic monitoring.* Children were periodically screened by staff at Children's Hospital Medical Center from age 2 weeks until entry into kindergarten.
3. *Education and enrichment.* The 2-year-old children attended weekly play group sessions in the BEEP project center.

In additon to these services, the BEEP program offered a parent center; consultants to answer questions; library books and pamphlets, films and videotapes on child development; a series of special events

A SPECIAL SECTION FOR DADDY

THINGS TO AIM AT!

Aiming and throwing at targets provide excellent practice in judging distance and coordinating the arm and hand with the eye. And any "balls" suggested here are indoor-safe so a wild pitch will cause no harm.

A tip about targets: Place the target close enough that your child experiences success (most of the time)—yet far enough away to provide a challenge. As your child's skill improves, move the target farther away and/or make the size of the target smaller.

PUNCHING BAG

Tightly stuff wadded-up newspapers in an old pillowcase, attach a sturdy string, and hang it from a door facing. Have your child hit the moving bag or balloon with his open hand or fist. Stress that he should keep his eyes on the moving bag.

As your child's batting average improves, reduce the size of the target—a paper cup, small sponge ball, or rubber toy. Sometimes have him toss a rolled-up sock at the target. That's harder still.

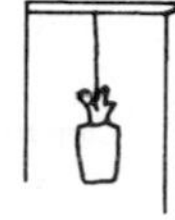

TARGET TOSS

A bean bag or rolled-up sock can be tossed in a box or grocery bag.

Or toss a bean bag or small weighted box (tightly taped) on big shapes chalked on the basement floor (or the sidewalk when the weather clears). Can she name the shapes she hits?

BASKETBALL

Have your child wad up newspaper into a ball (great for strengthening hand muscles) and toss it into a wastebasket or box.

BLEACH-BOTTLE TOSS

Cut out the bottom of a plastic bleach bottle (be sure to clean it out) and tie a whiffle ball or rolled-up sock to the handle with a piece of string about 2 feet long. Have your child hold onto the bottle's handle, give the ball a toss, and try to catch it in the bottle.

CATCH-AS-CATCH-CAN

Your child can play ball by himself by throwing it against the basement wall. To make it tougher, chalk a big circle on the wall for him to aim at. Sometimes, draw a chalked circle on the floor for him to bounce the ball in. Have him stand with his toes touching the circle's edge for easier catching after the bounce.

FIGURE 8.6 Fathers are an integral part of the Saturday School.

Source: Reprinted with permission from the Ferguson-Florissant School District, St. Louis, MO.

such as workshops, films, and lectures; and transportation for the parents of the children enrolled in BEEP (Pierson, Walker, & Tivnan, 1984).

A study begun in 1996 and published in 2002 found that the young adults who had participated in BEEP had higher incomes and reported higher health ratings and lower levels of depression. They attained more years of education and were more likely to be employed or in school than those who did not participate in the program. Home visits were reported as being the most valuable in terms of support for the parents. Over 95 percent of the mothers would recommend the BEEP program to their own children (Palfrey, Bronson, Hauser-Cram, & Warfield, 2002, pp. 1–2).

MATH AND SCIENCE ASSOCIATIONS THAT SUPPORT PARENT INVOLVEMENT

The National Council of Teachers of Mathematics (NCTM) recommend that parents get involved with their children in their success in and enjoyment of mathematics. They suggest that students discuss their classroom activities and what they

FIGURE 8.7 The hospital and school work together to provide for the child's health, education, and development.

have learned with their parents. Parents can help their student if they

- Provide a place for the student to do homework.
- Participate in parent–teacher conferences.
- Encourage their children to persist—not to do the work for them.
- Engage in activities such as games and puzzles during family time.
- Visit mathematics classes when given the opportunity.

Family Math

The Family Math classes include materials and activities for parents to use while they help their children with mathematics at home. Meetings two to three hours long take place one evening each week for 4 to 6 weeks. Children attend the meetings with their parents.

Families can use the Internet to obtain math activities that can be done at home. A book, *Helping Your Child Learn Math* is published by the U.S. Department of Education, and examples of the activities can be found at www.math.com/parents/articles/mathhome.html.

Family Science

An outgrowth of Family Math, Family Science encourages parents and children to work together on day-to-day science using inexpensive materials available in the home. The program's developers hope that minorities and girls—traditionally left behind or discouraged from scientific pursuits—will be encouraged to develop their abilities in math and science if they learn about them in a nonthreatening environment.

Education Resources Information Center

The Education Resources Information Center (ERIC) was an educational resource for areas of education including Elementary and Early Childhood Education, located at the University of Illinois under the direction of Lilian G. Katz. The service commenced in 1967 and continued until December 2003, when a new ERIC was established. At that time all the divisions of ERIC continued as a digital library of education resources under the Institute of Education Sciences of the U.S. Department of Education. The digital library was opened for public use in 2004 with a focus on providing current and archived resources. Access *eric.ed.gov*.

In the meantime, the Clearinghouse on Early Education and Parenting (CEEP), part of Early Childhood and Parenting (ECAP), was established within the College of Education at the University of Illinois, Urbana-Champaign, under the direction of Lilian G. Katz and Dianne Rothenberg.

REACHING ALL FAMILIES

Moles (1996a) describes methods and strategies to reach families that include (a) early fall mailings, (b) home–school handbooks, (c) open houses, (d) school-parent compacts, (e) personal contacts, (f) parent–teacher conferences, (g) home visits, (h) parent liaisons, (i) homework, (j) resource centers, (k) family gatherings, (l) special programs for children with special needs, and (m) positive communication.

Partnership for Family Involvement in Education

Family School Partnership was established to encourage families, local school board governance, administration, teachers, and school staff to form a partnership to affirm the importance in children's learning. They made the following pledge:

- We will share responsibility at school and at home to give students a better education and a good start in life.
- Our school will be welcoming to families; reach out to families before problems arise; offer challenging courses; create safe and drug-free learning environments; organize tutoring and other opportunities to improve student learning; and support families to be included in the school decision-making process.
- Our families will monitor student attendance, homework completion and television watching; take the time to talk and listen to their children; become acquainted with teachers, administrators and school staff; read with younger children and share a good book with a teen; volunteer in school when possible; and participate in the school decision-making process.
- We will promote effective two-way communication between families and schools, by schools reducing educational jargon and breaking down cultural and language barriers and by families staying in touch with the schools.
- We will provide opportunities for families to learn how to help their children succeed in school and for school staff to work with families.
- We will support family-school efforts to improve student learning by reviewing progress regularly and strengthening cooperative actions. (U.S. Department of Education, 1997, p. 12)

Communication Through Internet and/or Telephone

A telephone call to tell the family about the child's accomplishments or contributions can always be a positive interaction. Some children contribute with an unusual idea or a friendly smile. Others may have had a particularly successful day contributing to the class or finishing work. For the many parents who own a computer and have access to the Internet, communication can be easily accessible. E-mail addresses can be given to parents who want to contact the school or a particular teacher with questions or comments. Parents can furnish their child's or their own e-mail address for information that needs to go home such as an explanation of assignments or an invitation to a school event.

TITLE PROGRAMS

Title I

Federal programs funded under several titles also illustrate innovative use of parents as partners in the educational process. Needs assessments, parent advisory councils, conferences, and home–school activities are included in typical programs. Title I programs, active in most state school systems, heavily emphasize parent involvement, recognizing that the parent is the child's first teacher and that home environment and parental attitude toward school influence a child's academic success. A parent–resource teacher is provided to work solely with parents. Parents, paraprofessionals, teachers, and administrators work together to provide support and education for the children. Parents are trained to instruct their children at home and are also involved in the school program. These successful programs represent the best in curriculum development. Their concern for parent involvement illustrates the significance of parents in the successful education of their children.

Title 1—Sec 101

Improving the Academic Achievement of the Disadvantaged reflects the need to ensure high quality education for all children to have adequate and excellent education. If you want to locate these or other programs throughout the United States, call the U.S. Department of Education at 1–800-USA-LEARN and ask for the most recent publications about families and schools.

Suggestions for changes in Title I were included in the 2001 proposal of the No Child Left Behind Act. To meet the goal of reducing the achievement gap between disadvantaged and advantaged students, the report proposes maintaining high standards in reading and math and setting high standards in history and science, providing annual assessments in reading and math for third to eighth grades, reporting results of assessments to parents, and increasing flexibility by reducing the poverty threshold from 50 to 40 percent so that more schools can combine their federal money to improve quality. Federal funds would be available for technical assistance and to provide capacity building to schools that need improvement.

If an identified school still has not met adequate progress after 2 years, the district must implement corrective action and offer public school choice to all students in the failing school. If the school fails to make adequate progress after 3 years, disadvantaged students within the school may use Title I funds to transfer to a higher performing public or private school, or they may receive supplemental educational services from a provider of choice. All nonpublic providers receiving federal money will be subject to appropriate standards of accountability (U.S. Department of Education, 2001, p. 9).

Title IV

"The purpose of Title IV is to promote parental choice and to increase the amount of flexible funds available to states and school districts for innovative education programs" (U.S. Department of Education, 2001, p. 18). The proposal promotes charter schools, broadens education savings accounts, expands school choice, consolidates categorical grand programs, and expands private activity bonds to be used for public school construction (p. 19).

SCHOOL AND CENTER-BASED PARENT INVOLVEMENT

The Minnesota Early Childhood Family Education Program

The state of Minnesota offers support and information for parents and children, from birth to kindergarten. Some of the programs offered include:

1. *Early Childhood Screening* is for children before they enter kindergarten. Since it is important that any potential problems be identified early, it is recommended that screening be done by the time the child is 3.
2. *Early Childhood Family Education* is a program that parents of children, birth until enrollment in

kindergarten, can attend for information, activities, and support. A typical day has the parent and child doing an activity, followed by the parent and child doing their own activities, the child active in preschool and the parent attending a parent education session.

3. *The High-Five* kindergarten is a program for 4 year olds who will start kindergarten the following year.
4. *Early childhood special education* is for children from birth to kindergarten who have been identified as having a disability.
5. *Parents in Community Action (PICA)* has operated a Head Start program for over 30 years,
6. *Home-based programs* include Way to Grow, a program that builds school readiness for children 3 to 5. It focuses on future school success by focusing on cognitive, emotional, and social development and is delivered through home visits. In addition, Minneapolis offers Home Instruction Program for Preschool Youngsters (HIPPY). See chapter 9 for a description of HIPPY (Minneapolis Public Schools, 2005).

Minneapolis

Minneapolis is a good example of the greater involvement of parents with schools. The Early Childhood Family Education program welcomes the enrollment of all families living in Minneapolis who have children from birth to enrollment in kindergarten. Programs for the children include Early Reading First, a full-year program for children who are 3; Minneapolis Kids—Fours Explore is a full-day program for 4 year olds; and High-Five is a prekindergarten school year for children who are 4 years old. Programs are varied. Early Childhood Special Education serves children from birth to kindergarten. Screening is provided to assess if children need a special education program. The New Families Center is an all-day program for a year for families whose second language is English. There is also the Teenage Pregnant and Parenting Program, which provides services to support teenagers who are pregnant or parents. In Minneapolis, pledges or covenants are signed by all involved—students, parents or representatives, teachers and other staff members, the superintendent, school board members, and community members. All participants have specific ways in which they can help (Minneapolis Public Schools, 2006).

Reading First

Reading First provides funds and tools to states to ensure that children receive effective reading instruction from kindergarten through third grade. The National Reading Panel reported that

> Effective reading instruction includes teaching children to break apart and manipulate the sounds in words (phonemic awareness), teaching them that these sounds are represented by letters of the alphabet which can then be blended together to form words (phonics), having them practice what they have learned by reading aloud with guidance and feedback (guided oral reading), and applying reading comprehension strategies to guide and improve reading comprehension. (2000, p. 10)

"Building on a solid foundation of research, the program is designed to select, implement, and provide professional development for teachers using scientifically based reading programs, and to ensure accountability through ongoing, valid and reliable screening, diagnostic and classroom-based assessment" (Ed. Gov, 2004).

Institute for Responsive Education

The Institute for Responsive Education (2006) continues with its emphasis on connecting school, family, and community. In April 2005, the program moved to Cambridge College, School of Education, in Cambridge, Massachusetts. Its mission statement states:

> The Institute for Responsive Education (IRE) is a research, policy and advocacy organization that encourages and supports school, family, and community partnerships to enable high quality educational opportunities for all children. We believe that schools, families, and communities all share the responsibility to improve schools and raise educational standards.

The various activities of the Institute for Responsive Education includes the Parent Leadership Exchange, which provides networking for parent leaders in three New England states; the Boston Parent Organizing Network (BPON); and Family Involvement in After School Study, a study of family centers nationwide. The changes in the Institute illustrate the ebb and flow of family involvement with schools. New programs are developed, they flourish, meet the needs of the schools, change the environment, become a part of the total program, or diminish when they are no longer needed, something replaces them, or the funding source is lost (Institute of Responsive Education, 2006).

National Association of State Boards of Education

The National Association of State Boards of Education (NASBE, 1991, 2006) recommends that parents be involved in decision making on program policy, curriculum, and evaluation. There should be continual communication between parents and schools. Strong involvement of parents is important to accommodate the family in before- and after-school programs. Administrators try to have parents involved in the planning of before- and after-school programs through parent advisory committees, workshops, and orientation sessions. Parents should also be encouraged to tutor their children at home and to have opportunities to observe and volunteer in the classroom.

The task force of NASBE suggests inservice training on parent involvement for administrators and teachers. Time for teachers to plan and carry out home visits is recommended. Home activities and materials for parents to use with their children at home should be provided. Businesses should be encouraged to give parents time off to attend parent–teacher conferences and volunteer in the classroom. Schools should provide leadership in developing family support services in collaboration with existing community agencies. With this strong statement of cooperation between home and school, the task force supports provision of sufficient staff, training, and time to work together (National Association of State Board of Education, 1988).

The key state policies and case studies were reported in 2005 in *From Planning to Practice: State Efforts to Improve Early Childhood Education*. In 2001 NASBE, with financial support from the Kellogg Foundation, started Early Childhood Education Network, a project to increase the ability of six states (Kansas, Illinois, Massachusetts, Louisiana, Ohio, and Wyoming) to integrate early childhood education programs and services. The goal was to help states "increase their ability to create integrated, high-quality early childhood education policies, programs, and services to children" (National Association of School Boards of Education, 2006, p. 1). The results were outstanding, with the states able to define school readiness and unify their standards. It included an outreach to early childhood education programs in higher education and aligned the college course content to the program. In 2006, NASBE received a grant allowing the organization to add five new states to the Early Childhood Education Network (National Association of State Boards of Education, 2006, p. 1).

WORKSHOPS AT SCHOOL FOR PARENTS TO USE AT HOME

A workshop is one vehicle for introducing parents to home–school learning activities. Ann Grimes, a first-grade teacher, invited her students' parents to such a workshop. She greeted them, gave them name tags, and passed out a get-acquainted signature sheet for a signature game (see Figure 7.3A in chapter 7).

After the signature game, during which parents enthusiastically talked with one another, the make-and-take workshop began. Mrs. Grimes explained the program, its philosophy, and what the school expected of parents. She assured the parents that close, two-way communication helps ensure the program is meeting the needs of the child, parents, and school. If parents were interested in participating in a home–school learning project, she assured them that she would like to work with them as a member of the team.

Mrs. Grimes reminded the parents of how important it is to listen to children, ask open-ended questions, and allow children the opportunity to predict and problem solve. She also reminded the parents that children, like adults, work best when they have a quiet, private work area and a regular time to work. She stressed that children are expected to enjoy and succeed at home assignments. If a child struggles with more than 20 percent of the projects or problems, the activity selection should be reassessed and new activities better geared to the child's level can be chosen. Many home activities can be recreational and enriching to family life. As she concluded her talk,

Mrs. Grimes explained the plans for the evening. Parents were asked to participate in the activities located in different areas throughout the room. "If you will look at your name tag, you will find a number. Go to that activity first," she instructed the parents.

The centers included games and activities as well as directions on how to play them. Materials and guidelines were also available for activities that parents could make and take home. Some parents played Concentration (Figure 8.8) and made game boards. They found that game boards could be

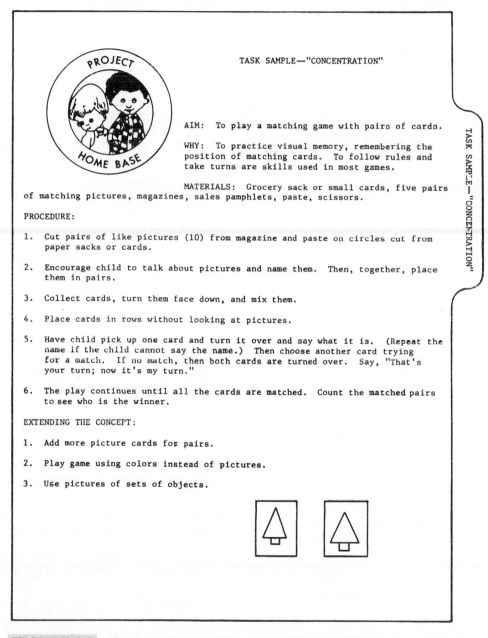

TASK SAMPLE—"CONCENTRATION"

TASK SAMPLE—"CONCENTRATION"

AIM: To play a matching game with pairs of cards.

WHY: To practice visual memory, remembering the position of matching cards. To follow rules and take turns are skills used in most games.

MATERIALS: Grocery sack or small cards, five pairs of matching pictures, magazines, sales pamphlets, paste, scissors.

PROCEDURE:

1. Cut pairs of like pictures (10) from magazine and paste on circles cut from paper sacks or cards.

2. Encourage child to talk about pictures and name them. Then, together, place them in pairs.

3. Collect cards, turn them face down, and mix them.

4. Place cards in rows without looking at pictures.

5. Have child pick up one card and turn it over and say what it is. (Repeat the name if the child cannot say the name.) Then choose another card trying for a match. If no match, then both cards are turned over. Say, "That's your turn; now it's my turn."

6. The play continues until all the cards are matched. Count the matched pairs to see who is the winner.

EXTENDING THE CONCEPT:

1. Add more picture cards for pairs.

2. Play game using colors instead of pictures.

3. Use pictures of sets of objects.

FIGURE 8.8 The game of Concentration may be designed, constructed, and played at home or at school.

Source: Project Home Base, Yakima, WA.

easily made from cardboard, poster board, or a file folder. Mrs. Grimes furnished decorative stickers that the parents could place on the game boards. To protect the completed board, some parents used the laminating machine, and others spread clear adhesive paper over their work. Each board was different, yet each was based on the same format, that is, squares on which the children placed symbols as they used a spinner or die to tell them how many spaces to move. Some parents wrote letters or numbers on the spaces; others developed cards that children could take as they had a turn. If the spaces were left empty, the board could be used for many skill activities by developing sets of cards for phonics, numbers, or other basic skills. Figure 8.9 illustrates a completed game board that can be used to develop many skills. While some parents were busy with the game boards, others worked on language and math concepts, constructed books, or plied their creativity at the art center.

After a busy 2-hour session the group met again, and an animated discussion of the activities began. Two parents volunteered to make canvas tote bags for the class, and another promised to make a silk-screened print of the class emblem on each. They decided the tote bags would be reserved for home-learning adventures. "Please be sure to evaluate the home-learning activities as you use them. And, please contribute your own ideas," encouraged Mrs. Grimes. "I'll keep track of each child's activities on these record sheets. If you have any questions, be sure to write or call me."

After refreshments, the parents began to leave. Some stopped by the table to sign up to volunteer in the program. Mrs. Grimes recognized that she would need help implementing the home-learning program and that she could use help in the room as well. A volunteer training session was planned for the next week; the work toward a productive home-school endeavor had just begun.

Implementation of Home-Learning Activities

Home-learning activities can be useful as enrichment projects, or they can be valuable as a sequential educational curriculum. If they are used to complement learning that is occurring simultaneously in the school, it is necessary to monitor the child's work at home and keep track of what is accomplished.

The process varies according to the availability of a parent coordinator. If parent coordinators are available, it will be their responsibility to keep track of the home-learning activities. They can contact parents, make home visits, and report on the progress of each child. It is the teacher's responsibility to advise the parent coordinator about the child's progress in school and recommend appropriate learning activities. If a parent coordinator is not available, a parent volunteer can help with record keeping and provide contact between the parents and the teacher. The following steps are appropriate for either situation:

1. Offer an orientation workshop.
2. Send learning activities home in a tote bag, deliver them personally, or give the responsibility of the delivery system to a parent coordinator.
3. Keep records of activity cards the child has taken home. Make a record card for each child with a space to indicate when each activity went home and a space for response to the activity. This way you will know which activity the child should be given next.
4. Get feedback from parents via notes, reports, phone calls, or visits. Find out their reactions to the activities and their assessments of their child's success.
5. Continue communicating with parents. Include supplemental ideas and activity sheets on a skill that proved difficult for a particular student. Ask parents to reinforce skills up to the too-difficult level. Have them refer to previous activity cards for related projects.
6. Diversify your program to meet the needs of the parents and keep interest levels high.
7. Meet occasionally with parents or make home visits to support the monitoring system.

Communication is a basic ingredient in the success of home–school cooperation. Through talking with parents, you will know whether they consider home-learning activities to be a joy or a threat. You will want to adapt your program according to each parent's desires.

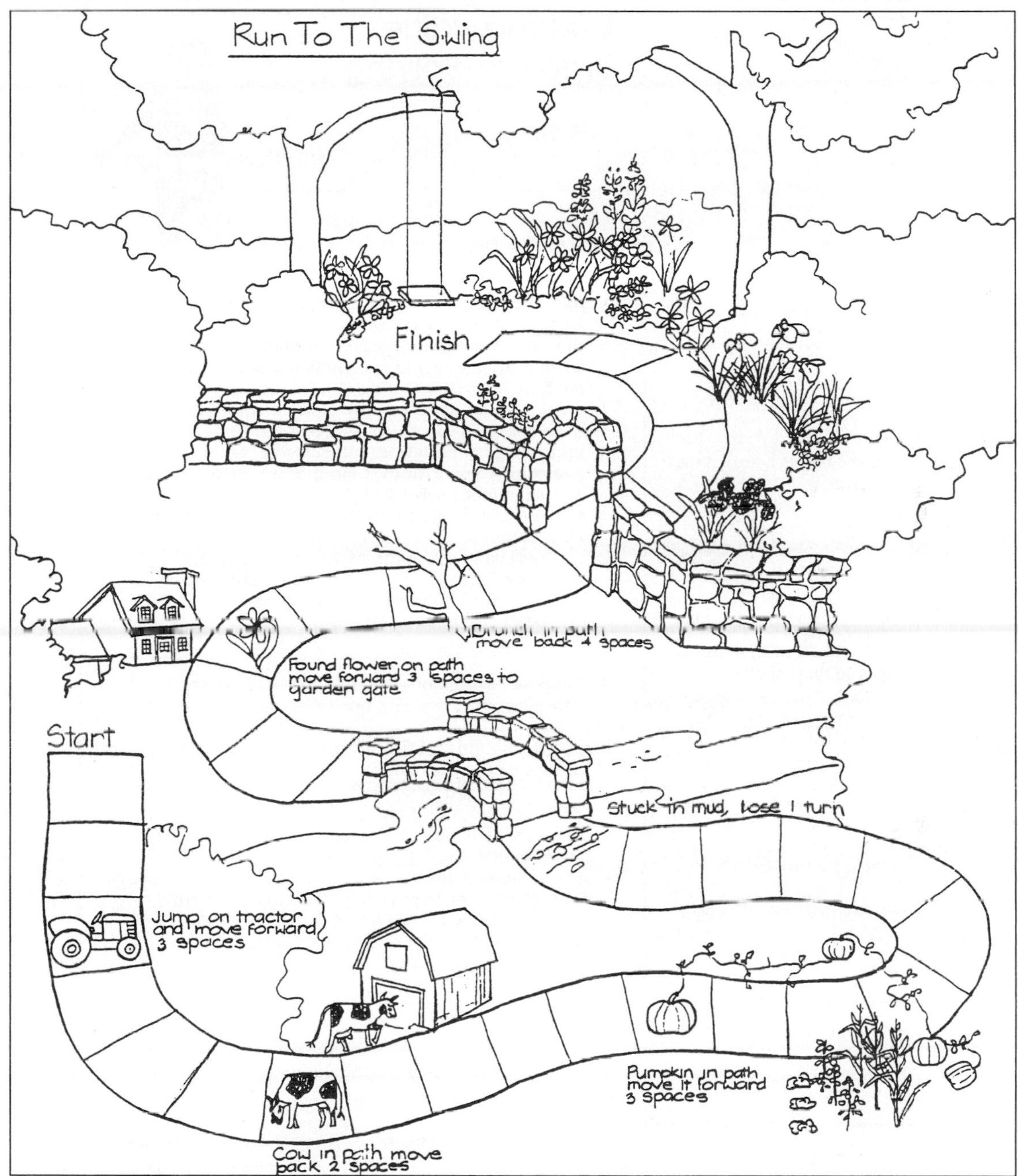
Run To The Swing
Finish
move back 4 spaces
Found flower on path move forward 3 spaces to garden gate
Start
Stuck in mud, lose 1 turn
Jump on tractor and move forward 3 spaces
Pumpkin in path move it forward 3 spaces
Cow in path move back 2 spaces

FIGURE 8.9 A "run to the swing" sets the theme for this game board. Children can suggest their special interests, and games can be developed from their ideas.

Source: Artwork by Debra McClave. Printed with permission.

Early Education
Ferguson-Florissant
School District

Lifelong Values
Problem-Solving

Problem-solving is the ability to take what you know and come up with a new solution to a problem. Problem-solving is the foundation that helps children think, reason, and make their own decisions. It enables children to accomplish the goals they choose in life.

One of the ways children learn is by watching and listening to others. As problems crop up in everyday life, by thinking out loud we are modeling problem-solving skills.

Examples:

- "We are having eight people for dinner, and there is only room for six people at the table. I wonder what we should do."
- "We have bird seed but our bird feeder broke. What can we use to build a new bird feeder?"

As you and your child are solving problems together you might ask:

- "Does it work?"
- "What else can I do?"
- "What's going to happen?"
- "How did we do?"

Ways to Encourage Problem-Solving:

1. **Age-appropriate activities and materials**
   Giving children materials that can be used in many different ways helps children understand that there is more than one way to accomplish a task. Materials such as Play-Doh (letting children decide what they want to make with the Play-Doh), blocks (how many different ways can the blocks be used to build with?), and collage materials (paint, scissors, tape, paper, paste) offer opportunities for children to explore, create and experience solving problems. Children are making judgments about size, cause and effect, and special relationships.
   "How can I make the paper stick together?"
   "What happens if I put this block on top?"
   "How can I build a ramp for my cars?"
   "What size does it need to be?"

2. **Take advantage of everyday opportunities**
   The following are just a few examples:

- You're planning a birthday party—"What can we use to decorate cupcakes for our party? What kind of decorations can we make?"
- It's time to clean up and your child can't reach the sink to wash his hands. You might ask, "What are you going to do?"
- You've been to the grocery store and you have a heavy bag of groceries to put away. You ask your child to help but the bag is too heavy for him to pick up. See if your child can think of a different way to get the bag of groceries to the pantry.

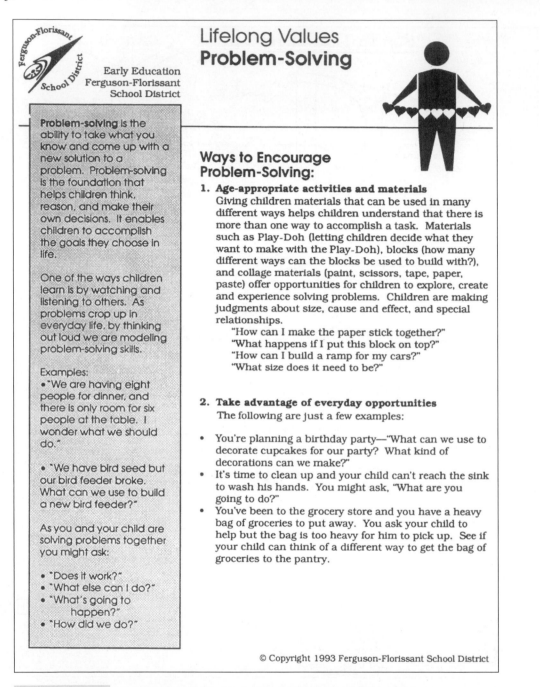

FIGURE 8.10 Home activities that help the child learn and solve problems.

Source: Reprinted with permission from the Ferguson-Florissant School District, St. Louis, MO.

Projects around the home can furnish experiences in math, language, art, music, science, and composition. The process of exploring an idea and carrying it to fruition requires problem solving. The Ferguson-Florissant School District developed a home curriculum to help parents of young children with problem solving (Figure 8.10). Ideas for activities around the home and in the community are restricted only by the imagination.

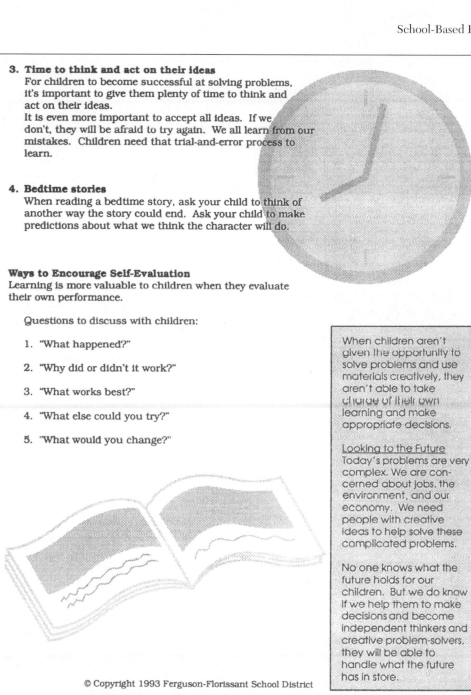

3. **Time to think and act on their ideas**
   For children to become successful at solving problems, it's important to give them plenty of time to think and act on their ideas.
   It is even more important to accept all ideas. If we don't, they will be afraid to try again. We all learn from our mistakes. Children need that trial-and-error process to learn.

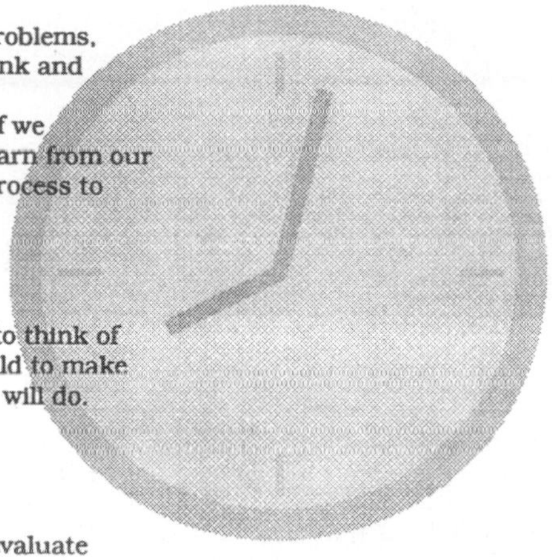

4. **Bedtime stories**
   When reading a bedtime story, ask your child to think of another way the story could end. Ask your child to make predictions about what we think the character will do.

Ways to Encourage Self-Evaluation
Learning is more valuable to children when they evaluate their own performance.

Questions to discuss with children:

1. "What happened?"
2. "Why did or didn't it work?"
3. "What works best?"
4. "What else could you try?"
5. "What would you change?"

When children aren't given the opportunity to solve problems and use materials creatively, they aren't able to take charge of their own learning and make appropriate decisions.

Looking to the Future
Today's problems are very complex. We are concerned about jobs, the environment, and our economy. We need people with creative ideas to help solve these complicated problems.

No one knows what the future holds for our children. But we do know if we help them to make decisions and become independent thinkers and creative problem-solvers, they will be able to handle what the future has in store.

FIGURE 8.10 Continued

REACHING RETICENT PARENTS

Parents who do not seem to fit into the "typical" parent role may not be encouraged by the school to take an active role. Are schools willing to open up to the group of parents who need help the most—low-income and minority families?

Which comes first, the parent's involvement in the child's success or the alienation of and lack of support for the parent, which results in no parental support for the school? Parents who feel good about themselves and who feel validated by the school participate. This situation is especially true for low-income, minority parents who may be made to feel inferior by school personnel, but it is also true for many middle- and upper-class parents who receive negative feedback on their involvement in the schools.

Families with two parents working and single parents may have difficulty being involved in daytime activities, but this does not mean that they don't care (Moles, 1987, 1996a). They might fit into the level of parents who are actively involved with their children's education at home. Most parents care about their children's progress in school irrespective of their background and want their children to do well (Epstein, 1987a, 1996; Moles, 1996a). The benefits from parent involvement that most middle-class parents receive cannot be closed to low-income and minority parents. The initiative of involvement by parents must come from the school; the school must reach out to the home.

Parent Involvement Program

New York City provided new incentives to accomplish family involvement. The Parent Involvement Program in the New York City Public Schools needed to change some underlying assumptions to collaborate with parents. The major misleading assumption was that parents did not care; they did. But beyond that, the schools needed to help the parents see how they could collaborate with leadership strategies. Ten factors seemed important in their efforts: (a) leadership from the schools, (b) accessibility—and open lines of communication, (c) time to plan and implement changes, (d) cultural awareness, (e) active teacher roles, (f) continuity, (g) public recognition of those involved, (h) broad-based support, (i) adolescent focus, and (j) recognition of parents as people (Jackson & Cooper, 1992).

Empowerment

A research project at Cornell University first worked with parents and later tied parent involvement to the schools. Working with 160 families, the parent teams helped parents become more confident of their abilities. The group used a series of activities, which included role playing, to help parents feel secure when they became involved with schools. They developed a program titled Cooperative Communication Between Home and School (CCBHS), which included teachers and administrators. Including the school along with the parents provided even more positive attitudes. Parents need to view themselves as worthwhile participants to truly be able to interact with teachers and administrators.

Eugenia Hepworth Berger

Perseverance, patience, and true interest in the parents are the most important factors in overcoming parents' reticence.

School personnel need to respect the parents and recognize their importance as they collaborate. School personnel and parents can be advocates for the children. In this way they work for the greater good of families, schools, and communities (Cochran & Dean, 1991).

Perseverance, patience, and true interest in the parent are the most important factors involved in overcoming parents' reticence. Understanding, support, and interest usually will encourage a parent to take that first step toward collaborating with a teacher for the good of the child. In every situation, a few parents may refuse to be involved. Some may have serious social adjustment problems and need professional help in that area. One difficult parent or one bad experience should not destroy the commitment of the home visitor or teacher toward working with others. Teachers should not expect to be 100 percent successful. Do what can be done and acknowledge the impossibility of reaching all parents. Do this with grace, understanding, and no recriminations. Work with the children and involve the parents who want to be involved.

Dunlap (2000) studied family empowerment in a preschool cooperative. Empowerment is a process of adult development, enhanced through participation. "Through involvement with the family component of this preschool, caregivers acquire cultural capital. Over time they translate cultural capital into human capital, or economic gain" (p. 5). The process of developing cultural capital into human capital is the process of empowerment. Dunlap found this can be accomplished without giving up the participant's sense of ethnic identity.

Necessary Communication and Support

A call from the teacher or home visitor should not always mean that a child is in trouble. If good communication and support have been established, that call could mean the child is a strong leader or is working hard on a research project. Involving parents may be difficult because of the following reasons:

1. *Families and parents might be under a lot of stress.* Problems might include lack of money, illness of a loved one, unemployment, or an argument with a friend. In our fast-paced society, many parents are under stress. It is possible that they cannot be actively involved during a time of hardship. They should not be made to feel guilty. Let them know you are supportive and whenever they want to be more actively involved, they may. Keep communication open through telephone calls.
2. *Many hard-to-reach parents feel out of their element whether coming to school or receiving home visitors.* They are unsure of themselves. They do not have confidence in their own ideas, or they believe someone else will not value them. They need their self-esteem and level of trust raised. If they have the time, let them contribute in a small way. Accept their ideas. Enlist their help in an activity at which they will succeed. Build slowly; it takes time to make a change.
3. *The parents do not realize their importance in their child's education.* Many parents, from those in special programs such as Home Start and Head Start to those who live in affluent areas, do not recognize their importance as educators. Starting with parent-teacher conferences or home visits, the teacher needs to reflect that the parent is a true partner. The parents' knowledge about the child is important; they are the best experts on their child. Their interaction with the child is part of the child's education.
4. *Many teachers do not know the parents' interests, strengths, and abilities.* Suggest projects and activities that lend themselves to the capabilities of the parent. In one program where a home visitor was working with an abusive parent, it was suggested that the child was not using the right arm enough. At the next week's class, the home visitor found bruises up and down the child's arm. The parent, who was concerned about the teacher's comment, was "developing" the child's arm! This may seem extreme, but the response demonstrated the parent's inability to cope with everyday problems and to nurture the child in appropriate ways. The parent actually wanted the child to do well. Some parents cannot work well with their children or help with schoolwork. They become frustrated and angry; the child responds with dejection and hurt. Rather than helping the child, the parent creates a battleground.

Teachers need to develop effective strategies for working with reticent parents. Honig (1979) suggested the use of a 24-hour crisis center with project staff, perhaps psychiatric interns, recruited to give telephone counseling, reassurance, and referrals. In 2008, the need for crisis lines for depressed persons continues to be necessary. There is a national line for those who are depressed or considering suicide: 1-800-SUICIDE (or 1-800-784-2433).

A second idea was a retreat house in the country where families could go to, under the guidance of staff members, discuss and learn as well as have fun. Honig's third suggestion described a workshop where new trust could be promoted. Family support centers located in the public schools can be a great assistance to parents at risk and in need of help. Coordinate with the center; use its resources and continue to be supportive of the family.

It is helpful to offer training sessions for parents where techniques and suggestions for working positively with the child are discussed. The STEP, PET, and Active Parenting programs suggest methods for communicating with children (see chapter 6), using planned programs for parents. Filmstrips, videotapes, CDs, and DVDs also illustrate parenting skills and the role of parents as teachers. These resources can serve as guides in setting up sessions on working with children. Parents also learn through modeling. Helping in the classroom can be an effective learning experience. Methods of teaching that permit observation, demonstration, and role playing prove useful. Parents, like children, learn best through active participation.

Minnesota Early Learning Design (MELD), based in Minneapolis, developed a program for parents that was disseminated throughout the United States. That program, started in 1973, was established to strengthen families. In 2005, it merged with Parents as Teachers National Center. Initially it focused on early childhood education, adult education, and family management (Parents as Teachers National Center, 2006). As needs emerged it expanded to include New Parents (for first-time parents); MELD Special (for parents of children with special needs); MYM, Young Moms; MELD for parents who are deaf; Nueva Familia/La Familia (for Hispanic parents); MELD's Young Dads; and MELD's Young Moms Plus, for parents of 3- to 6-year-old children (MELD, 1988). MELD's mission is to provide support and information that strengthens families at critical periods during the parenting process. To the merger with PAT (Parents as Teachers), it brought training for family service providers, 150 publications, and the education and support systems enumerated above. MELD increases parents' self confidence, supports parent's connection with their children. and helps families set goals in their work and family life (MELD, 2006).

Prevention is far better than a cure. That is why it is important to reach reticent parents when their children are young. If parents can be involved from the start, their resistance to programs and partnerships can be reduced or eliminated. The descriptions of varying kinds of programs and advocacy for children and parents illustrate that different approaches that meet the needs of the individual communities are essential.

PARENT EDUCATION FOR TEENAGERS

A powerful time for reaching new parents and parents-to-be is during adolescence. Although there is a reduction in teenage mothers, the number is still high. In 2003, the birthrate to teenagers decreased for the 12th straight year. It fell 3 percent in 2003 to 41.6 births for each 1,000 teenagers aged 15–19 years. From the high mark of 61.8 percent in 1991, that was a drop of 33 percent. The rate for teenagers 15 to 17 years of age fell 42 percent from 1991, while the rate for 18- to 19-year-olds declined 25 percent. This resulted in 134,384 births to 15- to 17-year-olds and 280,190 births to 18- to 19-year-olds (Martin et al., 2005, p. 5).

The changing birthrate for Black teenagers has been especially pronounced with a 50 percent decline for the 15- to 17-year-olds. Birthrates in 2003 were 93.2 per 1,000 Hispanic teenagers, 64.7 for non-Hispanic Black teenagers, 60.8 for Puerto Ricans, 53.1 for American Indians, 27.4 for non-Hispanic Whites, and 17.4 for Asian or Pacific Islanders (p. 5).

These figures point out the large number of young parents, married and unmarried, who need family life or parent education. The United States has the highest teen birthrate of the western industrial countries. Teenage pregnancy rates are four times higher than in France and Germany.

Over the years, individual school systems have developed excellent family life programs for their students, usually in home economics and sociology classes. Schools are beginning to recognize that human development courses and child care experiences are an essential part of the curriculum. In addition, schools are legally required to allow pregnant girls to attend classes. Title IX of the Education Amendments of 1972 prohibits exclusion of a student from any school receiving federal money on the basis of pregnancy or related conditions.

Factors involved in teenage pregnancies are poverty, low performance in school, and growing up in a single-parent family (more than one and a half to two times higher rates than in two-parent families; Maynard, 1997). Adolescent mothers are more likely to drop out of school, have dysfunctional families and behavior problems, and live in poverty (Children's Defense Fund, 1998). Lack of education makes assuming financial responsibilities more difficult for the young parent. Additionally, there is a higher mortality rate for baby and mother. Pregnant teenagers often receive inadequate prenatal health care, and their children run a greater risk of being born prematurely, having poor health, having no father in the home, suffering abuse, spending time in foster care, being less successful academically, and becoming pregnant in their teens (Children's Defense Fund, 1997). Infants born to teenage mothers may have neurological problems, mental retardation, low birth weight, or an infectious disease.

Teenage Pregnancy

These programs are needed to help teens take control of their lives. Teen pregnancy affects all economic groups of society. For example, two thirds of teen births occur to White teens who are not poor and do not live in large cities. The greatest pregnancy rate, however, is among poor, disenfranchised youth.

Agnes, age 15, is pregnant. Her mother is not aware of the impending birth, and Agnes, in tears, confides to her friend at school. Where should she turn? Mary, age 14 and pregnant, wants to marry her boyfriend, Tom, also 14. Tom is still in school. "If I quit," he says, "where will I get a job? Are you sure you want to have the baby?"

Problems and early teenage pregnancies go hand in hand. The young teenager who lives in a city with adequate facilities and programs geared to the young mother is very fortunate. Many public schools now offer special classes for pregnant teenagers and young mothers. Child care is provided while the young mothers attend classes. The programs provide health services and instruction in health care, nutrition, family living, child development, family planning, and homemaking.

Planned Parenthood and public health departments offer additional support systems for the young parent. Health departments are also available to schools as educational resources. Working together, these programs offer the support system needed by young parents.

What Teenagers Need

Young people, boys and girls alike, need to have knowledge and skills to prepare for their roles as adults. The Children's Defense Fund cited five needs that must be met if teenagers are to become successful, functioning adults (Children's Defense Fund, 1992).

The first need is a good education. The second need—nonacademic opportunities—is especially important for students who do not do well in school. They need a chance to feel successful and feel good about themselves. All people need a strong feeling of self and a good self-concept. The third need—work-related skills—is essential for participation in the job market. The fourth need—family-life education—helps the child continue to go to school rather than be derailed by parenthood or a sexually transmitted disease. The final need is comprehensive health services.

PARENTING SKILLS

Education to bolster parenting skills can be offered through center- or school-based programs, home visitors, or home-center based programs. Some schools operate child-care centers that allow new parents to bring their children to school with them. Bolstered by encouragement and understanding and equipped with knowledge of parenting skills, the young parents are better able to care for their infants. Teenagers without these opportunities and without positive models in their own homes face the enormous task of childrearing unprepared. Expectations by some young parents for their infant's development are often unreasonable. For example, some teenagers believe that infants should be completely toilet trained by 8 months. Understanding and knowledge of child development can smooth the way for effective childrearing. Providing support and mechanisms that allow teenagers to become self-sufficient parents is essential. The problems are evident; teenage parents need special attention, skillful direction, and sensitive support.

U.S. Department of Health and Human Services Programs

Programs funded by the U.S. Department of Health and Human Services to promote abstinence and help prevent teenage pregnancy and sexually transmitted diseases include:

1. *Abstinence Education Program.* Designed to promote abstinence from sexual activity before marriage.
2. *Community-Based Abstinence Education.* Funded for community-based abstinence education programs.
3. *Adolescent Family Life Program.* Funded for demonstration projects to develop programs to promote abstinence, prevent pregnancies and sexually transmitted diseases, and develop comprehensive health, education, and social services.
4. *Community Coalition Prevention Demonstrations.* Centers for Disease Control and Prevention (CDC) programs have been funded since 1995 to help prevent teen pregnancies. "These projects support coalition of local, public, and private agencies, and organizations in communities with high rates of teen pregnancy in order to develop community action plans, coordinate efforts to reduce teen pregnancy, identify gaps in current programs and services, target existing resources, and design evaluation plans" (p. 1).
5. *Working with Boys and Young Men.* Demonstration programs to ensure that boys and men secure the education and support necessary to postpone fatherhood.
6. *School-Based Prevention.* Centers for Disease Control and Prevention (CDC) works with the Joint Workgroup on School-Based Pregnancy. The JWG gives on-site two-day training sessions to state and local education and health policy makers to educate on how to prevent teen pregnancy. (U.S. Department of Health and Human Services, 2002.)

COMPREHENSIVE SERVICE DELIVERY

Family Support Programs

Family support programs have responded to the need for services and support across the United States by providing a wide range of services and help for families. Thirty-two percent of these programs are located in schools; 20 percent are located in day care, preschools, or Head Start (Family Support America States Initiative, 2002). The programs support families and reduce their isolation by giving them a gathering place and information they need to provide for their families. The 10 services most often provided are (a) 90 percent, information and referral; (b) 84 percent, parent education; (c) 73 percent, parent–child activities; (d) 70 percent, child development activities; (e) 66 percent, peer support (support groups, mentoring; (f) 48 percent, child abuse prevention; (g) 43 percent, community building activities; (h) 38 percent, child care during programmatic activities; (i) 37 percent, adult health care; and (j) 37 percent, emergency assistance for basic needs (p. 19). Three programs—Family Support America (formerly Family Resource Centers), Family and Child Education (FACE), and Family Literacy Projects—illustrate the types of services that support centers provide. Programs were developed because of families' obvious need for support to survive and provide the nurturing environment their children need. The National Center for Family Literacy focuses on literacy development for the total family. Family and Child Education is a support and literacy program for children who are Native Americans. The Family Support America is a national coalition of groups that work for resources and provisions to strengthen families. Family support centers are being developed throughout the United States, and models of centers developed and housed in public schools are increasing. School personnel are becoming increasingly aware that families are the underlying support for the child and that the school must work with both to be successful in the education of the child.

> Premises and principles of family support include the following:
>
> a. Primary responsibility for the development and well-being of children lies within the family, and all segments of society must support families as they rear their children.
>
> b. Ensuring the well-being of all families is the cornerstone of a healthy society and requires universal access to support programs and services.
>
> c. Children and families exist as a part of an ecological and reciprocal system.
>
> d. Child-rearing patterns are influenced by parents' understandings of child development and of their children's unique characteristics, personal sense of competence, and cultural and community traditions and mores.
>
> e. Enabling families to build on their own strengths and capacities promotes the healthy development of children.
>
> f. The developmental processes that make up parenthood and family life create needs that are unique at each stage in the life span.
>
> g. Families are empowered when they have access to information and other resources and take action to improve the well-being of children, families, and communities. (Family Support America's Shared Leadership Series, 2000, pp. 3–4)

These centers provide for young parents and mature parents alike. They help the families cope with stress; they offer prenatal classes, child development, and parent education to help them with their children; they work to prevent crises; they sponsor drop-in services; and they arrange opportunities for parents to develop support networks. The centers are staffed by empathetic professionals and paraprofessionals. Families are linked with social services that will help them meet their basic needs. The centers focus on families' strengths and respond to parents according to their needs.

Family and Child Education (FACE)

The Bureau of Indian Affairs, Office of Indian Education, desired an integrated program for early childhood parental involvement, from birth through third grade. Initiated in 1990, by 2001 the program had served 15,000 persons representing 5,000 families; 1,500 adults obtained employment and 400 adults received their GED. The program grew from 6 sites in 1992 to 32 in 2001.

Three recognized national programs—National Center for Family Literacy (NCFL), the Parents as Teachers (PAT) National Center, and High/Scope Research Foundation—have collaborated in a family education model for these children, birth through grade three. The Family and Child Education (FACE) training program provides training sessions and on-site assistance. Through the integration of the three programs, a strong support system of family and child education is implemented for American Indians (National Center for Family Literacy, 2002, p. 1).

Family Literacy

The U.S. Census Bureau (2004) reported that 10,255,623 persons, or 5.56 percent of those 25 years or older were illiterate in 2003. This was a reduction from the reported 10,813,147 persons, or 6.09 percent, who were illiterate in 2000. Education and services to reduce illiteracy are essential.

The federal definition of *family literacy* services is as follows:

> Services that are of sufficient intensity in terms of hours and of sufficient duration, to make sustainable changes in a family and that integrate all of the following activities:
>
> a. Interactive literacy activities between parents and their children.
>
> b. Training for parents regarding how to be the primary teacher for their children and full partners in the education of their children.
>
> c. Parent literacy training that leads to economic self-sufficiency.
>
> d. An age-appropriate education to prepare children for success in school and life experiences. (U.S. Department of Health and Human Services, 2000, p. 2)

Parents should engage in interactive literacy activities with their children, learn how to be the primary teacher for their children and to become full partners in their child's education, and become literate to ensure self-sufficient employment. Comprehensive family literacy programs and family-centered literacy programs provide the support that parents need to fulfill their parental roles.

The inability to read and write hinders men and women in fulfilling their role in society and their roles as parents. Those with children in school have an especially difficult time. Parents who cannot read books or notes their children bring home are unable to collaborate effectively with the school for the betterment of their children's education.

In reading about literacy, one finds more written on bilingual education and being literate in English than about literacy for all. Literacy programs should incorporate the person who does not speak English, but there is a great void in the recognition of the many English-speaking adults who cannot read or write.

Young men and women graduate from high school unable to read and write; many other adults drop out of school because of their inability to read and write. Illiterate adults live in a world that expects them to be literate. Employment is difficult; acknowledging their deficiency in the English language is embarrassing. They need adult literacy support as much as the person who does not speak English.

As stated earlier, recognition of the need for adults to be able to read has resulted in federal funding for literacy programs. Family literacy fits into the goals of Title I and Head Start programs. One way the federal government supports family literacy is through Even Start, which links adult literacy programs with a preschool program for parents who need to complete their education and who have children younger than 8. The Education and Human Services Consortium is a coalition interested in connecting families with the services they need. The National Institute on Early Childhood Development and Education is in the Office of Educational Research and Improvement, U.S. Department of Education.

Nonprofit organizations, workplace literacy programs, and colleges and universities also promote adult literacy. Two major nonprofit associations have made great strides in supporting families. Family Support (Family Resource Center) in Chicago spearheaded the move toward more centers, whether federally, state, or privately funded. The National Center for Family Literacy received a grant from the Kenan Trust in support of its efforts to promote family literacy through programs and training.

Family literacy includes the total family, rather than just the individual. "Literacy is defined as using printed and written information to function in society, to achieve one's goals, and to develop one's knowledge and potential" (National Center for Family Literacy, 2005, p. 1). Head Start was targeted to offer family literacy programs by 1992. Its focus on family literacy includes three goals: (a) helping parents realize their own needs and work to overcome their own literacy concerns; (b) helping them increase their access to literacy services, programs, and materials; and (c) supporting them in their role as their child's teacher (Potts, 1992).

The National Even Start Association supports literacy programs for families throughout the 50 states and territories. Even Start integrates early childhood education and parenting education into a program that has as its goal the reduction of illiteracy and poverty (National Even Start Association, 2006).

Family literacy programs focus on building family programs based on the strengths of families rather than on their deficits. It recommends that there should be sufficient duration of literacy programs so that the family is supported enough that it enables success. Literacy programs use methods of teaching adults that have been tested over time. In addition, a whole-language approach is often used, so language is learned in many ways. The curriculum is built around the strengths of families. High-interest, low-vocabulary books are used. Some theories that work for parents who do not speak English may apply to illiterate English-speaking adults, but it remains critical to involve the whole family, or at least the parent and child. They do activities together at school, usually after the parent has had a family literacy class and the child has reached preschool or first grade. Home visits are also used to bring activities and new books to the parents and visit with them on their home territory.

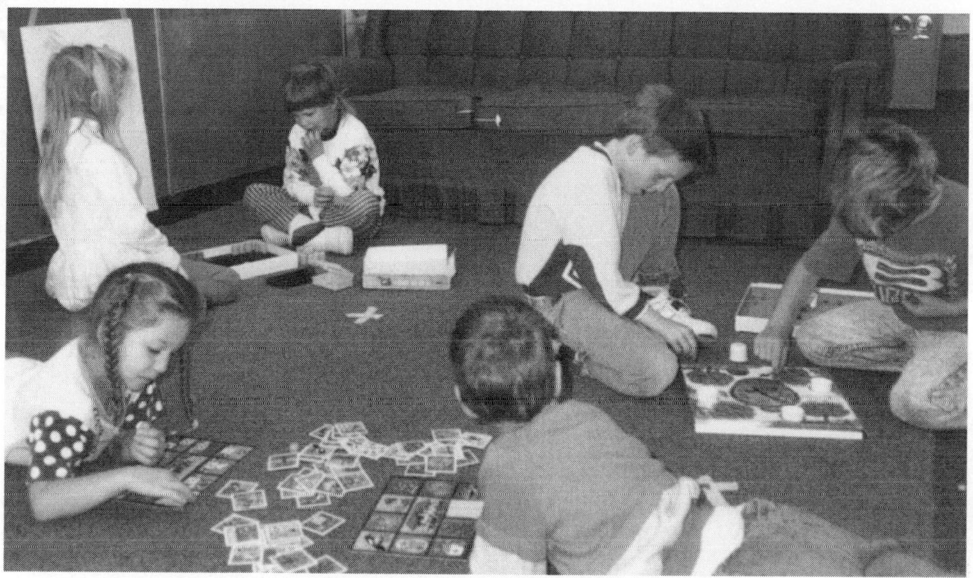
Eugenia Hepworth Berger

Involvement in activities carry over to home with an incentive to make plans, experiment, read directions, and construct.

MAKING PROGRAMS HAPPEN

"How can parent programs be started?" This question can be answered from two approaches, both related to financing. Funding can be obtained to establish a parent program, or the individual district, school, or teacher can design a program with or without financial support. This section presents information about funding sources as well as social agencies and other community resources.

Funding

Funding for school-related programs comes primarily from three major sources: (a) government grants, either federal or state; (b) private foundation awards; and (c) local school budgets. A public school's budget is based on local taxes and state distribution of funds. Private schools rely primarily on tuition and private sources to provide their budgets, although they are eligible for some federal grants. Current information on funding and grants can be obtained from your regional Department of Education or Department of Health and Human Services and your state social services or education department.

The most stable funding source for public schools is the local school board. As schools begin to view the parent component as worthwhile or essential, more programs will be implemented and funded through local support. Private foundations also fund special projects for parents and children. Local businesses and foundations are probably the best source of either funds or information about money available in your community.

Most grants have a specified duration, usually 3 years. If a program is dependent on the extra grant funding, plans must be made for financing after the grant runs out or the program will either deteriorate or disappear. The major importance of grants is the impetus they provide for developing programs, materials, and services. Many programs, now a permanent part of the community, were started on grants.

Try to obtain funding and grants, but if your efforts are not rewarded, consider parent involvement as an integral part of the school program and develop a unique approach to bring about a partnership. Using volunteers in a positive way can help teachers and enable the school to enrich its educational offerings. Volunteers can be an alternative to funding in making programs happen.

Resources and Social Agencies

Collaboration between schools and social agencies helps develop continuity and supply the support that families need. Teachers as well as administrators can make referrals to social services, recreation districts, libraries, and other public agencies. If the school district does not have a list, school personnel may contact the Department of Social Services, United Way, Chamber of Commerce, or other agencies or civic groups to obtain a list of community resources. Check to see if there is a clearinghouse in the area. The telephone book's white and yellow pages also have listings for the types of services listed here.

Reaching Out

It is apparent that families and children (infants to young adults) need supportive environments. Although it has been recognized that those in poverty have special needs, families at all income levels need a sense of community and commitment. Isolation, violence on television and through the Internet, and a sense of alienation affect many of the youth in America. Schools, family resource centers, and families must work together. If schools and community resources communicate and cooperate with one another, families and children with needs do not have to slip through the cracks.

SUMMARY

School-based programs that involve parents are varied. The chapter examines what parent involvement means and identifies nine levels of collaboraion. The Comer process is based on consensus, collaboration, and no-fault needed to develop a climate that allows children, parents, and schools to thrive. After describing a walk through a school committed to parent involvement, this chapter explores national efforts and school-based programs. Reggio Emilia is described and compared to the project approach.

Effective programs as selected by Rand Corporation were Head Start, Perry Prechool Project, Carolina Abecedarian Project, Project Care, Syracuse Family Development Research, Houston Parent–Child Development Center, Early Training Project, Chicago Child Parent Center, and Oklahoma Pre-K.

Programs included School on Saturday, Brookline, math and science programs, school- and center-based programs and workshops. How to reach reticent families was examined. School-based programs are diversified, but each type of involvement is essential if the needs of families are to be met. The changes in ERIC were noted. Teenage pregnancies are decreasing, but the issue is still important, and it is essential to try to find support and education for the teenage mother.

Ways to start home–school programs are discussed. Many programs are started with grants. If this monetary support is not available, schools can try to increase personnel support by soliciting volunteers. Efforts are being made to increase literacy and to support families so that all children can be successful in school and life.

SUGGESTED CLASS ACTIVITIES AND DISCUSSIONS

1. Visit a Title I program in a public school. Talk with the principal about the parent involvement specifically developed for the program. Or, if you work in a Title I program, develop a family literacy program.
2. Survey three or four schools that have federal funding. How do the schools differ in their approaches to parent involvement? How are they alike? Are there different responses to the various types of funding, for example, Title I, Title IV-C, Title VII, Follow Through, or Right to Read?
3. Visit schools in different areas and find out how they involve parents. Analyze the different approaches.
4. Design a parent bulletin board that illustrates the various components of the parent program in your classroom.
5. Develop a resource file of games, articles, books, and recycled materials.
6. Develop a workshop in which you have various learning centers—for example, early reading, sorting and classifying, problem solving, creativity, self-esteem, and language development.
7. Make a universal game board and a series of cards to be used with it.
8. Develop activities that parents can use with their children at home.
9. Search the community for resources that can be used in the school. Include specialists, materials, and places to visit.

WEB SITES

Clearinghouse on Early Education and Parenting (CEEP): ERIC/EECE Archive of Publications and Resources

http://ceep.crc.uiuc.edu/eecearchive

CEEP maintains the ERIC/EECE elementary and early childhood archive.

National Center for Education Statistics (NCES), U.S. Department of Education
www.nces.ed.gov
The NCES has researched and collected data on early childhood education.

National Center for Family Literacy
www.famlit.org
This site provides good tips and help to reduce illiteracy in America.

National Support America
www.familysupportamerica.org
Site includes resource centers throughout the United States that reach out to help parents.

9 Home-Based Programs

To work with a child and not with the parent is like working with only part of the pieces of a puzzle. It would be like a person who put a puzzle together with a thousand pieces, and then as he finished found the center part missing.

Winters, 1988, p. 8

In this chapter you will learn about home-based education, homeschooling, and homework. After completing the chapter, you should be able to do the following:

- Compare goals and services of several home-based programs.
- Describe a framework for developing activities to be used in a home-based program.
- Develop activities for use in home-based programs.
- Cite practices to avoid when working with parents in the home.
- Identify the reasons for homeschooling.
- Cite the public's response to homeschooling that supports cooperation between the homeschooler and the school.
- Describe the different strategies parents can use to support academic learning at home.

The home is the primary educational setting for children. Parents are responsible for nurturing and educating their infants and preschoolers. Some of them share this role with child-care centers and schools. They also work with schools by becoming involved in the school's education program. Some choose to educate their children at home. In this chapter the discussion will center first on children and the home-based offerings that can support the family. Learning at home is one area where parents and school personnel can support children's continued academic development. How can parents be the most helpful? Last, the move toward homeschooling—in which parents take responsibility for their children's entire education—will be considered.

ORIGINS OF HOME VISITING

Home visiting originally developed in Europe, especially in England. Assistance to families was provided by "friendly visitors," church members, and other nonprofessionals. Florence Nightingale, a nurse recognized for her caring of soldiers during the Crimean War, also was instrumental in promoting health and hygiene in rural areas, villages, and towns. Her efforts led to a school in Liverpool, England, for the training of nurses. She also encouraged health visitors who were not nurses to visit homes in rural areas (Wasik & Bryant, 2001).

When immigrants from southern and eastern Europe began to come in great numbers to the United States in the later 1800s, visiting nurses along with settlement houses became part of the response to "encourage" the new arrivals to use "proper" hygiene and health. As described in chapter 4, the growth of government intervention and services began in the 20th century. Parent education with parents attending meetings away from their homes became prominent in the 1920s. The trend toward home visiting was renewed after World War II and, since the 1970s, the programs have moved from working with individuals to working with and empowering families (Wasik & Bryant, 2001).

Eugenia Hepworth Berger

Home visitors sometimes provide an important contact, and sometimes the visits are the only contact the parent has with anyone outside the home.

HOME-BASED EDUCATION

Imagine yourself as the parent of two preschoolers living in the country at least a mile from the nearest neighbor. Or, pretend that you are a parent in a core-city apartment house. Some parents in urban and suburban areas have no more contact with supportive friends than those isolated by distance in the country. Both urban and rural residents, as the first teachers of their children, need the educational support and knowledge necessary to provide an enriched, positive environment for their children.

PROGRAMS THAT WORK

Numerous approaches have proved effective in a variety of projects throughout the United States. They range from programs specifically designed to educate children and bring good parenting practices into the home to those that provide support for the entire family's health, mental health, housing, income, child development, and education. Descriptions of selected programs illustrate the scope and variety of parent involvement in the educational process. Take from them the ideas and procedures that fit your situation.

It is evident, as illustrated by the research cited in chapter 1, that children's early experiences impact the rest of their lives. Brain development occurs incredibly fast during the first 3 years. Programs that help parents during these early years have great benefits for the cognitive and language development of these children. Many of these programs were developed to reduce the impact of child abuse (see chapter 11), by assisting parents to relate constructively to their children, and to guide parents to support the physical, emotional, and cognitive development of their children. Home-based programs were developed on the premise that parents are a child's first and most potent teacher, therefore, parents must be supported in order to reach this potential.

A recently published study by the Rand Corporation (Karoly, Kilburn, & Cannon, 2005) reported the benefits of early childhood education, and included a discussion of home visiting programs. A sample of the home-visiting program models that were included in the study were: Parents as Teachers (PAT), Home Instruction Program for Preschool Youngsters (HIPPY), Healthy Families America (HFA), Early Head Start (EHS), Nurse Family Partnership, the Parent–Child Home Program, and the Portage Project.

Parents as Teachers Program

Parents as Teachers Project (PAT) was developed in four districts in Missouri in the early 1980s and extended to the entire state in 1985. By 1999, the program had expanded to 2,197 sites in 49 states, the District of Columbia, and six other countries, serving 500,000 children. In addition to school districts, PAT is offered by churches, hospitals, social services, and as part of Head Start, Even Start, and Family Resource Centers.

PAT program services include four components:

1. Regularly scheduled personal visits by credentialed parent educators, who provide information on the child's development, model and involve parents in age-appropriate activities with the child, and respond to parents' questions and concerns.
2. Group meetings in which parents share insights and build informal support networks.
3. Monitoring of children's progress by both parents and home visitors to detect and treat any emerging problems as early as possible.
4. Linking of families with need of community services that are beyond the scope of the program. (Winter & McDonald, 1997, pp. 119–145).

> Home visits are usually one hour long and are scheduled monthly, biweekly, or weekly, depending on family needs and local program budgetary restrictions. For example, while most enrolled families receive monthly or bimonthly home visits in Missouri, state funds provide for 25 visits per year for high-needs families—that is, families with one or more of the following characteristics: teen parents, single parents, children or parents with disabilities, low educational attainment, English as a Second Language, unemployment, chemical dependencies, foster parents, numerous family relocations, high stress, or involvement with the corrections system or mental health, health, or social service agencies. Weekly visits are conducted at the 22 PAT program sites on Indian reservations which are administered by the Bureau of Indian Affairs. (*The Future of Children*, 1999, pp. 179–180)

Missouri conducted a school entry assessment project to study and create a plan in which all children come to school ready to succeed. A School Entry Profile was developed, organized around seven conceptual areas that reflect dimension of readiness for school. The "areas identified include symbolic development, communication, mathematical/ physical knowledge, working with others, learning to learn, physical development and conventional knowledge. . . ." The School Entry Profile is to identify and measure the equities and inequities of early life experiences known to promote school success or difficulty. It will be used to identify ways to address those inequities so all children will have access to opportunities that promote school success (Missouri Department of Elementary and Secondary Education, 1999, p. 2).

Research conducted in 1985 on first-time parents validated the parents' positive responses. It showed that children participating in the Parents as Teachers project scored significantly higher on all measures of verbal ability, intelligence, language ability, achievement, and auditory comprehension than did children in a comparison group. The program proved so successful that it was adopted by the Missouri Department of Elementary and Secondary Education for use by 543 school districts throughout the state. Revisions and updating of the PAT curriculum was accomplished in 1996 in addition to the development of the Born to Learn curriculum. It was field tested and became standard PAT for prenatal to 3 years curriculum for Missouri in 1999 and has now been used in programs around the United States.

In 1987, the National Center on Parents as Teachers was established in St. Louis. It offers technical assistance and training. The major goals for participants are not in the teaching of child development—it is expected that the trainees already have knowledge in that area. The 5-day training focuses instead on parent empowerment, parent strengths and how to build on them, and a combination of ways to observe parent–child interaction, respond, and demonstrate the curriculum (Winter, 1991).

Beginning in the third trimester of pregnancy and continuing until the child is 3, PAT home visitors meet with each family to provide the following:

- Information and guidance to help the parents-to-be prepare for the new arrival.
- Information on child development to foster cognitive, social, motor, and language development. Clearly written handbooks describing what the parents should expect during each phase of development are provided to parents. The phases are as follows:

  Phase 1—prenatal or birth to 6 weeks

  Phase 2—6 weeks to $3\frac{1}{2}$ months

  Phase 3—$3\frac{1}{2}$ months to $5\frac{1}{2}$ months

  Phase 4—$5\frac{1}{2}$ months to 8 months

  Phase 5—8 months to 14 months

  Phase 6—14 months to 24 months

  Phase 7—24 months to 36 months (Ferguson-Florissant School District, 1989b)
- Periodic hearing and vision checkups for the children.
- Parent resource center at the school that was available for parent meetings.
- Individualized parent conferences each month.
- Monthly group meetings with other parents.

The programs in Missouri and in other states have found that first-time parents are usually very receptive to guidance and so they developed a program for new mothers and infants. Mothers or fathers who do not work outside the home usually have a need to visit and socialize with others as well as a desire to learn how best to raise the child. Contact and support reduce the loneliness of a parent who is solely responsible for an infant. In addition, new parents have no preconceived ideas from their experiences in rearing other children that might conflict with the research design (Wagner, Spiker, & Linn, 2002; Wagner, Spiker, Inman, Linn, et al., 2003).

HIPPY—Home Instruction Program for Preschool Youngsters

The HIPPY program was developed in 1969 at the Hebrew University of Jerusalem in Israel, and it is now used in at least eight countries. The first U.S. programs were established in 1984. In 1999, there were 121 programs serving 15,000 families in 28 states, Guam, and the District of Columbia. The basic assumptions of the program are that all children can learn and that all parents want the best for their children. The skill areas included are tactile, visual, auditory, and conceptual discrimination, in addition to language development, verbal expression, eye–hand coordination, premath concepts, logical thinking, self-concept, and creativity. In 1994, a curriculum for 3-year-olds was added with storybooks and activity packets, so the program now serves 3- to 5-year-olds. The program has a detailed curriculum design, with each activity illustrated. The material for each year of 2 years has 9 storybooks, 30 activity packets, 20 manipulative shapes, and weekly instructions for the paraprofessional. Home visitors role play strategies for engaging children in learning activities. There are also group meetings with parents to encourage socialization. A professional coordinates the program, but home visitors are paraprofessionals selected from parents who were in the program. They visit bimonthly or at least 15 times a year to instruct the parents in the use of HIPPY educational materials (*The Future of Children,* 1999). Figures 9.1A and 9.1B illustrate the type of study materials offered to parents in the program (Baher, Piotrkowshi, & Brooks-Gunn, 1998; Bar-Hava-Monteith, Harre, & Field, 1999).

Healthy Families America

Healthy Families America (HFA) replicates the design of Hawaii's Healthy Start program (State of Hawaii, Department of Health, 1997). The HFA program was established by the National Committee to Prevent Child Abuse. The goals of the program include:

- Reduce incidents of neglect and abuse
- Ensure healthy children
- Encourage school readiness
- Promote family self-sufficiency
- Reduce maternal mental health treatment
- Demonstrate positive parenting

These goals support improved parenting skills, enhancement of child health and development, reduction of family stress, and improved family functioning, as well as prevention of child abuse and neglect.

THE CAT WHO LOOKED FOR A HOUSE (7)

WEEK: 10

DAY: 3

ACTIVITY SHEET: 2

1. (Cut out the animals below and put them on the table.)
(Point to the animals and to the houses and say):

   THESE ANIMALS LIVE IN THESE HOUSES.

2. I WILL PUT AN ANIMAL NEAR A HOUSE.

   YOU TELL ME IF IT IS THE RIGHT HOUSE.

   IF NOT, PUT THE ANIMAL NEXT TO A HOUSE THAT'S RIGHT FOR IT.

3. (Place each animal next to a house which is *not* appropriate for it.)

   NOW SEE IF I MADE ANY MISTAKES.
   (The child should be able to rearrange them all.)

4. (Now place 2 correctly and 2 *incorrectly*.)

   NOW IS EVERY ANIMAL IN THE RIGHT HOUSE?
   – no.

   SO PUT EACH ONE WHERE IT BELONGS.

5. PASTE EACH ANIMAL NEXT TO ITS HOME.

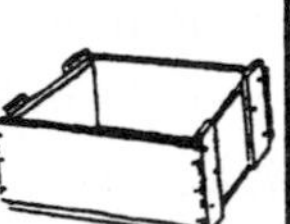

"HIPPY" — Age 4 (1991)

Published in The United States by The Dushkin Publishing Group, Inc. Revised Illustrations by the Averroès Foundation, Amsterdam.

10

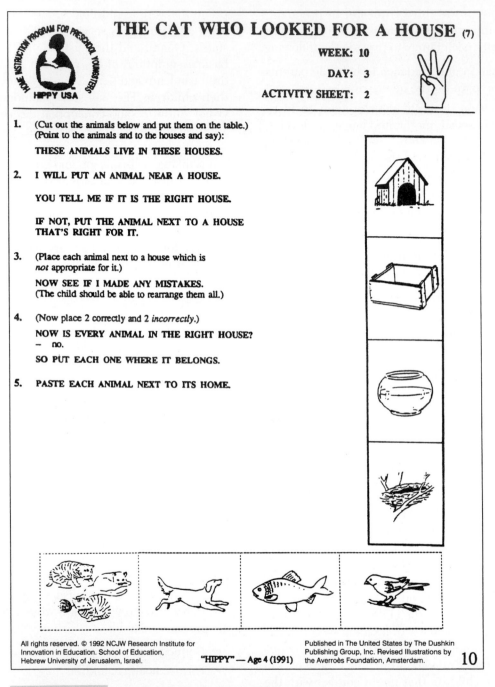

FIGURE 9.1A The cat who looked for a house.

Source: Printed with permission. All rights reserved © 1992 NCJW Research Institute for Innovation in Education. School of Education. Hebrew University of Jerusalem, Israel. Published in the United States by the Dushkin Publishing Group, Inc. Revised illustrations by the Averroès Foundation, Amsterdam.

SORTING (3)

WEEK: 10

DAY: 5

ACTIVITY SHEET: 1

(Materials on the table: an empty shoe box, 4 empty cups, 5 coins, 5 stones, toothpicks, 5 bottle caps and paste.)

1. (Sit next to a table.Place the 4 cups and the box with all the other objects in it on the table.)

   IN THIS BOX, THERE ARE MANY DIFFERENT THINGS. THEY ARE ALL MIXED TOGETHER. WE WILL ARRANGE THEM.

2. **GIVE ME A TOOTHPICK.**
   (Place it in a cup.)

   FIND ALL THE TOOTHPICKS AND PUT THEM IN THIS CUP.

   GIVE ME A COIN.
   (Put it in the second cup.)

   PUT ALL THE COINS IN THIS CUP.
   WHAT IS LEFT IN THE BOX?
   – stones and bottle caps.

   GIVE ME ALL THE BOTTLE CAPS.
   (Place them in the third cup.)

   NOW PUT ALL THE STONES IN THE EMPTY CUP.

3. (Put all the objects back in the large container.)

   NOW YOU SORT ALL THE THINGS.

   PUT ALL THE THINGS OF ONE KIND IN ONE CUP.
   (When the child has finished sorting the objects into the four cups, ask):

   WHAT DID YOU DO?
   – I arranged the things.
   – I sorted them
   – I put the ________ together, and the ________ together.

"HIPPY" — Age 4 (1991)

Published in The United States by The Dushkin Publishing Group, Inc. Revised Illustrations by the Averroès Foundation, Amsterdam.

17

FIGURE 9.1B Sorting.

Source: Printed with permission. All rights reserved © 1992 NCJW Research Institute for Innovation in Education. School of Education. Hebrew University of Jerusalem, Israel. Published in the United States by the Dushkin Publishing Group, Inc. Revised illustrations by the Averroès Foundation, Amsterdam.

Families are selected primarily through the use of a standardized assessment tool by participating hospitals or physicians, public health nurses, midwives, support groups in areas where access to hospital records is unavailable, or by self or family referral. The risk factors that are considered include (a) marital status of mother; single, separated, or divorced; (b) partner unemployed; (c) inadequate income or no information regarding source of income; (d) unstable housing; (e) no phone; (f) less than 12 years of education; (g) inadequate emergency contacts; (h) history of substance abuse; (i) late or no prenatal care; (j) history of abortions; (k) history of psychiatric care; (l) abortion unsuccessfully sought or attempted; (m) relinquishment for adoption sought or attempted; (n) marital or family problems; and (o) history of, or current, depression.

Assessment interviews are conducted if 7 of the 15 risk factors cannot be answered from information on medical charts; if 2 of the factors are present; or if any 1 of factors 1, 9, or 12 is present. The assessor scores the answers; families with scores of less than 25 are considered to be at low risk for child abuse; those above are considered at risk and are offered Healthy Start services.

Home visitors are trained to provide supportive, culturally appropriate services, beginning prenatally or at the birth of a child, and continuing until the child is 5. The program begins with level 1, weekly visits, progresses to level 2, which consists of 2 visits a month, and completes at levels 3 and 4 with monthly or quarterly visits.

Research findings published on the Prevent Child Abuse America Web site, www.prevent childabuse .org, provide results of program outcomes in various state settings. For example, in Pinellas County, Florida, the rate of child maltreatment for participants in the HFA program was 1.6, compared to 4.9 for the county as a whole. In Maryland there were only 2 reports of neglect among the 254 families served in 4 years (a rate of .8). In general, the Healthy Families program has demonstrated the following:

- Mothers achieving higher levels of confidence
- Home environment observed to be better organized
- Parents engaged in neglectful behavior less often
- Greater acceptance of their children's behavior
- Significantly lower levels of distress
- Significantly fewer reports of abuse and neglect within the first year of life

Considering the stress new parents face daily, especially without family/community supports, a key strategy to prevent child abuse and neglect is to provide the support that would otherwise be missing (Daro, McCurdy, Falconnier, & Stojanovic, 2003; Rogers & O'Connor, 2003).

Early Head Start

Early Head Start (EHS) is a federally funded program that serves low-income pregnant women and families with infants and toddlers. It is designed to serve children until their third birthdays, with transition plans made for preschool services, either in Head Start or other community services for which the families are eligible. Similar to the Head Start program, 10 percent of the children enrolled in EHS must have disabilities. The EHS program has four service areas in which outcomes are measured: child development, which includes health, language, cognitive and social–emotional development; family development which includes parenting skill development and economic self-sufficiency; staff development; and family/community partnerships, which include establishing collaborations between the EHS program and other community organizations. Services are provided through home visits by home visitors that represent the parent populations served by the program. Program services include:

- Weekly home visits that last $1\frac{1}{2}$ hours. Home visitors work with parents to guide them in using daily routines to promote child development. Parents are encouraged to plan each week's activities, which can include cooking to enhance nutrition habits, language and literacy skills, number awareness, and social skills such as turn-taking and sharing.
- Screening of children to determine if they are meeting developmental milestones in language, cognitive, and social–emotional development, physical growth and nutrition.
- Assessment of the home environment to determine if it is supportive of children's safe, healthy, cognitive, language and social–emotional development.

- Assessment of the children's and families' medical needs.
- Development of family partnership agreements through which parents plan strategies to develop self-sufficiency through participation in education/training activities, job search strategies, and advocacy skills, to attain services needed by their children.
- Assistance to parents in preparing their children for transitioning from the EHS program to preschool programs when their children reach 3 years of age.

Twice a month families have the opportunity to participate in group activities that encourage children and parents to socialize with others, and to observe staff modeling appropriate child–adult interactions. Parents also have the opportunity to identify other participants within the program with whom they can develop supportive relationships. Programming of parent–child socialization activities is decided by a Parent Committee, which is a subcommittee of the Parent Policy Council, a decision-making group overseeing the EHS program.

The EHS program must maintain a Parent Policy Council. The Policy Council is an elected group, made up of present and past parents, and some community representation. The Policy Council reviews the EHS budget, hiring and firing of staff, selection of curricula and screening tools to be used by home visitors, annual community needs assessment activities, and a federally mandated self-evaluation. Participation on the Parent Policy Council provides interested parents with many opportunities to develop skills in public speaking, committee work, business skills, communication skills, and enhanced understanding of the functioning of the program (Lane, Kesker, Ross, et al., 2005; McCallister, Wilson, Green, & Baldwin, 2005).

Nurse Family Partnership Program

The Nurse Family Partnership Program (formerly the Nurse Home Visitation Program) is a home visiting nurse program that serves low-income first-time mothers to improve their health and social functioning. Public health nurses begin providing service when mothers are 20–28 weeks into their pregnancy. The nurse provides support to the mother through the child's first 2 years of life. The program was begun as a research project in Elmira, New York, and was expanded to 6 demonstration cities. In 1999, the National Center for Children, Families and Communities was established to disseminate the program, which now operates in 22 states. The goals of the program are to:

- Improve prenatal, maternal and early childhood health
- Improve family functioning in health, home and neighborhood environment
- Build family and friend support
- Build parental roles
- Build skills to improve coping with major life events

Home visits target the following content areas:

- Health behaviors that affect preterm delivery, low birth weight and infant neurodevelopmental impairment such as tobacco and other substance abuse usage
- School dropout prevention
- Welfare dependence
- Unintended subsequent pregnancies

Nurse home visitors follow a structured intervention plan that involves assessing attitudes, skills, knowledge, and support available to the mother in the home environment. Mothers are encouraged to work toward personal goals, attain behavior changes, and cope with challenges. Activities are assigned between home visits. Visits are scheduled to coincide with the progression of the pregnancy and the child's development. Nurse home visitors use the Clinical Information System to track family characteristics, needs, services received, and progress attained by the mother.

A follow-up evaluation has demonstrated several positive outcomes. They include:

- A decrease in arrests and convictions of 15-year-old target children
- A decrease in sexual partners among 15-year-old target children
- Improved birth outcomes
- Reduced child abuse and neglect
- Savings of $4 for every dollar invested due to reduced welfare, fewer arrests, and lower health care costs (Karoly, Kilburn, & Cannon, 2005; Williams, 2004).

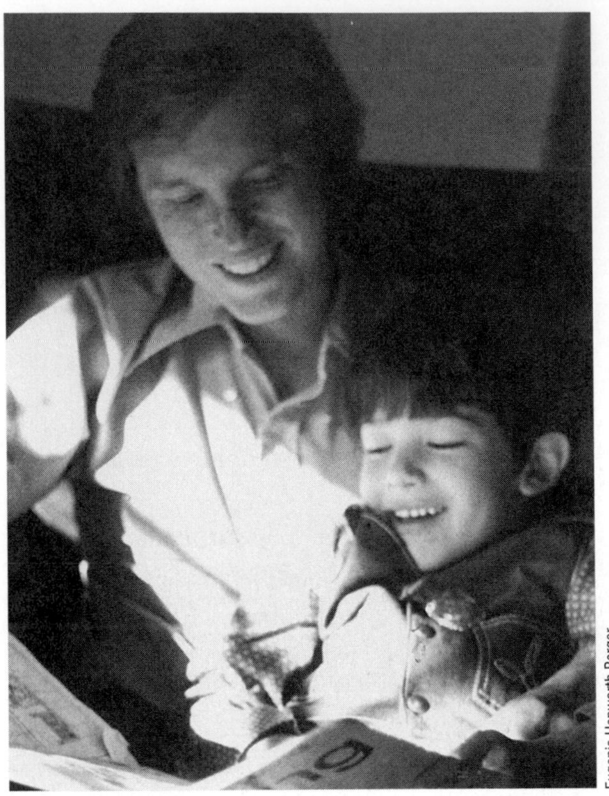
Eugenia Hepworth Berger

Young children gain through verbal interaction as they play and experiment. Books and toys are given to the families so that learning continues.

Parent–Child Home Program

The Parent–Child Home Program (PCHP) is a home-based family literacy program that relies on positive verbal interaction between the child, 2 to 4 years old, and the primary caregiver. It started as the Verbal Interaction Project in 1965 and was incorporated in 1982 as the National Center for the Mother–Child Home Program. It has continued with its name changed to Parent–Child Home Program. In 1998, there were 29 replications of PCHP in the United States and 10 in other countries. The caregiver may be any adult who has primary nurturing responsibilities for the child. The program is based in the child's home; trained home visitors ("toy demonstrators") come twice weekly for half-hour sessions from the time the child is 2 until the child is 4.

> The program's cognitive curriculum was derived from theories and empirical studies of investigators whose work had influenced the program at its inception. At its core are Vygotsky's links between thought and language (Vygotsky, 1962); Bruner's construct of "instrumental conceptualism," the idea that concept formation is fostered in the 2- and 3-year-old child through the child's experience with language (Bruner, 1966); and Sigel's (1971) "distancing hypothesis" in which the promotion of representational competence is given tangible meaning through the child's and parent's play focused around books and 3-dimensional toys as representations of reality, besides being intrinsically motivating curriculum materials. (Levenstein, Levenstein, Shiminski, & Stolzberg, 1998, p. 269)

The home visitor demonstrates toys and books in a play session with parent and child. Parenting behavior emphasizing verbal interaction is modeled instead of being taught directly. The parent and child participate as they learn through play. Books and toys are given to the families so that the learning can continue. There are no specific tasks other than enjoying the play and resultant verbal interaction. Guide sheets cover such concepts as colors, shapes, and sizes and such cognitive skills as matching, pretending, and differentiating. The twice-a-week visits to the home are set up at the parent's convenience (Levenstein et al., 1998).

The method, curricula, and delivery of the program include:

- 46 half-hour sessions twice a week spread over 7 months each year for 2 years
- A guide sheet, a one-page list of concepts, and developmentally appropriate labels for actions or words applied to the toy or book brought by the home visitor to the toddler
- A 20-item VIP-created instrument called "Child's Behavior Traits," a measure as well as a guide to the child's social–emotional goals
- A "Parent and Child Together" curriculum of 20 traits that measure and guide positive parent behavior, modeled by the home visitor and achieved by the parent
- Curriculum materials including 12 illustrated books and 11 toys—with a different set given each year of the 2-year program for a total of 46 books and toys, given to the family
- Parental involvement in the child's play modeled by the home visitor inviting the parent to be involved

- Home visitor modeling without directly teaching positive response to the child, pleasurable reading to the child, encouraging the family's literacy in addition to the child's
- Sessions arranged at the parent's convenience
- Program coordinators who are college graduates and work with home visitors to develop necessary nondidactic skills, respect for family privacy and lifestyles, and prepare written reports (Levenstein et al., 1998)

The goal of the program is to increase the caregiver's interaction with the child in a natural dialogue that enhances and enriches the child's home environment. By training toy demonstrators who are paraprofessionals with a high school education to demonstrate and model their toys without being didactic, the project facilitates relaxed, verbal interaction between parent and child (Levenstein et al., 1998).

A study (1996) conducted on the Pittsfield, Massachusetts, Parent–Child Home Program (Levenstein et al., 1998) included 123 students who, in 1976–1980, participated as toddlers in the program. The 1976–1980 participants were originally recruited by invitations sent to all parents of children attending Chapter I schools, also termed Title I schools. Those who responded were eligible if they met five of the following eight criteria:

1. Child's IQ score under 100 on the Peabody Picture Vocabulary Test (PPVT)
2. Single-parent family
3. Unemployment of mother
4. Unemployment of father
5. Family receives AFDC payments
6. Parent's education less than 12th grade
7. Family income qualifies for poverty status
8. Older sibling in a Chapter I remedial program (Levenstein et al., 1998)

The study looked at control groups of youngsters who would have been eligible for the Parent–Child Home Program but did not attend. All eligible respondents who were offered the Parent–Child Home Program accepted enrollment.

In a replication of the original PCHP program, high school graduation reached 84 percent for those students who had participated in the program. This is equivalent to the graduation rate among students from middle-income families. Only 15.7 percent of PCHP participants, as compared to 40 percent of the control group, dropped out of school.

Andrea Berger

Parents can devise a practical educational experience from everyday projects such as planting a garden.

PCHP research results show that the program is effective with at-risk parents, but it is not needed for families in which the parents already have strong verbal interaction with their children. The positive modeling along with books and toys enable at-risk parents to be positive parents (Mendel, 2004; Levenstein, Levenstein, & Oliver, 2002).

Portage Project

The Portage Project was developed in 1969 as a home-based, family-centered demonstration program providing service to children with disabilities and their families. The model worked with children from birth to age 6 and with their families through weekly home visits by a home teacher. The project originally covered 3,600 square miles in south-central Wisconsin. Successful evaluation of the model and validation by the National Diffusion Network led to other areas' setting up the program.

Over the years the Portage Project has adhered to the principles upon which it was based:

1. Intervention for children with disabilities should begin as early as possible. The earlier work begins, the greater the probability of having a significant effect on the child and the greater the chance that this effect will be maintained over time.
2. Parent/primary caregiver involvement is critical to successful early intervention.
3. Intervention objectives and strategies must be individualized for each child and support the functioning of the family.
4. Data collection is important to reinforce positive change and to make ongoing intervention decisions.

The Portage Project works in collaboration with community agencies to provide comprehensive services to children and families. Referral from individuals and local agencies leads to a play–based assessment conducted by a multidisciplinary team. This process is conducted in the family's home and is designed to provide information on parent–child interaction patterns, parent perceptions, and the developmental functioning level of the child.

If the team, including parents, determines that a child is eligible, the process to develop an Individual Family Service Plan is initiated. This process includes extensive observation and communication with the family. The plan might include weekly home visits by a member of the Portage Project transdisciplinary staff, therapy or counseling from community providers, consultation with child-care providers or other caregivers, participation in parent support groups or play groups, or other activities requested by the family.

Typically, one interventionist is the care coordinator for the family and maintains regular communication with other service providers. This interventionist may be an educator, a speech and language therapist, or a motor specialist, but his or her role in working with families is transdisciplinary.

The Portage Project staff has developed materials to support early childhood programs. These materials include the *Portage Guide to Early Education,* developed in the late 1970s and used in the United States and internationally, and *Growing: Birth to Three*.

The *Portage Guide* contains a checklist of 580 developmentally sequenced behaviors for children up to 6 years old. The behaviors are divided into 6 areas: infant stimulation, self-help, language, cognition, motor skills, and socialization. Ideas for teaching each of the behaviors are included to assist parents and teachers (see Figure 9.2).

Growing: Birth to Three offers materials to support family-centered interactive intervention. The materials are designed to be used as a package, as each piece contributes to the intervention process. Figure 9.3A describes an On the Move Behavior for children 3 to 6 months, and Figure 9.3B illustrates the Using My Senses Behavior for children 24 to 36 months. The materials are designed to encourage flexibility in working with families as well as a stimulus to expand beyond the specific suggested intervention strategies. A brief description of the components of *Growing* follows.

motor 87

AGE 3-4

TITLE: Pedals tricycle five feet

WHAT TO DO:

1. If the child cannot reach the pedals, build them up with blocks taped or screwed onto the pedals.
2. Push the child on the tricycle so that he gets the feel of pedaling.
3. Tape the child's feet to the pedals. Move the trike, so that the child can feel how the pedals work. Gradually reduce the amount of tape used. Straps from roller skates may serve the same purpose as tape.
4. Put pressure on the child's knees to help push the pedals down. Continue pushing each knee. Say "up," "down," etc. Decrease aid gradually.
5. Stand about one foot in front of the child on the tricycle. Show the child a goodie and tell him to come and get it. Praise and reward success.
6. Pull trike towards you with rope so child can concentrate on pedaling instead of steering.
7. Put trike in a stand to keep it stationary as child pedals.
8. Put trike on a slight incline so child won't have to use as much pressure at first.

motor 88

AGE 3-4

TITLE: Swings on swing when started in motion

WHAT TO DO:

1. Use a chair swing first that is likely to be found in a playground.
2. Push child in chair swing. Reassure him by keeping close to the swing, touching child often. Do not swing high.
3. Have the child watch other children swinging and show him that their legs move back and forth to make the swing go. Encourage him to lean "back" and "forward."
4. Don't push the child each time the swing comes back to you and tell him to move his legs back and forth with each swing.
5. As he becomes more independent switch to a swing without sides and have the child hold onto the chain. Be sure the swing is low enough for his feet to touch the ground. Continue encouraging him to swing on his own.
6. Stand in front of child and encourage him to reach out to you with the feet each time the swing comes forward to start a pumping motion.

FIGURE 9.2 Two examples from the card deck of the Portage Guide show the types of activities that parents can do with their children at home.

Source: From *Portage Project Readings*, by D. Shearer, J. Billingsley, A. Frohman, J. Hilliard, F. Johnson, & M. Shearer, 1976, Portage, WI: Portage Project.

ON THE MOVE J14
Three To Six Months

BEHAVIOR #14: Maintain Head In Midline When Pulled To Sit
AREA: On The Move

Why Is This Important?

When conscious effort is no longer required to maintain head control, the infant can attend to using her eyes, ears, hands, and mouth to explore the world.

Commentary:

I'm using my neck and tummy muscles to keep my head in a straight line with my body when you pull me up to sit. It requires some effort on my part, since these muscles are not yet that strong. With practice I will become stronger.

Information:

The amount of head lag which the child exhibits when pulled to a sitting position is a good indication of progression in the development of head control. At first, her head will lag behind her trunk when she is pulled up; later she will be able to keep her head in line with her trunk. Finally, she will develop enough strength to pull herself up while gripping your hands.

Interactive Activities:

Engaging: When I'm sitting on your lap facing you, place your hands over my shoulders with your fingers can supporting my head and my chin tucked. Hold me firmly so my head doesn't fall back. Slowly lower me slightly backward while you sing or talk to me. Watch to see if I can keep my head in line with my trunk; then bring me up again slowly. Repeat this activity several times while we play together. Caution: don't try this activity unless I can maintain head control while in a supported sitting position.

Expanding: Place me on my back. Grasp my hands and wrists and slowly pull me up into a sitting position. Please do not move faster than my head control allows. When I can keep my head in line with my trunk, pull me up halfway and let me pull myself the rest of the way. I'm getting so strong!

Giving Information: My tummy muscles need to be strong for me to pull myself up into a sitting position. You can help make these muscles stronger by gently rubbing or tickling (if I enjoy this) my tummy. Watch to see if I curl my body into flexion when you stimulate my tummy muscles in this way. Does my head tend to come forward so that my chin tucks down to my chest? Do my legs come up and pull in close to my body? If so, I am strengthening my tummy muscles with this playful activity.

Daily Routine Activities:

Diapering: If I'm in a playful mood after you change my diaper, try to pull me up into the sitting position. See how much I am able to help you. Make sure to smile and praise me for my attempts.

Caution:

Pay attention to the level of head control the child has and do not let her lose head control when you pull her up into a sitting position. It is frightening and potentially harmful to have her head fall back unexpectedly. Be prepared to catch her head when doing "pull to sit" activities.

FIGURE 9.3A On the Move: Three to Six Months. An example of activities from *Growing: Interactions/Daily Routines*.

Source: CESA 5, Portage Project (1998).

Ecological Planner

Part I of the *Ecological Planner* suggests guidelines for observation and communication, provides a way to document transactions across time, and offers a selection of formats for individualized intervention planning.

Part II of the *Ecological Planner* is called the *Developmental Observation Guide.* It provides an in-depth, developmentally sequenced series of behaviors that children frequently display from birth through 36 months.

USING MY SENSES C41
Twenty-Four To Thirty-Six Months

BEHAVIOR #41: Use Vision Effectively To Guide Hands
AREA: Using My Senses

Why Is This Important?

This behavior alerts the caregiver to the child's ability to effectively use eye-hand coordination.

Commentary:

What was once a complicated task for me, using my vision to guide what my hands do, is now becoming easier. Watch as I learn to put objects in containers, pegs in holes, and work switches on simple busy boxes. Aren't I clever!

Interactive Activities:

Turntaking: The game described in *Playtime* under Daily Routine Activities (see following section) could be lots of fun if we take turns. First, give me a chance to put something in the box, then you take a turn. Pause and wait so that I know it is my turn again.

Daily Routine Activities:

Doing Chores: As you are taking the clothes off the clothesline, you can occupy me by giving me a plastic milk jug or container with a large opening and some clothespins. Show me how to drop the clothespins into the milk jug, and then see if I will do this by myself.

Mealtime: As I begin to use utensils, am I able to scoop up the food, bring my hand all the way to my mouth, and pop it in? This is part of eye-hand coordination. You may need to guide me at first, then slowly let me try on my own.

Bedtime: As we look at a book together, see if I can start to flip the pages of the book by myself. Can I focus on the corner, place my hand on it and, with some help from you, turn the page?

Playtime: Shape boxes are a good way to help me to practice this skill. Find a shape box with 2 or 3 holes, or you may even want to tape up all but one hole at first. Show me how to drop the shapes in the box, then let me try to do this myself. Be sure to clap or praise all my attempts.

FIGURE 9.3B Using my Senses: Twenty-Four to Thirty-Six Months. An example of activities from *Growing: Interactions/Daily Routines*.

Source: CESA 5 Portage Project (1998).

Nurturing Journals

These journals are designed for use by parents or primary caregivers. Each book contains open-ended questions or statements to help parents reflect on the process of parenting.

Interactive Grow Pack

This section represents the heart of interactive intervention. It offers strategies for interactive communication with parents as well as ways to enhance and encourage mutually satisfying interactions between caregiver and child.

Interactions and Daily Routines Books

This collection offers activity suggestions for each skill or behavior listed in the *Developmental Observation Guide.* Activity suggestions are embedded in daily routines, rituals, play, and interactions.

Master Forms Packet

This packet of reproducible forms is designed to assist in family-guided intervention. The forms can be used to document communications and observations, develop a family-generated service plan, and develop intervention suggestions responsive to each individual family being served (CESA 5, Portage Project, 1998; CESA 5, Portage Project, 2000).

A variety of home-based programs are operating in the United States and in other countries. The programs included here are just a sample of them. While the basic premise is working with families and children in their own homes, there is great variety in the requirements for staff and the manner in which services are provided.

A DAY IN THE LIFE OF ONE HOME-BASED PROGRAM

A program initiated in Yakima, Washington, acknowledged the importance of parents as their children's first teachers. Although this home-based program is no longer funded, this article vividly illustrates how home-based programs make a difference in families' lives.

THE WINNING PLAY AT HOME BASE[1]

The Rochas's home, neat and attractive, is modest by almost anyone's standards. A few fall flowers brighten the gravel walk, and a small tricycle that has seen better days lies on its side in the grass announcing the presence of at least one preschooler. From under a bush the family's gray-striped cat lifts an eyelid as a visitor approaches.

Plump, dark-haired Mrs. Rochas responds immediately to the knock, hampered only slightly by her $2\frac{1}{2}$-year-old son, Benjie, who manages to cling to her knee while keeping one finger in his mouth.

"Hi, Jean. Come in," says Mrs. Rochas, with a smile almost as wide as the door she swings open to permit her caller to enter the small living room. As Mrs. Rochas gently eases Benjie back toward his toy collection in the corner, she tells Jean that Margaretta, her daughter who is almost 4, is still napping.

"That's fine, don't disturb her," Jean, a paraprofessional parent-educator, replies before she settles on the davenport and begins pulling some materials from her shopping bag—a stack of index cards, several old magazines, a pair of scissors, and a tube of glue.

The casual banter notwithstanding, some serious business is at hand: Mrs. Rochas is about to undergo a lesson that marks the beginning of her second "school year." She is one of 200 parents in Yakima, a central Washington community of 49,000, who are learning how to teach their own preschool children through Project Home Base, a pioneer early childhood education program. Depending on how well she learns her weekly lessons, she could have a positive and lasting effect on her child's performance in school.

Like many Home Base families, the Rochases were lured to the area from northern California during the previous fall by the promise of better wages in Yakima's fruit industry. Soon afterward they were visited by a representative from the Home Base project, who explained that all parents of children aged 8 months to 4 years in their neighborhood were being given an opportunity for special, federally sponsored training to enable them to help their preschoolers prepare for school. The Rochases were enthusiastic, but even while accepting the invitation, Mrs. Rochas had a number of doubts. Among them, her daughter (then 3 years old) did not always "take to strangers" and Benjie was still "just a baby." But as the weeks passed and the home-visitor became a familiar and friendly face, the doubts disappeared.

A half hour goes by and Margaretta awakens from her nap. Still sleepy, she enters the living room to find her mother busily engaged in a game of "Concentration." This particular exercise calls for pasting pictures of "like" objects, cut from magazines, onto cards to create a series of pairs. The cards, bearing pictures of various animals and buildings, are then shuffled and placed face down in rows. The game begins with a player picking up a card and trying to match it with a second. If no match results, both cards are returned to their original positions and a second player tries. When all the cards are matched, the player with the most pairs is the winner.

It is important, Mrs. Rochas knows from past experience, that she learn exercises like this one thoroughly before trying them with her children. Then she can become more comfortable in the unfamiliar role of "Teacher."

Before Margaretta plays the game after dinner that day and frequently during the remainder of the week, she will be encouraged to look at the cards and then talk—in complete sentences—about the pictures. As she gains a familiarity changes are made with the objects pictured and the exercise by adding more cards or, to keep the lessons fresh, changing the object of the exercise to matching pairs of colors rather than pictures. It may be just fun to Margaretta, but all the while she is playing, she is acquiring some important skills, including the ability to think logically. She is thus preparing to become a better learner when she enters kindergarten the following year.

Little Benjie, meanwhile, is an important part of the action, too. Before leaving that afternoon, Jean shows Mrs. Rochas how a small hand mirror and a full-length mirror can transform him into "The Most Wonderful Thing in the World."

Examining his face in the mirror, Benjie is helped to identify his most prominent physical characteristic,

[1] From "Winning Play at Home Base." By V. Hedrich and C. Jackson, 1977, *American Education*, pp. 27–30. Revised by Judy Popp, Early Childhood Director, Project Home Base.

such as his curly hair, bright brown eyes, and white teeth. Then he tries to figure out what makes him "special," what makes him different from everyone else in his family. He observes that one eyebrow is straighter than the other, and his ears are round. Then there are all the tricky things he can do with his face: he can squint, wrinkle his nose, and pucker his lips. He is encouraged to talk about how a smile is different from a frown. Before the full-length mirror in the bedroom, Benjie studies his posture and imitates various commonplace activities such as eating a hamburger or kicking a football. He and Margaretta look together into the mirror and discover how their appearances are different and how they are alike. The purpose? To help a child realize he or she is special and to feel good and confident about the discovery.

Although the allotted hour has flown by, Jean takes a few more minutes to discuss some new pamphlets on nutritious snacks for children she has brought along from the County Extension Office, and to confirm her appointment for next week.

The exercises for Margaretta and Benjie just described are only two drawn from more than 200 individual "tasks" for various age levels identified and developed by the Home Base staff. Each exercise has a specific goal or aim. Since most learning handicaps in the target population—preschoolers in the Yakima area—relate to language development, Home Base stresses conversations between parents and their children. There is no special significance attached to the activities' sequence. Tasks become more complex as the child's needs and intellectual capacity grow.

Parents are continually encouraged to adhere closely to a number of effective teaching techniques, such as eliciting questions from the learner, asking questions that have more than one correct answer, asking questions that require more than a one-word reply, praising the learner when he or she does well, urging the child to respond according to evidence instead of guesswork, allowing the child time to think out a problem before receiving assistance, and helping him or her to become familiar with the learning situation and materials.

"As we teach parents what to expect from their children in each situation and how to respond to their child's successes or failures, we find that the parents become stronger and more confident in their teaching role," project director Carol Jackson said. "When they understand the necessity for teaching skills like problem solving, they realize the time is well spent."

Home-visitor's workday may span from 8:30 to 4, with about an hour spent at each home. It is an emotionally demanding job and requires a valid driver's license, an available vehicle, and vehicle liability insurance. Fortunately, language problems are minimized because several of the home-visitors are bilingual. Their services are constantly being used to translate tasks into Spanish and to attend meetings to serve as interpreter for Spanish-speaking parents.

A great deal of role playing is used in the training of parent educators. They try out all of the activities scheduled.

Home Base is not without benefit for the rest of the family, too. "A father told me that being involved in Home Base has made a difference in his wife," reports another of the parent educators. "She's found out she has ability, and she is using it. Her opinion of herself has been greatly improved."

Keeping an otherwise isolated family in touch with the community is another valuable aspect of the Home Base program. "Instead of my feeling alone and all tied up by my problems," a woman told her visitor, "you help by just being a friend that I can talk to once a week." (Hedrich & Jackson, 1977; Popp, 1987)

The Yakima Home Base program illustrated how schools or centers can use the home as a teaching center. The emphasis was on practices that encourage the child's educational growth: (a) learning communication skills, (b) reasoning logically, (c) developing self-concept, (d) becoming nutritionally aware, (e) using developmental activity sequences, (f) employing effective teaching techniques, (g) using easily obtained play materials, and (h) extending new expertise and knowledge about parenting to other members of the family. This program responded to the individual requirements of the community from which it evolved, but many of the techniques of effective parenting and teaching are appropriate for any home-based program.

While the basic premise of home-based programs is working with families and children in their own homes, there is great variety in the requirements for staff and the manner in which services are provided. Table 9.1 compares the programs to enhance understanding as to who is eligible for service, how the programs operate, and who is responsible for providing services. This information can provide guidance for families if they have the

TABLE 9.1 Comparison of Home-Based Program Descriptions

	Populations Served			Goals	Provider Requirements		
Programs	Ages	Eligibility Requirements	Schedule		Background	Training	Materials Used
PAT Parents as Teachers	Prenatal to 5 yrs	Child under 3 yrs	Weekly	Child Development	Paraprofessional	Program specific	Program materials
HIPPY Home Instruction Program for Pre-school Youngsters	3–5 yrs	Any child and family	15× yr	School readiness	Parents	Program specific	Activity packet
EHS Early Head Start	Prenatal to 3 yrs	Low income & 1+infant	Weekly	School readiness, family self-sufficiency	Paraprofessional	Developmentally appropriate practice	Home materials
PCHP Parent–Child Home Program	2–4 yrs	Any child & family	2 × Week	Family literacy	Paraprofessional	Program specific	Toys
HFA Healthy Families America	Prenatal to 5 yrs	Meets specific criteria	Weekly	Child abuse prevention	Paraprofessional	Program specific	Home materials
Nurse–Family Partnership Program	Prenatal to 2 yrs	Low income At-risk mothers	Weekly	Improve family function	Registered nurse	Program specific	Program materials
Portage Project	Prenatal to 6 yrs	Children with disabilities	Weekly	Child development	Professional	Program specific	Program materials

option to choose support from one program or another, and for a community to decide which program to establish.

While some of the programs previously mentioned have explicit instructions for delivering services to children and families, the following guide to developing learning activities are generic guidelines that would result in the home visitor working with the parent to develop a learning environment based on the interests and availability of materials in or near the home.

FIVE-STEP GUIDE TO LEARNING ACTIVITIES

The Florida Parent Education Program developed by Gordon and his colleagues (Gordon & Breivogel, 1976) recommends the following five-step framework in the development of home activities:

Idea

The concept or idea emerges from the child, parent, home visitor, or special interests of the family. What does the family enjoy? Which experiences have been interesting and fun? What collections, toys, or materials are available around the home? Ideas are also shared among the staff—teachers, other home visitors, and curriculum specialists. When an idea occurs, a memo is jotted down to remind the home visitor of the activity.

Reason

Each idea is used for a reason. The reasons may range from learning experiences to self-concept development. After ideas are collected, examine the skills that can be associated with each. For example, if the child picks a leaf from one of the trees in the neighborhood, start a collection of fallen leaves that can be classified according to size, color, and shape. The child can make texture and outline rubbings of them. You might ask the child how many kinds of trees are represented by the variety of leaves, and instruct the child to put each kind of leaf in a separate pile and count the kinds. The many learning opportunities available from collecting leaves make this a worthwhile project for as long as the child's interest continues.

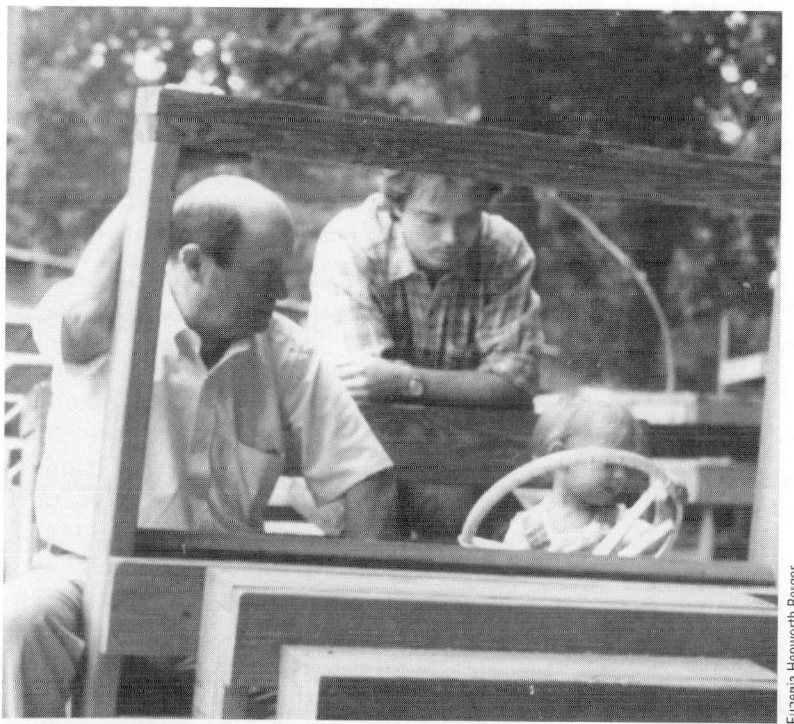

Eugenia Hepworth Berger

Intervention objectives and strategies must be individualized for each child and support the functioning of the family.

Materials

Implementing a reasonable idea requires available materials. Some experiences can be developed around materials commonly found in the home. If the idea requires special equipment and materials, make sure they are easily obtained. One of the main objectives of home visits is to involve the parent as the teacher. If parents do not realize that they have readily available teaching materials or if the learning activities are not furnished for them, part of the parental autonomy and subsequent success of the program is lost.

Action

Follow the child's lead and let the activity develop. If the child chooses something to explore that is different from your plans for the activity, vary your plans, take a detour, and enjoy the inquiry and discovery the child is experiencing. Your ideas may be brought up later or eliminated. Remember the objectives of the learning process. If they are being fulfilled, it does not matter which action brought about the learning.

Extension

Are there other activities related to this idea? If so, expand the action, follow the interest, and extend the learning (Packer, Hoffman, Bozler, & Bear, 1976). Try to help parents see how the activity can be adapted to the child's changing interests and skills. Figure 9.4 illustrates how a garden can be used as a learning experience.

DEVELOPMENT OF A HOME ACTIVITIES FILE

The development of a home activities file depends on the objectives and philosophy of the program. Materials and experiences are based on the home environment, the children's interests, and the parents' enthusiasm. This provides an excellent opportunity to involve parents in creating learning activities for their children. It can also enable the parents to change their approach to childrearing through encouragement and acceptance of their contributions. The idea for a garden described in Figure 9.4 could have originated with a suggestion from a parent.

Throughout the year, home visitors involve parents in teaching their children at home. As the home visitor suggests activities for the child, additional ideas may occur to both the visitor and the parent. In addition, children themselves may elaborate on old ideas or create new activities. The home visitor should bring these ideas back to the office where they can be classified and cataloged. Parents receive a boost if home visitors recognize their contributions. They will also continue to develop activities for children if they are reinforced. Write down their suggestions and file them for future use or include them in the program for the coming week.

Parent Involvement During Home Visits

Children learn best when they are actively involved. Piaget (1976) insists that learning stems from the active involvement of the person doing the inventing; once invented, the theory or steps are not forgotten. Piaget recommends "the use of active methods which give broad scope to the spontaneous research of the child or adolescent and require that every new truth to be learned be rediscovered or at least reconstructed by the student and not simply imparted to him" (pp. 15–16). Kamii (1985a, 1985b) recommends a Piagetian approach in constructivism. Children construct their own knowledge if given the opportunity.

Experiential activities that afford children an opportunity to learn by discovery are facilitated best in a relaxed, natural, and rich learning environment. The setting can be either in the home or in the community. It is important to guide and support parents so they can fulfill their role as their child's first teacher, and constant support system, to ensure that children are able to reach their full potential. The steps to developing a home-learning activity, as suggested by Gordon's program in Florida (Gordon & Breivogel, 1976), reflect the use of the natural environment. Most important is the attitude that learning is possible everywhere for the child.

The home is a learning center. Children learn to talk without formal instruction. They learn as they interact with others and participate in interesting events. Learning tasks at home can and should be intriguing rather than simply difficult. A parent who

UTAH HOME VISITOR GUIDE
April—1st week

Unit title: Gardens and Vegetables

With the high cost of living, it's important to grow your own fresh vegetables because they are so important in our daily diet. Homegrown vegetables are also healthier (less chemicals and fertilizers) and more nutritious. Families need information on how to store, preserve, and prepare fresh vegetables. Gardening is an excellent learning and sharing experience for families.

Specific objectives:

1. To help parents realize the economical benefits gained through home gardening
2. To give parents help with methods of food preparation and preservation
3. To stress the importance of vegetables to good nutrition

Activities

1. Discussion on growing a garden
   a. Why grow a garden?
   b. How to grow a garden
   c. How to store and preserve food from the garden
   d. Handout on food storage and preserving
   e. How to involve children in gardening
   f. Children will often eat more when they grow the food themselves
   g. Gardening is good exercise and teaches responsibility
   h. Handouts on planting times, spacing, what grows in this area (information from county agents)
2. Choose a garden site
3. Plan a garden
   a. What do you want to grow/like to eat?
   b. How much space, water, and time do you have?
   c. What will grow in your area?
   d. Is this to be a permanent site?
4. If no garden space, use boxes, crates, and flower beds
5. Take fruits and vegetables into home for snack/look, feel, and taste
   a. Cleanliness in handling food
6. Look at seeds and compare or match with vegetable
7. Snack tray of raw vegetables and cottage cheese dip
8. Sprout seeds
9. Plant seeds in plastic bag with wet paper towel
10. Plant seeds in egg carton
11. Grow plants from sweet potato and avocado seeds in water
12. Seed collage
13. Start your own tomato, green pepper, and cantaloupe plants indoors in cardboard cartons
14. Count seeds
15. Pop popcorn
16. Classify vegetables and fruits—cut out pictures from magazines
17. Stories and books
   a. Carrot seed
   b. Turnip seed
   c. Peter Rabbit—Mr. McGregor's Garden
   d. The Little Seed
18. Creative movement—germination and growth of seed
19. Tell parents where to get information and handouts
   a. County extension office
   b. Seed stores
20. Sprinkle grass on wet sponge
21. Print with vegetable or weed leaves
22. Talk about seeds you can eat and eat some for a snack
23. Talk about food that people and animals eat
24. Make a vegetable salad
25. Handouts on vegetables

Follow-up for positive reinforcement:

1. Show seeds—sprouted in bag or planted
2. How do you wash vegetables?
3. What did you decide about your garden?

FIGURE 9.4 The Utah Home Visitor Guide. The unit on gardens and vegetables illustrates how ordinary activities around the home can be used for education.

Source: U.S. Department of Health, Education, and Welfare (1978, pp. 68–69).

reads stories to children is actually teaching reading. The development of an interest in and love of reading is the first step toward acquisition of proficient reading skills.

Activities and Resources at Home

Brainstorm for a moment about all the learning opportunities in the home. Record the ideas that can be used during home visits or to share with parents. The following ideas may lead to many more:

- *Art and crafts.* Have tempera paint, watercolors, crayons, chalk, white paper, colored paper, scissors, glue or paste, Play-Doh, and modeling clay available for spontaneous art projects. Draw, paint, or make rubbings and collages. Try painting outdoors with water.
- *Read together.* Children begin learning to read at home. To help children with language and reading development, parents need to talk with and read to their infants. Include a range of literature from nursery rhymes and poems to stories that adults enjoy. Infants hear the voice, develop sensitivity to the sounds, and set out on their way to literacy. The proximity to the reader helps develop trust and attachment.

  Continue reading with preschoolers and school-age children. Discover and emphasize the many situations in which children can be engaged in reading and writing.
- *Publishing.* Make a publishing center and include paper, pencils, pens, typewriter or computer, and cardboard for backing of books.

  Create poetry, cinquains, haiku, free verse, rhyming, and limericks.

  For very young children, transcribe their stories for them and let them illustrate the story or book. If children are older, help them brainstorm ideas for a book or make a history book of their family. Let them write in journals or diaries. Encourage them to write to a relative, pen pal, or friend. Help them edit their work in a cooperative spirit.

  Write a cooperative newsletter for the neighborhood or relatives. Make a form with areas for writings by each person or descriptions of each project. Let someone fill in the information.
- *Games.* Take time to play games. The list is long: Concentration, hopscotch, jacks, jump rope, basketball, table tennis, toss a ball, Lotto, Monopoly, Boggle, word or letter bingo, anagrams, and matching.
- *Backyard science.* Examine the ground for insects and vegetation. Examine bugs with a microscope. Classify leaves by shape, size, and color. Categorize plants or animals.
- *Front yard business.* Have a garage sale and let your child be the cashier.
- *Listening center.* Collect read-along books, and buy tapes or make tapes of the story so the child can listen to the books and read along.
- *Music center.* Have a record player or tape recorder where the child can listen to various types of music. Use the center for singing, moving, and dancing. If you have songs with written words, the activity can also be a reading experience.
- *Communicate.* Talk with each other. Let children describe all the things that are happening. Help them predict and observe by showing interest in their predictions. Make the home a safe place to express feelings.
- *Homemaking activities.* Chores are not chores if you have fun doing them. Cooking is fun and can be used as an intellectual endeavor as well as a functional activity. Practice mathematics by dividing a recipe in half. Research where and how the ingredients were grown.

Activities Away from Home

Trips around and away from home can also be adventures.

- *Take a walk.* Collect water from a stream or puddle. Examine the water through a microscope when you return home. Describe or draw the creatures found in a drop of water.
- *Visit the library.* Go to the library. Help children get library cards if they don't have them. Choose and check out books. If the library has a storytime or program for older children, attending helps make the library a wonderful place to visit.

- *Visit a store.* It can be the grocery store, post office, department store, or hardware store. Before going, make out a shopping list together. Keep it simple. Let the child help with selection and cost of the products.
- *Explore museums.* Art, natural history, historical, or other specialty museums may have pictures or artifacts that lend themselves to artwork at home. To increase observation powers, let the child look for something specific, such as a color or materials. Talk about how the art materials were used or which shapes were selected.
- *Visit historical buildings.* Take along paper, pen, and crayons. Draw the shape of the building. Make a crayon rubbing of the placard that tells about the building's dedication.
- *Visit the airport and bus station.* Watch the people. Imagine where they are going. Count the people who walk by. Find out how the station or airport is managed. Note how many buses, trains, or airplanes you can see. How are they different from each other? Compare the costs of the different methods of travel.
- *Go to a garage sale.* Determine how many articles you can buy for $5 or $10.

Using intriguing and exciting activities benefits the family in two ways: (a) learning takes place, and (b) the parent-child relationship is enhanced. Parents need to know the importance of a rich home environment; they need to be reinforced for their positive teaching behaviors. Although good times together may be reinforcement enough, schools can help support productive parent-child interaction by encouraging parents, offering workshops, and supplying home-learning activities.

Home-Learning Strategies for the Home Visitor

Each home-based program has developed its own approach to home learning activities. The Portage Project developed a systematic program for its home visitors that can be used by others. HIPPY provides a specific curriculum design with storybooks and activity packets. The Nurse–Family Partnership Program includes a curriculum that emphasizes maternal health, mental health issues, and infant/toddler development. Other programs focus on giving the families support, building family self-sufficiency and encouraging improved parenting skills.

As parents and home visitors work together to develop the children's curriculum, the following tips will help.

- Choose an emerging skill that the child has shown an interest in or one in which an interest can be developed.
- Choose some skills that the parent considers important.
- Choose a skill the child needs to learn.
- Choose a developmentally appropriate task that is easily accommodated at home. (U.S. Department of Health and Human Services, 1985)

In the implementation of a home-based program, both home visitors and parents may develop activities related to individual families or they may be supported by learning activities developed by commercial companies and school districts. Appropriate learning activities can be purchased or found in the library.

Home visitors should remember that the relationship they establish with parents is the most critical means of helping parents support their children's development. They should acknowledge each parent's experience, be respectful at all times, and be a constant learner. While they may establish closer ties with some parents than others, objectivity and an awareness of professional boundaries are of equal importance for all families they serve (U.S. Department of Health and Human Services, 1987).

ESTABLISHING A HOME-BASED PROGRAM

Before a program is established, the reasons for and needs of such a program must be examined. The primary goals of home-based programs include the following:

1. To enable parents to become more effective teachers of their children
2. To support the parents in the roles of caregivers and homemakers

3. To strengthen the parents' sense of autonomy and self-esteem
4. To reach the child and family early in the child's formative years
5. To respond to the family's needs and thus improve the home environment

The overriding goal of educators is the effect of the program on the child. Desirable results are the child's increased sense of well-being, a more successful educational experience in school, and the realization of the child's potential for optimum development.

Goals for programs vary according to the needs of the area. For instance, an overriding concern in one area may be health; in another, language development; and in still another, nutrition. Although all three are important in varying degrees in every home-based program, the intensity of involvement may vary.

A number of studies have been conducted to determine the effectiveness of home-based programs, since the U.S. Advisory Board on Child Abuse recommended the design and implementation of a national, universal home-visiting program. Universal home-visiting was recommended to ensure that support to families would be available to all and, in particular, that universal access would not stigmatize the families most in need. The report also recommended that families should receive support from professionals and paraprofessionals, with weekly services being made available beginning in the neonatal period, in a manner that supported positive family interactions. Program evaluation was also recommended to determine the most effective strategies for serving children and families (Krugman, 1993). Subsequent reports have determined that the recommendations have not been realized for many programs. For some programs the reasons include scarcity of resources and other barriers. For others, outcomes have been child-focused or have assessed the home environment but not family functioning (Park, 2003). In order to fully determine a program's effectiveness, the long-term impact of family functioning is very important.

The concern for serving families and children in their homes as an intervention strategy has continued. A series of reports and policy briefs titled "Building Community Systems for Young Children" included a policy brief, "Home Visiting: A Service Strategy to Deliver First 5 Results," (Thompson, Kropenske, Heinicke, Gomby, & Halfon, 2003). The policy brief discussed strategies to strengthen program quality. Three principles identified as essential were: (a) interventions should be grounded in research that identify adverse outcomes to be addressed and factors necessary to change the outcome, (b) interventions should be based on theories of behavior change, and (c) interventions should be viewed as relevant and needed by the community. In addition, as in the U.S. Advisory Board recommendations, it was recommended as imperative that programs monitor the implementation of the program services by staff and monitor the impact of the interventions on holistic client outcomes. Program monitoring should be embedded in program implementation efforts in order to support continued funding and to determine what contributes to effective delivery of services to children and families.

DETERMINING THE NEED FOR A PROGRAM

Community groups, schools, and centers should consider the needs of children and their families and the availability of community resources as they determine the need for a home-based program. They should also examine the variety of programs available before embarking on a home-based program. The following questions can be used as guidelines for choosing a program:

1. Are there children and families who could be helped by early intervention in the home?
2. What can the community agency or school do in a home visitation program that cannot be accomplished through other programs?
3. Could early remediation reduce the number of retentions when children go to school?
4. Are there children with disabilities who could be diagnosed and given service before they enter school?
5. Will the preventive program help eliminate later educational problems, offsetting the cost to the public?

6. Will the prevention of later educational problems reduce emotional problems, also offsetting the cost to the public?
7. Are there parents who could be helped by an adult literacy program?
8. Do parents need support to develop self-sufficiency so they can provide for their children's long-term needs?

If "yes" is the answer to most of these questions, the next step is to consider the feasibility of a home-based program. The following questions must be addressed:

1. Has there been a thorough assessment of needs to establish community interest in home-based services?
2. Are there *enough* families in the community who are definitely interested and eligible to participate in a program that emphasizes home visits and the role of the parents?
3. Do staff members already have the skills and interests needed to work effectively with parents in their own homes? If not, does the program have, or can it obtain, the considerable training necessary to prepare staff members for their new roles? Is the staff willing to receive such training? Is the staff culturally and linguistically compatible with families to be served?
4. Can transportation needs be met? Public transportation is often an inefficient mode of travel and is not available in many areas. Home visitors need a car to get around quickly, transport materials, and take parents and children for special services needed from local resource agencies.
5. Will the program include family members who are away from home during the day? The answer to this usually involves meetings and home visits in the evenings and on weekends. In some ways, home-based programs require a staff selflessness and dedication that goes beyond the demands of the workload and schedules of center-based services (U.S. Department of Health and Human Services, 1985).

Before a questionnaire or needs assessment is devised, data should be gathered from school files, social service agencies, city surveys, or census reports. Social services will be particularly helpful in determining services and number of children in families. School figures, questionnaires, and surveys will supplement that data so that services can be offered to all those who want or need them. Make every effort to establish a good working relationship with the various agencies. You will need to coordinate your efforts later, and initial communication and rapport are essential to subsequent implementation of the program.

Parents to be served in a home-based program should be actively involved in the initial planning. Many schools and preschool programs have parent advisory councils or citizen advisory councils that can give input on the needs of the community and suggest relevant questions. If a council is not functioning in your area, it may be worth it to start one. You can work through the existing PTO or PTA, or you can establish an entirely new council with the parents you will serve.

The formation or election of the board should be advertised. Parents then have an opportunity to nominate themselves or others, and an election is scheduled to determine who will represent the community on the council. You could advertise the formation of an advisory council by sending notes home with children; explaining the council at meetings of Boy Scouts, Camp Fire Girls, PTA, YMCA, and YWCA; and distributing fliers throughout the community. All nominations should be accepted. If you use a democratic process, you will have to rely on the intelligence of the parents in the selection process.

Distinct advantages to using a democratic selection process rather than appointment to an advisory council include (a) interest in the program is generated and maintained, (b) the parents feel a sense of self-determination and autonomy, (c) the council becomes a source of relevant information and feedback from those affected, and (d) cooperation between school and parents increases.

Involving Others in the Program

The four components of an effective home-based program are (a) education, (b) social services, (c) health services (physical and mental health, dental care, nutrition, and safety), and (d) parent involvement. It is only through comprehensive services to children and their families that pervasive family-based problems can be solved. Although the project will be fully responsible for education and parent involvement, social and health services will need the support of other agencies.

Recruitment of Families

Many families can be identified through cooperative agreements with existing programs, such as Head Start, schools, and social service agencies. Articles in newspapers about the new home-based program will alert other parents, and fliers can be delivered by students. The most effective method, however, is a door-to-door canvass. Home visitors can go from house to house to chat with parents and explain the program and its benefits. This personal approach seems to encourage parents to participate when a notice through the mail may not. Families new to the area or unknown to social agencies probably will be reached only by a door-to-door campaign.

Published articles can increase parents' interest. Curriculum and child development may be communicated through newsletters as well as personal visits. It is also a good idea to combine the two and give the parent a handout at the end of a home visit.

Selection of Home Visitors

Before selecting home visitors, the choice must be made whether to use professionals, professional parent teachers, paraprofessionals, or volunteers. Although the director, coordinator, and special services specialists will probably be professionals, many programs use paraprofessionals or volunteers as the home-visit specialists. Criteria for selection will be determined by the needs of your program.

Five criteria often considered are:

1. Experience, age, and maturity—good judgment and flexibility
2. Race, ethnicity, and culture—key consideration should be to the home visitor who has respect for values and beliefs of other cultures
3. Professional education
4. Gender
5. Helping skills (Wasik, 1993, pp. 143, 147)

Communication Skills

The skills needed for an effective home visitor program (Figure 9.5) also include collaboration and effective communication in which the home visitor is able to:

1. Listen empathetically
2. Affirm the family
3. Recognize and affirm the family's strengths
4. Maintain appropriate boundaries
5. Individualize for each family's needs
6. Demonstrate and model effective parenting skills
7. Interpret the purpose of activities and child–parent interactions
8. Problem solve with the parents (Klass, Pettinelli, & Wilson, 1993)

Recruiting

When recruiting paraprofessional home visitors, the positions should be advertised throughout the community. Announcements must be clear and include the following:

1. *Explanation of the program.* Explain what your home-based program entails, indicating its goals and objectives.
2. *Job description of the position.* List the duties and responsibilities, workday schedule, salary range, and benefits.
3. *Qualifications required.* Indicate whether high school, college, or specific competencies are required.
4. *Equal opportunity employment announcement.* Make a statement of nondiscrimination.
5. *Instructions for applying.* Give instructions on how to apply, whom to contact, and the deadline for application.

The announcement should be posted in public places, such as libraries, schools, stores, and social agencies, such as Head Start. Telephone canvassing will alert many people to the new program. To

Are YOUR Home Visits Parent-Focused?

• Do you involve the parents in the assessment of the child?	Yes	No
• Do you provide the parent with a copy of the checklist for their own use?	Yes	No
• When you arrive for the weekly home visit, do you direct your attention and greeting toward the parent?	Yes	No
• Do you discuss the previous week's visit and follow up on the weekly activities with the parent?	Yes	No
• Does the parent co-plan the activities for the home visit?	Yes	No
• Do you make sure that the child is sitting beside the parent?	Yes	No
• Does the parent demonstrate EACH new activity?	Yes	No
• Do you review each activity with the parent before presenting it?	Yes	No
• Do you hand all materials to the parent?	Yes	No
• Do you identify and reinforce the parent's teaching strengths?	Yes	No
• When the parent has difficulty, do you intervene with the parent rather than the child?	Yes	No
• Do you let the parent be the primary reinforcing agent?	Yes	No
• Do you help the parent problem solve when problems do arise instead of jumping to the rescue?	Yes	No
• Do you work on activities the parent feels are important?	Yes	No
• Do you ask the parent to provide as many materials as possible?	Yes	No
• Do you give the parent the lead, when appropriate?	Yes	No
• Do you incorporate the parent's ideas into each activity?	Yes	No
• Do you let the parent present new and exciting experiences?	Yes	No
• Do you individualize parent education activities for each parent?	Yes	No
• Do you accept the parent's values?	Yes	No
• Do you involve the parent in evaluation of the home visit?	Yes	No

FIGURE 9.5 A self-evaluation form for home visitors.

Source: U.S. Department of Health and Human Services (1987).

reach a large population, advertise in the newspaper and distribute fliers. Wide dissemination of information about available positions encourages individuals in the community to become involved and alerts others to the upcoming home-based program.

Inservice Training After the Program Has Started

Learning by both the family and the home visitor comes to fruition during the development of the program. During this period, the home visitor responds to the needs, desires, and styles of the parents and children. Close contact with the program's coordinator or trainers supports the home visitor and allows administrators to keep track of what is happening in the field. Reports on each visit, with copies for the home visitor and for the program's administrators or trainers, will enable people from both levels of the program to keep in touch with developments and needs. In doing so, inservice training can be directed to enrich weak areas and clarify procedures. At the end of each visit, home visitors can reflect on the questions presented in Figure 9.5. A home visitor's answers to these questions can also provide the basis for inservice training.

Small Groups

Throughout the year, questions and needs for training will arise. Training sessions are more effective when small groups of home visitors—rather than all members of the program—meet together as needs emerge. The individualized meeting is beneficial because the session has been set up especially for the participants, and small numbers allow for a more personalized response by the trainer or coordinator.

Community Resources

Although lists of community resources are given to home visitors early in the program, more definite descriptions and procedures are useful when specific problems arise. During the year, specialists from a variety of community agencies can be invited to share their experiences and knowledge of procedures with the staff. Have them come to training meetings, meet the staff, and answer questions concerning use of their programs.

Program Evaluation

Ongoing evaluations of contacts, visits, and services rendered are essential. Home visit reports give data that can be used to measure progress. If the home visitor systematically completes each report, the administrator will be able to evaluate progress throughout the training period.

Parent Questionnaires

Statements by parents and responses to questionnaires concerning the effect of the program on the child and family are valuable in analyzing the effects of the program. Collect these throughout the program as well as at the completion of the year.

Evaluation is a tool to be used during the development of the program as well as a means to assess accomplishments. Include a variety of evaluations to improve the program and demonstrate its effectiveness.

SCREENING FOR BETTER UNDERSTANDING

As home visitors and parents work with children, they informally assess the child's characteristics and skills. Informal assessments with checklists can be used while the child is playing. It is always best to view the child in a natural setting unrestricted by contrived tasks. A portfolio containing collections of art activities and projects, teacher comments, and the child's comments can aid in assessing the child's development. These kinds of assessment are essential; they provide the parent and teacher with guidelines for developmentally appropriate activities for each child.

Parent educators also need to be able to recognize if families under their guidance need special help. Screening for potential problems in both the developmental status of children and the children's environment—especially if they are growing up in a low socioeconomic area—will help the parent-educator identify problems early and more effectively serve children and their families (Fandal, 1986).

Several instruments are available to screen the developmental progress of children. Two of the most widely used are the Denver Prescreening Developmental Questionnaire and the Denver Developmental Screening Test. There are also standardized methods of assessing the home environment of children, such as the Home Screening Questionnaire and the Home Observation for Measurement of the Environment.

Home Observation for Measurement of the Environment

The Home Observation for Measurement of the Environment (HOME) Inventory (Figure 9.6) is used by schools, child-care centers, and other social service agencies to help them determine the quality of the home environment as it relates to the child's development. "Although a child may appear to be developing at a normal rate early in life, the environment begins to either enhance or 'put a lid' on developmental progress within the first year or two" (Fandal, 1986).

The HOME Inventory was developed "to get a picture of what the child's world is like from his or her perspective—from where he or she lies or sits or stands or moves about and sees, hears, smells, feels, and tastes that world" (Caldwell & Bradley, 1984, p. 8). In addition to the standardized HOME Inventories for birth to 3-year-olds and 3- to 6-year-olds, an inventory for elementary school children also is available.

13

HOME Inventory for Families of Infants and Toddlers

Bettye M. Caldwell and Robert H. Bradley

Family Name________ Date________ Visitor________

Child's Name________ Birthdate________ Age____ Sex____

Caregiver for visit________ Relationship to child________

Family Composition________
(Persons living in household, including sex and age of children)

Family Ethnicity________ Language Spoken________ Maternal Education________ Paternal Education________

Is Mother Employed?________ Type of work when employed________ Is Father Employed?________ Type of work when employed________

Address________ Phone________

Current child care arrangements________

Summarize past year's arrangements________

Caregiver for visit________ Other persons present________

Comments________

SUMMARY

	Subscale	Score	Lowest Middle	Middle Half	Upper Fourth
I.	Emotional and Verbal RESPONSIVITY of Parent		0–6	7–9	10–11
II.	ACCEPTANCE of Child's Behavior		0–4	5–6	7–8
III.	ORGANIZATION of Physical and Temporal Environment		0–3	4–5	6
IV.	Provision of Appropriate PLAY MATERIALS		0–4	5–7	8–9
V.	Parent INVOLVEMENT with Child		0–2	3–4	5–6
VI.	Opportunities for VARIETY in Daily Stimulation		0–1	2–3	4–5
	TOTAL SCORE		0–25	26–36	37–45

For rapid profiling of a family, place an X in the box that corresponds to the raw score on each subscale and the total score.

14

HOME Inventory*

Place a plus (+) or minus (-) in the box alongside each item if the behavior is observed during the visit or if the parent reports that the conditions or events are characteristic of the home environment. Enter the subtotal and the total on the front side of the Record Sheet.

I. Emotional and Verbal RESPONSIVITY

1. Parent spontaneously vocalized to child twice.
2. Parent responds verbally to child's verbalizations.
3. Parent tells child name of object or person during visit.
4. Parent's speech is distinct and audible.
5. Parent initiates verbal exchanges with visitor.
6. Parent converses freely and easily.
7. Parent permits child to engage in "messy" play.
8. Parent spontaneously praises child at least twice.
9. Parent's voice conveys positive feelings toward child.
10. Parent caresses or kisses child at least once.
11. Parent responds positively to praise of child offered by visitor.

Subtotal

II. ACCEPTANCE of Child's Behavior

12. Parent does not shout at child.
13. Parent does not express annoyance with or hostility to child.
14. Parent neither slaps nor spanks child during visit.
15. No more than one instance of physical punishment during past week.
16. Parent does not scold or criticize child during visit.
17. Parent does not interfere or restrict child more than 3 times.
18. At least ten books are present and visible.
19. Family has a pet.

Subtotal

III. ORGANIZATION of Environment

20. Substitute care is provided by one of three regular substitutes.
21. Child is taken to grocery store at least once/week.
22. Child gets out of house at least four times/week.
23. Child is taken regularly to doctor's office or clinic.
24. Child has a special place for toys and treasures.
25. Child's play environment is safe.

Subtotal

IV. Provision of PLAY MATERIALS

26. Muscle activity toys or equipment.
27. Push or pull toy.
28. Stroller or walker, kiddie car, scooter, or tricycle.
29. Parent provides toys for child during visit.
30. Learning equipment appropriate to age--cuddly toys or role-playing toys.
31. Learning facilitators--mobile, table and chairs, high chair, play pen.
32. Simple eye-hand coordination toys.
33. Complex eye-hand coordination toys (those permitting combination).
34. Toys for literature and music.

Subtotal

V. Parental INVOLVEMENT with Child

35. Parent keeps child in visual range, looks at often.
36. Parent talks to child while doing household work.
37. Parent consciously encourages developmental advance.
38. Parent invests maturing toys with value via personal attention.
39. Parent structures child's play periods.
40. Parent provides toys that challenge child to develop new skills.

Subtotal

VI. Opportunities for VARIETY

41. Father provides some care daily.
42. Parent reads stories to child at least 3 times weekly.
43. Child eats at least one meal per day with mother and father.
44. Family visits relatives or receives visits once a month or so.
45. Child has 3 or more books of his/her own.

Subtotal

TOTAL SCORE

*For complete wording of items, please refer to the Administration Manual.

FIGURE 9.6 Home visitors can use the HOME Inventory to analyze the family's home environment.

Source: Caldwell & Bradley (1984).

When using the program, the interviewer should:

- Know the HOME Inventory well before using it.
- Contact the parents and arrange a visit.
- Visit when the child is awake and available.
- Start the interview with friendly, relaxed interaction.

A suggested technique for starting the interview is described by the following statement:

> You will remember that we are interested in knowing the kinds of things your baby (child) does when he is at home. A good way to get a picture of what his days are like is to have you think of one particular day—like yesterday—and tell me everything that happened to him as well as you can remember it. Start with the things that happened when he first woke up. It is usually easy to remember the main events once you get started. (Caldwell & Bradley, 1984, p. 3)

The administration and scoring of each item in the inventory are clearly described in the Administration Manuals, so the interviewer can make correct judgments on the scoring of HOME. For example, see Figure 9.6, Item 4, which states, "Parent's speech is distinct and audible." The score on this item is determined by whether the interviewer is able to understand what the parent says. This item should not be interpreted as meaning that dialect usage mandates a negative score; what is important is whether the interviewer can understand and communicate with the parent.

Home Screening Questionnaire (HSQ)

Coons, Gay, Fandal, Ker, and Frankenburg (1981) and Frankenburg and Coons (1986) recognized the value of an earlier version of the HOME Inventory but were concerned about the length of time needed for a skilled interviewer to make a home visit. They developed the Home Screening Questionnaire (HSQ), which could be answered by parents. With the cooperation of the authors of the HOME Inventory, items were selected and turned into two questionnaires that correspond to the 2 HOME scales (for children from birth to 3 years and those from 3 to 6 years of age). Each takes about 15 minutes for a parent to complete.

The questionnaires have been validated as effective screening tools to identify environments that would benefit from a more intensive assessment. "The HSQ Manual gives complete instructions for scoring the questionnaires. As with all suspect screening results, questionable HSQ results should be followed with a visit by a trained home interviewer to assure that the result of the screening test is accurate and that appropriate intervention can be planned" (Fandal, 1986).

HOMESCHOOLING

Homeschooling may be defined as "instruction and learning, at least some of which is through planned activity, taking place *primarily* at home in a family setting with a parent acting as teacher or supervisor of the activity" (Lines, 1991, p. 10). Homeschooling is not new. Many of our nation's early leaders were taught at home. The common school movement began about 1830 and 1840, but it was usual for children to attend for only 3 months out of the year for 3 or 4 years.

The last half of the 19th century saw a greater transformation of schooling. Eighty-six percent of children ages 5 to 14 were attending public schools by 1890 (Carper, 1992). During the 20th century, parents sent their children to public and private schools, and schools became more and more centrally administered. It was not until the 1980s that the increase in homeschooling began to be noticed.

Estimates of the number of children who were being schooled at home in the 1970s ranged from 1,000 to 15,000; in 1983, estimates ranged from 60,000 to 125,000; by 1988 the homeschool "student body" was thought to be 150,000 to 300,000 (Lines, 1991). It increased rapidly in the 1990s—estimates of homeschooled children ranged up to 2 million, but in 1999 the 95 percent confidence interval for the number of homeschoolers was 709,000 to 992,000. Subsequent data gathered has determined that homeschoolers account for 1.7 percent of the students in the United States (Kaplan-Leiserson, 2002; National Center for Education Statistics, 2001). It is anticipated that the number of children homeschooled will increase by 15% each year (Kaplan-Leiserson, 2002). The estimate of 1,096,000 homeschooled students shows an increase from 1.7 percent in 1999 to 2.2 percent in 2003 (National Center for Education Statistics, 2007).

Characteristics of Homeschooling and Homeschooled Children

Homeschoolers, when compared to nonhomeschoolers, are White, non-Hispanic, and have two parents with higher levels of education (25 percent college graduates compared to 16 percent). One of the parents was not employed full time outside the home. Both boys and girls are homeschooled, with slightly more girls. Eighty percent of homeschooled children lived in two-parent households compared to 66 percent of nonhomeschoolers. Sixty-three percent of the families had three or more children (National Center for Education Statistics, 2001).

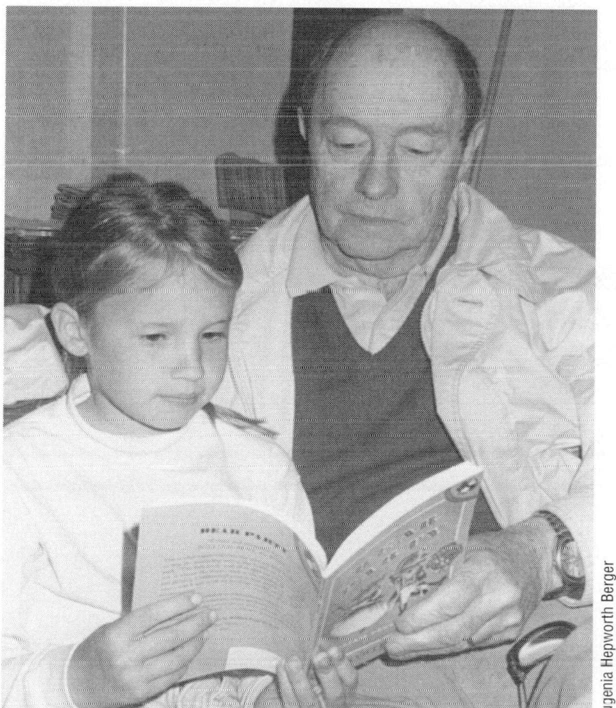

Eugenia Hepworth Berger

Children benefit from guidance offered by home-based educational programs. Follow the child's lead and let the activity develop. Reading, as well as indoor and outdoor activities, give children opportunities to increase their learning. Use the many learning opportunities there are at home.

In most cases of homeschooling, the mother is the teacher, and she usually teaches her own children, spending 20–30 hours each week in school activities. Homeschool teachers are reported to have a more controlling style of teaching than other teachers. They have fewers years of formal education and are more conservative in their political views (Cai, Reeve, & Robinson, 2002). There is no one curriculum that parents use, although they can buy curriculum programs from a variety of organizations.

Testing for academic achievement and effective development has indicated that most homeschooled children do well in academics. Scores on state-mandated tests indicate that although some score below average, "a large number test above that mark" (Lines, 1996). In 2002, the average SAT score for public school children was 1020, while it was 1092 for homeschooled children. In 2004 the average ACT score for public school children was 20.9, while it was 22.6 for homeschooled children (Beato, 2005). There also seems to be little risk to their socialization, psychological development, and self-esteem (Lines, 1996; Ray & Wartes, 1991).

The increasing number of homeschoolers has forced public schools and state legislators to analyze the coordination and cooperation needed between schools and parents who want to educate their children at home. In the past decade proponents have been successful in advocating for homeschools. When there have been court cases, the proponents of homeschooling are able to rely on court decisions and the Bill of Rights (Guterson, 1992).

State legislatures have been responding to parental demands. All states allow homeschooling. Typically, a state's statutes, through a court ruling, an attorney general's opinion, or a regulation that interprets a school attendance law to include homeschooling, consider homeschooling a legitimate option for meeting compulsory education requirements. Because each state regulates homeschooling differently, parents should examine local laws and consult other homeschoolers before proceeding. In every state, parents must, at a minimum, notify a state or local education agency of their intent to educate their children at home and identify the children involved (Lines, 1996, p. 1).

Technology—the use of the computer with educational resources, e-mail, and online communication—is becoming an important resource for homeschooled students. Students can research projects on the Internet and communicate with others about their interests (Natale, 1995). The Internet is continually providing new avenues, Websites, and research to the public. "Traditional publishers, corresponding schools, and dot-com startups are rushing to help overwhelmed parent-teachers offering everything from interactive classes to one-on-one tutoring" (Heurer, 2000, p. 1).

Reasons for Homeschooling

The largest single reason for homeschooling is the concern of parents about the environment of the school their child would attend (85 percent). Religious reasons follow (72 percent), with a dissatisfaction with the academic instruction being offered making up (68 percent) the third highest reason for selecting homeschooling. Figure 9.7 illustrates the reasons that homeschooling parents gave for homeschooling their children (National Center for Educational Statistics, 2003).

School–Parent Cooperation

The next step to help ensure the child's success will be cooperation between the home and school. How can parents and schools accommodate each other? Suggestions include part-time attendance in school by children who are homeschooled (Knowles, 1989; Mayberry, 1989).

Two examples of school districts illustrate how schools can respond to the collaboration between public schools and homeschoolers. The Cupertino Union School District in California has given parents options for over 25 years. Parents enroll their child in the district school system, but they educate the child at home. The school receives the revenue from the state, and parents are given curricula, money for books, services, materials, and software. Each family has a resource teacher who holds a conference with them monthly, or more often if desired. They also have access to a library of materials and books for homeschooling. They can use the school's supplies and equipment, and children can be enrolled in extended day class (Berger, 1997; Lamson, 1992).

Another example is the San Diego City School District, which offers support to homeschooled children. The school offers a structured curriculum for families to use. Educators are assigned as homeschool teachers who meet with the families on a trimester basis. Families can contact the teacher assigned to them as often as they desire. Parents can take advantage of services, field trips, special

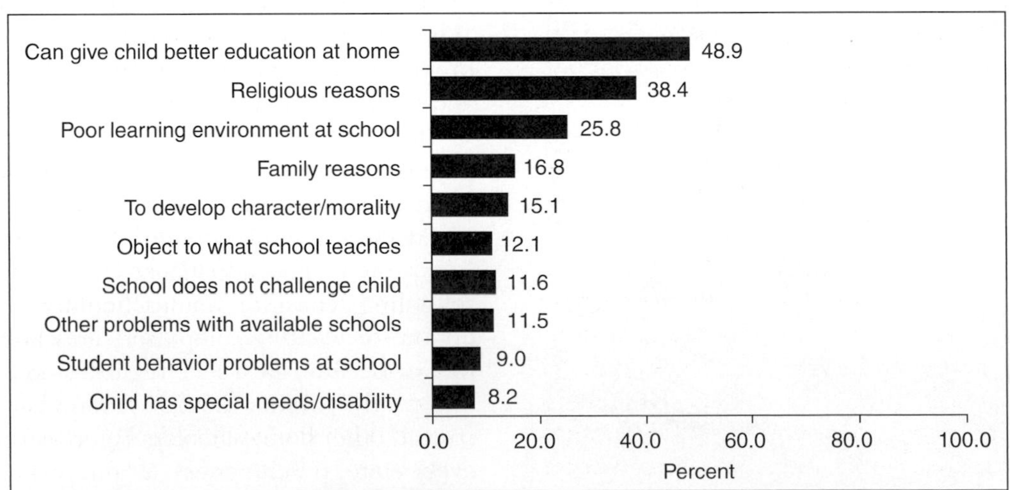

FIGURE 9.7 Ten reasons for homeschooling and the percentage of homeschooled students whose parents gave each reason: 1999.

Note: Percentages do not add to 100 percent because respondents could give more than one reason.

Source: From the *Parent Survey* of the National Household Education Surveys Program, 1999, by the U.S. Department of Education, National Center for Education Statistics.

education, and counseling, educating their own children with the support of the school district (Dalaimo, 1996).

In collaboration, schools can furnish resources and services for homeschool families. These may include offering the use of resource centers; enrollment in special classes such as music, art, and science; participation of homeschooled parents in school district programs; advisory and facilitating services; inservice workshops; and participation of homeschooled students in extracurricular activities, summer programs, and large group or team activities (Knowles, 1989). "As homeschooling grows, calls will continue for existing public schools to provide services that cannot be provided easily by home-school families themselves—such as advanced courses and extracurricular activities" (Bauman, 2001, p. 9).

By allowing the student to be schooled at home, but providing support and an opportunity to participate with other children in activities, the school helps parents achieve their goals of educating their children themselves while giving children opportunities to interact socially with other students. If the child later reenters school, the transition will be easier.

SUPPORTING CHILDREN'S LEARNING AT HOME

Children educated out of the home, in public or private school, need parental involvement to support their success in developing academic skills. Assisting children with homework is one way to build a bridge between home and school. Homework is defined as "tasks assigned to students by school teachers that are meant to be carried out during non-school hours" (Cooper, 1994, p. 2). A U.S. Department of Education report, *What Works: Research About Teaching and Learning* (1986), emphasized that the home environment and homework are essential for children to reach their full potential. Homework varies according to the age of the child. For young children, the home environment, the interaction, and intense work with toys make up the child's learning experience—the home is the child's school and what the child does is homework. As children get older and the location of school goes outside the home, suddenly what they do at home is not considered school unless they bring home an assignment. But the home is still part of the child's learning experiences, and parents can support children by learning about the child's school experience and what he/she is learning to do.

The need for homework for children in the early grades is questioned by both parents and educators. The Child Study Movement of 1890 and early 1900s believed that children should be children and not start school until they were 7. In the mid-1920s to 1940s homework was limited or abolished in New York City, Chicago, and San Diego. Reform of homework rather than elimination was the call after World War II. It should be "moderate in amount, creative in purpose and directed to each child's needs" (Winerip, 1999, p. 30). When the Soviet Union launched *Sputnik* in 1957, the educational system felt challenged and set out to educate the young so that the nation could compete. The result was increased homework nationwide (p. 31). A well-known report on education, *A Nation at Risk,* again alarmed the country. In 1986, the report mentioned earlier, *What Works,* stated that homework "worked." Since that time homework has been seen as necessary and beneficial. "Assignments become common as early as first grade, and some schools require it every day. Parents' grumbling is heard across the land" (p. 32).

Winerip (1999) describes the success that Chinese American parents have in home education. Chinese American children spend an average of 54 minutes each day studying at home. European Americans spend about 6 minutes. "At first and second grade, the Chinese-American families averaged 31 minutes in homework versus 11 for Euro-Americans" (p. 30). Chinese American parents also spent time working with their children on language. Since their parents spoke Chinese at home, the children were behind in their English. The Chinese American parents assigned 15 words each week and by the fourth grade, instead of being behind in English, they were ahead of the European American children (p. 30). Results such as these, even though the work Chinese American children do at home is not assigned by the school, make the demand for homework seem worthwhile.

An alternative to homework has been the development of after-school programs in which children can do schoolwork under supervision and with the help that they might need. This is especially helpful for families in which both parents work. Many after-school programs, however, have been careful to avoid being seen as an extension of the school day. The recurrent concern is how best to support and extend children's learning opportunities.

Home–School Collaboration

The satisfactory use of homework requires communication and planning on the part of the school and the parent. While homework has long been used as a tool by schools to reinforce classroom instruction, many teachers do not see the opportunity or responsibility to communicate with parents about homework. Much greater cooperation and collaboration will occur if a teacher communicates with parents about the importance of homework. Teachers must reach out to parents, as part of establishing a partnership with them, to find out how the parents respond to the opportunity to support their child's educational growth through homework. Teachers must also determine if parents have the language and educational background to understand information that comes from school. If necessary, written material sent to parents may need to be translated into the child's home language. If parents are not literate in their first language, school staff needs to attempt to make phone contact to speak with the parents in their first language. In many schools this may present quite a challenge as many languages may be represented in any particular elementary school. In addition, parents may have disabilities that require alternative methods of communication. If the school has a stated policy about homework, the school staff needs to make this information available to parents in a manner in which parents can understand. If the school leaves homework up to individual teachers, each teacher is responsible for communicating with parents, through translators if necessary, about specific requirements for homework in their classes.

Parents have a shared responsibility to communicate with their child's teacher. They need to ask: Will there be homework each night? How long should the average amount of homework take? Will the assignments be explained before the student is sent home with them? Will the student understand the assignment? What are the rules and regulations regarding homework? Can homework be made into "homefun," where both student and parent enjoy the challenge?

If parents resent homework or are not able to assist their children, it can become a negative experience. Instead of strengthening the family, it can become divisive and fail to strengthen the child's academic achievement. At a minimum, parents should be guided by the teacher to talk to their children, in their home language if appropriate, about their school day and what they are learning. This will convey a strong message to children that school is important, and that their parents care about their experience.

Homework must be handled with care. The teacher should do the following:

1. Send home work that reinforces or enriches what was learned in class. In either case the assignment should be something the child is able to accomplish. Assignments that are short and frequent rather than long and infrequent appear to have a more significant effect on the child's learning (Cooper, 1999).
2. Create meaningful assignments. Homework should not be haphazard busy work; instead, it should be well planned and well designed. Clearly explain the homework assignment. If it is new or extension material, review several of the issues or problems so the student knows what is expected.
3. Explain the rules and regulations of homework. Do you take off points for late homework? Is the homework grade figured into the grade for the grading period?
4. Provide a homework form that the student fills out in class that states the assignment, pages, or work sheets that go along with the homework. This could also include a signature line for the parent to sign so that the teacher knows the parent knows about the assignment.
5. Grade all homework personally. Display homework on the bulletin board to show the student that it is recognized and that it is important. Only assign homework on which students will be given feedback.
6. Communicate with parents to explain the process and respond to any difficulties that the family may be having with the homework.
7. Teach study skills (Canter & Hausner, 1987; Cooke & Cooke, 1988; Hodapp & Hodapp, 1992; Paulu, 1995; Radencich & Schumm, 1996).

A recent discussion of homework requirements compares the positives and negatives of homework (Cooper, 2001). Homework can provide immediate retention of recent learning, and can reinforce learning during leisure time. In addition, homework can support great self-direction, self-discipline and time organization. Homework can have negative outcomes, also. It can promote satiation of interest in learning, encourage parental interference in learning, cheating, and can increase the differences between low-income and more affluent students. Teachers and parent must work together to ensure that homework produces positive outcomes and avoids pitfalls.

How Can Parents Help?

Children of all ages can be helped with their homework. It is important that parents make sure that they observe their children and try to determine if the homework is developmentally appropriate. A rule of thumb is that homework should take about 10 minutes per grade level (Cooper, 2001). The following tips may be provided to parents by their child's teacher. However, teachers should recognize that parents who live in crowded quarters may not be able to provide a positive environment for homestudy. A staffed study hall for after school might be essential. For homework, parents can help by providing the following:

1. Set up a specific place to study that is
   a. Well lighted.
   b. Quiet, but not too isolated.
   c. Comfortable, with appropriate chair and table.
   d. Equipped with materials—paper, pencils, pens, erasers, pencil sharpener, clock, typewriter and/or computer.
2. Set aside a regular time for homework, or make a schedule for the week so that parents or children can fill in activities, study periods, dinner time, recreation, and bedtime for each school day.
3. Be supportive and give appropriate help. Parents should not do their children's homework, but parents can engage in problem solving with them, guide them, and help them over the rough spots.
   a. Consider the child's learning style. Does the child learn best through seeing, hearing, or manipulating the material?
   b. Talk about the assignments. Does the child understand the homework? What does the child need in order to complete the work?
   c. Help the child structure the time and assignment, and help the child get started. Recognize that the responsibility for completing the homework belongs to the student.
4. Show interest in and encourage the child's efforts.
5. Be a parent who is both loving and firm.
6. Refer the child to a homework hot line or Web site to get an explanation of the assignment if needed.
7. Contact the teacher if further help is needed (Canter & Hausner, 1987; Cooke & Cooke, 1988; Hodapp & Hodapp, 1992; Paulu, 1995; Radencich & Schumm, 1996).

Hong and Milgram (2000) state that the setting for homework should be determined by the learner's preferences and the conditions under which the student learns best. For example, some learners find background music helpful. Parents may adjust the study area to the child's preference of temperature, lighting, and sound. "It has been clearly established that higher academic achievement and improved attitude result from tailoring the learning experiences to the cognitive and personal social characteristics of the learner" (p. 17).

Conclusion

Because many homes have computers connected to information services and data banks, access to cable television classes, and videotapes and videodisks, the home is now widely recognized as a place where schoolwork can be supplemented and reinforced. Home-based education has many facets and will diversify and increase in the future. Methods may vary, but the home is still a primary educator of children.

SUMMARY

Home-based education, initiated in the 1960s, saw continued and increased use in the 1980s, 1990s, and the 21st century. Programs developed include Parents as Teachers, Home Instruction Program for Preschool Youngsters, Healthy Families America, and Early Head Start, which joined earlier programs such as Portage Project, Parent–Child Home Program (Verbal Interaction Project), and the Nurse Family Partnership Program.

If the school is interested in developing a home-based program, it should: (a) show a need for the program, (b) involve others in planning, (c) develop a parent advisory council, and (d) decide on a program format.

Home-learning activities to be used by the home visitor and the family can be obtained through development of individualized activities, commercial offerings, or activities developed by demonstration programs. Use materials that are readily available to the parents, because the parent is the primary teacher in the home-based program. The focus in a home-based program is on the parent interacting with and teaching the child after the home visitor is gone.

Screening instruments may be selected to guide teachers in their work with parents and children and to serve as a basis for referrals for more thorough evaluation.

Homeschooling has emerged as a growing option for parents and children.

Concern about excellence in education has brought added emphasis on homework and the question of what amount shows the greatest benefit. Parents and teachers must work together as partners to support and extend children's learning to ensure their success in school.

SUGGESTED CLASS ACTIVITIES AND DISCUSSIONS

1. Discuss the type of parent–child interaction that best promotes the child's emotional and intellectual growth.
2. Brainstorm home situations that would be positive experiences for children.
3. Itemize household equipment that can be used as home learning tools. How would you use each?
4. Write role-playing opportunities based on families in several home situations.
5. Discuss the guidelines related to home visits.
6. Discuss value systems that may vary from your own. How can you work with parents and refrain from infringing on their beliefs? Discuss.
7. Compare the strengths and weaknesses of home-based programs.
8. Discuss how to establish a working relationship with parents to support out of school learning.

WEB SITES

Early Head Start
www.acf.hhs.gov

The Early Head Start site is located within the Head Start Bureau site. Information includes publications, conferences, grant announcements and research. Links to a variety of Early Head Start resources are provided.

Healthy Families America
www.healthyfamiliesamerica.org

The site provides background information regarding network resources, advocacy activities and current research. It also provides parenting tips and a link that assists parents in locating programs near their homes.

HIPPY—Home Instruction Program for Preschool Youngsters
www.hippyusa.org

The site provides information regarding the HIPPY Model, research and public policy resources. It also provides a locator link to assist parents in contacting local programs.

Nurse Family Partnership Program
www.nursefamilypartnership.org

Information included on the Web site includes recognitions awarded to the program, outcome data and a program locator for parents. Employment opportunities and newsletter information is also provided.

Parent–Child Home Program
www.parent-child.org

The site provides information regarding training events, program news links, and research links. The program mission statement is included.

Parents as Teachers Program
www.patnc.org

The site provides parenting tips, announcements for conferences, training, and product sales. It provides links to an advocacy center, contact information, and a locator link for parents.

Portage Project
www.portageproject.org

Information included on the site includes links to information regarding a family service credential, a new Portage guide, and training and technical assistance information. Contact information is provided.

10 Working with Parents of a Child with Disabilities

Jo Spidel
Eugenia H. Berger

All about me may be silence and darkness, yet within me, in the spirit, is music and brightness, and color flashes through all my thoughts.

Keller, 1957

If our American way of life fails the child, it fails us all.

Buck, 1991

In this chapter on working with parents of children with exceptionalities you will find information and procedures that will enable you to do the following:

- Summarize the development of special education in the United States.
- Cite legislation that supports the needs of children with disabilities.
- Develop an Individualized Education Program (IEP) and an Individualized Family Service Plan (IFSP).
- Describe the types of students for whom special education should be provided.
- Cite the parents' rights in school and parent deliberations.
- List the levels-of-service continuum that provides placement options for students with exceptionalities.
- Discuss special concerns that must be met when working with parents of children with disabilities.

Parents are the most significant influence in the life of a child with exceptionalities. Children raised in proximity to parents or surrogate parents for the first 5 years of their lives, form emotional attachments, and bonding is established. When children begin school, their parents share them with teachers and peer groups. As they grow older, children are also affected by the community, but

Jo Spidel, M.Ed., was a professional advocate for special education for more than 25 years. She taught, presented papers on, and wrote about special education. Certifications included Learning Disabilities, Behavior Disorders, Mental Retardation, and Director of Special Education. Fifteen years were devoted to teaching in public schools, the last position at Northwest High School in Wichita, Kansas. In addition to teaching, she developed and directed an in-house school for adolescent patients in a psychiatric, drug, and alcohol abuse hospital and served as a case manager for the Kansas Elks Training Center for the Handicapped.

parents continue to influence and shape their development.

Teachers would be wise to listen to parents to learn about the child's background and to discuss concerns. Teachers will gain respect and cooperation from parents if they are willing to share objectives and goals for the child. If teachers allow the parents to accept some responsibility for the child's learning and share knowledge of teaching principles and methods of tutoring, the effectiveness of the learning experience can be doubled.

This chapter gives parents and regular classroom teachers techniques that can be used effectively with children with exceptionalities. There are many ways to solve problems, communicate with parents, and teach these children. The methods presented here have been proven effective. Take from them those ideas that will work for you.

DEVELOPMENT OF SPECIAL EDUCATION

Many labels have been placed on children with exceptionalities. One need only review titles of institutions for those with mental illness, retardation, or other mental or physical disabilities to find such descriptions as *imbecile, lunatic, crazy,* and *insane.* Such words are indicative of people's perceptions of the problem of exceptionality. Parents and professionals have voiced concern over and made efforts to correct such misconceived labels, most of which have been replaced by the term *exceptional.* The word is used to describe those who are different in some way from the majority of whatever group they belong to—adults, children, or youth. *Special education* refers to instruction specifically designed to meet the special needs of children with exceptionalities (Hallahan & Kauffman, 1997, 2006).

At the middle of the 20th century, the term *special education* commonly referred to the education of those who were mentally retarded. Since then, the term has properly become recognized as more open and inclusive. Children who have certain traits or disabilities or a combination thereof are encompassed by special education: giftedness; mental retardation; physical, neurological, or emotional disabilities; social maladjustment; speech and language impairments; hearing and visual impairments; learning disabilities; and developmental disabilities. It is significant that the condition of the child was once the labeling factor. The trend now is to label according to the educational needs of the child and to refer to the child first and the exceptionality second—"a child with a disability" rather than "a disabled child." "Use of the phrase *with disabilities* signifies that we think of the person first; the disabling condition is only one characteristic of an individual,

Krista Greco/Merrill

Children are pleased when they can accomplish their tasks successfully.

who has many other characteristics" (Hallahan & Kauffman, 1997, p. 29). The term *people first* has been adopted by professionals and parents as a reminder to all that it is important to acknowledge the "person" first and the "unique characteristics" of any person second (Heward, 2006; Snow, 2006).

Throughout history there have been many tales of cruel and inhumane treatment of people with exceptionalities. Recalling the story of *The Hunchback of Notre Dame* quickly brings to mind these cruelties. The Spartans were known to force parents to abandon imperfect babies by exposing them to the elements (Greenleaf, 1978). There are instances in very early history, however, of people who were more humane toward those who were different. Hippocrates, who lived around 400 B.C., believed that emotional problems were caused not by supernatural powers but by natural forces. Plato (375 B.C.) defended those with mental disabilities as not being able to account for their deeds as normal people could. They, therefore, required special judgment for their criminal acts. The temples built by Alexander the Great provided asylum for mentally ill persons. In 90 B.C. Asclepiades made the first attempt at classifying mental illness, advocating humane treatment of those with the illness.

The period of A.D. 1450 to 1700 was an especially difficult time for those who were mentally ill and people with other exceptionalities. Belief in demonology and superstition resulted in persecution of those who were mentally ill, retarded, or developmentally disabled, and those with any other form of exceptionality. John Locke, concerned about harsh discipline, cultivated the "blank tablet" concept of the newborn's mind to overcome the popular belief that a child was born full of evil ideas. He advocated that children be given empathic understanding (Cook, Tessier, & Armbruster, 1987).

Jean Jacques Rousseau stressed the importance of beginning the child's education at birth. He believed that strong discipline and strict lessons were inappropriate conditions for optimal learning. He advocated that children should be treated with sympathy and compassion as humans in their own right (Cook et al., 1987).

In the late 1700s Jean Marc Gaspard Itard (1775–1838) sought new methods to teach those with mental retardation. He was a physician and an authority on diseases of the ear and education of the deaf. He found a boy in the forest of Auvergne, France, naked and apparently without upbringing, whom he attempted to raise and educate. He produced behavioral changes in the boy, Victor, but was unable to teach him to talk or to live independently. Itard believed he was a failure, but others followed his methods, which began a movement in treatment and education that had a profound effect on the development of special education (Cook, Klein, & Tessier, 2004; Hallahan & Kauffman, 1997; Reinert, 1987).

The residential schools and asylums that were built in the United States were very much like those in Europe during the 19th century. The first American residential school for those who were deaf was established in 1817 at Hartford, Connecticut, by Thomas Hopkins Gallaudet (1787–1851). Most early schools avoided severely disabled students or those with multiple disabilities and worked only with those who were deaf, blind, or retarded. Those with more serious disabilities were often not eligible for admission to any school. Private schools were often expensive, and state-operated schools were often limited in their facilities (Hallahan & Kauffman, 1990).

The Perkins School for the Blind, founded in Watertown, Massachusetts, was the first school for people without sight. Samuel G. Howe (1801–1876) proved that those who were blind could be taught when Laura Bridgemen, who was blind and deaf, was educated (Hallahan & Kauffman, 1997). Seeking education for his daughter who was deaf and blind, Helen Keller (1880–1968), Arthur H. Keller consulted the director of the Perkins Institution. It was from this institution that Anne Mansfield Sullivan came to teach Helen, when Helen was almost 7 years of age (Keller, 1991). The fame of the successful life of this person with disabilities did much to persuade parents and professionals that, indeed, persons with disabilities could be educated.

It was not until the beginning of the 20th century that community-based programs for children with exceptionalities began to appear. Gallaudet College, the only college for those who were deaf, started a teacher training program in the 1890s. In 1904, summer training sessions for teachers of children who were retarded began at the Vineland Training School in New Jersey. The community-based programs, however, often became "sunshine" rooms, in which such activities as arts and crafts were pursued, with little attempt to educate the children. In some cases expectations were unrealistic and disappointment in the programs ensued. Few parents or professionals were optimistic about educating those who were exceptional (Hallahan & Kauffman, 1990).

Novelist Pearl S. Buck's frank and open discussion of her child and how she learned to accept her child's disability reached many parents when it was first published in 1950 after her daughter was grown (Buck, 1991). Her urging helped spur the massive movement to provide educational services for people with disabilities.

Educators from Europe who immigrated to the United States during World War II also affected the education of persons with disabilities. Marianne Frostig, a psychiatric social worker and rehabilitation therapist, trained in the United States as a psychologist and worked with children who were retarded, delinquent, or learning disabled (Hallahan & Kauffman, 1990).

The Association for Retarded Citizens (ARC), previously the National Association for Retarded Children, was chartered in 1950 and became active in influencing state legislatures and Congress. In 1957, along with other organizations, it supported such important legislative action as the federal establishment of national programs in the field of special education and governmental support of research and leadership training in mental retardation. In 1963 support was extended to other people with exceptionalities—except for people who were gifted, who did not receive support until 1979. The Bureau of Education for the Handicapped was established in 1966.

Another influence on the special education movement was the rehabilitation of World War II and Korean War veterans. Research into and efforts toward rehabilitation have carried over into the areas of working with people who are exceptional. For example, with expanded programs for mobility and occupational training, it was found that those who were blind or deaf did not have to be isolated and dependent upon fate. This philosophy spread to children's programs, and many schools began integrating children who were blind and deaf into regular classes for part of the day while separating them for the rest of their studies in a resource room with a special teacher.

The Kennedys, a powerful and influential family with a daughter with a disability, have done much to help the cause of people with disabilities. They established the Joseph P. Kennedy Jr. Foundation, a multimillion-dollar effort in support of those with mental retardation. The foundation's main objectives are "the prevention of mental retardation by identifying its causes and improving means by which society deals with its mentally retarded citizens" (The Foundation Center, 1990). It supports research, special projects, consulting services, technical assistance, conferences, and seminars. Special Olympics, established in 1968 by Eunice Kennedy Shriver, is an athletic program for people with intellectual disabilities. It is the world's largest sports program, with 150 countries, 2.25 million athletes and families, and 500,000 volunteers and coaches participating (McCarthy, 2006). Thus, parents, educators, and influential families reinforce the growing concern of all parents of children with disabilities: that their children should have opportunities to develop to their highest potential.

Children with disabilities receive a variety of services related to their needs. The Individuals with Disabilities Education Act Amendments of 1997 (reauthorized as the Individuals with Disabilities Improvement Act of 2004) emphasizes the practice of using the regular classroom to provide education as the "least restrictive environment" for children with disabilities. The act, known as IDEA 97 (now 2004) or PL 105-17 (now PL 108-446), provides education rights for children with disabilities.

LEGISLATION FOR PEOPLE WITH DISABILITIES

Legislation for people with disabilities has been developing since the 1960s. With each new law or amendment to existing legislation, the programs for children and adults with disabilities have become more encompassing. During the 1960s parents

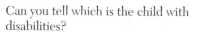

Can you tell which is the child with disabilities?

organized advocacy groups that became vocal, and attracted enough attention to result in legislation to provide educational support to children with disabilities. In 1971, the Pennsylvania Association for Retarded Children (PARC) won a landmark case against the Commonwealth of Pennsylvania. It was a decision based on the 14th Amendment, which assures all children, including those with disabilities, the right to a free and appropriate education. Decisions such as this one led to the passage of other important laws.

Vocational Rehabilitation Act of 1973, Section 504

Section 504 of the Vocational Rehabilitation Act of 1973, which relates to nondiscrimination under Federal Grant, PL 93-112, required that "no otherwise qualified handicapped individual in the United States shall, solely by reason of his handicap, be excluded from the participation in, be denied the benefits of, or be subjected to discrimination under any program or activity receiving Federal financial assistance" (29 U.S.C. § 794). At the time, Section 504 specifically applied to discrimination in employment. The Rehabilitation Act Amendments of 1974 extended coverage to all civil rights, including education, employment, health, welfare, and other social services programs.

Under Section 504, all recipients of Department of Education funds that operate public elementary and secondary programs must provide a free appropriate public education (FAPE) to each qualified individual with a disability who is in the recipient's jurisdiction, regardless of the nature or severity of the person's disability.

Since the legislation was passed, there has been confusion about implementation and compliance of the regulations. As a result of the confusion, the Office of Civil Rights has issued policies and rulings that clarify many issues.

A person is considered disabled under the definition of Section 504 if the individual:

1. Has a mental or physical impairment which substantially limits one or more of such person's major life activities
2. Has a record of such impairments
3. Is regarded as having such an impairment

Major life activities include functions such as caring for one's self, performing manual tasks, walking, seeing, hearing, speaking, breathing, learning, and working. When a condition does not substantially limit a major life activity, the individual does not qualify for services under Section 504.

Much confusion also exists regarding the relationship between Section 504 and special education laws and regulations. It must be emphasized that Section 504 falls under the management of regular education. Students who have disabilities, but who do not qualify for special education, may still be eligible for accommodations under Section 504.

Section 504, which covers a broader range of disabilities than the special education law, also requires public schools to provide students with a "free appropriate public education" and, in addition, ensures that students with disabilities are afforded an equal opportunity to participate in school programs. A student who is found to be disabled under Section 504 should be served by the resources provided through regular education. The exception to this standard would be a student who has been determined eligible as disabled under the Individuals with Disabilities Education Act (IDEA). Such a student could receive special education services under IDEA and accommodations required under Section 504 of the Rehabilitation Act of 1973.

For students with disabilities or who qualify for Section 504 services, this means that schools are required to make special arrangements so that the students have access to the full range of programs and activities offered, if needed, as determined at a multidisciplinary team meeting to determine students' service needs. At the meeting, the use of "evidence-based assistive technology," as mandated by IDEA 2004, is to be identified. Assistive technology, a means to provide the support needed to increase, maintain or improve a student's functioning, may include a range of devices, from "low tech," such as a pencil grip, to "high tech," such as a voice synthesizer or braille reader (Copenhaver, 2004; Families Together, 1993, p. lv.xxv).

Other students may need technology to provide physical access to the school facilities. An example may include a student who needs a wheelchair lift on a school bus to get to school must be provided with this technology. Other examples of modifications that might be required under Section 504 include installing ramps into buildings and modifying restrooms to provide access for individuals with physical disabilities.

Determination of a student's eligibility for Section 504 services must be based on the use of tests and other evaluations that evaluate specific areas of need, not solely a single intelligence quotient. They should not be culturally or linguistically biased. Subsequent assessment to determine progress made towards individualized goals should also provide appropriate accommodations so they reflect the student's achievement without the impact of the student's disability (Chicago Office of the Office for Civil Rights, 2005).

Enforcement of Section 504 of the Rehabilitation Act of 1973 in programs and activities that receive funds from the U.S. Department of Education, is provided by the Office for Civil Rights (OCR). There are 12 enforcement offices and a headquarters in Washington, DC. Section 504, like other civil rights laws, is monitored by OCR. It is a goal of OCR to foster partnerships between school districts and parents to address the special education needs of students attending programs that received federal funds. Enforcement procedures include administrative remedies, a private right of action in federal court, monetary damages, injunctive relief, attorney's fees, and defunding by the U.S. Department of Education (Chicago Office of the Office of Civil Rights, 2005).

The Americans with Disabilities Act

The Vocational Rehabilitation Act of 1973 was made more comprehensive by the Americans with Disabilities Act of 1990. In it, child-care centers were designated as public accommodations, which must be available to all who desire to use them. They must serve all children, including those who are disabled, unless (a) the child is a direct threat to self or others, (b) the facility cannot provide child care without it being an undue burden, or (c) the child-care center would have to change the services it provides.

The act specifically defines discrimination, including various types of intentional and unintentional exclusions, as the following: segregation, inferior or less effective services, benefits, or activities; architectural, transportation, and communication barriers; failure to make reasonable accommodations; and discriminatory qualifications and performance standards. Actions that do not constitute discrimination include unequal treatment unrelated to a disability or that result from legitimate application of qualifications and performance standards necessary and substantially related to the ability to perform or participate in the essential components of a job or activity.

The act stipulates that the Architectural and Transportation Barriers Compliance Board will issue minimum accessibility guidelines. Other regulations will be issued by the attorney general, the U.S. Equal Opportunity Commission, the secretary of Housing and Urban Development, the secretary of Transportation, the Federal Communication Commission, and the secretary of Commerce. The act does not repeal Sections 503 and 504 of the Vocational Rehabilitation Act of 1973, and all regulations issued under those sections remain in full force.

Education for All Handicapped Children Act of 1975—PL 94-142

The most far-reaching and revolutionary legislation related to education was PL 94-142, the Education for All Handicapped Children Act of 1975. All people between the ages of 3 and 18 must be provided with free and appropriate public education (FAPE). The term *appropriate* means suited to the disability age, maturity, and past achievements of the child and parental expectations. The education must be in a program designed to meet the child's needs in the least restrictive environment (Section 504 Regulations). This means that the child will be placed in the classroom that will benefit the child the most. If the student would benefit more from a regular classroom, the child is to be placed there.

The terms *mainstreaming* and *inclusion* have become synonymous with placing children with disabilities into the regular classroom. However, meeting the child's needs in the *least restrictive environment* can also refer to moving the child with disabilities out of a regular classroom into a resource room or self-contained special education room. The law requires diagnosis and individualization of the educational program. Additional terms that reflect the delivery of services in the least restrictive environment include "pull out" and "push in" services. "Pull out" services are those in which children with similar needs are "pulled out" of their base classroom to meet with a specialist for small group teaching. "Push in" services are those in which the specialist assigned to children with disabilities works in their base classroom. The specialists work with students with and without disabilities so that children with disabilities are not separated from their peers.

Amendments of 1983—PL 98-199

The Education of the Handicapped Act Amendments of 1983, PL 98-199, extended fiscal authorization for federal aid to state and local school systems through 1987; improved reporting and information dissemination requirements; increased assistance to children who are deaf and blind; provided grants for transitional programs; and expanded services for children from birth through 5 years of age (*Congressional Record*, 1983).

Amendments of 1986: Infants and Toddlers with Disabilities—PL 99-457

The Education of the Handicapped Act Amendments of 1986, PL 99-457, established statewide, comprehensive, coordinated, multidisciplinary, interagency programs of early intervention services for infants and toddlers with handicaps and their families (*Congressional Record,* 1986). This law addressed easily recognized needs of the very young with disabilities.

However, there are many conditions that are not immediately recognized, so services early in life may be delayed for those with genetic conditions associated with mental retardation, congenital syndromes associated with delays in development, sensory impairments, metabolic disorders, prenatal infections (AIDS, syphilis, cytomegalic inclusion disease), and low birth weight. There are also concerns for infants whose parents are developmentally delayed, have severe emotional disturbances, or are 15 years or younger.

Parents or caretakers may have difficulty finding the programs and services they need to help them care for these young children. These services are provided through the Department of Education in each state, so the first contact should be through the local school. Another group that may be able to offer information about services for rural families is:

American Council on Rural Special Education (ACRES)
Kansas State University
2323 Anderson Avenue, Suite 226
Manhattan, KS 66502
785-53-ACRES
www.ksu.edu/acres/

ACRES' goals foster quality services and education for individuals with disabilities who live in rural America. The Web site also offers links to other organizations serving children with disabilities, tips on advocacy and research related to services to children with disabilities.

PL 99-457 provided for public supervision at no cost (except where federal and state laws allow), meeting the needs of handicapped infants and toddlers, family training, counseling, special instruction, physical therapy, stimulation therapy, case management, diagnosis-qualified personnel, and conformation with the Individualized Family Service Plan.

INDIVIDUALS WITH DISABILITIES EDUCATION ACT AMENDMENTS 1997 PL 105-17 AND 2004 PL 108-446

This federal law—formerly the Education for All Handicapped Children Act, PL 94-142—mandated that all children receive an education regardless of the severity of their disability. An amended IDEA was reauthorized in June 1997 and went into effect on July 1, 1998, and was reauthorized again in 2004 and went into effect July 1, 2005. IDEA 97 and 2004 are organized into four parts: (a) general provisions; (b) school-aged and preschool—3- to 5- year-olds; (c) infants and toddlers, birth through 2; and (d) support. Part C relates to the education of infants and toddlers—birth to age 3. Although alike in many ways, the differences include "zero reject" in Part B. It requires that there be no exclusion of children aged 3 through 21, and public school systems are responsible for including all these children in an educational program, regardless of the extent or the kind of disability.

Part C for infants gives discretion to the states to develop a program that best serves the needs of infants and toddlers. Each state determines which agency can work most effectively with parents and their infants and toddlers. States use different agencies such as the Departments of Education or Health and Human Services. For infants and toddlers with identified disabilities, there must not be a break in service as they transition from Part C to Part B services.

Terms used in the act include:

1. The term *handicapped child* was changed to the *child with disabilities* because it was recognized that the children are handicapped by the limitations placed on them rather than by their abilities. The child has a disability, which may not be a handicap, depending on the situation.

Tom Watson/Merrill

IDEA requires that special education be provided to all who need it.

2. All children with disabilities will have an education that is individualized to meet their needs. This is written in an Individualized Education Program (IEP) for children 3 to 21, and in an Individualized Family Service Plan (IFSP) for infants and toddlers (Utah Parent Center, 1997). Teachers, special teachers, administrators, parents, and others who are concerned with the child's education are involved in the development of the IEP. If appropriate, the child is also included. The law provides for a hearing that can be initiated by the parents if they do not agree with the diagnosis of the child, the placement, and/or the IEP. This is due process, and it is the responsibility of the school to inform the parents of their rights.

The school district is responsible for serving or seeing that children aged 3 to 5 are served in preschools. The primary focus of the IEP is the education of the student, although the family may receive some services. The agenda for the IEP meeting is illustrated in Figure 10.1.

In the birth-to-3 program, an Individualized Family Service Plan (IFSP) is written to serve both student and family. "One of the requirements for the IFSP is to document family concerns, resources, and priorities and to provide the family with services, consistent with members' preferences, so the family can increase its capacity to meet the child's special needs" (Turnbull & Turnbull, 1997, p. 24).

3. Children with disabilities should receive education in an environment that promotes interaction with nondisabled peers to the maximum extent appropriate to that student's need, known as a "least restrictive environment" (Smith, 2005).

4. Parents are expected to be involved at all levels of the evaluation, decision-making process of meeting the needs of their children (Turnbull, 2005).

Highlights of the IDEA 2004 Reauthorization

In the reauthorization by Congress in 2004, the following changes have elicited a great deal of comment:

1. Children (ages 3–9) eligible to receive services are those who do not achieve appropriate to their age level, or appropriate to meet state-approved grade-level standards or demonstrates a pattern of delays in performance, achievement or both with relation to age and state standards (*Federal Register,* 2006).
2. Reduced the paperwork to be completed by special education teachers by deleting the requirement that IEPs should include short-term objectives, except for students using alternative assessment procedures.
3. Established a plan for allocating funding that specifically states funding levels for each year until 2011.
4. Discipline—if a child with disabilities violates school discipline code not related to the disability, the discipline should be applied consistent with the discipline for a child without disabilities. But no child should be denied appropriate education if discipline has a suspension of more than 10 days or expulsion. If, however, the child has a weapon or drugs or inflicts serious injury on someone, the child can be removed for up to 45 school days without regard to whether the behavior is related to the disability.
5. An increase in qualified special education teachers so children are taught by special education teachers certified in the content they teach the students with special needs.
6. School districts are required to reduce the overrepresentation of students from diverse backgrounds in special education (Turnbull, 2005).

Development of the Individualized Education Program (IEP)

The development of an Individualized Education Program (IEP) illustrates the goals that schools and parents want for their children with disabilities. An example of an IEP for a preschool child who was adopted from China in infancy is illustrated in Figures 10.2A, 10.2B, and 10.2C.

All children with disabilities receiving any type of special education services must have an Individualized Education Program (ages 3 through 21) prepared especially for them. It must be the

CONFIDENTIAL

Department of Special Services
Individualized Education Program

DRAFT UNTIL IEP IS SIGNED

IEP MEETING AGENDA
To be used at initial or annual IEP meetings

Student Name **Periwinkle** ID # ______ Date of IEP Meeting ______

Check each item after discussed:

I. ☐ Introduce IEP Team Members

II. ☐ State Purpose for the Meeting

III. ☐ Review *Rights and Procedural Safeguards Pertaining to Special Education*

IV. ☐ Review Information to be Considered by the IEP Team

Parent/family concerns regarding the student's education
Student's strengths and interests in the home, school, and community
Review progress on goals/objectives from current IEP
Review formal or informal assessment results

Additional factors for IEP team consideration (check after discussed):
- ☐ Impact of student's behavior and is it impeding his/her learning or that of others.
- ☐ Student's need for instruction in or use of Braille.
- ☐ Student's language needs, due to limited English proficiency.
- ☐ Student's communication and/or language needs.
- ☐ Student's assistive technology needs.
- ☐ Student's language and communication needs if deaf or hard of hearing.

*Any additional factor(s) that applies to the student must be addressed within the context of the IEP.

V. ☐ Identify Student Needs
—Annual Goals/Short-term Objectives
—Classroom Accommodations/Curriculum Modifications

VI. ☐ Determine Student's Participation in Assessment Programs
—Testing Accommodations
—Review of Information about State Assessments and Diploma Options for Students with Disabilities

VII. ☐ Discussion and Selection of the Least Restrictive Environment

VIII. ☐ Summary of Services Required to Meet Student's Areas of Need
—Transportation Needs

IX. ☐ Distribution of the ESY Information Form and Copies of the IEP

Information from the Fairfax County Public Schools student scholastic record is released on the condition that the recipient agrees not to permit any other party to have access to such information without the written consent of the parent or of the eligible student.

IEP 301 (06/05) IEP Meeting Agenda page _____ of _____

FIGURE 10.1 IEP agenda.

FAIRFAX COUNTY PUBLIC SCHOOLS

CONFIDENTIAL

Department of Special Services

Individualized Education Program

DRAFT UNTIL IEP IS SIGNED

Page ____ of ____

STUDENT Periwinkle ID # ____

4. Area of Need Personal/Social: Play Skills

5. Present Level Documentation: Teacher Observation

Periwinkle is now playing beside her classmates in structured play settings. She is beginning to demonstrate independent parallel play. She is also entering into some associative play when the activity is non-threatening to her (ie: free drawing with a friend). She is interested in playing with a wider variety of toys and she is capable of playing with these toys appropriately. She continues to need to broaden her play skills to include pretend play and dramatic play. She needs to acquire skills that will help her join in play with her peers.

How does this area of need impact this student's participation/ progress in the general education curriculum or for preschool children, the child's participation in age appropriate activities?

In order for Periwinkle to have successful relationships with her peers, she needs to acquire appropriate play skills.

7. Progress*

How will progress toward this annual goal be measured?

- ___ Classroom Participation
- ___ Checklists
- ___ Classwork
- ___ Criterion- referenced Test ____
- ___ Homework
- ___ Norm- referenced Test ____
- ___ Observation
- ___ Oral Reports
- ___ Special Projects
- ___ Tests and Quizzes
- ___ Written Reports
- ___ Other teacher notes

6. Annual Goal What does this student need to know or be able to do?

Periwinkle will exhibit cooperative play skills with three successes of four opportunities as evaluated three times per school year.

	Date			
Code				

Short-term Objectives What short-term objectives indicate progress toward this goal?

With three successes of four opportunities, Periwinkle will:

* exhibit parallel play skills in a variety of play activities.
* take turns with one teacher reminder.
* share toys with her classmates with one teacher reminder.
* clean up her toys/play materials with one teacher reminder.
* exhibit associative play skills in a variety of play activities.

Progress Comments

A copy of this form, indicating the student's progress toward this annual goal will be reported to parents at regular scheduled FCPS reporting periods. **The progress codes are: M** The student has met the criteria for this goal/ objective. **SP** The student is making sufficient progress toward achieving this goal/objective within the duration of the IEP. **EP** The student demonstrates emerging skill but may not achieve this goal/objective within the duration of this IEP. **NP** The student has not yet demonstrated progress toward achieving this goal/ objective and may not achieve this goal within the duration of this IEP. **NI** This goal/ objective has not been introduced.

Information from the Fairfax County Public Schools student scholastic record is released on the condition that the recipient agrees not to permit any other party to have access to such information without the written consent of the parent or of the eligible student.

FIGURE 10.2A Individualized Education Program (IEP)

FAIRFAX COUNTY PUBLIC SCHOOLS

CONFIDENTIAL

Department of Special Services

Individualized Education Program

DRAFT UNTIL IEP IS SIGNED

Page ____ cf ____

STUDENT Periwinkle ID # ____

4. Area of Need Personal/Social: Attention to Task

5. Present Level Documentation: Teacher Observation

Periwinkle is capable of attending to classroom activities for an age appropriate amount of time. While attending, she will jump up and come up to the teacher, wiggle in her chair, and make comments to her peers. She is easily influenced by her peers and may copy their behavior, not thinking about whether or not the behavior is appropriate.

How does this area of need impact this student's participation/ progress in the general education curriculum or for preschool children, the child's participation in age appropriate activities?

In order for Periwinkle to maximize her opportunities to learn, she needs to attend to a task without being distracted.

7. Progress*

How will progress toward this annual goal be measured?

- —— Classroom Participation
- —— Checklists
- —— Classwork
- —— Criterion- referenced Test ______
- —— Homework
- —— Norm- referenced Test ______
- —— Observation
- —— Oral Reports
- —— Special Projects
- —— Tests and Quizzes
- —— Written Reports
- —— Other Teacher notes

6. Annual Goal What does this student need to know or be able to do?

Periwinkle will attend to a variety of classroom activities for a 20 minute period, following activity directions with four successes of five opportunities as monitored three times during the school year..

	Date			
Code				

Short-term Objectives What short-term objectives indicate progress toward this goal?

With 4 successes of 5 opportunities, Periwinkle will:

* Use appropriate methods of responding as designated by her teacher during classroom activities.
* Participate appropriately, including remaining seated when appropriate, within a classroom activity as directed by the teacher.
* Focus on the content of the activity for a period of 15 minutes with one teacher reminder.
* Refocus on the classroom activity after being distracted by a classmate or any other distraction within the classroom setting.

Progress Comments

A copy of this form, indicating the student's progress toward this annual goal will be reported to parents at regular scheduled FCPS reporting periods. **The progress codes are: M** The student has met the criteria for this goal/ objective. **SP** The student is making sufficient progress toward achieving this goal/ objective within the duration of the IEP. **EP** The student demonstrates emerging skill but may not achieve this goal/ objective within the duration of this IEP. **NP** The student has not yet demonstrated progress toward achieving this goal/ objective and may not achieve this goal within the duration of this IEP. **NI** This goal/ objective has not been introduced.

Information from the Fairfax County Public Schools student scholastic record is released on the condition that the recipient agrees not to permit any other party to have access to such information without the written consent of the parent or of the eligible student.

FIGURE 10.2B Individualized Education Program (IEP)

FAIRFAX COUNTY PUBLIC SCHOOLS

CONFIDENTIAL

Department of Special Services

Individualized Education Program

DRAFT UNTIL IEP IS SIGNED

Page ____ of ____

STUDENT Periwinkle ID # ________

4. Area of Need Cognitive

5. Present Level Documentation: Brigance; Classroom Participation

Periwinkle is beginning to rote count, has a concept of the numbers one and two. She is showing emerging skills in counting out objects to four. Peri has a concept of one to one correspondence, but is inconsistent in demonstrating this knowledge. She needs to continue to acquire counting skills and the concept of number.

How does this area of need impact this student's participation/ progress in the general education curriculum or for preschool children, the child's participation in age appropriate activities?

In order for Periwinkle to be able to perform classroom activities that require the concept of number, she needs to acquire counting skills.

7. Progress*

How will progress toward this annual goal be measured?

—— Classroom Participation
—— Checklists
—— Classwork
—— Criterion- referenced Test ______
—— Homework
—— Norm- referenced Test ______
—— Observation
—— Oral Reports
—— Special Projects
—— Tests and Quizzes
—— Written Reports
—— Other Teacher notes

6. Annual Goal What does this student need to know or be able to do?

Periwinkle will count out five objects from a larger group of objects with three successes of four opportunities as monitored three times per school year.

	Date			
Code				

Short-term Objectives What short-term objectives indicate progress toward this goal?

With three successes of four opportunities, Periwinkle will:

* Rote count to 20.
* Demonstrate a one to one correspondence up to 8.
* Count out three objects from a larger group of objects.
* Answer questions requiring counting objects, etc. up to four objects.

Progress Comments

A copy of this form, indicating the student's progress toward this annual goal will be reported to parents at regular scheduled FCPS reporting periods. **The progress codes are: M** The student has met the criteria for this goal/ objective. **SP** The student is making sufficient progress toward achieving this goal/objective within the duration of the IEP. **EP** The student demonstrates emerging skill but may not achieve this goal/objective within the duration of this IEP. **NP** The student has not yet demonstrated progress toward achieving this goal/ objective and may not achieve this goal within the duration of this IEP. **NI** This goal/ objective has not been introduced.

Information from the Fairfax County Public Schools student scholastic record is released on the condition that the recipient agrees not to permit any other party to have access to such information without the written consent of the parent or of the eligible student.

FIGURE 10.2C Individualized Education Program (IEP)

product of the joint efforts of members of a child study team, which must include items (i) through (v) of the following:

Members of the IEP Team

1. Parents of the child with a disability
2. At least one regular education teacher of the child if the child is participating in the regular classroom environment
3. At least one special education teacher, or where appropriate, at least one special education provider of such child
4. A representative of the local educational agency who is (a) qualified to provide, or supervise the provision of, specially designed instruction to meet the unique needs of children with disabilities; (b) knowledgeable about the general curriculum; and (c) knowledgeable about the availability of resources of the local education agency
5. At least one individual who can relate the evaluation results to the goals and steps of the IEP (Turnbull, Turnbull, & Wehmeyer, 2007)
6. At the discretion of the parent or the agency, other individuals who have knowledge or special expertise regarding the child, including related services personnel as appropriate
7. Whenever appropriate, the child with the disability ([Section 614(d) (1)(B)] as cited in National Information Center for Children and Youth with Disabilities [NICHYC], 1998; Family and Advocates Partnership for Education Project, 2006).

The IEP should accomplish the following:

- The IEP meeting serves as a communication vehicle between parents and school personnel, and enables them, as equal participants, to jointly decide what the child's needs are, what services will be provided to meet those needs, and what the anticipated outcomes may be.
- The IEP process provides an opportunity for resolving any differences between parents and school personnel concerning the special education needs of a child with a disability; first, through the IEP meeting, and second, if necessary, through the procedural protections that are available to the parents.
- The IEP sets forth in writing a commitment of resources necessary to enable a child with a disability to receive needed special education and related services.
- The IEP is a management tool to help ensure that each child with a disability is provided special education and related services appropriate to the child's special learning needs.
- The IEP is a compliance and monitoring document that may be used by authorized monitoring personnel from each governmental level to determine whether a child with a disability is actually receiving the free appropriate public education agreed to by the parents and the school.
- The IEP serves as an evaluation device for use in determining the extent of the child's progress toward meeting the projected outcomes (Utah Parent Center, 1997, pp. 26–27; Gartin & Murdick, 2005; Turnbull, Turnbull, & Wehmeyer, 2007).

Ideally, the IEP:

- Specifies that the assessment yield information that will enable the student to be involved in and progress in the general curriculum or, for preschool children, to participate in appropriate activities.
- Requires that IEPs must now state how the student's disability affects academic achievement and functional performance in the general curriculum (Gartin & Murdick, 2005).
- Requires that annual, measurable academic and functional goals, including benchmarks, be related to helping the child be involved and progress in the general curriculum (Gartin & Murdick, 2005).
- Requires the IEP to state the "supplementary aids and services" needed by the student and the "program modifications or supports for school personnel" so that the student can be involved and progress in the general curriculum and participate in extracurricular and other nonacademic activities.
- Requires IEP teams to consider positive behavioral intervention strategies and supports for students whose behavior impedes their own learning or that of others.

- Requires that the IEP include an "explanation of the extent, if any, to which the child will not participate with nondisabled children in regular class" and in extracurricular and nonacademic activities (Utah Parent Center, 1997).
- Adds the regular education teacher to the IEP team as a required member.
- Requires that the IEP state how the parents will be regularly informed of the student's progress toward the annual goals (as often as parents of other students receive progress reports).
- Allows local districts to use IDEA funds to support students in general education classrooms without concern that students without disabilities might also benefit (PEAK Parent Center, 1997).

(See Figures 10.2A and 10.2B.)

Many requirements must be met when dealing with the child with disabilities. The IEP should be reviewed periodically, but not less than annually, to determine if progress toward the goals is advancing as expected and to reevaluate and assess the program. The 2004 IDEA reauthorization changed attendance requirements so that all members of the IEP do not need to attend a reevaluation meeting if the area they represent is not being discussed. Administrators and teachers must be aware of all procedures that the schools are responsible for administering. These procedures include the following types of subjects: definitions, opportunity to examine records, independent educational evaluation, prior notice, parent consent, procedures when parent refuses consent, content of notice, formal complaint resolution, impartial due-process hearing, reasonable attorney's fees, impartial hearing officer, appointment of hearing officer, access rights, records, children's rights, and more (Burns, 2006; Family and Advocates Partnership for Education, 2006; Gartin & Murdick, 2005).

Rights and Responsibilities for Parents—IDEA 2004

IDEA 97 and 2004 addressed the participation of parents in the development of their child's program. It states that the Local Education Agency (LEA) or the State Education Agency (SEA) will ensure that parents are members of any group that makes decisions on the educational placement of their child. Parents can examine all records and participate in meetings regarding the evaluations, placement, and the free and appropriate public education that the child will receive. Specifications include:

- Public agencies must notify parents when the agencies propose or refuse to initiate or change the identification, evaluation, or educational placement of the child or the provision of FAPE to the child.
- Parents have the right to inspect and review all records relating to their child that a public agency collects, maintains, or uses regarding the identification, evaluation, or educational placement of the child or the provision of FAPE to the child.
- Parental consent is required before a child may be evaluated for the first time.
- Parents have the right to obtain an independent educational evaluation (IEE) of their child.
- Parental consent is required for a child's initial special education placement.
- Parents have the right to challenge or appeal any decision related to the identification, evaluation, or educational placement of their child or the provision of FAPE to their child.
- Parents are responsible for notifying the public agency if they plan to remove their child from the public agency for placement in a private school at public expense.
- Parents are responsible for notifying the public agency if they intend to request a due-process hearing (Family and Advocates in Education Project, 2006; PEAK Parent Center, 1997).

Notification

There are also procedural safeguards that require written notification to parents prior to any proposed action. The notification must be in the parents' native language or preferred mode of communication—for example, braille or sign language. There is protection of the child's rights when parents cannot be located.

Mediation

If disagreements arise, a mediation system employing a qualified, impartial mediator must be available. Parents may be required to attend a mediation meeting.

Developmental Delay

The developmental delay category, previously used for placement of children three to five years old, was recognized as appropriate for those three to nine and was therefore extended to cover that age group.

Charter Schools

Charter schools, new since the original IDEA, were included in the provisions. They must follow the same guidelines as other publicly funded schools.

POSITIVE COLLABORATION OF PARENTS AND SCHOOL

Through collaborating with one another, parents and school professionals have the opportunity to:

- Secure a full understanding of the student's needs and strengths
- Take into account the observations of parents and others (including educators) as they develop that understanding
- Make sure to acknowledge the feelings of parents and their need to be empowered to care for their child
- Ensure that the evaluation is useful to and used by the student's teachers and other involved professionals and by the family as they work together to provide a free appropriate public education (Family and Advocates in Education Project, 2006; Turnbull & Turnbull, 1997, p. 21; Turnbull, Turnbull, Erwin, & Soodak, 2006).

STUDENTS WHO ARE GIFTED AND TALENTED

Students who are gifted and talented have the potential for superior performance. This can include intellectual achievement, special aptitudes, or creative thinking and performing abilities.

The Gifted and Talented Children's Education Act, PL 95-561, gave states and local education agencies financial incentives to identify and educate students who are gifted and talented, provide inservice training, and conduct research (Heward & Orlansky, 1988). None of the federal legislation has mandated educational opportunities for children who are gifted. Approximately 30 states mandate educational opportunities for youngsters who are gifted, and other states have legislation permitting establishment of such classes (Karnes & Marquardt, 1997).

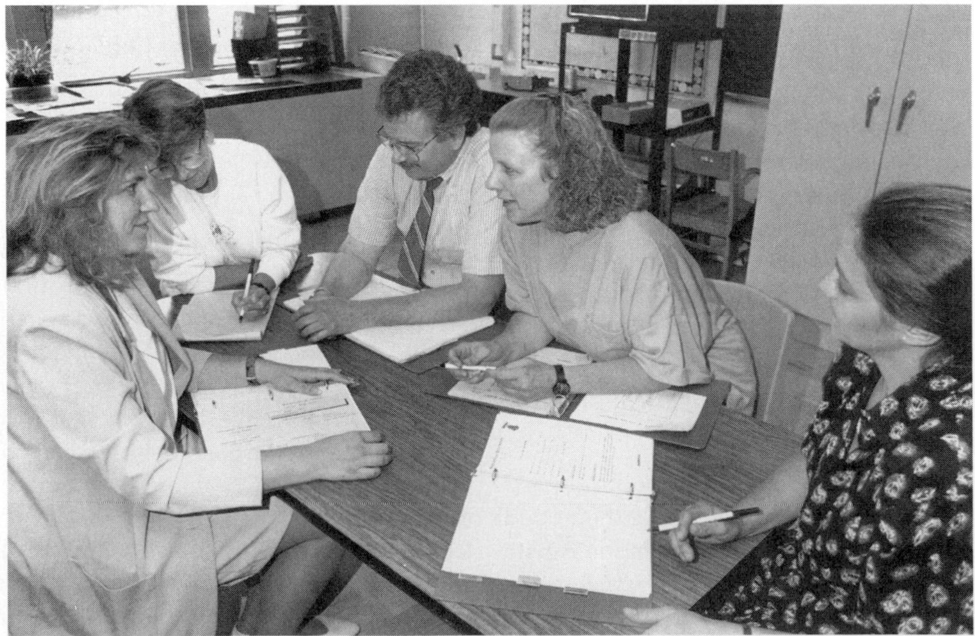

Todd Yarrington/Merrill

An IEP or IFSP meeting is a time to discuss the child's plan. Whenever feasible, the child should be included.

The Jacob K. Javits Gifted and Talented Students Education Act of 1988 was followed by the Jacob K. Javits Gifted and Talented Education Act of 1992. In 1998 the Javits Act was the only federal funding earmarked for gifted education. Funding not earmarked for gifted education may be used to benefit students who are gifted. In funding for children with disabilities, meeting the child's needs is required, but children with gifts and talents do not have legislation that requires support. The purpose of the federal acts is to encourage rich education for gifted and talented students and to have special programs broadened and expanded into the regular classroom (Boren, 1994).

According to the Council of State Directors of Programs for the Gifted, 20 states administer gifted and talented under special education or exceptional children divisions. Others administer programs under curriculum and instruction, general education or gifted and talented divisions. Twenty-one states provide funding for gifted children, however most other states do not require school divisions to provide services to children with high abilities (Council of State Directors of Programs for the Gifted, 2002).

According to analysis by The Davidson Institute for Talent Development, more states are offering gifted education. These include the following:

1. Six states offered gifted programming mandated and fully funded: Nebraska, Oklahoma, Alaska, Iowa, Mississippi, and Georgia.
2. Twenty-one states mandated partially funded gifted programs: Montana, Idaho, Wyoming. Utah, Arizona, New Mexico, Kansas, Texas, Arkansas, Louisiana, Tennessee, Kentucky, Ohio, West Virginia, Virginia, Maine, North Carolina, South Carolina, Florida, Maryland, and Hawaii.
3. Four states mandated gifted programs but had no gifted funding available: Oregon, Pennsylvania, Alabama, and New Jersey.
4. Eleven states do not require gifted programs but gifted funding is available: Washington, California, Nevada, Colorado, North Dakota, Minnesota, Wisconsin, Missouri, Indiana, Michigan, and Massachusetts.
5. Eight states do not mandate gifted programs and no gifted funding is available: South Dakota, Illinois, New York, Vermont, New Hampshire, Rhode Island, Connecticut, Delaware, and the District of Columbia.

Each state makes its own decision on gifted education, but with the help of foundations and the Jacob K. Javits Gifted and Talented Students Education Act, there is an increase in gifted education. It continues to need support.

The increase of children that speak languages other than English in the education system has created an additional burden for educators of children with high abilities. Children that have limited English proficiency are assumed to be less able. They feel alienated from teachers, peers, and the curriculum. They are often lost in remedial programs, and therefore are not able to reach their full potential. Many leave the education system prematurely. Appropriate testing tools, multiple sources of assessment information and strong parental involvement are strategies educators must use in order to fully meet the needs of gifted, limited English proficiency students (Council for Exceptional Children, 2001, 2003).

DEFINITIONS OF DISABILITIES OR EXCEPTIONALITIES

The following descriptions of children with exceptionalities as defined in IDEA (34 Code of Federal Regulations, Section 300.7) clarify those who need special programs. If a student in a classroom fits into any of the following categories, special services should be provided.

1. *Autism.* A developmental disability significantly affecting verbal and nonverbal communication and social interaction, generally evident before age 3, that adversely affects educational performance.
2. *Deafness.* A hearing impairment so severe that a child is impaired in processing linguistic information through hearing, with or without amplification, which adversely affects educational performance.
3. *Deafness–blindness.* Simultaneous hearing and visual impairments, the combination of which causes such severe communication and other

developmental and education problems that a child cannot be accommodated in special education programs solely for children who are deaf or for children who are blind.

4. *Hearing Impairment.* An impairment in hearing, whether permanent or fluctuating, that adversely affects a child's educational performance but is not included under the definition of "deafness."
5. *Mental retardation.* Significantly subaverage general intellectual functioning existing concurrently with deficits in adaptive behavior and manifested during the developmental period, which adversely affects a child's educational performance.
6. *Multiple disabilities.* Simultaneous impairments (such as mental retardation and blindness or mental retardation and orthopedic impairment), the combination of which causes such severe educational problems that the child cannot be accommodated in a special education program solely for one of the impairments. The term does not include children with deafness–blindness.
7. *Orthopedic impairment.* A severe orthopedic impairment that adversely affects a child's educational performance. The term includes impairments caused by a congenital anomaly (e.g., clubfoot or absence of a limb), impairments caused by disease (e.g., poliomyelitis or bone tuberculosis), and impairments from other causes (e.g., cerebral palsy, amputations, or fractures or burns that cause contractures).
8. *Other health impairment.* Having limited strength, vitality, or alertness, due to chronic or acute health problems—such as a heart condition, tuberculosis, rheumatic fever, nephritis, asthma, sickle cell anemia, hemophilia, epilepsy, lead poisoning, leukemia, or diabetes—that adversely affects a child's educational performance. According to the Office of Special Education and Rehabilitative Services' clarification statement of September 16, 1991, eligible children with Attention Deficit Disorder may also be classified under "other health impairment."
9. *Tourette syndrome.* A neurological disorder that includes repetitive, stereotyped involuntary movements or tics. The average age of onset is 7 to 10 years of age. Vocal tics include sniffing, snorting, and barking. Involuntary motor movements include self-harm, such as punching oneself. The movements become worse when there is a high degree of excitement (National Institute of Neurological Disorders and Stroke, 2006).
10. *Emotional disturbance.*
    a. A condition exhibiting one or more of the following characteristics over a long period of time and to a marked degree and that adversely affects educational performance: (a) an inability to learn that cannot be explained by intellectual, sensory, or health factors; (b) an inability to build or maintain satisfactory interpersonal relationships with peers and teachers; (c) inappropriate types of behavior or feelings under normal circumstances; (d) a general pervasive mood of unhappiness or depression; or (e) a tendency to develop physical symptoms or fears associated with personal or school problems.
    b. The term includes children who have schizophrenia. The term does not include children who are socially maladjusted, unless it is determined that they have an emotional disturbance.
11. *Specific learning disabilities.* A disorder in one or more of the basic psychological processes involved in understanding or in using language, spoken or written, that may manifest itself in an imperfect ability to listen, think, speak, read, write, spell, or to do mathematical calculations. The term includes such conditions as perceptual disabilities, brain injury, minimal brain dysfunction, dyslexia, and developmental aphasia. The term does not include children who have learning problems that are primarily the result of visual, hearing, or motor disabilities, of mental retardation, of emotional disturbance, or of environmental, cultural, or economic disadvantage (Hallahan & Kauffman, 2006; NICHCY, 2002b).
12. *Speech or language impairment.* A communication disorder, such as stuttering, impaired articulation, a language impairment, or a voice impairment, that adversely affects a child's educational performance.

13. *Traumatic brain injury.* An acquired injury to the brain caused by an external physical force, resulting in total or partial functional disability or psychosocial impairment, or both, that adversely affects educational performance. The term does not include brain injuries that are congenital or degenerative, nor does it include brain injuries induced by birth trauma.
14. *Visual impairment, including blindness.* A visual impairment that, even with correction, adversely affects a child's educational performance. The term includes both children with partial sight and those who are completely blind (Hallahan & Kauffman, 2006; NICHCY, 1997).

    Visually impaired children and youth shall be identified as those whose limited vision interferes with their education and/or developmental progress. Four divisions for the visually impaired shall be made:

    "Partially sighted" indicates some type of visual problem has resulted in a need for special education.

    "Low vision" generally refers to a severe visual impairment, not necessarily limited to distance vision. Low vision applies to all individuals with sight who are unable to read the newspaper at a normal viewing distance, even with the aid of eyeglasses or contact lenses. They use a combination of vision and other sense to learn, although they may require adaptations in lighting or the size of print, and sometimes, braille;

    "Legally blind" indicates that a person has less than 20/2000 vision in the better eye or a very limited field of vision (20 degrees at its widest point); and

    Totally blind students learn via braille or other nonvisual media.

    Visual impairment is the consequence of a functional loss of vision, rather than the eye disorder itself. Eye disorders that can lead to visual impairments can include retinal degeneration, albinism, cataracts, glaucoma, muscular problems that result in visual disturbances, corneal disorders, diabetic retinopathy, congenital disorders, and infection.
15. *Pervasive developmental disorders (PDD).* A delay in social/language/motor and/or cognitive development. The child may have social development delays, and delays in one or more other categories. PDD is a category of delays in different magnitudes and different domains (Council for Exceptional Children, 2000).

Attention-Deficit Disorder—Attention-Deficit/Hyperactivity Disorder

A policy developed in the 1990s resulted in children with attention-deficit disorder (ADD) or attention-deficit/hyperactivity disorder (AD/HD) being classified under other health impairment, making them eligible to receive special education and related services. *Other Health Impairment* is defined as "having limited strength, vitality, or alertness, including a heightened alertness to environmental stimuli, that results in limited alertness with respect to the educational environment, that is due to chronic or acute health problems such as asthma, attention deficit disorder or attention deficit hyperactivity disorder, diabetes, epilepsy, a heart condition, hemophilia, lead poisoning, leukemia, nephritis, rheumatic fever, and sickle cell anemia; and adversely affects a child's educational performance" (NICHCY, 2001). A federal policy issued by the Office of Special Education and Rehabilitative Services, U.S. Department of Education, September 16, 1991, specified that a child no longer needs to be labeled as having a specific learning disability or as being seriously emotionally disturbed to receive special education services. Under the policy, a child who is identified as having ADD or AD/HD to the extent that it adversely affects education "performance" can now be served.

Symptoms that are a sign of AD/HD are (a) problems with paying attention, (b) being very active (called hyperactivity), and (c) acting before thinking (called impulsivity). Three types of AD/HD are:

- Inattentive type, in which the person cannot seem to focus on a task or activity
- Hyperactive-impulsive type, in which the person is very active and often acts without thinking
- Combined type, in which the person is inattentive, impulsive, and too active

A Brief Look at Autism, Learning Disabilities, and Mental Retardation

Autism

Characteristics. Children will vary in intelligence, abilities, and behaviors. They adjust best in steady and predictable environments. While some do not speak, others may have limited language that includes repeated phrases. Children with autism often have difficulty with abstract concepts, have a limited range of interests, and a small range of topics, and they commonly have unusual responses to sensory information such as lights, loud noises, and some textures of food or fabrics. The NICHCY (2001) described the following characteristics of autism:

- Communication problems (e.g., using and understanding language)
- Difficulty in relating to people, objects, and events
- Unusual play with toys and other objects
- Difficulty with changes in routine or familiar surroundings
- Repetitive body movements or behavior patterns (p. 2)

Autism can be characterized by a broad range of behaviors, which has led diagnosticians to describe autism as a broad spectrum disorder. This has resulted in the need for teachers and parents to recognize the differences in the needs of children, depending on how their disability manifests itself (Hallahan & Kauffman, 2006).

Recommendations. The child with autism responds best in a predictable and consistent program.

> Behavior and communication problems that interfere with learning sometimes require the assistance of a knowledgeable professional in the autism field who develops and helps to implement a plan which can be carried out at home and school. . . . Students learn better and are less confused when information is presented visually as well as verbally. Interaction with nondisabled peers is also important, for these students provide models of appropriate language, social, and behavior skills. To overcome frequent problems in generalizing skills learned at school it is very important to develop programs with parents, so that programs of learning activities, approaches, and experiences can be carried over into the home and community. (NICHCY, 2001, p. 2)

Learning Disabilities

Characteristics.

1. Children with learning disabilities are primarily intact children. They are not primarily visually impaired, hearing impaired, environmentally disadvantaged, mentally retarded, or emotionally disturbed. In spite of the fact that these children have adequate intelligence, adequate sensory processes, and adequate emotional stability, they do not learn without special assistance.
2. Children with learning disabilities show wide discrepancies of intra-individual differences in a profile of their development. This is often shown by marked discrepancies in one or more of the specific areas of academic learning or a serious lack of language development or language facility. These disabilities may affect the child's behavior in such areas as thinking, conceptualization, memory, language, perception, reading, writing, spelling, or arithmetic.
3. The concept of deviation of a child with learning disabilities implies that the child deviates so markedly from the norm of the child's group as to require specialized instruction. Such specialized instruction required for these children may be of value to other children. However, the population to be served with special education funds authorized for children does not include children with learning problems that are the result of poor instruction or economic or cultural deprivation (Kearns, 1980).

Signs of Learning Disabilities. Learning disabilities are generally recognized when the child enters school and specific learning tasks are expected. Watch for the difference between what a child accomplishes in school and what that child should be able to do given the child's intellect and ability. There is no one sign that says that the child has a learning disability.

Silver and Hagin (2002) describe and discuss learning disorders, research, and the various curriculum designs used to help students develop. Planning for students requires an understanding of the factors that affect them including cognitive, emotional, social, neuropsychological, and educational. "Learning disorders are complex conditions. The characteristics vary from person to person and from stage to stage in the development of an individual. . . . People responsible for educational planning with learning disabilities must understand these differences and provide for them appropriately" (p. 218).

Identification of the problems that disable a child's learning need to be analyzed by a specialist, but if a child has several of the following problems, a learning disability should be considered by the parent or teacher. Clues include the following:

- May have trouble learning the alphabet, rhyming words, or connecting letters to their sounds
- May make many mistakes when reading aloud, and repeat and pause often
- May not understand what he or she reads
- May have real trouble with spelling
- May have very messy handwriting or hold a pencil awkwardly
- May struggle to express ideas in writing
- May learn language late and have a limited vocabulary
- May have trouble remembering the sounds that letters make or hearing slight differences between words
- May have trouble understanding jokes, comic strips, and sarcasm
- May have trouble following directions
- May mispronounce words or use a wrong word that sounds similar
- May have trouble organizing what he or she wants to say or not be able to think of the word he or she needs for writing or conversation
- May not follow the social rules of conversation, such as taking turns, and may stand too close to the listener
- May confuse math symbols and misread numbers
- May not be able to retell a story in order (what happened first, second, or third)
- May not know where to begin a task or how to go on from there (NICHCY, 2002b p. 3)

Tips for Teachers and Parents

1. Learn as much about learning disabilities as you can.
2. Observe the child playing and "working." Make note of progress the child has made and tell the child what you have seen. This helps to confirm for the child that you know when he or she works hard or does well. Give positive feedback.
3. Recognize the child's strengths and interests. Find out how the child learns best. Give the child opportunities to use his or her talents and strengths.

Tips for Teachers

1. Review the student's records and ask specialists about the best method for working with the child. This may include:
   a. Giving students more time to take tests
   b. Breaking tasks into smaller units
   c. Providing directions verbally and in writing (NICHY, 2002b)
   d. Having a peer or classroom assistant take notes or write answers on a test
   e. Providing tutors in order to individualize teaching
   f. Providing audio-taped textbooks
   g. Providing supplementary video materials that relate to the classroom topic

   For students who have listening difficulties, allow them to use a tape recorder or to borrow notes. For students who have difficulty writing, furnish a computer with specialized software that recognizes speech, and let the student use grammar checks and spell checks on a computer.
2. Teach study skills, organizational skills, and learning strategies. Study various ways to assess a student's learning so that students with learning disabilities can show what they have learned.
3. Communicate and become partners with the parents.

Tips for Parents

1. Give your child with learning disabilities the opportunity to excel or just enjoy activities outside the classroom such as dancing, music, sports, or computers. Give your child opportunities to participate in areas of interest or/and talent. Encourage friendships with children whom they meet in these activities.
2. Help your child learn through areas of strengths. Talk with your child's teacher and observe for yourself how the child learns best. Establish a special place where the child can do homework and prioritize its importance.
3. Meet other parents who have children with learning disabilities. Share concerns and successes with others as well as advice and emotional support.
4. Help develop an educational plan for your child with the school. Establish a positive working relationship and communicate regularly with your teacher, discuss questions, and exchange information about successes and progress (NICHCY, 2002b).

Mental Retardation

Mental retardation is diagnosed by determining (a) the ability of a person's brain to learn, think, solve problems, and make sense of the world (called intelligence quotient [IQ] or intellectual functioning); and (b) whether the person has the skills he or she needs to live independently (called adaptive behavior, or adaptive functioning) (NICHCY, 2002a).

The average score of an IQ test is 100, and those classified as mentally retarded score 70 to 75 or below. To look at the skills needed to live independently, the child is compared to others of the same age. The adaptive skills are (a) daily living skills, dressing, using the bathroom, and feeding oneself; (b) communication skills—understanding what is said and being able to respond; and (c) social skills with adults, friends, and family (NICHCY, 2002a).

More than 614,000 children with mental retardation, ages 6 through 21, have need for special education. "One out of every 10 children who need special education has some form of mental retardation" (NICHCY, 2002a, p. 3).

Tips for Parents

- Learn about mental retardation in order to give your child the help he or she needs.
- Encourage your child to be independent, learning daily care skills such as dressing, grooming, eating, and using the bathroom.
- Give your child chores, but make the chores one in which she or he can be successful. Use them as teaching tools. For example, in setting the table have the child count out the number of napkins. Give the child one task at a time and help when assistance is needed.
- Praise, praise, praise when the child has worked hard and accomplished the task. Give feedback and build your child's abilities.
- Have your child join in outside activities such as scouts, sports, and recreational activities.
- Work with the school and your child's teacher. Apply what he or she is learning at school with activities at home and in the community (NICHCY, 2002a).
- Volunteer in the classroom or in another classroom. See how the teachers work with the children. Contribute to the success of the class by cooperating with the teacher.

Tips for Teachers

- Learn as much as you can about mental retardation. Check with organizations such as NICHCY and the Council for Exceptional Children.
- "Recognize that you can make an enormous difference in this student's life! Find out what the student's strengths and interests are, and emphasize them. Create opportunities for success" (NICHCY, 2002a, pp. 5–6).
- "Be as concrete as possible. Demonstrate what you mean rather than just giving verbal directions. Rather than just relating new information verbally, show a picture. And rather than just showing a picture, provide the student with hands-on materials and experiences and the opportunity to try things out" (NICHCY, 2002a, pp. 5–6). The greater the specificity, the greater the likelihood that the goals can be achieved (Burns, 2006).

- "Break longer, new tasks into small steps. Demonstrate the steps. Have the students do the steps, one at a time. Provide assistance as necessary" (NICHCY, 2002a, pp. 5–6). Make sure to acknowledge the student's strengths, as well as needs, when operationalizing steps to reach the student's goals (Burns, 2006).
- Have an IEP that will give the educational goals for the child. Check with the special education teacher for effective ways of teaching this student (NICHCY, 2002a). If possible, observe the special education staff to see for yourself what they do with the child.
- Work with the parents; make a partnership for the welfare of the student.

Implications of Disabilities on Learning

For years, the popular philosophy has been that we could best motivate young people in pleasing and attractive settings. The lesson would stimulate interest, be fun, and be relevant to the learner. Because students enjoyed doing it, they would be willing to learn. This is an excellent theory, and there is no quarrel with its premise. However, we have produced some youths who have not met their potential because, in real life, work is not always pleasing and for children with disabilities it is even more of a challenge to achieve.

Work involves diligence, tenacity, endurance, sacrifice, discipline, and repetition. It requires deep concentration and dedication. Work is *not* always fun. It is often boring! Most of us spend our lives doing work. We are willing to make this sacrifice not only for the extrinsic values of status, income, and fringe benefits but also for the intrinsic values of self-worth, dignity, and contribution to society. It is important to help children identify the intrinsic value of what they are learning. It is important for teachers and parents to communicate explicitly with children how what they are learning relates to what is important to them. This will help establish a pattern of life-long learning—a very valuable lesson indeed.

Children with disabilities often work harder and longer to accomplish what other children do easily and quickly. It is not always easy for them to accept this. It is hard for parents to refrain from expecting the school and the teacher to lighten the load, to expect less because the child has a disability. But this deprives the child of the feeling of accomplishment, of striving for and reaching full potential. The Individualized Education Program provides for the appropriate level of accommodation. Use this tool effectively to ensure that all exceptional children are given the opportunity to reach their goals.

Just as the parent feels warmth and joy at the progress of a child with a disability, so will the professional whose help and guidance leads to better family relations, improved schoolwork, and an ability to participate in life more fully for the child with a disability. It is a worthy and mighty undertaking.

CHILD FIND PROJECT

Concern about reaching parents and their children with disabilities resulted in the federal funding of the Child Find Project. In this program:

> All children with disabilities residing in the State, including children with disabilities attending private schools, regardless of the severity of their disabilities, and who are in need of special education and related services are identified, located, and evaluated and a practical method is developed and implemented to determine which children with disabilities are currently receiving needed special education and related services. (NICHCY, 1998; Smith, 2005)

Child Find is designated to locate children with disabilities using any feasible methods available such as door-to-door surveys, media campaigns, dissemination of information from the schools, and home visits by staff and/or volunteers (Cook et al., 2004; Lerner, Mardell-Czudnowski, & Goldenberg, 1987). Figure 10.3 summarizes the special education process starting from Child Find or other referrals to the placement and evaluation team meeting.

In recent years other names such as Count Your Kid In and Make a Difference have been used to designate this type of program. In many cases this program is funded by both federal and state governments. Preschool screenings have been very successful in finding children in need and informing parents that help is available.

EVALUATION

When parents believe that their child needs special assistance, or if a child is identified through Child Find, the subsequent evaluations must be evaluated in a fair and unbiased manner. Figure 10.3 summarizes the education process. Parents must be informed and must give their consent to have the original evaluation.

For initial evaluations:

- Notice must be provided to evaluate a child, and informed consent of parents must be obtained.
- No single procedure shall be the sole criterion for determining eligibility.
- The child must be assessed in all areas of suspected disabilities.
- Determination of eligibility shall be made by a team of qualified professionals and the child's parents. Children are not eligible if the only deciding factor is a limited English proficiency or a lack of math or reading instruction (National Association of State Directors of Special Education, 1997; Turnbull, 2005).

Figure 10.4 illustrates the special education cycle. For insight and a detailed discussion of the major issues in education for children with disabilities see *Free Appropriate Public Education: The Law and Children with Disabilities* (Turnbull & Turnbull, 1998; Turnbull, Turnbull, Stowe & Wilcox, 2000). The text discusses the law as well as the zero reject principle, nondiscriminatory evaluation, individualized appropriate education, least restrictive environment, procedural due process, and parent participation.

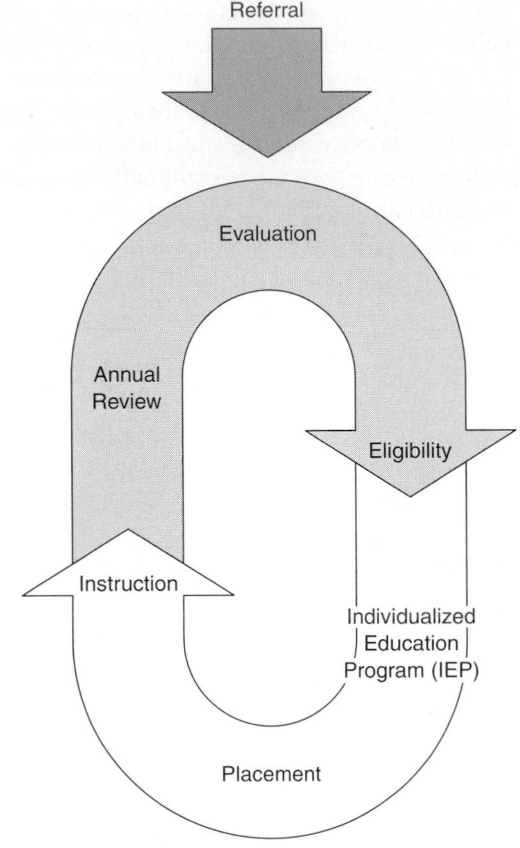

FIGURE 10.4 The special education cycle.

Source: Utah Parent Center, Salt Lake City, UT.

A Summary of the Special Education Process

Child Find/Referral	Referral of child for diagnosis may be formal or informal; may come from parent or from others.
Assessment/Diagnosis	Multidisciplinary, non-biased comprehensive battery of tests. (Complete reevaluation for classification required every 3 years.)
Classification (includes parent)	Team reviews assessment/diagnostic data and classifies for special education based on test results. Parent signature required.
IEP Meeting (includes parent)	Individualized Educational Plan developed by team. Must be updated yearly, but team or parent may request as needed. Parent signature required.
Placement (includes parent)	Team decides placement based on the IEP. Parent signature required.
Evaluation Team Meeting	Team evaluates child's total special education program and (includes parent) progress at least yearly. (Teacher evaluates daily as child works on short-term objectives.)

FIGURE 10.3 A summary of the special education process.

Source: Utah Parent Center, Salt Lake City, UT.

REACHING INFANTS AND TODDLERS WITH DISABILTIES

The importance of development while a child is an infant or a toddler is increasingly recognized. All children require a nurturing and positive environment beginning at birth. The importance of attachment and brain development was discussed in Chapter 1. Recently developed brain-scan techniques have made it possible to see how synapses and connections develop during the first years of life. If this is a critical time for children without disabilities, one can immediately recognize how important it is for a child with a disability. This is a period in which great change and remediation can be made.

Child Find, discussed in the previous section, is one method of reaching parents of infants or toddlers with disabilities. Health agencies, doctors, visiting nurses, and hospitals are important sources in finding infants who need services.

PART C OF IDEA 97 AND 2004

Part C of the Individuals with Disabilities Education Act Amendments of 1997 and 2004 focuses on infants and toddlers with disabilities. An at-risk infant or toddler is an individual younger than 3 who would be at risk of experiencing substantial developmental delay if early intervention services were not provided to the individual. Each state sets up its own program, but the program is expected to have the following:

1. A comprehensive child-find system, including a system to make referrals to service providers.
2. An Individualized Family Service Plan, including service coordination.
3. A comprehensive, multidisciplinary evaluation of the infant or toddler with a disability.
4. A family-directed identification of the needs of each family with an at-risk infant or toddler to assist the child's development.
5. A public awareness program that focuses on early identification of infants and toddlers with disabilities. This emphasizes that hospitals and physicians need to be provided with information about the services so that parents will know about their availability.
6. A comprehensive system of personnel development. Qualified personnel include special educators, speech-language pathologists and audiologists, occupational therapists, physical therapists, psychologists, social workers, nurses, nutritionists, family therapists, orientation and mobility specialists, and pediatricians and other types of physicians. Part C also includes the training of paraprofessional and primary

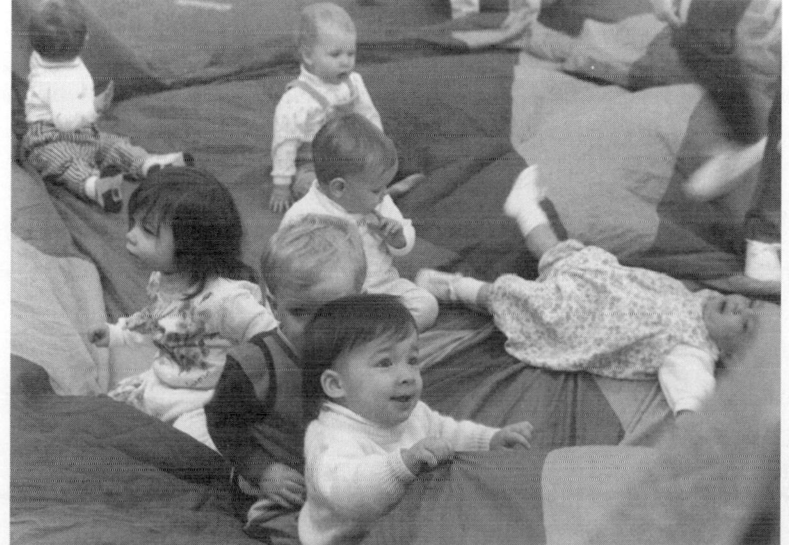

Anne Vega/Merrill

Play and interaction with others are important for infants and small children.

referral sources—recruitment and retention of early education service providers; early intervention providers, fully and appropriately qualified to provide early intervention; personnel to work in rural and inner-city areas; and personnel to coordinate transition services for infants and toddlers to preschool or other appropriate services. Nothing prohibits the use of paraprofessionals and assistants who are appropriately trained and supervised, and states were given 3 years to develop the qualified staff.

These services are provided at no cost to families, except where federal or state law provides for a system of payment by families, including a schedule of sliding fees.

Identifying the Infant and Toddler with Disabilities

The phrase *infant or toddler with a disability* means any child under 3 who needs intervention services because the child is at risk of substantial developmental delays if intervention is not provided to the child. The areas of delay may be in cognitive development, physical development, communicative development, social or emotional development, adaptive development, or a diagnosed physical or mental condition that would probably cause developmental delay (National Association of State Directors of Special Education, 1997).

Conditions that are associated with significant delays in development include:

- Chromosomal conditions (such as Down syndrome, Fragile X)
- Congenital syndromes or conditions (such as spina bifida)
- Sensory impairments (such as hearing or visual impairments)
- Metabolic disorders (such as PKU or lactic acidosis)
- Prenatal and/or perinatal infections or conditions (such as AIDS, CMV, or exposure to toxic substances)
- Significant medical problems (such as cerebral palsy)
- Babies weighing less than 1,200 grams (less than 2 lbs., 10 oz.)
- Postnatal conditions (such as attachment disorder) (Colorado Department of Education, Early Childhood Initiatives, the Arapahoe Early Childhood Network, PEAK Parent Center, the Colorado Consortium of Intensive Care Nurseries, 1997, p. 3)

THE INDIVIDUALIZED FAMILY SERVICE PLAN AND FAMILY SURVEY

The Individualized Family Service Plan (IFSP) differs from the IEP in format because it is designed to focus on programs for infants and young children. IDEA 97 and 2004 places preschoolers under the school system and does not differentiate between preschooler programs and elementary and secondary programs, which leave the IEP as the format to decide on the child's program. If it appears that a family would benefit from services, it seems appropriate to continue to use the IFSP for that family as was indicated in previous IDEA legislation. Each state may make its own determination. The intent is the same—to serve individuals with disabilities. The IFSP gives attention to family concerns and needs as well as services for the child.

The IFSP is designed to be flexible, family-focused, and unintrusive for families. It includes the following elements:

1. A statement of the infant's or toddler's present levels of attainment in physical or motor, sensory, cognitive, communication, social–emotional, and adaptive development. The law requires that this statement be based on objective criteria acceptable to both parent and provider.
2. A statement of the family's resources, priorities, and concerns related to enhancing the development of the child with special needs and/or related to broader family issues.
3. A statement of the major outcomes expected for the child and family, including how and when the team will evaluate whether progress is being made and whether changes or updates in outcomes or services are needed.

4. A statement of specific supports and services necessary to meet the unique strengths and needs of the infant/toddler and family, including options and a variety of all community supports and services available.
5. A statement describing the environments in which services will be provided and the location of services.
6. Dates when services will start and how long services will be used.
7. The name of the service coordinator. This person is responsible for seeing that the IFSP is carried out and coordinating the process among all involved parties.
8. The steps to be taken to support the child's transition to home, community, or preschool services, if appropriate. (Colorado Department of Education et al., 1997, p. 7)

The IFSP is evaluated once a year, and the family is provided a review of the plan at 6-month intervals or more often, if appropriate, based on the infant's and family's need.

A number of states have established statewide mandated forms for IFSPs. Examples of these forms, and guidance for completing them, can be found at www.nectac.org/topics/families/stateifsp.asp. There are many commonalities, however, there are a few specific individual differences.

Procedural Rights for Infants and Toddlers

Each state has flexibility in how it sets up Part C for Infants and Toddlers, IDEA 97, and 2004. Most programs should have the following components:

First, a program should have *multidisciplinary evaluations.* A team consisting of the family and two or more qualified professionals looks at how the child is doing in the following areas: physical or motor, sensory, cognitive, communication, social–emotional, and adaptive development. This evaluation is the procedure used to determine initial and continuing eligibility for services.

Second, an *Individualized Family Service Plan* (IFSP) is needed, consisting of a team of people, including family members, who jointly plan supports and services and identify resources that will meet the family's concerns and priorities about the child's development. This plan is documented.

Other components include a *service coordinator,* who works with the family to identify resources, supports, and services and coordinates agencies and people involved. Parents are given *prior notice* about any changes that service providers want to make, and parents are given the chance to say "yes" or "no" to those changes.

Information, both written and spoken, will be given in the child's native language or, if that is impossible, will be translated orally or by another mode of communication so that parents understand the information. Parents have the right to accept or deny service and must have *informed consent. Confidentiality* is ensured by keeping private any information about the child and the family. Parents will have *access to records* with the ability to change incorrect information.

Support and services are provided in a *natural environment,* the environment typically used for children who are the same age but do not have disabilities. Parents will also have *access to services,* helped by the service coordinator.

Parents may use an *appeals process* to resolve any disagreements they have with providers. The appeals process can involve mediation and due process. Finally, *mediation* will be used to find a solution satisfactory to all involved in the dispute. Due process is employed in resolving complaints (Colorado Department of Education et al., 1997).

CHILDREN WITH DISABILITIES IN HEAD START AND CHILD CARE

In 1974, with the passage of the Community Services Act (PL 96-644), Congress stipulated that 10 percent of Head Start's enrollment must be children with disabilities. Head Start developed procedures and policies to answer the needs of these children by offering individualized and appropriate education. When Early Head Start was initiated, the same requirement for 10 percent enrollment of children with disabilities was mandated for that program.

The Local Education Agency (LEA) is responsible for ensuring that services are provided to children with disabilities from birth to 21 years of age, but it is not responsible for providing all services. IDEA's policy is to ensure that all children with disabilities beginning as soon as diagnosed for infants and toddlers, and continuing through age 21 have the right to a free, appropriate education in either public or private institutions. This includes Early Head Start, Head Start and private child-care facilities. Early Head Start and Head Start facilities were directed to use IDEA's definition of children with disabilities.

The coordinator of services for children with disabilities must have a plan containing: (a) procedures for timely screening; (b) procedures for making referrals to the LEA for evaluation; (c) procedures to determine whether there is a need for special education and related services for a child as early as the child's third birthday; (d) provisions to ensure accessibility of the facilities and appropriate special furniture, equipment, and materials as needed; and (e) transition of children from Early Head Start to Head Start or into other appropriate preschool placements.

The Early Head Start and Head Start's service delivery plans must include options to meet the needs and take into consideration the strengths of each child based upon the IFSP or IEP so that a continuum of services available from various agencies is considered.

Eligibility requirements are similar to those cited in the discussion of IDEA 2004, with the addition of developmental delays. These include health impairment, hearing impairment, orthopedic impairment, visual impairment including blindness, learning disabilities, autism, and traumatic brain injury. The developmental delays are in physical development, cognitive development, communicative development, social–emotional development, or adaptive development as discussed in IDEA 97 and 2004's Part C for Infants and Toddlers.

Parent Involvement in Early Head Start and Head Start

Parents must be involved in the program for their child. The Early Head Start and Head Start staff must:

1. Support parents of children with disabilities
2. Provide information to parents on how to foster their child's development
3. Provide opportunities for parents to observe large-group, small-group, and individual activities described in their child's IFSP or IEP
4. Provide follow-up assistance and activities to reinforce program activities at home
5. Refer parents to groups of parents of children with similar disabilities who can provide peer support
6. Inform parents of their rights under IDEA
7. Inform parents of resources that may be available from the Supplemental Security Income (SSI) Program, the Early and Periodic Screening,

Anthony Magnacca/Merrill

Parents are receptive to open and direct communication.

Diagnosis and Treatment (EPSDT) Program, and other sources as well as assist them with initial efforts to access such resources

8. Identify needs (caused by the disability) of siblings and other family members
9. Provide information that might help prevent disabilities among younger siblings
10. Build parents' confidence, skill, and knowledge in accessing resources and advocating to meet the needs of their children (*Federal Register*, 1993, p. 5509)

Special Quest

In 1997, a special partnership was begun between the Hilton Foundation and Early and Migrant Head Start programs. It is the first public/private partnership with the Administration for Children, Youth, and Families. This partnership was established to improve services to infants and toddlers with disabilities. From 1997 to 2004, 250 teams of service providers to include Early Head Start administrators, teachers, early intervention specialists, parents and community members met for 4-year intervals to receive training, develop plans and monitor improvements to the service delivery systems in their respective communities. In February 2004, the Conrad Hilton Foundation was given an award by the Administration for Children, Youth, and Families (ACF) for its contribution to infants and toddlers (Press release, ACF Press Office, February 5, 2004).

PARENT–SCHOOL PARTNERSHIPS

Helping the Young Child Develop

Infants and toddlers need opportunities to interact with the environment, including parents and others who respond to their cues. Developmental delays need special consideration, but very young children in particular benefit from a nurturing and responsive home or child-care center. Individual concerns for such things as autism, Fragile X, and Down syndrome need to be addressed in relation to appropriate intervention. Because there is not enough space in this text to include all the information and recommendations, care providers should contact the Special Education Early Childhood program and the parent center for children with disabilities in their home state. Call or write the National Information Center for Children and Youth with Disabilities (NICHCY). (See the end of the chapter for Web sites.) NICHCY can furnish information on each area of the child's disability and can also furnish the names of other references.

Children ages 3 to 5 should attend a good, developmentally appropriate class that has supplemental intervention that meets the needs of each child. They need an appropriate nurturing environment where language, movement, creativity, and discovery support their physical, social–emotional, and cognitive development.

Communicate with the Child

Communication is how children learn their language, and they must be given opportunities to practice that skill. Talk naturally so the child can understand and develop language. When your child talks, listen. How do you feel when you talk to someone who will not listen to what you are saying? Most adults don't waste time talking to people who do not listen to them. Children don't either. If you want your children to express themselves, let them initiate conversations and respond by giving them your attention.

Give Praise and Encouragement

Praise reinforces learning and behaviors, and encouragement helps children continue working. Let children know when you are pleased with what they are doing. We all work for rewards, and praise is one of the most important rewards you can give. Be patient with children. It takes many trials and many errors to learn skills. Adults forget over the years how it was to be a child. If the situation gets out of hand and you become impatient or angry, leave the situation, do something else, and come back to it when you are in control of yourself.

Never Compare

Don't compare your children with others. Allow for individuality. Every child is different, with special characteristics that make up his or her personality and no one else's.

Offer Enrichment Activities

Help increase your children's knowledge by taking them to places such as zoos, libraries, or airports. Use television as a learning tool by selecting appropriate programs, viewing them together, and discussing them afterward. Another learning experience that is often overlooked is the family mealtime. Sharing experiences, talking about interesting subjects, and improving conversational skills can happen around the dining table.

Encourage Play

Play is as important for children with disabilities as it is for children without. It is especially important for children who are deaf or blind. These disabilities do not interfere with the natural phenomenon of learning about the world and growing and developing while doing so. Activities that are appropriate for normal babies are appropriate for the infant with disabilities, too. Clapping hands, cooing, playing peekaboo, and cuddling are necessary and helpful. Provide the baby or small child with objects to grasp. Firm cushions may be used for crawling babies. Rock children back and forth or play with them on a swing so they will have the experiences needed to develop. Babies and small children must have the opportunity to think, experiment, investigate, and learn about their environment. Of course, infants should never be left unsupervised.

Read and Talk Together

Read to your children, have them read to you, and listen to them read. Let them tell you about what they have been reading. Magazines, newspapers, comics, and books can all be used to increase a child's knowledge and reading ability.

For school-age children add the following:

Develop Good Work Habits

Set the stage for good homework habits. A well-lighted place to study that is quiet, with room for books, pencils, and papers, helps. Schedule regular home study.

Get Sufficient Rest

Set a bedtime and stick to it. Children need a lot of rest to be able to do good mental work. Rest is necessary for proper growth.

Attend School Regularly

See that your child attends school regularly and on time. Visit with teachers to learn how your child is getting along in school and listen to what they have to tell you about your child.

HOW PARENTS CAN HELP THE SCHOOL-AGE CHILD AT HOME

For teachers and parents alike, the goal is to have all children reach their full potential. Students with disabilities may need extra help at home to keep up their schoolwork. Special tutoring by someone outside the family might be very effective. If the parents are planning to work with their child, the following suggestions should help guide them.

What Parents Can Do

Know your child. You are your child's first teacher and often know better about his or her capabilities than anyone else. Communicate your hopes and plans to your child's teacher.

Actively participate in your child's school. Treat all students and other members of the school community with respect (Educational Resources Information Center, National Library of Education, Office of Educational Research and Improvement, U.S. Department of Education, 1996, p. 32).

First, Visit with the Teacher

Explain that you want to help your child at home with schoolwork. Ask the teacher to explain the material the class will be covering and how assignments should be done. Try to get a schedule for assignments if your child doesn't already have one.

Set a Definite Time for the Child

Set a time to work with your child. Go over the day's experiences and listen to how your child felt about them. Discuss how the assignments can be completed and turned in on time.

Monitor Progress

Keep a record of the assignments handed in and the scores received, so you can tell how your child is doing in school. If the grades are low or you do not understand them, visit with the teacher to find out exactly what the teacher expects.

Promote Success

Your child will be more likely to succeed in home–school collaboration if you do the following:

1. Use a pleasant, firm approach that says, "Yes, this must be done, and we'll do it as quickly and pleasantly as we can."
2. Set up a reward system. Few of us will work hard at a job we do not receive satisfaction from or get paid for. Your praise and approval are the students' pay for a job well done. If they get scolded all the time, they are unlikely to want to work for another scolding.
3. Make sure your child has time for work, play, and rest. There has to be some work, play, and rest in everyone's life. If we do too much of one, the other two will suffer. Parents are the best ones to determine how to keep this balance.

Parents may be the most important force in seeking the correct educational placement for their children. It is important that they are aware of the various ways their children may be served. Different labels for placement may exist in different regions. The *interrelated classroom* is a popular term for a classroom in which children are placed according to their level of academic achievement rather than according to their diagnosed disabilities.

Parent Involvement in the Classroom

In addition to an advocacy role, parents should also take an active role in the education of their children. Parent involvement in the classroom is an asset that is often overlooked or mismanaged. The parent is involved in planning the IEP and has the right of input and due process. Although parents are aware of these rights, many probably do not feel self-assured enough to fully capitalize on them. They rely on the teacher, the administrator, or the psychologist to keep them informed of what they, as parents, should be doing. Many parents believe the teacher, or some other person in an authority role, knows what is best and that it is up to that person to decide whether the parent can be of assistance. The counterpart is the teacher who fears parent involvement, perhaps because of misconceptions or a bad experience. Thus, there may be a lack of communication or overt action that prevents application of an influential force—the parents—for the education of the student with disabilities.

An Example of Parent Involvement

Precise Early Education for Children with Handicaps (PEECH) involves parents by offering conferences, group meetings, home visits, classroom observations, and a lending library, as well as by being receptive to their questions and suggestions. This program integrates children with disabilities in a classroom with children who have no special education needs. The children, ages 3 to 6, attend the program half a day, 5 days a week (National Dissemination Association & National Diffusion Network, 1993).

Merle Karnes, director of the project, emphasizes the importance of family involvement and the necessity of skillful staff interaction with parents. She finds that parents are interested in their children with disabilities and want to learn how to work with them. Karnes offers the following advice to the professional educator working with these parents:

To ensure success in your work with parents, give specific directions and objective feedback on their contributions. Respect them as individuals and be flexible in responding to their needs and value systems. If parents are included in decision making, if the program makes sense to them, if their goals and values are compatible with those of the school, if they are approached as individuals and are convinced that you, the professional, are interested in helping them, they will join you in developing their abilities and contributing their time.

Parents can work effectively in the classroom, and they will extend their newfound understanding to other members of the family. They may become so knowledgeable and skillful that they can reach out to help other parents of children with disabilities.

How Parents Can Support Children's Schoolwork at Home

Parents may find that the cassette recorder is one of the most valuable instruments available in helping the student learn at home or at school. With a recorder, parents can put exactly what they want in a lesson and determine its format. A set of headphones further enhances the learning situation.

The cassette recorder is excellent for recording spelling words and for having children practice taking spelling tests as they would in a classroom. If the children can read the words, have them record the words on the tape and take them as in a spelling lesson. When the students listen to the words, they automatically monitor the sound of the word, the inflection, and the phrasing. Corrections are made unconsciously as the mind corrects errors that the ear hears.

The cassette recorder is also valuable for taping messages. It is particularly useful for giving directions. Instructions on how to set a table, mix pudding, or make a bed can be recorded to give a child valuable experience in learning to follow directions.

Another important use is letting children record a reading lesson on the tape and then asking them to correct their own errors. A chart of the time, number of words read, and errors made can be kept to show progress.

Suggestions for Putting Lessons on Cassettes

1. Make the length of your lesson 5 minutes shorter than the period you want the lesson to last. This gives flexibility for handling interruptions.
2. Arrange the tasks sequentially. Check the order by doing the lesson once yourself.
3. Speak more slowly than your normal rate of speech. Children with learning disabilities do not process words and thoughts as quickly as most people do. Check to see if children know what the tape is saying by asking them to repeat what they hear. Be careful not to ask if they understand the information. They may think they do, but testing may reveal they don't.
4. Include a set of questions at the end of the taped lesson for immediate review of the material. (This is also helpful for the teacher with students who have missed reading lessons or lectures.)

A Few Things to Remember

When teaching children with disabilities, teachers and parents should follow these suggestions:

1. Encourage correct responses—wrong responses have to be relearned.
2. Use tests as learning instruments. More learning takes place when tests are answered and corrected soon after being given.
3. Learning occurs more effectively when more channels of learning are involved. Involving the visual and hearing channels is more effective than involving just vision or just hearing.
4. Putting what has been learned into action through verbal or physical reaction increases the learning experience.
5. Learning is reinforced by repetition, that is, reviewing often at first and then again at varying intervals.
6. Begin with concrete items and move gradually to teaching abstract concepts. Make sure to model expectations for children that need to learn by observing before they can internalize expectations.
7. Ask the child to help make a list of to do's so the child begins to practice organizing what needs to be done, and the most efficient order in which to do them. The child can dictate them, or record them, if writing is a problem. Checking off completed tasks is very rewarding.
8. Color-code folders at home and school to help children organize their materials: homework, worksheets, notes, and so forth. Make sure to put the folders in the same place so children can consistently get and put their materials away.
9. Establish a consistent schedule so children can pace themselves and can anticipate how much time it takes to complete tasks. Time management is an issue, whether a child has disabilities or not! Help the child become aware of time spent doing tasks by using an egg or clock timer.
10. Children with disabilities, like all children, need down time. It is important to plan unstructured time that allows the child to make constructive leisure choices. Life is about balancing needs, and an overworked child will be resentful and unproductive. Children should be encouraged to work hard and play hard.

COMMUNICATION BETWEEN PROFESSIONALS AND PARENTS OF CHILDREN WITH DISABILITIES

Teachers may be confronted with dispirited parents experiencing considerable doubt, confusion, and anxiety about their child with a disability and their reactions to her. A troubled parent may enlist the help of

Silver Burdett Ginn

Helping children requires a partnership between family and school.

a teacher to discuss problems that are related to a child's performance at school or other, more personal concerns that bear a relationship to the child. A parent's inability to cope effectively with a child is often a motivating factor in seeking help. (Seligman, 2000, p. 9)

It takes skill, tact, and ingenuity for a professional to communicate with people who have different needs. Mistakes to avoid include "talking down" to the parents, assuming an understanding exists where in fact none may, and using jargon or technical language.

Parents react differently and sometimes unpredictably to the birth or the diagnosis of a child with a disability. Reactions are a result of feelings; parents may experience frustration, hurt, fear, guilt, disappointment, ambivalence, or despair. For the professional to work effectively with parents of children with disabilities, there must be an ability to recognize these feelings and a willingness to honor them (Chinn, 1984; Chinn et al., 1978). It is also very important to choose the best words to assist in conveying an understanding of parents' feelings. People First Language (Snow, 2006) offers suggestions for phrases and terms that can facilitate lines of communication.

It is usually easier for the professional to view the child with a disability objectively than it is for the parents. The professional deals with the child day to day or only occasionally, whereas the parents deal with the child before and after school and on weekends. Parents of a child with a severe disability may be faced with a lifetime of caring for the child. There is a need to offer parents relief from the constant care that is often required. Foster parents, substitute grandparents, and knowledgeable volunteers are becoming more available to give these parents helpful breaks (Chinn, 1984; Chinn et al., 1978).

Parents are receptive to open and direct communication. Messages should be clear and in language the parents can understand. The teacher or professional will deal with a wide variance of language efficiency, so they should acquaint themselves with the parents' backgrounds. Listen to the words parents use to guide how to best communicate information about their child. The professional should also be receptive to clues from the parents to determine if the message is being received and accommodated as intended. Ask a leading question to let the parents express their understanding of the topic being discussed. You might be surprised to find the interpretations are different from what you intended.

The professional should include the support and consultation of the medical and theological professions if the parents exhibit a need for these services. Be aware of the agencies and organizations that assist parents and professional workers in the community as well as national organizations.

Communication Sources

Although two-way communication is essential, important tips and information can be relayed to parents through books, newsletters, personal letters, and charts. These can be used in conjunction with a conference, or they can be separate forms of communication.

Sources for learning more about communicating with parents include Turnbull and Turnbull's *Families, Professionals, and Exceptionality: A Special Partnership* (1997) and Turnbull and Turnbull's *Parents Speak Out: Then and Now* (1985). *Two-way Talking with Parents of Special Children, A Process of Positive Communication* (Chinn et al., 1978) discusses in-depth communication, semantics, transactional analysis, stroking, family interactions, and transactions. Case studies may be read in *Case Studies About Children and Adolescents with Special Needs* (Halmhuber & Beauvais, 2002) and *The Parental Voice* (Holzberg & Walsh-Burton, 1996). Both books describe the trials and concerns of individuals who have a variety of disabilities.

Mullins (1987) chose 60 books written by parents of children with disabilities and analyzed them for issues and concerns that were prominent in their lives. Parents of children with disabilities paint a picture of parenthood as one with "exceptional parenting, with its attendant special problems, pain, and pleasure" (p. 31).

Although the authors of the books presented their concerns in a variety of ways and used different approaches, the same four themes were repeated: (a) realistic appraisal of the disability, (b) extraordinary demands on families, (c) extraordinary emotional stress, and (d) resolution:

1. The parents who wrote the books were realistic about the disabilities. Many shared their manner of coping and information about their child's disability. Mullins pointed out Jablow's (1982) book about her child with Down syndrome, Parks's (1982) discussion on the autistic child, and the Turnbulls' book, *Parents Speak Out* (1985).
2. Rearing a child with a disability affects the whole family and in much greater depth than one that has not had a child with a disability can imagine. Some siblings worry that they might have a child with a disability themselves. They also have to share a greater amount of their parents' time and may find the obligation of caring for the child overwhelming. Parents have greater difficulty deciding on the best way to handle the child with a disability, and many marriages fail. The books show that parents use creative ways to handle the challenge, but having a child with a disability places "extraordinary demands on the physical and financial resources of the family" (Mullins, 1987, p. 31).

   Concerns included inaccurate or ambiguous diagnosis in which families have had to search for the answers to their concerns. A great deal of insensitivity to the parents was exhibited by some professionals who worked with them. Some parents had to work for years to get their children placed in appropriate schools. On the other hand, parents were forever grateful for professionals who were helpful and caring.
3. Parents express emotional ambivalence and grieve for the ideal child they did not have. Children may also wish for what could have been. Sometimes parents blame themselves for their child's disability. Parents who live with a child who has a degenerative condition are under constant stress about the future. These intense emotional concerns, joined with the physical and financial stress on the family, have an extraordinary effect on family life.
4. After gaining insights and living with their child with a disability, most parents believe their lives were "enriched and made more meaningful" by their child (Mullins, 1987, p. 32). Visit the www.fathersnetwork.org for expressions of feelings about being the father of a child with disabilities.

Additional Ways to Reach Parents

Newsletters

Use a newsletter to offer tips for parents. There are things that all parents can do to help their children in school that are important to parents of both children with disabilities and without.

Letters

Letters are another effective means of communicating an idea or message to parents. Letters should state the concern, then present methods or suggestions for dealing with or changing the situation, include any guidelines or datelines that are pertinent, and finally, end with a conclusion and an offer for assistance if needed.

There are as many ways to write the message you wish to convey as there are teachers. Each will need to adapt the contents to the concerns of the situation.

Reaching Out with Programs

When parents are confronted with the task of rearing a child with a disability, they need both emotional support and specific information. One program for fathers of infants with disabilities illustrates an innovative way to reach out to parents (Delaney, Meyer, & Ward, 1980). The first step is the establishment of attachment between father and infant. The second step is the development of parenting qualities in the father. This ability is acquired when the father is able to read cues and understand the baby's behavior. The cues and behavior patterns of a child with a disability may not be the same as those of a typically developing infant. If misinterpreted by the parents, a certain behavior may confuse and frustrate the parents, causing them eventually to withdraw from meaningful relationships. The end result may be that the attachment process between parent and child is disturbed.

The state of Washington emphasizes fathers and their children with disabilities. The Fathers Network Web site, www.fathersnetwork.org, shares information on fathers and their children. Included are current news articles from sources such as the *Seattle Times*, *Seattle Post Intelligencer*, the *New York Times*, and the Associated Press that provide information pertinent to fathers with children with disabilities. Topics include: planning for the future of children with disabilities, experiences of siblings of children with disabilities, and personal experiences of fathers coping with their children's disabilities. The Fathers Network provides resources for fathers, family members, and care providers. Also on the Web site are current articles that deal with issues of fathers as caregivers. An events calendar list upcoming conferences and seminars offered in Washington state, the Northwest, the rest of the United States, and Canada.

PARENTAL REACTIONS TO DISABILITIES

Parents of a child with a disability typically go through a series of steps or stages in dealing with their concerns. First, they become aware of and recognize the basic problem. Then they become occupied with trying to discover a cause and later begin to look for a cure. Acceptance is the last stage (Chinn, 1984; Chinn et al., 1978). The usual progression to acceptance may vary, but most parents experience guilt and grief before they reach acceptance and compassion.

Parents' Initial Response

Denial

Parents who deny the existence of a child's disability feel threatened. Their security is uncertain, and they are defending their egos or self-concepts. This is a difficult reaction for the professional to deal with. Time, patience, and support will help these parents see that much can be gained through helping children with disabilities realize their potentials.

Projection of Blame

A common reaction is to blame the situation on something or someone else—the psychologist, the teacher, the doctor. Often parents' statements begin with "If only. . . . " Again, patience, willingness to listen to the parent, and tact will help the professional deal with a potentially hostile situation.

Fear

The parents may not be acquainted with the cause or characteristics of the disability. They may have unfounded suspicions or erroneous information, which causes anxiety or fear. Information, in an amount that the parent can handle, is the best remedy for fear of the unknown. A positive communication process helps the professional judge the time to offer additional information.

Guilt

Parents' feelings of guilt—thinking they should have done something differently or believing the disability is retribution for a misdeed—are difficult to deal with. The professional can help by encouraging guilt-ridden parents to channel their energies into more productive activities after genuine communication has been established.

Grief

Grief is a natural reaction to a situation that brings extreme pain and disappointment. Parents who have not been able to accept their child as having a disability may become grief-stricken. In such a case it is necessary to allow the parents to go through a healing process before they can learn about their child and how the child can develop.

Withdrawal

Being able to withdraw and collect oneself is a healthy, necessary response. It is when one begins to shun others, avoid situations, and maintain isolation that it becomes potentially damaging.

Rejection

There are many reasons for rejection and many ways of exhibiting it. It may be subtle, feigning acceptance, or it may be open and hostile. Some forms of rejection are failing to recognize positive attributes, setting unrealistic goals, escaping by desertion, or presenting a favorable impression to others while inwardly rejecting the child.

Acceptance

Finally, the reaction of parents may be acceptance that the child has a disability—acceptance of the child and of themselves. This is the goal and realization of maturity. The parents and the child can then grow and develop into stronger, wiser, and more compassionate human beings (Chinn, 1984; Chinn et al., 1978).

Although parents may have some of these feelings, one of the most important components in handling their feelings is the knowledge that there are things they can do to help their child. When parents are able to focus on the positive and able to design a program that will enable their child to develop to full potential, they have a challenge and an answer to the crisis that they may have felt initially. Too often, professionals and friends respond with sympathy rather than suggestions for ways to face the future and meet the challenges.

Students Speak Out

The National Council on Disability (2002) asked youth to respond to questions about their school experiences in IDEA. The questions included were:

1. When you think about your years in school, what comes to mind about special education and related services?
2. If your school was reluctant to provide special education services because of financial concerns, which services were disputed? Did you receive the services that your IEP team said you needed?
3. If the discipline procedures under IDEA need to be clearer, how would you change the way the discipline policy is explained to students and their parents?
4. How could schools do a better job before students leave high school to help you and other young people with disabilities prepare in areas such as: Employment, Transportation, Housing, Managing my finances, Health care, Independent living, Connecting to resources in my community, and/or Postsecondary (college or vocational) education? (pp. 8–9)

One student's experience:

> I am a 12-year-old who has been diagnosed with Chronic Fatigue Syndrome (CFS) and Postural Orthostatic Tachycardia Syndrome (POTS). I am currently finishing the 6th grade and have been ill with these illnesses for most of my life. By the 3rd grade I was unable to attend school at all and my parents worked with the school to have me classified as Other Health Impaired so that I could receive services under the IDEA. The problem that they had initially was that my test scores showed that I was at the high end of my ability, even though my education was being severely affected by the illness. . . . I have been very fortunate in my school system because once my eligibility was accepted the CSE has been very supportive. They have been very open to our suggestions and those of the tutor to services that may benefit me, and have stuck by my IEP in following through with services. My parents have had to maintain an active role and remind the school of things we needed, such as extra textbooks, or use of a word processor, but the school has accommodated when reminded. Individual teachers have been our great allies and our worst enemies. If they try to understand my illness and limitations they bend over backwards to help me out. But some teachers have been totally unwilling to teach me via a tutor. They will not grade my work and resist modifying my workload. We have been fortunate to be able to find ways to work around

> these situations. . . . Most of my teachers have been willing to offer help in modifying and consolidating the workload to a manageable level for me to complete. (pp. 11–12, 17)

While not all students interviewed had positive experiences, positive communication that acknowledges an understanding of a student's experience can make a significant impact on a student's performance.

PARENTS SHARE THEIR FEELINGS

Suzanne Crane is the mother of a child with a disability. She has shared her feelings and thoughts about this so that others may benefit from her experiences.

> Having a handicapped child was not what we expected. I remember the feelings likened to having run into a brick wall, the heartbreak of having a broken doll and no one able to fix her. The uncertainties were even more of a struggle due to fragmented medical care and follow-up on her development. We were told of the absolute and immediate necessity of finding special help for her and then sent home with no guidance as to who and where we could turn to for this help. However, through community support and the efforts of other parents we were able to secure services for our child. I do not believe our daughter would be walking or talking now if we hadn't persevered in this. She presently is 7 years old and being served by special education in the public school system. However, I will always crusade for the infants, toddlers, and preschoolers with special needs and their families who are faced with the overwhelming situation of no help available.
>
> I feel that we are more like other families than set apart. I have seen other children accept her with open arms, bridging the gap. Our daughter's celebrative spirit, her love for music, her essence have affected us, her parents, and our second child in positive ways. She has shaped our perspective on the world and life. She has taught us to be happy. We hope that her future will enhance her internal spirit and allow her to be accepted by others. (Crane, 1986)

In 1994, Crane offered an update on her child:

> My daughter is now 15, a friendly, outgoing young lady with much promise. She will be able to live semi-independently in the community. It is my hope that her future will be happy and fulfilling. Our family focus is on vocational skills, community work experience, and supportive community living. (Crane, 1994)

Parents of Twin Boys with Cerebral Palsy Share

Bruce and Kelly Stahlman did not expect their twins to be born 3 months early at 28 weeks gestation.

BRUCE'S LETTER

Relativity.

> *Whenever we discuss speed or velocity (an object's speed and its direction of motion), we must specify precisely who or what is doing the measuring . . . each observer feels stationary and perceives the other as moving. Each perspective is understandable and justifiable. As there is symmetry between the two space-dwellers, there is, on quite fundamental grounds, no way of saying one perspective is "right" and the other "wrong." Each perspective has an equal claim on truth.* (Greene, 2000, p. 28)

Special needs kids weren't visible during the 60s and 70's when I progressed through public school. Once in a while, you'd see bus No. 16 making an afternoon run, shorter than all the other buses and rumored to be carrying retards. We didn't really understand what that meant, of course, any more than we understood what it meant to be Negro or Jewish or Communist. We gave no thought, shallow or otherwise, to what having a disabled sibling or child might imply.

They'd always been out there, unseen, hidden away by parents and convention, probably ashamed or afraid. More likely out of exhaustion and confusion from having nowhere to turn, no one to help and no one to empathize out of personal experience.

Mike's brother, Tom, had Down's Syndrome. Strong as an ox, he was never without his beloved tinker toy wheel on the end of a coat hanger. We'd always see him while playing cards in Mike's basement. There was a sense of loss, years later, when I heard Tom had passed away. I wish I'd known him better.

Rob was transformed from a cocky high school student to a drooling semi-vegetable as a result of a boating accident. He'd play cards, too, but he was unintelligible most of the time and he moved so slowly. His parents got divorced. I lost track of Rob in short order.

That pretty much covers my formative experience with disabilities. So it's fair to say I wasn't overly prepared for the arrival of our second and third sons, Mark and Eric, 28-week preemies. One alone would have been a shock, two crossed the line into farce. It started with an extended stay in the Intensive Care Nursery. When Eric, the younger twin, finally arrived home he sported a newly repaired heart, apnea monitors, oxygen tanks, and joined his brother in fussing most every night due to their inability to consume enough calories. Sleep deprivation was the worst because it precipitated a cascade of dysfunctionality throughout the house.

I could go on and on. Cerebral palsy is a complicated disorder. Both boys have gastrointestinal tubes for feedings, a regimen of medications and supplements to help with everything from muscle spasm to bowel movement, and a fleet of assistive devices. Hospital trips for specialist review, surgeries, botox injections, and an endless stream of therapist and nursing assistants invading our privacy have become something of a routine that's emotionally draining yet monotonous. A sales professional by training, my wife has become an expert at navigating the private and public health care systems out of necessity, an educational consultant out of conviction and an advocate out of desire.

It would have flatly been impossible to survive this institutionalized anarchy any other way than by simply growing into it, over the years, one day at a time. In the process, the twins have gone from pre-med thesis material to become our sons with rich, individual personalities, idiosyncrasies and foibles just like "normal" kids. While we wish for them more than is presently possible, we take great pride in their many and significant accomplishments: Eric babbling away at dinner and sitting by himself in his red rocker; Mark learning to use his talker; Eric driving his power chair and endlessly playing and rewinding the Lion King with a remote controller all by himself, and Mark laughing hysterically whenever his older brother gets in trouble. We love them as any parent loves his children. We love reading at bedtime, tickling and teasing, going to a baseball game and swimming. And Eric's Make-A-Wish trip to Give Kids the World Village and Disney World in Florida to meet his favorite Radio Disney DJ was one of the most inspirational events of my life.

People in the disability community threw us a lifeline early on by acting as guides through the maze of public services access. It's beyond astonishing that the richest society on earth makes people traverse a gauntlet to receive even the most basic services. It's worse when you realize how many more get no help or respect from agencies purportedly designed for that purpose. In the process, my politics have changed from conservative to liberal. Both my wife and I have served in various charitable capacities to give something back to the community because it's important to remember you're in a lifeboat with others.

Our oldest son, Jay, gets a lot of credit. I assume he's been impacted in ways I can't comprehend, but mainly for the good. He produced a video of his brothers and spent a day in a wheel chair for a school project last year, something that would never have occurred to me when I was his age.

Our marriage has become stronger over the years as we've grown with the family. My wife is fond of saying life is what you do every day. That's true, but I could certainly live without changing my ten-year-olds' diapers, administering tube feeds, doing the "clean and jerk" whenever they need to be moved and watching Barney tapes for the umpteenth million time and counting. This last point is particularly heinous—no parent should be made to endure Barney for ten years without receiving a Congressional medal.

The emotions, surgeries, finances, the life overall certainly isn't what I'd expected or planned. Does God work in mysterious ways? Probably. Do I put more stock in theology versus philosophy? Depends on the day. Are Mark and Eric better off than Chinese, Bosnian, or Rwandan kids with CP? Unquestionably. Do other people see it that way? I guess it's relative.

Bruce R. Stahlman
Littleton, Colorado
September 26, 2002

Kelly follows with a letter which she hopes will clarify the relationship between parent and teacher and help teachers understand parents better.

A letter to teachers, current and future:

As a mother of twins with cerebral palsy, I want to thank you for taking the time and making great efforts to care for my children. Without you I would be lost.

Next, I would like to explain, one by one, some of my actions and reactions. Please be patient.

First. After reading the vignette "Story" in the book, *Changed by a Child,* I finally understood why I keep telling you the same story over and over and over. The vignette talks about the excruciating details that I need to convey, because it is all still so real and so raw to me. That, like a spider spinning its web, retelling my story allows me to connect my old life to this new, overwhelming reality.

My story is the vehicle that makes the trip of survival and allows me to cope with the present.

Second. In caring for children with disabilities, a large part of the care is emotional, so the teacher/parent relationship is, by definition, also emotional. We are both investing all that we can into my children, yet we frequently seem to be at odds. Please work WITH me. Give careful consideration to the information that I bring to the table, because it comes as the result of sweat and tears. It is also my role in your system, as a parent, to push the envelope, to be looking ahead, and to be asking for everything that I can to support my child. I will still be here when I am 80 and they are 50, and we shall still be "doing the best we can."

Third. Asking "how are things going" at the start of our meetings gives necessary information. My sleep, the children's health, and life overall will be things that affect our conversation and how effectively I am able to communicate.

Last. Never forget that I am grateful for all that you do. It becomes tiring to always say thank you, because that is the nature of our life. In fact, one of the blessings of a disability is that it frequently brings out the best in others. I never forget a kindness, even years later, but it still gets old saying "thank you" as a way of life. Nevertheless, THANK YOU.

Kelly Stahlman
Mother 3 sons, Jay, 13, Mark and Eric, 10 year-old twins with cerebral palsy due to prematurity

Addendum to Bruce Stahlman's letter:

August 10, 2000

Mark and Eric turned 14 this past weekend and their first day of high school is tomorrow. No doubt all parents think time passes quickly, but I still have vivid memories of their stay in the ICCN. They remain great kids with some unique challenges for our family as they inexorably become young adults. These fall into three general categories:

1. Logistic—The physical exertion to move them through space has increased dramatically over time. Simply, they continue to grow and gain weight while my wife and I and the attending CNAs age, so lifting them for wheel chair positioning, hygiene, sleep, etc. while avoiding injury to them and us has become more difficult. We are presently in the final stages of home modification project that involves combining bedrooms; enlarging the bathroom and installing a ceiling lift system to address these concerns. Finally, we continue to explore evolving technology for communication purposes for both boys including Dynavox upgrades for Mark, who is non-verbal, to PC applications for Eric to afford him greater access to the Internet.
2. Behavior—Coupled with the normal hormone changes of adolescence are overlay symptoms of ADD particularly in Eric, the more mobile twin. We suspect there's also a growing psychological awareness of their general situation vis-à-vis other kids, for example, as their older brother enters his junior year of high school. We're seeing a lower tolerance of schedule changes, higher demand for activity repetition, and increased incidence of temper tantrums accompanied by hitting, both outward and self-directed. Behavior modification techniques have been at the forefront of ongoing discussions with school personnel and the CAN, but results have been mixed. This is a challenging problem given the paradox of life skill training to set appropriate boundaries vs. the need to actively parent through these important years.
3. Medical—My wife estimates each boy has had nine or ten surgeries over the course of their lives and more are on the horizon. Recently some disturbing changes in Eric's spine have been observed and he'll likely require an involved stabilization procedure. Mark will likely have non-weight bearing ankle bones fused to counteract the effects of overpronation. Thankfully, the logistics changes noted about should be a big help here for recuperation and ongoing care.

Of course this type of clinical situation analysis doesn't capture the daily joy of parenting kids with special needs. They are exceptional, funny, loving, and interactive in their own ways, and I can't imagine the family without them.

A FEW JEWELS FROM THE STAHLMAN FAMILY SURVIVAL SKILLS

Why me?
Why not me?
Ignorance is bliss; knowledge is power.
Kids with disabilities take much longer to go to the next stage. They wear you out. Patience and endurance are required, with lots of support!
In some ways it gets easier; in some ways it gets harder, and in some ways it just gets different as you go through stages and ages.
God never gives you more than you can handle.
He did at our house! The miracle is to watch God's grace at work in the midst of all the chaos.
My kids teach the art of being with the gift of presence, the miracle of doing, and the priority of having.
No matter where you are, someone is better off and someone is worse off.
Equipment is the quintessential mixed blessing: It can be social barrier which prevents the community from seeing the child/person, a management nightmare and just plain awkward while being vital to the child's participation in life. My greatest nightmare is that Eric and Mark will learn the low expectation of observing life instead of participating in it.[1]

[1]Reprinted by permission from Bruce and Kelly Stahlman (2002, 2006).

CONCERN FOR THOSE WHO WORK WITH CHILDREN WITH DISABILITIES

Burnout

Burnout is a term applied to the loss of concern and emotional feeling for people you work with or live with (Maslach, 1982). Both teachers and parents experience burnout. It is felt most when what you are trying to do seems unproductive, or you may think you have few alternatives that would change or improve the course of events. This frustration can lead to a feeling of being trapped. It can happen to any teacher and any parent. The obligations of teaching and parenting are similar. Both are in an authoritarian role and are responsible for setting up the child's program. Balancing the student's needs with time constraints, the mechanical constraints of running a classroom or a home, and the constraints of the personal needs of the authoritarian figure is a role for a magician. Indeed, when parents and teachers are successful, the result does seem to be magical. Both teacher and parent know, however, that their success was produced by hard work, good planning, cooperation, and perseverance.

Those who set high standards and aim for perfection are more likely to experience burnout, as are those who feel a need to be in control. Feelings of anger, guilt, depression, self-doubt, and irritability are symptoms of burnout. When these occur, take a hard look at what is really going on and what needs to be going on. Are you neglecting yourself? Are the things you want to do essential? Do some things need to be changed? Learn to accept the fact that change can occur. Be willing to give yourself and others credit where credit is due. Build in rewards so that you and others feel good about what you are doing. Always have some goals that are short-term and accessible. Nothing feels better than success. This is one of the best methods to combat burnout. Remember, burnout is reversible.

Depression and Suicide

People who parent or work with exceptional children need to know that these children are in a high-risk group for depression and suicide. Children with learning disabilities are particularly at risk because of the frustration they often encounter in trying to learn. Children with giftedness often find it difficult to feel comfortable in the school and home environment.

Parents and teachers must recognize the child's symptoms of depression and impending suicide and be willing to take appropriate action. Generally, the child will be depressed or irritable, lacking enjoyment in usually pleasurable activities. Changes in weight, appetite, or eating habits may be signals. Sleeplessness, hyperactivity, loss of energy, or fatigue are also signals that something is wrong. Loss of self-esteem and feelings of inadequacy or decreased ability to concentrate should alert teachers and parents to a very real need for help. Thoughts of death or suicide should not be taken lightly. Recognize these as very serious symptoms and get professional help. Mental health centers and public schools have programs for crisis intervention and can give guidance and help in a time of need.

RIGHTS AND SERVICES AVAILABLE TO PARENTS

Many parents of children with exceptionalities are unaware of the rights they have and the services available to them. The Buckley Amendment, described here, is a right for all parents, but it is especially important for parents who have children with disabilities.

Family Educational Rights and Privacy Act (FERPA)—The Buckley Amendment

The Buckley Amendment, written for all citizens, greatly affected record keeping for people with disabilities. Please refer to chapter 12 for a description of FERPA.

How to File a Complaint of Discrimination

No one enjoys being a complainer. Most of us do not enjoy confrontations. But every U.S. law was written because someone cared enough to speak up and work to get the law passed. Then the legislature built in procedures for citizens to protect their rights. If parents and friends of the disabled do not stand up for these rights, they will be lost. Whenever discrimination occurs, it hurts not just the people involved, but our nation as well. Complaints should be directed first to the person in charge. If a satisfactory conclusion is not reached, take the complaint to the next higher level of responsibility. Follow the chain of command. If this is not satisfactory, contact the Regional Office of Civil Rights for your area. The following items are important to include in a complaint:

- Your name and address (a telephone number where you can be reached during business hours is helpful, but not required).
- A general description of the person or class of people injured by the alleged act or acts (names are not required).
- The name and location of the institution that allegedly committed the discriminatory act or acts.
- A description of the alleged discriminatory act(s) in sufficient detail to enable OCR to understand what occurred, when it occurred, and the basis for the alleged discrimination (race, color, national origin, sex, disability, age, or the Boy Scouts of America Equal Access Act). (Office for Civil Rights, 2007, p. 1)

MASLOW'S HIERARCHY OF NEEDS

When schools become involved with parents, it is wise to list the basic needs that must be satisfied before parents can effectively assist in the education of their children with disabilities. Coletta (1977) elaborates on Maslow's hierarchy of needs in *Working Together: A Guide to Parent Involvement.*

How does Maslow's hierarchy apply to these children? When teachers or administrators work with parents, it is helpful if they understand the parents' feelings, motivations, and concerns. Maslow's hierarchy of needs serves as a guide to this understanding. Parents who are poor and struggling to provide the necessities of life have different views of their problems from those of affluent parents. That is, physiological needs such as food and shelter must be satisfied before individuals can attend to higher order needs such as success and fulfillment. All parents' love and concern for their children will be the same. Therefore, all parents—regardless of economic standing—must be treated with dignity and respect.

The various levels of Maslow's hierarchy are discussed in the following sections.

Physical Needs

The needs for sustaining life—nourishment, protection from the elements, and sexual activity—are physical. There must be protection from the cold, wind, and rain, which usually means a shelter, such as a house, and clothing. There must be food, and to be effective, it must be nourishing. There is a need for companionship and sexual activity.

Psychological Needs

People need to feel secure. It is important to know that you will awake each day to go to a job. It is difficult to handle change, conflict, and uncertainty. It is important to reduce these frustrations. Much emphasis is placed on norms and rules, which results in little flexibility at this level.

Emotional Love and Belonging

At this level there is a need to feel a part of a group where you are accepted, wanted, loved, and respected. When these needs are met or satisfied, then there can be love, respect for others, and consideration for or helpfulness to others. When these needs are not met, there may be self-defeating, attention-getting behaviors, such as suspicion and aggression.

Self-Esteem

Basic needs must be met before the need for self-esteem can be satisfied. When you are regarded as valuable and competent by others, you have self-esteem. Growth in awareness of self-worth leads to less dependence upon another's judgment of one's worth. The key for the professional is to find ways to help parents see themselves as worthwhile contributors to their children's education.

Fulfillment

This is referred to as self-actualization and is achieved only after the previous levels have been reached. The person strives for self-development, directs energies toward self-established goals, and takes risks willingly.

This hierarchy of needs is applicable to children, teachers, and administrators as well as to parents. It is wise to note where we and the people we would like to help are in the hierarchy. If there is an understanding of needs, then our expectations and suggestions for helping may be more valid.

SUMMARY

Parents, teachers, and other professionals are effective forces in influencing the life of the exceptional child. It is important that all be able and willing to work together for the benefit of the child with disabilities. Special educational terms, once crude, have been replaced with more inclusive educational terms.

During the 20th century the special education movement grew, and in 1971 the Pennsylvania Association for Retarded Children (PARC) won a court case against the Commonwealth of Pennsylvania affirming the right of all children to a free and appropriate education. This includes children with disabilities. The Vocational Rehabilitation Act of 1973, the Education of All Handicapped Children Act of 1975 (Public Law 94-142), the Education of the Handicapped Act Amendments of 1983 (PL 98-199), Americans with Disabilities Act, Individuals with Disabilities Act, and IDEA 97 are some of the far-reaching laws passed in the last quarter of the century.

From the Education of All Handicapped Children Act of 1975 to IDEA 97 (PL 105-17), and IDEA 04 reauthorization, the Individualized Education Program (IEP) and the Individualized Family Service Program (IFSP) have been instrumental in addressing the needs of children with disabilities. They are plans developed by the parents, the child, teachers, administrators, special teachers, psychologists, and any others involved with the child's education. The plans ensure a continuum of services, appropriate to age, maturity, handicapping condition, achievements, and parental expectations. The child or student with a disability includes those with autism, deafness, deafness–blindness, hearing impairments, mental retardation, multiple disabilities, orthopedic impairments, other health impairments (including ADD), emotional disturbances, learning disabilities, speech or language impairments, traumatic brain injury, and visual impairments. For children 3 to 9 years old, developmental delays are also used for placement. IDEA 97 and 04 also provide for due process—the right to a hearing—if parents disagree with the educational placement.

Parents have been effective forces in securing this legislation. Parents should and do have an important role in the life and education of their exceptional children. The parent's role begins as one of nurturing in the home but can become an effective force in the school as the parent supports the teacher at home as a tutor or at school as a volunteer.

SUGGESTED CLASS ACTIVITIES AND DISCUSSIONS

1. Write a brief review of the development of special education.
2. Describe in your own words what "least restrictive" means.
3. List and describe briefly the 13 categories of exceptional students.
4. A *staffing* refers to the meeting that takes place when an exceptional student's IEP is developed or changed. Who is included on the IEP team? What are their responsibilities?
5. *Mainstreaming and inclusion* are terms used quite frequently. Read carefully about them and write in your own words what you think they mean.
6. List ways that the general classroom can adapt to and support a child with a disability.
7. Study the legislation that has developed for children with disabilities. How has it progressed? List changes.
8. Using Maslow's hierarchy of needs, assess yourself and five acquaintances. Try to select people in different professions. Use this as background material for a general class discussion to increase awareness of these needs.
9. Choose one of the problems a parent of an exceptional child may encounter and describe how you as a professional would try to help that parent.

WEB SITES

Council for Exceptional Children
www.cec.sped.org

Provides updates on legislation related to children with special needs and their families, resource information related to specific disabilities, and links to organizations serving children with special needs and their families.

National Council on Disabilities
www.ncd.gov

The council is an independent federal agency that makes recommendations to the President of the U.S. The council Web site provides resource information and links to agencies and programs, including contact information for legislators and state vocational and rehabilitation agencies.

National Information Center for Children and Youth with Disabilities (NICHCY)
www.nichcy.org

Provides resource information of agencies serving children with disabilities, including phone numbers, addresses and e-mail addresses. Links are provided to information regarding specific disabilities.

Special Quest
www.specialquest.org

Provides information related to infants and toddlers with special needs, especially those being served by early intervention programs and Early Head Start. Resources and links for families and providers are also provided.

11 The Abused Child

Children who live through years of assault, degradation, and neglect bear emotional scars that can last for years. We all pay the price of their suffering.

Besharov, 1990, p. 2

Then there is the pain. A breaking and entering when even the senses are torn apart. The act of rape on an eight-year-old body is the matter of the needle giving because the camel can't. The child gives, because the body can, and the violator cannot.

Angelou, 2002, p. 76

In this chapter, you will learn about recognizing and intervening in cases of child abuse and neglect. After completing the chapter, you should be able to:

- Acknowledge the moral responsibility and legal requirement that teachers and school personnel have to report suspected maltreatment of children.
- Identify ways schools can help ameliorate the crisis of child abuse and neglect.
- Describe when and how abuse of children was identified and brought to the attention of the public.
- List and describe the characteristics that may indicate child abuse of preschool, elementary, and secondary students.
- Identify types of abuse: physical, emotional, and sexual.
- Identify neglect, and differentiate between neglect and poverty.
- List the psychological characteristics of abused children.
- Describe possible characteristics of the abusive parent.
- List guidelines for interviewing children and parents about abuse.
- Recognize the danger of violence in the schools and the importance of working to eliminate it.
- Discuss the climate of the school and school offerings that would help abusive families.

What is child abuse? According to the Child Abuse Prevention and Treatment Act of 1974, or PL 93-247 (1977), it is:

> The physical or mental injury, sexual abuse, negligent treatment or maltreatment of a child under the age of 18 by a person who is responsible for the child's welfare under circumstances which indicate that the child's health or welfare is harmed or threatened thereby. (p. 1826)

RESPONSIBILITY TO REPORT

School personnel and child-care staff members have more than a moral responsibility to report suspected abuse. Laws in each state require them to report it (Besharov, 1990, 1994; Horton & Cruise, 2001). Some states identify categories of school personnel such as teachers, psychologists, or administrators; others have a general category of

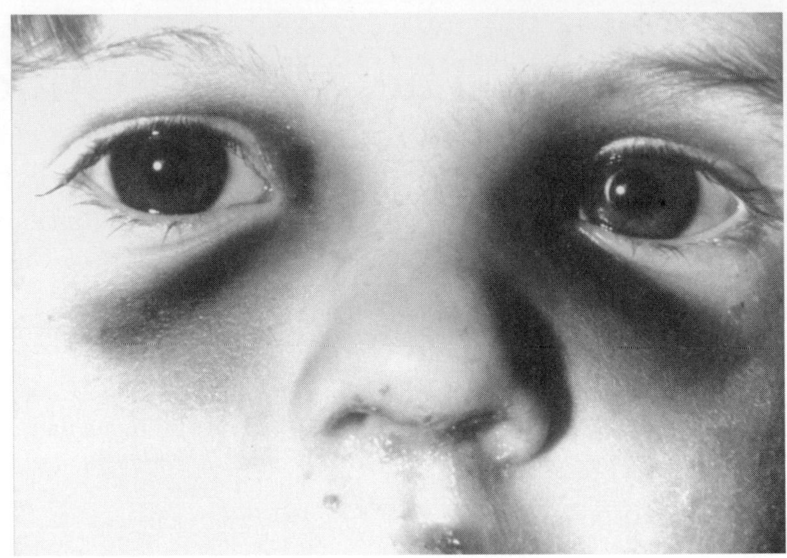

It is difficult to understand this kind of physical abuse against children.

Courtesy of Barton D. Schmitt, M.D., C. Henry Kempe National Center for Prevention and Treatment of Child Abuse and Neglect.

school personnel. Four categories of professional-mandated reporting are medical, legal, and human service professionals, and educators (Lowenthal, 2001). No states require proof of the abuse before reporting, and the reporters must report if they have suspicions of maltreatment. Teachers, child-care professionals, and others who report in good faith are immune from legal action.

Schools are essential agencies in the reduction of the national crisis of child abuse and neglect. Recommendations from the U.S. Advisory Board on Child Abuse and Neglect (1990) illustrate the national crisis:

> The Board has concluded that child abuse and neglect in the United States represents a national emergency.
>
> The Board bases this conclusion on three findings: 1) each year hundreds of thousands of children are being starved and abandoned, burned and severely beaten, raped and sodomized, berated and belittled; 2) the system the nation has devised to respond to child abuse and neglect is failing; and 3) the United States spends billions of dollars on programs that deal with the results of the nation's failure to prevent and treat child abuse and neglect.
>
> Not only are child abuse and neglect wrong, but the nation's lack of an effective response to them is also wrong. Neither can be tolerated. Together they constitute a moral disaster.
>
> All Americans share an ethical duty to ensure the safety of children. Protection of children from harm is not just an ethical duty: it is a matter of national survival.
>
> Although some children recover from maltreatment without serious consequences, the evidence is clear that maltreatment often has deleterious effects on children's mental health and development, both short- and long-term.
>
> Although most victims of serious and fatal child abuse are very young, to regard older children and adolescents as invulnerable to the severe consequences of abuse and neglect is a mistake.
>
> All Americans should be outraged by child maltreatment. (pp. vii–viii)

The responsibilities are great, and an affirmative response by schools is vital to the well-being of thousands of children throughout the United States. Because of required school attendance and an increase in the use of child-care centers, caregivers and teachers have an expanded opportunity for contact with families and children. These professionals work closely with children and families over extended periods. In so doing, they are also the people most able to detect and prevent abuse and neglect.

School has not always been recognized as an important agency in the detection of child abuse. At one time it was believed that most cases of child abuse involved infants who are vulnerable to serious injury or death. But it is now recognized that older children are also victims. More than 70 percent of the children who are abused or neglected may have contact with schools or child-care centers. Through Parents as Teachers, Early Head Start and Head Start, and private and public preschool programs, it has become easier to detect abuse of 2- to 6-year-olds. Increasingly, the detection and prevention of child abuse and neglect is recognized as a concern and responsibility of the schools. Denver Public Schools (1998), under the topic "legal responsibilities," states:

> suspicion or knowledge of abuse/neglect must be reported to the Denver Department of Social Services (DDSS) Child Abuse Hotline or the Police depending on the situation. School personnel have a legal and moral obligation to make a report if child abuse or neglect is suspected. *No one within the school district has the authority to veto reporting.* If it is necessary for school personnel to examine a student for evidence of physical abuse, two adults should be present during the examination.

Abuse and neglect include many degrees and varieties of neglect, physical abuse, emotional abuse, and sexual abuse. The effect on the child differs by age and development, degree of intensity, duration, the relationship between abused and abuser (Steele, 1986), and the intervention that the child receives.

Physical abuse that causes permanent damage to a child is generally easy to recognize and evokes outrage. The damage to a child's psychological development is more difficult to recognize and assess. Unpredictable parental behavior gives the child a "sense of insecurity and difficulty trusting other human beings" (Steele, 1986, p. 285). Parents who lack appropriate parenting behavior exhibit inconsistent caregiving; they most often learned their parenting methods during their own formative years when they were themselves neglected or abused.

Besharov (1994) recommends that better information and education on reporting responsibilities is needed in order to encourage more accurate and more complete reporting. "Training efforts should be both expanded and improved. Professional education programs should sensitize all child-serving professionals to the occurrence of child abuse and neglect, and should instruct them in how and when to report" (p. 143).

The U.S. Advisory Board on Child Abuse and Neglect (1991) made 27 recommendations for responding to this crisis. Recommendation D-4a refers to Child Protection and the Schools as follows:

> *Strengthening the Role of Elementary and Secondary Schools in the Protection of Children*
>
> The Federal Government should take all necessary measures to ensure that the nation's elementary and secondary schools, both public and private, participate more effectively in the prevention, identification, and treatment of child abuse and neglect. Such measures should include knowledge building, program development, program evaluation, data collection, training, and technical assistance. The objective of such measures should be the development and implementation by State Educational Agencies (SEAs) in association with Local Educational Agencies (LEAs) and consortia of LEAs, of:
>
> - Inter-agency multidisciplinary training for teachers, counselors, and administrative personnel on child abuse and neglect;
> - Specialized training for school health and mental health personnel on the treatment of child abuse and neglect;
> - School-based, inter-agency, multidisciplinary supportive services for families in which child abuse or neglect is known to have occurred or where children are at high risk of maltreatment, including self-help groups for students and parents of students;
> - Family life education, including parenting skills and home visits, for students and/or parents; and
> - Other school-based inter-agency, multidisciplinary programs intended to strengthen families and support children who may have been subjected to maltreatment, including school-based family resource centers and after-school programs for elementary and secondary school pupils which promote collaboration between schools and public and private community agencies in child protection. (p. 164)

Both public and private schools are considered essential to the child protection system and have responsibilities to effectively provide for the children who attend schools.

The school professionals must consider legal considerations (mandated reporting), ethical considerations (confidentiality), and moral considerations (commitment to the child's well-being) (Horton & Cruise, 2001). When a professional reports suspicions of maltreatment, "families may move away from the school or at least cancel their children's participation in any counseling relationships" (p. 55). The parents may feel that their belief and trust in the school has been destroyed. Reporting, however, may prevent severe physical injury, psychological harm, or inadequate nourishment and health care. "On a case-by-case basis, reports may protect children from severe physical injury or even death. Psychological suffering may be lessened and dysfunctional patterns interrupted. Families may get needed services" (p. 56).

The school must serve as a defense against child abuse in three basic ways: (a) as a referral agency to child protection agencies—reporting suspected abuse is required by law; (b) as an educational institution offering parent education, family-life education, and home visitations to adults and students; and (c) as a support system for families and as a collaborator with other agencies in providing a total protection system.

BACKGROUND

Child abuse and neglect have been social phenomena for centuries. Childhood is described by deMause (1988) in a history of child abuse. The child was considered property of the father to be worked, sold, loved, or killed as the father willed. The child had no rights (Crosson-Tower, 2002; Gelles & Lancaster, 1987; Helfer & Kempe, 1987; Nagi, 1977). "The notion that parents have the right to rear children as they see fit, in the privacy of their home, is a deeply rooted tradition in American history" (Vondra & Toth, 1989, p. 18). Actions that would be called child abuse today were overlooked or considered to be the parent's right to discipline.

In the 1800s it was common for children to work 12 hours a day under the threat of beatings. They were cheap and useful laborers. Children "continued to be the property of their parents who could choose to beat them, neglect them, or send them out to work" (Crosson-Tower, 2002, p. 4). It was not until 1874, in New York City, that the first case of abuse was reported. It involved a 9-year-old girl, Mary Ellen, who was beaten daily by her parents and was severely undernourished when found by church workers. Because there were no agencies to deal with child abuse, the workers turned to the American Society for the Prevention of Cruelty to Animals.

One year later the New York Society for the Prevention of Cruelty to Children was organized (Fontana & Besharov, 1979; Lazoritz, 1990). The Children's Division of what is now the American Humane Association began addressing the issues in 1878 (American Humane Association, 1998). There were other early indications of growing concern for children. A paper published in 1888, for example, discussed acute periosteal swelling in infants, which can indicate injury (Nagi, 1977). Periosteal swelling is the inflammation and swelling of fibrous connective tissue. National groups such as the Child Study Association of America and the National Congress of Parents and Teachers were formed. Mounting concern over working conditions and care of children culminated in 1909 in the first White House Conference on Children, which resulted in the 1912 legislation establishing the Children's Bureau.

In recent years, widespread concern over and protective action for the child at risk of maltreatment has become a mandate to schools, and medical care agencies have recognized the prevalence of children who are abused. This relatively recent overwhelming concern resulted in the nearly unanimous passage of the federal Child Abuse Prevention and Treatment Act of 1974.

What happened between 1913 and recent decades to focus attention on the child at risk? Dr. John Caffey, a radiologist, began collecting data that indicated child abuse in the early 1920s, but he was not supported in his beliefs by his associates. Thus, it was not until after World War II that he published the first of several studies relating to fractures in young children (American Humane Association, 1978; Elmer, 1982). Caffey's first medical paper, written in 1946, reported the histories of six traumatized infants and questioned the cause of their injuries. In it he reported that fractures of the long bones and subdural hematomas occurring concurrently were not caused by disease (pp. 163–173).

Dr. Frederick Silverman, who had been a student of Caffey's, followed in 1953 with an article that indicated that skeletal trauma in infants could be the result of abuse (American Humane

Association, 1978; Elmer, 1982). Reports began appearing more frequently (Altman & Smith, 1960; Bakwin, 1956; Fisher, 1958; Silver & Kempe, 1959; Woolley & Evans, 1955), but it was an article by Kempe, Silverman, Steele, Droegemueller, and Silver (1962), "The Battered-Child Syndrome," that brought national attention to the abused child. The authors began their article with the following charge to physicians:

> The battered-child syndrome, a clinical condition in young children who have received serious physical abuse, is a frequent cause of permanent injury or death. The syndrome should be considered in any child exhibiting evidence of fracture of any bone, subdural hematoma, failure to thrive, soft tissue swellings or skin bruising, in any child who dies suddenly, or where the degree and type of injury is at variance with the history given regarding the occurrence of the trauma. Psychiatric factors are probably of prime importance in the pathogenesis of the disorder, but knowledge of these factors is limited. Physicians have a duty and responsibility to the child to require a full evaluation of the problem and to guarantee that no expected repetition of trauma will be permitted to occur. (Kempe et al., p. 17)

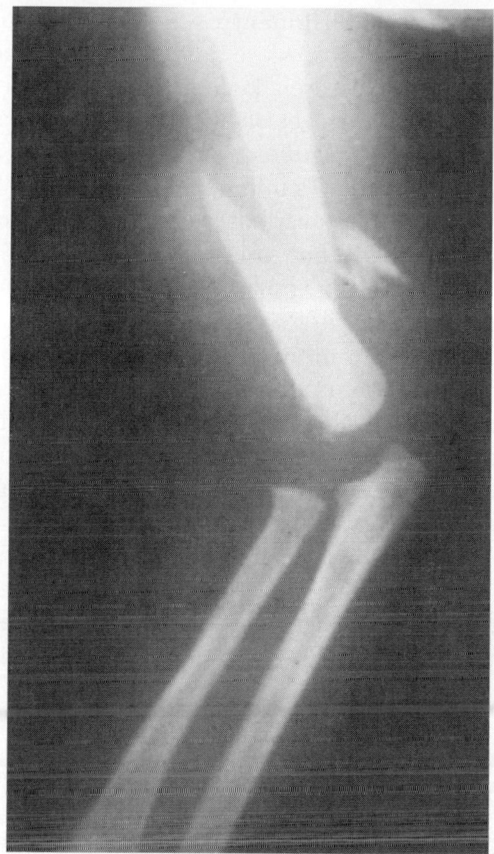

When X-rays became available, doctors began noticing recurring breaks that revealed abuse.

Courtesy of Barton D. Schmitt, M.D., C. Henry Kempe National Center for Prevention and Treatment of Child Abuse and Neglect.

The article described the status of child abuse in the nation and pointed out the effectiveness of X-ray examinations in determining abuse. The term *battered* came from the description of bruises, lacerations, bites, brain injury, deep body injury, pulled joints, burns and scalds, fractures of arms, legs, skull, and ribs, and other injuries that resulted from beating, whipping, throwing the child about, or slamming the child against something. Fontana (1973b) described battering by parents as follows:

> Parents bash, lash, beat, flay, stomp, suffocate, strangle, gut-punch, choke with rags or hot pepper, poison, crack heads open, slice, rip, steam, fry, boil, dismember. They use fists, belt buckles, straps, hairbrushes, lamp cords, sticks, baseball bats, rulers, shoes and boots, lead or iron pipes, bottles, brick walls, bicycle chains, pokers, knives, scissors, chemicals, lighted cigarettes, boiling water, steaming radiators, and open gas flames. (pp. 16–17)

National Response

The term *battered* and the picture it evoked aroused the nation. By 1967, all 50 states had legislation to facilitate the reporting of child abuse. There was, however, no provision for the coordination of procedures, nor was there a standard definition of abuse and neglect. Other conditions that precluded standardized reporting included the inconsistent ages of children covered by law, hesitation of professional and private citizens to report cases, different systems of official record keeping, and varied criteria on which to judge abuse.

National Center on Child Abuse and Neglect

The National Center on Child Abuse and Neglect (NCCAN) was created in 1974 by PL 93-247. The NCCAN disseminates information through the Clearinghouse on Child Abuse and Neglect.

After the establishment of NCCAN, regional centers on child abuse were funded. Their purpose was to conduct research to determine the cause of child abuse and neglect, its identification and prevention, and the incidence of child abuse in the nation. Reporting of child abuse and neglect has been conducted by a variety of organizations. From 1973 until 1986 the American Association for Protecting Children (now the American Humane Association) supplied data on abuse and neglect. The National Committee for the Prevention of Child Abuse did a survey of the 50 states in 1991. At that time, NCCAN established the National Child Abuse and Neglect Data System (NCANDS) to be responsible for providing comprehensive data on abuse and neglect.

Reports by states have always been voluntary. Each state develops its own procedures for analyzing and reporting, but because it is important to have data that is useful throughout the United States, NCANDS provides forms for states to use. These forms ask for report source; number of investigations; number of children by disposition; victim data that includes the type of maltreatment, age, gender, and ethnicity; number of victims from each home; number of victims removed from homes; number of victims for whom court action was initiated; number of victims who died; number of victims and families who received additional services; and the relationship of the victim to the perpetrator (U.S. Department of Health and Human Services, Children's Bureau, 1998).

EXTENT OF CHILD ABUSE AND NEGLECT

In 2000, child protection agencies (CPA) throughout the United States reported to the National Child Abuse and Neglect Data System (NCANDS). Out of approximately 5 million children there were 3 million referrals identified, with 62 percent needing to be "screened in" and 38 percent "screened out." "Screened-in referrals alleging that a child was being abused or neglected received investigations and assessment to determine whether the allegations of maltreatment could be substantiated" (National Child Abuse and Neglect Data System [NCANDS], 2002, p. 1).

Of these referrals, 879,000 children were identified as victims of maltreatment. The maltreatment categories include neglect, physical abuse, sexual abuse, medical neglect, and psychological or emotional maltreatment. The largest category was neglect, including medical neglect, with almost two thirds (63 percent) being neglected.

Figure 11.1 compares the incidence of child maltreatment in 1990, 1996, and 2000. As shown in Figure 11.1, in addition to the 63 percent who were neglected, 19 percent were physically abused, 10 percent were sexually abused, and 8 percent were emotionally abused (NCANDS, 2002). The other maltreatment in the 1990 and 1996 reports includes abandonment, congenital drug addiction, and threats.

Who Are the Victims?

Child abuse strikes children at all ages. Figure 11.2 compares the rate of maltreatment of children by age in 2002. The figure demonstrates that children from birth to age 7 are at the greatest risk of maltreatment, but even teenagers still are not immune to the ravages of abuse.

Children birth to 3 years of age account for 16.1 victims per 1,000, whereas youths 16 to 17 years of age account for 6.1 victims per 1,000. Children ages 4 to 7 account for 13.4 victims per 1,000; combining children under 7 results in 29.5 victims per 1,000.

Who Are the Abusers?

Most of the victims (84 percent) were abused by their parents. Mothers were responsible for 32 percent of the physical abuse and 47 percent of the neglect.

Nonrelatives were the perpetrators of 29 percent of sexual abuse. Fathers acting alone were responsible for 22 percent, whereas other relatives accounted for 19 percent of sexual abuse. Most sexual abuse was committed by someone who continued to be near the child, placing the child at high risk for repeat attacks.

Perpetrators of maltreatment are defined by most states as parents and other caregivers including other relatives, foster parents, and baby-sitters. Females account for 60 percent of the perpetrators. The median age of perpetrators was 34 for males and 31 for females (NCANDS, 2002).

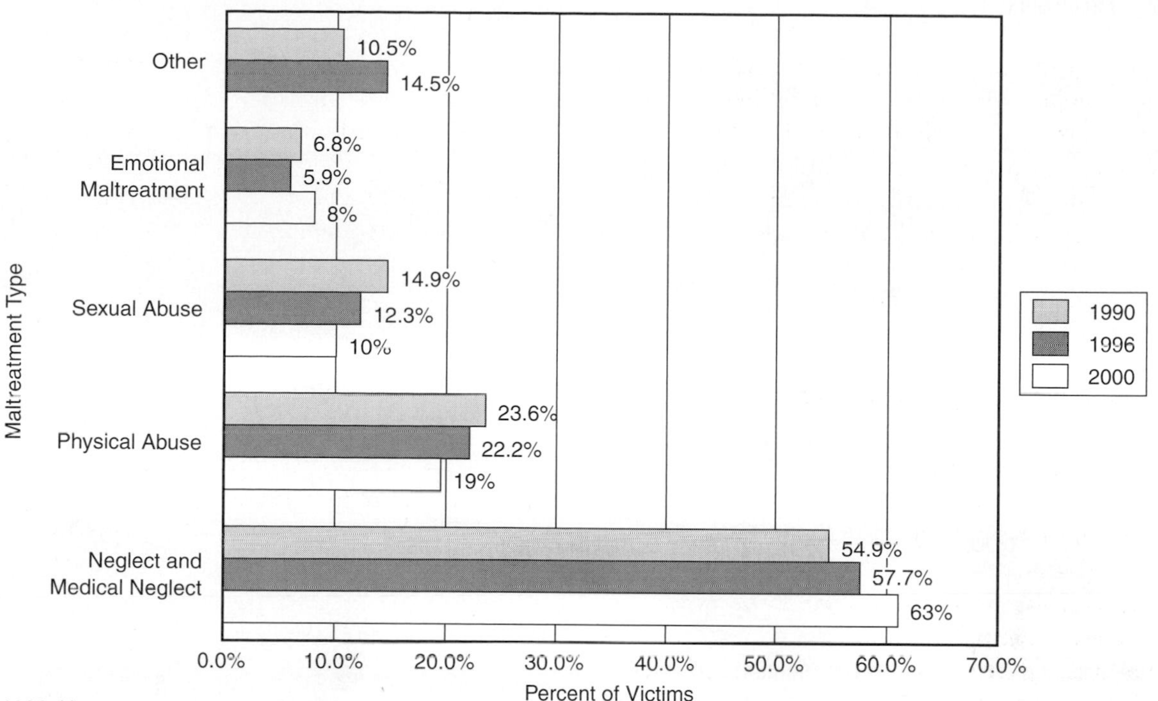

FIGURE 11.1 Types of maltreatment, 1990, 1996, 2000.

Neglect, as manifested in deprivation of necessities, is the most frequently reported form of abuse and neglect.

Sources: From *Child Maltreatment, 1996: Reports from the States to the National Child Abuse and Neglect Data System,* by the U.S. Department of Health and Human Services, Children's Bureau, 1998, Washington, DC: U.S. Government Printing Office.

Summary of Key Findings from Calendar Year 2000, by the U.S. Department of Health and Human Services, Children's Bureau, Administration on Children, Youth and Families, National Child Abuse and Neglect Data System (NCANDS), retrieved May 22, 2002, from www.calib.com/nccanch/prevmnth.scope/ncands.cfm.

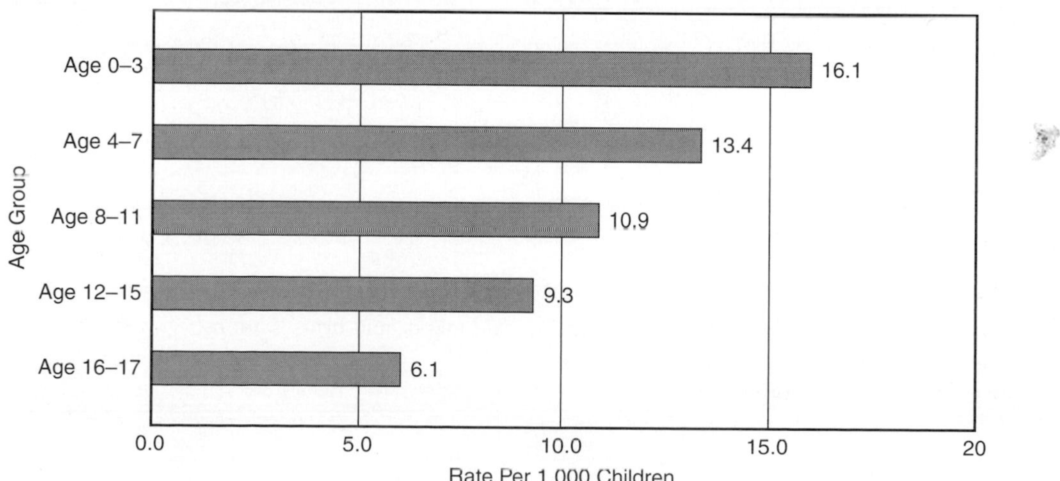

FIGURE 11.2 Victimization rates by age group, 2004, Child Maltreatment 2004.

This bar graph breaks the victim population into age groups as follows: 0–3, 4–7, 8–11, 12–15, and 16–17. According to this chart, the most largely victimized age group is the youngest, with a rate of 16.1 per 1,000 children of the same age group. The oldest children were victimized the least frequently.

Source: U.S. Department of Health and Human Services, Administration for Children and Families, Children's Bureau. Retrieved September 20, 2006, from www.acf.hhs.gov/programs/cb/pubs/cm04/figures_1.htm.

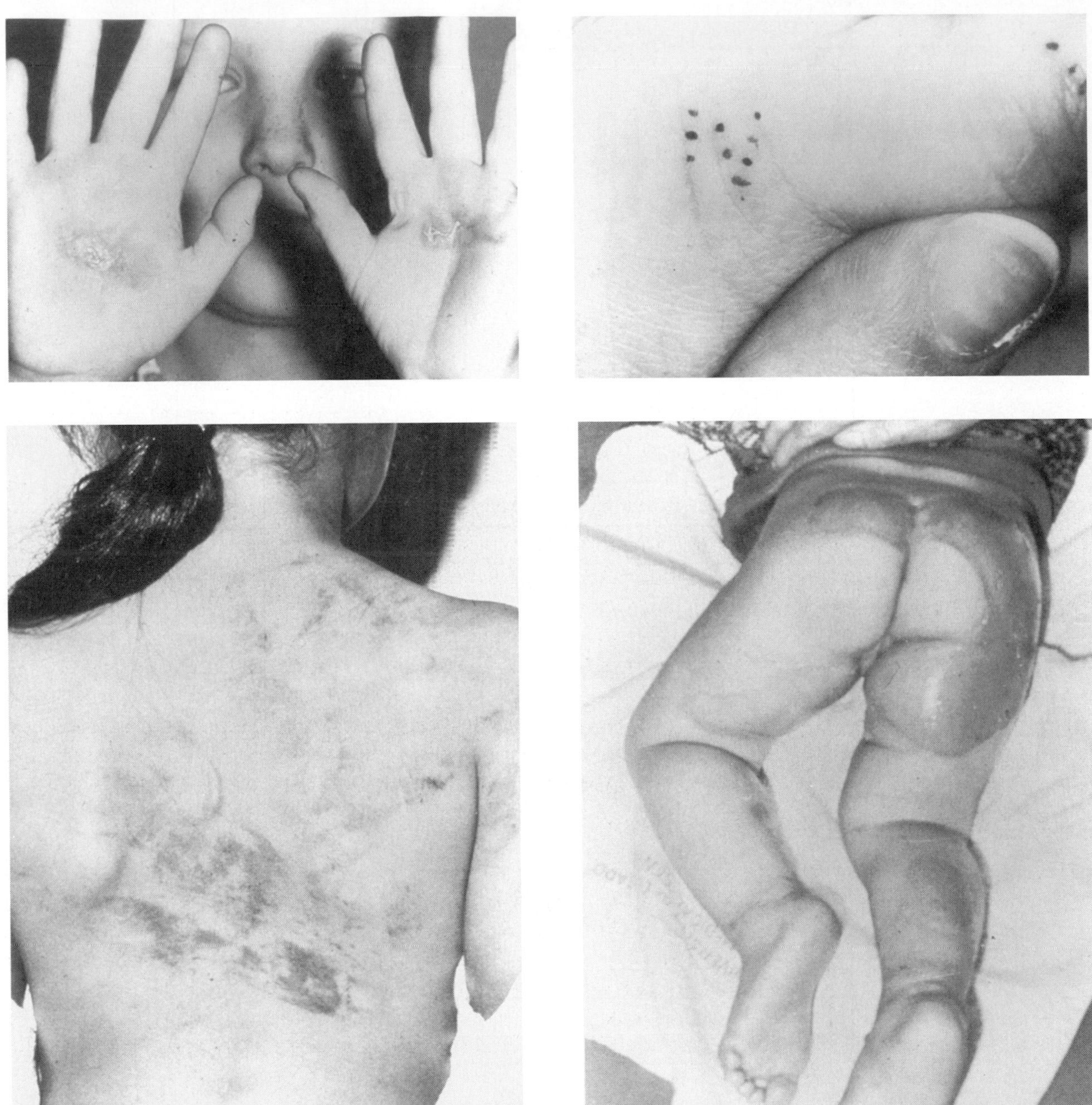

Cigarette burns on the hands or body, puncture wounds, scald marks, and bruises are recognizable signs of physical abuse.

Courtesy of Barton D. Schmitt, M.D., C. Henry Kempe National Center for Prevention and Treatment of Child Abuse and Neglect.

Fatalities of the Young

Young children are most at risk for fatal attacks. In 2003, 1,400 children died of abuse or neglect, a rate of 1.98 victims per 100,000 children. Of these, 44 percent were infants. Eighty-five percent of the fatalities were for children under 6 years of age. The large increase in fatalities in early childhood appears to be the consequence of better reporting (Child Welfare Information Gateway, 2003). The figures in Table 11.1 have slightly different age

TABLE 11.1 Child fatality victims by sex and age, detailed case data component (DCDC).

Age Group	Child Sex: Male	Female	Totals
0–3	128 (74.4%)	106 (78.5%)	234 (76.2%)
4–7	23 (13.4%)	21 (15.6%)	44 (14.3%)
8–11	15 (8.7%)	4 (3.0%)	19 (6.2%)
12 and over	6 (3.5%)	4 (3.0%)	10 (3.3%)
Totals	172 (100.0%)	135 (100.0%)	307 (100.0%)

Note: Over 76 percent of fatalities occurred to children 3 or younger.

Source: From *Child Maltreatment, 1996: Reports from the States to the National Child Abbuse and Neglect Data System,* by the U.S. Department of Health and Human Services, Children's Bureau, 1998, Washington DC: U.S. Government Printing Office.

categories, but the incidence of fatalities of the young are evident. Seventy-six percent were infants under the age of 3. Infants and young children are much more vulnerable to fatal injuries than older children because their skull, muscles, and bones are in the early stages of development.

Every state and the District of Columbia were mandated to establish Child Fatality Review Teams as a part of the Child Abuse Prevention Initiative by the Office of Child Abuse and Neglect, the Children's Bureau, and the Administration of Children and Families in 2003. The teams coordinate investigations into child deaths at state, local, or state/local levels. These teams include prosecutors, coroners or medical examiners, law enforcement officers, child protective services and public health workers and other appropriate personnel. The goal is to improve interagency communication, identification of gaps in community child protective services and the development of data information systems to guide public policy (National Center on Child Fatality Review, 2005). Figure 11.3 illustrates that neglect causes the most fatalities with multiple maltreatment and physical abuse causing a significant number.

Shaken Baby Syndrome

Parent educators and teachers should discuss shaken baby syndrome with parents and those who care for infants, because violent shaking is extremely dangerous for infants and young children. Children under 2 have undeveloped neck muscles, and sudden motion can result in the brain pulling away and tearing blood vessels and brain cells. The force with which an angry person might shake a child is 5 to 10 times greater than if the child had simply fallen (American Humane Association, 2001). In the U.S. every year, 1,200–1,400 children are shaken, and 25 percent to 30 percent die as a result (National Center for Shaken Baby Syndrome, 2006).

Even pushing a young child on a swing is cause for concern. Is the baby able to hold its head upright? Is the head bobbing back and forth? If it is, the jarring of the brain might cause injury. Tossing a baby in the air results in jarring and should be avoided. Shaken baby syndrome appeared in medical literature about 1972 and has since been recognized as a cause of injury or death for young children. Shaking can cause subdural hemorrhage, brain swelling, and damage that may result in developmental delays, mental retardation, blindness, paralysis, hearing loss, or death (American Humane Association, 2001).

Shaking usually occurs when a frustrated caregiver loses control with a crying child. Parents and caregivers need to know that it is all right for a baby to cry if the caregiver checks and knows that all the child's needs are met. It is also very important to acknowledge that some children cry more than others. When this is the case, respite needs to be given to caregivers so they can maintain control of their own emotions. Three states (Texas, New York,

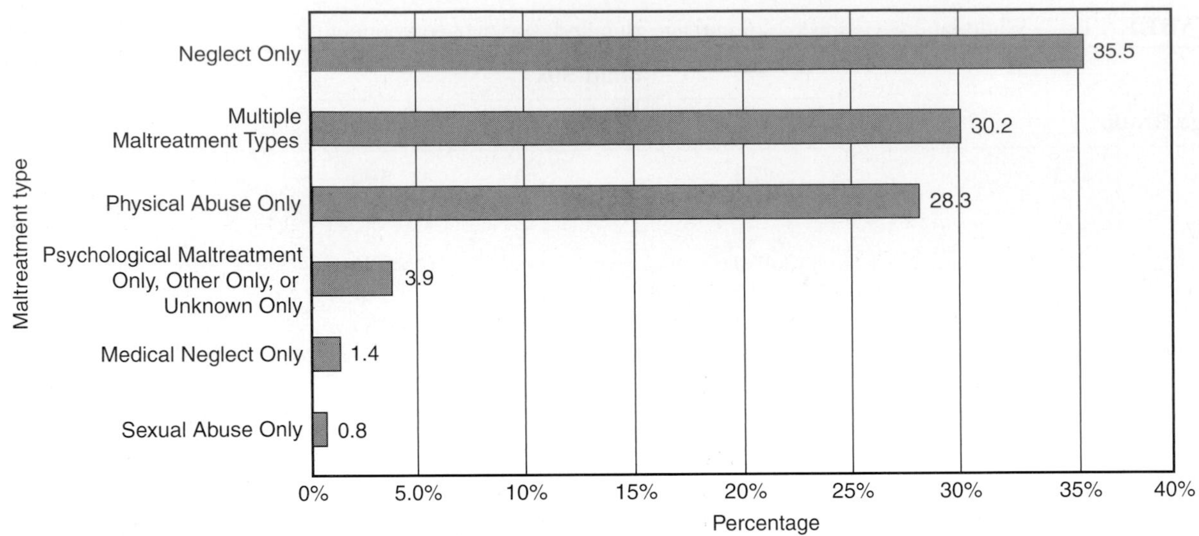

FIGURE 11.3 Maltreatment types of fatalities, 2004; Child Maltreatment 2004.

This graph breaks down the fatality victims by type of maltreatment. Each bar represents a type of maltreatment in the following order: neglect only; multiple maltreatment types; physical abuse only; psychological maltreatment only, other only, or unknown only; medical neglect only; and sexual abuse only. Most fatalities were associated with neglect only (35.5%), combinations of maltreatment types (30.2%), and physical abuse only (28.3%). www.acf.hhs.gov/programs/cb/pubs/cm04/figures_5.htm

and Utah) have legislation regarding the prevention of shaken baby syndrome. Training regarding the dangers of shaking infants and young children is mandatory for caregivers to maintain their license (National Center for Shaken Baby Syndrome, 2006).

Incidence of Child Abuse

Although some may believe the incidence of abuse is exaggerated, doctors who see children every day believe that child abuse occurs more often than the data indicate and that statistics reveal merely the tip of the iceberg (Fontana, 1973b; Gelles & Lancaster, 1987; Green, 1988). Fontana, a pediatrician who works with abused children, believes that one or two children are killed and thousands are permanently injured by their parents each day in the United States. He states, "In New York City two children per week die at the hands of their care providers" (Green, 1988, p. 10).

It was not until the 1980s that people began to realize the extent of sexual abuse. The lingering aftermath of being sexually abused was not previously acknowledged by the medical community. There were 150,000 confirmed cases of child sexual abuse reported in 1993 (Finkelhor, 1994). Adults who suffered sexual abuse as children have begun to report their plight and seek help.

The story is clear: There is a great deal of child abuse and neglect in our society. For many, violence has become an accepted mode of behavior. Sexual abuse is increasing. Television often depicts violence and force as the normal way of life. Physical punishment has long been condoned and is sanctioned by schools in many states as an alternative to other forms of discipline. The long acceptance of physical abuse makes its detection and control more difficult.

Response by Schools

> It is very important to distinguish between willful neglect and a parent's or caretaker's failure to provide necessities of life because of poverty or cultural norms. (U.S. Department of Health and Human Services, 1992, p. 2)

Schools can be part of the child abuse and neglect prevention system when they identify families that have difficulties due to poverty or cultural norms. The school can provide clothing exchanges, free breakfasts and lunches, and educational support for families at risk of abuse and neglect because of poverty. The school can offer workshops to help families understand the importance of nurturing their children. It can help parents who do not speak English by offering interpreters and educational opportunities. Positive interactions in the classroom where each child has a partner—someone to help them feel a part of the classroom—can reduce children's isolation and depression.

Besharov (1990) wrote a book, *Recognizing Child Abuse,* to help professionals recognize child abuse. There is concern that the flood of unsubstantiated claims makes it difficult to care for the children who are being abused. Child protection agencies are overwhelmed with reports. Families wrongly accused can go through a very traumatic experience. For example, Besharov points out that reasonable corporal punishment, such as spanking a child, should not be reported, but a suspicious injury or a "forceful assault to the head of a child of any age is so dangerous that it is usually considered 'unreasonable' (p. 67). Consider whether the injury was accidental—the intent of the parent or other person—and the condition of the child. Refer to *Recognizing Child Abuse* for detailed information. When in doubt, you must report.

Communication with Families

Just as there are varieties and levels of abuse and neglect, there should be variations in the school's interaction with parents. Child-care workers and school personnel who want to help an abused child must exercise good judgment. Their first response may be to want to call the parent to determine how the injury occurred. In the case of violent abuse, the child may be in danger of being permanently injured or killed. Calling the family to discuss the problem not only fails to help the family but also may precipitate more abuse. In addition, the family may become alarmed and move away. Then the child may be abused for many more months before a new school or center detects the problem. *With serious abuse, do not call the parents or try to handle the situation by yourself. Contact the appropriate authorities immediately.*

If you are working with a child you think might be enduring physical punishment at home, but who is disruptive in class, it is better to have a conference and discuss the situation. Offer appropriate discipline ideas, such as timeouts or restrictions on free time or television viewing, and continue communication with the parents. Include the child in the conference. A contract between parents, child, and teacher might be helpful. Merely calling and talking with the parent about misbehavior at school may result in the child being severely punished.

When the problem appears to be neglect rather than abuse, as when a child comes to school hungry or inappropriately dressed, a supportive visit or call to the family is in order. The school can provide emotional support and food and clothing. Working *with* parents shows them they are not alone with their overwhelming problems. If providing services is beyond the capability of the school, or if the family needs professional help, social services should be called.

CATEGORIES OF MALTREATMENT

Factors in Child Abuse

Three factors are almost always present for child abuse to occur. The first is parents or caregivers who have the potential to abuse. The second is a child the parents regard as different. The third factor is a stress situation that brings on a crisis.

According to Helfer and Kempe (1987), abusive parents or caregivers tend to acquire the potential to abuse over many years. These people usually had deprived childhoods. They lacked a consistent, loving, nurturing environment when they were young. They have a poor self-image, and their mates are passive and do not or cannot give their spouses the emotional support they need. The family probably has isolated itself; the parents have no support system from neighbors or community. Because few of them understand child development, they have unrealistic expectations of their children.

Such parents are most likely to abuse children they consider different. Child abuse also occurs against a child who actually is different from the norm—for example, a child with hyperactivity or mental retardation or another disability.

TABLE 11.2 Race of victim by maltreatment type, 2004, Child Maltreatment 2004.

	Physical Abuse Only		Neglect Only		Medical Neglect Only		Sexual Abuse Only		Psychological, Other or Unknown Maltreatment Only		Multiple Maltreatments		Total
Race	**Number**	**%**	**Number**	**%**	**Number**	**%**	**Number**	**%**	**Number**	**%**	**Number**	**%**	**Number**
African American	24,115	14.7	84,507	51.6	2294	1.4	9,350	5.7	22,684	13.8	20,906	12.8	163,856
American Indian or Alaska Native	646	8.1	5,477	68.7	45	0.6	307	3.9	515	6.5	981	12.3	7,971
Asian	1,167	17.3	3,348	49.5	49	0.7	322	4.8	1,049	15.5	825	12.2	6,760
Pacific Islander	216	12.3	517	29.4	6	0.3	99	5.6	657	37.3	265	15.1	1,760
White	39,119	11.0	180,608	51.0	2430	0.7	29,716	8.4	49,173	13.9	53,173	15.0	354,219
Multiple Race	1,140	9.7	6,217	53.1	97	0.8	465	4.0	1,877	16.0	1,903	16.3	11,699
Hispanic	14,736	11.7	65,261	51.9	953	0.8	8,905	7.1	18,763	14.9	17,102	13.6	125,720
Unknown or Missing	5,029	13.1	21,585	56.2	312	0.8	3,183	8.3	3,405	8.9	4,911	12.8	38,425
Total	86,168		367,520		6186		52,347		98,123		100,066		710,410
Weighted Percent		12.1		51.7		0.9		7.4		13.8		14.1	

The first column of this table lists the type of race or ethnicity. The next column lists the total number of victims for each race. The next five columns lists the number and percentage of victims by maltreatment type. With the exception of Pacific Islander, approximately one-half of all reces experienced neglect. Data source: Child File. Based on data from 44 states.

Source: U.S. Department of Health and Human Services, Administration for Children and Families, Children's Bureau. Retrieved from www.acf.hhs.gov/ programs/cb/pubs/cm04/figure 3_5.htm

Before the abusive act occurs, there is a precipitating event—one that does not directly cause the specific act against the child, but a minor or major crisis that sets the stage for the parent to lose control. This crisis may be physical (e.g., a broken washing machine) or personal (e.g., spouse desertion, a death in the family). With these three factors the stage is set. The parent or caregiver loses control and abuses the child (Helfer, 1975).

Table 11.2 is an interesting table with its separation of psychological, other unknown maltreatment, medical neglect, and multiple maltreatment separate from the earlier typical separation of physical abuse, neglect, sexual abuse, and emotional abuse. It illustrates the percentage and number of each abuse by race. The weighted percentage totals 100 percent and the data is collected from 44 states.

NEGLECT

Child neglect occurs when there is failure to care for the child's basic needs. This type of maltreatment is reported most often (see Figure 11.1 and Table 11.2). Physical neglect is the area most frequently identified, but there are also emotional and educational neglect. Parents may not be indifferent. Instead, they may not recognize the importance of medical care or a developmental environment, or they may be incapable of furnishing them.

Physical neglect refers to the parents' failure to provide the necessities—adequate shelter, care and supervision, food, clothing, and protection. Neglect is the most common type of child abuse, accounting for more than half of maltreatment. The child shows signs of malnutrition, usually is irritable, and may need medical attention. The child often goes hungry and needs supervision after school. The parents are either unable or unwilling to give proper care. Neglect is often the result of the parent's inability to supply necessary care in 90 percent of those cases reported. Insufficient income is cited as the greatest cause of neglect (Cupoli & Sewell, 1988; Horton & Cruise, 2001).

Neglect may include medical neglect, abandonment, and not allowing a runaway to return home. When a child is abandoned, it represents renunciation and total rejection of the child by the parent.

Educational neglect occurs when parents permit chronic truancy, fail to make sure their child attends school, or fail to tend to any special educational needs of the child. Both medical neglect and educational neglect result in the child's inability to develop fully.

Emotional neglect includes refusal to provide psychological help if the child needs it, exposure of the child to abuse of someone else (e.g., spousal abuse in the child's presence), and permission for use of drugs and alcohol by the child (U.S. Department of Health and Human Services, 1992).

Parents may be psychologically unavailable to the child, ignoring their child's need for comfort. This results in some children who fail to thrive. The child does not continue to grow or develop at a rate expected for their age. These instances of failure to thrive may be the result of this emotional neglect (Brier, Berliner, Bulkley, Jenny, & Reid, 1996).

Table 11.2 differentiates between neglect and medical neglect. The figures are weighted so that the total percentages total 100 percent, thus giving clear proportions. Neglect makes up 51.7 percent of the total neglect with an additional 9 percent medical neglect, for a total of 52.6 percent of maltreatment related to neglect. If we disregard the unknown or missing items, the totals for neglect group around 51 percent with the American Indian or Alaska Native higher at 68.7 percent and the Pacific Islander lower at 29.4 percent. Note that insufficient income is cited earlier in this discussion as a probable cause of neglect.

Physical Abuse and Neglect

The *physically abused* child shows signs of injury—welts, cuts, bruises, burns, or fractures. Educators should be aware of repeated injuries, untreated injuries, multiple injuries, and new injuries added to old.

Multiple maltreatment often occurs in a child who suffers abuse or neglect. Although emotional maltreatment can be isolated, instances of physical abuse or neglect usually are accompanied by emotional abuse.

Recognizing Physical Abuse

Although many bruises and abrasions are accidental, others give cause for the teacher to believe that they were intentionally inflicted. Bruises are the most common symptoms of physical abuse. Other symptoms include welts, lumps, or ridges on the body, usually caused by a blow; burns, shown by redness, blistering, or peeling of the skin; fractured bones; scars; lacerations or torn cuts; and abrasions.

Head Start personnel are given guidelines with four criteria for identifying abuse of the preschool child. These guidelines are useful for detection of abuse in children of any age. The first is location of the injury. As illustrated in Figure 11.4, bruises on the knees, elbows, shins, and—for the preschool child—the forehead are considered normal in most circumstances. "If these bruises were found on the back, genital area, thighs, buttocks, face or back of legs, one should be suspicious" (U.S. Department of Health, Education and Welfare, 1977, p. 67).

The second criterion is evidence of repetition of injury. A significantly large number of bruises or cuts and injuries in various stages of healing should be suspect. There are instances, however, when repetition could be accidental: The child could be accident-prone, so the correlation between the injury and an explanation of its cause—the fourth criterion, described later—needs to be kept in mind.

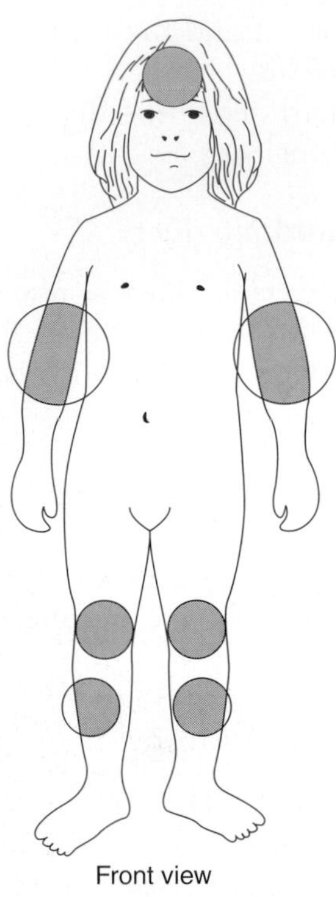

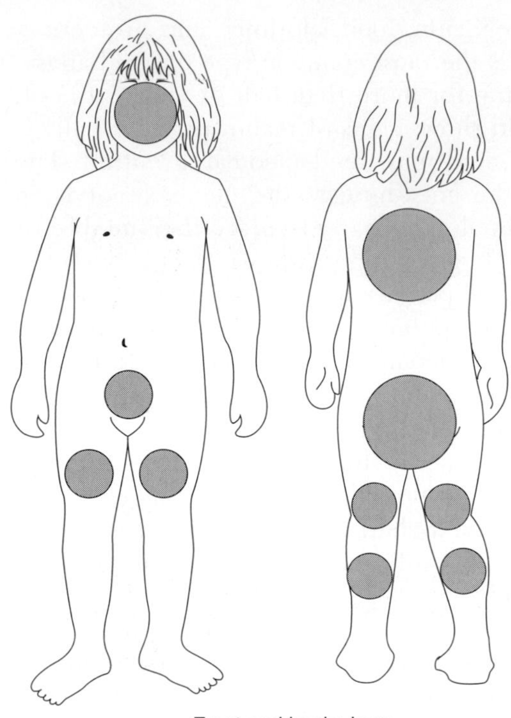

FIGURE 11.4 Comparison of typical and suspicious bruising areas.

Note: The bruises children receive in play are depicted on the left. The bruises on the right would not normally happen in everyday play.

Source: From *Child Abuse and Neglect: A Self-Instructional Text for Head Start Personnel,* by the U.S. Department of Health, Education and Welfare, Head Start Bureau and Children's Bureau, 1977, Washington, DC: U.S. Government Printing Office.

The third criterion is the injury. If it is obvious that the bruise, cut, or burn was inflicted by an object, such as a belt, stick, or cigarette, the caregiver or teacher should suspect abuse.

The fourth criterion is the correlation between the injury and the explanation given by the child or the parent. The accident as described should be likely to produce the resultant injury. For example, could round burns shaped like the end of a cigarette be caused by the child playing too near the stove?

Parents who were victims of maltreatment as children are more likely to resort to abuse when confronted with other risk factors (Horton & Cruise, 2001). According to Table 11.2 the race with the highest rate of physical abuse is Asian with a 17.3 percent, while the lowest is American Indian or Alaska Native at 8.1 percent. The weighted percentage is 12.1 with the other races falling a little below or above that rate (U.S. Department of Health & Human Serves, 2004).

In ascertaining the extent of suspected physical abuse, the teacher should not remove any of the child's clothing. That should be done only by such personnel as a nurse or doctor who would undress a child as part of their professional responsibilities.

After reviewing the four criteria and checking school policy—the suspicious placement of injury, the severity and repetition of injuries, evidence of infliction by an object, and inconsistent explanation (or consistent if the child reports the abuse)—the educator must report a suspected injury to the appropriate authorities.

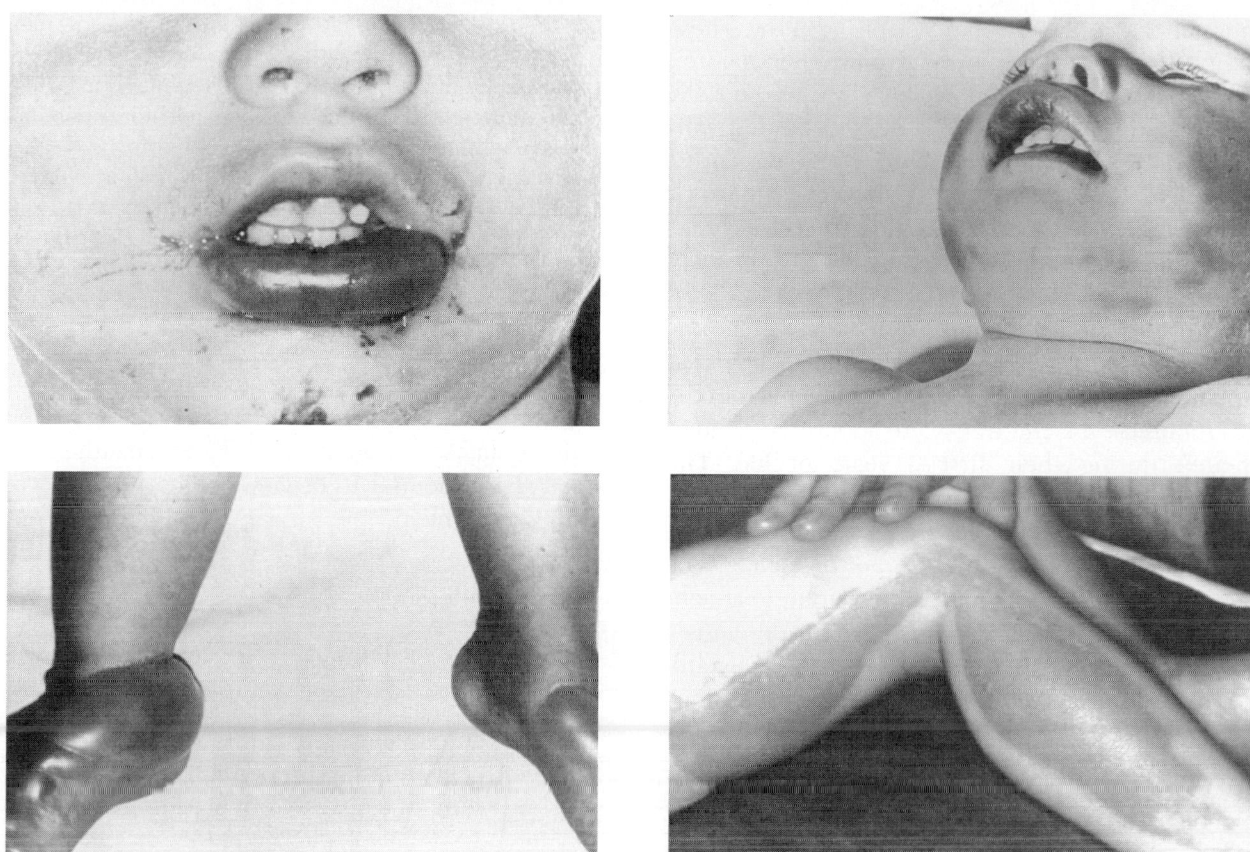

Scalded and battered, these children were victims of child abuse.
Courtesy of Barton D. Schmitt, M.D., C. Henry Kempe National Center for Prevention and Treatment of Child Abuse and Neglect.

EMOTIONAL ABUSE

Compared to physical neglect and abuse, it is more difficult to identify *emotional neglect and abuse,* defined as a "pattern of behavior that can seriously interfere with a child's positive emotional development" (American Humane Association, 1992c).

Parents of emotionally abused children are usually overly harsh and critical. They withhold love and acceptance and do not give the child either physical or verbal encouragement and praise. Although they expect performance, they do not support the child's endeavors. Physical abuse damages a child's body, and emotional abuse damages a child's psyche. "Children who are constantly shamed, terrorized, humiliated, or rejected suffer at least as much if not more than if they had been physically assaulted" (p. 1). Patterns can include the following:

- Terrorizing
- Continued rejection of the child
- Refusal to provide needed nurturance
- Refusal to provide help for a child's psychological problems
- Lack of needed mental or physical stimulation
- Forced involvement with drugs, criminal activities, and other corruptive forces (American Humane Association, 1992b)

Chapter 1 discusses the importance of attachment during the first years of life. Spitz (1945) reported on children who developed marasmus—progressive emaciation—and died from lack of nurturing. These are obvious cases of emotional abuse, but children who are not nurtured and who live in an emotionally insecure environment may show signs of low self-esteem, slow educational growth, and insecurity. Table 11.2 identifies psychological, other, or unknown maltreatment, indicating that it includes emotional as well as other factors. Most of the races center around 15 to 16 percent.

Egeland (1988) reported on the Minnesota Mother–Child Project, a longitudinal study that worked with at-risk children and their families. In the 267 families, 44 children were identified as maltreated during their first 2 years of life. The researchers assessed four maltreatment groups: physical abuse, neglect, verbal rejections, and psychological unavailability at 12, 18, 24, 41, and 54 months. The infancy period was examined in relation to attachment, the "relationship that the infant develops a sense of trust and confidence" (p. D-12). The children were followed through the periods until they were in school. At each level it was apparent that psychological unavailability affects the child's development, self-esteem, and confidence. The children who were neglected (psychological unavailability) displayed greater problems in attention. They were:

> uninvolved, reliant, lacking creative initiative, and having much more difficulty comprehending the day-to-day schoolwork than children in the control group. They were impatient, disrespectful, expressed anxiety about their schoolwork and were more likely to make irrelevant response in the classroom. . . . On the individual scales, the neglected children were rated as anxious, withdrawn, unpopular, aggressive, and obsessive-compulsive. Not only did they present far more problems than children in the control group, but they also presented more problems than children in the physical abuse group. (p. D-15)

The difficulty of identifying psychological unavailability and emotional neglect makes it doubly difficult for the schools to respond to the concern. It also is impossible for teachers to overcome a student's childhood devoid of emotional security. However, there are incidents and examples of teachers who have had a positive effect on children who were emotionally neglected.

> I don't think my fourth-grade teacher, Mr. Evans, had any idea what an impact he had on my life. He was my father's opposite and taught me much about how men could be. He was consistent and concerned while my father was drunk or ignoring me. He praised me while my father criticized. He prized my mind and my accomplishments; my father cared only about abusing my body. I learned a great deal from that teacher about who I was and that I was an important person. I think I became a teacher myself to be like him, so that I could make a difference for some other child. (Tower, 1992, p. 57)

Teachers have a great deal of power over how the students in their classes feel about themselves. Children's self-confidence and self-esteem can be either enhanced or diminished. They can either feel good about themselves or view themselves as incapable, unlikable people.

SEXUAL ABUSE

Sexual abuse is defined under the Child Abuse Prevention and Treatment Act (CAPTA) as:

- The employment, use, persuasion, inducement, enticement, or coercion of any child to engage in, or assist any other person to engage in, any sexually explicit conduct or simulation of such conduct for the purpose of producing a visual depiction of such conduct
- The rape, and in cases of caretaker or interfamilial relationships, statutory rape, molestation, prostitution, or other form of sexual exploitation of children, or incest with children (NCCAN, 2001, p. 2)

As illustrated in Table 11.2, white people have the highest rate of sexual abuse at 8.4 percent. The next highest rate is Hispanic with 7.1 percent, followed by African American with 5.7 percent.

Keep in mind that although the child might be forced to cooperate, he or she is (by legal definition) not capable of giving consent (Hagans & Case, 1988, p. 21).

Categories of sexual abuse include:

1. *Incest.* Physical sexual activity between members of the extended family.
2. *Pedophilia.* Sexual preference by an adult for prepubertal children.
3. *Exhibitionism.* Exposure of genitals to someone of the opposite gender.

4. *Molestation.* Fondling, touching, masturbation, or kissing child, especially on breast and genital areas.
5. *Sexual intercourse (statutory rape).* Includes penile–vaginal intercourse, fellatio (oral–genital contact), and sodomy (anal–genital contact).
6. *Rape.* Sexual intercourse or attempted sexual intercourse without consent.
7. *Sexual sadism.* Infliction of bodily harm for sexual gratification.
8. *Child pornography.* Photographs, videos, or films showing sexual acts featuring children. An estimated 300,000 children are involved in child pornography.
9. *Child prostitution.* Children in sex acts for profit. (Kempe & Kempe, 1984)

Sexual conduct becomes abuse when activities are instigated through trickery or force with the instigator—one who has caretaking relations with the child or has age and maturational advantage over the child. The situation includes a perpetrator who has a power advantage over a child (Finkelhor, 1994).

Abuse may be categorized as contact and non contact sexual abuse. Contact includes touching sexual parts of a child's body or having the child touch parts of the sexual partner's body, which may include penetration (into the vagina, mouth, or anus) and nonpenetration. Nonpenetration contact involves fondling, kissing, or touching sexual parts of the body by either the child or the partner.

Noncontact sexual abuse may involve exhibitionism, voyeurism, or the making of pornographic materials, and it may also include verbal harassment (Finkelhor, 1994).

Sexual abuse is difficult to detect. About 80 percent of the offenders are known to the family or are family members. The victims are most often girls (77 percent) ranging from infants to adolescents (U.S. Department of Health and Human Services, Children's Bureau, 1998).

Although historically most societies have had taboos against such behavior, sexual abuse and incest have always existed. But sexual abuse generally has been concealed, mythicized, or ignored. Not until the late 1970s and early 1980s did its existence become realistically recognized. Even then, most people gathering information on the problem believed that, as in reported incidents of other kinds of child abuse, only the tip of the iceberg had been revealed.

Incest and other sexual abuse occurs in all socioeconomic groups, and therefore, teachers in all schools or child-care settings should be aware of the indicators. Sexually abused children often exhibit some of the following physical and behavioral characteristics (Krugman, 1986; Riggs, 1982):

Physical signs

- Bruises or bleeding in external genitalia or anal area
- Uncomfortable while sitting
- Difficulty walking
- Pregnancy
- Torn, bloody, or stained underclothing
- Sexually transmitted disease

Behavioral signs

- Appetite disorders
- Phobias
- Guilt
- Temper tantrums
- Neurotic and conduct disorders
- Truancy
- Suicide attempts
- Confides with teacher or nurse that he or she has been sexually mistreated
- Reports by other children that their friend is being sexually mistreated
- Displays precocious sexual behavior and/or knowledge
- Unwilling to change for gym
- Withdrawn, engages in fantasy
- Depressed, sad, and teary eyed
- Confused about own identity
- Frequent absences justified by male caregiver or parent
- Acts out in a seductive manner
- Reluctant to go home

- Young child regresses to earlier behavior by thumb sucking, bed wetting, difficulty in eating, sleeping, and fear of the dark
- Older child turns to drugs, tries to run away, and has difficulty doing schoolwork

Concern about sexual abuse has steadily risen because of its deleterious effects on the child and, later, the adult. Psychological and emotional reactions are common. Children feel trapped, confused, betrayed, and disgraced. They may have fears, phobias, somatic complaints, mood changes, anxieties, hysterical seizures, multiple personalities, or nightmares. They may become prostitutes, self-mutilating, or suicidal. At school they may show developmental lags, communication problems, and apparent learning deficiencies (Finkelhor, 1986; Krugman, 1986; Ryan, 1989; Wodarski & Johnson, 1988).

After a 15-year increase (from 1977 until 1992), substantiated cases of child sexual abuse have declined from 149,890 substantiated cases in 1992 to 103,600 cases in 1998, a 31 percent reduction. There may be a variety of reasons for this. Public awareness, prevention programs, incarceration of offenders, and treatment programs may have had an effect on the reduction of incidence of abuse (Jones & Finkelhor, 2001).

Boys and girls have similar responses to sexual abuse, both long term and short term, including fears, sleep problems, and distractedness (Finkelhor, 1990). The differences show boys are less symptomatic when evaluated by teachers and parents, but the same when evaluated by themselves. Whereas boys may act out more aggressively, girls may act more depressed.

Children who are being sexually abused often go through five phases: (a) secrecy; (b) helplessness; (c) entrapment and accommodation; (d) delayed, conflicted, and unconvincing disclosure; and (e) retraction (Summit, 1983). To understand a child's predicament, one must understand the helplessness the child feels in responding to the adult who is more physically powerful and supposedly more knowledgeable. The adult first approaches the child with the need for secrecy: "Everything will be all right if you do not tell. No one else will understand our secret." "Your mother will hate you." "If you tell, it will break up the family." "If you tell, I'll kill your pet." "If you tell, I'll spank you."

Whatever the secret, the child is in a no-win position. The child fears being hurt if he or she tells the secret. When the child does tell, the reaction is often disbelief. "Unless the victim can find some permission and power to share the secret and unless there is the possibility of an engaging, nonpunitive response" the child may spend a life of "self-imposed exile from intimacy, trust and self-validation" (Summit, 1983, p. 182).

The teacher or child caregiver who suspects sexual abuse must report those suspicions—social service and child protection agencies are established in every state.

The teacher's role is a supportive one. Continue to have normal expectations for the child, keep a stable environment for the child, and do not make the child feel ostracized or different. Treat the child with understanding, be sensitive to the child's needs, and help build the child's self-esteem. Several programs have been developed to help the child develop defenses against personal abuse.

Reviewers and teachers have asked for more help in responding to a child who shares about an abusive situation. An article by Austin (2000) gives suggestions to help teachers respond to a sexually abused child. The topics include:

- Remain calm and reassuring. Speak quietly; do not panic.
- Take the child to a private place like the nurse's office.
- Position yourself at the child's eye level.
- Speak on the child's level. Use language the child understands.
- Listen intently.
- Take the child seriously.
- Obtain only the information necessary to make a report.
- Do not put words in the child's mouth.
- Do not use words that the child has not already used. (Don't use words describing the sex that are not in the child's vocabulary.)
- Allow the child to have feelings.
- Reassure the child that the abuse is not his or her fault.
- Start your conversation with general open-ended questions and allow the child to tell the story without interrupting.

- Do not condemn the abuser.
- Let the child know that he or she is not alone and that you are willing to help.
- Do not touch the child without permission.
- Tell the truth—do not make promises you will not be able to keep.
- Tell the child about the process, that others will be told about the abuse.
- Thank the child for confiding in you.
- Help the child devise a safety plan if abuse occurs again. Have the child tell someone immediately—a reliable person at home or a teacher or school professional.
- Assure the child that she or he will remain with someone safe until authorities come. Do not allow the child to return to the home of the abuser (pp. 4–5).

Internet Safety

In recent years children using the Internet have become vulnerable to pedophiles and pornographers. Children can inadvertently become exposed by simply typing the word *legs*, for Legos. Several steps must be taken to protect children, by teachers, parents, and children themselves. First, parents and teachers must monitor children's use of the computer. At school, teachers can set up safe Web sites that control what children will be able to access. Parents can contact their Internet service providers to block certain materials from coming into a child's computer. The filtering programs can also restrict personal information from being sent online. In addition, children can be guided to discriminate between appropriate sites, and those that make them feel uncomfortable. All three steps are necessary to safeguard children (Kids Health, 2006).

BULLYING AND VIOLENCE IN SCHOOLS

"Bullying refers to repeated, unprovoked, harmful actions by one child or children against another" (Bullock, 2002, p. 130). Bullying can be physical or emotional. The emotional bullying includes being teased, threatened, taunted, called names, or having negative rumors started about one. Equally devastating is being rejected and excluded from other groups of children (Banks, 1997; Bullock, 2002; Garrity, Baris, & Porter, 2000).

Physical bullying can include hitting, pushing, rough and intimidating actions, a quick jab, or a head shoved into a locker (Bullock, 2002; Garrity et al., 2000). There is a difference between girl bullying and boy bullying. Boys use more physical along with verbal aggression, whereas girls add social intimidation to verbal aggression.

Two types of victims are chosen by the aggressor. One is the passive victim who seems to be helpless and unable to fight back. Afraid and alone, the child is an easy victim of the aggressor. The victim may convey his or her vulnerability through body language.

The second type of victim is the child who is a provocative victim. This child is impulsive, acts without thinking, and responds to the attack by fighting back (Bullock, 2002; Garrity et al., 2000). "Soon the bully has far more children on his or her side and the victim feels even more helpless. When a scene such as this plays itself out day after day, the victimized child grows more miserable, desperate, and incapable of handling the situation. If the cycle has grown this serious, it will not turn itself around without adult help" (Garrity et al., 2000, p. 7).

Bullies tend to be children whose parents use physical discipline; these children strike back physically to handle problems. They may break school rules and are oppositional to authority (Banks, 1997). Bullies enjoy dominating others; they also have little empathy for others. As mentioned, boy bullies usually have physical strength that helps them dominate others. Girls use their ability to control other girls through intimidation and exclusion.

Research conducted by Arseneault et. al. (2006), examined the impact of early school bullying experiences on the mental health of 5- and 7-year-olds. The results indicated that there was a long-term impact, both socially and cognitively on children's development, even years after the experience. It was recommended that programs targeted to meet the mental health needs of children should include bullying as a risk factor.

Work by the National Youth Violence Prevention Resource Center (2006) indicates that bullying has long-term consequences on children's behavior. If bullying behavior continues into the teen years, they (especially boys) are more likely to be involved in vandalism, truancy, and drug abuse into adulthood.

Sixty percent of bullies have at least one criminal conviction by age 24. Victims of bullies are more likely to do poorly in school and have a number of behavior problems. They generally have few friends and poor peer relationships. Some victims have been driven to suicide. Observers of bullying are also victims. They feel helpless and experience guilt. They may be drawn into bullying themselves, or avoid relationships with the bullied victims.

Awareness of Abuse, Child to Child

Another area of concern that has been evident in schools and playgrounds for many years, but which is most often overlooked as a process of growing up, is degradation of one child by another whether it is defined as bullying or teasing. Research by the Family and Work Institute, conducted from October to December 2001, found that the issue of being teased or gossiped about in a mean way within the past month reached 67 percent. The study cannot say which came first, the being hurt or hurting, but 68 percent of those who were gossiped about or teased in the past month turned around and did the same to others. Sixty-one percent of the Colorado students in the study had been rejected or ignored, and 32 percent had been bullied (Galinsky & Salmond, 2002).

"Many kids believe that insensitivity and meanness can be triggers for more harmful kinds of violence" (p. 15). The study involved students in Grades 5 through 12. More children are bullied, hit, kicked, shoved between 5th and 8th grade than high school, where there is more gossip and students are more often teased. Programs designed to reduce devastating experiences for children in school need to be implemented in schools. Action steps to end violence include:

1. Help establish norms where differences are not put down but are celebrated
2. Work toward the creation of a civil society where there is more caring and respect
3. Improve the relationships that children have in all aspects of their lives—at home and at school
4. Include young people's views of how to end violence in violence prevention efforts
5. Establish, invest in, and evaluate violence prevention efforts, as well as positive youth development efforts (Galinsky & Salmond, 2002, pp. 57–63)
6. Do *not* victimize the child who has already been bullied and victimized

Can Teachers Make a Difference?

Teachers are extremely important to a child's feeling adequate, competent, and cared for. One way teachers can lose this and add to a child's insecurity is by using children as scapegoats in a class. They control the rest of the class by focusing on one or two children who are targeted for discipline and negative reinforcement. This author has observed classrooms in which teachers cause emotional abuse in their efforts to control the classroom. Teachers can have an attitude toward a child that fosters prejudice and discrimination against that child by the child's classmates. They do not recognize that they are, in effect, emotionally abusing the child. Their actions are not occasional disciplinary decisions; they are caused by a repeated pattern as described by James Garbarino, executive director of the Erikson Institute, "the chronic pattern that erodes and corrodes a child . . . that persistent, chronic pattern of behavior toward a child" (American Humane Association, 1992c, p. 2).

Garbarino was speaking about parents and children, but this chronic pattern is also damaging when it is used in the schools. An occasional loss of control by parents (or teachers) does not indicate emotional abuse. Human beings may lose control and say hurtful things, but the person who consistently destroys a child's self-esteem is the one who is being extremely hurtful to the child and is emotionally abusing the child.

Programs to Combat Bullying and Violence in Schools

The National Education Association Professional Library has published teacher guides to prevent bullying and sexual harassment. The one for students kindergarten through grade three is titled *Quit It.* Educational Equity Concepts, Inc., Wellesley College Center for Research on Women, and the NEA Professional Library cooperated in producing the teacher's guide, which discusses procedures and activities in detail (Froschi, Sprung, & Mullin-Rindler, 1998).

The second guide, *Bullyproof: A Teacher's Guide on Teasing and Bullying,* was developed for fourth- and fifth-grade students and was a joint publication of the Wellesley College Center and NEA Professional Library (Stein, 1996). One activity illustrates an example of a letter written to the person who is bullying. Lesson 8, which is one or two class sessions, is titled "What Are Your Rights" and is a review and discussion of sexual harassment and relevant laws. Lesson 10, an action alert, allows the students to brainstorm to answer how to end bullying and teasing among the students. The guides include materials, a teacher's guide, and many references (Stein & Sjostrom, 1994).

The third guide, titled *Flirting or Hurting? A Teacher's Guide to Student-to-Student Sexual Harassment in Schools*, gives examples and discussion points to clarify what sexual harassment is and what can be done if a student thinks he or she is being harassed (Stein & Sjostrom, 1994).

The International Bullying Prevention Association, P.O. Box 2288, Falmouth, MA, also provides conferences, resources and training to guide adults in effective strategies to develop environments to protect victims of bullying. The organization also recognizes the need to guide and redirect children that bully others, so they have the chance to develop constructive interpersonal relations (International Bullying Prevention Association, 2006).

CORPORAL PUNISHMENT IN SCHOOLS

Does there seem to be an element of inconsistency in our work to eliminate abuse in the schools with the policy of corporal punishment still in place in many schools? Every industrialized country in the world prohibits school corporal punishment except the United States, and one state in Australia (Center for Effective Discipline, 2006). The paddle is the primary instrument of physical discipline in the schools that still had corporal punishment. In the United States 301,016 students were physically punished in the 2002–2003 school year. Black students were hit at more than twice their make-up in the population. Black students received 38 percent of paddlings but make up 17 percent of the population. Teachers in Texas account for 19 percent of all school paddlings in the country (U.S. Department of Education, 2005).

Zigler, a noted Yale University psychologist, who was instrumental in establishing Head Start, noted that "the widespread acceptance of physical abuse as an appropriate disciplinary technique implicitly condones the physical abuse of children" (Green, 1988, p. 10). "Not only can children be injured, but the practice perpetuates the cycle of child abuse. . . . Children abused at school as well as at home further incorporate the message that violence is the only way to ensure compliance with rules laid down by another individual or group of individuals" (Tower, 1992, p. 56). Although we have made considerable progress since the 1700s and 1800s, when child labor was rampant, our cultural values, socialization patterns, and resultant discipline still support the use of physical force with children.

The National Committee for Prevention of Child Abuse adopted the following policy statement in 1983:

> Since corporal punishment in schools and custodial settings contradicts our national policy dedicated to the eradication of child abuse from our society, and since appropriate disciplinary alternatives can be made available, we will work toward the elimination of corporal punishment in the schools and toward the adoption of alternatives to corporal punishment. (Green, 1988, pp. 9–10)

More than 40 national organizations have policies that oppose corporal punishment in the schools. Among them are the American Academy of Pediatrics, American Association for Counseling & Development, American Bar Association, American Medical Association, American Psychiatric Association, American Psychological Association, American Public Health Association, Association for Childhood Education International, Council for Exceptional Children, National Association for the Advancement of Colored People, National Association of Elementary School Principals, and the National Association of School Nurses, National Association of School Psychologists, National Association of State Boards of Education, National Congress of Parents and Teachers, National Education Association, and the National Mental Health Association.

Almost every other industrialized nation in the world has abolished corporal punishment: American Samoa, Austria, Belgium, Britain, Denmark, Fiji, Finland, France, Germany, Holland, Ireland, Italy, Kenya, Namibia, New Zealand, Norway, Poland, Portugal, Romania, Russia, South Africa,

Spain, Sweden, Switzerland, Thailand, Tobago, Trinidad, Turkey, Zambia, and Zimbabwe. Poland was the first to abolish it in 1783 (End Violence Against the Next Generation, n.d.). Iceland is the only country that banned corporal punishment during its foundation (Center for Effective Discipline, 2006).

By 2007, 29 states and the District of Columbia had banned corporal punishment. They were Alaska, California, Connecticut, Delaware, Hawaii, Illinois, Iowa, Maine, Maryland, Massachusetts, Michigan, Minnesota, Montana, Nebraska, Nevada, New Hampshire, New Jersey, New York, North Dakota, Oregon, Pennsylvania, Rhode Island, South Dakota, Utah, Vermont, Virginia, Washington, West Virginia, and Wisconsin. Many cities in states that have not abolished corporal punishment have abolished the practice in their schools (Center for Effective Discipline, 2007; U.S. Department of Education, 2005). In general, schools have been alarmingly slow to join the national movement to reduce abuse—a movement that began in the 1960s and has continued into the 21st century. Thus, schools perpetuate the use of force to discipline children. In addition, schools that use ridicule, fear, and ostracism to discipline children may cause emotional abuse in the classroom (Krugman & Krugman, 1984).

Parents can impact the school culture to protect their children from corporal punishment. According to the Center for Effective Discipline (2006), parents can do the following:

1. Get a copy of the school's discipline code to determine school policy.
2. Write a letter requesting that their child not be physically punished and if possible have the child's pediatrician sign the letter.
3. If the child has a disability, ask to have a statement included in the IEP that prohibits the child from receiving corporal punishment.
4. If a child is injured, take the child to a physician or emergency room and ask that pictures be taken of the injury.
5. Talk with the child to make sure he/she doesn't feel to blame for the punishment.
6. Organize a ban in the school district on corporal punishment.

Parents and educators working together can make a difference in ensuring that children experience human treatment in their school settings.

WHO REPORTS MALTREATMENT CASES?

Cases of child maltreatment are reported by both nonprofessionals and professionals. Educators have become much more aware of their responsibility, and most reports come from this group (16.5 percent in 2004), as shown in Figure 11.5. Professionals—including educators as well as law enforcement, social services, and medical personnel—made 55.7 percent of the reports. Friends and family members reported 19.6 percent of the cases (U.S. Department of Health and Human Services, 2004). As Figure 11.5 illustrates, 9.4 percent of the reports were made anonymously and 8.4 percent were classified as "other"; both probably contain some of the same groups.

Situations related to teachers and schools are described in *Child Abuse and Neglect: A Shared Community Concern* (U.S. Department of Health and Human Services, 1992). Two examples follow.

REPORT

When Cindy was 8 years of age, her teacher called Child Protection Services (CPS). Cindy was the only child in her family who wore old, tattered clothing to school and was not given the same privileges and opportunities as her brothers and sisters. The other children were allowed to join in after-school activities; however, Cindy was not allowed to participate in any outside activities. Cindy became very withdrawn at school. She stopped speaking in class and would not engage in play activities with her classmates. Her academic performance declined rapidly. Finally, Cindy became incontinent and had "accidents" in class.

REASONS

The reasons the teacher reported this case to CPS were:

- Serious differential treatment of one child in the family.
- Marked decline in academic performance and class participation.
- Incontinence.

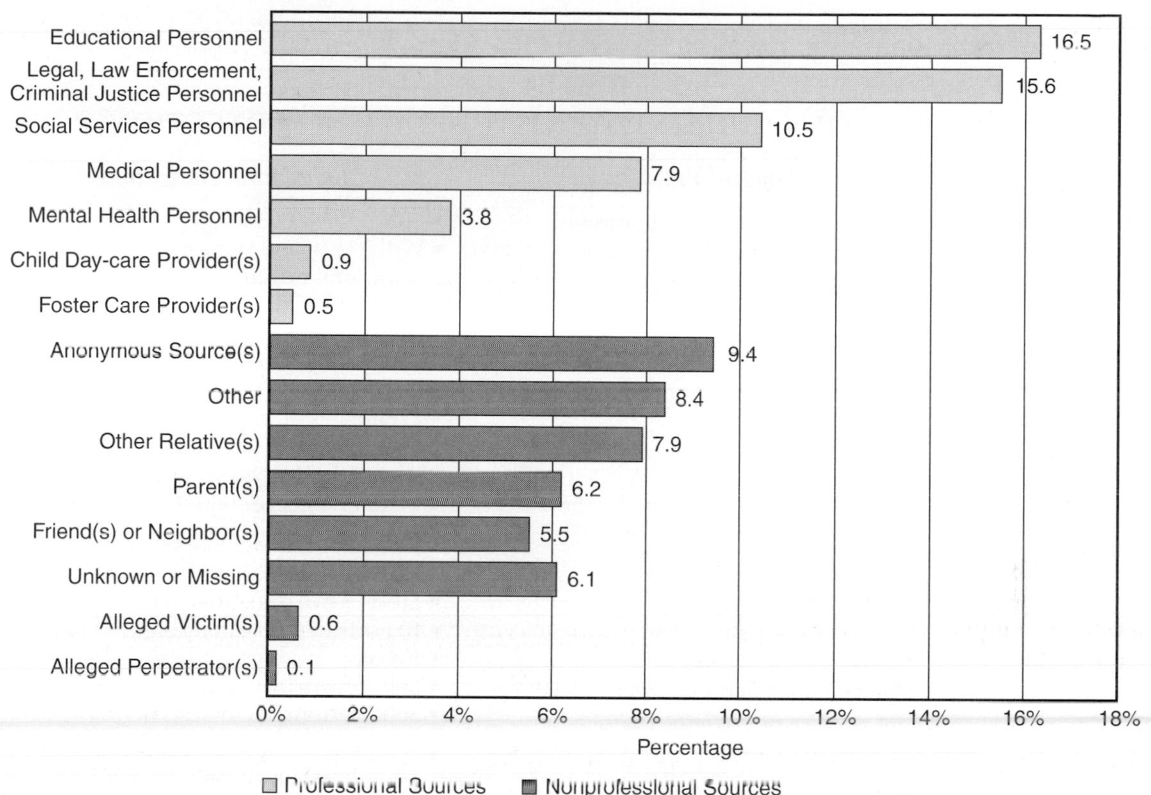

FIGURE 11.5 Report sources, 2004, Child Maltreatment 2004.

Report Sources, 2004

This graph indicates the percentages of reports received by source, broken into two main categories—professionals and nonprofessionals. Professionals submitted more than half (56.0%) of the reports. The categories of professionals include educators, legal and law enforcement personnel, social services personnel, medical personnel, mental health personnel, child day-care providers, and foster care providers. The three most common sources of reports in 2004 were from professionals--educational personnel (16.5%), legal or law enforcement personnel (15.6%), and social services personnel (10.5%). Nonprofessional report sources submitted the remaining 44 percent of reports. These included parents, other relatives, friends and neighbors, alleged victims, alleged perpetrators, anonymous callers, and "other" sources. Anonymous (9.4%), "other" sources (8.4%), and other relatives (7.9%) accounted for the largest groups of nonprofessional reporters.

Source: U.S. Department of Health and Human Services, Administration for Children and Families, Children's Bureau. Retrieved. September 20, 2006, from www.acf.hhs.gov/programs/cb/pubs/cm04/figures_2.htm

REPORT

Susan, aged 7, was in her first-grade class when her teacher noticed that she had difficulty sitting and had some unusually shaped marks on her arm. Susan was sent to the school nurse to be examined. The nurse noted approximately 12 linear and loop-shaped marks on her back and buttocks. These marks ranged in length from 6 to 10 inches. The nurse believed that the marks were inflicted by a belt and belt buckle. The marks were purple, blue, brown, and yellow, indicating that the bruises were sustained at different times. Susan said she did not know how she got the bruises. The nurse spoke with the principal, who called CPS.

REASONS

The school principal reported this case to CPS because:

- The child had sustained a physical injury.
- The bruises were inflicted at different times, perhaps days apart. (Even if the bruises had been inflicted at one time this case should still be reported. The fact that the bruises were in different stages of healing raises greater concern for the child's safety.)
- The nurse's clinical opinion was that the injuries were inflicted by a belt and belt buckle. (U.S. Department of Health and Human Services, 1992)

Box 11.1
INDICATORS OF A CHILD'S POTENTIAL NEED FOR PROTECTION

	Physical Indicators	*Behavioral Indicators*
Physical Abuse	• Unexplained bruises (in various stages of healing), welts, human bite marks, bald spots • Unexplained burns, especially cigarette burns or immersion burns (glovelike) • Unexplained fractures, lacerations or abrasions	• Self-destructive • Withdrawn and aggressive—behavioral extremes • Uncomfortable with physical contact • Arrives at school early or stays late as if afraid to be at home • Chronic runaway (adolescents) • Complains of soreness or moves uncomfortably • Wears clothing inappropriate to weather, to cover body
Physical Neglect	• Abandonment • Unattended medical needs • Consistent lack of supervision • Consistent hunger, inappropriate dress, poor hygiene • Lice, distended stomach, emaciated	• Regularly displays fatigue or listlessness, falls asleep in class • Steals food, begs from classmates • Reports that no caretaker is at home • Frequently absent or tardy • Self-destructive • School dropout (adolescents)
Sexual Abuse	• Torn, stained or bloody underclothing • Pain or itching in genital area • Difficulty walking or sitting • Bruises or bleeding in external genitalia • Venereal disease • Frequent urinary or yeast infections	• Withdrawal, chronic depression • Excessive seductiveness • Role reversal, overly concerned for siblings • Poor self-esteem, self-devaluation, lack of confidence • Peer problems, lack of involvement • Massive weight change • Suicide attempts (especially adolescents) • Hysteria, lack of emotional control • Sudden school difficulties • Inappropriate sex play or premature understanding of sex • Threatened by physical contact, closeness
Emotional Maltreatment	• Speech disorders • Delayed physical development • Substance abuse • Ulcers, asthma, severe allergies	• Habit disorders (sucking, rocking) • Antisocial, destructive • Neurotic traits (sleep disorders, inhibition of play) • Passive and aggressive—behavioral extremes • Delinquent behavior (especially adolescents) • Developmentally delayed

Source: From *Guidelines for Schools to Help Protect Abused and Neglected Children,* by the American Association for Protecting Children (n.d.), Denver, CO: American Humane Association. Adapted in part from *Early Childhood Programs and the Prevention and Treatment of Child Abuse and Neglect,* by D. D. Broadhurst, M. Edmunds, and R. A. MacDicken, 1979, The User Manual Series, Washington, DC: U.S. Department of Health, Education and Welfare.

Indicators that a child has the potential need for protections is described in Box 11.1.

BEHAVIORS AND ATTITUDES OF PARENTS AND CHILDREN THAT MAY INDICATE CHILD ABUSE

Specialists working with child abuse (Fontana, 1973a; Helfer & Kempe, 1987) have also developed some guidelines to help educators determine the existence of child abuse. The following are modified from publications by Head Start, the U.S. Department of Health and Human Services, and the American Humane Association.

The Child of Preschool Age

1. Does the child seem to fear his or her parents?
2. Does the child miss preschool or the child-care center often?
3. Does the child bear evidence of physical abuse? Are there signs of battering, such as bruises or welts, belt or buckle marks, cuts, or burns?
4. Does the child exhibit extreme behavior changes? Is the child very aggressive at times and then fearful, withdrawn, and/or depressed?
5. Does the child have sores, bruises, or cuts that are not adequately cared for?
6. Does the child come to school inadequately dressed? Does the child look uncared for?
7. Does the child take over the parent role and try to "mother" the parent?
8. Does the child seem to be hungry for affection?

The Child of Elementary School Age

1. Does the child exhibit behavior that deviates from the norm? Is the child (a) aggressive, destructive, and disruptive or (b) passive and withdrawn? The first may be a child who is shouting for help, demanding attention, and striking out, whereas the second may be out of touch with reality, remote, submissive, and subdued, but crying for help in another way.
2. Does the child miss classes, or is the child often tardy? Does the child come to school too early and stay around after hours? In the first instance, the child's behavior suggests problems at home. In the second, the child may be pushed out in the morning and have nowhere to go after school.
3. Does the child bear evidence of physical abuse? Are there obvious signs of battering: bruises, belt or buckle marks, welts, lacerations, or burns?
4. Does the child lack social skills? Is the child unable to approach other children and play with them?
5. Does the child have learning problems that cannot be diagnosed? Does the child underperform? If intelligence tests show average academic ability and the child is not able to do the work, there may be problems at home.
6. Does the child show great sensitivity to others' feelings? Does the child get upset when another person is criticized? Abused children often have to "mother" their abusive parents, and some are overly sensitive to the feelings of others.
7. Does the child come to school inadequately dressed? Is the child unwashed and uncared for? These may be signs of neglect.
8. Does the child seem tired or fall asleep in class?
9. Does the child appear undernourished? Does the child attempt to save food? Is there real poverty in the home, or do the parents not care?
10. Does the child seem to be afraid of his or her parents?

The Secondary-Level Student

Most of the traits just mentioned are relevant to detection of abuse in the middle school and high school student, but there are additional signs to watch for in the upper levels. In addition to evidence of physical abuse, neglect, truancy, and tardiness, the older student may experience the following:

1. Does the student have to assume too much responsibility at home?
2. Does the parent expect unrealistic and overly controlled behavior?
3. Does the student have difficulty conforming to school regulations and policies?
4. Does the student have problems communicating with his or her parents?
5. Does the student have a history of running away from home or refusing to go home?

6. Does the student act out sexually?
7. Does the student lack freedom and friends?

BEHAVIORAL AND PSYCHOLOGICAL CHARACTERISTICS OF THE CHILD IN SCHOOL

The largest group of children who chronically act out in the classroom is not a group with psychotic or cognitive impairments, but children with behavior disorders. Hochstedler categorizes three disorders: attention-deficit disorder, conduct disorder, and adjustment disorder (Sandberg, 1987). Although disorders do overlap, each disorder needs an individualized analysis to determine the appropriate intervention plan. *In each case, however, it is harmful to punish and make the child feel even more inadequate.* In conduct disorders the "alarming process is fueled by punishment approaches, when what is needed is to hold the child responsible for his/her destructive behavior without branding the child 'bad'" (p. 11). Acting out is a coping mechanism used by children who do not have an appropriate response repertoire.

Children with attention-deficit disorder (ADD) or attention-deficit/hyperactivity disorder (ADHD) are found in almost every classroom. These children do not seem to be able to stay on task, concentrate, or complete their assignments. Children who are hyperactive probably have ADD, but it is not necessary to be hyperkinetic or hyperactive to be unable to concentrate and sit still. Every teacher has experienced the child who disrupts the room, fails to progress, and is constantly distracted, going from the assigned task to watch another child, flitting from one task to another and, thus, failing to progress in the academic program. Some of these children may have too much energy, or they may be hyperactive. ADD is distinguished by poorly organized, haphazard, and nongoal-directed activities. It is 10 times more likely to happen in a boy than to a girl.

In addition, without early intervention, ADD and ADHD are precursors to more intense problems. Hochstedler observed that "the pattern we see over and over with ADD children in the early years is their inability to pay attention and behave properly, followed by parents and teachers viewing the child as bad or unacceptable" (Sandberg, 1987, p. 10). This hurts the child's self-esteem and leads to a worsening of the condition. If these patterns continue, the child may become conduct disordered, a child who breaks rules and is "calloused toward the needs and rights of others" (p. 10).

Conduct-disordered children are at risk of developing adult personality disorders. A comprehensive intervention plan that limits the acting-out behavior needs to be developed. Multiple factors may affect the child. Some of these factors are child abuse, family violence, adoption, divorce, and harsh discipline. The child may live in a family with an antisocial lifestyle, or the parents may be engaged in criminal activity. The factors related to each child need to be addressed by the therapist (Sandberg, 1987).

Adjustment disorder is connected to either single or multiple traumatic events that affect the child. The treatment and prognosis for success varies with the social–emotional condition of the child. Children who do not have persistent psychiatric and social impairment may be helped by therapy and by talking through the critical event to help them understand and resolve their pain.

"A significant body of child abuse research suggests that child abuse precipitates disorders in children" (Sandberg, 1987, p. 12). Teachers should not assume child abuse is present just because the child has attention deficiencies. However, the school must be "involved with identifying and remediating assorted problems, including child abuse, that severely jeopardize a child's opportunity to learn" (p. xvi). It is important for teachers to help the child learn appropriate behaviors at an early age. They should use disciplinary methods that help the child learn self-control rather than discipline that is actually punishment. Classrooms should give support and continuity to children. They should provide special help for children with learning deficiencies, use special education services to help socially and emotionally deficient children get the help they need, and above all else, make sure these children do not feel inadequate.

How can teachers accomplish this? Teachers need parent volunteers or aides in the classroom plus a support system to meet the needs of each child and make sure that each child has more successes than failures.

Halperin (1979) cites practical guidelines for teachers to follow in identifying the child who needs attention. He cautions against jumping to conclusions, however. Marks on a body may come from many circumstances. "Only when school personnel have gathered substantial information on the family and its internal functioning are they in a position to assess if a child is being maltreated at home" (p. 67). Educators who bear in mind that children are unique, may respond to the same treatment in opposite ways, and display a wide range of behaviors will be cautious in labeling a child.

When educators recognize Halperin's clues for children who need attention, whether or not there is any suspicion of maltreatment, they will be doing a great service to all children in their classrooms. Individualization of the academic program as well as individualization for emotional needs will result in a well-rounded educational program for each child. As the teacher gets to know a child better and responds to the child with needed praise or reinforcement, as well as with an individualized curriculum, the result will be improved education. The following descriptions are modified from Halperin (1979).

Aggressive Child

Typical Characteristics

- Defiant
- Domineering
- Blames others

Possible Reasons for Actions

- Little self-esteem
- Cannot control impulses
- Unhappy
- Little self-discipline

Show-Off

Typical Characteristics

- Extremely extroverted
- Answers questions without knowing the answer
- May appear hyperactive
- Wants to be center of attention

Possible Reasons for Actions

- Masks insecurity
- Little attention at home
- Shows off to compete for praise and love
- May be attention-deficit disorder (ADD) or attention-deficit/hyperactive disorder (ADHD)

Disobedient Child

Typical Characteristics

- Purposely breaks rules
- Impolite and insolent
- Struggles against authority

Possible Reasons for Actions

- Unhappy
- Disobeys to get attention
- Models parental attitude toward authority
- Inconsistent discipline at home
- Prefers punishment to indifference
- Has internalized feelings of worthlessness

Child Who Lies, Cheats, and Steals

Typical Characteristics

- Tells lies
- Cheats in games and on tests
- Steals from stores, classmates, others

Possible Reasons for Actions

- Lies to escape punishment
- Wants to get away with action without being caught
- Gains attention
- Little supervision at home
- Actions of dishonesty are condoned at home

Child Nobody Likes

Typical Characteristics

- Sullen
- Depressed
- Jealous
- Blames others for acts
- Frequently absent

Possible Reasons for Actions

- Little warmth from parents
- Unable to establish healthy relationship with others
- Lives an isolated life
- Not fond of self
- Poor self-concept
- May be bullied and not able to handle it

Unkempt Child

Typical Characteristics

Soiled clothes

Unkempt hair and body

General lack of care in work

Possible Reasons for Actions

Lack of adult supervision and concern

Poor self-image

Fearful Child

Typical Characteristics

Anxious

Uneasy

Emotionally unstable

Possible Reasons for Actions

Neurotic family life

Harsh punishment from caregivers

Unpredictable home environment

Afraid of bullying or violence in the school

Shy Child

Typical Characteristics

Fearful in contacts with others

Sits quietly with lowered head

Seldom defends self

Seldom expresses self

Possible Reasons for Actions

Lacks encouragement and acceptance at school

Excessively critical parents

Fears failure

May share same timid characteristics as parents

Withdrawn Child

Typical Characteristics.

Isolates self

Appears tense, nervous, and unhappy

Easily discouraged and frustrated

Abandons tasks if they prove difficult

Possible Reasons for Actions

Unsatisfactory experiences in past

Unsatisfactory experiences at school

Excessive demands from parents

Frequently lacks love, affection, and praise

Parents may be unpredictable and unable to establish relationships

Emotionally Unstable Child

Typical Characteristics

Volatile and unpredictable

Attitude toward life is negative

Appears agitated, worried, or preoccupied

Possible Reasons for Actions

Little attention or affection

Inadequate supervision or psychological support at home

Under tremendous pressure

Low-Achieving Child

Typical Characteristics

Short attention span

Withdrawn from classroom activities

Disobedient and disruptive

Rarely completes assignments

Possible Reasons for Actions

Brain damage

Physically neglected

Medical problems

Educational neglect

If these characteristics and causes are kept in mind when working with children, along with the realization that typical factors may not affect a particular child, the educator can adapt the educational program to the needs of the child.

With the increase of violence in the schools, children who have needs should be identified. Programs that help children become increasingly and positively involved, as well as programs that help children see alternatives to rage, must be a part of the schools. These include learning how to resolve conflicts with peers, handle anger, recognize consequences, and seek alternatives to violence.

The development of the ability to make friends as well as the ability to control anger begins at a young age—preschool. At an early age some children need guidance in the appropriate way to interact with classmates. Children continue to need support throughout their school years.

Teachers are very powerful in their influence on children. They can make children into scapegoats by ridiculing them before classmates. It is better to help children develop the skills they need to interact with others and give them opportunities to be positive participants than it is to shame them into obedience.

The opportunity to raise a child's self-esteem will often improve the child's behavior. It is a safe beginning.

WHY DO ABUSE AND NEGLECT CONTINUE TO HAPPEN?

The National Center on Child Abuse and Neglect identified the following factors to determine which contribute to ongoing abuse and neglect of children:

- *Family income.* Children who come from families with incomes below the poverty level are seven times more likely to be abused than those at a higher income level.
- *Gender.* A child's gender has no effect on whether the child is neglected. However, girls are more likely to be abused than boys. The rate of sexual abuse is three times higher for girls than for boys.
- *Family size.* Children in families with four or more children are more likely to be neglected or abused.
- *Race or ethnicity.* There was no significant difference among children of different ethnic groups.
- *Type of community.* Abuse and neglect occur in rural, suburban, and urban communities (U.S. Department of Health and Human Services, 1992).
- *Exposure to violence.* Personal experience, and exposure to media reports, television programs, Internet, and movies exposes the child and the school to excessive violence.

CHARACTERISTICS AND RISK FACTORS OF ABUSIVE PARENTS

Three approaches for understanding abusive parents have been investigated: the psychological model, the sociological model, and the parent–child interaction model.

In the psychological model, lack of empathy distinguishes the abusive parent. In the sociological model, cultural attitudes toward violence, social stress, family size, and social isolation are factors that relate to child abuse. Prevention and treatment based on the sociological model focus on the effect the community and society have on the family. Environmental stress is a sociological risk factor in abuse of children. Stress from poverty or in the workplace may cause anxiety in parents, and they may lash out at their child.

In the parent–child interaction model, the parents lack skill in interacting with their children, disciplining them, and teaching them appropriate behavior (Wiehe, 1989). Parents may have had inadequate exposure to positive parenting and lack information on child development. If raised by maladaptive parents or if raised with cultural beliefs that are compatible with mistreatment, the parent may not be capable of adapting to the child's needs. "Just as beliefs about child development and behavior arise from prior experience, parenting skills and strategies must be learned at some time in an individual's life" (Iverson & Segal, 1990, p. 42).

The U.S. Department of Health and Human Services (1992) discusses parents who are more likely to abuse their children:

> Parents may be more likely to maltreat their children if they abuse drugs or alcohol (alcoholic mothers are three times more likely and alcoholic fathers are eight times more likely to abuse or neglect their children than are nonalcoholic parents); are emotionally immature or needy; are isolated, with no family or friends to depend on; were emotionally deprived, abused or neglected as children; feel worthless and have never been loved or cared about; or are in poor health. Many abusive and neglectful parents do not intend to harm their children and often feel remorse about their maltreating behavior. However, their own problems may prevent them from stopping their harmful behavior and may result in resistance to outside intervention. It is important to remember that diligent and effective intervention efforts may overcome the parents' resistance and help them change their abusive and neglectful behavior.
>
> Children may be more likely to be at risk of maltreatment if they are unwanted, resemble someone the parents dislike, or have physical or behavioral traits which make them different or especially difficult to care for.

- *Family interactions.* Each member of a family affects every other member of that family in some way. Some parents and children are fine on their own, but just cannot get along when they are together, especially for long periods of time. Some characteristics commonly observed in abusive or neglectful families include social isolation and parents turning to their children to meet their emotional needs.
- *Environmental conditions.* Changes in financial condition, employment status, or family structure may shake a family's stability. Some parents may not be able to cope with the stress resulting from the changes and may experience difficulty in caring for their children. (U.S. Department of Health and Human Services, 1992, p. 5)

The National Center on Child Abuse and Neglect suggests these guiding principles:

- Child maltreatment is a family problem. Consequently our treatment efforts must focus on the family as a whole as well as the individual family members. Treatment must be provided to abused and neglected children as well as their parents. Unless children receive the support and treatment for the trauma they have suffered, they may suffer permanent physical, mental, or emotional handicaps, and as adults they may continue the cycle of abuse with their own family or other children. In addition, abused and neglected children are more likely than other children to have substance abuse problems.
- Although we cannot predict with certainty who will abuse or neglect their children, we do know the signs indicating *high risk.* People at high risk include parents who abuse drugs and alcohol, young parents who are ill-prepared for the parenting role, families experiencing great stress who have poor coping skills and have no one to turn to for support, and parents who have difficulty with or who have not developed an emotional bond with their infant. We need to be alert to these and other high risk indicators and offer assistance, support, counseling, and/or parent education to families at risk before their children are harmed.
- Families at risk may be most receptive to help soon after the birth of their first child.
- Child sexual abuse prevention programs aimed at school-aged children appear to be useful in helping children avoid sexually abusive situations and to say no to inappropriate touch by adults. However, prevention programs must be carefully examined and selected. These programs must be responsive to the learning capacities and developmental stages of the children involved. Inappropriately designed programs may frighten young children or fail to teach them what they can do to protect themselves.
- Volunteers can be very effective with some abusive and neglectful parents—especially with those parents who are experiencing stress, who have been emotionally deprived, and who lack knowledge of child development and effective parenting skills. Volunteers must be carefully screened, trained, and supervised.

Clearly, if we are going to stop child abuse and neglect and help the child victims and their families, we all must work together. Efforts must occur at the Federal, State, and local levels. (U.S. Department of Health and Human Services, 1992, pp. 10–11)

The following behavioral characteristics can help the professional determine the likelihood of abuse or neglect:

1. Do the parents fail to show up for appointments? Do they stay away from school? When they come to school, are they uncooperative and unresponsive?
2. Do the parents have unrealistically high expectations for themselves and their child? Do the parents describe the child as "different" or "bad"?
3. Do the parents have expectations for the child that are inconsistent or inappropriate for the child's age?
4. Do the parents become aggressive or abusive when school personnel want to talk about the child's problems?
5. Do the parents isolate themselves? Do they know other parents in the school? Are they known by other parents?
6. Do they lack knowledge of child development and the child's physical and psychological needs?
7. Do the parents report that they were abused or neglected as children?
8. Do the parents refuse to participate in school events?
9. Do the parents ignore the child and avoid touching?
10. Do the parents show little interest in the child's activities or concern for the child's well-being?

ROOTS OF VIOLENCE

The authors of *Ghosts from the Nursery: Tracing the Roots of Violence* give compelling evidence of the importance of a caring environment for the infant and young child and of the effects of being abused or neglected. It is especially important to have a rich, loving environment for the child prenatal until 5 years of age. "When environmental experiences early in life cause noradrenaline levels to be too high and serotonin levels too low, the result, in the presence of later emotional triggers, may be impulsive violence" (Karr-Morse & Wiley, 1997, p. 44).

Children who are ignored or physically mistreated are at risk. The effects of abusive early experiences without intervention or change put the child at risk, unable to trust others or feel connected. The book chronicles the life of Jeffrey, a young man on death row, who grew up in a sterile, disorganized family, with one short period of a caring foster family. His reactions were impulsive, and at the age of 16 he killed another. A youth who is neglected or abused has a 53 percent increased likelihood of being arrested and a 38 percent increased likelihood of the arrest being for a violent crime (Karr-Morse & Wiley, 1997, p. 262). Violence breeds violence.

Jeffrey wrote the following in August 1996:

> Everybody has to deal with anger. . . . When I get mad, I borderline up there, then I follow my impulses. . . . If I can't control my impulses, then I do things that I regret later. . . . I do follow my impulses. . . because that was the way I learned to survive when I was little. (p. 152)

School-age children also show their fear, concern, and sadness through drawings that reveal the violence they have encountered. "With education and support, adults can recognize children's aggressive or withdrawn behavior, or their dulled emotions, as symptoms of posttraumatic stress disorder" (Osofsky & Fenichel, 1996, p. 7). These children need special support from the school professionals.

Infant and Toddler Exposure to Abuse

It is often believed that infants and toddlers do not remember their exposure to violence. Infants and toddlers are not able to remember the details of their life when they were 1 or 2 years old, but the impact is still there. "In fact, infants and young children can be overwhelmed by their exposure to violence, especially—as is likely to be the case with very young children—when both victims and perpetrators are well-known and emotionally important to the child and the violence occurs in or near the child's own home" (Osofsky & Fenichel, 1996, p. 7). Factors that relate to the severity of the exposure to violence include *intensity* (a killing versus a pushing); *proximity* (how close the child is to the violence); *familiarity* (if the victim or perpetrator is known by the child); *developmental status* (ability to cope with the violence); and *chronicity of exposure* (if the child is exposed to violence again and again). "It is likely that experiencing violence repeatedly over the years may be devastating to the social and emotional development of young children, who learn, from what they see, that violence is a usual and acceptable way to respond to other people" (p. 8). Infants and toddlers exhibit the same type of symptoms that adults and older children exhibit. They reexperience the violence, a traumatic experience, by numbing their response and avoidance of the remembrance and signs of hypervigilance and hyperarousal (Zeanah & Scheeringa, 1996).

Brain Damage Risk Linked to Child Abuse and Neglect

Research at the McLean Hospital identified four types of brain abnormalities related to child abuse and neglect. The abnormalities caused are permanent; the solution is elimination of abuse and neglect.

- *Limbic irritability:* The limbic system, a network of brain cells that "controls many of the emotions and drives for survival. The McLean researchers found evidence that abuse may cause disturbances in electrical impulses as limbic nerve cells communicate, resulting in seizures or significant abnormalities on an EEG, a diagnostic test that measures brain waves" (McLean Hospital, 2000, p. 2).
- *Arrested development in the left hemisphere:* Studies show that there is deficient development in the left brain of abused persons, which may contribute to depression and the increased risk of memory impairment.

- *Deficient integration between the left and right hemispheres:* "In abused children the corpus callosum was smaller than in healthy children" (p. 2).
- *Increased vermal activity:* The vermis is the division between the left and right hemispheres of the brain where vermal activity occurs. "The researchers theorize that the abused patients had higher vermal activity in order to quell electrical irritability within the limbic system. They hypothesize that the cerebellar vermis helps to maintain emotional balance, but that trauma may impair this ability" (p. 3).

The researchers examined animal studies and came to the following conclusion: "We know that an animal exposed to stress and neglect early in life develops a brain that is wired to experience fear, anxiety and stress. . . . We think the same is true of people" (p. 3).

Children, Youth, and Gun Violence

More than 20,000 children and youth under age 20 are killed or injured by guns each year, the second leading cause of death of young people ages 10 to 19 (Behrman, 2002). Children exposed to gun violence often experience psychological disturbances that include sleep distortion, withdrawal, and posttraumatic stress disorder (Garbarino, Bradshaw, & Vorrasi, 2002). "Studies suggest that children exposed to gun violence at home, at school, in the community, or through the media can experience negative psychological effects including posttraumatic stress, poor school performance, increased delinquency, risky sexual behaviors, substance abuse, and desensitization to violence. All of these effects can make child and youth more prone to violence themselves" (The Future of Children, 2002, p. 1). The four strategies to reduce gun violence include

- Reducing children's unsupervised exposure to guns
- Engaging communities and strengthening law enforcement
- Changing the design of guns (requiring safety features and personalizing guns)
- Limiting the flow of illegal guns to youth (Reich, Culross, & Behrman, 2002)

WHY IS THERE ABUSE?

Children learn parenting patterns from their parents (Iverson & Segal, 1990). With few exceptions, abusive parents experienced some form of maltreatment when young (Steele, 1986). These parents did not have a childhood that allowed them to become independent, productive, functioning adults. Generally they had to disregard their own needs and desires for the wishes of an authority figure. They were unable to develop inner controls and looked to outside figures for direction. Such parents also exhibit dependence on others in their search for love and affection. They are still affected by maternal deprivation. Their parents were their only models. "Learned patterns of abusive parenting are transmitted from parent to child and are replicated by the child upon becoming a parent in his/her own right"(Bavolek, 1989, p. 99). These practices include:

1. *Inappropriate expectations*. Abusive parents often perceive the child's abilities to be greater than they are. Parents expect children to take on responsibilities that are not appropriate for their ages. These parents may have expectations such as toilet training the child at 6 to 12 months, talking by age 2, and taking on housekeeping chores at an early age. Young or inexperienced parents, who do not know child development, may interpret an infant or toddler's appropriate behavior as stubbornness and rebellion. Combine this with a belief that physical punishment will help the child behave, and you have the conditions for abuse. Children in these families develop a poor self-concept, and feel incapable, unacceptable, and worthless (Bavolek, 1989; Hamilton, 1989).
2. *Lack of empathy*. Abusive parents often did not experience loving care when they were growing up, so they do not have a model to follow. They cannot change their own personality traits until they receive the support and love they need. These parents usually have dependency needs and are unable to empathize with their children. The child's basic needs are ignored. Such parents may justify cruel and abusive behaviors under the guise of teaching and guiding their children. Mothers who were brought up by uncaring, inattentive mothers will tend to mother their own children in the same way. Their children grow up with a low sense of

self-esteem and inadequate identity (Bavolek, 1989; Hamilton, 1989; Steele, 1986, 1987).

3. *Belief in physical punishment*. Abusive parents often believe that physical punishment is necessary to rear their children without spoiling them. This is a common belief in the United States, but abusive parents go to extremes and believe that babies and children should not be allowed to get away with anything. They punish to correct perceived misbehavior or inadequacy on the part of their child. The child does not live up to expectations and is considered "bad." The parents think they have the moral duty to correct their child's behavior any way they choose.

4. *Parent–child role reversal*. In these abusive families, children are looked upon by the parents as providing the love and support that the parent needs. The parent is like a needy child, so the child must play the role of the adult. If the child is able to take on some of the parental roles, abuse may be avoided, but only at the expense of the child's normal development. This is destructive to children—they do not go through normal developmental stages, do not develop their own identities, and see themselves as existing to meet the needs of their parents (Bavolek, 1989; Hamilton, 1989).

5. *Social isolation*. Social isolation is recognized by most child abuse researchers as a factor that perpetuates neglect and abuse. Either the absence of social support or inability to accept any support has the same effect. The abusive family isolates itself, attempts to solve its problems alone, and avoids contact with others. Isolation is a defense against being hurt and rejected. Although abusive parents may act self-sufficient and sure of themselves, they are dependent, frightened, and immature. Cross-cultural research indicates that child maltreatment occurs less often in cultures with multiple caregivers, including extended families (Hamilton, 1989).

6. *Difficulty experiencing pleasure*. In other abusing families, the parents do not enjoy life. Their social relationships are minimal and unrewarding. They do not feel competent, have difficulty planning for the future, and do not trust their own performances. Children in these families exhibit similar behavior.

7. *Intergenerational ties*. Although a history of maltreatment and lack of parenting skills set the scene for more neglect and abuse, the "majority of maltreated children do not maltreat their own children" (Hamilton, 1989, p. 38). According to Vondra and Toth (1989), one third of the maltreated are abusive to their children (p. 13). If abuse and neglect are viewed in a broad sense, however, an alarming number of parents did not receive adequate parenting or develop a positive attachment to their parents and other loved ones and thus have a difficult time providing the kind of environment that nourishes and cares for a child adequately (Steele, 1986).

The American Association for Protecting Children, a division of the American Humane Association, has developed a flier that briefly describes parental attitudes, the child's behavior, and the child's appearance. This flier succinctly focuses on the highlights of the foregoing discussion. Schools may purchase this flier from the American Humane Association for a nominal fee and distribute it to staff and teachers. The flier is illustrated in Box 11.1.

DEVELOPMENT OF POLICIES

School districts and child-care centers need to develop the policies and training programs vital to successful child abuse intervention. If there is no policy, the teacher should see the school nurse, psychologist, director, counselor, social worker, or principal, depending on the staffing of the school. Even in a school district with a policy statement, each school or child-care center should have one person who is responsible for receiving reports of child abuse. Making one person responsible results in greater awareness of the problem of abuse and facilitates reporting. It is also helpful to establish a committee to view evidence and support the conclusions of the original observer. A written report contains the details of the situation.

All states require reporting of suspected child abuse. Evidence of violent physical abuse must be reported immediately. If school officials refuse to act, you should call social services, law enforcement, or a family crisis center. The person making the report should have the right to remain anonymous. When reporting in good faith, the person reporting is protected by immunity described in state legislation. Colorado law, for example, specifically states: "Any person participating in good faith in the making of a report or in a judicial proceeding held pursuant to this title shall be immune from any liability, civil or criminal, that otherwise might result by reason of such reporting" (Denver Public Schools, 1992).

Needs Assessment

Schools and child-care centers first must determine the prevention and protection delivery systems that are already available in the community. They should consider social service departments, child protection teams, child welfare agencies, law enforcement, juvenile court system, Head Start, child-care centers, hospitals, clinics, public health nurses, mental health programs, public and private service groups, fund-raising agencies such as United Way, and service organizations that might be unique to their community.

Following assessment of the community, the schools and child-care centers have to determine their roles in an integrated approach to abuse and neglect. Communication lines must be kept open at all times. A representative of the schools should serve on the child protection team. One role that is mandated is identification of abuse and neglect. Other roles will be individualized according to the needs of the community, the resources in the schools and child-care centers, and the commitment of the personnel.

Policy

Child abuse is found in all socioeconomic groups in the United States, so all school districts must be prepared to work with interdisciplinary agencies in the detection and prevention of this national social problem.

Policies should be written in compliance with the requirements of each state's reporting statute, details of which may be learned by consulting the state's attorney general. Because reporting is required in all states, the policy should include a clear statement of reporting requirements. The policy should also inform school personnel of their immunity and legal obligations. Dissemination of the policy should include the community as well as all school employees. Not only is it important that the community realize the obligation of the school or child-care center to report suspected abuse or neglect, it also is vital that the community become aware of the extent of the problem.

HOW TO TALK WITH CHILDREN AND PARENTS

When planning to talk with the parents and/or children of suspected abuse or neglect, plan a productive meeting focused first on the needs of the family and how the school might be able to help them. Although you should report your concerns of abuse to the authorities first, if there is obvious suspected abuse, offering support to the family is always appropriate.

Care must be taken in talking with or interviewing children or parents. The conversation should take place in a private, relaxed, and comfortable atmosphere. Children should not feel threatened, nor should they be pressed for information or details they do not want to reveal. Parents should be aware of the school's legal obligation to report suspected neglect and abuse. If they believe the school is supportive of the family, the interaction between parents and school will be more positive. Tower (1992) provides some guidelines:

When Talking with the Child

Do:

Make sure the interviewer is someone the child trusts.

Make sure the educator is the most competent person in the school to talk with children.

Conduct the interview in private.

Sit beside the child, not across a table or desk.

Tell the child that the interview is confidential, but that child abuse and neglect must be reported.

Conduct the interview in language the child understands.

Ask the child to clarify words or terms that you do not understand.

Tell the child if any future action will be required.

Don't:

Allow the child to feel "in trouble" or "at fault."

Disparage or criticize the child's choice of words or language.

Suggest answers to the child.

Probe or press for answers the child is unwilling to give.

Display horror, shock, or disapproval of parents, the child, or the situation.

Pressure or force the child to remove clothing.

Conduct the interview with a group of interviewers.

Leave the child alone with a stranger (e.g., a CPS worker).

When Talking with the Parents

Do:

Select the person most appropriate to the situation.

Conduct the interview in private.

Tell the parents why the interview is taking place.

Be direct, honest, and professional.

Tell the parents the interview is confidential.

Reassure the parents of the support of the school.

Tell the parents if a report has been made or will be made.

Advise the parents of the school's legal responsibilities to report.

Don't:

Try to prove abuse or neglect; that is not an educator's role.

Display horror, anger, or disapproval of parents, the child, or the situation.

Pry into family matters unrelated to the specific situation.

Place blame or make judgments about the parents or child.

PROGRAMS TO PREVENT ABUSE

Parent Education

Parent education can be delivered in high school, provided by hospitals when parents have their first child, offered through adult education, or provided by social services. The STEP, Parent Effectiveness Training, and Active Parenting courses have been effective. Building Family Strengths programs reinforce the positive aspects of a family. Specially designed programs are also appropriate.

Caring Programs

Home visitation programs have demonstrated that early intervention is effective. First-time parents are especially receptive to help from visiting nurses or nonprofessionals who model, support, and help them with their infant (Justice & Justice, 1990). Programs that were developed to offer this support included the Prenatal/Early Infancy Project in Rochester, New York; the AVANCE Parent-Child Education Program in San Antonio, Texas; the Pre-School Intervention Program in Bloomfield, Connecticut; MELD in Minnesota; the Parents as Teachers program; and Healthy Start (see chapter 9). The emphasis in the last three programs—MELD, Parents as Teachers, and Healthy Start—is broader than home visitations for parenting skills, but the programs include these areas and demonstrate that larger groups can benefit from a national response. In Great Britain, newborns and their parents are visited by public health nurses. Although the parents do not have to accept the visit, most do, and after the initial visit there are follow-ups with periodic assessments of intellectual, emotional, and physical development.

The Community Caring Project

A joint project of the Center and the Junior League of Denver (C. Henry Kempe National Center for the Prevention and Treatment of Child Abuse and Neglect, n.d.) is based on the concept of intervention and was developed after Kempe and others found that home visitations for at-risk parents could prevent abuse. It provides support and parenting skills to new mothers. These mothers, selected from four hospitals in the Denver area, are matched with a community volunteer, who offers assistance, modeling, and education to new mothers.

The Caring Program is an offshoot of programs developed by researchers at the University of Colorado Medical School. Mothers who are at high risk for abnormal parental practices (following observations made during and after labor and delivery) are offered special programs. When identified as high-risk, the family receives a pediatric follow-up by a physician, lay health visitor, and/or public health nurse.

Support Offered by Schools

The position statement by the American School Counselor Association supports programs to help eliminate child abuse. The association hopes to provide children with coping skills; help teachers understand abuse; provide continuing counseling to the child and the family; and offer workshops for parents that focus on handling anger, parenting skills, and methods of discipline other than corporal punishment (American School Counselor Association, 1988). Some of the school-based programs include life skills training, socialization skills, problem solving, and coping skills (Tower, 1992).

If the public were aware of how essential it is for teenagers who have not received these skills at home to be able to learn and model life skills, there would not be the demand to eliminate these types of courses. Although academic basics (reading, writing, and arithmetic) are essential, the focus away from life skills could be detrimental to the next generation. Offering of workshops or courses on conflict resolution, consequences of actions, and seeking alternatives should be recognized as essential. It should be possible for schools to provide all the needed academic skills as well as the necessary skills for parenthood, self-protection, and life skills.

Many schools are developing family resource centers, as described in chapter 8. Offerings for parents who are no longer students include parent education and family literacy.

Programs After Abuse Is Recognized

Professionals who work with the abusive parent must first understand themselves and their values so they can come to peace with their feelings toward abuse and neglect of children. To help the family, professionals should not have a punitive attitude toward the parents. It may help to remember that many abusive or neglectful parents are rearing their children the same way they were reared. It is a lifelong pattern that must be broken (Bavolek, 1989; Reppucci, Britner, & Woolard, 1997; Steele, 1987; Vondra & Toth, 1989).

Although the parents may resist intrusion or suggestion, they desperately need help in feeling good about themselves. They need support, comfort, and someone they can trust and lean on. They need someone who will come when they have needs. Instead of criticism, they need help and assurance that they are worthwhile. Because they are unable to cope with their child, someone must help them understand the child. Parents need to feel valuable and adequate.

Parents Anonymous

Parents Anonymous (2006) is a self-help program that gives parents the chance to share their feelings with others who have had similar experiences. Parents can use Parents Anonymous (PA) and its crisis-intervention hotlines without fear of public disclosure.

The members help one another avoid abuse by providing the opportunity to talk out problems. Each group has a group facilitator, who is trained in Parents Anonymous standards and practices. They also have a parent group leader, selected by the group. Weekly meetings are held and both the group leader and group facilitator are available between the weekly meetings. PA believes that abuse happens because parents have unresolved issues about their own childhood, stressful current problems and unmet needs, and a precipitating crisis that brings about the abuse.

Community Help

Help from social services or nonprofit organizations may include treatment that is offered by parent-aides, homemakers, and health visitors (Hamilton, 1989). The helper may serve as an advocate for the family to get the extra assistance it needs. This might include family therapy (Pardeck, 1989), assertiveness training, Healthy Start, Parents as Teachers, Community Resource Centers, Family Resource Centers, and Building Family Strengths programs. These programs try to bolster the positive elements in the family and eliminate the destructive elements. "Treatment may require in-depth, long-term therapy and a lot of permanent social support systems" (Hamilton, 1989, p. 41).

Many abusive parents want help. When they reveal their desires, they indicate that they want another parent to help them develop childrearing skills through modeling and friendship. Professionals can give them psychiatric help and other support, but because these parents may have missed a childhood with nurturing parents, their greatest need is the opportunity to have an active experience with a nurturing model. The importance of bonding and of a close relationship between parent and infant has been recognized as necessary for the child's emotional and physical growth. Severe deprivation can result in failure to thrive and marasmus (Skeels & Dye, 1939; Spitz, 1945). Failure to develop close and trusting bonds as infants and children results later in parents who need special help in learning to relate to their own child. These parents are still looking for someone to mother them. The supportive help of another parent can function as a nurturing model for both parent and child.

Preschool Settings

Youngsters who have been abused adapt in two ways, according to Pearl (1988). They either internalize and over control their behavior, or they externalize and under control their actions. Children in the first category will be easy to overlook their behavior is often fearful, withdrawn, depressed, and shy. The externalized child will demand attention, be aggressive, and act out (Pearl, 1988; Steele, 1986). Both types of children have low self-esteem. Aggressive, externalized children see themselves as unlovable and bad. The withdrawn child tries to please but feels little pleasure. Abused children will scan their surroundings often, avert their eyes, and stare away to avoid eye contact. Preschool teachers can help both types of children if they:

1. Use a quiet clear voice.
2. Have good eye contact.
3. Stand near the child when giving directions.
4. Use body language that says the same thing as the oral message.
5. Give directions that tell the child the appropriate behavior using specific instructions.
6. Set limits and have expectations for behavior.
7. Accept all feelings, but be consistent with behavioral expectations (Pearl, 1988).

INTERVENING IN SEXUAL ABUSE

Programs that help children say "no" to sexual abuse have been developed throughout the nation. Teachers and social services personnel who use the methods suggested in these programs need to be careful to ensure that the child does not become fearful, however (Binder & McNiel, 1987).

Programs for preschool children should avoid causing children to become fearful of every stranger. An example of a program that works well is the Safe Child Personal Safety Training Program. Safe Child uses a scripted videotape curriculum for training teachers and parents, with segments for children ages 3 through 10. It demonstrates role-playing techniques and teaches basic life skills such as communication, assertiveness, problem solving, and decision making.

Young children need to know how to respond. Programs should be experientially based. Teaching children the concepts of safety from abuse is not as effective as teaching them the skills they need to prevent the abuse. In Safe Child, the children practiced the preventive skills and were taught to resist "unwanted touch, even in the face of bribery, emotional coercion, rejection, and intimidation" (Kraizer, Witte, & Fryer, 1989, p. 25). The study suggests:

1. Preschool children did as well as older children in the program, so prevention education should begin in preschool.
2. Prevention programs should give the information needed and nothing more. Labels of *good* and *bad* need not be used, nor the suggestion that someone they love might hurt them.
3. Evaluation of the programs should continue.
4. Children with very low self-esteem may not respond to the program. Ten percent of the children did not benefit from this program.

A government pamphlet shares tips to parents concerning sexual abuse. See Figure 11.6 for suggestions on how to listen and talk to children, how to choose a child-care center, and what to do if you think your child may have been abused.

Another concern of sexually abused children is their need for concerned intervention. The intervention should address the issue and help the child overcome feelings of unworthiness. The high rate of victims becoming victimizers also makes it

Listen and Talk to Your Children

Perhaps the most critical child sexual prevention strategy for parents is good communication with your children. This is not only challenging to every parent but also can be difficult, especially for working parents and parents of adolescents.

☐ Talk to your child every day and take time to really listen and observe. Learn as many details as you can about your child's activities and feelings. Encourage him or her to share concerns and problems with you.

☐ Explain to your children that their bodies belong only to them alone and that they have the right to say no to anyone who might try to touch them.

☐ Tell your child that some adults may try to hurt children and make them do things the child doesn't feel comfortable doing. Often these grownups call what they're doing a secret between themselves and the child.

☐ Explain that some adults may even threaten children by saying that their parents may be hurt or killed if the child ever shares the secret. Emphasize that an adult who does something like this is doing something that is wrong.

☐ Tell your child that adults whom they know, trust and love or someone who might be in a position of authority (like a babysitter, an uncle, a teacher or even a policeman) might try to do something like this. Try not to scare your children—emphasize that the vast.majority of grownups never do this and that most adults are deeply concerned about protecting children from harm.

Choosing a Preschool or Child Care Center

Although the vast majority of this nation's preschools and child care centers are perfectly safe places, recent reports of child sexual abuse in these settings are a source of great concern to parents.

☐ Check to make sure that the program is reputable. State or local licensing agencies, child care information and referral services, and other child care community agencies may be helpful sources of information. Find out whether there have been any past complaints.

☐ Find out as much as you can about the teachers and caregivers. Talk with other parents who have used the program.

☐ Learn about the school or center's hiring policies and practices. Ask how the organization recruits and selects staff. Find out whether they examine references, background checks, and previous employment history before hiring decisions are made.

☐ Ask whether and how parents are involved during the day. Learn whether the center or school welcomes and supports participation. Be sensitive to the attitude and degree of openness about parental participation.

☐ Ensure that you have the right to drop in and visit the program at any time.

☐ Make sure you are informed about every planned outing. Never give the organization blanket permission to take your child off the premises.

☐ Prohibit in writing the release of your child to anyone without your explicit authorization. Make sure that the program knows who will pick up your child on any given day.

If You Think That Your Child Has Been Abused...

☐ Believe the child. Children rarely lie about sexual abuse.

☐ Commend the child for telling you about the experience.

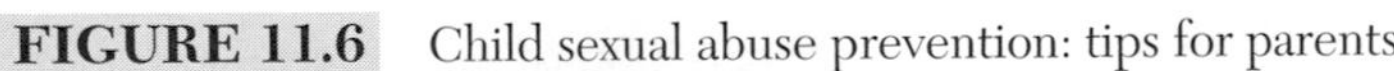

FIGURE 11.6 Child sexual abuse prevention: tips for parents.

Source: U.S. Department of Health and Human Services, Administration for Children, Youth and Families. National Center on Child Abuse and Neglect, 1986, Washington, DC: U.S. Government Printing Office.

necessary to work with children who have been sexually abused so they will not victimize others. An alarming finding is the number of young sexual abusers—20 percent of sexual abusers are adolescents. Victims tend to become victimizers. Ryan (1989) cites studies suggesting that as many as 80 percent of adult sexual abusers were abused themselves as children.

Checklist for Schools and Centers

- Does the school have a policy on reporting child abuse and neglect?
- Did the school do a needs assessment that shows the resources in your area and the status of child abuse and neglect in the school district?
- Does the school or center coordinate activities and resources with other social agencies?
- Does the school or center hold periodic meetings for improved communication and coordination among agencies?
- Does someone in the school district serve on the child protection team?

☐ Convey your support for the child. A child's greatest fear is that he or she is at fault and responsible for the incident. Alleviating this self-blame is of paramount importance.

☐ Temper your own reaction, recognizing that your perspective and acceptance are critical signals to the child. Your greatest challenge may be to not convey your own horror about the abuse.

☐ Do not go to the school or program to talk about your concern. Instead, report the suspected molestation to a social services agency or the police.

☐ Find a specialized agency that evaluates sexual abuse victims—a hospital or a child welfare agency or a community mental health therapy group. Keep asking until you find a group or an individual with appropriate expertise.

☐ Search for a physician with the experience and training to detect and recognize sexual abuse when you seek a special medical examination for your child. Community sexual abuse treatment programs, childrens' hospitals and medical societies may be sources for referrals.

☐ Talk with other parents to ascertain whether there are unusual behavior or physical symptoms in their children.

☐ Remember that taking action is critical because if nothing is done, other children will continue to be at risk. Child sexual abuse is a community interest and concern.

Finally, do not blame yourself. Sexual abuse is a fact in our society. Many individuals who molest children find work through employment and community activities which give them access to children. The vast majority of abuse occurs in situations where the child knows and trusts the adult. Do your homework well, but remember a community and national consciousness is needed before we can stamp out sexual molestation in our society.

We encourage photocopying or reprinting this information.

☐ Make sure that your children know that if someone does something confusing to them, like touching or taking a naked picture or giving them gifts, that you want to be told about it. Reassure them and explain that they will not be blamed for whatever an adult does with them.

Observe Physical and Behavioral Signs

Children who may be too frightened to talk about sexual molestation may exhibit a variety of physical and behavioral signals. Any or several of these signs may be significant. Parents should assume responsibility for noticing such symptoms including:

☐ Extreme changes in behavior such as loss of appetite.

☐ Recurrent nightmares or disturbed sleep patterns and fear of the dark.

☐ Regression to more infantile behavior such as bedwetting, thumb sucking, or excessive crying.

☐ Torn or stained underclothing.

☐ Vaginal or rectal bleeding, pain, itching, swollen genitals, and vaginal discharge.

☐ Vaginal infections or venereal disease.

☐ Unusual interest in or knowledge of sexual matters, expressing affection in ways inappropriate for a child of that age.

☐ Fear of a person or an intense dislike at being left somewhere or with someone.

☐ Other behavioral signals such as aggressive or disruptive behavior, withdrawal, running away or delinquent behavior, failing in school.

FIGURE 11.6 *continued.*

- Does the school or center have a training program?
- Do parents feel welcome in the school?
- Does the school or center have a parent education program for parents of preschoolers?
- Does the school or center have a parent education program for parents of infants and toddlers?
- Is the PTA or any other parent group involved with the school or center in a meaningful way for parents?
- Is there a parent resource room in the school?
- Do parents feel welcome to visit the school?
- Is there regular contact with parents, the teacher, and the school or center? Do the teachers have frequent communication with parents when there is something good to report?

Rights of the Child

The U.S. Advisory Board on Child Abuse and Neglect (1993), using statements (shown in italics) taken from the United Nations Convention on the

Rights of the Child (United Nations, 1989), declares the following rights for the child:

> Respect for the inherent dignity and inalienable rights of children as members of the human community requires protection of their integrity as persons.
>
> Children have a right to protection *from all forms of physical or mental violence, injury or abuse, neglect or negligent treatment, maltreatment or exploitation, including sexual abuse, while in the care of parent(s), legal guardian(s) or any other person who has the care of the child, including children residing in group homes and institutions* (art. 19, 1).
>
> Children have a right to *grow up in a family environment, in an atmosphere of happiness, love and understanding* (preamble).
>
> The several Governments of the United States share a profound responsibility to ensure that children enjoy, at a minimum, such protection of their physical, sexual, and psychological security.
>
> The several Governments of the United States bear a special duty to refrain from subjecting children in their care and custody to harm.
>
> Children have a right to be treated with respect as individuals, with due regard to cultural diversity and the need for culturally competent delivery of services in the child protection system.
>
> Children have a right to *be provided the opportunity to be heard in any judicial and administrative proceedings* affecting them (art. 12), with ample opportunity for representation and for provision of procedures that comport with the child's sense of dignity.
>
> The duty to protect the integrity of children as persons implies a duty to prevent assaults on that integrity whenever possible. (p. 84)

SUMMARY

The wave of child abuse cases reveals a phenomenon that is not new. Child abuse has been with society since very early times, but it was not recognized as a problem until the second half of the 20th century, and no concerted effort was made to stem the crisis until the 1960s.

Legislation requires schools to report cases of abuse and neglect. Schools work with children more than any other agency, so they need to be in the forefront in preventing child abuse.

The chapter defines and describes child abuse and neglect—physical, sexual, and emotional. It includes characteristics of families who tend to be abusive, ways to identify the abused or neglected child, and psychological characteristics of abusive parents and abused children. Points useful for interviewing the child and/or parents are given.

The recognition of the incidence of abuse has increased since the early reports and Kempe's article on the battered child. The chapter includes a discussion of what precipitates abuse, and typical characteristics of abusers.

Greater concern for gun control and reduction of violence in schools, communities, and media is recognized throughout the nation.

School district policy and responsibility are described and illustrated by a typical policy statement. Ways schools can work to help potentially abusive parents are discussed. Recognition of and response to the problem by financial support from the school, parent education groups, school curricula, resource rooms, crisis nurseries, and/or parent-to-parent support groups are necessary.

SUGGESTED CLASS ACTIVITIES AND DISCUSSIONS

1. Attend a meeting of the Child Protection Council or similar group. What is the composition of the council—for example, doctors, educators, social workers, or judges? How does the wide spectrum of specialists show the need for cooperation among agencies working with families?
2. Discuss the signs that teachers may observe in suspected child abuse and neglect cases.
3. What are the steps teachers should take if they suspect child abuse or neglect?
4. Develop a policy for dealing with child abuse and neglect in a hypothetical school.
5. Talk to teachers about how they feel about reporting child abuse. What policies do they follow in reporting suspected child abuse or neglect cases?
6. Identify and describe the local community agencies that help parents learn parenting skills.
7. Identify and describe the agencies in the local community that counsel victims and perpetrators of child abuse.
8. Investigate the manner in which the courts handle child abuse and neglect cases. How do they manage out-of-home placements? Which rights are guaranteed the parents?
9. Make a list of guidelines for identifying maltreated children. Base your discussion on Halperin's descriptions of these children. What are some ways a teacher can support maltreated children?
10. Visit a school and determine what action the teachers and administrators take to reduce and prevent bullying and school violence.

WEB SITES

Child Welfare Information Gateway
http://childwelfare.gov
Provides links and resources for professionals, parents and community personnel on child abuse and neglect. It provides toll-free phone numbers for crisis and abuse. It consolidates information and services from National Clearinghouse for Child Abuse and Neglect Information and National Adoptive Information Clearinghouse. The Web site is a service of the Children's Bureau, the Administration of Children and Families and the U.S. Department of Health and Human Services.

Child Welfare League of America (CWLA)
www.cwla.org
CWLA is the oldest and largest membership-based child welfare organization. It was established to promote the well-being of children, youth, and families.

I-SAFE
www.i-safe.com
A nonprofit organization that works to protect online experiences of youth worldwide. Programs are offered to teach children Internet safety in school. The Web site includes a calendar of events, educational resources, and outreach resources.

National Data Analysis System
http://ndas.cwla.org
Provides reports and links to child abuse data from a nationwide and state-by-state perspectives.

12 Rights, Responsibilities, and Advocacy

G. R. Berger
Clark E. Myers
Eugenia Hepworth Berger

Who advocates for the children? If it is not the parents, it must be someone in the community—teachers, coaches, neighbors. A child's ability to grow and develop is not only a responsibility of parents and community, it also is essential for the survival of the culture and society.

America has an undeniable stake in the economic well-being of families with children. Families with an adequate income are better able to provide the emotional and intellectual, as well as physical, care children need to become healthy, productive adults. Failure to prevent poverty and address the economic needs of families will inevitably lead to other social ills—more crime and delinquency, more teenage childbearing, more unhealthy babies, more failure in school, more substance abuse and mental illness, more child abuse and neglect, and lower productivity among the working-age population.

National Commission on Children, 1991, p. 80

In this chapter on rights and responsibilities you will study the customs and judicial decisions that will guide you and enable you to:

- Cite the Bill of Rights and other amendments to the U.S. Constitution, as well as administrative laws, that form the basis for rights in schools.
- List rights that students and parents have under the Family Educational Rights and Privacy Act (Buckley Amendment).
- Cite the rights of students related to freedom of speech, expression, and press; suspension and due process; search and seizure; flag salute and Pledge of Allegiance; religion; racial and sexual discrimination; disability issues; corporal punishment; text selection; and use of languages other than English.
- Discuss the responsibilities students have in their roles as members of the school community.
- Develop a school behavior code.
- Develop an advocacy program.

- Describe advocacy in other countries.
- Describe the power of advocacy and collaboration.

With rights come responsibilities for parents, children, educators, and society. Could mutual recognition of privileges and obligations provide guidelines for productive dialogue between schools and families? Today the school and the family, two of our most important social institutions, face a challenge to provide what is best for the child.

ORIGIN OF PARENTS' AND CHILDREN'S RIGHTS

Parents have long been recognized as having guardianship rights over their biological children. Parents of adopted children are guaranteed those same rights, which can be terminated only by court action or voluntary relinquishment. At the same time parents have responsibilities to their children. They have the right and responsibility to socialize their children; choose and provide health services for them; discipline and rear them; choose whether they will be educated in private or public schools; and give them care, shelter, and nourishment. It is only when they ignore or misuse these responsibilities that authorities have the right to intervene.

The rights and responsibilities of parents are derived from the U.S. Constitution and its amendments, social customs, legislation, and opinions of state and federal courts. In most of the United States, English common law also often reflects customs through several centuries in Great Britain; in Louisiana laws are traceable to French customs, including Napoleon's codes of law for his empire. Customs as well as law have influenced the manner in which a child's rights are viewed. Basic to this view are two assumptions: (a) children need to be protected and taught until they are mature enough to make wise decisions, and (b) parents can be trusted to protect children's rights (Caldwell, 1989) and care and provide for their children.

But all one has to do to see that parents do not always protect and provide for their children is to look at history (chapter 4) and current child abuse (chapter 1). As far back as the 15th century there was concern in Britain for the protection and rights of children. The government could intervene if the family did not act properly in rearing their children. The concept of *parens patriae* became a part of British custom and law, and so became law in North America as well, underlies the state's right to

Margy Dudley

The rights that guard these children are derived from the U.S. Constitution, the Bill of Rights, social customs, legislation, and rulings of state and federal courts.

intervene for the child because ultimately the state is the child's parent (Caldwell, 1989; Hawes, 1991).

The founders of the United States were concerned about protecting people's rights when they wrote the Constitution and the first 10 amendments. At a minimum, the basis for legal rights in the United States are the Bill of Rights (the first 10 amendments to the Constitution) and the Fourteenth Amendment. The First Amendment states: "Congress shall make no law respecting an establishment of religion, or prohibiting the free exercise thereof; or abridging the freedom of speech, or of the press; or the right of the people peaceably to assemble, and to petition the Government for a redress of grievances." Thus, all citizens, including parents and their children, are guaranteed freedom of religion, freedom of speech, the right to assemble peacefully, a free press, and the right to petition for redress of grievances. The Fourteenth Amendment, enacted after the American Civil War, has been interpreted to make the rights found in the Bill of Rights applicable, at least in a general way, against the individual states as well as against Congress. For example in the early Republic a state could establish a religion, but after the Fourteenth Amendment neither Congress nor any state can establish a religion.

Constitutional Law

The Constitution forms the framework that guides the federal government. Each state also has its own constitution. Rights are guaranteed by the federal Constitution and by individual state constitutions. The U.S. Constitution and the Supreme Court hold precedence over lower courts and states. Some powers, such as education, are delegated completely to the states. According to the Tenth Amendment: "The powers not delegated to the United States by the Constitution, not prohibited by it to the States, are reserved to the States respectively, or to the people." Education was not included as a responsibility of the federal government and was designated as an obligation and right of the individual states. Today, the national government will sometimes take some power over local school systems in exchange for some funding. See, for example the discussion below of Title IX and sex discrimination in secondary schools.

The federal Constitution provides basic rights that are common throughout the United States. "Constitutions are adopted by the people, statutes by legislatures, regulations by agencies, and the common law is created by courts" (Imber & van Geel, 2000, p. 4). Because regulations and laws vary from state to state, people concerned about their rights should check the state constitution, common law, and rules and regulations in their state. State legislatures delegate authority to school boards who must conform to the "limitations of relevant constitutional provisions, statutes, regulations and common law" (p. 5).

Statute Law

The legislative branch of government enacts statutes that affect individual rights. These laws extend from Congress to state legislatures, down to county or city governments, and may be reviewed by the courts to determine their constitutionality.

The state constitution usually provides for the establishment of the public school system. The structure and operation of the school system are provided, revised, and supplemented by legislative enactment of education statutes (Valente, 1987). The federal statutory laws that provide funding to schools and prohibit discrimination are also significant (Imber & van Geel, 2000).

Most state legislatures have statutes that

- Establish and dissolve local school districts and boards
- Determine the selection process, responsibilities, and duties of the local board of education
- Designate the requirements for public school teachers and administrators to be qualified for school positions
- Determine who is eligible for school and who must attend
- Prescribe the curriculum that must be offered
- Specify requirements for high school graduation
- Establish regulations for discipline
- Determine and/or create funding for education

(Adapted from Imber & van Geel, 2000)

Court Law

Court decisions handed down by judges at the federal, state, or local level are called court law, common law, or case law. The Supreme Court is the highest court in the land, and its decisions are binding on all lower courts. For a state constitution, the state supreme court has full power to make a final decision, although the state constitution may not contradict the national constitution. The state may not deny a right guaranteed at the national level, but the state may extend rights beyond those guaranteed by the Bill of Rights. For example, in June 2002 a Supreme Court decision interpreting the Constitution of the United States allowed vouchers to be used by parents or guardians who want their child to attend a school administered by a religious organization. Such vouchers may or may not be legal under state or local laws. Court decisions are binding only within their jurisdiction of the court. The jurisdiction of the U.S. Supreme Court is nationwide; state courts have more limited jurisdiction, and local courts even more limited jurisdiction.

Administrative Law

Regulations and rules of federal and state agencies also affect the rights of parents and families. The *Federal Register* publishes the regulations of federal administrative agencies. Check in your state for specific regulations guiding your rights as a parent or teacher.

Rights vary, depending on the rights and authority of the courts and administrative agencies. Check with the attorney general's office or ask your legal counsel to find out the laws and regulations in your state.

PARENTS' RIGHT TO SELECT THEIR CHILD'S EDUCATION

Parents' traditional right to choose and guide their children's education is supported by several court decisions. In 1923 the *Meyer v. Nebraska* decision ruled that parents have the right to teach their own children.

In 1925 it was ruled that parents have the right to choose parochial rather than public schools to teach their children. The Supreme Court in *Pierce v. Society of Sisters of the Holy Name* (1925) ruled that an Oregon law requiring children to attend public school was unconstitutional. The requirement for an educated citizenry could be met by acceptable private schools, whether parochial or secular, as well

Eugenia Hepworth Berger

Parents are responsible for seeing that their children attend school, but there are a variety of alternatives such as public, private, parochial, and charter schools, as well as homeschooling.

as public schools. On November 7, 1922, Oregon had adopted a Compulsory Education Act. The Society of Sisters was an Oregon corporation established in 1880 that cared for orphans, established schools and academies, and educated students primary through junior college. When the act was passed, parents removed their children from the private schools causing a loss of income and property to the Society. The Fourteenth Amendment states, "nor shall any State deprive any person of life, liberty, or property, without the due process of law." The court ruled that the Fourteenth Amendment guaranteed them protection against the loss of their property without due process of law. "It declared the right to conduct schools was property, and that the parents and guardians, as part of their liberty, might direct the education of their children by selecting reputable teachers and places" (Imber & van Geel, 2000, p. 18).

All states have compulsory attendance laws. Children usually must start school by the age of 6 or 7 and attend until they are 16 or 17. Parents are responsible for seeing that their children attend school. All states have free public schools. Children must attend them, or their parents must provide acceptable and approved schooling at home or in a private school. A growing number of children receive their education at home.

A few exceptions to school attendance have been approved by the courts. In *Wisconsin v. Yoder* (1972), the Supreme Court ruled in favor of Amish parents—Messrs. Yoder, Miller, and Yutzy in Green County, Wisconsin—who refused to send their children to school after the eighth grade. The Amish religion emphasizes a life separate from worldly influences. The parents did not object to their children learning basic reading, writing, and mathematics because basic education is necessary for them to be able to read the Bible and work on the communal farms.

They did object, however, to their children attending school until age 16. In high school, their children would learn values that conflict with Amish religious beliefs. Secondary schools are based on competitiveness, self-achievement, and success, quite different from the cooperative, simple life goals of the Amish. The adolescent years are viewed as formative years that could influence young adults and take them away from the ways of the church. Amish children did not need to learn modern science, claimed the parents; their work on their farms could be taught at home in their own shops under the supervision of the Amish.

Chief Justice Warren E. Burger delivered the majority opinion that Wisconsin's compulsory attendance laws were invalid for the Amish. The decision was based primarily on the First Amendment, which states: "Congress shall make no law respecting an establishment of religion, or prohibiting the free exercise thereof."

Justice William O. Douglas wrote a dissenting opinion, arguing that if a child "is harnessed to the Amish way of life by those in authority over him or if his education is truncated, his entire life may be stunted and deformed." A mature child "may well be able to override the parents' religiously motivated objections."

Two concerns were in conflict: the free exercise of religious beliefs and the need and right of states to have an educated citizenry. In cases where both of these issues are involved, the courts may find in favor of the parents as they did in the *Yoder* case. In 1980, in an Ohio case, *Nagle v. Olin*, the *Yoder* provision prevailed. In this case a father wanted to send his daughter to Kopperts' Korner, an Amish school that did not meet state standards. The school was the only one close enough to the family's home that met the family's religious beliefs. Although the father was not Amish, the court found in favor of him because the school met his religious needs (Lines, 1982a).

Other cases have not met the Yoder test. In *State v. Faith Baptist Church* (1981) the Nebraska high court rejected a request for exemption from compulsory education. In *State v. Shaver* (1980), a North Dakota court found that, though the religious beliefs were sincere, attending public school did not preclude free exercise of those beliefs. In North Carolina, Peter Duro refused to send his children to school because he believed his children's religious beliefs would be undermined by secular humanism and exposure to beliefs contrary to theirs. The Duros, Pentecostals, were not members of an established, self-sufficient community as the Amish were, nor had the children attended school for 8 years as the Amish children had, so the courts ruled against Duro. The state overrode the parent's request. In situations such as these, both concerns must be addressed: the need for an educated citizenry and established religious tenets that might be undermined by the school (LaMorte, 2001; Schimmel & Fischer, 1987).

Public Money for Private Schools

The 1990s saw the use of public money to support students in private schools as well as a growing number of other alternatives to public schools. Private schools have been a legally recognized alternative to public education since 1925 *(Pierce v. Society of Sisters of the Holy Name)*, but the public and the courts had resisted the use of tax money to support private schools. This changed in 2002.

On June 27, 2002, the Supreme Court by a vote of 5 to 4 issued a ruling that vouchers, which use taxpayer money, can be used by parents or guardians to send their children to private (secular or religious) schools. The case concerned a school-voucher program in Cleveland, Ohio. The ruling came after a challenge to a 6-year-old voucher program in Cleveland that allowed low-income children a $2,250 voucher to attend private schools.

Opponents to the use of vouchers to attend religious schools argue that they violate the First Amendment, which guarantees a separation of church and state. The opinion written by Chief Justice Rehnquist said that the voucher program did not breach the First Amendment because it offers private choice by the parents rather than payment directly to the religious schools. The parent is able to choose whether to send the child to private, charter, a school outside their district, magnet, or religious school.

The Road to Use of Vouchers

Several states passed legislation in the mid-1990s to permit vouchers to be used at public or private schools. These allow parents to use public money in the form of vouchers to pay tuition at private schools. Opponents of the voucher system claim that the system is unfair, that it would hurt people financially who are not well-to-do, and that it would ruin the public school system. Supporters of the voucher system think the public school system has failed and should be competitive or should be replaced. The voucher system allows parents to choose the school in which they enroll their child. That could be a private school or a public school in or outside the family's attendance district.

In *Zobrest v. Catalina Foothills School District*, the Supreme Court ruled in a 5–4 vote that public schools could use a public employee to provide sign-language interpretation for a student attending a religious school ("The Supreme Court's Decisions of Note," 1993).

Charter Schools

A public school alternative to the voucher system, charter schools, gives parents greater choice in the type of school they have in their community. Charter schools may allow parents to help plan the school, determine the curriculum, and select teachers with the expectation that the school will be more responsive to the parents and community. Other charter schools offer different choices depending on the chartering organization.

Homeschooling

Another trend is for parents to educate their children at home. Chapter 9 discusses homeschooling in more detail. Although parents have no constitutional right to educate their children at home, state law can determine the regulations for home education or refuse to allow home education. Most states permit parents to teach their own children, but the states have varied requirements. To learn of current regulations, contact your state's Department of Education.

STUDENT RECORDS—OPEN RECORD POLICY

In 1974 Congress passed the Family Educational Rights and Privacy Act (FERPA), often referred to as the *Buckley Amendment*, which gives parents of students younger than 18 and students 18 and older the right to see and control their school records, except for information placed in the file before January 1, 1975. Be sure to check your own school's rules, the Code of Federal Regulations, or another source before dealing with different circumstances. Records, including health files, grades, school records, and other documents concerning the person and kept by the school, must be available within 45 days of the request.

Eugenia Hepworth Berger

The Buckley Amendment (Family Educational Rights and Privacy Act) gives this child's parents the right to see her school records.

Directory information is given to newspapers and others who request it unless the parents or person over 18 years old request that their name or the child's name be removed from the directory information list.

> Directory information means information contained in an education record of a student that would not generally be considered harmful or an invasion of privacy if disclosed. It includes, but is not limited to, the student's name, address, telephone listing, electronic mail address, photograph, date and place of birth, major field of study, dates of attendance, grade level, enrollment status (e. g., undergraduate or graduate; full-time or part-time) participation in officially recognized activities and sports, weight and height of members of athletic teams, degrees, honors and awards received, and the most recent educational agency or institution attended.
>
> 34 CFR Sec. 99.3 as of 2005
> (Authority: 20 U.S.C. 1232g(a)(5)(A))

Notice that the current regulations include e-mail addresses in the directory records, something hardly thought of in 1974 when the Buckley Amendment passed Congress as FERPA.

Privacy Procedures

1. Schools must permit eligible students or parents to inspect student records.
   a. The teacher's grade book when shared only with a substitute teacher is exempt. Student aides or volunteer parents should not enter grades or otherwise share the book. There are special concerns when the grade book is on a computer, especially a networked computer. The grade book is exempt from inspection only when properly maintained and safeguarded because the grade book would not be an education record under the act.

      > The term [education record] does not include:
      >
      > (1) Records that are kept in the sole possession of the maker, are used only as a personal memory aid, and are not accessible or revealed to any other person except a temporary substitute for the maker of the record.
      >
      > 34 CFR Sec. 99.3 as of 2005
      > (Authority: 20 U.S.C. 1232g(a)(4))

   b. Schools must provide an explanation of records when requested by parents or students.
   c. Records may be destroyed before a request, but once a request has been made, the records may not be destroyed until the parent or eligible student has seen them.
   d. Psychiatric or treatment records may be available only to a medical doctor who can review them for the parent or eligible student. The Health Insurance Portability and Accountability Act of 1996 (HIPAA) applies new federal rules for many medical records. These rules are called "Standards for Privacy of Individually Identifiable Health Information," and found in the *Federal Register* at 45 CFR Parts 160, 162, and 164. No disclosure can be made

contrary to national rules and some states and school districts may have stricter rules. Under federal law and regulations individual treatment records may, in some cases, be denied to parents and to students. Even for students over 18 (who otherwise have the rights of the parent as well the rights of the individual patient) access to some records may be limited to a professional community.

   e. If parents are unable to come to school, the school should send the records to them. The school may charge a reasonable amount for making copies, but not for the time spent preparing and obtaining the records.

2. Schools must let parents or eligible students correct misleading or false information.
   a. If the school administrator agrees with the parent's or student's request, the official may remove questionable data.
   b. If the official refuses to change or remove the questionable information, a hearing may be requested. This hearing must take place within a reasonable time, although the law does not specify a deadline. Parents and students may bring a lawyer or friend to present evidence for them. Both sides may present evidence at a meeting presided over by an impartial hearing officer. If the decision is against the parents, they may insert a written statement about why they disagree with the information.
3. Schools must inform eligible students and parents of their rights to record disclosure and privacy.
4. Schools must obtain written permission from parents or eligible students before giving information to others, with some exceptions. Even when an exception exists care should be taken about individually identifiable information. For instance a reporting agency, typically a school or district, may report information for statistical purposes. However, the school should take great care in sending a list of subgroups and records for a subgroup when the subgroup is very small. Individual identity may be discovered when the subgroup is small. Typically fewer than 5 members is considered small. Remember too, that if a grade book is disclosed to anyone but a temporary substitute for the teacher, the grade book is no longer an exception to the general educational record rule.

   Exceptions generally include:

   a. School officials and teachers with a legitimate, what some people call a need-to-know, educational interest. If there is no need to know, the interest may not be legitimate despite membership in the educational community.
   b. Federal and state officials for use in an audit or evaluation of state or federally supported programs.
   c. Accreditation associations doing accreditation work.
   d. Financial aid officials seeking information for processing financial aid requests.
   e. Administrators of another school district to which the student is transferring. Parents and eligible students have the right to review the file before it is processed.
   f. People doing research, but only if the individuals are not and cannot be identified. Teachers must be very careful in not identifying students by numbers, especially Social Security numbers or any part of a Social Security number or e-mail addresses or Web sites that might be used to identify individuals.
   g. Officials responding to emergencies in which the information is necessary to protect the health of the student.
5. No information about a student may be kept secret from everybody. Medical information generally and special needs students often have special requirements. Schools are allowed and expected to recognize court orders

If these requirements are met, eligible students and their parents can be sure that student records are accurate and that the records are not used for any purpose other than those stated above without their approval (Berger & Berger, 1985).

Situation

Melissa had not done well in her second-grade class. Her parents thought the teacher did not appreciate Melissa's talents because she had difficulty staying in her seat and refraining from talking to her neighbors.

When they moved to another school district, the teacher had Melissa sit in a carrel to help her concentrate on her work and avoid talking when she was supposed to be studying. Mrs. Jones, Melissa's mother, was furious. "Why should she be isolated from the rest of the children?" she complained to her husband. "This is going to ruin her self-confidence. I won't stand for it! I am going to make an appointment with the principal."

The following week both Mr. and Mrs. Jones were sitting in the principal's office waiting to talk. "May we see Melissa's record?" asked Mr. Jones. "What is in there that would make her teacher segregate her from the rest of the class on the first day of school?" The principal responded, "It will take several days to obtain her record. I also would like to talk with her teacher to find out why she separated her from the rest of the class. We have a wonderful school here; teachers work hard and are devoted professionals. I am sure there was a reason. Did Melissa have trouble at her former school? Ask the secretary to set up another appointment for you. I'm sure we can straighten this out and give you a satisfactory explanation."

1. What rights do Melissa's parents have?
2. Why do you think the teacher separated Melissa from the rest of the class?
3. What should happen next?

RIGHTS AND RESPONSIBILITIES OF STUDENTS AND PARENTS

Students and their parents have rights and responsibilities while the child is attending school. This section includes a discussion of these rights and responsibilities. Because laws change and vary, you should check the most recent law in your state if a specific incident occurs within your district.

Free Speech and Expression

The First Amendment provides that "Congress shall make no law . . . abridging the freedom of speech or of the press; or the right of the people peaceably to assemble. . . " The Fourteenth Amendment applies the Bill of Rights in a general fashion to the states. Thus, the Fourteenth Amendment prevents the states and local jurisdictions from making any law that Congress itself could not make under the First Amendment. Students have the right, therefore, to express themselves, verbally or symbolically (armbands, symbols on clothing, salutes), even if their position is in disfavor. However, most students are children under the law. The school may act in place of the parent—in loco parentis—that is be "charged, factitiously, with a parent's rights, duties and responsibilities" *Wetherby v. Dixon* (19 Ves. 412) and repeated many times since. "[M]inors often lack the experience, perspective, and judgment to recognize and avoid choices that could be detrimental to them" (*Bellotti v. Baird,* 443 U.S. 622, 635 [1979]). Students have the responsibility, however, to not slander another or disrupt the operation of the school. Misconduct in the guise of free expression need not be tolerated. Student rallies may have prescribed times and places. Students do not have the right to commandeer the school and intrude on the rights of others (Valente, 1987). Time, place, and manner of speaking may be regulated and may be regulated more strictly for minors and in schools.

Freedom of Expression

The landmark decision on freedom of expression came in 1969 during the Vietnam War. In *Tinker v. Des Moines Independent Community School District* (1969), the Supreme Court ruled that students had the right to expression while they were at school: "It can hardly be argued that either students or teachers shed their constitutional rights to freedom of speech or expression at the schoolhouse gate."

The case involved a protest against the Vietnam War. The petitioners, John F. Tinker, Christopher Eckhardt, and Mary Beth Tinker, were among a group of adults and students who held a meeting at the Eckhardt home. They determined that they would wear black armbands during the holiday season commencing December 16, 1965, to protest the war in Vietnam. The parents, who were Quakers, supported their children's actions. The school administrator heard of the plan and instituted a rule that students who wore black armbands would be asked to remove them and, if they refused, would be suspended (Schimmel & Fischer, 1987).

The students refused to remove their armbands and were subsequently suspended. Their parents protested the suspension and took the case to court. Both the U.S. District Court and the U.S. Court of Appeals for the 8th Circuit found in favor of the schools, stating that their action prevented a disturbance. When the Supreme Court wrote its decision, the justices emphasized that schools must have the right "to prescribe and control conduct in the schools," but to prohibit an expression of opinion, the school must show that it substantially interfered with "appropriate discipline in the operation of the school." The court found that there was no evidence that it interfered "with the school's work or with the rights of other students to be secure or left alone" (Fischer, Schimmel, & Kelly, 1999, p. 173). The passive use of armbands was not disruptive in this situation. The principal had put the suspension policy in place because he opposed the students' action, not because he feared a disturbance.

The threat of a disturbance influences court decisions. In *Guzick v. Drebus* (1971), Guzick, a student at Shaw High School in East Cleveland, Ohio, wore a button that was a symbol against the Vietnam War. Shaw High School, with a ratio of 70 percent Black and 30 percent White students, had a long-standing rule against wearing symbols and buttons because they had promoted racial disturbances. The court ruled against Guzick in this case because of the danger of a racial disturbance in the school.

Gang activity has caused concern about students wearing clothes or colors to school to signify their allegiance to a gang. Would this be considered freedom of speech? In *Olesen v. Board of Education of School District No. 228* (1987), the courts found that dress in this case was not "speech" protected by the First Amendment but was individualization or membership in a group, and schools could restrict the displaying of gang apparel because of student safety. If the wearing of certain colors or clothes might cause disruption of the schools, then barring their display probably would be found to be reason for prohibiting those clothes or colors.

A disruptive speech was held to be unprotected speech in *Bethel School District No. 403 v. Fraser* (1986). The speech was not obscene, and every word of the speech might have been used properly. The language as spoken was metaphorical and indecent by implication. The student was warned in advance by teachers not to make his speech. In some sense the student defied legitimate instructions by his school. In this case a minor student in a school setting had some rights but not all the rights of an adult in a public forum.

The trial court found for the respondent following the rule of *Tinker*, but the Supreme Court reversed it. The court distinguished *Tinker*, holding:

> 1. The First Amendment did not prevent the School District from disciplining respondent for giving the offensively lewd and indecent speech at the assembly. *Tinker v. Des Moines Independent Community School Dist.*, 393 U.S. 503, distinguished. Under the First Amendment, the use of an offensive form of expression may not be prohibited to adults making what the speaker considers a political point, but it does not follow that the same latitude must be permitted to children in a public school. It is a highly appropriate function of public school education to prohibit the use of vulgar and offensive terms in public discourse. Nothing in the Constitution prohibits the states from insisting that certain modes of expression are inappropriate and subject to sanctions. The inculcation of these values is truly the work of the school, and the determination of what manner of speech is inappropriate properly rests with the school board.

Freedom of the Press

The Supreme Court case *Hazelwood School District v. Kuhlmeier* (1988) has affected schools' supervisory capacity over publications. Until that time the governing theory was that a school could regulate the grammar and technical quality of a newspaper produced in connection with a high school journalism class, but that it could not remove articles because they might be controversial or unpopular. The *Hazelwood* case involved a journalism II class producing a newspaper that had traditionally been reviewed by the principal before publication. In 1983 the principal rejected two stories, one on pregnancy and one on divorce. The principal felt that the students in the article on pregnancy were identifiable, and printing the story was an invasion of privacy. In the one on divorce, a student complained about her father's behavior without the father having an opportunity to respond.

The trial court upheld the principal's action, stating that his deletions were "legitimate and reasonable," based on invasion of privacy issues. A federal appeals court reversed that, holding that a journalism class newspaper is a public forum for students and not just an academic project and therefore deserved the protection of the First Amendment (Fischer et al., 1999; Schimmel & Fischer, 1987). The Supreme Court decision placed the newspaper as a curriculum project connected to academics, so the principal could oversee the work. Justice Byron White, writing for the Court, drew a fine line between *Tinker*'s guarantee of free speech in general and *Hazelwood*'s new rule that schools could forbid speech to promote education. The *Hazelwood* rule is "A school need not tolerate speech that is inconsistent with its basic education mission, even though the government could not censor similar speech outside the school."

Search and Seizure

The Fourth Amendment states:

> The right of the people to be secure in their persons, houses, papers, and effects, against unreasonable searches and seizures, shall not be violated, and no warrants shall issue, but upon probable cause, supported by oath or affirmation, and particularly describing the place to be searched, and the persons or things to be seized.

The idea that children do not leave their constitutional rights at the schoolhouse gate, expressed in *Tinker v. Des Moines Independent Community School District* (1969), means that school personnel need some reasonable cause before they search individual lockers or individuals. In *New Jersey v. T.L.O.*, officials had reason to believe the student possessed marijuana. Justice White, writing for the court, noted that "T. L. O. confessed that she had been selling marihuana at the high school" and reached this conclusion: "Our review of the facts surrounding the search leads us to conclude that the search was in no sense unreasonable for Fourth Amendment purposes." The court went on to write a rule such that the search in *T.L.O.* follows the rule. The rule in *New Jersey v. T.L.O.* (1985) states that "first, one must -consider whether the 'action was justified at its inception,' . . . second, one must determine whether the search as actually conducted 'was reasonably related in scope to the circumstances which justified the interference in the first place'" (Kierstead & Wagner, 1993, p. 76). The minority opinion by Justice Brennan, joined by Justice Marshall, makes the search-without-a-warrant issue in *T. L. O.* perhaps more clear:

> Today's decision sanctions school officials to conduct full-scale searches on a "reasonableness" standard whose only definite content is that it is *not* the same test as the "probable cause" standard found in the text of the Fourth Amendment. In adopting this unclear, unprecedented, and unnecessary departure from generally applicable Fourth Amendment standards, the Court carves out a broad exception to standards that this Court has developed over years of considering Fourth Amendment problems. Its decision is supported neither by precedent nor even by a fair application of the "balancing test" it proclaims in this very opinion.

Three years later *Irby v. State of Texas* (1988) set forth the principle that school officials who want to search a child or the child's locker must have a reason. "Under ordinary circumstances, a search of a student by a teacher or other school official will be justified at its inception when there are reasonable grounds for suspecting that the search will turn up evidence that the student has violated or is violating either the law or the rules of the school" (Kierstead & Wagner, 1993).

Testing for Drugs

A decision by the Supreme Court (Lindsay Earls vs. Board of Education) issued on June 27, 2002, expanded the right for schools to randomly test students for drug use if the students participate in extracurricular activities. The school district began random drug tests for students who wanted to participate in extracurricular activities such as Future Farmers of America, playing chess, band, choir, and Academic Teams (Greenberger, 2002; Holland, 2002). This expanded a ruling in 1995 that allowed random testing of high school athletes. Lindsay Earls, an Oklahoma honor student, was subjected to a random drug test when she was a sophomore in high school. Two students and their parents challenged the testing, stating that it violated their Fourth Amendment protection against unreasonable searches. The Supreme Court rejected their case 5–4. Justice Clarence Thomas stated that testing of students "is a reasonably effective means of addressing the school district's legitimate concerns in detecting and preventing drug use."

The use of drug-sniffing dogs, where drugs means illegal drugs, is usually considered not a search; there is no right to private possession of illegal drugs. Likely enough, the use of, say, chocolate-sniffing dogs would be considered a search. An indication that a drug-sniffing dog has in fact found drugs may then make a further search reasonable. Examples include having dogs sniff all lockers for illegal drugs or for explosives and other contraband, followed by the search of individual lockers.

Suspension and Due Process

The Fourteenth Amendment guarantees the right to due process for all citizens—"nor shall any State deprive any person of life, liberty, or property without due process of law." When a student is suspended, the act affects the parents' rights as well as the child's. An early case concerning due process, *Dixon v. Alabama State Board of Education* (1961), involved college students who were expelled or placed on probation after they staged a sit-in at a lunch counter. The students had not been given a hearing or notice of the charges against them. The court established the right to notice and to a hearing before suspension or expulsion.

A landmark case, *Goss v. Lopez* (1975), resulted from a disturbance at a school lunchroom in Ohio during the winter of 1971. Seventy-five students were suspended. In Ohio, a principal could suspend students for up to 10 days if parents were notified within 24 hours and told the reason for the suspension. To get a hearing, the parents or students had to appeal. Nine students, including Dwight Lopez, filed a lawsuit in federal district court citing the lack of due process. The court ruled in favor of the students, and the school administration appealed to the U.S. Supreme Court. The Supreme Court also found in favor of the students, holding that students are entitled to a public education under Ohio law and that state right could be taken away from them only after due process, as guaranteed by the national constitution even for rights created outside that constitution. Justice White wrote:.

> Those young people do not "shed their constitutional rights" at the schoolhouse door. "The Fourteenth Amendment, as now applied to the States, protects the citizen against the State itself and all of its creatures—Boards of Education not excepted." The authority possessed by the State to prescribe and enforce standards of conduct in its schools although concededly very broad, must be exercised consistently with constitutional safeguards.

The court used the same principle as the one in *Tinker:* Students "do not shed their constitutional rights at the schoolhouse door." The court saw no need to footnote so obvious a principle. Notice, however, that the constitutional rights of young people inside the schoolhouse door are not identical to the rights of adults outside the schoolhouse. Justice Powell, writing for the four dissenters, wrote: "Moreover, to the extent that there may be some arguable infringement, it is too speculative, transitory, and insubstantial to justify imposition of a *constitutional* rule."

Students who are suspended for a short time (up to 10 days) must be given (a) notice of the charges, (b) an explanation of the charges and reasons for the suspension, and (c) an opportunity to explain their side of the situation. The Supreme Court opinion recognized that formal, adversarial proceedings would take too much of the school's time, but "effective notice and informal hearing permitting the student to give his version of the events will provide a meaningful hedge against erroneous action" (Fischer et al., 1999; Schimmel & Fischer, 1987, p. 251).

Students who present a danger to the school can be removed immediately. In the *Goss v. Lopez* decision, the court limited the rules to short suspensions, stating that longer suspensions or expulsions may require more formal hearings. The Supreme Court has not addressed the procedures for longer suspensions, but notice, the right to counsel, presentation of evidence, and cross-examination of witnesses should be permitted in any such hearing. The student and parents should also have a statement of findings, conclusions, recommendations, and the right to appeal (Fischer et al., 1999; Schimmel & Fischer, 1987). There have been many longer-term suspensions, including some for a full year and even expulsions, in recent years under zero-tolerance policies in the public schools. Many of these have seemed excessive to the general public. Some such cases have received national publicity and have been resolved in the court of public opinion following threats of litigation.

Valente (1987) points out that brief in-school sanctions do not require prepunishment hearings. Nor does *Goss v. Lopez* apply in corporal punishment cases (*Ingraham v. Wright*, 1977) because corporal punishment does not require a student to miss school. "The student's right to demand an *open hearing* is not settled" (Valente, 1987, p. 307).

Flag Salute and Pledge of Allegiance

Students do not have to salute the U.S. flag or say the Pledge of Allegiance if it violates their religious beliefs. In *West Virginia State Board of Education v. Barnette* (1943), Jehovah's Witnesses parents objected to their children being required by state law to salute the flag. The U.S. Supreme Court found in their favor. Children did not have to salute the flag if the salute violated their beliefs or values.

The decision that students do not have to salute the flag has since been extended to cases in which a person objects as a matter of conscience. In Coral Gables, Florida, a high school student objected to having to stand during the Pledge of Allegiance as a matter of conscience. The Florida court found in favor of the student: "Standing is an integral portion of the pledge ceremony and is no less a gesture of acceptance and respect than is the salute or the utterance of the words of allegiance" (Fischer et al., 1999, p. 206).

Other cases have reaffirmed that students cannot be required to say the Pledge of Allegiance or stand during the pledge. A New York honor student refused to pledge allegiance because he did not believe there was freedom and liberty for all. Although the school board had offered to let him leave the room or stand up during the pledge, he preferred to remain seated. The act of standing was an affirmation. "Therefore, the alternative offered plaintiff of standing in silence is an act that cannot be compelled over his deeply held convictions. It can no more be required than the pledge itself" (Fischer et al., 1999, p. 207).

The school has an affirmative duty to protect the student's rights. The school and the classroom teacher in particular must prevent any harassment on account of a student asserting his or her rights.

Racial Discrimination

The Fourteenth Amendment states:

> All persons born or naturalized in the United States, and subject to the jurisdiction thereof, are citizens of the United States and of the State wherein they reside. No State shall make or enforce any law which shall abridge the privileges or immunities of citizens of the United States; nor shall any State deprive any person of life, liberty, or property, without due process of law, nor deny to any person within its jurisdiction the equal protection of the laws.

The *Brown v. Topeka Board of Education* (1954) decision on racial discrimination set the stage for implementing racial equality in the schools. The U.S. Supreme Court stated:

> Today, education is perhaps the most important function of state and local governments. Compulsory school attendance laws and the great expenditures for education both demonstrate our recognition of the importance of education to our democratic society. It is required in the performance of our most basic public responsibilities, even service in the armed forces. It is the very foundation of good citizenship. (p. 493)

Congress enacted the Civil Rights Act of 1964 as an instrument to eliminate continued discrimination. Recipients of federal funds, including schools, must meet its guidelines to receive government support. Title VI of the act states:

> that no person in the United States shall, on the grounds of race, color, or national origin, be excluded from participation in, be denied the benefits of, or be otherwise subjected to discrimination under any program or activity receiving Federal financial assistance from the Department of Education. (Civil Rights Act, § 601 [1964])

A "recipient under any program to which this part applies may not, directly or through contractual or other arrangements, on the basis of race, color, or national origin" engage in the following discrimination practices (*Federal Register*, 1990,

p. 30918). Because most schools receive federal financial support and are therefore recipients, they must abide by these regulations and cannot:

> 1. Deny an individual any service, financial aid or other benefit provided under the program;
> 2. Provide any service, financial aid or other benefit to an individual which is different or is provided in a different manner from that provided to others under the program;
> 3. Subject an individual to segregation or separate treatment in any matter related to his receipt of any service, financial aid or other benefit under the program;
> 4. Restrict an individual in any way in the enjoyment of any advantage or privilege enjoyed by others receiving any service, financial aid or other benefit under the program;
> 5. Treat an individual differently from others in determining whether he satisfies any admission, enrollment, quota, eligibility, membership or other requirement or condition which individuals must meet in order to be provided any service, financial aid or other benefit provided under the program;
> 6. Deny an individual an opportunity to participate in the program through the provision of services or otherwise afford him an opportunity to do so which is different from that afforded others under the program. . . .
> 7. Deny a person the opportunity to participate as a member of a planning or advisory body which is an integral part of the program;
> 8. . . . Utilize criteria or methods of administration which have the effect of subjecting individuals to discrimination because of their race, color, or national origin, or have the effect of defeating or substantially impairing accomplishment of the objectives of the program as respect individuals of a particular race, color, or national origin. (*Federal Register*, 1990, pp. 30918–30919)

Schools must not, therefore, separate students based on race, determine services for students using methods that in effect discriminate against a student, or in any way discriminate against students based on race, color, or national origin.

Situation

Rex came to school ready to learn. He was an African American child with poor but interested parents. The first day the teacher assigned him to a seat in the back of the room. She was pleased that he seemed alert and smiled at her a lot, but she was sure that he would probably need a lot of help, and she had 32 children in her class already. "Why did they have to assign another student to me in the middle of the year? Don't they know that I have as much as I can handle?"

She assigned him to the polar bear group. Everyone in the room knew that was the low group, but Miss Barton thought Rex would be better off there than in the other groups.

During reading groups, Rex read unhesitatingly and with great expression. When Miss Barton asked him questions, he was able to describe the plot and the ending of the story. "He seems to be ready for a higher group, but I think I will keep him in this group until I really find out," thought Miss Barton.

During math Rex raised his hand ready to answer questions, but Miss Barton did not call on him. "I want to give him time to adjust," she said. This continued for the first 2 weeks that Rex was in the classroom, but by the third week, he no longer smiled; he no longer raised his hand; he no longer wanted to attend school; and his parents worried that something was terribly wrong. They called the school and made an appointment with Miss Barton.

1. Do you think the parents were right in asking for an appointment?
2. Why did Miss Barton continue to ignore Rex?
3. How can Miss Barton turn the situation around?
4. What should Rex do to help his school experience?

Sex Discrimination

Title IX of the Educational Amendments of 1972 provides that "no person in the United States shall, on the basis of sex, be excluded from participation in, be denied the benefits of, or be subjected to discrimination under any program or activity receiving Federal financial assistance" (U.S. Department of Education, n.d.).

For more information, see the Code of Federal Regulations Title 34 Education Part 106: Nondiscrimination on the Basis of Sex in Education

Programs or Activities Receiving Federal Financial Assistance (www.ed.gov/policy/rights/reg/ocr/edlite-34 cfr106.html).

The Office for Civil Rights based in the Department of Education enforces the laws that apply to elementary, secondary, and postsecondary schools. In 1975 a federal regulation required schools to examine their programs to see if discriminatory policies were in effect. Military schools, religious organizations in which the regulations would be at variance with the groups' beliefs, and single-sex colleges are exempt. Other than these, educational institutions receiving federal funds cannot "assign students to separate classrooms or activities, or prevent them from enrolling in courses of their choice, on the basis of sex. This includes health, physical education, industrial arts, business, vocational, technical, home economics, music and adult education courses" (U.S. Department of Education, n.d., p. 1).

Educational institutions that receive federal funds cannot do the following:

1. Exclude students of one sex from participation in any academic, extracurricular, research, occupational training or other educational program or activity.
2. Subject any student to separate or different rules of discipline, sanctions or other treatment.
3. Apply different rules of appearance to males and females (for example, requiring males to wear their hair shorter than females).
4. Aid or perpetuate discrimination against any person by providing significant assistance to any agency, organization, or person which discriminates on the basis of sex in providing any aid, benefit, or service to students.
5. Assign pregnant students to separate classes or activities, although schools may require a student to obtain a physician's certificate as to her ability to participate in the normal educational program or activity so long as such a certificate is required of all students for other physical or emotional conditions requiring the attention of a physician.
6. Refuse to excuse any absence because of pregnancy or refuse to allow the student to return to the same grade level that she held when she left school because of pregnancy.
7. Discriminate against any person on the basis of sex in the counseling or guidance of students or the use of different tests or materials for counseling unless such different materials cover the same occupation and interest areas and the use of such different materials is shown to be essential to eliminate sex bias.

Exceptions include:

1. In music classes, schools may have requirements based on vocal range or quality, which may result in all-male or all-female choruses.
2. In elementary and secondary schools, portions of classes that deal exclusively with human sexuality may be conducted in separate sessions for boys and girls.
3. In physical education classes or activities, students may be separated by sex when participating in sports where the major purpose or activity involves bodily contact (for example, wrestling, boxing, rugby, ice hockey, football, and basketball).
4. Students may be grouped in physical education classes by ability if objective standards of individual performances are applied. This may result in all-male or all-female ability groups.
5. If the use of a single standard to measure skill or progress in a physical education class has an adverse effect on members of one sex, schools must use appropriate standards that do not have such an effect. For example, if the ability to lift a certain weight is used as a standard for assignment to a swimming class, application of this standard may exclude some girls. The school would have to use other, appropriate standards to make the selection for that class. (U.S. Department of Education, n.d., pp. 1–2)

Children with Disabilities

Section 504 of the Rehabilitation Act of 1973 provides that "no qualified handicapped individual shall, on the basis of handicap, be excluded from participation in, be denied the benefits of, or otherwise be subjected to discrimination under any program or activity receiving Federal financial assistance" (U.S. Department of Education, 1980, pp. 30937–30938). The Education for All Handicapped Children Act of 1975, PL 94–142, ensures that children with disabilities have an appropriate public education. Amendments of 1986, PL 94–457, extend the concept to preschool children. The Individuals with Disabilities Education Act (IDEA), PL 101–476, and Individuals with Disabilities

When this child gets involved in extracurricular sports, Title IX will ensure that she has an opportunity to participate.

Education Act Amendments 1997 (IDEA 97), PL 105–17, clarified requirements and increased parent involvement in the education choices for their children. The child is to be educated in the least restrictive environment—one that fits the child's needs. An Individualized Education Program or Individualized Family Service Plan, developed by professionals and parents, protects the child's interest. Refer to chapter 10 for more complete information.

Corporal Punishment

Although parents may object to corporal punishment, schools do not always honor their request. Punishment must not be harsh and excessive. If it is, teachers and administrators may be subject to civil and criminal liability. Bans on corporal punishment exist in 28 states and the District of Columbia. In addition, Ohio and Utah have limited bans. Even where not banned by the state there may be local bans and restrictions (Center for Effective Discipline, 2005). The Supreme Court in *Ingraham v. Wright* (1977) found that paddling students as a means of maintaining school discipline in schools was not cruel and unusual punishment and that to the extent paddling is permissible there is no due process requirement for prior notice and opportunity to be heard. The Court thus upheld paddling as a means of control in public schools, so schools in a minority of states have the right to use corporal punishment without hearings or other components of due process.

Situation

Melvern was late for school that day. When he swaggered into class, he grinned at his buddy across the room, made a motion with his hand, and began to go to the teacher's desk. The teacher greeted him by telling him that his work was late and would not count. "Sorry," said Mr. Beller, "if your work had been here at 9:00 A.M. I would have accepted it, but it is now 9:20, and you'll just have to take the consequence. This just might change your grade from a C to a D. I'm afraid you won't be able to go out for the track team."

Melvern glared at Mr. Beller, threw down his book, kicked at his desk, and made inaudible comments under his breath. "To the office this minute, Melvern, I will not tolerate that kind of behavior. This is your third offense in this class. Mrs. Markam will handle the physical punishment."

1. Did Mr. Beller handle the situation correctly?
2. How do you evaluate Melvern's response?
3. Should physical punishment be allowed in the schools? Does it help control the school?
4. Is corporal punishment allowed in the state where you reside?
5. Are there any offenses that you think might require corporal punishment? Why?

Rights of Non-English-Speaking Students

In 1965, the Elementary and Secondary Act supported bilingual education for students who do not speak English. This was followed in 1974 by a Supreme Court decision in *Lau v. Nichols* that children who could not speak English did not have equal educational opportunity if they did not receive education in their own language. In this case, 1,800 ethnic Chinese children in San Francisco attended classes conducted in English. The parents contended that the children were discriminated against because no classes were provided that would benefit them. The Supreme Court agreed and stated that schools must take affirmative action and provide classes for students who do not speak English by providing bilingual education or English as a Second Language programs. The court did not offer regulations concerning language programs and left the decision of provisions up to the states.

Later cases implementing and interpreting *Lau v. Nichols* include *Castañeda vs. Pickard* 648 F.2d 989; 1981 U.S. App 1981. The Court of Appeals for the 5th Circuit suggested a three-step test. The court said:

> Congress has provided us with almost no guidance, in the form of text or legislative history, to assist us in determining whether a school district's language remediation efforts are "appropriate." . . . The court's responsibility, insofar as educational theory is concerned, is only to ascertain that a school system is pursuing a program informed by an educational theory recognized as sound by some experts in the field or, at least, deemed a legitimate experimental strategy. . . .
>
> The court's second inquiry would be whether the programs and practices actually used by a school system are reasonably calculated to implement effectively the educational theory adopted by the school. . . .
>
> Finally, a determination that a school system has adopted a sound program for alleviating the language barriers impeding the educational progress of some of its students and made bona fide efforts to make the program work does not necessarily end the court's inquiry into the appropriateness of the system's actions. If a school's program, although premised on a legitimate educational theory and implemented through the use of adequate techniques, fails, after being employed for a period of time sufficient to give the plan a legitimate trial, to produce results indicating that the language barriers confronting students are actually being overcome, that program may, at that point, no longer constitute appropriate action as far as that school is concerned. We do not believe Congress intended that under § 1703(f) a school would be free to persist in a policy which, although it may have been "appropriate" when adopted, in the sense that there were sound expectations for success and bona fide efforts to make the program work, has, in practice, proved a failure.

Also in 1981, *Idaho Migrant Council v. Board of Education*, 647 F.2d 69 (9thCir. 1981), held that state as well as local agencies are responsible for seeing that the student's need for bilingual education is met. *Denver v. School District No. 1 (Denver) 1983* applied the three rules of *Castañeda v. Pickard* to test the Denver program. *Teresa P. v. Berkeley Unified 1987* applied the three rules of *Castañeda v. Pickard* to test the Berkeley Unified program. In *Illinois v. Gómez* (1987), the Court of Appeals for the 7th Circuit concluded, much like the 9th Circuit in *Idaho Migrant Council*, that the state was obligated to establish minimums and additional requirements. This area of law remained unsettled as late as 2007.

Situation

Kim Sung came into the fourth-grade classroom. She had arrived just the week before from Venezuela, where her family had lived for the last 10 years. She was a lovely young lady with dark hair and beautiful eyes. She could speak Spanish and Chinese fluently, but she had no experience with English. The teacher, Miss Zingle, had not expected to have a student this term who could not speak English, and she could not speak Spanish or Chinese. By using body language she was able to direct Kim to a seat in the back of the classroom. As soon as Kim was seated, Miss Zingle continued to tell the class what the assignment was. School progressed slowly for Kim. She sat there unable to understand what was going on, and wondering if she were behaving correctly.

1. How could Miss Zingle have handled the situation differently?
2. What would be the best arrangement and learning situation for Kim?
3. What could a teacher and classmates do to help Kim adjust to the new surroundings?
4. What could Miss Zingle have done to help Kim that first day?

Selection of Texts

In general, schools choose text materials to achieve their educational objectives and goals. When parents object to the use of particular books, the courts make decisions based on each individual circumstance and how the book relates to the school's objectives. Courts determine the constitutionality of a position; legislatures may set curriculum requirements to be achieved by public schools.

One 2006 case, *No. 05–11725*, which involved evolution in biology texts and which was heard in the U.S. Court of Appeals for the 11th Circuit by a three-judge panel, shows the difficulties courts have in deciding disputes that are properly legislative and administrative. The Court was unable to reach a decision on the merits and remanded for further proceedings and fact finding saying, "because in this area of the law the devil is in the details. Facts and context are crucial and they, of course, must be determined from the evidence, which presupposes that a court knows what the evidence is."

Private schools and early childhood centers that are not connected to the public school system have autonomy in text selection. However, it is wise for both public and private schools to include parents in book selection to prevent later disagreements.

Obscenity is not protected by the First Amendment, but the Supreme Court has not defined obscenity. When the issue over a book or other medium becomes so heated that it ends up in court, the court will judge whether it lacks serious literary, artistic, political, or scientific value and whether it is obscene because it appeals to prurient interests (*Miller v. California*, 1973). Whether it is obscene will be judged by contemporary local standards.

DEVELOPING CRITERIA TOGETHER

Only when parents and teachers work together does the opportunity for optimum education exist. A delineation of three levels of involvement for home and school will clarify and help establish procedures that support positive home-school interaction:

1. Development and periodic review of a code of rights and responsibilities for each class, school, or school district.
2. Selection of and active involvement with a parent or citizen advisory council.
3. Implementation of the educational program in a classroom community.

The first two levels can be accomplished by administrators and parents working together; however, individual classrooms can develop codes and advisory councils as well. The third level of teacher–parent involvement is that essential area where the benefits of positive relationships most make a difference—the classroom. The teacher–child–parent relationship nourishes the opportunity for learning. The clarification of issues and development of codes, a two-way communication system, and advisory councils are but means of supporting direct involvement with the classroom and its most important member, the child.

Development of a Code

The formation of a school or classroom code creates an opening for participating in a democratic decision-making process. If parents and students join school staff in developing a code for their class or school, both rights and responsibilities are learned through a democratic process. *The Rights and Responsibilities of Students: A Handbook for the School Community* (U.S. Department of Health, Education, and Welfare, 1979) suggests a model code and a procedure for implementing a code. Recommended steps include:

1. *Identification of the level of interest.* Determine the interest in and awareness of codes with a questionnaire or informal survey of the school community. Include teachers, administrators, students, parents, and interested community residents. If there is a lack of understanding of the purpose of a code, you must launch an awareness campaign to explain the code, its benefits, and why it is needed.
2. *Research.* Background information on the current rules and regulations should be gathered before writing a code. Samples of codes from other schools or states, legal groups, professional associations, and civil liberty organizations are helpful in the process. Key issues that need to be addressed in your individual area should be identified.
3. *Formulation of a draft code.* The actual writing of the code needs to be done by a committee of parents, teachers, students, and administrators. Include the regulations that are important for your school and community. If guidance is needed, base your draft on the samples obtained.

4. *Feedback.* After the code is drafted, distribute copies or publish the document in the newsletter. Schedule an open forum or ask for written comments on the code. The responses will reveal questions and areas of confusion or vagueness, which will guide revisions of the draft.

5. *Approval and implementation.* The code should be approved by the student body as well as the school staff. If the code is being developed for the entire district, the school board should review and approve the code. Their support is essential for implementation. At the preschool level the students will not need to approve the code, but their parents should be involved, and discussion of rules and regulations with the children is appropriate.

6. *Review.* Each year the student body or governing committee should review the code. If needed, items may be revised. The review makes the code relevant to the current student body and is a learning as well as a decision-making process.

The three levels of involvement—the code, the parent advisory council, and the classroom—strengthen a school–home partnership. The parent advisory council is discussed in more detail in chapter 5; good classroom relations are discussed in chapters 5, 6, and 8. The code can be developed on a formal level in the entire school district, or individual teachers may modify it and use it in an informal way in their classrooms.

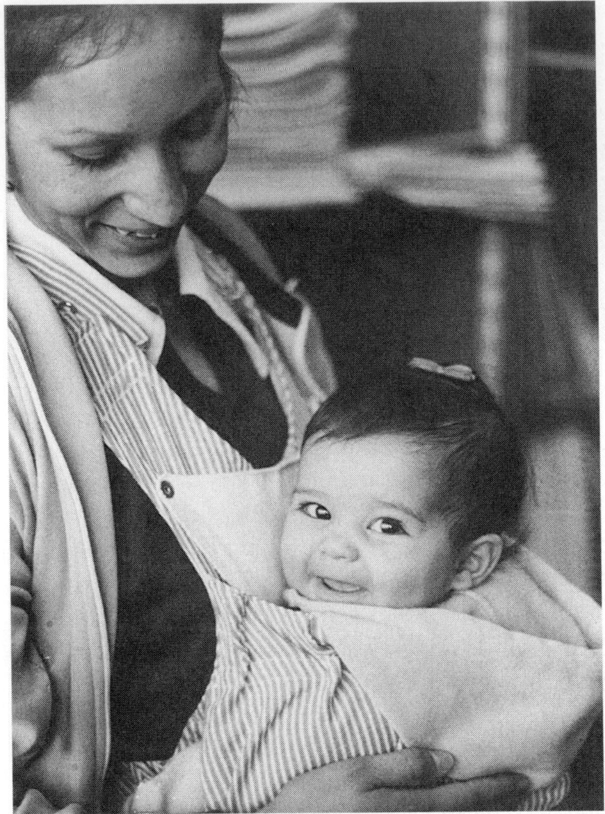

Parents are their child's first advocates. No one can escape the responsibility of being an advocate.

CHILD ADVOCACY

Child advocacy grows from an emotional involvement in the lives of children, a caring, a recognition of need, and a willingness to do something about that need. On both an individual level (micro) and a social level (macro), the opportunity for advocacy is ever present for teachers. It is there when the teacher assesses the children's abilities and life situations. How can children be protected so that they grow into productive adults? How can children be enabled to achieve their potential?

Was there a sudden realization of children's need for protection that caused the child's rights movement and civil rights movement? No. As described in this text, through the ages there have been movements to help the child, although sometimes the answers seemed to remove children's rights rather than help them. Asylums for children during the Roman days, for example, were intended to save children from death or disfigurement. Locke's plan to take children from their parents to train and educate them, though harsh, was meant to help the children survive and become productive adults.

Rights, in the form of the doctrine *parens patriae*, were established in law and custom in Britain as early as the 15th century. Parents were not allowed to treat their children in any manner desired because the state could "exercise 'paternal rights' when evidence existed that parents were jeopardizing the welfare of their minor offspring" (Caldwell, 1989, pp. 4–5). This custom followed the settlers to the colonies. The state also began to act as guardian for disabled adults. Today, a court as an agent of the state may appoint a *guardian*.

The *Body of Liberties*, passed in Massachusetts in 1641, provided that youths 16 and older could be put to death if they cursed or smote their parents.

The youths had some protection, however. If there was evidence that the parents were extremely harsh and cruel, it could be demonstrated that the youth were forced to act that way to save themselves (Hawes, 1991). The youths had the responsibility to obey their parents, but the government could intervene if the parents were not raising their children properly.

The family was a very strong unit in the colonies, and survival required that each person contribute to the welfare of the family. Most families lived on farms that required numerous chores to manage the production of food and other provisions. Children obeyed their parents, and parents had responsibilities to the children. In spite of the importance of the family, *parens patriae* allowed the state to intervene in the family on behalf of the child. "In the colonial world the concept of *parens patriae* was so pervasive that it scarcely received comment" (Hawes, 1991, p. 6).

As the nation developed, beliefs about childhood changed. Rousseau, Locke, Pestalozzi, and Froebel had developed philosophies based on the child as a developing person who needed nurturance. Their beliefs influenced the notion of childhood in America. During the 1800s Elizabeth Peabody and Henry Barnard campaigned for the Froebelian concept of education in the United States. In the late 19th century, G. Stanley Hall began his studies on children, and children began to be viewed relative to their development.

Community-based services for children were established between 1890 and 1920. Lightner Witmer's psychological clinic was started in 1896. The National Committee for Mental Hygiene was founded in 1909. Other associations for young people were formed, such as the Young Women's Christian Association (1906), Camp Fire Girls (1910), and Girl Scouts (1912). To deal with adolescents with problems, the juvenile courts were started in Chicago and Denver about 1899. The visiting teacher movement began in 1906. The National Federation of Settlements was formed in 1912 (Levine & Levine, 1992). Family interests, governmental activities, and new organizations illustrated the strong feelings for children at the turn of the century.

Concern about children and how they should be reared continued throughout the 20th century. The civil rights movement and the rights of people with disabilities focused on fair and equal treatment in the 1960s, and both movements continued to work for equality into the 1990s.

Currently the Children's Defense Fund, founded and headed by Marion Edelman, advocates vehemently for children's rights. Other associations—such as the Center on Families, Communities, Schools and Children's Learning; Family Resource Coalition; Institute for Responsive Education; National Association of Elementary School Principals; National Center for Family Literacy; and National Parent and Teacher Association—work to provide equal educational opportunities for children of all abilities, ethnicity, and gender.

Government agencies such as social services and mental health agencies continue to provide services for those who are at risk and in need. Although we seem concerned, the United States does not rank high in health or social services for children.The percentage and number of children (people under 18 years old) without health insurance in 2004 was 11.2 percent and 8.3 million, both unchanged from 2003 (DeNavas-Walt, Proctor, & Lee, 2004, p. 21). How does the United States compare with other nations in child advocacy?

A Sleeping Giant: The Child Advocate

Children have neither the skills nor the power to advocate for themselves. It rests with parents and teachers to recognize their needs and advocate for them. The issues of the new century vividly illustrate why children need advocates. The growing demand for child care, along with increases in poverty, homelessness, and reports of incest and child abuse, shout to the public. These social problems need a great deal of action to overcome the obstacles that children face. But children also need advocates at a personal level. Many children who come to child-care centers or schools lack self-esteem. They need advocates—individual teachers who may be able to help such children feel important and wanted. Advocacy is needed at all levels; both teachers and parents must stand up for the children. If they do not, who will?

As a group, parents of students with disabilities have been particularly successful advocates for their children's education. Strong parental involvement resulted in passage of PL 94-142 (The Handicapped Children Act of 1975) and has continued since that time. The 1986 amendments in PL 99–457 include education for very young children and provisions for an Individualized Family Service Plan (IFSP) similar to the Individualized Education Program (IEP) of PL 94-142. In 1997 the Individuals with Disabilities Education Amendments of 1997, PL 105-17 (IDEA), and the reauthorization in 2002 strengthened the rights of children with disabilities and participation in decision making by parents. (See chapter 10 for additional information.)

Levels of Advocacy

Advocacy can be done on the case or class level, at administrative or legislative levels, or on the public level.

Case or Class Action

Advocates may work with individual cases or in class actions. The individual or case advocate works on behalf of a specific child. The class or social advocate works for a whole group of children who need special or basic services (e.g., the Children's Defense Fund works for child rights; the Pennsylvania Association for Retarded Children began advocacy for the rights of children with mental retardation). Lay advocates must obtain the necessary services and help. When legal issues and court cases are involved, legal counsel from a lawyer, a professional advocate, is needed. The Family Leave Bill, which languished but was finally passed by Congress and signed into law by President Clinton, is an example of the persistence demanded of those who advocate for families.

Administrative or Legislative Levels

Advocates can bring change at the administrative and legislative levels. The advocate may work toward change in regulations and guidelines at the administrative level, or toward change in the laws through legislative advocacy (Goffin & Lombardi, 1988).

Advocacy on the Public Level

Individuals work together and separately to advocate on the public level. Most successful advocacy requires a broad-based approach, whether it is achieved through the responses of many individuals, the advocacy work of professional organizations, or the lobbying efforts of political action committees. The issue of child care affects many people: parents, children, grandparents, employers, schools, and society as a whole.

Youngsters who go through a troubled childhood—abusive, poverty-stricken, or the like—become adults who are unable to hold a job, who use alcohol or other drugs to mask their pain, or who serve time in prison. In the long run, adequate and fulfilling child care is very cost effective.

THE CHILD ADVOCATE

An advocate is a parent, teacher, or citizen—alone or in a group—who speaks or acts on behalf of a child's welfare. The advocate must grasp the needs of the child, the resources available within the school system, and the alternative resources outside the school system. Advocates may be involved at many levels:

1. *Leaders* —people with vision who help keep advocacy efforts on track
2. *Advisers* —people who share their expertise with advocates and policymakers
3. *Researchers* —people who collect data and synthesize research reports to support advocacy efforts
4. *Contributors* —people who make phone calls, stuff letters and make visits or write letters to legislators (National Association for Education of Young Children, 2004)

Making a Personal Contribution

The most common kind of advocacy is one that many teachers and parents do every day. If parents and teachers look upon positive intervention that helps children live full and meaningful lives as advocacy and recognize that children cannot advocate for themselves, they will accept the responsibility and challenge of advocacy as a necessary role. Individual advocates who work for children in their own child-care programs or classrooms can have a huge effect on children's lives. No one can escape the responsibility of being an advocate, whether as a parent, classroom teacher, friend, or child-care worker. If everyone who works or lives with a child would assume the important role of an advocate for the child, the lives of all children would be improved.

Child care is also affected by personal advocacy. About one third of the children in the United States are cared for in their own homes or in the homes of others. More than half of all children are cared for at school; many are latchkey children before and after school and in the summer.

If working parents have the opportunity to use grandparents, other relatives, neighbors, and friends for child care, it is important that the community offer parent support, education, enrichment, and recreation to help these caregivers provide an excellent environment that will benefit the children. This can be addressed at the grass-roots level. Private agencies can help, as can churches, recreation districts, and schools. They may provide crisis child care, parent education, and drop-in child care. Parents who provide their own care could also benefit from this community support, as could child-care centers. Children are the responsibility of country and community as well as parents.

Parents and teachers can advocate on a personal level in the following ways.

- Provide a stimulating, appropriate environment so the child can play and work productively.
- Advocate for a child in a classroom or for their own children.
- Spend time with children, listening to what concerns or interests them.
- See that children are in educationally and socially appropriate classes.
- Seek out interesting excursions and activities that will benefit the child.
- Determine the best facilities for a child who needs special help.
- Take time to give proper care to their own children.
- Report physical and sexual abuse.
- Become an ombudsman and share resources with or develop resources for a parent who is neglectful because of lack of resources.
- Share information about good childrearing practices.
- Communicate with the teacher if you are a parent, and with the parents if you are a teacher.
- Attend meetings and speak out on issues (for example, the school board, child-care institutions, PTA, League of Women Voters).
- Become active in professional organizations (for example, the local affiliate of the Association for the Education of Young Children, the National Association for the Education of Young Children, or the National Council on Family Relations).
- Write and contact your legislator about upcoming legislation.

What Is a Personal Advocate's Role?

Situation

Joyce, a small child with big brown eyes and a pixie haircut that frames her face, is usually an outgoing, pleasant child. She has many friends and is a leader during class and at recess. But for the past 4 weeks, she has come to school with a worried look and has avoided the other children during recess. Instead of participating in class, she sits and stares. Her teacher has reacted to her lack of class participation by having her stay in during music class in an attempt to get her to finish her work.

"I don't know what has gotten into you," Miss Lerch complains. "I used to be able to depend on you, but you have become so lazy lately. You'll never learn if you don't get busy. If you don't straighten out, I'll have to send you to the principal and contact your parents."

1. Is Miss Lerch advocating for Joyce?
2. What could she do to help Joyce?
3. Should she communicate with Joyce's parents?

On a personal level, the classroom teacher can advocate every day for all the children in the classroom.

Situation

One day, Robbie came to school with his hair uncombed and his clothes torn and dirty, but with a smile on his handsome face. Miss Eller knew his mother had died the previous spring and his father was out of work but doing his best to get the children to school.

"Am I late?" Robbie asked as he rushed into the room. "Dad told me that if I didn't hurry I would be late for class."

"You are fine, Robbie," Miss Eller responded. "In fact, you are 15 minutes early—just in time for a snack in the lunchroom. Have you looked at the weekly class organization board? You are in charge of lunch count and taking the money to the office this week. I know you will do a good job. Robbie, I talked with your father yesterday and he said it would be all right if you stayed after school tonight, because I have a special treat for you. I won't tell you what it is right now, but if you do your work well today, I know you will be pleasantly surprised. Now, off with you. Go to the lunchroom with this note. They will give you a snack."

1. Did Miss Eller advocate for Robbie?
2. Was it appropriate for her to call Robbie's father?
3. Do you think the morning snack was a good idea? Why?
4. What do you think the after-school surprise is going to be?

Qualifications for Personal Advocates

Essentially what qualifies a person to be a good child advocate is the intrinsic quality of being truly motivated to help children. The help must be systematic, knowledgeable, and thorough. The advocate must be committed to finding out all the needs of the child or children being helped. Although it is time consuming and difficult, advocacy, when supported by the best available data, is helpful to the community, parents, and schools.

PREPARING FOR ADVOCACY

To be a successful advocate, one needs to be knowledgeable about the case at hand. The Child Care Employee Project has developed curriculum to be used with persons to help them develop their advocacy skills. These are some of the suggestions to better prepare advocates for long-term advocacy:

- Know about the history of child care, child abuse, and the rights of children.
- Recognize the process of social change—how change happens and the history of change in the nation.
- Recognize the effect that social and economic conditions and the organization of society have on the advocate and other families and children.
- Become aware of the effect that technology, power, class, and race have on families in a given society.
- View children as the future of society and as a protected class, with children of all races and classes having needs.
- View child care in a positive light, as a profession with ethical guidelines and practices.
- Identify and use resources in the community, state, and nation. (Whitebook & Ginsburg, 1984)

Procedure

Teachers advocate for their students when they see that the children's needs are met. At times, this seems to be just part of the role of a teacher. At other times, objectives and preparation must be established to advocate effectively.

To achieve their objectives, advocates must systematically study and proceed with a sound foundation. They first list the needs of the child and justify these needs by making certain they have been professionally determined. They read the literature and speak to experts in the field so that their views are supported by reputable observations. Good advocates make sure their positions are based not on their own beliefs alone but on the true needs of the child, the group of children, and society at large.

The following guidelines describe the steps to take when working on an individual advocacy case.

1. *Know your facts.* Be sure they are correct. Find out: Who? What? Where? When? and Why?
2. *Know the rights* of the child, the parent, or other parties in the case. Contact an advocacy organization or lawyer if you have any questions.
3. *Know the policy* and/or procedures that relate to the problem. Get it in writing; don't accept just an oral version.

4. *Keep accurate notes.* Document as much evidence as possible. Date everything. Remember when notes kept as a personal memory aid are not educational records and when educational records must be shared.
5. *Discuss various options* with the child or parents you are assisting. Do not tell the young person or parent what to do. Rather, let the people you are helping choose the option and course of action that is wisest and that they are willing to live with.
6. *Never go alone* (except in unusual circumstances) to a meeting with officials. Take the young person, the parent, or another concerned person with you.
7. *Keep to the point* when meeting with officials. Be firm but not antagonistic and keep focused on the problem and the need to resolve it. Steer clear of personality conflicts.
8. *Follow channels.* Don't go over someone's head without first talking to that person about the problem. It is wise to let the person know you are dissatisfied with the result of your meeting and that you intend to go to the next person in authority.
9. *Send a letter,* if appropriate, to indicate your understanding of what took place at a meeting with officials or administrators. (Fernandez, 1980, p. 83)

National Advocacy

Three prime areas that can be addressed by advocates are child abuse and neglect, child care, and education. Education may include parent education, brain development, attachment, Goals 2000, and being ready to learn. Quality in child-care centers and early education is discussed in this chapter. See chapter 11 for a discussion of child abuse and neglect.

The National Center for Early Development & Learning and the Frank Porter Graham Child Development Center compiled research on child-care centers. This research gives child-care advocates information that is useful as they advocate for improved child care. Contact the centers in Chapel Hill, North Carolina, or the U.S. Department of Education for more information.

The following studies emphasize the importance of high-quality child care.

- The survey of centers found that quality in child-care centers around the country is often mediocre. For example, of more than 400 centers studied in 4 states, only 8 percent of infant classrooms and 24 percent of preschool classrooms were of good or excellent quality. Ten percent of preschool programs and 40 percent of infant programs were rated as having poor quality (Cost, Quality, and Child Outcomes Study Team [CQO], 1995).
- A significant correlation exists between program quality and outcomes for children. Outcomes related to quality include cooperative play, sociability, creativity, ability to solve social conflicts, self-control, and language and cognitive development (CQO, 1995; Frede, 1995; Love, Schochet, & Meckstrom, 1996).
- Research suggests that education of staff is positively related to quality of care. However, two recent studies found that only a small percentage of teachers in child-care programs have a bachelor's degree or higher (CQO, 1995).
- Child-care center staff turnover is high, ranging from 25 to 50 percent a year. This means that children are constantly adapting to new caregivers and administrators are constantly orienting and training staff.
- Child-care center staff compensation, including wages and benefits, is exceptionally low, with child-care staff among the lowest paid of all classes of workers in the United States.
- Research suggests that quality is important for all children, regardless of family income level (CQO, 1995; Love et al., 1996).

Advocacy for Child Care and Education

Steps can be taken to improve the quality of child care. They include the following policy changes:

- Strengthen standards and regulations for child-care programs.
- Require initial and ongoing training for staff working in child-care programs.

- Recruit and retain more highly educated and skilled staff.
- Continue efforts to inform parents about the importance of good-quality child care and its effects on children.
- Provide funds sufficient to support the costs of high-quality child care. (National Center for Early Development & Learning, 1997)

The quality of care in centers and other child care settings must be excellent for young children to receive nourishing and nurturing care and be ready to learn when they attend public or private schools. Children's readiness to learn is a goal that is ever present.

Help Parents Become Advocates and Active Partners in the Schools

How can professionals ensure that parents will feel empowered and become involved? The following suggestions are adapted from a book on community mobilization from the Families and Work Institute (Dombro, O'Donnell, Galinsky, Melcher, & Farber, 1996).

- If you provide ongoing support to parents from the beginning—showing respect, using a buddy system, encouraging them to ask questions, and introducing them into the school program—you will promote feelings of competence and empowerment. The parents will be more comfortable and confident and will see how they can contribute.
- Help parents see that they are important as part of the organization. Parents come to the table with different skills and experiences. "When parents define roles with which they are comfortable, they are more likely to be effective and remain involved in the process" (Dombro et al., 1996).
- Parents have unique skills, but you can offer them training and workshops to develop their skills and leadership potential.
- Recognize that parents have limited time. If possible, reimburse them for expenses such as transportation or try to assist with their transportation needs so they can participate. Provide child care to permit parents with younger children to attend meetings. Reach out to single parents with their special needs and help them get representation in the political process (Dombro et al., 1996).

If you include parents as partners in the education process, you are advocating for them and their children.

Steps to Take for Public Advocacy

These are the basic steps involved in advocacy at the public level:

1. *Write to federal officials.* Individual letters written by constituents are more effective than form letters with many signatures. You can also use e-mail and telephone contact. Send letters about national issues and legislation to:

   President of the United States: The White House, Washington, DC 20500.

   Representatives: The Honorable *(name)*, U.S. House of Representatives, Washington, DC 20515.

   Senators: The Honorable *(name)*, U.S. Senate, Washington, DC 20515.

   For representatives' and senators' telephone numbers and e-mail addresses, call the Capitol switchboard, 202–224–3121, or go to www.house.gov or www.senate.gov.

2. *Talk with and write to state legislators.* On the state level, write or call your state representative or state senator. Work with your representative before the assembly or legislature meets if you or your group has a bill that you want introduced.

   If you plan to write to your state representative or senator, there are a few tips to follow:

   - State your purpose in the first paragraph, including the number of the legislation, such as HR _______ or S _______.
   - Be courteous, but to the point.
   - Address only one issue in the letter.
   - Follow-up your letter with a phone call (Children's Defense Fund, 2006).

If you will be communicating with the media remember to:

- Know what you want to say.
- Say it well by using a brief but powerful anecdote.
- Say it clearly. Avoid jargon.
- Say it again, clearly and simply (National Association of Education of Young Children, 2004).

3. *Get involved before elections.* Campaign for legislators who agree with your position on child care, families, and children.
4. *Stay involved after elections.* After an election, invite elected officials to meet with your organization.
5. *Join professional organizations in your region.* For example, the National Association for the Education of Young Children, the Council for Exceptional Children, the National Association for Children with Learning Disabilities, your local Association for the Education of Young Children, and National Council on Family Relations.
6. *Get firsthand experience.* Visit child-care centers, homeless shelters, schools, and other facilities.

FACTS ABOUT CHILDREN AND FAMILIES

Facts can be used by persons to advocate for improvement in children's lives and conditions.

Population

- In 2002 there were 288 million persons in the United States, an increase of nearly 33 million persons over the 1990 population count. Sixty percent of the increase was natural, birth over death; immigration was responsible for the remaining 40 percent (Kent & Mather, 2002). The population reached 300 million in October 2006.
- Of the 74 million children in the United States, over 40 percent belong to a racial or ethnic minority (National Center for Children in Poverty, 2006c).

Poverty

- The poverty rate for everyone in 2005 was 12.6 percent. Thirty-seven million were poor (U.S. Census Bureau, 2005b).
- The poverty rate for Hispanic families with a mother and no husband was 38.9 percent; for Native American families it was 38.3 percent, and for Black families it was 37.3 percent (U.S. Census Bureau, 2005b).
- The poverty level in 2005 for a family of four was $19,971 and for a family of three, $15,338 (U.S. Census Bureau, 2005b).
- In 2005, 28.4 percent of families headed by women were below the poverty level (U.S. Census Bureau, 2005b).
- It is not until a family of four reaches twice the poverty level ($40,000) that parents can provide children with sufficient housing, food, and health care (National Center for Children in Poverty, 2006c).
- In 2005 child poverty stood at 17.6 percent, up from 16.2 percent, as determined by the 2000 U.S. Census (U.S. Census Bureau, 2005b).
- Children make up 37 percent of the poor but only 26 percent of the population.
- Children from poor families are at higher risk for poor health, inadequate maternal care, and poor education experiences. They are more likely to die in childhood, score poorly on standardized tests, drop out of school, fall victim to violence, and continue the poverty cycle (Levit, Terman, & Behrman, 1997).
- More than 1 million children (8 percent) live in extreme poverty (a family of three with an annual income of $7,870), which is a 22 percent increase over the first five years of the 21st century (Children's Defense Fund, 2005; Kids Count, 2004).
- Black families have the lowest median income of racial groups, at $30,858, or 36 percent of Black families. Next on the continuum are Hispanic families, at $35,967 or 29 percent of Hispanic families, then non-Hispanic White families at $50,784 or 11 percent of White families. Asian families' median income is the highest at $61,094 or 9 percent of Asian families (U.S. Census, 2005b; Kids Count, 2004).

- One in three Black children lives in poverty (Children's Defense Fund, 2005).
- Long-term poverty for children was greatest for African American children; 29 percent were in poverty for 10 or more years and half were in poverty for 5 years. By comparison, 1 percent of Whites were poor for 10 or more years and 6 percent were for 5 years (Corcoran & Chaudry, 1997).

Young Parents

- An infant is born to a teenager every minute of the day in the United States.
- Teen mothers' birthrate was 22 percent for teens 15–17, 71 percent for teens 18–19, and 42 percent for teens 15–19 in 2003 (Kids Count, 2004). The birthrate for teens who were already mothers was 19.9 percent in 2003 (U.S. Census, 2005a).

Working Parents

- Enrollment in nursery school increased from less than 8 percent in 1970 for children 3 to 6 years of age to 28 percent by 1998 (Population Reference Bureau, AmeriStat, 2000; U.S. Census, 2005a).
- The unemployment rate for persons 16 and over was 4.7 percent in 2005, down from 6.1 percent in 2005 (U.S. Census, 2005b).
- The Consumer Product Index, a measure of average change over time in the prices paid by urban consumers for consumer goods and services, was at an all-time high of 600.9 percent in the middle of 2006 (Bureau of Labor Statistics, 2006).
- Forty-four percent of Black families and 40 percent of Hispanic families have low incomes, even if the parents have some college education. These family remain at low income levels even if the parents attain a college degree (National Center for Children in Poverty, 2006a).
- Black and Hispanic parents, working full-time year round with some college education, are more than twice as likely to be low income as non-Hispanic White and Asian families (National Center for Children in Poverty, 2006a).

Single-Parent Families

- The percentage of children living in two-parent families in the United States declined from 76 percent in 1990 to 69 percent in 2004, whereas the percentage of children in one-parent families increased from 20 to 31 percent. Families that included a father only made up 6 percent of the population, and with a mother only made up 24 percent (U.S. Census, 2005a).
- The increase in percentage of births to unmarried mothers increased from 5 percent in 1970 to 14.2 percent in 1975, and from 18 percent in 1980 to 32.8 percent in 2001.
- Sixty-four percent of Black children were most likely to live in single-parent homes. Forty-seven percent of American Indian children, 35 percent of Hispanic children, and 23 percent of non-Hispanic White children live in single-parent homes (U.S. Census, 2005a).

Health

- African Americans have a 5 percent higher risk of low birth weight compared to the U.S. population as a whole. They are also more likely to be born preterm (Goldman, 2005).
- Seventeen percent of U.S. children are born with developmental disabilities. Three percent of all developmental defects are related to exposure to toxic chemicals and environmental factors, and 25 percent may be due to genetic and environmental factors combined (Goldman, 2005).
- Environmental associations with childhood asthma include exposure to dust mites, molds, cockroaches, pets, tobacco smoke, and poorly vented stoves (Goldman, 2005). Exposure to these irritants is a function of poor living conditions and lack of knowledge of alternative activities.
- Exposure to methamphetamines is an increasing problem in rural areas. Users of methamphetamines are more likely to live in harsh neighborhoods and have a lower socioeconomic status. They also used more alcohol, tobacco, and marijuana than non–methamphetamine

users during pregnancy. Exposed infants had lower birth weight, had poorer quality of movement, more signs of stress, and more lethargy than nonexposed children (Lester et al., 2006).

Homelessness

- Three and a half million persons (men, women, and children) were homeless in 2003 (National Law Center on Homelessness and Poverty, 2004).
- Data on homeless showed that 40 percent are families with children, 84 percent are single-parent families, 57 percent have mental disabilities, 44 percent work, and 22 percent have been forced to leave home (National Law Center on Homelessness and Poverty, 2004).
- Of these, 35 percent are White, 12 percent are Hispanic, 2 percent are Native American, and 1 percent are Asian (Adapted from National Law Center on Homelessness & Poverty, 2002a, Overview, p. 1).
- Homeless people lack a support network—families and friends—that could help them through a crisis. Becoming homeless also takes them away from whatever network they may have established with former neighbors, friends, churches, or communities.
- Compared to children in higher income families, poor children have triple the risk of lead poisoning, which causes neurological damage (Children's Defense Fund, 1998).
- Ninety-three percent of White students, 89 percent of Black students, and 62 percent of Hispanic students complete high school (Children's Defense Fund, 2001).
- Thirty-eight percent of fourth-grade students are below the proficient reading level, and 21 percent are below basic math proficiency (Kids Count, 2004).
- Almost 7 million children, 5 to 14 years of age, care for themselves without supervision (Children's Defense Fund, 2001).
- Children in foster care increased from 262,000 children in 1982 to 568,000 in 1999. Almost one third were in foster homes with relatives (Children's Defense Fund, 2001).
- The drop-out rate for American Indians was 13 percent, for Black Americans 8 percent, for Hispanics 8 percent, for non-Hispanic Whites 6 percent, and for Asians and Pacific Islanders 3 percent (Children's Defense Fund, 2005). Seventeen percent of children live in households where a high school dropout is the head of household (Children's Defense Fund, 2005).

Violence

- Juvenile crime peaks between 3 and 7 P.M., endangering nearly 5 million latchkey children (Children's Defense Fund, 1998).
- In 2004, more than 750,000 young people ages 10–24 were treated in emergency rooms for injuries due to violence (Centers for Disease Control, 2006a).
- In 2003, 5,570 young people ages 10–24 were murdered, an average of 15 each day. Eighty-two percent were killed with firearms (Centers for Disease Control, 2006a).
- An estimated 906,000 children were confirmed by children protective services to have been maltreated (Centers for Disease Control, 2006b).
- Victims of child maltreatment who were physically assaulted by caregivers, are twice as likely to be physically assaulted as adults (Centers for Disease Control, 2006b).
- Children incarcerated in adult prisons are five times more likely to be sexually assaulted, eight times more likely to commit suicide, and twice as likely to be sexually assaulted by staff as those who serve time in a juvenile facility (Children's Defense Fund, 1998).

When needing current data on the status of children, check the references for information in the library or on the Internet.

ADVOCACY FOR CHILDREN AROUND THE WORLD

Europe has been a leader in advocacy for children. The Council of Europe has been active since after World War II, 50 years of work, much of it concerned with children and their rights. European states also adopted the United Nations Convention on the Rights of the Child, and there is movement in recognizing the need for rights for children. The United States has tended to be slower than Western Europe in implementing legislation and policies to support and protect children, but the United States is now making many of the same policy changes. For example, two more states have banned corporal punishment in schools since the last edition of this book, and many school districts have banned paddling.

European Network

> In Sweden an Ombudsman was first appointed in 1809. In 1919 Finland adopted the idea, but it was not until after 1954, when Denmark established an Ombudsman's Office, that the idea of an Ombudsman started to attract world-wide attention (Office of the Ombudsman, 1998, p. 2).

The European Network of Ombudsmen for Children (ENOC) reports on the achievements of the nations in Europe. This includes Austria, Belgium, Denmark, France, Georgia, Hungary, Iceland, Lithuania, Macedonia, Northern Ireland, Norway, Poland, Portugal, Romania, Russia (Volgograd), and Sweden. Some nations, such as Finland, Norway, and Sweden, have had ombudsman systems for many years. Other countries, having adopted the United Nations Convention on the Rights of the Child, are developing their children's ombudsman program.

Office of Children's Ombudsman in United States

In the United States many individual states are in the process of creating Ombudsmen for Children on the European model (see Table 12.1). *Ombudsman* is a Scandinavian word first used in the current form in Sweden when Sweden ruled much of Scandinavia. The root is from Old Norse and means *representative.* The word is commonly used today to mean a people's advocate in dealing with government. The mission statement for Michigan's ombudsman is:

> MISSION OF THE OFFICE OF CHILDREN'S OMBUDSMAN
>
> The mission of the office of the Children's Ombudsman is to assure the safety and wellbeing of Michigan's children in need of foster care, adoption, and protective services and promote public confidence in the child welfare system. This will be accomplished through independently investigating complaints, advocating for children, and recommending changes to improve law policy and practice for the benefit of current and future generations.

Many other states have ombudsmen for children in one form or another. The remaining states have offices dealing with family issues but not specifically for children.

Finland, Israel, Norway, and Sweden

In Finland, the ombudsman is the legal aspect of the Mannerheim League for Child Welfare, a private advocacy group, and in Israel the ombudsman is under the direction of the Jerusalem Children's Council (Rauche-Elnekave, 1989). In Norway the system was created by national legislation. In Sweden, it was run by Radda Barnen (Save the Children), a large, private organization until 1993, when Sweden established an Office of Children's Ombudsman (Mork, 1998; Rauche-Elnekave, 1989). In each of these countries, in addition to working on behalf of individual children, the ombudsmen work toward betterment for groups of children and answer general complaints.

Norway

Norway and Sweden have highly developed systems of ombudsmanship—a comprehensive child advocacy office. Norway's involvement with families reaches back several centuries. In 1621, a Norwegian law required parents to find a useful occupation for their children. If the children were found idle, public guardians would take over the responsibility of the parents. Now Norway has one of the first national ombudsman programs for children—the Ombudsman for Children office, established in 1981 (Flekkoy, 1989). "The Ombudsman for Children is by law regarded as an independent, non-partisan, politically neutral which neither the national Assembly nor the Government have the power to instruct" (Barneombudet, 2002, p. l).

The Ombudsman for Children advocates for children's education based on international conventions, including the United Nations Convention on the Rights of the Child. Children have rights to

TABLE 12.1 Child Advocates by State

Sources: National Conference of State Legislatures Web sites for individual states	Alabama	Alaska	Arizona	Arkansas	California	Colorado	Connecticut	Delaware	Florida	Georgia
Ombudsman or advocate		Yes	Yes	Yes	Yes and by county		Yes	Yes	Yes	Yes
Within state divisions of children and family services				Yes	Yes					
Independent ombudsmen specifically handling children's issues—not necessarily exclusively							Yes	Yes		Yes
Ombudsmen or offices that represent children (not necessarily exclusively) or Offices of the Child Advocate		Office of the Ombudsman Box 102636 Anchorage AK 99510-2636	Arizona Ombudsman/ Citizen's Aide Office 3737 N. Seventh Street, Ste. 209 Phoenix, AZ 85014	Office of Youth Advocate (re: Children) Division of Children and Families Department of Human Services P.O. Box 1437, Slot 700 Little Rock, AR 72203-1437	"Californias programs administered by the 58 individual counties" website below. Example: LA County Department of Ombudsman 510 S. Vermont, Suite 215, Los Angeles, CA 90020	"Colorado is a state-supervised, county-administered system for social services, including child welfare services."	The Office of the Child Advocate 18–20 Trinity Street Hartford, CT 06106	The Office of the Child Advocate 900 King Street Suite 210 Wilmington, DE 19801	Florida Statewide Advocacy Council 2727 Mahan Drive, MS-57 Tallahassee, FL 32308	The Office of the Child Advocate 3312 Northside Drive Building D Suite 250 Macon, GA 31210-2591
URL		www.state.ak.us/ local/akpages/ LEGISLATURE/ ombud/home.htm	www.azleg. state.az.us/ ombudsman/ default.htm	www.arkansas .gov/dhhs/ chilnfam/	www.childsworld .ca.gov/ Example: LA County: http://ombudsman .lacounty.info/ default.asp		www.ct.gov/ oca/site/ default.asp	courts.dela ware.gov/ childadvocate/ index.htm	www.floridasac .org/	www.state.ga.us/ gachildadvocate/
For children but not ombudsman	Department of Children's Affairs					Complaint Resolution Process Colorado Department of Social Services 1575 Sherman Street Denver, CO 80203				
URL	www.dca .state.al.us/					www.cdhs. state.co.us/				

TABLE 12.1 Child Advocates by State

Sources: National Conference of State Legislatures Web sites for individual states	Hawaii	Idaho	Illinois	Indiana	Iowa	Kansas	Kentucky	Louisiana	Maine	Maryland
Ombudsman or advocate	Yes		Yes		Yes	Yes	Executive order	Yes		
Within state divisions of children and family services			Yes			Yes	Yes	Yes		
Independent ombudsmen specifically handling children's issues—not necessarily exclusively	Yes								Yes (state contract)	
Ombudsmen or offices that represent children (not necessarily exclusively) or Offices of the Child Advocate	Office of the Ombudsman 465 South King Street, 4th Floor Honolulu, H1 96813		Advocacy Office (Ombudsperson's Office) for Children and Families, DCFS, 406 East Monroe Street, Springfield, IL 62701	PROPOSED Child Advocate Bureau, within the Indiana Department of Administration	Office of Citizens' Aide/Ombudsman Ola Babcock Miller Building, 1112 East Grand, Des Moines, IA 50319	Ombudsman Program Social & Rehabilitation Services (re: children), Perry Building, 300 SW Oakley, Topeka, KS 66606	The Office of the Ombudsman Cabinet for Health and Family Services, 275 East Main Street, 1E-B Frankfort, KY 40621	Family Ombudsman Office of Youth Development, P. O. Box 66458, Audubon Station Baton Rouge, LA 70896	Maine Children's Alliance. Ombudsman Program, 303 State St., Augusta, ME 04330-7037	Governor's Office for Children, (also for Youth & Families) 301 W. Preston St. Baltimore, MD 21201
URL	www.ombudsman.state.hi.us		www.state.il.us/dcfs/index.shtml		www.legis.state.ia.us/ombudsman/	www.srskansas.org	chfs.ky.gov/omb/	www.oyd.louisiana.gov	www.mainechildrensalliance.org/am/publish/ombudsman.shtml	www.ocyf.state.md.us
For children but not ombudsman		Traditional State Services by Regions Regional Director: Kathleen Allyn, 1720 Westgate Drive, Suite A, Boise, ID 83704								
URL		www.state.id.us/		www.state.in.us/						

TABLE 12.1 Child Advocates by State

Sources: National Conference of State Legislatures Web sites for individual states	Massachusetts	Michigan	Minnesota	Mississippi	Missouri	Montana	Nebraska	Nevada	New Hampshire	New Jersey
Ombudsman or advocate	Yes	Yes	Yes		Yes		Yes		Yes	Yes
Within state divisions of children and family services	Yes				Yes				Yes	
Independent ombudsmen specifically handling children's issues—not necessarily exclusively		Yes					Yes			Yes
Ombudsmen or offices that represent children (not necessarily exclusively) or Offices of the Child Advocate	Governor's Office of Constituent Services Department of Social Services Ombudsman State House, Room 159 Boston, MA 02133	Children's Ombudsman P.O. Box 30026 Lansing, MI 48909	Ombudsman for Mental Health and Mental Retardation (re: children) Governor's Office Metro Square Building 7th & Robert Streets, Ste. 202 St. Paul, MN 55101		Office of Child Advocate P.O. Box 809 Jefferson City, Missouri 65102	Department of Family Services P.O. Box 8005 Helena, MT 59604	State Ombudsman's Office P.O. Box 94712 Room 807 State Capitol Lincoln, NE 68509-4712		New Hampshire Department of Health and Human Services Ombudsman Office 6 Hazen Drive Concord, NH 03301	Child Advocate P.O. Box 92 Trenton, NJ 08625
URL	www.mass.gov/gov	www.michigan.gov/oco	www.ombudmhmr.state.mn.us/contact/ombuds.htm		www.cca.mo.gov	www.dphhs.mt.gov	http://www.nebraskalegislature.gov/web/public/ombudsman		www.dhhs.state.nh.us/DHHS/OMBUDSMAN/default.htm	www.childadvocate.nj.gov
For children but not ombudsman				Family and Children's Services, Mississippi Department of Human Services, 750 North State Street, Jackson, MS 39202				Domestic Violence Ombudsman Office of the Attorney General, Nevada Department of Justice Carson City Office, 100 North Carson Street, Carson City, NV 89701-4717		
URL				www.mdhs.state.ms.us/index.html				ag.state.nv.us/menu/action_bttn/units/domestic/ombud.htm		

TABLE 12.1 Child Advocates by State

Sources: National Conference of State Legislatures Web sites for individual states	New Mexico	New York	North Carolina	North Dakota	Ohio	Oklahoma	Oregon	Pennsylvania	Rhode Island	South Carolina
Ombudsman or advocate	Executive order	By county	Yes		By county	Yes	Yes		Yes	Yes
Within state divisions of children and family services	Yes		Yes			Yes	Yes			Yes
Independent ombudsmen specifically handling children's issues—not necessarily exclusively									Yes	
Ombudsmen or offices that represent children (not necessarily exclusively) or Offices of the Child Advocate	Social Services Client Relations Liaison (re: children) Children Youth & Families, P.O. Drawer 5160, P.E.R.A. Room 254, Santa Fe NM 87502	Public Advocate for the City of New York, 1 Centre Street, Room 1500, New York, NY 10007	North Carolina Department of Health and Human Services' (NCDHHS) Ombudsman Program, 2001 Mail Service Center Raleigh, NC 27699-2001, Location: Adams Building, 101 Blair Drive, Raleigh		Executive Director/ Ombudsman, Citizens of Cuyahoga County Ombudsman, 2800 Euclid Avenue, Suite 207, Cleveland, OH 44113; Children's Ombudsman/ Lucas County, 705 Adams Street, Toledo, OH 43624	Advocate General Office of Client Advocacy, Office of Advocate Defender, Oklahoma Department of Human Services, P.O. Box 25352, Oklahoma City, OK 73125	Oregon Department of Human Services 500 Summer Street NE E15 Salem, OR 97301-1097	Governor's Cabinet and Commission for Children and Families, P.O. Box 2675, Harrisburg, PA 17105-2675	Office of the Child Advocate, 272 West Exchange Street, Suite 301, Providence, RI 02903 (ABA Model Legislation)	Governor's Office of Children's Affairs, 1200 Senate Street, Suite 104, Columbia, SC 29201, and Governor's Office of Ombudsman, 1200 Senate Street, Room 104 Columbia, SC 29201
URL	www.newmexico.gov	www.pubadvocate.nyc.gov	www.dhhs.state.nc.us/ocs/ombudsman.htm		ohio.gov	www.okdhs.org/divisionsoffices/oca/	www.oregon.gov/DHS/aboutdhs/gao.shtml	www.pachildren.state.pa.us/ccf/site/default.asp?dsftns=32261	www.state.ri.us/govtracker/index.php?page=DetailDeptAgency&eid=3867	www.govoepp.state.sc.us/ca/
For children but not ombudsman				The public child welfare system in North Dakota is county administered and state supervised						
URL				www.nd.gov/humanservices/services/childfamily/						

TABLE 12.1 Child Advocates by State

Sources: National Conference of State Legislatures Web sites for individual states	South Dakota	Tennessee	Texas	Utah	Vermont	Virginia	Washington	West Virginia	Wisconsin	Wyoming
Ombudsman or advocate		Yes	Yes				Yes	Yes		
Within state divisions of children and family services			Yes	Yes				Yes		Yes
Independent Ombudsmen specifically handling children's issues—not necessarily exclusively		Yes					Yes			
Ombudsmen or offices that represent children (not necessarily exclusively) or Offices of the Child Advocate		Gerald Papica or Michael Cash, Ombudsman for Children and Families, Tennessee Commission on Children and Youth, Andrew Johnson Tower, 9th Floor, 710 James Robertson Parkway, Nashville, TN 37243-0800	Texas Health and Human Services Commission Office of the Ombudsman Mail Code: H-700 P. O. Box 85200, Austin, TX 78708	Office of Child Protection Ombudsman (OCPO) 120 North 200 West, Room 422, P. O. Box 45500, Salt Lake City, UT 84145-0500			Office of the Family and Children's Ombudsman 6720 Fort Dent Way, Suite 240, Mail Stop TT-99, Tukwila, WA 98188	Office of the Ombudsman for Behavioral Health, State Capitol Complex, Building. 6, Room 850, Charleston, WV 25305	Office of the Milwaukee Ombudsman for Child Welfare, 1442 North Farwell Avenue, Suite 300, Milwaukee, WI 53202	Wyoming Department of Family Services Ombudsman Division, 2300 Capitol Avenue, 3rd Floor, Cheyenne, WY 82002
URL		www.tennessee.gov/tccy/ombuds.html	www.hhs.state.tx.us/OMB	www.ocpo.utah.gov			www.governor.wa.gov/ofco/index.html	www.wvdhhr.org/bhhf/ombudsman.asp	www.ombudsmanmilw.org	dfsweb.state.wy.us
For children but not ombudsman	South Dakota Department of Social Services 500 East Capitol, Pierre, SD 57501-5070				Vermont Agency of Human Services, 103 South Main Street, Waterbury, VT 05671-0204	Virginia Department of Social Services Attention: (Department or Person mail is to be directed to), 7 N. Eighth Street, Richmond, VA 23219				
URL	dss.sd.gov/cps/				www.vermont.gov/health-safety/children.html	www.dss.state.va.us/family/children.html				

education, rights in education, and rights through education. The rights to education include: (a) the right of refugees to obtain education without regard to the length of their stay in the country or their legal status; (b) the right to a religious and moral education (Norway has a state church); and (c) the right to come and go to school without extra costs—"right to go to school in the closest environment" (Hauge, 1998, p. 53).

Three rights in education provide for quality of education with stimulating education and child care. These rights also include the right to be protected from bullying or abuse by teachers, with the right to complain and to have the situation resolved in a "secure procedure" (p. 53).

The rights through education include participation and democracy. Schools have a dialectic process leading to democracy and school development with input from the children.

The ombudsman has particularly focused on:

Environment: learning environment, environment of labor to increase opportunities of growth and learning, directly and indirectly.

Participation: children's competence, participation in school-democracy and in the community.

Equality: equal access to schooling and to quality in education by means of participation (p. 54).

Sweden

The Office of Children's Ombudsman, referred to in Swedish as Barnombudsmanner (BO), was established in Sweden in 1923 and followed the United Nations Convention on the Rights of the Child (Children's Ombudsman, 1998) for the purpose of ensuring children's rights. "The Ombudsman has the task of ensuring that the Rights of the Child [are] respected, as well as promoting good formative condition, a good psychosocial environment and a good standard of child safety" (Mork, 1998, 21).

Austria

The Federal Youth Welfare Act of 1989 was established through child welfare legislation. By 2002, each of the nine provinces had an ombudsman for children and youth. Each office is in direct contact with children and young people: "We provide information and give advice, we mediate between them and the parents or other professionals. We try to represent their interest, to find amicable solutions. We help them to solve their problems" (Centre for Europe's Childen, 2001b, p. 3). Notice that like the United States there are provincial ombudsmen for children but, unlike the United States, also a federal ombudsman.

France

The ombudsman for children was established March 6, 2000, as an independent agency vested with authority to defend and promote children's rights as defined by law or an international agreement such as the United Nations Convention of the Rights of the Child (Centre for Europe's Children, 2001a).

Latin America

Although Latin American countries do not have an Office of Ombudsman for Children, children's rights are advocated by either a broader ombudsman office or a commissioner for human rights. Honduras has a National Commissioner for Human Rights Office. Costa Rica has an Ombudsman Office for the Inhabitants of the Republic. Guatemala has an Ombudsman Office for the Rights of the Child within the Human Rights Ombudsman Office. In Colombia, within the Defensoria del Pueblo there is a delegate for Children, Women, and Seniors. Panama has an Office of the General Ombudsman. Ecuador and Peru have Commissions of State, which include a defender of children. Mexico's National Commission of Human Rights includes Coordination of Woman, the Child and the Family (Centre for Europe's Children, 2001d). Latin America has begun to recognize the special needs and rights of women and children, but much greater development needs to be accomplished.

Ombudsmanship

The United Nations Convention on the Rights of the Child has made a strong impact on the development of programs concerned about children's rights and the need to be protected. The need for protection ranges from slavery and sexual violence, to provision of a home and nourishment. The European Network of Ombudsmen for Children (ENOC) is working to end all corporal punishment of children in Europe. ENOC states: "Hitting children is disrespectful and dangerous. Children deserve at least the same protection from violence that we as adults take for granted for ourselves." (Centre for Europe's Children, 2001b, p. 3). What a giant step it would be if the same practices could be considered and implemented throughout the world.

In 2006, the Council of Europe launched a 3-year campaign to increase protection of children affected by violence, this followed a summit of heads of state in May 2005. The European Community contemplated appointing a European Defender of the Rights of the Child as the highest-level coordinator. Also in 2006 the Department of Freedom, Security and Justice of the European commission circulated a draft of the Communication on the Rights of the Child. The rights of children throughout the world is a goal that all nations and all citizens should applaud and serve.

SUMMARY

Legal rights and responsibilities of parents, students, and professional educators are explored in this chapter. Criticisms of schools make cooperation between home and schools even more essential than in previous times.

Rights and responsibilities of parents and students are expressed on the following topics: suspension and expulsion, speech and expression, flag salute and Pledge of Allegiance, racial discrimination, sex discrimination, students with disabilities and special education, corporal punishment, and the Buckley Amendment on open-record policy.

Three levels of involvement between home and school help clarify and delineate procedures that support positive home–school relationships. These include: (a) development and periodic review of a code of rights and responsibilities for each class, school, or local school district; (b) election of and active involvement with a parent or citizen advisory council; and (c) implementation of the educational program in a classroom community. Development of a code involves identification of interests, research and gathering of background material, formulation of a draft code, feedback, approval, implementation, and review.

Parents and teachers must advocate for children's rights. This can be accomplished by organizing, planning, and advocating for a more caring and healthy environment. Parents and schools working together can provide a wholesome, intellectually stimulating, and challenging environment for families and children.

Ombudsman programs for children have been recognized as needed in Sweden for over two hundred years. In recent years more countries have started ombudsman programs. Since 1950 programs have been developed in the United States. The chapter includes a discussion of ombudsman programs in some countries in Europe and the program's development in the 50 United States.

SUGGESTED CLASS ACTIVITIES AND DISCUSSIONS

1. What is free speech? How are the boundaries defined? Discuss.
2. What rights do parents and students have to see school records?
3. Discuss the concept that rights are also accompanied by responsibilities.
4. How have schools responded to the need to eliminate racial discrimination? Investigate the changes that have occurred in schools in your area because of affirmative action.
5. Contact a school in your area and find out what alternative education programs exist.
6. Follow the legislative action in your state, choose a bill that you strongly support, and advocate for its passage.
7. Brainstorm and come up with a list of needs that should be addressed by an advocate or advocacy groups.
8. Research the status of the United Nations Convention on the Rights of the Child in the United States.
9. Design a ombudsman program for children. What would be needed?

WEB SITES

Child Advocate
www.childadvocate.net

The goal of this Web site is to develop resources for advocacy for children and parents. It seeks to address educational, legal and medical issues, and to support local, state and national legislative action.

Child Welfare League of America (CWLA)
www.cwla.org/advocacy/advocacyresources.htm

The CWLA provides links to other advocacy organizations and government sites, advocacy tips, links to nonpartisan, nonprofit voter information with factual information about elected officials and a link to a youth policy action center, which is a resource that helps youth and concerned adults contact elected officials about programs and initiatives related to children and families.

Children's Defense Fund
www.childrensdefense.org

This site provides information that assists concerned adults with contacting legislators regarding current and pending legislation, data regarding the status of children in the United States and the world, and resources available to assist advocacy initiatives for children and families.

Bibliography

Achord, B., Berry, M., Harding, G., Kerber, K., Scott, S., & Schwab, L. O. (Eds.). (1986). *Building family strengths.* Lincoln: Department of Human Development and Family, University of Nebraska.

Adams, R. L. (1991). *Great negroes: Past and present* (Rev. 3rd ed.). Chicago: Afro-Am.

Administration for Children, Youth, and Families. Conrad Hilton Foundation Award. (2004, February 5). Press release.

Ahlburg, D. A., & De Vita, C. J. (1992). New realities of the American family. *Population Bulletin, 47*(2), Washington, DC: Population Reference Bureau.

Ainsworth, M. D. (1973). The development of infant–mother attachments. In B. M. Caldwell & H. N. Ricciuti (Eds.), *Review of child development research.* Chicago: University of Chicago Press.

Allen, M. L., Brown, P., & Finlay, B. D. (1992). *Helping children by strengthening families.* Washington, DC: Children's Defense Fund.

Altman, D. H., & Smith, R. L. (1960). Unrecognized trauma in infants and children. *Journal of Bone and Joint Surgery, 42A*(1), 407–413.

Amato, P. R. (1994). Life-span adjustment of children to their parents' divorce. *The Future of Children: Children and Divorce 4*(1), 143–164.

American Academy of Child & Adolescent Psychiatry. (2004, July). Stepfamily problems. Retrieved February 14, 2006, from *www.aacap.org/publications/factfam/stepfmly.htm*

American Association for Protecting Children. (n.d.). *Guidelines for schools to help protect abused and neglected children.* Denver, CO: American Humane Association.

American Association of School Administrators. (1991). *America 2000: Where school leaders stand.* Arlington, VA: Author.

American Bar Association Presidential Working Group on the Unmet Legal Needs of Children and Their Families. (1993, July). *America's children at risk: A national agenda for legal action.* Washington, DC: The ABA Center on Children and the Law.

American Humane Association. (1978). *National analysis of official child neglect and abuse reporting.* Denver, CO: Author.

American Humane Association. (1992b, July). *Fact sheet: Shaken baby syndrome.* Englewood, CO: Author.

American Humane Association. (1992c, October). *Fact sheet: Child abuse and neglect data.* Englewood, CO: Author.

American Humane Association. (1998). *Children's division.* Englewood, CO: Author.

American Humane Association. (2001). Fact sheet: Shaken baby syndrome. Retrieved December 6, 2001, from *www.americanhumane.org/children/factsheets/shake.htm*

American Institute for Research. (1994). *Educational innovation in multiracial contexts: The growth of magnet schools in American education.* Palo Alto, CA: U.S. Department of Education.

American School Counselor Association. (1988). The school counselor and child abuse/neglect prevention. *Elementary School Guidance & Counseling, 22*(4), 261–263.

Anastasiow, N. (1988). Should parenting education be mandatory? *Topics in Early Childhood Special Education, 8*(1), 60–72.

Anderson, R. C., Hiebert, E. H., Scott, J. A., & Wilkinson, I. A. G. (1985). *Becoming a nation of readers: The report of the Commission on Reading.* Champaign, IL: Center for the Study of Reading.

Angelou, M. (2002). *I know why the caged bird sings.* New York: Random.

Annie E. Casey Foundation. (2001). *Kids count data book, 2001.* Baltimore: Author.

Annie E. Casey Foundation. (2002a). *Kids count data book, 2002.* Baltimore: Author

Annie E. Casey Foundation. (2002b). *Kids count pocket guide.* Baltimore: Author.

Annie E. Casey Foundation. (2005). *Kids count indicator brief: Reducing the teen birth rate.* Baltimore: Author.

Applbaum, R. L., Bodaken, E. M., Sereno, K. K., & Anatol, K. W. E. (1979). *The process of group communication* (2nd ed.). Palo Alto, CA: Science Research Associates.

Arseneault, L., Walsh, E., Trzesniewski, K., Newcombe, R., Caspi, A., Muffit, T. (2006). Bullying victimization uniquely contributes to adjustment problems in young children: A nationally repesentative cohort study. *Pediatrics, 118* (1), 130–138.

Aries, P. (1962). *Centuries of childhood.* New York: Vintage Books.

Asher, L. J., & Lenhoff, D. R. (2001). Family and medical leave: Making time for family is everyone's business.

The Future of Children: Caring for Infants and Toddlers, 11(1), 115–121.

Austin, J. S. (2000). When a child discloses sexual abuse: Immediate and appropriate teacher responses. *Childhood Education, 77*(1), 2–5.

Baker, A. J. L., & Piotrkowski, C. S. (1998). The effects of the home instruction program for preschool youngsters (HIPPY) on children's school performance at the end of the program and one year later. *Early Childhood Research Quarterly, 13,* 571–588.

Baker, A. J. L., Piotrkowski, C. S., & Brooks-Gunn, J. (1998). The effects of the Home Instruction Program for Preschool Youngsters on children's school performance at the end of the program and one year later. *Early Childhood Research Quarterly, 13*(4), 571–589.

Bakwin, H. (1956). Multiple skeletal lesions in young children due to trauma. *Journal of Pediatrics, 49*(1), 7–15.

Ballantine, J. H. (1999/2000, Winter). Figuring the father factor. *Childhood Education, 76*(2), 140–145.

Banks, J. A. (1991). *Teaching strategies for ethnic studies* (5th ed.). Boston: Allyn & Bacon.

Banks, J. A. (1997). *Teaching strategies for ethnic studies* (6th ed.). Boston: Allyn & Bacon.

Banks, J. A. (2003). *Teaching strategies for ethnic studies* (7th ed.). Boston: Allyn & Bacon.

Banks, J. A. (Ed.) (2004). *Diversity and citizenship education.* San Francisco: Jossey-Bass.

Banks, J. A. (Ed.) & Banks, C. (Assoc. Ed.). 2001. *Handbook of research on multicultural education*. San Francisco: Jossey-Bass.

Barbour, N. H., & Seefeldt, C. (1993). *Developmental continuity across the preschool and primary-grades.* Wheaton, MD: Association for Childhood Education International.

Bar-Hava-Montieth, G., Harre, N., & Field, J. (1999, July). Hippy New Zealand: An evaluation overview. *Social Policy Journal of New Zealand,* 106–122.

Barneombudet. (2002). The ombudsman for children in Norway. Retrieved June 29, 2002, from *www.barneombudet.no/ html/english/factsheet.html*

Barton, P. E. (2002, January). Raising achievement and reducing gaps. Retrieved February 5, 2002, from *www.negp.gov*

Bassuk, E., & Rubin, L. (1987). Homeless children: A neglected population. *American Journal of Orthopsychiatry 57*(22), 279–285.

Bassuk, E. L. (1991). Homeless families. *Scientific American, 264*(6), 66–74.

Bauman, K. J. (2001, August). *Home schooling in the United States: Trends and Characteristics.* Washington, DC: U.S. Census Bureau Population Division.

Bavolek, S. J. (1989). Assessing and treating high-risk parenting attitudes. *Early Child Development and Care, 42,* 99–111.

Beal, G., Bohlen, J. M., & Raudabaugh, J. N. (1962). *Leadership and dynamic group action.* Ames: Iowa State University.

Beato, G. (2005). Homeschooling alone. *Reason, 36*(11), 32–39.

Becker, H. J. (2000, Fall/Winter). Who's wired and who's not: Children's access and use of computer technology. *The Future of Children: Children and Computer Technology, 10*(2), 44–75.

Behrman, R. E. (2000). Statement of purpose. *Future of Children: Children, Youth, and Gun Violence, 12*(2), 1.

Bell, R. Q., & Harper, L. V. (1980). *Child effects on adults.* Lincoln: University of Nebraska Press.

Benne, K. D., & Sheets, P. (1948). Functional roles of group members. *Journal of Social Issues, 4*(2), 41–49.

Berck, J. (1992). No place to be: Voices of homeless children. *Public Welfare, 5*(2), 28–33.

Berger, E. H. (1968). *Mature beginning teachers: Employment, satisfaction, and role analysis.* Unpublished doctoral dissertation, University of Denver.

Berger, E. H. (1996a). Don't leave them standing on the sidewalk. *Early Childhood Education Journal, 24*(2), 131–133.

Berger, E. H. (1996b). Communication: The key to parent involvement. *Early Childhood Education Journal, 23*(3), 179–183.

Berger, E. H. (1997). Home schooling. *Early Childhood Education Journal, 24*(3), 205–208.

Berger, E. H. (1998). Reaching parents through literacy. *Early Childhood Education Journal, 25*(3), 211–215.

Berger, E. H., & Berger, G. R. (1985). Parents and law: Rights and responsibilities. In L. Sametz & C. S. McLoughlin (Eds.), *Educators, children and the law.* Springfield, IL: Charles C. Thomas.

Berliner, D. (1987, May). Parents can be great summer tutors. *Instructor,* 20–21.

Berrueta-Clement, J. R., Schweinhart, L. J., Barnett, W. S., Epstein, A. S., & Weikart, D. P. (1984). *Changed lives: The effects of the Perry Preschool Program on youths through age 19. (Monograph of the High/Scope Educational Research Foundation,* No. 8). Ypsilanti, MI: High/Scope Press.

Besharov, D. J. (1990). *Recognizing child abuse.* New York: Free Press.

Besharov, D. J. (1994). Responding to child sexual abuse: The need for a balanced approach. *The Future of Children: Sexual Abuse of Children, 4*(2), 135–155.

Bethel School District No.403 v. Fraser No. 84-1667. 478 U.S. 675, July 7, 1986.

Bianchi, S. M., & Spain, D. (1996). Women, work, and family in America. *Population Bulletin, 51*(3). Washington, DC: Population Reference Bureau.

Biddle, B. J., & Thomas, E. J. (1979). *Role theory: Concepts and research.* Melbourne, FL: Robert E. Krieger.

Bigner, J. J. (1985). *Parent–child relations.* New York: Macmillan.

Billingsley, A. (1992). *Climbing Jacob's ladder.* New York: Simon & Schuster.

Binder, R. L., & McNiel, D. E. (1987). Evaluation of a school-based sexual abuse prevention program: Cognitive and emotional effects. *Child Abuse and Neglect, 11*(4), 497–506.

Binkley, M. R. (1988). *Becoming a nation of readers: What parents can do.* Lexington, MA: D. C. Heath.

Bjorklund, G., & Burger, C. (1987). Making conferences work for parents, teachers, and children. *Young Children, 42*(2), 26–31.

Bloom, B. S. (1964). *Stability and change in human characteristics.* New York: Wiley.

Bloom, B. S. (1981). *All our children learning.* New York: McGraw-Hill.

Bloom, B. S. (1986). The home environment and school learning. In Study Group of National Assessment of Student Achievement, *The nation's report card.* Washington, DC: U.S. Department of Education. (ERIC Document Reproduction Service No. ED279663).

Blow, S. E., & Eliot, H. R. (1910). *The mottos and commentaries of Friedrich Froebel's mother play.* New York: D. Appleton.

Board on Children and Families. (1995). Immigrant children and their families: Issues for research and policy. *The Future of Children: Critical Issues for Children and Youth, 5*(2), 72–89.

Bodrova, E., & Leong, D. J. (2007). *Tools of the mind: The Vygotskian approach to early childhood education (2nd ed.).* Upper Saddle River, NJ: Merrill/Prentice Hall.

Bogolub, E. B. (1995). *Helping families through divorce: An eclectic approach.* New York: Springer.

Bond, J. T., Galinsky, E., & Swanberg, J. E. (1998). *The 1997 national study of the changing workforce.* New York: Families and Work Institute.

Borchers, T. (1999). Small group communication: Roles in groups. Retrieved August 28, 2002, from *www.abacon.com/ commstudies/groups/roles.html*

Boren, S. (1994). *Education of the gifted and talented reauthorization fact sheet.* Washington, DC: (ERIC Document Reproduction Service Nos. ED371526 and EC303113).

Bossard, J. H. S., & Boll, E. S. (1966). *The sociology of child development.* New York: Harper & Row.

Bove, C. (1999), L'inserimento del bambino al nido *Young Children.* 54(2), 32–34.

Bower, T. G. R. (1982). *Development in infancy* (2nd ed.). San Francisco: W. H. Freeman.

Bowlby, J. (1966). *Attachment.* New York: Basic Books.

Bowlby, J. (1982). *Maternal care and mental health.* New York: Schocken Books.

Bowlby, J. (1988). *A secure base.* New York: Basic Books.

Boyer, E. L. (1991). *Ready to learn: A mandate for the nation.* Princeton, NJ: The Carnegie Foundation for the Advancement of Teaching.

Boyer, E. L. (1995). *The basic school: A community for learning.* Princeton, NJ: Carnegie Foundation for the Advancement of Teaching.

Brazelton Institute. (2005). The Newborn Behavioral Observation system: What is it? Retrieved November 17, 2005, from www.touchpoint.brazelton-institute.com/clnbas.html

Brazelton Touchpoint Cemter. (2005). Early child care & education training. Retrieved November 17, 2005, from *www.touchpooints.org/ecet.html*

Brazelton, T. B. (1987). *Working and caring.* Reading, MA: Addison-Wesley.

Brazelton, T. B., & Greenspan, S. I. (2000). *The irreducible needs of children: What every child must have to grow, learn, and flourish.* Cambridge, MA: Perseus.

Brazelton, T. B., & Greenspan, S. I. (2001). The irreducible needs of children. *Young Children, 56*(2), 6–14.

Brazelton, T. B., & Yogman, M. W. (1986). *Affective development in infancy.* Norwood, NJ: Ablex.

Bredekamp, S. (Ed.). (1987). *Developmentally appropriate practice in early childhood programs serving children from birth through 8* (expanded ed.). Washington, DC: National Association for the Education of Young Children.

Bredekamp, S., & Rosegrant, T. (1992). *Reaching potentials: Appropriate curriculum and assessment for young children* (Vol. 1). Washington, DC: National Association for the Education of Young Children.

Brier, J., Berliner, L., Bulkley, J. A., Jenny, C., & Reid, T. (1996). *The APSAC handbook on child maltreatment.* Thousand Oaks, CA: Sage.

Bright, J. A. (1994). Beliefs in action: Family contributions to African-American student success. *Equity and Choice, 10*(2), 5–3.

Brim, O. (1965). *Education for child rearing.* New York: Free Press.

Broderick, C. B. (1993). *Understanding family process: Basics of family systems theory.* Newbury Park, CA: Sage.

Bronfenbrenner, U. (1979). *The ecology of human development.* Cambridge, MA: Harvard University Press.

Bronfenbrenner, U. (1986). Ecology of the family. Research perspectives. *Developmental Psychology, 22*, 723–742.

Brook-Gunn, J., & Duncan, G. J. (1997). The effects of poverty on children. *The Future of Children: Children and Poverty, 7*(2), 55–71.

Brougham, Lord. (1828). Speech to the House of Commons. In B. Evans (1978), *Dictionary of quotations* (p. 193). New York: Avenel Books.

Brown v. Topeka Board of Education, 347 U.S. 483 (1954).

Bruckey, S. (Ed.). (2000). *Children of poverty.* New York: Garland.

Bruner, J. S., & Greenfield, P. (1996). *Studies in cognitive growth.* New York: Wiley.

Bryson, K. (1996, October). Household and family characteristics. March 1995. *Current Population Reports* (P20-488). Washington, DC: Bureau of the Census.

Buck, P. S. (Reprint, 1991). *The child who never grew.* Cutchogue, NY: Buccaneer Books.

Buell, M. J., Hallam, R. A., & Beck, H. L. (2001, May). Early Head Start and child care partnerships: Working together to serve infants, toddlers, and their families. *Young Children, 56*(3), 7–12.

Bullock, J. R. (2002). Bullying among children. *Childhood Education, 78*(3), 130–133.

Bureau of Labor Statistics. (2006). Unemployment. Retrieved on September 3, 2006, from *www.bls.gov/data/home.htm*

Burns, E. (2006). *IEP-2005. Writing and Implementing Individual Education Plans (IEPs).* Springfield, IL: Charles Thomas Ltd.

Burr, W. R. (1990). Beyond I-statements in family communication. *Family Relations, 39*(3), 266–273.

Butts, R. F., & Cremin, L. A. (1953). *A history of education in American culture.* New York: Holt, Rinehart and Winston.

Byrne, G. (1997, October). Father may not know best, but what does he know? *Population Today, 15*(10), 1–3.

C. Henry Kempe National Center for the Prevention and Treatment of Child Abuse and Neglect. (n.d.). *Kempe Center programs.* Denver, CO: Author.

Caffey, J. (1946). Multiple fractures in long bones of infants suffering from chronic subdural hematoma. *American Journal of Roentgenology, 56*, 163–173.

Cai, Y., Reeve, J., & Robinson, D. T. (2002). Homeschooling and teaching style: Comparing motivational styles of homeschool and public school teachers. *Journal of Educational Psychology, 94*(2), 372–380.

Caldwell, B. (1968). The fourth dimension in early childhood education. In R. Hess & R. Bear (Eds.), *Early education: Current theory, research, and action.* Chicago: Aldine.

Caldwell, B. M. (1989). Achieving rights for children: Role of the early childhood profession. *Childhood Education, 66*(1), 4–7.

Caldwell, B. M. (1991). Continuity in the early years: Transitions between grades and systems. In S. L. Kagan (Ed.), *The care and education of America's young children: Obstacles and opportunities. Ninetieth Yearbook of the National Society for the Study of Education.* Chicago: University of Chicago Press.

Caldwell, B. M., & Bradley, R. H. (1984). *Administration manual: Home observation for measurement of the environment.* Little Rock: University of Arkansas.

Calhoun, A. W. (1960). *A social history of the American family* (Vols. 1–3). New York: Barnes & Noble.

California Task Force on School Readiness. (1988). *Here they come: Ready or not.* Sacramento: California Department of Education.

Candoli, I. C. (1991). *School systems administration: A strategic plan for site-based management.* Lancaster, PA: Technomic.

Canter, L., & Hausner, L. (1987). *Homework without tears.* New York: Harper & Row.

Carlson, C. I. (1992). Single-parent families. In M. E. Procidano & C. B. Fisher (Eds.), *Contemporary families: A handbook for school professionals.* New York: Teachers College Press.

Carlson, M. (2002, January). Developing self and emotions in extreme social deprivation. In panel: The effect of emotions: Laying the groundwork in childhood. Retrieved February 5, 2002, from *www.lcweb.loc.gov/loc/brain/emotion/Carlson*

Carnegie Corporation of New York. (1994). *Starting points: Meeting the needs of our youngest children.* New York: Author.

Carper, J. C. (1992). Home schooling: History and historian: The past and present. *The High School Journal, 75*(4), 252–257.

Carroll, L. (1968). *Through the looking-glass and what Alice found there.* New York: St. Martin's Press.

Casanova, U. (1987, May). Parents can be great summer tutors. *Instructor*, 20–21.

Casper, L. M. (1997, November). Who's minding our preschoolers? Fall 1994 (Update). *Current Population Reports* (P70-62). Washington, DC: Bureau of the Census.

Casper, L. M., & Bianchi, S. M. (2002). *Continuity & change in the American family.* Thousand Oaks, CA: Sage.

Casper, L. M., & Bryson, K. R. (1998, March). Co-resident grandparents and their grandchildren: Grandparent maintained families. Washington, DC: Population Division, U.S. Bureau of the Census.

Retrieved April 2, 2002, from *www. census.gov/population/www/documentation/twps0026.html*

Cataldo, C. Z. (1987). *Parent education for early childhood.* New York: Teachers College Press.

Center for Effective Discipline (2000, July). *Facts about corporal punishment.* Retrieved January 14, 2003, from *www.stophitting.com/disatschool/facts.php*

Center for Effective Discipline. (2006, July). *Facts about corporal punishment worldwide.* Retrieved August 25, 2006, from *www.stophitting.com/disatschool/facts.php*

Center for Effective Discipline. (2007). U.S.: Corporal punishment and paddling statistics by state and race. Retrieved January 11, 2007, from *www.stophitting.com/disatschool/statesBanning.php*

Center for Family Strengths. (1986). *Building family strengths: A manual for facilitators.* Lincoln, NE: University of Nebraska.

Center for Immigration Studies. (2005). Immigration at Mid-Decade. Retrieved January 9, 2006, from *www.cis.org/articles/2005/back1405.pdf*

Center for the Future of Children, The David and Lucile Packard Foundation. (1995). The Future of Children. *Critical Issues for Children and Youth, 5*(2).

Center for Substance Abuse. (2003). Houston Parent–Child Development Center. Building a successful prevention program. Retrieved April 14, 2006, from *www.casat.unr.edu/bestpractices/view.php?program=49*

Centers for Disease Control. (2006a). Youth violence: Fact sheet. Retrieved September 3, 2006, from *cdc.gov/hcipe/factsheets/yvfacts.htm*

Centers for Disease Control. (2006b). Child maltreatment: Fact sheet. Retrieved September 2, 2006, from *cdc.gov/hcipc/fctsheets/yvfacts.htm*

Centre for Europe's Children. (2001a, December 13). Annual report on the activities of the French ombudsman for children/Defenseur des enfants. Retrieved June 29, 2002, from *www.ombudsnet.org/Ombudsmen/France/Activities_00_01.htm*

Centre for Europe's Children. (2001b, December 13). Austrian report for the annual meeting of ENOC. Retrieved June 29, 2002, from *www.ombudsnet.org/Ombudsmen/Austria/austria.htm*

Centre for Europe's Children. (2001c, December 13). Standards for human rights. Retrieved June 29, 2002, from *www.ombudsnet.org/WhatsNew.htm*

Centre for Europe's Children. (2001d, March 30). Latin America. Retrieved June 29, 2002, from *www.ombudsnet.org/ombudsmen/RestOfWorld/LatinAmerica/LatinAmerica.htm*

Centre for Europe's Children. (2002, April 4). History of the office. Retrieved June 29, 2002, from *www.ombudsnet.org/ombudsmen/Hungary/hungary.htm*

CESA 5, Portage Project. (1998). *Growing: Interactions/Daily routines.* Portage, WI: Author.

Chambliss, R. (1982). *Social thought.* New York: Irvington Press.

Chapman, W. (1991). The Illinois experience: State grants to improve schools through parent involvement. *Phi Delta Kappan, 72*(5), 355–358.

Chicago Longitudinal Study. (2004). Parent program. Retrieved December 28, 2006, from *www.waisman.wisc.edu:8000/cls/parent.htm*

Chicago Office of the Office for Civil Rights. (2005). Protecting students with disabilities: Chicago: Author.

Child Abuse Prevention and Treatment Act of 1974. (1977). *United States Code, 1976, The Public Health and Welfare, Section 5101* (Vol. 10). Washington, DC: U.S. Government Printing Office.

Child Trends Data Bank. (2004). Child maltreatment rate (per 1,000) by Age, 2002. Retrieved September 2006, from *www.childtrendsdatabank.org*

Child Trends Data Bank. (2004). Number and rate of victims of child maltreatment, 2002. Retrieved September 2006, from *www.childtrendsdatabank.org*

Child Welfare Information Gateway. (2003). Child fatalities resource listing. Retrieved April 1, 2004, from *www.childwelfare.gov/pubs/reslit/rl_dsp.cfm?subjiD=1*

Children's Ombudsman in Sweden. (1998). Children's ombudsman in Sweden report. Retrieved June 29, 2001, from *www.bo.se/eng/engelsk.asp*

Children's Defense Fund. (1989). *A vision for America's future.* Washington, DC: Author.

Children's Defense Fund. (1992). *The state of America's children, 1991.* Washington, DC: Author.

Children's Defense Fund. (1997). *The state of America's children: Yearbook 1997.* Washington, DC: Author.

Children's Defense Fund. (1998). *The state of America's children: Yearbook 1998.* Washington, DC: Author.

Children's Defense Fund. (2001). *Children in the states.* Washington, DC: Author

Children's Defense Fund. (2005). State of America's children, 2005. Retrieved September 2, 2006, from *www.childrensdefensefund.org.*

Chinn, P. C. (Ed.). (1984). *Education of culturally and linguistically exceptional children.* Reston, VA: Council for Exceptional Children.

Chinn, P. C., Winn, J., & Walters, R. H. (1978). *Two-way talking with parents of special children: A process of positive communication.* St. Louis, MO: C. V. Mosby.

Citizens for Parental Rights v. San Mateo County Board of Education, 124 Cal. Reptr. 68 (1975).

Civil Rights Act of 1964, 42 U.S.C. 601, 78 Stat. 252; 2000d. Cited in the *Federal Register, 45*(92).

Clark, R. M. (1983). *Family life and school achievement.* Chicago: University of Chicago Press.

Clewell, B. C., Brooks-Gunn, J., & Benasich, A. A. (1989). Evaluating child-related outcomes of teenage parenting programs. *Family Relations, 38*(2), 201–209.

Coan, D. L., & Gotts, E. E. (1976). *Parent education needs: A national assessment study.* Charleston, WV: Appalachia Educational Laboratory. (ERIC Document Reproduction Service No. ED132609).

Cochran, M., & Dean, C. (1991). Home–school relations and the empowerment process. *Elementary School Journal 91*(3), 261–269.

Coleman, J., Campbell, E. Q., Hobson, C. J., McPartland, J., Mood, A. M., Weinfeld, F. D., et al. (1966). *Equality of educational opportunity.* Washington, DC: U.S. Government Printing Office.

Coleman, J. S. (1987). Families and schools. *Educational Researcher, 16*(1), 32–38.

Coleman, J. S. (1994). Family involvement in education. In C. L. Fagnano & B. Z. Werber (Eds.), *School, family and community interaction: A view from the firing lines.* Boulder, CO: Westview Press.

Coleman, J. S. (1997). *Redesigning American education.* Boulder, CO: Westview Press.

Coleman, J. S., & Schneider, B. (Eds.). (1993). *Parents, their children and schools.* Boulder, CO: Westview Press.

Coletta, A. J. (1977). *Working together: A guide to parent involvement.* Atlanta, GA: Humanics Limited.

Colorado Department of Education, Early Childhood Initiatives, The Arapahoe Early Childhood Network, PEAK Parent Center, & The Colorado Consortium of Intensive Care Nurseries. (1997). *From one parent to another.* Denver, CO: Author.

Comeau, C. (2006) *Working together.* ASD Online. Retrieved March 3, 2006, from *www.asdk12.org/parents/involvement*

Comenius, J. A. (1967). *The great didactic of John Amos Comenius* (M. W. Keatinge, Ed. & Trans.). New York: Russell & Russell. (Original work published 1657)

Comer, J. P. (1988). Educating poor minority children. *Scientific American, 259*(5), 42–48.

Comer, J. P. (1997). *Waiting for a miracle.* New York: Dutton.

Comer, J. P. (2004). *Leave no child behind: Preparing today's youth for tomorrow's world.* New Haven: Yale University Press.

Comer, J. P., & Haynes, N. M. (1991). Parent involvement in schools: An ecological approach. *The Elementary School Journal, 91*(3), 271–277.

Comer, J. P., Haynes, N. M., & Joyner, E. T. (1996). The school development program. In J. P. Comer, N. M. Haynes, E. T. Joyner, & M. Ben-Avie (Eds.), *Rallying the whole village: The Comer process for reforming education* (pp. 1–26). New York: Teachers College Press.

Comer, J. P., Haynes, N. M., Joyner, E. T., & Ben-Avie, M. (Eds.). (1996). *Rallying the whole village: The Comer process for reforming education.* New York: Teachers College Press.

Commissioner's Task Force on Parent Involvement in Head Start. (1987). *Final report: Commissioner's task force on parent involvement in Head Start.* Washington, DC: U.S. Department of Health and Human Services, Office of Human Development Services, Administration for Children, Youth and Families, Head Start Bureau.

Congressional record. (1983). 98th Congr., Vol. 129, pt. 24: 33310–33329, 98–199.

Congressional record. (1986). 99th Congr., Vol. 132, pt. 125: H7908–H7912, 457.

Consortium for Longitudinal Studies. (1983). *As the twig is bent.* Hillsdale, NJ: Erlbaum.

Cook, R. E., Klein, M. D., & Tessier, A. (2004). *Adapting early childhood curricula for children in inclusive settings* (6th ed.). Upper Saddle River, NJ: Merrill/Prentice Hall.

Cook, R. E., Tessier, A., & Armbruster, V. B. (1987). *Adapting early childhood curricula for children with special needs* (2nd ed.). Upper Saddle River, NJ: Merrill/Prentice Hall.

Cooke, G., & Cooke, S. (1988). Homework that makes a difference in children's learning. Personal communication.

Cooley, H. C. (1964). *Human nature and the social order.* New York: Schocken Books.

Coons, C. E., Gay, E. C., Fandal, A. W., Ker, C., & Frankenburg, W. K. (1981). *Home Screening Questionnaire.* Denver, CO: JFK Child Development Center.

Cooper, H. (1994, Summer). *Homework research and policy: A review of the literature.* Center for Applied Research and Education Improvement. Retrieved June 21, 2002, from *education.umn.edu/carei/Reports/Rpractice/Summer94/homework.htm*

Cooper, H. (2001). Homework for all. *Educational Leadership, 58*(7), 34–38.

Cooper, J. M. (1999). *Classroom teaching skills* (6th ed.). Boston: Houghton Mifflin.

Copenhaver, J. (2004). *Assistive technology for students with disabilities: Information for parents and educators.* Logan, UT: U. S. Department of Education.

Corcoran, M. E., & Chaudry, A. (1997). The effects of poverty on children. *The Future of Children: Children and Poverty* 7(2), 40–54.

Cost, Quality, and Child Outcomes Study Team (CQO). (1995). *Cost, quality, and child outcomes in child care centers.* Denver, CO: Department of Economics, University of Colorado at Denver.

Council for Exceptional Children. (2000). Pervasive Developmental Disorders (PDD). Retrieved July 31, 2006, from *www.cec.sped.org*

Council for Exceptional Children. (2001). Nurturing young children. Retrieved July 31, 2006, from *www.cec.sped.org*

Council for Exceptional Children. (2002). Public policy and legislative information. IDEA reauthorization recommendations. Retrieved June 22, 2002, from *www.cec.sped.org/pp/*

Council for Exceptional Children. (2003). GT-English as a second language. Retrieved July 31, 2006, from *www.cec.sped.org*

Council of State Directors of Programs for the Gifted. 2001–2002. State of the States. Dr. Kristy Ehlers, State Director, Gifted and Talented Education. Oklahoma Department of Education, 2500 North Lincoln Bld., Suite 316, Oklahoma City, OK 73105.

Crane, S. (1986). Personal communication.

Crane, S. (1994). Personal communication.

Crosbie-Burnett, M., & Giles-Sim, J. (1994). Adolescent adjustment and step-parenting styles. *Family Relations, 43*(4), 394–399.

Crosbie-Burnett, M., & Skyles, A. (1989). Stepchildren in schools and colleges: Recommendations for educational policy changes. *Family Relations, 38*(1), 59–64.

Crosson-Tower, C. (2002). *Child abuse and neglect* (5th ed.). Boston: Allyn & Bacon.

Cupoli, J. M., & Sewell, P. M. (1988). One thousand fifty-nine children with a chief complaint of sexual abuse. *Child Abuse and Neglect, 12*(2), 151–161.

Currie, J. (2000). Early Childhood Intervention Programs: What do we know? Retrieved April 22, 2006, from *www.jcir.org/wpfiles.currie.EARLYCHILDHOOD.Psd*

Dainton, M. (1993). The myth and misconceptions of stepmother identity. *Family Relations 42*(1), 93–98.

Dalaimo, D. M. (1996). Community home education: A case study of public school-based home schooling program. *Education Research Quarterly, 19*(4), 3–21.

Daresh, J. C. (1986). Effective home-school-community relations for secondary school improvement. *The Clearing House, 59*(7), 312–315.

Daro, D., McCurdy, K., Falconier, L., Stajanovie, D. (2003). Sustaining new parents in home visitation services: Key participation and program factors. *Child Abuse and Neglect, 27*(10), 1101–1126.

DaSilva, B., & Lucus, R. D. (1974). *Practical school volunteer and teacher-aide programs.* West Nyack, NY: Parker.

Davidman, L., & Davidman, P. T. (2001). *Teaching with a multicultural perspctive,* 3rd ed. New York: Longman.

Davidson Institute for Talent Development. (2007). Genius denied: How to stop wasting our brightest young minds. Retrieved January 9, 2007, from *www.geniusdenied.com/Policies/StatePolicy.aspx*

Davies, D. (1987). Parent involvement in the public schools. *Education and Urban Society, 19*(2), 147–163.

Davies, D. (1990). Shall we wait for the revolution? A few lessons from the Schools Reaching Out project. *Equity and Choice, 6*(3), 68–73.

Davies, D. (1997). Crossing boundaries: How to create successful parnerships with families and communities. *Early Childhood Education Journal, 25*(1), 73–77.

Day, J. C. (1996a). Population projections of the United States by age, sex, race, and Hispanic origin: 1995–2050. *Current Population Reports* (P25-113). Washington, DC: Bureau of the Census.

De Gaetano, Y., Williams, L. R., & Volk, D. (1998). *Kaleidoscope: A multicultural approach for the primary school classroom.* Upper Saddle River, NJ: Merrill/Prentice Hall.

Delaney, S. W. (1980, March 12–16). Fathers and infants class: A model program. *Exceptional Teacher.*

Delaney, S. W., Meyer, D. J., & Ward, M. J. (1980). *Fathers and infants class: A model for facilitating attachment between fathers and their infants.* Seattle, WA: Experimental Education Unit, Child Development and Mental Retardation Center, University of Washington.

Deloria, P. J., & Salisbury, N., (Eds.) (2002). *A companion to American Indian history.* Malden, MA: Blackwell.

deMause, L. (Ed.). (1974). *The history of childhood.* New York: Psychohistory Press.

deMause, L. (Ed.). (1988). *The history of childhood: The untold story of child abuse.* New York: Harper & Row.

DeNavas-Walt, C., Proctor, B. D., & Lee, C. H. (2004). Income, poverty, and health insurance coverage in the United States. Retrieved September 5, 2006, from *www.sph.umn.edu/img/assets/18528/CPS2004summary_Sep2005.pdf*

Denver Public Schools. (1998). *Child abuse bulletin.* Denver, CO: Author.

Denver Public Schools. (n.d.). *For VIPs only. Volunteers in public schools.* Denver, CO: Author.

Denver Public Schools, Emily Griffith Opportunity School. (n.d.). *Parent education and preschool department leadership handbook.* Denver, CO: Author.

Derman-Sparks, L. (2004). Culturally relevant anti bias education with young children. In W. G. Stephan and

W. P. Viogt (Eds.), *Education programs for improving intergroup relations.* New York: Teachers College Press.

Derman-Sparks, L., & A.B.C. Task Force. (1989). *Anti-bias curriculum: Tasks for empowering young children.* Washington, DC: National Association for the Education of Young Children.

Dervarics, C. (2001). Charter school catching on. *Population Today,* 29(6). Washington, DC: Population Reference Bureau.

Deutsch, C. P., & Deutsch, M. (1968). Brief reflections on theory of early childhood enrichment programs. In R. Hess & R. Bear (Eds.), *Early education: Current theory, research, and action.* Chicago: Aldine.

Devaney, B. L., Ellwood, M. R., & Love, J. M. (1997). Programs that mitigate the effects of poverty on children. *The Future of Children: Children and Poverty* 7(2), 88–112.

Dewey, J. (1916). *Democracy and education: An introduction to the philosophy of education.* New York: Macmillan.

Diffily, D. (2004). *Teachers and families working together.* Boston: Allyn & Bacon.

Dinkmeyer, D., & McKay, G. D. (1989). *STEP: Systematic training for effective parenting.* Circle Pines, MN: American Guidance Service.

Dinkmeyer, D., McKay, G. D., Dinkmeyer, J. S., & Dinkmeyer, D., Jr. (1992). *Teaching and leading children.* Circle Pines, MN: American Guidance Service.

Dinkmeyer, D., McKay, G. D., & Dinkmeyer, D., Jr., (1997). *Parent's handbook. Systemic training for effective parenting.* Circle Pines, MN: American Guidance Service.

Dixon v. Alabama State Board of Education, 368 U.S. 930 (1961).

Dombro, A. L., O'Donnell, N. S., Galinsky, E., Melcher, S. G., & Farber, A. (1996). *Community mobilization: Strategies to support young children and their families.* New York: Families and Work Institute.

Dornbusch, S., Ritter, P., Leiderman, P. H., Roberts, D. F., & Fraleigh, M. (1987). The relation of parenting style to adolescent school performance. *Child Development, 58*(5), 1244–1257.

Duggan, A. K., McFarlane, E. C., Windham, A. M., Rohde, C. A., Salkever, D. S., Fuddy, L., et al. (1999). Evaluation of Hawaii's Healthy Start program. *The Future of Children: Home Visiting: Recent Program Evaluations,* 9(1), 73.

Dunlap, K. M. (2000). *Family empowerment: One outcome of parental participation in cooperative preschool education.* New York: Garland.

Earls, F. (2002, January). Studying the causes of delinquency and violence. In panel: The effect of emotions: Laying the groundwork in childhood. Retrieved February 5, 2002, from *www.lcweb.loc.gov/loc/brain/emotion/Earls.html*

Earley, J. (2000). *Interactive group therapy.* Philadelphia: Brunner/Mazel.

Ed.gov. (2004). Reading first purpose. Retrieved April 17 from *www.ed.gov/print/programs/readingfirst/index.html*

Eddowes, E. A. (1992). Children and homelessness: Early childhood and elementary education. In E. H. Stronge (Ed.), *Educating homeless children and adolescents: Evaluating policy and practice.* Newbury Park, CA: Sage.

Education Commission of the States. (1996). *Bridging the gap between neuroscience and education.* Denver, CO: Author.

Educational Resources Information Center, U.S. Department of Education. (1996, Fall). Inclusion. *ERIC Review, 4*(3).

Edwards, C. P., & Gandini, L. (2001). Conclusions for now, questions and directions for the future. In L. Gandini & C. P. Edwards (Eds.), 2001. *Bambini: The Italian approach to infant/toddler care.* New York: Teachers College Press.

Edwards, P., & Young, L. (1992). Beyond parents: Family, community, and school involvement. *Phi Delta Kappan, 74,* 72–78.

Egeland, B. (1988). The consequences of physical and emotional neglect on the development of young children. In U.S. Department of Health and Human Services, Children's Bureau, *National Center on Child Abuse and Neglect: Research symposium on Child Neglect,* February 23–25. (D-10–D-21)

Ehrle, J., Adams, G., & Tout, T. (2001). *Who's caring for our youngest children: Child care patterns of infants and toddlers.* Washington, DC: The Urban Institute.

Elam, S. M., Rose, L. C., & Gallup, A. M. (1992). The 24th annual Gallup Phi Delta Kappa Poll of the public's attitudes toward public schools. *Phi Delta Kappan 74*(1), 41–53.

Elkind, D. (1987a). The child yesterday, today, and tomorrow. *Young Children, 42*(4), 6–12.

Elmer, E. (1982). Abused young children seen in hospitals. In S. Antler (Ed.), *Child abuse and child protection: Policy and practice.* Silver Springs, MD: National Association of Social Workers.

Emmons, C. L., Comer, J. P., & Haynes, N. M. (Eds.). (1996). Translating theory into practice: Comer's theory of school reform. In J. P. Comer, N. M. Haynes, E. T. Joyner, & M. Ben-Avie (Eds.), *Rallying the whole village: The Comer process for reforming education* (pp. 27–41). New York: Teachers College Press.

End Violence Against the Next Generation. (n.d.). *Child abuse in schools: A national disgrace.* Berkeley, CA: Author.

Engle, P. L., & Breaux, C. (1998). Fathers' involvement with children: Perspectives from developing countries. *Social Policy Report, 12*(1). Ann Arbor, MI: Society for Research in Child Development.

Epstein, A. S. (1998). Is the High/Scope educational approach compatible with the revised Head Start performance standards? *High/Scope Resource, 17*(2), 1, 8–11.

Epstein, J. L. (1986). Parents' reactions to teacher practices of parent involvement. *The Elementary School Journal, 86*(3), 277–294.

Epstein, J. L. (1987a). Parent involvement: What research says to administrators. *Education and Urban Society, 19*(2), 119–136.

Epstein, J. L. (1987b). What principals should know about parent involvement. *Principal, 66*(3), 6–9.

Epstein, J. L. (1994). Theory to practice: School and family partnerships lead to school improvement and student success. In C. L. Fagnano & B. Z. Werber (Eds.), *School, family, and community interaction: A view from the firing lines.* Boulder, CO: Westview Press.

Epstein, J. L. (1995b). School/family/community partnerships: Caring for the children we share. *Phi Delta Kappan, 76*(9), 701–712.

Epstein, J. L. (1996). Perspective and previews on research and policy for school, family and community partnerships. In A. Booth & J. F. Dunn (Eds.), *Family-school links: How do they affect educational outcomes?* Mahwah, NJ: Erlbaum.

Epstein, J. L. (2001). Schools, family, and community partnerships: Preparing educators and improving schools. Boulder, CO: Westview Press.

Epstein, J. L. (2005a). Developing and sustaining research-based programs of school, family, and community partnerships: Summary of five years of NNPS research. Retrieved April 6, 2006, from *www.csos.jhu.edu/p2000/Research%20Summary.pdf*

Epstein, J. L. (2005b). Attainable goals? The spirit and letter of the No Child Left Behind Act on parental involvement. *Sociology of Education, 78,* 179–182.

Epstein, J. L., & Dauber, S. L. (1991). School programs and teacher practices of parent involvement in inner-city elementary and middle schools. *The Elementary School Journal, 91*(3), 289–305.

Epstein, J. L., Sanders, M. G., Simon. B. S., Salinas, K., Jansom, N. R., & Van Voorhis, F. L. (2002). *School, family and community partnerships: Your handbook for action* (2nd ed.). Thousand Oaks, CA: Corwin Press.

Epstein, J. L., & Sheldon, S. B. (2002). Present and accounted for: Improving student attendance through family and community involvement. *Journal of Educational Research, 95,* 308–318.

EQUALS. (1986). *Family math.* Berkeley: University of California.

Erikson, E. (1986). *Childhood and society.* New York: W. W. Norton.

Executive summary: Children, youth and gun violence: Analysis. (2002). *The Future of Children: Children, Youth, and Gun Violence, 12*(2). The David and Lucile Packard Foundation.

Fagan, P. F., & Rector, R. E. The Heritage Foundation. (2000, June). The effects of divorce on America. Retrieved February 13, 2006, from *www.heritage.org/Research/Family/BG1373.cfm*

Fagnano, C. L., & Hughes, K. N. (1993). *Making schools work: A view from the firing lines.* Boulder, CO: Westview Press.

Families and Work Institute. (1994). *Employers, families, and education: Facilitating family involvement in learning.* New York: Author.

Families together. (1993, Summer). Newsletter. Topeka, KS: Author.

Family and Advocates Partnership for Education Project. (2006). *The IEP process.* Minneapolis, MN: Pacer Center.

Family and Child Education. (2002). *Family and child education (FACE).* Retrieved May 27, 2002, from *www.famlit.org/faqs/faqface.html*

Family Resource Coalition. (1993a). *Family support programs and family literacy.* Chicago: Author.

Family Resource Coalition. (1993b). *Family support programs and the prevention of alcohol and other drug abuse (AOD).* Chicago: Author.

Family Resource Coalition. (1993c). *Family support programs and school readiness.* Chicago: Author.

Family Resource Coalition. (1993d). *Family support programs and school-linked services.* Chicago: Author.

Family Support America's Shared Leadership Series. (2000). *From many voices: Consensus what American needs for strong families and communities.* Chicago: Family Support America.

Fandal, A. (1986, February). Personal correspondence. Denver: University of Colorado Medical Center.

Federal Register. (1990, May 9). *Part II Department of Education, 45*(92), 30918–30965.

Federal Register. (1993, January 21). *Part VI Department of Health and Human Services: Administration for Children and Families, 58*(12), 1304–1305, 1308.

Federal Register. (2006). Rules and regulations assistance to states for the education of children with disabilities and preschool grants for children with disabilities. *Department of Education, 71*(156), 46544.

Fehrmann, P. G., Keith, T. Z., & Reimers, T. M. (1987). Home influence on school learning: Direct and indirect effects of parental involvement on high school grades. *Journal of Educational Research, 80*(6), 330–337.

Fenichel, E., & Mann, T. L. (2001). Early Head Start for low-income families with infants and toddlers. *The Future of Children: Caring for Infants and Toddlers, 11*(1), 135–141.

Ferguson-Florissant School District. (1989b). *Parents as first teachers.* Ferguson, MO: Author.

Fernandez, H. C. (1980). *The child advocacy handbook.* New York: The Pilgrim Press.

Fierman, A. H., Dreyer, B. P., Quinn, L., Shulman, S., Courtland, C. D., & Guzzo, R. (1991). Growth delay in homeless children. *Pediatrics, 88*(5), 918–925.

Finkelhor, D. (1986). *A sourcebook on child sexual abuse.* Beverly Hills, CA: Sage.

Finkelhor, D. (1990). Early and long-term effects of child sexual abuse: An update. *Professional Psychology: Research and Practice, 21*(5), 325–330.

Finkelhor, D. (1994). Current information on the scope and nature of child sexual abuse. *The Future of Children: Sexual Abuse of Children, 4*(2), 31–53.

Finkelhor, D., & Ormrod, R. (2000, June). Characteristics of crimes against juvenile. *Juvenile Justice Bulletin.*

Fischer, L., Schimmel, D., & Kelly, C. (1999). *Teachers and the law* (5th ed.). New York: Longman.

Fisher, M. (1933). Parent education. In *Encyclopedia of the social sciences* (Vol. 2). New York: Macmillan.

Fisher, S. H. (1958). Skeletal manifestations of parent-induced trauma in infants and children. *Southern Medical Journal,* 956–960.

Flekkoy, M. G. (1989). Child advocacy in Norway: The ombudsman. *Child Welfare, 68*(2), 113–122.

Fontana, V. (1973a). The diagnosis of the maltreatment syndrome in children. *Pediatrics, 51,* 780–782.

Fontana, V. (1973b). *Somewhere a child is crying.* New York: Macmillan.

Fontana, V. J., & Besharov, D. J. (1979). *The maltreated child: The maltreatment syndrome in children.* Springfield, IL: Charles C. Thomas.

Foundation Center, The. (1990). *The foundation directory.* New York: Author.

Fox, S. J. (1988). A whole language approach to the communication skills. In H. Gilliland (Ed.), *Teaching the Native American.* Dubuque, IA: Kendall/Hunt.

Frank, L. R. (Ed.). (2001). *Quotationary.* New York: Random House.

Franklin, C. J. (1993, June). Dealing with concerns throughout the year. Personal correspondence. Colorado Springs, CO.

Frede, E. C. (1995). The role of program quality in producing early childhood program benefits. *The Future of Children: Long-Term Outcomes of Early Childhood Programs, 5*(3), 115–132.

Froschi, M., Sprung, B., & Mullin-Rindler, N. (1998). *Quit it: A teacher's guide on teasing and bullying for use with students in grades k–3.* Washington, DC: NEA Professional Library.

Frost, S. E., Jr. (1966). *Historical and philosophical foundations of Western education.* Upper Saddle River, NJ: Merrill/Prentice Hall.

Furstenberg, F. F., Jr. (1994). History and current status of divorce in the United States. *The Future of Children: Children and Divorce 4*(1), 29–43.

Future of Children, The. (1999, Spring/Summer). *Home visiting: Recent program evaluations* (Vol. 9). Los Gatos, CA: The David and Lucile Packard Foundation.

Galinsky, E. (1987). *The six stages of parenthood.* Reading, MA: Addison-Wesley.

Galinsky, E., & Salmond, K. (2002, July). *Youth & violence.* Denver: Colorado Trust and Families and Work Institute.

Gamble, T. K., & Gamble, M. (1982). *Contacts: Communicating interpersonally.* New York: Random House.

Gandini, L. (1993, November). Fundamentals of the Reggio Emilia approach to early childhood education. *Young Children 49*(1), 4–8.

Gandini, L., & Edwards, C. P., (Eds.). (2001). *Bambini: The Italian approach to infant/toddler care.* New York: Teachers College Press.

Gandini, L., & Goldhaber, J. (2001). Two reflections about documentation. In Gandini, L. & Edwards, C. P., (Eds.). *Bambini: The Italian approach to infant/toddler care.* New York: Teachers College Press.

Garbarino, J., Bradshaw, C. P., & Vorrasi, J. A. (2002). Mitigating the effects of gun violence on children and youth. *The Future of Children: Children, Youth, and Gun Violence, 12*(2), 73–85.

Gardner, N. D. (1974). *Group leadership.* Washington, DC: National Training & Development Service Press.

Garrett, S. (2004). *Oklahoma #1 in pre-kindergarten program participation.* Retrieved June 17, 2006, from *www.sde.state.ok.us/pro/prek/default.htm*

Garrity, C., Baris, M., & Porter, W. (2000). *Bully proofing your child: A parent's guide.* Longmont, CO: Sopris West.

Gartin, B., and Murdick, N. (2005, November/December). IDEA 2004: the IEP. *Remedial and Special Education, 26*(6), 327–332.

Gelles, R. J., & Lancaster, J. B. (Eds.). (1987). *Child abuse and neglect: Biosocial dimensions.* New York: Aldine de Gruyter.

Gilliland, H. (Ed.). (1988). *Teaching the Native American.* Dubuque, IA: Kendall/Hunt.

Ginott, H. G. (1965). *Between parent & child.* New York: Macmillan.

Ginsberg, E. (Ed.). (1960). *The nation's children* (Vols. 1–3). New York: Columbia University Press.

Goffin, S. G., & Lombardi, J. (1988). *Speaking out: Early childhood advocacy.* Washington, DC: National Association for the Education of Young Children.

Goldhaber, J., & Smith, D. (2002). The development of documentation strategies to support teacher reflection, inquiry, and collaboration. In Fu, V. R., Stremmel, A. N., & Hill, L. T. (Eds.). (2002). *Teaching and learning: Collabora-tive exploration of the Reggio Emilia approach.* Upper Saddle River, NJ: Merrill/Prentice Hall.

Goldman, L. (2005). Child health and the environment, a review of evidence. *Zero to Three,* November, 2005, 11–19.

Goldman-Rakic, P. (1996). What can neuroscience contribute to education? In Education Commission of the States, *Bridging the gap between neuroscience and education.* Denver, CO: Author.

Gomby, D. S., Culross, P. L., & Behrman, R. E. (1999, Spring/Summer). Home visiting: Recent program evaluations. *The Future of Children, 9*(1), 4–26.

Gomby, D. S., Larson, C. S., Lewit, E. M., & Behrman, R. E. (1993). Home visiting: Analysis and recommendations. *The Future of Children: Home Visiting, 3*(3).

Gonzalez-Mena, J. (1998). *The child in the family and the community* (2nd ed.). Upper Saddle River, NJ: Merrill/Prentice Hall.

Goodson, B. D., & Hess, R. (1975). *Parents as teachers of young children: An evaluative review of some contemporary concepts and programs.* Stanford, CA: Stanford University Press.

Goodson, B. D., Swartz, J. P., & Millsap, M. A. (1991). Working with families: Promising programs to help parents support children's learning. *Equity and Choice, 7*(2–3), 97–107.

Goodykoontz, B., Davis, M. D., & Gabbard, H. F. (1947). Recent history and present status in education for young children. In *National Society for the Study of Education, 46th yearbook, part II.* Chicago: National Society for the Study of Education.

Gordon, I. J., & Breivogel, W. F. (Eds.). (1976). *Building effective home-school relationships.* Boston: Allyn & Bacon.

Gordon, T. (1975). *P.E.T.: Parent effectiveness training.* New York: Wyden.

Gordon, T. (2000). *P.E.T.: Parent effectiveness training: The proven program for raising responsible children.* New York: Three Rivers Press.

Gormley, W. T. Jr., Gayer, T., Phillips, D., & Dawson, B. (2004). The effects of universal pre-k on cognitive development. Retrieved June 14, 2006, from *www.crocus.georgetowm.edu/reports/oklahoma9z.pdf*

Goss v. Lopez, 419 U.S. 565 (1975).

Gotts, E. E. (1989, February). *HOPE revisited: Preschool to graduation, reflections on parenting and school-family relations: Occasional paper 28.* Charleston, WV: Appalachia Educational Laboratory.

Governor Romer's Responsible Fatherhood Initiative. (1997). *Colorado fathers' resource guide.* Denver, CO: Author.

Gray, S. W., & Klaus, R. A. (1965). An experimental preschool program for culturally deprived children. *Child Development, 36*(4), 887–898.

Gray, S. W., Ramsey, B. K., & Klaus, R. A. (1982). *From 3 to 20: The early training project.* Baltimore: University Park Press.

Graziano, A. M., & Diament, D. M. (1992). Parent behavioral training: An examination of the paradigm. *Behavior Modification, 16,* 3–38.

Green, F. (1988). Corporal punishment and child abuse. *The Humanist, 48*(6), 9–10, 32.

Green, S. (2002, October). Involving fathers in children's literacy development: An introduction to fathers reading every day (FRED) program. *Journal of Extension.* Retrieved February 14, 2006, from *www.joe.org.joe/2002october/iw4.shtml*

Greenberg, P. (1989). Parents as partners in young children's development and education: A new American fad? Why does it matter? *Young Children, 44*(4), 61–75.

Greenberger, R. S. (2002, June 28). Supreme Court expands right to drug-test students. The *Wall Street Journal, 239*(126) p. 4.

Greene, B. (2000). *The elegant universe.* New York: Vintage Books.

Greenleaf, B. (1978). *Children through the ages: History of childhood.* New York: McGraw-Hill.

Greenspan, S. (2002, January). Emotional origins of intelligence. Special presentation. Retrieved February 5, 2002, from *www.lcweb.loc.gov/loc/brain/emotion/Greenspan.html*

Grissom, C. E. (1971). Listening beyond words: Learning from parents in conferences. *Childhood Education 48*(3), 138–142.

Grossman, S. (1999, Fall). Examining the origin of our beliefs about parents. *Childhood Education, 76*(1), 24–27.

Gruenberg, B. C. (Ed.). (1927). *Outlines of child study.* New York: Macmillan.

Gruenberg, S. (1940). Parent education: 1930–1940. In W. B. Grave (Ed.), *Annals of the American Academy of*

Political and Social Sciences. Philadelphia: American Academy of Political and Social Sciences.

Gutek, G. L. (1968). *Pestalozzi and education.* New York: Random House.

Guterson, D. (1992). *Family matters: Why homeschooling makes sense.* New York: Harcourt Brace Jovanovich.

Guzick v. Drebus, 401 U.S. 948 (1971).

Hagans, K. B., & Case, J. (1988). *When your child has been molested: A parent's guide to healing and recovery.* Lexington, MA: Lexington Books.

Hale, J. E. (1994). *Unbank the fire: Visions for the education of African American children.* Baltimore: The Johns Hopkins University Press.

Hale-Benson, J. E. (1986). *Black children: Their roots, culture, and learning styles.* Baltimore: The Johns Hopkins University Press.

Hallahan, D. P., & Kaufman, J. M. (1997). *Exceptional learners: Introduction to special education* (7th ed.). Boston: Allyn & Bacon.

Hallahan, D. P., & Kauffman, J. M. (2006). *Exceptional learners: Introduction to special education* (10th ed.). Boston: Allyn & Bacon.

Halmhuber, N., & Beauvais, K. J. (2002). *Case studies with children and adolescents with special needs.* Boston: Allyn & Bacon.

Halperin, M. (1979). *Helping maltreated children: School and community involvement.* St. Louis, MO: C. V. Mosby.

Hamilton, L. R. (1989). Child maltreatment: Prevention and treatment. *Early Child Development and Care, 42,* 31–56.

Hamilton, M. E., Roach, M. A., & Riley, D. A. (2003). Moving toward family-centered early care and education. The past, the present, and a glimpse of the future. *Early Childhood Education Journal, 30*(4), 225–232.

Handel, G. (Ed.). (1988). *Childhood socialization.* New York: Aldine de Gruyter.

Hanson, R. A. (1975). Consistency and stability of home environmental measures related to IQ. *Child Development, 46*(2), 470–480.

Hauge, E. (1998). Promoting children's interests and rights in education. In A. Curtis (Ed.), *International Journal of Early Childhood: 50th anniversary issue OMEP, 30*(1), 52–55.

Hawes, J. M. (1991). *The children's rights movement.* Boston: Twayne.

Haynes, N. M., Ben-Avie, M., Squires, D. A., Howley, J. P., Negron, E. N., & Corbin, J. N. (Eds.). (1996). It takes a whole village: The SDP school. In J. P. Comer, N. M. Haynes, E. T. Joyner, & M. Ben-Avie (Eds.), *Rallying the whole village: The Comer process for reforming education* (pp. 42–71). New York: Teachers College Press.

Hazelwood School District v. Kuhlmeier, 484 U.S. 592 (1988).

Head Start Family Literacy Project. (2002). Federal definition of family literacy. Retrieved May 27, 2002, from *www.famlit.org/headstart/hsdefine.html*

Hedrich, V., & Jackson, C. (1977, July). Winning play at home base. *American Education, 13*(6), 27–30.

Helfer, R. E. (1975). *The diagnostic process and treatment programs.* Washington, DC: U.S. Department of Health, Education and Welfare.

Helfer, R. E., & Kempe, R. S. (Eds.). (1987). *The battered child* (4th ed.). Chicago: University of Chicago Press.

Helm, J., Huebner, A., & Long, B. (2000). Quiltmaking: Perfect project for preschool and primary. *Young Children, 5*(3), 44–49.

Helm, J. H., & Lang, J. (2003) Overcoming the ill effects of poverty. In C. Copple (Ed.), *A world of difference.* Washington DC: National Association for the Education of Young Children.

Henderson, A. T. (Ed.). (1987). *The evidence continues to grow.* Columbia, MD: National Committee for Citizens in Education.

Henderson, A. T., & Berla, N. (1994). *A new generation of evidence. The family is critical to student achievement.* Washington, DC: National Committee for Citizens in Education.

Hess, R. D., & Holloway, S. D. (1984). Family and school as educational institutions. In R. D. Parke, R. N. Emde, H. P. McAdoo, & G. P. Sackett (Eds.), *Review of child development research: Vol. 7. The family.* Chicago: University of Chicago Press.

Heward, W. L. (1992). *Exceptional children: Introduction to special education.* (4th ed.). Upper Saddle River, NJ: Merrill/Prentice Hall.

Heward, W. L. (2006). *Exceptional children: An introduction to special education* (8th ed.). Upper Saddle River, NJ: Merrill/Prentice Hall.

Heward, W. L., & Orlansky, M. D. (1988). *Exceptional children: An introductory survey of special education* (3rd ed.). Upper Saddle River, NJ: Merrill/Prentice Hall.

Hewett, V. M. (2001, Winter). Examining the Reggio Emilia approach to early childhood education. *Early Childhood Education Journal, 28*(4), 95–99.

Hildago, N. (1994). Profile of a Puerto Rican family's support for school achievement. *Equity and Choice 10*(2), 14–22.

Hill, R. (1960). The American family today. In E. Ginsberg (Ed.), *The nation's children.* New York: Columbia University Press.

Hill, R. B. (1992). Dispelling myths and building on strengths: Supporting African American families. *Family Resource Coalition Report, 12*(1), 3–5.

Hodapp, A. F., & Hodapp, J. B. (1992). Homework: Making it work. *Intervention in School and Clinic, 27*(4), 233–235.

Hodges, J. (1996). The natural history of early non-attachment. In B. Bernstein & J. Brannen (Eds.), *Children, research and policy: Essays for Barbara Tizard.* London: Taylor & Francis.

Holland, G. (2002, June 28). Students who compete subject to drug testing. *Rocky Mountain News,* p. 2A.

Holmes, S. (1982). Parents Anonymous: A treatment method for child abuse. In S. Antler (Ed.), *Child abuse and child protection.* Silver Springs, MD: National Association of Social Workers.

Holzberg, R., & Walsh-Burton, S. (Eds.). (1996). *The parental voice.* Springfield, IL: Charles C. Thomas.

Hong, E., & Milgram, R. M. (2000). *Homework: Motivation and learning preference.* Westport, CT: Bergin & Garvey.

Honig, A. S. (1979). *Parent involvement in early childhood education.* Washington, DC: National Association for the Education of Young Children.

Horn, W. F. (1997, July, August). You've come a long way, daddy. *Policy Review,* No. 84, 24–30.

Horton, C. B., & Cruise, T. K. (2001). *Child abuse and neglect.* New York: Guilford Press.

Howe, W. J. (1988). Education and demographics: How do they affect unemployment rates? *Monthly Labor Review, 111*(1), 3–9.

Hunt, D. (1970). *Parents and children in history.* New York: Basic Books.

Hunt, J. M. (1961). *Intelligence and experience.* New York: Wiley.

Hurd, T. L., Lerner, R. M., & Barton, C. E. (1999). Integrated services: Expanding partnerships to meet the needs of today's children and families. *Young Children, 54*(2), 74–80.

Hyde, D. (1992). School-parent collaboration results in academic achievement. *NASSP Bulletin, 76*(543), 39–42.

Hymes, J. L., Jr. (1974). *Effective home-school relations.* Sierra Madre: Southern California Association for the Education of Young Children.

Hymes, J. L., Jr. (1987). *Early childhood education: The year in review: A look at 1986.* Carmel, CA: Hacienda Press.

IEP Process. (2006). Family and Advocates Partnership of Education Project (FAPE). Minneapolis, MN: Pacer Center.

Imber, M., & van Geel, T. (2000). *Education law* (2nd ed.). Mahwah, NJ: Erlbaum.

Ingraham v. Wright, 430 U.S. 651 (1977).

Institute for Responsive Education. (2006). IRE: Connecting school, family and community. Retrieved April 17, 2006, from *www.responsiveeducation.org*

International Bullying Prevention Association. (2006). *Our mission.* Retrieved August 26, 2006, from *stopbullyingworld.com/*

Irby v. State of Texas, 751 S.W.2d 670 (p. 1002) [Tex. Ct. App.] 1988).

Iverson, T. J., & Segal, M. (1990). *Child abuse and neglect: An information and reference guide.* New York: Garland.

Jablow, M. M. (1982). *Cara: Growing with a retarded child.* Philadelphia: Temple University Press.

Jackson, B. L., & Cooper, B. S. (1992). Involving parents in improving urban schools. *NAASP Bulletin, 76*(543), 30–38.

Jacobson, S. W., & Frye, K. F. (1991). Effect of maternal social support on attachment: Experimental evidence. *Child Development, 62*(3), 572–582.

Jayson, S. (2005). Feds: 1.5 million babies born to unwed moms in '04. Retrieved February 15, 2006, from *www.futureofchildren.org/newsletter2861/newsletter_show.htm?doc_id=313009*

John, R. (1988). The Native American family. In C. H. Mindel, R. W. Habenstein, & R. Wright, Jr. (Eds.), *Ethnic families in America* (3rd ed.). New York: Elsevier.

Johnston, J. H. (1990). *The new American family and the school.* National Middle School Association. Macon, GA: Panaprint.

Jones, L., & Finkelhor, D. (2001, January). The decline in child sexual abuse cases. *Juvenile Justice Bulletin.* Washington, DC: Office of Juvenile Justice and Delinquency Prevention.

Justice, B., & Justice, R. (1990). *The abusing family.* New York: Plenum Press.

Kagan, S. L., & Cohen, N. E. (Eds.). (1996). *Reinventing early care & education: A vision for a quality system.* San Francisco: Jossey-Bass.

Kagan, S. L., Moore, E., & Bredekamp, S. (Eds.). (1995). National Education Goals Panel. *Reconsidering children's early development and learning: Toward common views and vocabulary.* Washington, DC: U.S. Government Printing Office.

Kagan, S. L., & Zigler, E. F. (1987). *Early schooling.* New Haven: Yale University Press.

Kamii, C. (1985a). Leading primary education toward excellence: Beyond worksheets and drills. *Young Children, 40*(6), 3–9.

Kamii, C. (1985b). *Young children reinvent arithmetic.* New York: Teachers College Press.

Kaplan, G. P., Van Valey, L., & Associates. (1980). *Census '80: Continuing the factfinder tradition.* U.S. Bureau of the Census. Washington, DC: U.S. Government Printing Office.

Kaplan-Leiserson, E. (2002). Education evolution: How many other institutions look exactly as they did 40 years ago? *T&D, 56*(4), 16–18.

Karnes, F. A., & Marquardt, R. (1997, February). Know your legal rights in gifted education. Reston, VA: The ERIC Clearinghouse on Disabilities and Gifted Education, The Council for Exceptional Children.

Karoly, L. A., Kilburn, R., & Cannon, J. (2005). *Early childhood interventions: Proven results, future promise.* Santa Monica, CA: Rand Books & Publication.

Karr-Morse, R., & Wiley, M. S. (1997). *Ghosts from the nursery: Tracing the roots of violence.* New York: Atlantic Monthly Press.

Katz. L. G. (n.d.). *Clearinghouse on early education and parenting.* The project approach catalog. The importance of projects. Retrieved April 2, 2006, from *ceep.crc.ululc.edu eecearchive/books/projappl/ initial.html# incorporating*

Kaufman, H. O. (2001, July). Skills for working with all families. *Young Children 56*(4), 81–83.

Kawin, E. (1970). *A manual for group leaders and participants.* Lafayette, IN: Purdue University.

Kearns, P. (Ed.). (1980). *Your child's right for a free public education: Parent's handbook.* Topeka: Kansas Association for Children with Learning Disabilities.

Kellaghan, T., Sloane, K., Alvarez, B., & Bloom, B. S. (1993). *The home environment and school learning: Promoting parental involvement in the education of children.* San Francisco: Jossey-Bass.

Keller, H. (1957). *The open door.* Garden City, NY: Doubleday.

Keller, H. (1991). *The story of my life: With her letters (1887–1901) and supplementary account of her education including passages from the reports and letters of her teacher, Anne Mansfield Sullivan.* CA: Temecula American Biography Series, Reprint Services Co.

Kelley, M. L. (1990). *School-home notes: Promoting children's classroom success.* New York: Guilford Press.

Kelly, P. (1995). *Developing healthy stepfamilies: Twenty families tell their stories.* New York: Haworth Press.

Kempe, C. H., & Kempe, R. (1984). *The common secret: Sexual abuse of children and adults.* San Francisco: W. H. Freeman.

Kempe, C. H., Silverman, F. N., Steele, B. F., Droegemueller, W., & Silver, H. (1962). The battered-child syndrome. *Journal of the American Medical Association, 181,* 17–24.

Kent, M. M., & Mather, M. (2002, December). What drives U.S. population growth? *Population Bulletin, 57*(6).

Kent, M. M., Pollard, K. M., Haaga, J., & Mather, M. (2001, June). First glimpses from the 2000 U.S. census. *Population Bulletin 56*(2), 3–8.

Kids Count. (2001, May 14). Promising progress yet troubling trends face kids in the new millennium. Retrieved April 2, 2002, from *www.accf.org/ kidscount/Kc2001/kc2001_press.htm*

Kids Count. (2004). Kids Count state-level data outline: Children in povety. Retrieved September 2, 2006, from *www.aecf.org*

Kids Health. (2006). Internet safety. Retrieved August 27, 2006, from *kidshealth.org/kid/*

Kierstead, F. D., & Wagner, P. A., Jr. (1993). *The ethical, legal, and multicultural foundations of teaching.* Madison, WI: Brown & Benchmark.

King, C. E. (1962). *The sociology of small groups.* New York: Pageant Press.

Kirk, S. A. (1989). *Educating exceptional children* (5th ed.). Boston: Houghton Mifflin.

Klass, C., Pettinelli, D., & Wilson, M. (1993). Home visiting: Building linkages. Personal correspondence.

Klaus, M. H., & Kennell, J. S. (1982). *Parent–infant bonding.* St. Louis, MO: C. V. Mosby.

Klein, T., Bittel, C., & Molnar, J. (1993). No place to call home: Supporting the needs of homeless children in the early childhood classroom. *Young Children, 48*(6), 22–31.

Knapp, P. A., & Deluty, R. H. (1989). Relative effectiveness of two behavioral parent training programs. *Journal of Clinical Child Psychology, 18,* 314–322.

Knowles, J. G. (1989, January). Cooperating with home school parents: A new agenda for public schools? *Urban Education, 23*(4), 392–411.

Koch, P. K., & McDonough, M. (1999, March). Improving parent–teacher conferences through collaborative conversations. *Young Children 54*(2), 11–15.

Kontos, S. (1992). The role of continuity and context in children's relationships with nonparental adults. In R. C. Pianta (Ed.), *Beyond the parent: The role of other adults in children's lives.* San Francisco: Jossey-Bass.

Kozol, J. (1991). *Savage inequalities: Children in American schools.* New York: Crown.

Kraizer, S., Witte, S. S., & Fryer, G. E., Jr. (1989, September–October). Child sexual abuse prevention programs: What makes them effective in protecting children? *Children Today,* 23–27.

Krall, C. M., & Jalongo, M. R. (1998–1999). Creating a caring community in classrooms. *Childhood Education, 75*(2), 83–89.

Kristensen, N., & Billman, J. (1987). Supporting parents and young children. *Childhood Education, 63*(4), 276–282.

Krugman, R. D. (1986). Recognition of sexual abuse in children. *Pediatrics in Review 8*(1), 25–30.

Krugman, R. D. (1993). Universal home visiting: A recommendation from the U.S. Advisory Board on Child Abuse and Neglect. *The Future of Children, 3*(3), 185–201.

Krugman, R. D., & Krugman, M. K. (1984). Emotional abuse in the classroom. *American Journal of Diseases of Children, 138,* 284–286.

Kruse, T. (2006). Classroom corner—Partnerships with parents. *High Scope Resource, 25*(1), 26–27.

Kuhl, P. K. (1996). How babies map their native languages. In Education Commission of the States, *Bridging the gap between neuroscience and education.* Denver, CO: Author.

Kullen, A. S. (1994). *The peopling of America: A timeline of events that helped shape our nation.* Beltsville, MD: Americans All: The Portfolio Project.

LaConte, R. T. (1981). *Homework as a learning experience.* Washington, DC: National Education Association of the United States.

Lally, J. R. (2001). Infant care in the United States and how the Italian experience can help. In L. Gandini & C. P. Edwards (Eds.), *Bambini: The Italian approach to infant/toddler care.* New York: Teachers College Press.

Lamb, M. E. (Ed.). (1997). *The role of the father in child development.* New York: Wiley.

Lamison-White, L. (1997, September). Poverty in the United States, 1996. *Current Population Reports: Consumer Income.* (P60–198). Washington, DC: Bureau of the Census.

LaMorte, M. W. (2001). *School law: Cases and concepts* (7th ed.). Boston: Allyn & Bacon.

Lamson, P. A. (1992). Home schooling: A choice the Cupertino district supports. *The School Administrator, 49*(1), 26–27.

Lane, J., Kesker, E. E., Ross, C., et al. (2005). The effectiveness of Early Head Start for 3 year old children and their parents. *Developmental Psychology, 41*(6), 885–902.

Language and Orientation Resource Center. (1981). *Indochinese students in U.S. schools: A guide for administrators.* Washington, DC: Center for Applied Linguistics.

Larner, M. (1996). Parents' perspective on quality in early care and education. In S. L. Kagan & N. E. Cohen (Eds.), *Reinventing early care and education: A vision for a quality system.* San Francisco: Jossey-Bass.

Lazar, I. (1983). Discussion and implications of the findings. In Consortium of Longitudinal Studies, *As the twig is bent.* Hillsdale, NJ: Erlbaum.

Lazar, I., Darlington, R., Murray, H., Royce, J., & Snipper, A. (1982). Lasting effects of early education: A report from the Consortium for Longitudinal Studies. *Monographs of the Society for Research in Child Development, 47*(2–3).

Lazoritz, S. (1990). Whatever happened to Mary Ellen? *Child Abuse and Neglect, 14*(2), 143–149.

LeDoux, J. (1996, September). *Response. Bridging the gap between neuroscience and education.* Denver, CO: Education Commission of the States.

Lee, S. M. (1998, June). Asian Americans: Diverse and growing. *Population Bulletin, 53*(2).

Leipzig, J. (1987). Parents as partners. *Day Care and Early Education, 15*(2), 36–37.

Leon, K., & Cole, K. (March, 2004). Helping children understand divorce. University of Missouri Extension retrieved February 13, 2006, from *muextension.missouri.edu/xplor/hesguide/humanrel/gh600.htm*

Lerner, J., Mardell-Czudnowski, C., & Goldenberg, D. (1987). *Special education for the early childhood years.* Upper Saddle River, NJ: Prentice Hall.

Lester, B. M., Arria, A., Derauf, C., LaGasse, L., Newman, E., Shah, R., Steward, S., & Wouldes, T. (2006). Methamphetamine exposure. A rural early intervention challenge. *Zero to Three* (March), 30–36.

Lester, B. M., & Tronick, E. Z. (2004). History and description of the neonatal intensive care unit network. *Pediatrics, 113*(3), 634–640.

Levenstein, P. (1988). *Messages from home: The mother-child program.* Columbus: Ohio State University Press.

Levenstein, P., Levenstein, S., & Oliver, D. (2002). First grade school readiness of former child participants in a South Carolina replication of the Parent-Child Home Program. *Journal of Applied Developmental Psychology, 23*(3), 331–354.

Levenstein, P., Levenstein, S., Shiminski, J. A., & Stolzberg, J. E. (1998). Long-term impact of a verbal interaction program for at-risk toddlers: An exploratory study of high school outcomes in a replication of the mother-child home program. *Journal of Applied Developmental Psychology, 19*(2), 267–285.

Levine, J. A., Murphy, D. T., & Wilson, S. (1993). *Getting men involved: Strategies for early childhood programs.* New York: Scholastic.

Levine, J. A., & Pittinsky, T. L. (1997). *Working fathers: New strategies for balancing work and family.* Reading, MA: Addison-Wesley.

Levine, M., & Levine, A. (1992). *Helping children: A social history.* New York: Oxford University Press.

Levit, E. M., Terman, D. L., & Behrman, R. E. (1997). Children and poverty: Analysis and recommendations. *The Future of Children: Children and Poverty* 7(2), 40–54.

Lewis, J. K. (1992). Death and divorce: Helping students cope in single-parent families. *NASSP Bulletin, 76*(543), 55–60.

Lichter, D. T., & Crowley, M. L. (2002). *Poverty in America: Beyond welfare reform.* Washington, DC: Population Reference Bureau.

Lindsey, R. B., Roberts, L. M., & Campbelljones, F. (2005). Culturally proficient school. Thousand Oaks, CA: Corwin Press.

Lines, P. (1991). Home instruction: The size and growth of the movement. In J. Van Galen & M. A. Pitman (Eds.), *Home schooling: Political, historical, and pedagogical perspective* (pp. 9–42). Norwood, NJ: Ablex.

Lines, P. (1996). *Homeschooling*. Washington, DC: Office of Educational Research and Improvement, U.S. Department of Education. (ERIC Document Reproduction Service No. ED965033)

Lines, P. M. (1982a). *Compulsory education laws and their impact on public and private education.* Denver, CO: Education Commission of the States.

Liontos, L. B. (1992). *At risk families and schools: Becoming partners.* Eugene, OR: ERIC Clearinghouse on Education.

Lipsky, D. K., & Gartner, A. (1989). Overcoming school failure: A vision for the future. In F. J. Macchiarola & A. Gartner (Eds.), *Caring for America's children, 37*(2). New York: The Academy of Political Science.

Little Soldier, L. (1985). To soar with the eagles: Enculturation and acculturation of Indian children. *Childhood Education, 62*(2), 185–191.

Locke, J. (1989). *Some thoughts concerning education* (J. W. Yolton & J. S. Yolton, Eds.). Oxford: Clarendon.

Lombardi, J. (1992). Beyond transition: Ensuring continuity in early childhood services. *ERIC Digest.* Urbana, IL: ERIC Clearinghouse on Elementary and Early Childhood Education (ED345867).

Lorence, B. W. (1974). Parents and children in eighteenth century Europe. *History of Childhood Quarterly: The Journal of Psychohistory, 2*(1), 1–30.

Loucks, H. (1992). Increasing parent/family involvement: Ten ideas that work. *NASSP Bulletin, 76*(543), 19–23.

Love, J. M., Schochet, P. Z., & Meckstrom, A. (1996). *Are they in any real danger? Children's well-being.* Princeton, NJ: Mathematica Policy Research.

Lowenthal, B. (2001). *Abuse and neglect.* Baltimore: Brookes.

Lyons, P., Robbins, A., & Smith, A. (1983). *Involving parents in schools: A handbook for participation.* Ypsilanti, MI: High/Scope Press.

Macchiarola, F. J., & Gartner, A. (Eds.). (1989). *Caring for America's children.* 37(2). New York: The Academy of Political Science.

Malaguzzi, L. (1993, November). For an education based on relationships. *Young Children, 49*(1), 9–12.

Manning, B. H. (1985). Conducting a worthwhile parent-teacher conference. *Education, 105*(4), 342–348.

Manning, D. T., & Wootten, M. D. (1987). What stepparents perceive schools should know about blended families. *The Clearing House, 60*(5), 230–235.

Manning, M. L. (1992). Parent education programs at the middle level. *NASSP Bulletin, 76*(543), 24–29.

Mantovani, S. (2001). Infant-toddler centers in Italy today: Tradition and Innovation. In L. Gandini & C. P. Edwards (Eds.), *Bambini: The Italian approach to infant/toddler care.* New York: Teachers College Press.

Margolis, H., & Brannigan, G. G. (1986). Relating to angry parents. *Academic Therapy, 21*(3), 343–346.

Markow, D., & Martin, S. (2005). *The MetLife survey of the American teacher.* Retrieved March 26, 2006, from *www.harrisinteractive.com*

Marsh, D. (1992). Enhancing instructional leadership: Lessons from the California School Leadership Academy. *Education & Urban Society, 24*(3), 386–409.

Martin, J. A., Hamilton, B. E., Sutton, P. D., Ventura S. J., Menacker, P. H., & Munson, M. L., Division of Vital Statistics. (2005, September 8). *Births: Final data for 2003, 58*(2) Washington DC: U.S. Department of Health and Human Services, Centers for Disease Control and Prevention, National Center for Health Statistics. Retrieved April 23, 2006, from *www.childstats.gov/americaschildren/index/asp*

Martin, P., & Widgren, J. (2002, March). International migration: Facing the challenge. *Population Bulletin,* 57(1). Washington, DC: Population Reference Bureau.

Marvasti, A., & McKinney, K. D. (2004). *Middle eastern lives in America.* Lanham, MD: Rowman & Littlefield.

Maslach, C. (1982). *Burnout: The cost of caring.* Upper Saddle River, NJ: Prentice Hall.

Maslow, A. H. (1968). *Toward a psychology of being.* Princeton, NJ: D. Norstrand.

Mauldin, T. A. (1990). Women who remain above the poverty level in divorce: Implications for family policy. *Family Relations* 39(2), 141–146.

Mayberry, M. (1989). Home-based education in the United States: Demographics, motivations, and educational implications. *Educational Review, 41*(2), 171–180.

Maynard, R. A. (Ed.). (1997). *Kids having kids: Economic costs and social consequences of teen pregnancy.* Washington, DC: Urban Institute Press.

McCallister, C., Wilson, P., Green, B., & Baldwin, J. (2005). "Come take a walk": Listening to Early Head Start parents on school readiness as a matter of child, family and community health. *American Journal of Public Health, 95*(4), 617–626.

McCormick, L., & Holden, R. (1992). Homeless children: A special challenge. *Young Children, 47*(6), 61–67.

McLean Hospital. (2000, December). McLean researchers document brain damage linked to child abuse and neglect. Retrieved May 20, 2002, from *www.mcleanhospital.org/PublicAffairs/20001214_child_abuse.htm*

McLearn, K. T., Davis, K., Schoen, C., & Parker, S. (1998). Listening to parents: A national survey of parents with young children. (Reprinted from the *Archives of Pediatrics and Adolescent Medicine, 152*, March 1998.) New York: The Commonwealth Fund.

Mead, M., & Wolfenstein, M. (1963). *Childhood in contemporary cultures.* Chicago: University of Chicago Press.

Meadows, B. J., & Saltzman, M. (2000). *Building school communities: Strategies for leaders.* Golden, CO: Fulcrum Resources.

MELD. (1988). *MELD's Young Moms (MYM): Information and support for teen mothers.* Minneapolis, MN: Author.

MELD. (1990). *Blending information and support for parents.* Minneapolis, MN: Author.

MELD. (2006). *What is MELD?* Retrieved May 8, 2006, from *www.meld.org*

Mendel, D. (2004). Leave no parent behind. *Early Childhood.* (November), 8–10.

Meyer v. Nebraska, 262 U.S. 390, 399 (1923).

Meyerhoff, M. K., & White, B. L. (1986). New parents as teachers. *Educational Leadership, 44*(3), 42–46.

Meyers, K., & Pawlas, G. (1989). Simple steps assure parent-teacher conference success. *Instructor, 99*(2), 66–67.

Michel, G. J. (1996). *Building schools: The new school and community relations.* Lancaster, PA: Technomic.

Middlekauff, R. (1969). Education in colonial America. In J. A. Johnson, H. W. Collins, V. L. Dupuis, & J. H. Johansen (Eds.), *Foundations of American education: Readings.* Boston: Allyn & Bacon.

Miller v. California, 413 U.S. 15 (1973).

Miller, S., Wackman, S., Nunnally, E., & Miller, P. (1988). *Connecting with self and others.* Littleton, CO: Interpersonal Communication Programs.

Minneapolis Public Schools. (2006). School Readiness. Retrieved April 17, 2006, from *schoolchoice.mpls.k12.mn.us/School_Readiness.html*

Mischley, M., Stacy, E. W., Mischley, L., & Dush, D. (1985). A parent education project for low income families. *Prevention in Human Services, 3,* 45–57.

Missouri Department of Elementary and Secondary Education (1999). *School entry assessment project.* Jefferson City, MO: Author.

Moles, O. C. (1987). Who wants parent involvement? Interest, skills, and opportunities among parents and educators. *Education and Urban Society, 19*(2), 137–145.

Moles, O. C. (Ed.). (1996a). *Reaching all families: Creating family-friendly schools.* Washington, DC: U.S. Department of Education, Office of Educational Research and Improvement.

Moles, O. C. (1996b). New national directions in research and policy. In A. Booth & J. F. Dunn (Eds.), *School–family links: How do they affect educational outcomes?* Mahwah, NJ: Erlbaum.

Moody, E. (1775/1972). The school of good manners: Composed for the help of parents in teaching children how to behave during their minority. In D. J. Rothman & S. M. Rothman (Eds.), *The colonial American family: Collected essays.* New York: Arno Press.

Moore, R. L. (1974). Justification without joy: Psychohistorical reflections on John Wesley's childhood and conversion. *History of Childhood Quarterly: The Journal of Psychohistory, 1*(3), 31–52.

Mork, O. (1998). Playing processes—Art processes. In A. Curtis (Ed.), *International Journal of Early Childhood: 50th Anniversary Issue OMEP 30*(1), 20–26.

Morrison, G. S. (1991). *Early childhood education today* (5th ed.). New York: Macmillan.

MSU Extension. (1999). Group effectiveness: Under standing group member roles. Retrieved August 27, 2002, from *www.msue.msu.edu/msue/imp/modii/ii719202.html*

Mullins, J. B. (1987). Authentic voices from parents of exceptional children. *Family Relations, 36*(1), 30–33.

Nagi, S. Z. (1977). *Child maltreatment in the United States.* New York: Columbia University Press.

Nagle v. Olin, 415 N.E.2d 279 (Ohio, 1980).

Napier, R. W., & Gershenfeld, M. K. (1981). *Groups, theory, and experience* (2nd ed.). Boston: Houghton Mifflin.

Natale, J. A. (1995, July). Home, but not alone: Home schoolers are linking up with e-mail and on-line classes. *American School Board Journal 182*(7), 34–36.

National Association for the Education of Young Childen (2004). NAEYC affiliate public policy tool kit, 2004. Retrieved September 1, 2006, from *www.naeyc.org*

National Association for the Education of Young Children (NAEYC) & National Association of Early Childhood Specialists in State Departments of Education. (1991). Guidelines for appropriate curriculum content and assessment in programs serving children ages 3 through 8. *Young Children, 46*(3), 21–38.

National Association of Elementary School Principals. (1990). *Early childhood education and the elementary school principal: Standards for quality programs for young children.* Alexandria, VA: Author.

National Association of Elementary School Principals. (1994). *Best ideas from America's blue ribbon schools.* Thousand Oaks, CA: Corwin Press.

National Association of State Boards of Education (NASBE). (1988). *Right from the start.* Alexandria, VA: Author.

National Association of State Boards of Education. (1991). *Caring communities: Supporting young children and families.* Alexandria, VA: Author.

National Association of State Boards of Education. (2001). *NASBE Projects: Early Childhood Education Network.* Alexandria, VA: NASBE.

National Association of State Boards of Education. (2006). NASBE awarded grant to replicate successful early childhood learning strategies. Alexandria, VA: NASBE.

National Association of State Directors of Special Education. (1997). *1997 amendments to the Individuals with Disabilities Education Act.* Washington, DC: Author.

National Campaign to Prevent Teen Pregnancy. (2002). Fast Facts: Pregnancy among sexually experienced teens, aged 15–19. Washington, DC: Author.

National Center on Child Fatality Review. (2005). A "How-To" guide for child fatality review teams. Retrieved August 25, 2006, from *www.icanncfr.org/documents/How_To.pdf*

National Center for Children in Poverty. (2006a). Parent's low education leads to low income, despite full employment. Retrieved September 2, 2006, from *www.nccp.org/fact.html*

National Center for Children in Poverty. (2006b). Basic facts about low income children: Birth to age 18. Retrieved September 2, 2006, from *www.nccp.org/fac.html*

National Center for Children in Poverty. (2006c). Basic facts about low income on children in the U.S. Retrieved September 2, 2006, from *www.nccp.org/fact.html*

National Center for Early Development & Learning. (1997). *Early childhood research and policy briefs, 1*(1). Chapel Hill, NC: Frank Porter Graham Child Development Center.

National Center for Education Statistics. (2001, March). National Assessment of Educational Progress History—Time spent on homework. Retrieved June 21, 2002, from *nces.ed.gov/nationsreportcard/ushistory/findhomework.asp*

National Center for Education Statistics. (2002). Children's reading and mathematics achievement in kindergarten and first grade. Retrieved May 25, 2002, from *nces.ed.gov/pubs2002/kindergarten/5.asp?nav=1*

National Center for Educational Statistics. (2003). National Household Education Surveys Program. Homeschooling in the U.S.

National Center for Education Statistics. (2007). 1.1 million homeschooled students in the United States in 2003. Retrieved January 7, 2007, from *http://nces.ed.gov/nhes/homeschool*

National Center for Family Literacy. (2002). *Family and child education (FACE).* Retrieved January 11, 2003, from *www.famlit.org/faqs/faqface.html*

National Center for Family Literacy. (2005). *Family literacy programs targeting Hispanics prove successful.* Louisville KY: Author.

National Center on Child Abuse and Neglect (NCCAN). (2001). Child abuse and neglect state statutes elements. Definitions of child abuse and neglect. Retrieved May 20, 2002, from *www.calib.com/nccanch/pubs/stats01/define/indes.cfm*

National Center on Fathers and Families. (2002). *Fathering indicators framework; a tool for quantitative and qualitative analysis.* Philadelphia: Author.

National Center on Shaken Baby Syndrome. (2006). Prevention and legislation. Retrieved August 29, 2006, from *www.dontshake.com*

National Child Abuse and Neglect Data System (NCANDS). (2002, April). *Summary of key findings from calendar year 2000.* Washington, DC: U.S. Department of Health and Human Services, Children's Bureau, Administration on Children, Youth and Families, National Clearinghouse on Child Abuse and Neglect Information. Retrieved July 9, 2002, from *www.calib.com/nccanch/pubs/factsheets/canstats.cfm*

National Child Abuse Coalition. (1991). *Corporal punishment.* Washington, DC: Author.

National Commission on Children. (1991). *Beyond rhetoric: A new American agenda for children and families.* Washington, DC: Author.

National Commission on Excellence in Education. (1983). *A nation at risk: The imperative for educational reform.* Washington, DC: U.S. Department of Education.

National Council on Disability. (2002, July). Individuals with disabilities education act reauthorization: Where do we really stand? Retrieved August 2, 2002, from *www.ncd.gov/newsroom/publications/synthesis_07–05–02.html*

National Dissemination Association & National Diffusion Network. (1993). *Educational programs that work.* Longmont, CO: Sopris West.

National Education Goals Panel. (1991). *The national education goals report: Building a nation of learners, executive summary.* Washington, DC: Author.

National Information Center for Children and Youth with Disabilities. (1997). *NICHCY documents on disabilities.* Washington, DC: Author.

National Information Center for Children and Youth with Disabilities. (1998). IDEA amendments of 1997. *NICHCY News Digest 26* (Rev. ed.). Washington, DC: Author.

National Information Center for Children and Youth with Disabilities. (2000, February). Reading and learning disabilities. Retrieved August 7, 2002, from *www.nichy.org/pubs/factshe/fs17text.htm*

National Information Center for Children and Youth with Disabilities. (2001, December). Attention deficit/hyperactivity disorder (AD/HD). Retrieved August 7, 2002, from *www.nichcy.org/pubs/factshe/ fs19txt.htm*

National Information Center for Children and Youth with Disabilities. (2002a, January). Mental retardation. Retrieved August 7, 2002, from *www.nichcy.org/pubs/factshe/fa8txt.htm*

National Information Center for Children and Youth with Disabilities. (2002b, April). Learning disabilites. Retrieved August 7, 2002, from *www.nichcy.org/pubs/factshe/fs7txt.htm*

National Information Center for Children and Youth with Disabilities, Early Childhood Research Network. (1996). Characteristics of infant child care: Factors contributing to positive caregiving. *Early Childhood Research Quarterly, 11,* 269–306.

National Institute of Neurological Disorders and Stroke. (2006). *What is Tourette syndrome?* Retrieved August 18, 2006, from *www.hinds.nih.gov.disorders/tourette/detail_tourette.htm*

National Law Center on Homelessness & Poverty. (2002a). Homelessness and poverty in America. Retrieved March 18, 2002, from *www.nlchp.org/FA_HAPIA/*

National Law Center on Homelessness & Poverty. (2002b). *McKinney-Vento 2001 reauthorization—at a glance.* Retrieved March 18, 2002, from *www.nlchp.org/FA_Education/mckinneyGlance.cfm*

National Law Center on Homelessness and Poverty. (2004, July). Key data concerning homeless persons in America. Retrieved September 3, 2006, from *www.nlchp.org*

National Reading Panel. (2000). *Teaching children to read: An evidence based assessment of the scientific research literature on reading and the implication for reading instruction reports of the subgroups.* Washington, DC: National Institute of Child Health and Human Development.

National Society for the Study of Education. (1929). *Twenty-eighth year book. Preschool and parent education (parts 1 and 2).* Bloomington, IL: Public School Publishing.

National Youth Violence Prevention Resource Center. (2006). Retrieved August 24, 2006, from *www.safeyouth.org/scripts/teens/bullying.asp*

New, R. S. (1999). Here, we call it "drop off and pickup": Transition to childcare, American-style. *Young Children, 54*(2), 34–35.

New Jersey State Federation. (1989, May). *CEC newsletter.* New Brunswick, NJ: Council for Exceptional Children.

New Jersey v. T. L. O., 469 U.S. 325 (1985).

Newman, F. (1996). Introduction. In Education Commission of the States, *Bridging the gap between neuroscience and education.* Denver, CO: Author.

Newman, L. (1996). Response. In Education Commission of the States, *Bridging the gap between neuroscience and education.* Denver, CO: Author.

Nimnicht, G. P., & Brown, E. (1972). The toy library: Parents and children learning with toys. *Young Children, 28*(2), 110–116.

Noller, P., & Taylor, R. (1989). Parent education and family relations. *Family Relations, 38*(2), 196–200.

Northwest EQUALS. (1988). *Family science.* Portland, OR: Portland State University.

Norton, A. J., & Glick, P. C. (1986). One parent families: A social and economic profile. *Family Relations, 35*(1), 9–17.

Nuñez, R.D. (1996). *The new poverty: Homeless families in America.* New York: Plenum Press.

Nuñez, R. D. (2004). A shelter is not a home . . . Or is it? Lessons from family homelessness in New York City. Retrieved November 30, 2006, from *www.homesforthehomeless.com*

O'Callaghan, J. B. (1993). *School-based collaboration with families.* San Francisco: Jossey-Bass.

O'Connell, M., & Bloom, D. E. (1987). *Juggling jobs and babies: America's child care challenge. Population Bulletin,* No. 12. Washington, DC: Population Reference Bureau.

Office of Civil Rights, U.S. Department of Education. (2007). How to file a discrimination complaint with the Office for Civil Rights. Retrieved January 10, 2007, from *www.ed.gov/about/offices/list/ocr/docs/howto.html*

Office of the Ombudsman (1998). *Information manual.* Retrieved June 29, 2002, from *www.ir/gov.ie/ombudsman/2362156.htm*

Olesen v. Board of Education of School District No. 228, 676 F. Supp. 820 D.C. N.D.III. (1987).

Osborn, A. F. (1957). *Applied imagination.* New York: Scribner's.

Osborn, D. K. (1991). *Early childhood education in historical perspective* (3rd ed.). Athens, GA: Education Associates. PL 94–142, Part B of the Education of All Handicapped Children Act, Title 20 of the United States Code, Sections 1400–1420. Regulations, Title 34 of the Code of Federal Regulations, Sections 300.1–300.754 and Appendix C, IEP Notice of Interpretation.

Osofsky, J. D., & Fenichel, E. (1996). *Islands of safety: Assessing and treating young victims of violence.* Washington, DC: Zero to Three.

Pacer Center (2006). *Family and advocates partnership for education project (FAPE). The IEP process.* Minneapolis MN: Author.

Packer, A., Hoffman, S., Bozler, B., & Bear, N. (1976). Home learning activities for children. In I. Gordon & W. F. Breivogel (Eds.), *Building effective home-school relationships.* Boston: Allyn & Bacon.

Palfrey, J., Bronson, M. B., Hauser-Cram, P., Warfield, M. E. (2002). *Beepers come of age. The Brookline early education project follow-up study.* Retrieved March 30, 2006, from *www.bc.edu/bc_org/avp/ soe/ beep/ bpmajorfindings.htm*

Papernow, P. (1998). *Becoming a stepfamily. Patterns of developent of remarried families.* Mahwah, NJ: Analytic Press.

Papernow, P. L. (1993). *Becoming a stepfamily.* San Francisco: Jossey-Bass.

Pardeck, J. T. (1989). Family therapy as a treatment approach to child maltreatment. *Early Child Development and Care, 42,* 151–157.

Parents Anonymous. (1985). *The program development manual.* Los Angeles: Author.

Parents Anonymous. (2006). Strengthening families around the world. Retrieved October 7, 2006, from *www.parents anonymous.org*

Parents as Teachers National Center. (2002). What's new. Retrieved September, 2002, from *www.patnc.org/ forpatprograms-whatsnew.asp*

Parents as Teachers National Center (2006). Fact sheet. Retrieved July 10, 2006, from *www.parentsasteach ers.org/site/pp.asp?c=eklRLcMZJxE&B=1802131*

Parks, C. C. (1982). *The siege: The first eight years of an autistic child with an epilogue, fifteen years after.* Boston: Little, Brown.

Paulu, N. (1995). *Helping your child with homework for parents of elementary and junior high school-aged children.* Washington, DC: Office of Educational Research and Improvement, U.S. Department of Education.

PEAK Parent Center. (1997). IDEA 97 and the tie to the general curriculum. Module 9–1. Colorado Springs, CO: Parent Education and Assistance for Kids (PEAK).

Pearl, P. (1988). Working with preschool-aged child abuse victims in group settings. *Child and Youth Care Quarterly, 17*(3), 185–194.

Pennsylvania Association for Retarded Children v. Commonwealth of Pennsylvania, 343 F. Supp. (E.D. Penn. 1972).

Pennsylvania Department of Public Instruction. (1935). *Parent education.* Bulletin 86. Harrisburg: Author.

Pestalozzi, F. J. (1915). *How Gertrude teaches her children.* London: Allen & Unwin.

Pestalozzi, F. J. (1951). *The education of man.* New York: Philosophical Library.

Piaget, J. (1976). *To understand is to invent.* New York: Penguin Books.

Pierce v. Society of Sisters of the Holy Name, 268 U.S. 510 (1925).

Pierson, D. E., Bronson, M. B., Dromey, E., Swartz, J. P., Tivnan, T., & Walker, D. K. (1983). The impact of early education: Measured by classroom observations and teacher ratings of children in kindergarten. *Evaluation Review,* 7(2), 191–216.

Pierson, D. E., Walker, D. K., & Tivnan, T. (1984). A school-based program from infancy to kindergarten for children and their parents. *The Personnel and Guidance Journal, 62*(8), 448–455.

Plato. (1953). *The dialogues of Plato* (4th ed., B. Jowett, Trans.). London: Oxford University Press. (Original work published 1871.)

Popkin, M. H. (2002). *Active parenting now.* Marietta, GA: Active Parenting. Retrieved September 12, 2002, from *www.activeparenting.com/xapn.htm*

Popp, J. (1987, October). Personal correspondence. *Revision winning play at first base.* Yakima, WA: Author.

Population Reference Bureau, AmeriStat. (2000). *The class of 2010: Nursery school enrollment soars.* Washington, DC: Author.

Population Reference Bureau, AmeriStat. (2002). Single mothers still a small fraction of the U.S. labor force. Retrieved March 16, 2002, from *www.prb.org/ AmeristatTemplate.cfm?Section=Labor_Employment& template=/Contentmanagement/ContentDispla y.cfn&ContentID=2731*

Portage Project Outreach. (2000). Portage Project of Cooperative Education Agency #5: Final Report. Portage, WI: Author.

Porter P. (December 5, 2003). Early Brain Development. Retrieved January 4, 2006, from *educarer.com/brain.htm*

Post-Kammer, P. (1988). Does Parents Anonymous reduce child abuse? *Education Digest, 54*(3), 33–39.

Potts, M. (1992, March). Strengths model. *National Center for Family Literacy, 4*(1), 5.

Powell, D. R. (1986). Parent education and support programs. *Young Children, 41*(3), 47–53.

Promising Practices Network (n.d.) Syracuse family development research program. Retrieved March 1, 2006, from *www.promisingpractices.net/program.asp? programid=133#overview*

Pruett, K. D. (1996). Child development: The difference a dad makes. *Family Resource Coalition Report, 15*(1), 8–10.

Puckett, M., Marshall, C. S., & Davis, R. (1999, Fall). Examining the emergence of brain development research: The promises and the perils. *Childhood Education, 74*(1), 8–12.

Radencich, M. C., & Schumm, J. S. (1996). *How to help your child with homework* (2nd ed.). Minneapolis, MN: Free Spirit.

Ramey, C. T., & Ramey, S. L. (1993). Home visiting programs and the health and development of young children. *The Future of Children: Home Visiting, 3*(3), 129–139.

Rauche-Elnekave, H. (1989). Advocacy and ombudswork for children: Implications of the Israeli experience. *Child Welfare, 68*(2), 101–112.

Ray, B. D., & Wartes, J. (1991). The academic achievement and affective development of home-schooled children. In H. Van Galen & M. A. Pitman (Eds.), *Home schooling: Political, historical, and pedagogical perspective* (pp. 43–62). Norwood, NJ: Ablex.

Reed, J. (1991). Grass roots school governance in Chicago. *National Civic Review, 80*(1), 41–45.

Reich, K., Culross, P. L., & Behrman, R. E. (2002, Summer/Fall). Children, youth, and gun violence: Analysis and recommendations. *The Future of Children: Children, Youth, and Gun Violence, 12*(2), 5–23.

Reinert, H. R. (1990). *Children in conflict: Educational strategies for the emotionally disturbed and behaviorally disordered* (3rd ed.). Upper Saddle River, NJ: Prentice Hall.

Reppucci, N. D., Britner, P. A., & Woolard, J. L. (1997). *Preventing child abuse and neglect through parent education.* Baltimore: Brookes.

Rich, D. (1988). *Megaskills: How families can help children succeed in school and beyond.* Boston: Houghton Mifflin.

Rich, D., & Mattox, B. (1977). *101 activities for building more effective school-community involvement.* Washington, DC: Home and School Institute.

Riggs, R. C. (1982). Incest: The school's role. *The Journal of School Health, 52,* 365–370.

Rigsby, L. C., Reynolds, M. C., & Wang, M. C. (Eds.). (1995). *School-community connections: Exploring issues for research and practice.* San Francisco: Jossey-Bass.

Rioux, J. W., & Berla, N. (1993). *Innovations in parent and family involvement.* Princeton, NJ: Eye on Education.

Rogers, C. (1983). *Freedom to learn for the '80s.* Upper Saddle River, NJ: Merrill/Prentice Hall.

Rogers, C., & Freiberg, H.J. (1994). *Freedom to learn* (3rd ed.). Upper Saddle River, NJ: Merrill/Prentice Hall.

Rogers, P., & O'Connor, R. E. (2003). How to build a better mother: A successful program prevents child abuse by teaching the art of being a mother. *People Weekly, 59*(15), 137.

Ronstrom, A. (1989). Sweden's children's ombudsman: A spokesperson for children. *Child Welfare, 68*(2), 123–128.

Rose, L. C., & Gallup, A. M. (2000). The 32nd annual Phi Delta Kappa/Gallup Poll of the public's attitudes toward the public schools. *Phi Delta Kappan.* Retrieved July 31, 2002, from *www.pdkintl.org/kappan/kpol0009.htm#2a*

Rose, L. C., & Gallup, A. M. (2001). The 33rd annual Phi Delta Kappa/Gallup Poll of the public's attitudes toward the public schools. *Phi Delta Kappan.* Retrieved July 31, 2002, from *www.pdkintl.org/kappan/k0109gal.htm*

Rose, L. C., & Gallup, A. M. (2005). The 37th annual Phi Delta Kappa/Gallup Poll of the public's attitudes toward the public schools. *Phi Delta Kappan.* Retrieved March 25, 2006, from *www.Pdkintl.org/kappan/k0509pol.htm*

Rose, L. C., Gallup, A. M., & Elam, S. M. (1997). The 29th annual Phi Delta Kappa/Gallup Poll of the public's attitudes toward public schools. *Phi Delta Kappan, 79*(1), 41–56.

Rosenblatt, P. C. (1994). *Metaphors of family systems theory: Toward new constructions.* New York: Guilford Press.

Rotter, J. C., & Robinson, E. H. (1986). *Parent-teacher conferencing: What research says to the teacher.* Washington, DC: National Education Association of the United States.

Rousseau, J. J. (1979). *Emile: Education* (A. Bloom, Trans.). New York: Basic Books. (Original work published 1762.)

Rutter, M. (1981). *Maternal deprivation reassessed.* Harmondsworth, England: Penguin Books.

Rutter, M. (1985). Family and school influences on cognitive development. *Journal of Child Psychology and Psychiatry, 26*(5), 683–704.

Ryan, G. (1989). Victim to victimizer: Re-thinking victim treatment. *Journal of Interpersonal Violence, 4*(3), 325–341.

Sandberg, D. N. (1987). *Chronic acting-out students and child abuse: A handbook for intervention.* Lexington, MA: Lexington Books.

Sanders, M. G. (1999). Schools' programs and progress in the National Network of Partnership Schools. *Journal of Educational Research, 92*(4), 220–229.

Save the Children. (2000). The history of children @risk. Retrieved June 29, 2002, from *www.reddbarna.no/english/children_at_risk/history/*

Schimmel, D., & Fischer, L. (1987). *Parents, schools and the law.* Columbia, MD: National Committee for Citizens in Education.

Schlossman, S. L. (1976). Before Home Start: Notes toward a history of parent education in America, 1897–1929. *Harvard Educational Review, 46*(3), 436–467.

Schorr, L. B., & Schorr, D. (1988). *Within our reach: Breaking the cycle of disadvantage.* New York: Doubleday.

Schweinhart, L. J., Barnes, H. V., & Weikart, D. P. (1993). *Significant benefits: The High/Scope Perry Preschool student through age 27.* Ypsilanti, MI: High/Scope Press.

Schweinhart, L. J., Montie, J., Xiang, Z., Barnett, W. S., Belfield, C. R., & Nores, M. (2005). Lifetime effects: The High/Scope Perry Preschool study through age 40. *Monographs of the High/Scope Educational Research Foundation 14.* Ypsilanti, MI: High/Scope Press.

Schweinhart, L. J., & Weikart, D. P. (1997). The High/Scope preschool curriculum study through 23. *Early Childhood Research Quarterly, 12*(2), 117–143.

Section 504 Regulations, Title 34 of the Federal Regulations, Sections 104.1–104.61, and Appendix A: Analysis of Final Regulations (29 U.S.C. § 794).

Seefeldt, C. (1985). Parent involvement: Support or stress. *Childhood Education, 62*(2), 98–102.

Seeley, D. S. (1989). A new paradigm for parent involvement. *Educational Leadership, 47*(2), 46–48.

Seligman, M. (2000). *Conducting effective conferences with parents of children with disabilities.* New York: Guilford Press.

Shapiro, I., & Greenstein, R. (1988). *Holes in the safety net.* Washington, DC: Center on Budget and Policy Priorities.

Shaw, D. S. (1992). The effects of divorce on children's adjustment. In M. E. Procidano & C. B. Fisher (Eds.), *Contemporary families: A handbook for school professionals.* New York: Teachers College Press.

Shearer, D., Billingsley, J., Frohman, A., Hilliard, J., Johnson, F., & Shearer, M. (1976). *Portage Project readings.* Portage, WI: Portage Project.

Shields, M. K., & Behrman, R. E. (2000). Children and computer technology: Analysis and recommendations. *The Future of Children: Children and Computer Technology, 10*(2), 4–30.

Shiono, P. H., & Quinn, L. S. (1994). Epidemiology of divorce. *The Future of Children: Children and Divorce, 4*(1), 15–28.

Shipman, V. C., Boroson, M., Bidgeman, B., Gart, J., & Mikovsky, M. (1976). *Disadvantaged children and their first school experiences.* Princeton, NJ: Educational Testing Service.

Shonkoff, J. P., & Phillips, D. H. (2000). *From neurons to neighborhoods: The science of Early Childhood Development.* Washington, DC: National Academy Press.

Shore, R. (1997). *Rethinking the brain.* New York: Families and Work Institute.

Sigel, I. E. (1971). Language and the disadvantaged: The distancing hypothesis. In C. S. Lavatelli (Ed.), *Language training in early childhood education.* Urbana: University of Illinois Press.

Silver, A. A., & Hagin, R. A. (2002). *Disorders of learning in childhood.* New York: Wiley.

Silver, H. K., & Kempe, C. H. (1959). Problems of parental criminal neglect and severe physical abuse of children. *American Journal of Diseases of Children, 95,* 528.

Silverman, F. (1953). Roentgen manifestations of unrecognized skeletal trauma in infants. *American Journal of Roentgenology, 69,* 413–427.

Silvern, S. B. (1988). Continuity/discontinuity between home and early childhood education environments. *The Elementary School Journal, 89*(2), 147–159.

Simmons, T., & Dye, J. L. (2003, October). *Grandparents living with grandchildren: 2000.* Washington, DC: U.S. Department of Commerce, Economics and Statistics Administration, U.S. Census Bureau.

Skeels, H. (1966). Adult status of children with contrasting early life experiences: A follow-up study. In *Monographs of the Society for Research in Child Development* (Vol. 31). Chicago: University of Chicago Press.

Skeels, H. M., & Dye, H. B. (1939). A study of the effects of differential stimulation on mentally retarded children. *Proceedings and Addresses of the American Association on Mental Deficiency, 44,* 114–136.

Smith, T. (2005, November/December). IDEA 2004: Another round in the reauthorization process. *Remedial and special education, 26*(6), 314–320.

Smith, V. (1986). Listening. In O. Hargie (Ed.), *A handbook of communication skills* (pp. 246–265). Washington Square: New York University Press.

Spidel, J. (1980, March). *Exceptional students in the regular classroom: How we help them learn.* Paper presented at Showcase Kansas, Wichita State University, Wichita, KS.

Spitz, R. A. (1945). Hospitalism: An inquiry into the genesis of psychiatric conditions in early childhood. In A. Freud et al. (Eds.), *The psychoanalytic study of the child* (Vol. 2). New York: International Universities Press.

Spitz, R. A. (1965). *The first year of life.* New York: International Universities Press.

Spock, B. (1957). *Baby and child care.* New York: Pocket Book.

Spodek, B. (Ed.). (1982). *Handbook of research on early childhood education.* New York: Free Press/Macmillan.

St. Pierre, R. G., Layzer, J. I., & Barnes, H. V. (1995). Two generation programs: Design, cost, and short-term effectiveness. *The Future of Children: Long-Term Outcomes of Early Childhood Programs* 5(3), 76–93.

Stahlman, B. R. (2002). Personal communication.

Stahlman, K. (2002). Personal communication.

State of Hawaii, Department of Health. (1997, October). *Innovations in American government recognizes Hawai'i Healthy Start for Program Excellence.* Honolulu: Author.

State v. Faith Baptist Church, 107 Neb. 802, N.W.2d 571 (1981).

State v. Shaver, 294 N.W.2d 883 (N.D. 1980).

Steele, B. F. (1986). Notes on the lasting effects of early child abuse throughout the life cycle. *Child Abuse and Neglect, 10,* 283–291.

Steele, B. F. (1987). C. Henry Kempe memorial lecture. *Child Abuse and Neglect, 11,* 313–318.

Stein, M. R. S., & Thorkildsen, R. J. (1999). *Parental involvement in education: Insights and applications from the research.* Bloomingham, IN: Phi Delta Kappa International.

Stein, N. (1996). *Bullyproof: A teacher's guide on teasing and bullying for use with fourth and fifth grade students.* Washington, DC: Wesley College Center for Research on Women and NEA Professional Library.

Stein, N., & Sjostrom, L. (1994). *Flirting or hurting? A teacher's guide to student-to-student sexual harassment in schools (grades 6 through 12).* Washington, DC: NEA Professional Library.

Stendler, C. B. (1950). Sixty years of child training practices. *Journal of Pediatrics, 36*(1), 122–134.

Stephan, W. G., & Vogt, W. P. (Eds.). (2004). *Education programs for improving intergroup relations.* New York: Teachers College Press.

Stevens, J. H., Jr. (1982). Support systems for black families. In J. D. Quisenberry (Ed.), *Changing family lifestyles.* Wheaton, MD: Association for Childhood Education International.

Stinnett, N., & DeFrain, J. (1985). *Secrets of strong families.* Boston: Little, Brown.

Stouffer, B. (1992). We can increase parent involvement in secondary schools. *NASSP Bulletin, 75,* 5–8.

Stronge, J. H. (Ed.). (1992). *Educating homeless children and adolescents: Evaluating policy and practice.* Newbury Park, CA: Sage.

Stronge, J. H., & Helm, V. A. (1991). Legal barriers to the education of homeless children and youth: Residency and guardianship issues. *Journal of Law & Education, 20*(2), 201–218.

Sui, S. (1994). Taking no chances: A profile of Chinese-American family support for school success. *Equity and Choice, 10*(2), 23–32.

Suleiman, M. W. (Ed.). (1999). *Arabs in America.* Philadelphia: Temple University.

Summit, R. C. (1983). The child sexual abuse accommodation syndrome. *Child Abuse and Neglect, 7,* 177–193.

Sunley, R. (1955). Early nineteenth-century American literature on child rearing. In M. Mead & M. Wolfenstein (Eds.), *Childhood in contemporary cultures* (pp. 150–163). Chicago: University of Chicago Press.

The Supreme Court's decisions of note. (1993, July 19–25). *The Washington Post National Weekly Edition,* p. 9.

Swap, S. M. (1990). Comparing three philosophies of home-school collaboration. *Equity and Choice, 63,* 9–19.

Swick, K. J. (1983, April). Parent education: Focus on parents' needs and responsibilities. *Dimensions,* 9–12.

Swick, K. J. (1986). Parents as models in children's cultural development. *The Clearing House, 60*(2), 72–75.

Swick, K. J. (1997). A family-school approach for nurturing caring in young children. *Early Childhood Education Journal 25*(2), 151–154.

Swick, K. J. (1999). Empowering homeless and transient children/families: An ecological framework for early childhood education. *Early Childhood Education Journal, 26*(3), 195–201.

Swick, K. J. (2001). Nurturing decency through caring and serving during the early childhood years. *Early Childhood Education Journal, 23*(2), 131–137.

Swick, K. J., Da Ros, D. A., & Kovach, B. A. (2001). Empowering parents and families through a caring inquiry approach. *Early Childhood Education Journal, 29*(1), 65–71.

Swick, K. J., & Manning, M. L. (1983). Father involvement in home and school settings. *Childhood Education, 60*(2), 128–134.

Swick, K. J., Varner, J., & McClellan, S. (1991, November). *Toward an evaluation framework for statewide parent education.* Paper presented at the meeting of the National Association for the Education of Young Children, Denver, CO.

Taylor, K. W. (1981). *Parent and children learn together: Parent cooperative nursery schools.* New York: Teachers College Press.

Teachersfirst.com. (n.d.). Involving fathers at school. Adapted from Fathers involvement in children's learning. U.S. Department of Education. Retrieved February 8, 2006, from *www/teachersfirst.com/fathers.html*

Tebes, J. K., Grady, K., & Snow, D. L. (1989). Parent training in decision-making facilitation: Skill acquisition and relationship gender. *Family Relations, 38*(3), 243–247.

The Children's Ombudsman. (1998). *The children's ombudsman in Sweden.* Retrieved June 29, 2002, from *www.bo.se/eng/engelsk.asp*

Thompson, F. (1988). Shelley. In D. C. Browning (Ed.), *Dictionary of quotations and proverbs.* Secaucus, NJ: Chartwell Books.

Thompson, R. W., Grow, C. R., Ruma, P. R., Daly, D. L., & Burke, R. V. (1993). *Family Relations, 42*(1), 21–25.

Thornton, A., & Freedman, D. (1983). The changing American family. *Population Bulletin,* No. 38, 4. Washington, DC: Population Reference Bureau.

Thompson, L., Kropenske, V., Heinicke, C., Gomby, D., & Halfon, N. (2003, July). Home visiting: A service strategy to delivery first 5 results. *Policy Brief Number 15, Building Community Systems for Young Children.* Los Angeles: UCLA Center for Healthier Children, Families and Communities, California Policy Research Center.

Tinker v. Des Moines Independent Community School District, 393 U.S. 503 (1969).

Tizard, J., & Hodges, J. (1978). The effect of early institutional rearing on the development of eight-year-old children. *Journal of Child Psychology and Psychiatry, 19*(2), 99–118.

Tower, C. C. (1992). *The role of educators in the protection and treatment of child abuse and neglect.* Washington, DC: U.S. Department of Health and Human Services, National Center on Child Abuse and Neglect.

Turbiville, V., Umbarger, G. T., III, & Guthrie, A. C. (2000, July). Fathers' involvement in programs for young children. *Young Children, 55*(4).

Turnbull, A. P., & Turnbull, H. R., III. (1997). *Families, professionals, and exceptionality: A special partnership* (3rd ed.). Upper Saddle River, NJ. Merrill/ Prentice Hall.

Turnbull, A. P., Turnbull, R., Erwin, E. & Soodak, L. (2006). *Families, professionals, and exceptionality:* Positive outcomes through partnership and trust (5th ed.). Upper Saddle River, NJ: Merrill/ Prentice Hall.

Turnbull, H. R., Turnbull, A. P., Stowe, M. J., & Wilcox, B. (2000). *Free appropriate public education.* Denver: Love.

Turnbull, H., III. (2005, November/December). Individuals with Disabilities Education Act reauthorization: Accountability and personal responsibility. *Remedial and special education, 26*(6), 320–327.

Umansky, W. (1983). On families and the re-valuing of childhood. *Childhood Education, 59*(4), 259–266.

UNICEF. (2006). State of the World's Children 2006. Retrieved September 3, 2006, from *www.childinfo.org*

United Nations. (1989). *United Nations convention on the rights of the child.* New York: Author.

University of North Carolina FPG Child Development Institute. (2004). The Carolina Abecedarian Project. Retrieved March 3, 2006, from *www.fpg.unc.edu/-abc/index.cfm* and *www.childcareresearch.org/location/ccrca4716*

U.S. Advisory Board on Child Abuse and Neglect (1990, August). Department of Health and Human Services: Office of Human Development Services, Child Abuse and Neglect. *Critical first steps in response to a national emergency.* Washington, DC: U.S. Government Printing Office.

U.S. Advisory Board on Child Abuse and Neglect. (1993, April). In Department of Health and Human Services, Administration for Children and Families, *The continuing child protection emergency: A challenge to the nation.* Washington, DC: U.S. Government Printing Office.

U.S. Bureau of the Census. (1991). *The Census and You, 26*(12). Washington, DC: U.S. Government Printing Office.

U.S. Bureau of the Census. (1995, June). *Who receives child support? Statistical briefs* (SB 95-16). Washington, DC: Author.

U.S. Bureau of the Census. (1997, Spring). Who's minding the kids? Child care arrangements. Retrieved August 22, 2002, from *www.census.gov/prod/w2002pubs/p70–86.pdf*

U.S. Bureau of the Census. (1998). Money income in the United States: 1997 (with separate data on valuation of noncash benefits). *Current Population Reports* (P60-200). Washington, DC: U.S. Government Printing Office.

U.S. Census Bureau. (2000a). Current Population Reports (P20–515) and unpublished data. Households, families, sub/families and married couples: 1980 to 2000. Retrieved March 5, 2002, from *www.census.gov/prod/2001pubs/statab/sec01.pdf*

U.S. Census Bureau. (2000b). *Current Population Survey (March 1950–2000). Poverty rates by race and Hispanic origin: 1959 to 2000.* Retrieved March 5, 2002, from *www.census.gov/hhes/poverty/poverty00/ povrac00.html*

U.S. Census Bureau. (2000c). *Historical poverty tables.* Retrieved March 18, 2002, from *www.census.gov/hhes/poverty/hispov/hispov4.html*

U.S. Census Bureau. (2000d). *Income and poverty, 2000.* Retrieved February 25, 2002, from *www.census.gov/hhes/income/income001/prs01/asc.html*

U.S. Census Bureau. (2000e). *Real median household income holds steady between 1999 and 2000.* Retrieved February 25, 2002, from *www.census.gov/hhes/www/img/incpov00/fig01*

U.S. Census Bureau. (2000). *The American Indian and Alaska Native Population.* Washington, DC: Author.

U.S. Census Bureau. (2001, April 25). Administrative and Customer Services Division, Statistical Compendia Branch. *Population by race and Hispanic/Latino status.* Retrieved February 21, 2002, from *www.census.gov/statab/www/partla.html*

U.S. Census Bureau (2001, July). *Population briefing, National Population estimates for July, 2001.* Retrieved February 25, 2002, from *www.census.gov/popest/data/national/popbriefng.php*

U.S. Census Bureau, U.S. Department of Commerce News. (2001, September 25). *Nations household income stable in 2000. Poverty rate virtually equals record low.* Census Bureau Reports. Retrieved March 16, 2002, from *www.census gov/PressRelease/www/2001/cb01–158.html*

U. S. Census Bureau (2002). *Historical poverty tables.* Retrieved December 18, 2002, from *www.census.gov/hhes/poverty/hispoolfamindex.html*

U. S. Census Bureau. (2004). *ACS Congression Toolkit.* Washington, DC: Author.

U.S. Census Bureau, (2005a, August 15). 2005 American community survey data. Retrieved September 2, 2006, from *factfinder.census.gov*

U.S. Census Bureau. (2005b). Income, poverty and health insurance coverage in the U.S. 2005. Retrieved September 3, 2006, from *www.census.gov*

U.S. Census Bureau. (2005). American Fact Finder. *Ancestry for People with One or More Ancestry Categories Reported.* Retrieved February 16, 2006, from *factfinder.census.gov*

U.S. Department of Commerce, U.S. Bureau of the Census. (2000). *Statistical Abstract of the United States, Education.* Washington, DC: Author.

U.S. Department of Education. (1980, May 9). Establishment of Title 34, Section 504, Rehabilitation Act of 1973, Rules and Regulations. *Federal Register 45*(92), 30937–30938.

U.S. Department of Education. (1986). *What works: Research about teaching and learning.* Washington, DC: U.S. Government Printing Office.

U.S. Department of Education. (1987). *Schools that work: Educating disadvantaged children.* Washington, DC: U.S. Government Printing Office.

U.S. Department of Education. (1991a). *America 2000: An education strategy.* Washington, DC: U.S. Government Printing Office.

U.S. Department of Education. (1991b). *Preparing young children for success: Guideposts for achieving our first national goal.* Washington, DC: Author.

U.S. Department of Education. (1993). *Goals 2000: Educate America.* Washington, DC: Author.

U.S. Department of Education. (1994). *Strong families, strong schools: Building community partnerships for learning.* Washington, DC: Author.

U.S. Department of Education. (1996, October 3). *United States Department of Education news: Riley announces $17 million in support for charter schools.* Washington, DC: Author.

U.S. Department of Education. (1997). *America goes back to school: The partnership for family involvement in education.* Washington, DC: Author.

U.S. Department of Education. (1998a). Partnership for family involvement in education. *Community Update.* Washington, DC: Office of Intergovernmental and Interagency Affairs.

U.S. Department of Education, Office for Civil Rights. (n.d.). *Student assignment in elementary and secondary schools and Title IX.* Washington, DC: Author.

U.S. Department of Education, Office for Civil Rights, 2002 Elementary and Secondary School Civil Rights Compliance Report. (2005, November). *Corporal Punishment in U.S. Public Schools, 2002–2003 School Year.* Washington, DC: U.S. Government Printing Office.

U.S. Department of Education, Office of Intergovernmental and Interagency Affairs. (1998b). America's public opinion on education and budgets. *Community Update.* Washington, DC: Author.

U.S. Department of Education, Office of Intergovernmental and Interagency Affairs. (2002, January/ February). No child left behind plan becomes law. *Community Update.* Washington, DC: Author.

U.S. Department of Education, Office of Intergovernmental and Interagency Affairs, Educational Partnerships and Family Involvement Unit. (2003). *Reading tips for parents.* Washington, DC: Author.

U.S. Department of Education, Office of the Secretary. (2001, February). *No child left behind.* Washington, DC: Author.

U.S. Department of Education, Office of Educational Research and Improvement, Office of Educational Technology. (1997). *Parents' guide to the Internet.* Washington, DC: Author.

U.S. Department of Education, Office of Special Education and Rehabilitative Services. (1997, September). *Resource 10–4.* Washington, DC: Author.

U.S. Department of Education, Title I of the Elementary and Secondary Education Act of 1965. (2002). *Improving the academic achievement of the disadvantaged.* Washington, DC: Author.

U.S. Department of Health and Human Services. (2002). *Head Start promoting early childhood development.* Retrieved January 11, 2002, from *www.hhs.gov/news/press/2002pres/headstart.html*

U.S. Department of Health and Human Services, Administration for Children, Youth and Families, (2004). *Child Maltreatment,* 2002. Washington, DC: U.S. Government Printing Office.

U.S. Department of Health and Human Services, Office of Human Development Services. (1985). Administration for Children, Youth and Families, Head Start Bureau. *A guide for operating a home-based child development program.* Washington, DC: U.S. Government Printing Office.

U.S. Department of Health and Human Services, Office of Human Development Services. (1987). Administration for Children, Youth and Families, Head Start Bureau. *The Head Start home visitor handbook.* Washington, DC: U.S. Government Printing Office.

U.S. Department of Health and Human Services, Administration for Children and Families, Administration on Children, Youth and Families, National Center on Child Abuse and Neglect. (1992, March). *Child abuse and neglect: A shared community concern.* Washington, DC: U.S. Government Printing Office.

U.S. Department of Health and Human Services, Administration for Children and Families (2000). *Information memorandum: Family literacy services in Head Start and Early Head Start programs.* Retrieved January 11, 2003, from *www.headstartinfo.org/publications/im00/m00_25.htm*

U.S. Department of Health and Human Services, Administration for Children and Families. (2004). *Child Maltreatment. 2002.* Washington, DC: U.S. Government Printing Office.

U.S. Department of Health and Human Services, Children's Bureau. (1998). *Child maltreatment 1996: Reports from the states to the National Child Abuse and Neglect Data System.* Washington, DC: U.S. Government Printing Office.

U.S. Department of Health, Education and Welfare, Children's Bureau. (1949). *Your child from 6 to 12.* Washington, DC: U.S. Government Printing Office.

U.S. Department of Health, Education and Welfare. (1962). *Your child from one to six.* Washington, DC: U.S. Government Printing Office.

U.S. Department of Health, Education and Welfare. (1974). *Home Start/Child and family resource programs. Reports of a joint conference—Home Start, child, and family resource programs.* Washington, DC: U.S. Government Printing Office.

U.S. Department of Health, Education and Welfare, Head Start Bureau, Children's Bureau, Administration for Children, Youth and Families, Office of Human Development. (1977). *Child abuse and neglect: A self-instructional text for Head Start personnel.* (Publication No. OHDS 8–31103) Washington, DC: U.S. Government Printing Office.

U.S. Department of Health, Education and Welfare, Office of Human Development. (1978). Administration for Children, Youth and Families; Head Start Bureau. *Partners with parents.* Kathryn D. Hewett et al. for Abt Associates and High/Scope Educational Research Foundation. Washington, DC: U.S. Government Printing Office.

U.S. Department of Health, Education and Welfare, Office of Human Development Services. (1979). *The rights and responsibilities of students: A handbook for the school community.* Washington, DC: U.S. Government Printing Office.

U.S. General Accounting Office. (1992, August). Report to the chairman, Oversight of Government Management Subcommittee, U.S. Senate Committee on Governmental Affairs. *Child abuse: Prevention programs need greater emphasis. Appendix I: Hawaii's Healthy Start program.* Washington, DC: Author.

Utah Parent Center. (1997). *Parents as partners in the IEP process: Information booklet.* Salt Lake City, UT: Author.

Utriainen, S. (1989). Child welfare service in Finland. *Child Welfare, 68*(2), 129–130.

Valente, W. D. (1987). *Law in the schools* (2nd Ed.). Upper Saddle River, NJ: Merrill/Prentice Hall.

Van Voorhis, F. L. (2003). Interactive homework in middle school: Effects on family involvement and students' science achievement. *Journal of Educational Research, 96(9),* 323–339.

Vandewalker, N. C. (1971). *The kindergarten in American education.* New York: Arno Press.

Venezky, R. L. (1995). *Read write now: The partners tutoring program.* Washington, DC: U.S. Department of Education.

Vincent, C. E. (1951). Trends in infant care ideas. *Child Development, 22*(3), 199–209.

Visher, E. B. (2001). Paper presented at the first annual Ohio State University Extension Family Life Electronic Inservice: A Systemic Examination of Stepfamily Relationships. Columbus, OH, May 8–10, 2001.

Visher, E. B., & Visher, J. S. (1979). *Stepfamilies: A guide to working with stepparents and stepchildren.* Secaucus, NJ: Citadel Press.

Vondra, J. I., & Toth, S. L. (1989). Child maltreatment research and intervention. *Early Child Development and Care, 42,* 11–24.

Vygotsky, L. S. (1978). *Mind in society: The development of psychological processes.* Cambridge, MA: Harvard University Press.

Wadsworth, B. (1712/1972). The well-ordered family: Or relative duties. In D. J. Rothman & S. M. Rothman (Eds.), *The colonial American family: Collected essays.* New York: Arno Press.

Wagner, M., Spiker, D., Inman, M., Linn, D., et al. (2003). Dimensions of parental engagement in home visiting programs, exploratory study. *Topics in early childhood special education, 4,* 171–188.

Wagner, M., Spiker, D., & Linn, M. (2000). The effectiveness of the PAT program with low-income parents and children. *Topics in early childhood special education, 22*(2), 67–82.

Walberg, H. F. (1984). Families as partners in educational productivity. *Phi Delta Kappan, 65*(40), 397–400.

Wallerstein, J. (1985). Effect of divorce on children. *The Harvard Medical School Mental Health Letter, 2*(3).

Wallerstein, J. S., & Kelly, J. B. (1980). The effects of parental divorce: Experience of the child in later latency. In A. Skolnick & J. H. Skolnick (Eds.), *Family in transition.* Boston: Little, Brown.

Walsh, M. E. (1992). *Moving to nowhere.* Westport, CT: Auburn.

Wanat, C. L. (1992). Meeting the needs of single-parent children: Schools and parent views differ. *NASSP Bulletin, 76*(543), 43–48.

Wardle, F. (2003). Supporting multiracial and multiethnic children and their families. In C. Copple (Ed.), *A world of difference.* Washington, DC: National Association for the Education of Young Children.

Warner, I. (1991). Parents in touch: District leadership for parent involvement. *Phi Delta Kappan, 73*(5), 372–375.

Warren, V. B. (1963). *Tested ways to help your child learn.* Upper Saddle River, NJ: Prentice Hall.

Wasik, B. H. (1983, August). *Teaching parent problem-solving skills: A behavioral-ecological perspective.* Paper presented at the American Psychological Association Meeting, Anaheim, CA.

Wasik, B. H. (1993). Staffing issues for home visiting programs. *The Future of Children: Home Visiting, 3*(3), 140–157.

Wasik, B. H., & Bryant, D. M. (2001). *Home visiting: Procedures for helping families* (2nd ed.). Thousand Oaks, CA: Sage.

Watson, T., Brown, M., & Swick, K. J. (1983). The relationship of parents' support to children's school achievement. *Child Welfare, 72*(2), 175–180.

Weatherford, J. (1988). *Indian givers: How the Indians of the Americas transformed the world.* New York: Fawcett Columbine.

Weatherford, J. (1991). *Native roots: How the Indians enriched America.* New York: Fawcett Columbine.

Weaver, H. N. (2005). *Explorations in cultural competence.* Belmont, CA: Thomas Brooks/Cole.

Weber, E. (1969). *The kindergarten.* New York: Teachers College Press.

Webster's encyclopedic unabridged dictionary of the English language. (1989). New York: Portland House.

Webster-Stratton, C., & Hammond, M. (1990). Predictors of treatment outcome in parent training for families with conduct problem children. *Behavior Therapy, 21,* 319–337.

Weikart, D. R., & Lambie, D. A. (1968). Preschool intervention through a home teaching program. In J. Hellmuth (Ed.), *Disadvantaged child. Vol. 2: Head Start and early intervention.* New York: Brunner/Mazel.

West Virginia State Board of Education v. Barnette, 319 U.S. 624 (1943).

Westinghouse Learning Corporation & The Ohio State University. (1969). *The impact of Head Start: An evaluation of the effects of Head Start on children's cognitive and affective development.* Springfield, VA: Clearinghouse for Federal Scientific and Technical Information.

What Works Clearinghouse, Institute of Education Sciences, U.S. Department of Education. Retrieved December 12, 2006, from *www.whatworks.ed.gov*

Wheeler, P. (1992). Promoting parent involvement in secondary schools. *NASSP Bulletin, 76*(543), 28–35.

White, B. L., Kaban, B. T., Attanucci, J., & Shapiro, B. B. (1973). *Experience and environment: Major influences on the development of the young child* (Vol. 1). Upper Saddle River, NJ: Prentice Hall.

Whitebook, M., & Ginsburg, G. (Eds.). (1984). *Beyond "just working with kids": Preparing early childhood teachers to advocate for themselves and others.* Berkeley, CA: Child Care Employee Project.

Wiehe, V. R. (1989). Child abuse: An ecological perspective. *Early Child Development and Care, 42,* 141–148.

Wiehe, V. R. (1996). *Working with child abuse and neglect: A primer.* Thousand Oaks, CA: Sage.

Williams, D. L., Jr. (1992). Parental involvement teacher preparation: Challenges to teacher education. In L. Kaplan (Ed.), *Education and the family.* Boston: Allyn & Bacon.

Williams, K. J., Sheldon, S. B., & Epstein, J. L. (2005) Summary 2005 update data from schools in NNPS. Retrieved April 6, 2006, from *www.csos.jhu.edu/p2000/Research/Schools%Summary%202005.pdf*

Williams, R. (2004, Summer/Fall). The nurse-family partnership: Pennsylvania investment in family. *The Link: Connecting juvenile justice and child welfare, 3*(3), 5–7.

Wilson, M. (1991). Forging partnership with preschool parents: The road to school success begins in the home. *Principal, 70*(5), 25–26.

Winerip, M. (1999, January 3). Homework bound. *Education Life.* New York: New York Times.

Winter, M. (1991, February). An overview and discussion of Parents as Teachers: A parent education project for the state of Missouri. Speech given for First Impressions, Denver, CO.

Winter, M., & McDonald, D. (1997). Parents as Teachers: Investing in good beginnings for children. In G. Albee & T. Gullotta (Eds.), *Primary prevention works* (pp. 119–145). Thousand Oaks, CA: Sage.

Winter, M. M. (1999, Spring/Summer). Parents as teachers. *The Future of Children,* 9(1), 179–181.

Winters, D. G. (1988). *Parents: The missing link in education reform.* (Hearing before the Select Committee on Children, Youth, and Families. House of Representatives 100th Congress. November 16, 1987.) Washington, DC: U.S. Government Printing Office.

Winters, W. G. (1993). *African American mothers and urban schools: The power of participation.* New York: Lexington Books.

Wisconsin v. Yoder, 406 U.S. 205, 233 (1972).

Wodarski, J. S., & Johnson, S. R. (1988). Child sexual abuse: Contributing factors, effects and relevant practice issues. *Family Therapy, XV*(2), 157–173.

Wolfenstein, M. (1953). Trends in infant care. *American Journal of Orthopsychiatry,* 23(1), 120–130.

Woolley, P. V., Jr., & Evans, W. A. (1955, June). Significance of skeletal lesions in infants resembling those of traumatic origin. *Journal of American Medical Association,* 539–543.

World Health Organization. (2006). World Health Report, 2006. Working together, within and across countries. Retrieved September 3, 2006, from *www.who.int/*

Yankelovich, Skelly, & White, Inc. (1976). *Raising children in a changing society: The General Mills American family report, 1976–1977.* Minneapolis, MN: General Mills.

Youngblade, L. M., & Belsky, J. (1989). Child maltreatment, infant-parent attachment security, and dysfunctional peer relationships in toddlerhood. *Topics in Early Childhood Special Education,* 9(2), 1–15.

Zeanah, C. H., & Scheeringa, M. (1996, April/May). Evaluation of posttraumatic symptomatology in infants and young children exposed to violence. In J.D. Opofsley & E. Fenichel (Eds.). *Islands of safety: Assessing and treating young victims of violence. Zero to Three, 16*(5), 9–14.

Zero to Three. (1998–2001). *Brain Wonders.* Retrieved January 10, 2006, from *zerotothree.org/brainwonders/faq.html*

Zill, N. (1996). Family change and student achievement: What we have learned, what it means for schools. In A. Booth & J. F. Dunn (Eds.), *Family-school links: How do they affect educational outcomes?* Mahwah, NJ: Erlbaum.

Index